NTOA 36

Leo Mildenberg

Vestigia Leonis

# NOVUM TESTAMENTUM ET ORBIS ANTIQUUS (NTOA)

Im Auftrag des Biblischen Instituts
der Universität Freiburg Schweiz
herausgegeben von Max Küchler
in Zusammenarbeit mit Gerd Theissen

*Der Autor:*

Leo Mildenberg, geb. 14. Februar 1913 in Kassel; Schulzeit in Bad Mergen-
theim und Schwäbisch Hall; Studium der Alten Geschichte und Semitistik
in Frankfurt, Leipzig und Dorpat bei Lazar Gulkowitsch; 1939–1941
Dozent für Orientalische / Altsemitische Sprachen in Dorpat; 1941–1946
Deportation nach Kasachstan; nach dem Krieg Direktor des Münzhandels
der Bank Leu; 1966–1979 Hrsg. der «Schweizerischen Numismatischen
Rundschau»; 1980 Ehrenmitglied des Internationalen Münzhändlerver-
bandes (AINP); 23. Mai 1995 Dr. phil. h.c. der Universität Tübingen. Festschrift zum 70. Geburtstag: A. HOUHGTON – S. HURTER – P.E. MOTTAHADEH –
J.A. SCOTT, Festschrift für / Studies in Honor of Leo Mildenberg (Wetteren
1984); Buchveröffentlichung: The Coinage of the Bar Kokhba War (Typos 6),
Aarau – Frankfurt a.M. – Salzburg 1984.

*Die Herausgeber:*

Ulrich Hübner (geb. 1952) ist Professor für Altes Testament und Biblische
Archäologie in Kiel. Buchveröffentlichungen: Die Ammoniter (ADPV 16;
1992); Spiele und Spielzeug im antiken Palästina (OBO 121; 1992)

Ernst Axel Knauf (geb. 1953) ist Professor für Altes Testament und
Biblische Archäologie in Bern. Buchveröffentlichungen: Midian (ADPV;
1988); Ismael (ADPV; ²1989); Die Umwelt des Alten Testament (NSK AT
29; 1994).

L. Mildenberg

Leo Mildenberg

# Vestigia Leonis

Studien zur antiken Numismatik
Israels, Palästinas
und der östlichen Mittelmeerwelt

Herausgegeben von
Ulrich Hübner und Ernst Axel Knauf

UNIVERSITÄTSVERLAG FREIBURG SCHWEIZ
VANDENHOECK & RUPRECHT GÖTTINGEN
1998

Die Deutsche Bibliothek – CIP-Einheitsaufnahme

**Mildenberg, Leo:**
Vestigia Leonis. Studien zur antiken Numismatik Israels, Palästinas und der östlichen Mittelmeerwelt / Leo Mildenberg. Hrsg. von Ulrich Hübner und Ernst Axel Knauf. – Freiburg, Schweiz: Univ.-Verl.; Göttingen: Vandenhoeck und Ruprecht; 1998
  (Novum testamentum et orbis antiquus; 36)
  ISBN 3-525-53907-X (Vandenhoeck & Ruprecht).
  ISBN 3-7278-1155-2 (Univ.-Verl.).

Herausgegeben mit der Hilfe des Hochschulrates Freiburg Schweiz,
des Rektorats der Universität Freiburg Schweiz
und der Leu Numismatik AG


Die Druckvorlagen wurden von den Verfassern
als reprofertige Dokumente zur Verfügung gestellt

© 1998 by Universitätsverlag Freiburg Schweiz
Paulusdruckerei Freiburg Schweiz
ISBN 3-7278-1155-2 (Universitätsverlag)
ISBN 3-525-53907-X (Vandenhoeck und Ruprecht)
ISSN 1420-4592

# Inhalt

# Vorwort

Münzen sind Text-, Bild- und Sachquellen zugleich. Für die Geschichte Israels und Palästinas von Kyros bis Bar Kochba sind sie eine Primärquelle, deren Bedeutung oft noch nicht wahrgenommen wird, für den zweiten jüdischen Aufstand oder, wie LEO MILDENBERG formulieren würde, den zweiten jüdischen Krieg gegen Rom sind sie die Hauptquelle. Diese Einsicht und die erste sachgerechte Rekonstruktion der Ereignisse von 132 bis 135 verdankt die Forschung LEO MILDENBERG. Wie es im Laufe der Jahrzehnte gelang, die ersten festen Punkte in Raum und Zeit zu gewinnen, wie das immer vollständiger erschlossene Material half, frühere Irrtümer und Fehlannahmen zu korrigieren, bis schließlich das gegenwärtige Geschichtsbild entstand, läßt sich an den hier versammelten Aufsätzen noch einmal nachvollziehen. Die Bar-Kochba-Münzen stellen den Löwenanteil des bisherigen Werkes von LEO MILDENBERG dar. Mit den Münzen der achämenidischen Satrapie Transeuphratesien führt uns der Autor auf Neuland. Diese Studien stellen *work in progress* vor; wer sie bei der Rekonstruktion der Wirtschafts-, Verfassungs-, Verwaltungs- und Mentalitätsgeschichte des perserzeitlichen Palästina unbeachtet läßt, läuft aber schon jetzt Gefahr, vermeidbare Irrtümer zu kolportieren.

Steht die Bedeutung der Forschungen LEO MILDENBERGs für die historisch engagierte Bibelwissenschaft außer Frage, so dürften doch zahlreiche seiner einschlägigen Veröffentlichungen diesem Leserkreis nicht ohne Weiteres zur Hand sein. So verfolgt der vorliegende Band ein doppeltes Ziel: einerseits, LEO MILDENBERG den Dank abzustatten, den ihm gerade die historisch-kritische Exegese seit langem schuldet; andererseits den Kreis seiner dankbaren Rezipienten nach Kräften zu erweitern. Auch klassische und vorderorientalische Archäologen, Numismatiker und Althistoriker, die das Werk LEO MILDENBERGs längst kennen und schätzen, werden, so hoffen wir, von dieser Zusammenstellung von Aufsätzen ihren Nutzen haben. Wieweit die Liebe zur kleinformatigen Tierdarstellung der Antike den Autor bei der Auswahl seiner Studienobjekte geleitet hat, wissen wir nicht; doch lohnt es sich, auch in dieser Hinsicht der Spur des Löwen von Taf. I 2 bis Taf. LXX 3 zu folgen.

Die Aufsätze sind nahezu unverändert wieder abgedruckt; insgesamt wurden sie äußerlich, z.B. in Bezug auf Abkürzungen, Transkriptionen, Stempelstellung (11 h – 12 h), Anmerkungsziffern und Zitierweise vereinheitlicht. Kleinere Versehen wie etwa Druckfehler wurden stillschweigend verbessert, einige Querverweise hinzugefügt. In ganz wenigen Fällen sind nicht alle Abbildungen der Erstpublikation wiederholt, sondern durch Querverweise auf Abbildungen anderer Aufsätze ersetzt. Die Her-ausgeber bedauern sehr, daß angesichts des bereits beträchtlichen Umfangs einige Arbeiten, die während der Druckvorbereitung erschienen sind, nicht mehr aufgenommen werden konnten. Für die Erlaubnis zum Wiederabdruck haben wir vor allem M. Amandy (Bibliothèque Nationale de France, Paris), Antike Kunst (Basel), D. Barag (Israel Numismatic Society, Jerusalem), dem C. H. Beck Verlag (München), A. Burnett (International Numismatic Commission, London), P. Calmeyer (Deutsches Archäologisches Institut, Abt. Teheran, Berlin), T. Hackens und Gh. Moucharte (Département d'Archéologie et d'Histoire de l'Art, Université Catholique de Louvain), der Israel Explotation Society (Jerusalem), M. II. Martin (American Numismatic Society, New York), Peeters Publishers (Leuven), dem Philipp von Zabern Verlag (Mainz), dem D. Reimer Verlag (Berlin), B. Schärli (Circulus Numismaticus Basiliensis), Ch. Segal (Department of the Classics, Harvard University, Cambridge/MA), Spink Publishers (London), S. Hurter (Schweizerische Numismatische Gesellschaft, Zürich), A. P. Tzamalis (Hellenic Numismatic Society, Athen), den Herausgebern von Transeuphratène, J. Elayi und J. Sapin sowie dem J.-P. Gabalda Verlag (Paris), S. Sorda (Istituto Italiano di Numismatica, Rom), H. Voegtli (Internal Association of Professional Numismatists, Basel) und U. Westermarck (Swedish Numismatic Society, Stockholm) zu danken. Besondere Dank gilt Sonja Schröer (Kiel) für ihre Hilfe beim Eingeben der Vorlagen in den Computer und M. Küchler (Fribourg) für seine Bereitschaft, den Band in die Reihe NTOA aufzunehmen. A. Bromberg (London) danken wir für eine namhafte Beihilfe zu den Druckkosten.

LEO MILDENBERGs 85. Geburtstag ist ein passender Anlaß, dem Jubilar einen Teil seines Lebenswerks in einem Band vereint zu überreichen und ihn *VOT LXXXV – MVLT LXXXX* zu grüßen.

Doch genug des Vorwortes: *lectores ad leonem* !

Im Dezember 1997

Ulrich Hübner (Kiel)              Ernst Axel Knauf (Bern und Zumikon ZH).

# Abkürzungsverzeichnis

| | |
|---|---|
| AA | Archäologischer Anzeiger |
| AASOR | Annual of the American School of Oriental Research |
| ACNAC | Ancient Coins in North American Collections |
| AIIN | Annali del'Istituto Italiano di Numismatica |
| AINP | Association Internationale des Numismates Professionels |
| AJN | American Journal of Numismatics |
| AK (.B | Antike Kunst (Beiheft) |
| AMI (Ergbd.) | Archäologische Mitteilungen aus Iran (Ergänzungsband) |
| AMUGS | Antike Münzen und Geschnittene Steine |
| ANET$^3$ | Ancient Near Eastern Texts, ed. J.B. Pritchard, Princeton/NJ $^3$1969 |
| ANRW | Aufstieg und Niedergang der Römischen Welt |
| ANS | American Numismatic Society |
| ANSMN | ANS Museum Notes |
| ANSNNM | ANS Museum Notes and Monographes |
| BA | Biblical Archaeologist |
| BAR.IS | British Archaeological Reports, International Series |
| BASOR | Bulletin of the American School of Oriental Research |
| BDBAT | Beihefte zu den Dielheimer Blättern zum Alten Testament |
| BMC | British Museum Catalogue |
| CAH | Cambridge Ancient History |
| CHI | Cambridge History of Iran |
| CHJud | Cambridge History of Judaism |
| CIN | Congrès International de Numismatique (International Congress of Numismatics) |
| CNP | Corpus Nummorum Palaestinensium |
| Coin Hoards | M.J. Price et al. (ed.), The Royal Numismatic Society, London 1975ff |
| DJD | Discoveries in the Judaean Desert |
| ErIs | Eretz-Israel |
| FS | Festschrift / Studies / Essays in Honour |
| Gorny | D. Gorny, Münchner Auktionen |
| HdA | Handbuch der Archäologie |
| Hess-Leu | A. Hess AG - Bank Leu, Luzerner Auktionen |
| Hist.Jud. | Historia Judaica |
| HSCP | Harvard Studies in Classical Philology |
| HSM | Harvard Semitic Monographs |
| HUCA | Hebrew Union College Annual |
| IAPN | s. unter AINP |
| IGCH New | M. Thompson et al. (ed.), An Inventory of Greek Coin Hoards, York 1973 |
| IMN | Israel Museum Notes |

| | |
|---|---|
| INB | Israel Numismatic Bulletin |
| INJ | Israel Numismatic Journal |
| IstForsch | Istanbuler Forschungen |
| JIAN | Journal International d'Archéologie et de Numismatique |
| JBL | Journal of Biblical Literature |
| JHS | Journal of Hellenic Studies |
| JNES | Journal of Near Eastern Studies |
| JNG | Jahrbuch für Numismatik und Geldgeschichte |
| JbÖByz | Jahrbuch der Österreichischen Byzantinistik |
| JPOS | Journal of the Palestine Oriental Society |
| JQR | Jewish Quarterly Review |
| JRS | Journal of Roman Studies |
| KAW | Kulturgeschichte der Antiken Welt |
| Leu | Bank Leu und Leu Numismatik, Zürcher Auktionskataloge |
| MMAG | Münzen und Medaillen AG, Basler Auktionen |
| MUSJ | Mélanges de l'Université Saint-Joseph |
| NAAG | Numismatic and Ancient Art Gallery AG, Z‚rich |
| NC | The Numismatic Chronicle (The Royal Numismatic Society, London) |
| NFA | Numismatic Fine Arts, Los Angeles/CA |
| Num.Lov. | Numismatica Lovaniensia |
| OrLovA | Orientalia Lovaniensia Analecta |
| QDAP | Quarterly of the Department of Antiquities of Palestine |
| PEQ | Palestine Exploration Quarterly |
| PRE | Paulys Real-Encyclopädie der Classischen Alterthumswissenschaft |
| QTic | Quaderni Ticinesi di Numismatica e Antichità Classiche |
| RB | Revue Biblique |
| RBN | Revue Belge de Numismatique et de Sigillographie |
| RÉA | Revue des études anciennes |
| RIC | Mattingly H. et al., The Roman Imperial Coinage |
| RN | Revue numismatique |
| RNS | The Royal Numismatic Society, London |
| RSF | Rivista di Studi Fenici |
| ScrH | Scripta Hierosolymitana |
| SKA | Monetarium der Schweizerischen Kreditanstalt Zürich |
| SM | Schweizer Münzblätter |
| SNG | Sylloge Nummorum Graecorum |
| SNR | Schweizerische Numismatische Rundschau |
| Sternberg | F. Sternberg, Zürcher Auktionskataloge |
| StJAL | Studies in Judaism in Late Antiquity |
| Stud. Phoen. | Studia Phoenicia |
| Traité | Babelon E., Traité de monnaies grecques et romaines, Paris 1910-1932 |
| VT | Vetus Testamentum |

# Bibliographie Leo Mildenberg*

## I. Monographien

The Coinage of the Bar Kokhba War (Typos 6), Aarau - Frankfurt a.M. - Salzburg 1984

## II. Aufsätze in Fachzeitschriften und Buchbeiträge

Eine Ueberprägung des 2.Aufstandes der Juden gegen Rom, in: SNR 33 (1947) 17-24

Die alten jüdischen Münzen auf den neuen Briefmarken Israels, in: Das Neue Israel 2 (Zürich 1948) 12-13

Die erste Münze des Staates Israel, in: Das Neue Israel 22 (Zürich 1949) 7

*Numismatische Evidenz zur Chronologie der Bar Kochba-Erhebung, in: SNR 34 (1948-1949) 19-27

*The Eleazar Coins of the Bar Kochba Rebellion, in: Hist. Jud. 11 (1949) 77-108

Alte jüdische Staatlichkeit im Spiegel der Münzprägung, in: Das Neue Israel, 1949, 10

Von der eigenen Münzprägung der Juden in der Antike, in: Omanut. Verein zur Förderung Jüdischer Kunst in der Schweiz, Zürich 1949, 1-2

Nachruf: In Memoriam Dr. Jacob Hirsch, in: AINP-Bulletin 1955, 1-3

*Les inscriptions des monnaies Carthaginoises, in: CIN Paris 6-11 Juillet 1953, Actes, Tome II, Paris 1957, 149-151

---

* Die mit * gekennzeichneten Aufsätze sind hier wieder abgedruckt.

*Mithrapata und Perikles, in: Congresso Internazionale di Numismatica Roma 11-16 Settembre 1961, Vol. 2: Atti, Rom 1965, 45-55

Great Art in Small Greek Coins, in: INB 2 (1962) 35-38

*The Monetary System of the Bar Kokhba Coinage, in: International Numismatic Convention Jerusalem 27-31 December 1963: The Patterns of Monetary Development in Phoenicia and Palestine in Antiquity. Proceedings, ed. A.KINDLER, Tel-Aviv - Jerusalem 1967, 41-48 *

R - RR - RRR - ... De degrès de rareté dans la description des monnaies antiques / R - RR - RRR - ... On the degree of rarity in describing ancient coins, in: AINP-Bulletin 39 (1964) 1-5 und 6-10

*Florinus Mildenbergensis, in: Charisteion für Herbert A. Cahn. SM 51-54, Jg. 13-14 (1964) 106-108

*Von der Kunst der griechischen Kleinmünzen, in: FS für E. Madsack zum 75.Geb., Hannover 1964, 95-106

Quelques réaux d'or inédits de Charles I$^{er}$ d'Anjou, Roi de Sicilie (1266-1285), in: RN 6$^e$ série, Tome 7 (1965) 306-309

Ancient Hebrew Inscriptions translated for Numismatists, in: World Coins 55 (1968) 618-619

*Nergal in Tarsos. Ein numismatischer Beitrag, in: Zur griechischen Kunst. FS für H. Bloesch zum 60.Geb. (AK.B 9), Bern 1973, 78-80

Kimon in the Manner of Segesta, in: Actes du 8$^{ème}$ CIN, New York - Washington Septembre 1973, Paris - Basel 1976, 113-121

Collections des monnaies - placement de capitaux?, in: Agence économique et Financière 11-12, Janvier 1976, XXVIII

Die Schrift auf den souveränen Münzen der jüdischen Antike, in: Ausstellungskatalog «Hebräische Schrift» im Kunstgewerbemuseum Zürich 1976, 12-13

Eternal Bar Kochba Forgeries, in: AINP-Bulletin 2,3 (1977) 59-60

*Bar Kochba in Jerusalem?, in: SM Jg. 27, H. 105 (1977) 1-6

Die Tradition der Münzauktion in der Schweiz, in:  Der Münzen- und Medaillensammler. Berichte 107, 18.Jg. (1978) 763-764

*Yehud: A Preliminary Study of the Provincial Coinage of Judaea, in:  Greek Numismatics and Archaeology. Essays in Honor of  M. Thompson, ed. O. MØRKHOLM – N.M. WAGGONER, Wetteren 1979, 183-196

*Bar Kokhba Coins and Documents, in:  HSCP 34 (1980) 311-335

Der Bar Kokhba-Krieg und seine Münzprägung, in:  Geldgeschichtliche Nachrichten 95, 18.Jg. (1983) 117-118

Zum 70.Geburtstag von D.W.H. Schwarz, in:  SM 130, 33.Jg. (1983) 51

*The Bar Kokhba Wars in the Light of the Coins and Document Finds 1947-1982, in:  INJ  8 (1984-1985) 27-32

*A Bar Kokhba Didrachm, in:  INJ  8 (1984-1985) 33-36

*Schekel-Fragen, in:  FS für H.A. Cahn zum 70.Geb., ed. Circulus Numismaticus Basilensis, Basel 1985, 83-88

Aufstandsprägungen im römischen Kaiserreich, in:  Numismatics - Witness to History (La Numismatique - Témoin de l'Histoire). Articles by members of the IAPN to commemorate its 35th anniversary (Articles de membres de l'AINP pour le 35 anniversaire de l'association), AINP-Publication 8 (1986) 41-50

Nachruf: Eric von Schulthess Rechberg, in: Helvetische Münzenzeitung 10, 21.Jg. (1986) 433-434

*Baana. Preliminary Studies of the Local Coinage in the Fifth Persian Satrapy: Part 2, in: ErIs (M. Avi-Yonah Memorial Vol.) 19 (1987) 28*-35*

*Numismatic Evidence, in:  HSCP 91 (1987) 381-395

*Über das Kleingeld in der persischen Provinz Judäa: Die Yehud-Münzen, in:  H. Weippert, Palästina in vorhellenistischer Zeit (HdA, Vorderasien II, Bd. 1), München 1988, 719-728

מטבעות מורדים בעימפריה הרומנית, in: Qatedrah 52 (1989) 90-99

*Punic Coinage on the Eve of the First War against Rome. A Reconsideration, in: Punic Wars, ed. H. DEVIJER - E. LIPINSKI (Stud.Phoen. 10; OrLovA 33), Leuven 1989, 5-14

*Über Kimon und Euainetos im Funde von Naro, in: Kraay - Mørkholm Essays. Numismatic Studies in Memory of C.M. Kraay and O. Mørkholm, ed. G. LE RIDER - K. JENKINS - N. WAGGONER - U. WESTERMARK (Publications d'Histoire de l'Art et d'Archéologie de l'Université Catholique de Louvain 59, Num. Lov. 10), Louvain-la-Neuve 1989, 182-189

*«Those ridiculous arrows». On the meaning of the die position, in: Nomismatika Chronika 8 (1989) 23-27

*Der Bar-Kochba-Krieg im Lichte der Münzprägungen, in: H.-P. KUHNEN, Palästina in griechisch-römischer Zeit (HdA, Vorderasien II, Bd. 2), München 1990, 357-366

Nachruf: Mario Ratto, in: Helvetische Münzenzeitung 4 (1990) 180

*Gaza von 420 bis 332 nach den Sachquellen, in: Akten des XIII. Internationalen Kongresses für Klassische Archäologie, Berlin 1988, Mainz 1990, 431-432 *

*Rebel Coinage in the Roman Empire, in: Greece and Rome in Eretz Israel. Collected Essays, ed. A. KASHER - U. RAPPAPORT - G. FUKS, Jerusalem 1990, 62-74

*Gaza Mint Authorities in Persian Time. Preliminary Studies of the Local Coinage in the Fifth Persian Satrapy, Part 4, in: Transeuphratène 2 (1990) 137-146

*Notes on the Coin Issues of Mazday, in: INJ 11 (1990-1991) 9-23

*Palästina in der persischen Zeit, in: A Survey of Numismatic Research 1985-1990, ed. T. HACKENS et al. (AINP, Special Publication No. 12), Brussels 1991, 102-105

Die Bedeutung der Bar Kochba Münzprägungen, in: Luchot. Mitteilungsblatt der Jüdischen Liberalen Gemeinde Or Chadasch 143 (Zürich 1992) 3-6

*The Philisto-Arabian Coins. A Preview. Preliminary Studies of the Local Coinage in the Fifth Persian Satrapy. Part 3, in: Numismatique et histoire économique phéniciennes et puniques. Actes du Colloque tenu à Louvain-la-Neuve, 13-16 Mai 1987, ed. T. HACKENS - GH. MOUCHARTE (Num.Lov. 9; Stud.Phoen. 9), Louvain 1992, 33-40

*The Mint of the First Carthaginian Coins, in: Florilegium Numismaticum. Studia in honorem U. Westermark edita (Svenska Numismatiska Föreningen), Stockholm 1992, 289-293

*Ršmlqrt, in: Essays in Honour of R. Carson and K. Jenkins, ed. M. Price - A. Burnett - R. Bland, London 1993, 7-8

*Sikulo-punische Münzlegenden, in: SNR 72 (1993) 5-21

*Über das Münzwesen im Reich der Achämeniden, in: AMI 26 (1993) 55-79

*On the Money Circulation in Palestine from Artaxerxes II till Ptolemy I. Preliminary Studies of the Local Coinage in the Fifth Persian Satrapy. Part 5, in: Transeuphratène 9 (1994) 63-71

Burton Y. Berry: The Man and the Collector, in: A Golden Legacy. Ancient Jewelry from the B. Y. Berry Collection at the Indiana University Art Museum, ed. L. Baden, Bloomington/IN 1995, VII

Description of the Ancient Weights in the Fleischman Collection, in: A Passion for Antiquities. Ancient Art from the Collection of Barbara and Lawrence Fleischman. Exhibition Catalogue, The J. Paul Getty Museum in Association with The Cleveland Museum of Art, Malibu/CA 1994, Nos. 25-26. 93-99. 140 (zusammen mit K. Hamma). 141-142. 160. 166

*Bes on Philisto-Arabian Coins, in: Transeuphratène 9 (1995) 63-65

*On the Cyzikenes: A Reappraisal, in: AJN Second Series 5-6 (1993-1994) [1996] 1-12

Petra on the Frankincense Road?, in: Transeuphratène 10 (1995) 69-72, fig. 1

yəhūd und šmryn. Über das Geld der persischen Provinzen Juda und Samaria im 4. Jahrhundert, in: H. CANCIK – H. LICHTENBERGER – P. SCHÄFER ed., Geschichte – Tradition – Reflexion (FS M. Hengel zum 70. Geburtstag; Tübingen 1996), Band I: Judentum, 119-146

Zu einigen sikulo-punischen Münzelegenden, in: Italiam fato profugi Hesperinaque venerunt litora (FS V. und E.E. Clain-Stefanelli; Numismatica Lovaniensia 12; Louvain-la-Neuve 1996), 259-270; 272

On the Money Supply under Artaxerxes II, in: Memory Volume M.J. Price, im Druck

Once Again: Petra on the Francincense Road, in: ARAM Colloquium Papers, Oriental Institute, Oxford University, im Druck

On the So-called Satrapal Coinage, in: Institut Français d'Archéologie d'Istanbul, Colloque 1996, im Druck

A Note on the Coinage of Hierapolis-Bambyce, in: FS L. Rider, im Druck

A Note on the Persian Great King in the Jagged Crown, in: FS A. Kindler, INJ, im Druck

## III. Mitarbeit an Sammlungs- und Auktionskatalogen

Geld, Münze und Medaille. Von den Anfängen bis zur Gegenwart. Ausstellungskatalog des Kunstgewerbemuseums der Stadt Zürich, 19.November - 18.Dezember 1949, zusammen mit F. BURCKHARDT und D. SCHWARZ, Zürich 1949

A. Hess AG Luzern und Bank Leu & Co AG Zürich, 1-50, 1954-1971

Bank Leu & Co AG Zürich, 1-41, 1971-1986

Geld als Kunstwerk. Katalog der Münzausstellung zum 200jährigen Bestehen der Bank Leu & Co AG 1755-1955, Zürich 1955

Jewish Coins. Auction Catalogue Leu & Co - Adolph Hess, Lucerne 3.April 1963, 1-18, Pl. 1-10 [ dt. Ausgabe: Jüdische Münzen. Bellum Iudaicum, Iudaea Capta, Bar Kochba-Krieg, Auktionskatalog Bank Leu & Co AG - Adolph Hess 3.April 1963, Luzern 1963, 1-20, Taf. I-VIII]

Mitarbeit an: Bedeutende Kunstwerke aus dem Nachlass Dr. Jacob Hirsch. Auktionskatalog 7.Dezember 1957 Luzern Adolph Hess - William H. Schab, Luzern 1957

Aus einer Sammlung griechischer Münzen (zusammen mit D. SCHWARZ), Zürich 1961

Sammlung Walter Niggeler, I-IV, 1965-1967

Mitarbeit an: Kunstfreund, 1974

Zürcher Münzen und Medaillen. Ausstellungskatalog Haus zum Rechberg Zürich 12.Oktober - 22.November (zusammen mit H.-U. GEIGER und D. SCHWARZ), Zürich 1969

CAHN, H.A. / MILDENBERG, L. / RUSSO, R. / VOEGTLI, H., Griechische Münzen aus Großgriechenland und Sizilien (Antikenmuseum Basel und Sammlung Ludwig), Basel 1988

MILDENBERG, L. / HURTER, SILVIA (ed.), The Arthur S. Dewing Collection of Greek Coins I-II - Text and Plates (Ancient Coins in North American Collections 6; ANS), New York 1985

MILDENBERG, L. / RYNEARSON, PAUL (ed.), The Abraham Bromberg Collection of Jewish Coins I-II, Beverly Hills/CA - Zürich 1991-1992

## IV. Herausgeber-Tätigkeit

SNR 44-59, 1966-1980

## V. Bibliographie Leo Mildenbergs

Numismatik, Kunstgeschichte, Archäologie. FS für Leo Mildenberg zum 70.Geb. [Numismatics, Art History, Archaeology. Studies in Honor of Leo Mildenberg], ed. A. HOUGHTON - S. HURTER - P. E. MOTTAHEDEH - J. AYER SCOTT Wetteren 1984, VII

## VI. Anhang: Publikationen zu der Leo Mildenberg-Sammlung antiker Tier-Darstellungen

Animals in Ancient Art from the Leo Mildenberg Collection, ed. A.P. KOZLOFF (The Cleveland Museum of Art), Cleveland 1981 [Deutsche Ausgabe: Tierbilder aus vier Jahrtausenden. Antiken der Sammlung Mildenberg, ed. U. GEHRIG, Mainz 1983]

More Animals in Ancient Art from the Leo Mildenberg Collection, ed. A.P. KOZLOFF - D.G. MITTEN - M. SGUAITAMATTI, Mainz 1986

Animals in Ancient Art from the Leo Mildenberg Collection Part III, ed. A.S. WALKER, Mainz 1996

Aus Noahs Arche. Tierbilder der Sammlung Mildenberg aus fünf Jahrtausenden, ed. G. ZAHLHAUS, Mainz 1996.

# I.

Münzprägungen
innerhalb der achämenidischen Satrapie
Transeuphratesien

# Über das Münzwesen im Reich der Achämeniden

## (Tf. I - XIV)

*Silvia Hurter zum 23.Juli 1993*

## Einleitung (Tf. I 1-12)

Im Perserreich wurde mit ungeprägtem Silber und einer kaum übersehbaren Masse von Münzen bezahlt. Ist eine Gruppierung möglich, also die Struktur des Münzwesens erfaßbar? Sind dabei die Bezeichnungen der einzelnen Gruppen treffend, die verwendeten Begriffe eindeutig?

Unbestritten und vielfach belegt ist die Tatsache, daß bis tief ins 5.Jahrhundert und insbesondere in den Randgebieten des Reiches Tauschhandel überwog, Abgaben und Entlohnungen in Naturalien erfolgten und Silbermetall noch im Osten verwendet wurde, als der Westen bereits ein hochentwickeltes Münzwesen kannte[1]. Ebenso geläufig ist die Feststellung, daß alle Großkönige in ihren Schatzhäusern große Mengen von Gold und Silber horteten, die schließlich Alexander in die Hände fielen[2]. Die Frage, wie die Wirtschaft mit diesem drastischen Mittelentzug fertig wurde, scheint bisher nicht beantwortet worden zu sein.

## 1. Das Reichsgeld (Tf. II 13-21)

Es ist erstaunlich und bemerkenswert, daß Darius I. um 500 v.Chr. Gold- und Silbermünzen einführte[3]. Es ist offensichtlich, daß dies keine Erfindung des Großkönigs war, aber fragen sollte man sich, warum er dies tat und wieweit er dabei von der Prägung der lydischen Könige beeinflußt war[4]. Dienten die Golddareike und der Silbersiglos dem gleichen Zweck, und waren sie von gleicher Bedeutung?

---

[1] Siehe L. MILDENBERG, Transeuphratène 2 (1990) 140, Anm. 6 [hier S. 80].

[2] Nach F. DE CALLATAY, REA 91 (1989) 259-276, bes. 261, betrug der persische Königsschatz, der Alexander in die Hände fiel, insgesamt 468 Tonnen Gold und 4680 Tonnen Silber. P.R. FRANKE, in: Akten des XIII. Internationalen Kongresses für Klassische Archäologie Berlin 1988, Mainz 1990, 465-466 kommt in Silber gerechnet auf 10'000 Tonnen.

[3] L. MILDENBERG, Transeuphratène 2 (1990) 139, Anm. 9 [hier S. 80] zur wichtigen Entdeckung von M.C. ROOT, die den Zeitpunkt der Einführung des Reichsgeldes sichert.

[4] C.M. KRAAY, Archaic and Classical Greek Coins, London 1976, 31 nimmt die Weiterprägung des lydischen Geldes während ungefähr 30 Jahren unter persischer Herrschaft an, bis sie dann durch das Reichsgeld unter Darius I. ersetzt wurde. I. CARRADICE, The regal coinage of the Persian empire (BAR.IS 343), Oxford 1987, 92 sagt

Die Golddareike war in erster Linie eine eminent achämenidische Münze, deren Bild keine Entsprechung im Westen hatte und also auch nicht von dort beeinflußt war (Tf. II 14. 16. 17. 21). Der Zusammenhang, in dem die Dareiken in der griechischen Literatur vorkommen, zeigt dies deutlich. Sie wurden für politische Zwecke im Westen eingesetzt[5]. Der Bogenschütze auf dem Persergold blieb fast 200 Jahre unverändert, wurde selbst zu Alexanders Lebzeiten noch gebraucht. Ebenso bemerkenswert war die Wertbeständigkeit. Gewicht und Goldgehalt blieben unantastbar. Die Dareiken überschritten die Grenzen des Reichs. Sie galten und wirkten nicht nur in Griechenland, sondern erscheinen auch in sizilischen Funden[6]. Sie wurden zur anerkannten Weltwährung, die erst von Alexanders Goldstateren im gleichen Gewicht abgelöst werden sollte.

Besonders auffällig ist das von Darius I. gewählte Gewicht der Dareike, das der Silbereinheit des altehrwürdigen Schekels entsprach[7]. Hatte er ursprünglich Großes im Sinn, nämlich das Metallgeld durch geprägtes Geld zu ersetzen, also eine einheitliche Reichswährung zu planen[8], oder dachte er praktisch, ja politisch, und schuf sich ein wertvolles, im Westen für Finanzierungen, Apanagen und Bestechungen passendes Instrument, das dann in der Tat große Wirkung zeitigte? Jedenfalls sind Dareikenfunde im Osten des Reichs äußerst selten, was selbst für die Levante gilt[9].

---

nur, die späteren Krösusmünzen und die frühesten Sigloi lägen zeitlich nahe beieinander und seien beide möglicherweise unter Darius I. eingeführt worden. Wenn sich die Perser für die Prägung ihrer Sigloi der bestehenden Münzstätte der lydischen Könige bedienten – siehe M. PRICE / N. WAGGONER, Archaic Greek Silver Coinage. The «Asyut» Hoard, 1975, 97 – , so bedeutet dies nicht, daß das Produkt lokales Geld darstellt. Es ist vielmehr mit den neuen Bildern und Gewichten persisches Reichsgeld.

[5] Plutarch, Artaxerxes 20. Siehe I. CARRADICE, The regal coinage of the Persian empire, 1987, 76 und 92.

[6] IGCH 2122, Avola 1914 («contents c. 200 AV with 43 darics»); IGCH 2124 («34 AV, 4 darics»). Neuerdings hat H. NICOLET-PIERRE die publizierten Dareiken-Funde in NC 1992, 7-22, Appendix 1, zusammengestellt.

[7] Gewicht des babylonischen Schekels unter Darius I. 8.40 g und der Dareike 8.35 g. Siehe A.D.H. BIVAR, Achaemenid Coins, Weights and Measures, CHI 2 (1985) 610-639, bes. 635-636.

[8] Darius I. dürfte die Bedeutung des Münzwesens erkannt haben, sonst ist die Bilderwahl des Reichsgeldes und die Hinterlegung griechischer Silbermünzen gemeinsam mit lydischen Goldmünzen unter den steinernen Behältern mit den Gründungsurkunden in Persepolis schwer verständlich (dazu IGCH 1789 mit Literatur). Neuere numismatische Kommentare zu den «Persepolis Apadana Deposits» finden sich bei M. PRICE / N. WAGGONER, Archaic Greek Silver Coinage. The «Asyut» Hoard, 1975, 16 und I. CARRADICE, The regal coinage of the Persian empire, 1987, 80-81. Zur Einführung des Reichsgelds siehe M.C. ROOT, in: Achaemenid History 7 (1991) 16: «It was created to look the way it looks precisely because in style and imagery it was a quintessentially Persian, Achaemenid, manifestatic)n of imperial power.» Für den Schreibenden ist sie in erster Linie eine finanzpolitische Maßnahme, «a grandiose financial reorganisation» (E.S.G. ROBINSON, NC 1958, 191).

[9] In IGCH ist keine einzige Dareike aus dem Osten verzeichnet und nur wenige aus Ägypten (1654-1656). Eine einzige Dareike kam aus einer Grabung in Samaria, vgl. J. ELAYI / A. LEMAIRE, Transeuphratène 1 (1989) 163.

Im Osten wurden die Dareiken von den Großkönigen nicht eingesetzt[10], aber als unersetzlich erwiesen sie sich im Westen.

Auch auf dem etwa gleichzeitig eingeführten Silbersiglos (Tf. II 13. 15. 18. 20) erscheint der Bogenschütze. Der Siglos ist ebenso wertbeständig und langlebig wie die Dareike, also gewiß ebenfalls Reichsgeld, aber Reichsgeld für Sonderzwecke, insbesondere für die Bezahlung der in Kleinasien stationierten Söldner[11]. Die Sigloi kommen fast nur in anatolischen Funden vor, und zwar dort in sehr großen Mengen[12]. Die Dareike wurde zum Zahlungsmittel der großen Politik, der Siglos zum Soldgeld.

Man kann nicht genug betonen, daß der Bogenschütze auf Dareike und Siglos eine Zackenkrone trägt. Auf dem für Darius I. repräsentativen Relief von Bisutun hat er sich selbst mit der Zackenkrone abgebildet[13]. Auch auf dem Relief mit dem Sonnenschirm auf einer Türe seines Palastes, des Apadana von Persepolis, sind die Zacken über dem Stirnreif deutlich zu erkennen[14]. «Kronen mit Zinnenmuster waren nicht nur dem König vorbehalten»[15]. Dies ist gewiß zu beachten, zumal es zeigt, daß den Achämeniden jedes Verständnis für Monopolmaßnahmen abging. Wenn aber der Großkönig auf den für ihn wichtigen Monumenten sich selbst in der Zackenkrone darstellt, so ist nicht daran zu zweifeln, daß er sich selbst auf den von ihm eingeführten Reichsmünzen zeigen will[16]. Die universale Dareike und das kleinasiatische

---

[10] Es ist immer zu bedenken, daß alle Werte im Osten, also in den Gebieten östlich des Euphrats, von altersher bis ins angehende 4.Jh., in Silber gemessen wurden, sofern nicht immer noch reiner Warenverkehr herrschte.

[11] Dies wurde zum ersten Mal von D. SCHLUMBERGER, L'argent grec dans l'empire aché- ménide, 1953, 3-62 erkannt. Für I. CARRADICE, The regal coinage of the Persian empire, 1987, 73-94 bilden Dareike und Siglos «The regal coinage of the Persian empire». Er behandelt auch ebendort auf S. 83 und im Katalog auf S. 94-95 die erstaunliche Aufwertung des Siglos im 5.Jh. von 5.30-5.39 g auf 5.55-5.60 g. – C. TUPLIN, auch BAR 343, 1987, 112, spricht aber, indem er sich auf CARRADICE beruft, von «a standardized royal coinage which was not, however, the coinage of the empire.» Was denn? Kommt C. TUPLIN zu diesem Schluß, weil er die Sigloi und deren begrenztes Umlaufgebiet im Auge hat? Jedenfalls, Dareike und Siglos waren von der Verwaltung der achämenidischen Großkönige ausgebrachte Münzen und deshalb Reichsgeld.

[12] Im westlichen Kleinasien die großen Funde IGCH 1178. 1197. 1201. 1224. 1225. – Nur je ein einziger Siglos kommt aus den Levante-Funden IGCH 1481. 1482. 1483, die zwischen 450 und 420 v.Chr. vergraben wurden. – Für das 4. Jahrhundert siehe auch Coin Hoards I, 1975, Nos. 34. 35 und 36.

[13] R. GHIRSHMAN, Iran (Universum der Kunst), 1964, Abb. 284; H. KOCH, Es kündet Dareios der König (KAW 45), Mainz 1992, Tf. 3 und vorderer Umschlag.

[14] R. GIRSHMAN, Iran (Universum der Kunst), 1964, Abb. 233; H. KOCH, Es kündet Dareios der König, 1992, Abb. 88. – Zur «Zinnenkrone» siehe H. VON GALL, AMI NF 7 (1974) 145ff und J. BORCHARDT, AMI Ergbd. 10 (1983) 208.

[15] H. KOCH, Es kündet Dareios der König, 1992, 213.

[16] Der Großkönig an der Apadanafassade in Persepolis (Xerxes?) trägt eine hohe, zylinderförmige Kopfbedeckung, auf der keine Zacken zu sehen sind (H. KOCH, Es kündet Dareios der König, 1992, Abb. 45). Es fällt aber auf, daß mehrere Anführer der Gesandtschaften an der Osttreppe sehr ähnliche, fast ebenso hohe Hüte tragen, und daß keiner der großen Würdenträger eine Zackenkrone trägt. Nach KOCH, Es kündet, 213, Anm. 132 zeigt sich nur ein Diener am Darius-Palast mit einer solchen Krone. Sonst

Silbergeld des Siglos dokumentieren die Macht des Reichs. Wer immer die Vision hatte, neben der Natural- und Silbermetall-Währung des Ostens das geprägte Reichsgeld in Gold und Silber zu schaffen, es geschah unter Darius I. etwa in der Mitte seiner Regierungszeit. Die Einführung neuer Münzsorten in der Antike[17] ist immer ein folgenschwerer Schritt. Wenn ein Herrscher eines Weltreiches ihn tut, so ist die Wirkung um so größer.

Es ist verständlich, daß sich die iranistische Forschung mit den aufschlußreichen Tontäfelchen von Persepolis und anderen Schriftquellen beschäftigt und die monumentalen Bauten der frühen Achämeniden behandelt. Aber es ist unbegreiflich, daß man der heute gesicherten Einführung der Dareike und des Siglos oft nicht die gebührende Beachtung schenkt[18]. Daß die lydischen Herrscher mit ihrer Edelmetall-Doppelwährung vorangingen (Tf. I 6-12), macht die Maßnahme des Großkönigs nicht weniger bedeutsam. Wenn die Heeresorganisation, das Steuerwesen und der Straßendienst große Errungenschaften waren, so ist es die Schaffung des Reichsgeldes nicht weniger. Ohne die Dareike und den Siglos wäre die Konsolidierung des Reichs im Westen nicht möglich gewesen.

---

bleibt die Zacken- oder Zinnenkrone dem Großkönig vorbehalten.

[17] Man denke nur an die Eulen von Athen, die Reichswährung Alexanders in Gold und Silber, das Billon- und Bronzegeld in Ägypten, die Einführung des römischen Denars, ferner an die dicken Schekel des Bellum Iudaicum, den Argenteus des Diokletian und den Wechsel vom Aureus zum Solidus unter Konstantin I.

[18] A.D.H. BIVAR, CHI 2 (1985) 610ff äußert sich nicht zur Ursache, Bedeutung und Bildwahl von Dareike und Siglos. Ähnliches gilt für M.A. DANDAMAEV, A political history of the Achaemenid empire, 1989, und H. KOCH, Es kündet Dareios der König, 1992. R.N. FRYE, The history of ancient Iran, München 1984, 116 hingegen nennt die Einführung «an event in world history of great significance», und M.C. ROOT, The king and kingship in Achaemenid Art, 1979, behandelt die Bildwahl als Teil des künstlerischen Programms des Königs. Zum Bogenschützen hält sie fest «The image of the king as archetypal archer carried a symbolic value of real significance to the Achaemenids» (165). H.T. WALLINGA, in: Achaemenid History 1, Leiden 1987, 72. 74 betont, daß Darius «monetized system was clearly centered on Western Asia Minor», und weist dabei auf die Bedeutung der von Darius eroberten Minen in der Ägäis für dieses System hin. Beizufügen wäre, daß diese Minen Silber produzierten; über Herkunft des Goldes und die Ausmünzung der Dareiken ist damit noch nichts ausgesagt.

## 2. Die sogenannten Satrapenmünzen[19] (Tf. II 22-24; III 25.26)

In der achämemenidischen Hierarchie ist die gültige Reihenfolge: Großkönig – Satrap[20] – Provinzstatthalter – lokale Autoritäten[21]. Man könnte also meinen, daß das Münzwesen entsprechend strukturiert sei: Geld des Reichs, der Satrapen, der Gouverneure und der lokalen Machthaber. Andernorts hat der Schreibende die bedeutsame Tatsache festgehalten, daß der Satrap von Transeuphratesien («Abarnahara») auch nicht eine einzige Satrapenmünze geprägt hat, weil in seinem großen Gebiet die Münzversorgung durch die Könige auf Zypern, die Gouverneure von Samaria und Judäa, die Städte am Meer, ja sogar durch die Herren der südlichen Grenzwüste gesichert war[22]. Wenn dem aber so ist, dürfte es die in der früheren Forschung angenommenen «Unterstatthalterschaften» nicht gegeben haben[23]. Und dann muß man sich auch fragen, ob, wann, wo und wie andere Satrapen wirklich Satrapengeld geschaffen haben. Es gibt nun aber keine Münzgruppe, die den Namen und Titel des Satrapen sowie den seiner Satrapie nennt und die ausschließlich eigene für diese gültige Bilder zeigt. Offensichtlich muß ferner diese Satrapenprägung aus einer Münzstätte kommen, die im Verwaltungsbereich des Satrapen liegt und jedenfalls hauptsächlich für ihn arbeitet. Es müßte sich also um eindeutig achämenidische Zahlungsmittel handeln und dem Satrapen als vom Großkönig bevollmächtigten oder

---

[19] Die Liste der «satrapal coins» in B.V. HEAD, Historia Numorum, Oxford [2]1911, 606-608 ist kurz und mit aller Vorsicht konzipiert: Tissaphernes, Pharnabazos (in Kyzikos), Orontas und Spithridates. Die Soldprägungen der überregional aktiven Granden Tiribazos, Pharnabazos, Datames und Mazaios werden als Erzeugnisse der lokalen Münzstätten behandelt. Es ist zu vermerken, daß der Titel der Dissertation von C.M. HARRISON von 1982, gedruckt Ann Arbor 1992, lautet: The Coinage of the Persian Satraps, nicht: The Persian Satrapal Coinage. Noch beachtenswerter ist, daß sie ihre Arbeit mit der Feststellung auf S. 445 schließt: «The overall picture of coins minted on behalf of Persians does not warrant the assumption that Persian commanders brought to the mint along with their bullion, demands that special designs be used for their coins, much less that their personal images be used as types».

[20] «Satrap» und «Satrapie» sind schillernde Begriffe. Als Satrap bezeichnet werden persische Funktionäre auf sehr verschiedenen Ebenen und in Landschaften, deren Zusammensetzung und Ausdehnung sich ändern kann. Der Schreibende nennt die höchsten Würdenträger wie Tissaphernes, Tiribazos, Pharnabazos, Datames und Mazaios, die Oberkommandierende und eigentliche Vizekönige waren, persische Granden, die Regierenden in der einzelnen größten Verwaltungseinheit, wie Tattenaï und Bēlšunu von Transeuphratesien, Satrapen und die Funktionäre in der nächstfolgenden Einheit, der Provinz (*mdynt* ), wie Bagôhî und Yehezkiyah von Juda, Statthalter oder Gouverneure (*pḥh* oder *pḥt* ). Siehe insbesondere E. LIPINSKI, Transeuphratène 3 (1990) 96-97. 106-107; P. CALMEYER, ebd. 110-112 und J. WIESEHÖFER, Achaemenid History 6, 1991, 309.

[21] Siehe hierzu L. MILDENBERG, Transeuphratène 2 (1990) n. 3 [hier S. 80]; ders., Notes on the Coin Issues of Mazday, INJ 11 (1990-1991) 9, Anm. 2. 13-15 [hier S. 43; 46f].

[22] Siehe L. MILDENBERG, Transeuphratène 2 (1990) 138-144 [hier S. 80-86].

[23] O. LEUZE, Die Satrapieneinteilung in Syrien und im Zweistromland (1935 und 1972) 40. Man beachte dagegen die überzeugende Analyse der Verwaltungsstruktur von «Abarnahara» durch J.M. COOK, CHI 2 (1985) 272. Sie deckt sich vollumfänglich mit der Struktur des Münzwesens, ohne daß sie sich darauf bezieht.

geduldeten Münzherrn. Es liegt keinesfalls bereits eine «Satrapenprägung» vor, wenn auf einer Münze ein Kopf in persischer Tiara erscheint[24], selbst wenn der Name eines Satrapen ausgeschrieben oder abgekürzt dazu gesetzt ist.

Auf der Tetradrachme und Drachme von Kyzikos um 400 v.Chr. findet sich das Portrait und der Name des mächtigen Satrapen Pharnabazos (Tf. II 22-23; XII 107). Die Münzstätte liegt in seinem Gebiet. Er wäre auch ohne Zweifel ein legitimer Münzherr, aber diese Emission dürfte nicht dem Münzumlauf in seiner Satrapie gedient haben, sondern sicherte einmalige Soldzahlungen nach einer erfolgreichen Militäraktion des Satrapen zu Land und zur See[25]. Dafür wurde die lokale Münzstätte benutzt, und deshalb steht das Wappen der Stadt, der Thunfisch, an prominenter Stelle. Es handelt sich also um lokales Geld und nicht um Satrapengeld.

Auch Tissaphernes, der andere Grande um 400 v.Chr., erscheint mit seinem abgekürzten, griechischen Namen $TI\Sigma\Sigma A$ auf Bronzemünzen von Astyra (Tf. III 25) in Mysien[26]. Auffällig ist nicht nur die frühe Verwendung von Bronze in einer kleinasiatischen Münzstätte, wenn die Serie vor 395 entstanden ist, sondern auch das Fehlen der Tiara. Der eindrucksvolle Kopf der Vorderseite mit dem Namen unter dem Halsabschnitt ist barhäuptig. Auf der Rückseite dieser Bronzemünzen steht der Name

---

[24] Zu den von Herodot VII, 61 und Xenophon, Kyropaidia VIII, 3,13, erwähnten Formen der Tiara in weicher und steifer Gestaltung siehe H. VON GALL, in: Akten des XIII. Internationalen Kongresses für Klass. Archäologie, 1990, 320-322, bes. die Feststellung, daß sich die «Satrapentiara... von der weichen Tiara der persisch-medischen Normaltracht höchstens durch den verwendeten Stoff unterschieden haben kann». Also stellt nicht jeder Kopf in der Tiara einen Satrapen dar. Man vergleiche C.M. HARRISON, The Coinage of the Persian Satraps, 87-93, die sich auf die schon von F. IMHOF-BLUMER, Portraitköpfe, 1885, 4f, geäußerte Auffassung beruft, daß «jene Köpfe alle als bloße Varietäten eines stehenden Satrapentypus, ohne jede absichtliche Portraitähnlichkeit mit den prägenden Münzherren, aufzufassen sind". Dagegen betont H.A. CAHN, SM 100 (1975) 84-87, Anm. 13: «Auf einem hochoffiziellen Dokument wie der Münze ist die Tiara Hoheitszeichen des Vertreters des Großkönigs». Dies mag für das späte Königsgeld gelten (siehe Text unten Abschnitt 6), auf dem die Tiara der Würdenträger mit dem auf der Stirn geknüpften Band gehalten ist; vgl. dazu J. ZAHLE, in: Akten Berlin 1988, 1990, 169, und Akten des Berner Numismatischen Kongresses 1979 (1982) 110. Für das Lokalgeld, zu dem nach dem Schreibenden auch die Satrapenprägung gehört, kann es nicht in Betracht kommen.

[25] Der Schiffsbug auf der Rückseite wird in diesem Sinne gedeutet. Nach E.S.G. ROBINSON, NC 1948, 33 befreite Pharnabazos [zum Namen R. SCHMITT, AMI Ergbd. 10 (1983) 84-85] im Jahre 396 v.Chr. den athenischen Admiral Konon aus der Blockade von Kaunos an der karischen Küste. Nach P.H. MARTIN, Jahrbuch der Staatl. Kunstsammlungen in Baden-Württemberg II, 1974, 218, wurden die Portraitmünzen für Soldzahlungen nach Pharnabazos' Sieg über die Athener bei Kyzikos 410 v.Chr. gebraucht. Es muß sich bei diesen Prägungen, Lokalgeld von Kyzikos, um eine einmalige und begrenzte Emission handeln; denn für Vorder- und Rückseite ist nur ein Bild bekannt. Die begleitende Drachme mit denselben Bildern ist lokales Kleingeld, was die Einreihung der Tetradrachmen in die Kyzikener Stadtprägung stützt. Wenn man die ganze Gruppe als «zu Ehren des Pharnabazus» emittiert versteht (Katalog F. Sternberg 26, 1992, 93), dann ist der Stadtmagistrat und nicht der Grande der Münzherr. - Zu einem bärtigen Kopf in der Tiara auf einer Hekte von Mytilene stellt A. FURTWÄNGLER, SNR 61 (1982) 22 fest, «daß dies nur als offizielle Huldigung an den persischen Satrapen verstanden werden kann».

[26] H.A. CAHN, AA 1985, 587-594 und Numismatics-Witness to History (1986) 11-14.

*AΣTYPH* neben dem Kultbild der Artemis von Astyra. Es ist also offensichtlich, daß es sich um Lokalgeld handelt, nicht um eine Satrapenprägung; denn die soeben genannten Voraussetzungen sind nicht gegeben. Ja selbst, daß Tissaphernes der Auftraggeber für dieses periphere Kleingeld war, steht nicht fest. Eine Prägung zu seinen Ehren ist nicht auszuschließen. Auch auf Lykisch erscheint der Name des Granden auf einer Emission von Xanthos (Tf. II 24) mit Reiter und Kopf der Pallas Athene[27]. Auch das Gewicht weicht nicht ab. Alles entspricht der Norm der lykischen Dynastenprägungen. Der Grande läßt nichts ändern, wenn er die Ausmünzung überhaupt veranlaßt hat. Auch hier kann nicht von einer Satrapenmünze die Rede sein.

Der Name des Spithridates findet sich auf Griechisch, und zwar in drei verschiedenen Abkürzungen, auf Silber- und Bronze-Kleingeld, das im kleinasiatischen Nordwesten entstanden ist (Tf. III 26)[28]. Die abgekürzten Namen stehen aber nicht neben dem konventionellen, bärtigen Kopf auf der Vorderseite, sondern auf der Rückseite bei dem beliebten Bild der Pferdeprotome. Dieser Befund und die niedrigen Münzwerte kennzeichnen auch diese Gruppe als Lokalgeld.

Es gibt eine Prägung von Tarsos (Tf. X 93) mit zwei einander gegenüber stehenden Figuren[29]. Die eine ist mit Datames, die andere mit Ana benannt, beides in aramäischer Schrift. Datames ist griechisch, nicht persisch, bekleidet. Ana ist nackt, stellt also ein Kultbild griechischer Art dar. Die Vorderseite zeigt den als solchen bezeichneten, sitzenden Baal von Tarsos, wie er auch auf der tarsischen Datames-Münze mit dem sitzenden persischen Krieger auf der Rückseite vorkommt (Tf. X 92). Beide Emissionen erweisen sich durch diese Baaltars-Vorderseite als lokales Geld aus dem großen kilikischen Atelier. Datames hat seine Herstellung in Auftrag gegeben.

Es gibt eine andere Münzserie, bei der fast alle Voraussetzungen für eine Satrapenprägung gegeben sind[30], ebenfalls in Tarsos, die Serie des Mazaios mit der kilikischen Pforte und mit dem Namen des Granden im gleichbleibenden aramäischen Duktus und seinem Titel in umschriebener Form («Mazday, der über Kilikien und Transeuphratesien ist») (Tf.XI 96). Die große Münzstätte Tarsos liegt in Kilikien, einer seiner beiden Satrapien. Die kilikische Pforte findet sich auch nur auf der Gruppe mit dieser langen, kennzeichnenden Inschrift. Aber das Rückseitenbild des Löwen über dem Stier schmückt auch andere tarsische Münzgruppen des Mazaios. Und auf der Vorderseite erscheint der Baal von Tarsos in Bild und Schrift, wie auf allen Münzen, für deren Prägung die persischen Granden von Tiribazos und Pharnabazos über Datames bis Mazaios die Münzstätte von Tarsos benutzten[31].

---

[27] S. HURTER, in: Greek Numismatics and Archaeology. Essays in Honour of M. Thompson, 1979, 100-101.

[28] E. BABELON, Traité des monnaies grecques et romaines. 2[e] partie: description historique, Paris 1910-1912, Pl. 89, 1-5.

[29] E. BABELON, Traité, Pl. 109,13.

[30] Siehe zum Folgenden L. MILDENBERG, INJ 11 (1990-1991) 11, Pl. 2,7 [hier S. 46, Tf. XVII 7].

[31] C.M. HARRISON, The Coinage of the Persian Satraps, 96: «The clear evidence that it was the custom of satraps to adhere closely to local numismatic practises has great significance of interpretation of their coins».

Letztlich handelt es sich also auch hier um tarsisches Lokalgeld, wie und für welchen Zweck es auch immer emittiert worden ist.

Ähnliches gilt für Mazaios' «Löwen»-Tetradrachmen von Babylon (Tf. XI 99). Natürlich kann er nach dem bei Gaugamela besiegelten Untergang des Reiches[32] seinen persischen Titel nicht mehr verwenden. Von persischem Satrapengeld kann also nicht mehr die Rede sein. Zudem fehlt jeder Hinweis auf Babylon durch ein Symbol oder Monogramm. Es ist für den Granden kennzeichnend, daß er die alten Bilder von Tarsos beibehält, nicht nur den Löwen, sondern immer noch den Baal von Tarsos. Mazaios war Alexanders Verwalter in Babylon, und erstaunlicherweise ließ der Makedone ihn in der Münzprägung gewähren, wobei der Eroberer auch auf diesem heiklen Gebiet in der pragmatischen Tradition der achämenidischen Großkönige steht. Ihrem Wesen nach gehören Mazaios' «Löwen»-Tetradrachmen ebenfalls zu den einstmaligen, auch von Alexander immer noch geduldeten Lokalprägungen[33].

Das Fehlen einer eigentlichen Satrapenprägung läßt sich dadurch erklären, daß dafür keine Notwendigkeit bestand; denn die Geldversorgung war ohnehin gesichert. Im Osten galt das Silbermetall als Geld, in der Levante nahe der Küste zirkulierten bisweilen Provinzialmünzen, aber immer und überall finden sich Lokalprägungen sowie die vielen importierten griechischen Silbermünzen, teils als «Hacksilber», teils unversehrt.

## 3. Das Provinzialgeld (Tf. III 27-34)

Gab es Provinzialgeld im Perserreich, also Geld, das von einem Provinzialstatthalter mit der Nennung seines Namens und dem seiner Provinz und innerhalb derselben sowie für deren Geldumlauf emittiert wurde? Zwei Funde jüngster Zeit aus der Provinz Samaria (Tf. III 27-30) in der Satrapie Transeuphratesien erbrachten diese Evidenz[34]. All diese Voraussetzungen hat auch ein ähnliches Fundgut in der Nähe von Jerusalem in der Nachbarprovinz Judäa erfüllt (III 31-34)[35]. Bemerkenswert ist

---

[32] Gaugamela war gewiß eine entscheidende Schlacht, aber A. KUHRT, in: Achaemenid History 5, 1990 zeigt auf Grund der literarischen Quellen, daß Alexander auch danach noch in Schlachtordnung auf Babylon vorrückte. Um so verständlicher wird Mazaios' darauf folgende Kapitulation, zumal er nur Reste seiner Truppen in die Stadt bringen konnte und das Schicksal von Tyros und Gaza kannte.

[33] M.J. PRICE, Circulation at Babylon in 323 B.C., in: Mnemata. FS N. Waggoner, 1991, 69: «There is clear evidence that he blended his imperial coinage with others that were more fitted to the traditions of the areas over which he held sway».

[34] Y. MESHORER / S. QEDAR, The coinage of Samaria in the fourth century BCE, Jerusalem 1991, 13-17. Zum Titel des Gouverneurs von Samaria *pḥt* und des lokalen Präfekten *sgn* siehe F.M. CROSS, in: P.W. LAPP / N.L. LAPP, Dicoveries in the Wâdī ed-Dâliye (AASOR 41), Cambridge/MA 1974, 18, Anm. 10.

[35] Von der bereits weitläufigen Literatur s. insbesondere: L. MILDENBERG, Yehud: a preliminary study of the provincial coinage of Judaea, in: FS M. Thompson, 1979, 183-196 [hier S. 67-76]; Y. MESHORER, Ancient Jewish Coinage I, 1982, 13-34; D. BARAG, A silver coin of Yoḥanan the High Priest and the coinage of Judaea in the fourth century B.C., INJ 9 (1986-1987) 4-21; A. SPAER, Jaddua the High Priest, INJ 9 (1986-1987) 1-3; L. MILDENBERG, Über das Kleingeld in der persischen Provinz Judaea, in: H. WEIPPERT,

das Erscheinen des Gouverneurstitels, in semitischer Sprache und Schrift (Tf. III 33), und die Wahl von ganz bestimmten Bildern für dieses Silberkleingeld, die zusammen so sonst nicht vorkommen. Der Gouverneur hat so Provinzialgeld par excellence geschaffen. Die höheren Instanzen, die Satrapen oder gar die Großkönige, mögen dies gebilligt haben, geduldet wurde es von ihnen jedenfalls, wofür schon allein das Auftauchen des Königskopfes in der Zackenkrone (Tf. III 32) spricht[36]. Jedenfalls sind auch diese Provinzprägungen keinesfalls nur in den Zeiten der Schwäche des Reichs möglich gewesen. Die Drachme mit der Inschrift Yehud für Judäa neben dem «Gott auf dem Flügelrad»[37] ist ungefähr zur Zeit entstanden, als der Großkönig den Antalkidas-Frieden von 387 v.Chr. diktierte. Die Yehud-Kleinsilbermünzen setzten um 360, also vor dem Aufstand der phönizischen Städte, ein und dauerten, auch nach der Rückeroberung Ägyptens um 343 v.Chr., bis auf Alexander an. Die Yehud-Kleinmünzen der persischen Zeit errangen sich einen solch starken Sitz im Leben, daß sie noch unter Ptolemaios I. von etwa 300 bis 282 v.Chr. weiter geprägt wurden, und zwar mit dem Namen der Provinz Judäa auf Hebräisch und in hebräischer Schrift und mit seinem Portrait und dem seiner Königin Berenike I. (Tf. III 33-34)[38].

## 4. Der Münzimport (Tf. IV 35-38)

Das über ein Jahrhundert andauernde Einströmen griechischer Silbermünzen ins Perserreich[39] dürfte schon zu Kyros II. Zeiten, spätestens unter Kambyses, begonnen haben. Der Ausgräber von Ras Shamra / Ugarit, C.F.A. SCHAEFFER, hob dort einen Fund von 38 früharchaischen, meist makedonischen Stateren und einer frühen Tetradrachme von Abdera, die bereits um 525-520 v.Chr. in die Erde gekommen sein müßte[40]. Der starke Zustrom griechischen geprägten Silbergeldes, meist aus Athen, dauerte jedenfalls bis ins letzte Viertel des 5.Jahrhunderts und versiegte dann im Laufe des Peloponnesischen Krieges.

Die griechischen Münzen aus dem Westen gelangten als Silbergeld in den Osten und wurden dort wieder zum Silbermetall. Ihre Zerstückelung in kleine Brocken, das oft registrierte «Hacksilber», und ihre Verstümmelung durch tiefe Einhiebe, ja ihre begleitenden Barren oder kuchenförmige Klumpen sind dafür beredte Zeugen[41]. Dafür

---

Palästina in vorhellenistischer Zeit (HdA Palästina II 1), München 1988, 721-728.

[36] L. MILDENBERG, in: FS M. Thompson, 1979, 183-196 [hier S. 67-76], Pl. 22,12-13 [hier Tf. XXIII 12-13].

[37] Titel der Veröffentlichung von H. KIENLE (GOF VI,7), Wiesbaden 1975, des Unikums BMC Pl. XIX,1.

[38] L. MILDENBERG, in: FS M. Thompson, 1979, 183-196 [hier S.67-76], Pl. 23,13-15 [hier Tf. XXIII 13-15].

[39] Siehe D. SCHLUMBERGER, L'argent grec dans l'empire achéménide, 1953, 1-64.

[40] IGCH 1478; J.M.F. MAY, The Coinage of Abdera (540-345 BC), 1966, 96. – Eine ähnliche Münze findet sich im «Persepolis NE Deposit»: Nr. 36 in E. SCHMIDT, Persepolis II. Contents of the Treasury, Chicago 1957, 113f. Siehe J. KAGAN, An Archaic Greek Coin Hoard from the Eastern Mediterranean and Early Cypriote Coinage. Excursus A, NC 1994.

[41] Siehe D. SCHLUMBERGER, L'argent grec dans l'empire achéménide, 1953, 11. 17; C.M.

spricht insbesondere der Gesamtbefund des großen, vielgestaltigen Hortes von «Asyut» im persischen Ägypten, der um 475 v.Chr. in die Erde kam[42].

Zum Import der griechischen Münzen muß es gekommen sein, weil man das Silber als Metall im Perserreich benötigte und weil es dabei einfacher gewesen sein muß, es in Münzform zu beziehen. Hier erhebt sich aber die wesentliche Frage nach der Gegenleistung. Was erhielt man für das in den Osten gebrachte Silbergeld? Dienstleistungen sind ausgeschlossen. Persische Söldner im griechischen Westen hat es jedenfalls nicht gegeben. Man konnte an Weihrauch denken, der aus Südarabien über die autonome, im persischen Transeuphratesien liegende Hafenstadt Gaza in den Westen gelangte[43]. War der «Asyut»-Hort der Gegenwert für geliefertes ägyptisches Getreide? Oder bezahlte man gar für die importierten griechischen Silbermünzen mit persischem Gold, den Dareiken? Tribute und Steuern aus den westlichen Satrapien in Kleinasien und auf Zypern konnten jedenfalls in Münzen abgeliefert worden sein, die dann teilweise in den Schatzkammern verschwanden. Eine schlüssige Erklärung für den Massenimport aus dem Westen gibt dies aber noch nicht.

## 5. Das Lokalgeld (Tf. IV 39 - XI 103)

### 5.1. Die Eulen des Ostens (Tf. IV 39-42)

Von den vielen aus Griechenland importierten Münzen waren im 6.Jahrhundert die meisten aus Makedonien gekommen. Im 5.Jahrhundert überwogen die Eulen aus Athen. Offensichtlich wurden ihre gleichbleibende Erscheinung und Hochwertigkeit sowie die ständige Verfügbarkeit im Osten besonders geschätzt. Als der Zustrom zu versiegen begann, mußte man sie nachahmen, um die Nachfrage befriedigen zu können. Deshalb wurden von etwa 420 an vom Nil bis zum Indus und von Nordsyrien bis Südarabien die Eulen des Ostens geprägt. Ende des 5.Jahrhunderts müssen Produkte aus der attischen Münzstätte gemeinsam mit östlichen Prägungen zirkuliert haben. Damals wie heute waren diese Kopien von den Originalen nur schwer auseinanderzuhalten[44], wie von den publizierten Materialien aus dem Riesenfund von Tell el-Mashūṭa abzulesen ist[45]. Wenn man sich anfangs bemühte, die Athener Tetradrachmen möglichst genau zu imitieren, und dabei keinen Wert darauf legte, ihre Provenienz zu dokumentieren, so ging man doch bald dazu über, die Herkunft durch Einstempelungen, Ortsangaben oder Beizeichen zu betonen. Schließlich erhielt der

---

KRAAY / P.R.S. MOOREY, RN 10 (1968) 181-235; M. PRICE / N. WAGGONER, Archaic Greek Silver Coinage. The «Asyut» Hoard, 1975, Nrn. 11. 15. 30. 32. 44. 60. 142. 149. 160. 170. 257. 748. 806. 814. 860. 861.

[42] M. PRICE / N. WAGGONER, The «Asyut» Hoard, 1975, Pl. 1-31. Etwa die Hälfte der 873 Münzen dieses wichtigen Fundes sind verstümmelt.

[43] Siehe L. MILDENBERG, Akten Berlin 1988, 1990, 431-432 mit Karte auf Abb. 1 [hier S. 77-78].

[44] Vgl. TH.R. MARTIN, Sovereignty and coinage in classical Greece, 1985, 21-47, bes. 25.

[45] IGCH 1649 mit Literatur; ursprünglich etwa 7000 Athener «Eulen».

lokale Stempelschneider freie Hand, auf seine Weise den Kopf der Pallas Athene sowie die Eule zu gestalten. Der Einfluß des athenischen Geldes war so groß, daß nicht nur beide Bilder der Tetradrachmen gemeinsam, sondern diese auch einzeln kopiert wurden. Der Kopf der Pallas Athene in Tetradrachmen-Manier findet sich auf vielen Prägungen in verschiedenen Nominalen in Kleinasien und der Levante. Ähnliches gilt für die athenische Eule, die allein, ohne den Kopf der Göttin, erscheint. Besonders ist dies bei den philisto-arabischen Prägungen zu beobachten.

Die Eulen des Ostens waren ein geschickt konzipierter Ersatz für die athenischen Originale. Das eigentliche Lokalgeld[46] ist aber das Rückgrat des achämenidischen Münzwesens. Es gibt lokale Münzprägungen, die vor der persischen Herrschaft emittiert wurden, und solche, die viel später entstanden. Die Münzherren sind ebenso verschieden wie die Münzsorten - und Bilder. Es ist wie ein bunter Fleckenteppich, der sich über die riesigen Flächen ausbreitet, von der Westküste Kleinasiens über Zypern, die Levante und Vorderasien bis Nordafrika. Eine Konstante ist auszumachen: das Silbergeld in sehr großen bis sehr kleinen Einheiten überwiegt. Eine Gesamtdarstellung des Lokalgeldes liegt außerhalb der vorliegenden Strukturanalyse[47]. Bisher wurde das persische Münzwesen der altehrwürdigen ECKHELschen Methode unterworfen, indem man die einzelnen Münzstätten geographisch von West nach Ost und dann wieder von Ost nach West behandelte[48], also den Küsten des Mittelmeeres im Uhrzeigersinn entlang ging. Diesem für die griechischen Münzen entworfenen Schema folgten getreulich HEADs «Historia Numorum» und die meisten Sammlungs- und Auktionskataloge sowie das wichtige neue Gemeinschaftsunternehmen der «Sylloge Nummorum Graecorum», während BABELONs großer «Traité» anders geordnet war. KRAAY in seinen «Archaic and Classical Greek Coins» verbindet die geographische mit der chronologischen Ordnung[49]. In all diesen Werken werden also aus griechischer Sicht die Materialien,

---

[46] Der Begriff «Lokalgeld» betrifft die an einem bestimmten und genannten Ort durch eine lokale Behörde mit lokalen Bildern geschaffene Ausmünzung, wobei diese Behörde auch im Auftrag einer übergeordneten Amtsstelle gehandelt haben kann. Diese lokale Behörde prägt also in Ausübung ihres eigenen Prärogativs, ist demnach Münzherr in Ergänzung zum Großkönig, der das Reichsgeld prägt, und zum Gouverneur, der die Provinzialmünzen schlagen läßt. Der Begriff «Autonomie» trifft den Sachverhalt nicht genau; denn es gibt eklatante Unterschiede in der «Autonomie» der Selbstverwaltung. Die «Autonomie» der karischen Hekatomniden bei ihrer Münzprägung reicht nach der Auffassung des Schreibenden bis zur Souveränität (siehe Text unten S. 12). Davon kann bei der gesamten, großen Prägung des kilikischen Ateliers von Tarsos nicht die Rede sein. (Siehe Text unten 5.5). Lokalgeld sind beide Emissionen.

[47] In einem neueren und aufschlußreichen Versuch einer Strukturanalyse gliedert D. SCHLUMBERGER, L'argent grec dans l'empire achéménide, 1953, 25 den Gesamtbefund in zwei große Gruppen: «La monnaie d'empire» und «L'argent Grec dans l'empire jusqu'à vers 425». Alle anderen Prägungen im Reich der Achämeniden sind für ihn nur «monnaies complementaires». Diese im Grunde graekozentrische Sicht verwehrt dem bedeutenden Iranisten den Blick für Umfang, Eigenart, Struktur und Bedeutung der lokalen Prägungen im Westen. - Zu einer frühen Analyse siehe B.V. HEAD, The coinage of Lydia and Persia, 1876, 35.

[48] J. ECKHEL, Doctrina Numorum Veterum, 9 Bände, 1792-1839.

[49] In seinem Hauptwerk, das er ein Handbuch nennt, behandelt C.M. KRAAY, Archaic and

nämlich die Erzeugnisse der einzelnen Münzstatten im Reich der Achämeniden, vorgelegt. Über das Münzwesen bei den Persern ist damit noch nichts ausgesagt[50]. Bei allem sind die Gründe für den Einsatz des Lokalgeldes im persischen Reich offensichtlich. Die Möglichkeit zur lokalen Geldschöpfung ist überall dort gegeben, wo die finanziellen, organisatorischen und technischen Voraussetzungen vorhanden waren. Lokale Prägungen entstanden während rund 200 Jahren, also von Kyros II. bis auf Alexander III., an vielen Orten des Reichs[51]. Gesetze oder Verordnungen des Großkönigs wurden dafür nicht benötigt. Man ließ diese Geldschöpfung zu, ohne sich in Einzelheiten einzumischen, während der ganzen Dauer der persischen Herrschaft - zu Zeiten der Stärke und der Schwäche des Reichs.

## 5.2. Die Prägungen der Herrscher (Tf. V 43 - VI 58)

Die Stadtkönige auf Zypern emittierten ihre Münzen (Tf. VI 55-58) meist in Silber, in der Spätzeit bisweilen in Gold, aber immer ohne irgendwelche Einflußnahme seitens der achämenidischen Verwaltung. Bilder aus der Levante und der griechischen Welt stehen neben solchen aus der großen Insel selbst, auf der längst vor der persischen Zeit Geld geprägt wurde. Die Legenden sind zypriotisch und aramäisch, nicht griechisch[52].

Noch näher an die volle Souveränität der Münzschöpfung kommt die Prägung der Hekatomniden in Karien (Tf.V 43-48). Die Herrscher dieser Dynastie haben zwar stets als Satrapen gehandelt, nicht nur in Karien, sondern auch in Lykien[53], aber ihre lang andauernde und umfangreiche Münzprägung zeigt eigene, griechisch beeinflußte Darstellungen und nennt ihre Namen griechisch. Erscheinungsbild und Qualität

---

Classical Greek Coins, 1976, preface X «The Persian Empire» am Schluß als eine der «peripheral areas of the Greek World». Niemand wird die Bedeutung und den Einfluß der griechischen Münzen leugnen, aber mit dieser Ausrichtung auf das Geld der Griechen kann das achämenidische Münzwesen als ein Ergebnis der persischen Münzpolitik nicht erfaßt werden.

[50] Selbstverständlich ist die Darstellung des Materials eine conditio sine qua non, aber die Forschung ist ebenso der Deutung verpflichtet, was interdisziplinäres Arbeiten verlangt. Hier muß aufgezeigt werden, wie es zu dem einzigartigen Erscheinungsbild des achämenidischen Münzwesens kam und warum und worin sich die Münzpolitik des Perserreiches von der aller anderen Großreiche der Antike scharf unterscheidet.

[51] Die Schöpfung von Lokalgeld wurde in der Levante zu einer Notwendigkeit, als der Zustrom der athenischen Eulen versiegte. I. CARRADICE, The regal coinage of the Persian empire, 1987, 93 weist zudem darauf hin, daß das stärkere Aufkommen von lokalem Silbergeld in Kilikien zusammenfällt mit der offensichtlichen Produktionsverminderung der Sigloi um 400.

[52] BMC Cyprus, 1904, by G.F. HILL; C.M. KRAAY, Archaic and Classical Greek Coins, 1976, Nos. 1078-1110. Vgl. I. MICHAELIDOU-NICOLAU, Cyprus, in: A Survey of Numismatic Research 1985-1990, Vol. I, 1991, 91-93. – Die Herrscher der kleinen Königreiche zur Perserzeit sind mit griechischen und phönizischen Namen bekannt. Aber griechische Buchstaben finden sich nur selten: in Abkürzungen und nur in den Jahrzehnten vor Alexander, etwa in Salamis. - Vgl. J. WIESEHÖFER, Achaemenid History 4, Leiden 1990, 239-252, mit neuerer Literatur.

[53] P. FREI, Transeuphratène 3 (1990) 168, Nr. 26 mit Literatur in Anm. 34.

wirken unverändert von Anfang des 4.Jahrhunderts bis auf Alexander - in Karien und den angrenzenden Gebieten[54]. Obwohl die Hekatomniden auch Satrapen waren, prägten sie keine Satrapenmünzen. Und obwohl man sie als souveräne Münzherren auffassen kann, gehörte ihr Gebiet zum persischen Großreich. Demnach kann man ihre Münzen aus der eigenen Münzstätte Halikarnassos als souverän ansehen, aber Lokalgeld sind sie allemal.

Auch in der Münzprägung der lykischen Dynasten (Tf. V 49-52; VI 53-54) in der persischen Zeit[55] sind die Bilder griechisch beeinflußt, sogar direkte Kopien syrakusanischer Werke des ausgehenden 5. Jahrhunderts finden sich[56]. Die Legenden sind lykisch. Einzelne Münzserien in Lykien sind kurzlebiger als in Karien. Die lykischen Emissionen des 6. und 5. Jahrhunderts sind grenzüberschreitend[57], was im Laufe des zweiten Viertels des 4.Jahrhunderts kaum mehr vorkommt. Jedenfalls stellen die Dynastenprägungen Lokalgeld dar.

## 5.3. Lokale Elektron- und Goldprägungen (Tf. VII 59 - VIII 80)

Die Elektronprägung der Hafenstadt Kyzikos am südlichen Marmarameer (Tf. VII 59-67) ist eine res sui generis. Sie dauerte ununterbrochen über 200 Jahre, war umfangreich und kannte nur eine Metallzusammensetzung, ein Rückseitenbild, eine Herstellungstechnik sowie ein Haupt- und ein Nebennominal[58]. Die ständig wechselnden Vorderseiten zeigen eine Fülle verschiedenster Bilder in meist hervorragendem Stempelschnitt. Die Kyzikener[59] zirkulierten im weiten Schwarzmeerraum, aber auch im westlichen Kleinasien. Ihre Akzeptanz war allgemein.

Es ist nicht verwunderlich, daß sich die numismatische Forschung eingehend mit dieser erstaunlichen Münzgruppe beschäftigte[60]. So sammelte man das Material[61],

---

[54] BMC Caria etc., 1897, by B.V. HEAD; S. HORNBLOWER, Mausolus, 1982, 339-340 und explizit 155: «The Hekatomnids are unique at this date in issuing a regular, copious, dynastic coinage».

[55] In den letzten Jahrzehnten gab es große Funde und wichtige Publikationen auf diesem Gebiet. Neben BMC Lycia etc., 1897, by G.F. HILL, s. insbesondere: SNG H. VON AULOCK, 1957-1968; O. MØRKHOLM, JNC, 1964, 65-78; O. MØRKHOLM / J. ZAHLE, Acta Archaeologica 43 (1972) 57-113; L. MILDENBERG, CIN Rom 1961, II Akten, 45-55 [hier S. 105-109]; N. OLÇAI / O. MØRKHOLM, NC 1971, 1-29; O. MØRKHOLM / J. ZAHLE, Acta Archaeologica 47 (1976) 47-90; S. HURTER, in: FS M. Thompson, 1979; O. MØRKHOLM / G. NEUMANN, Die lykischen Münzlegenden, 1978.

[56] L. MILDENBERG, CIN Rom 1961, II Akten, Nrn. 20-29 und 32 [hier Tf. XXXVI]; N. OLÇAI / O. MØRKHOLM, NC 1971, Nos. 2-21. 272-388. 389-447.

[57] Im ägyptischen Fund von «Asyut», vergraben um 475, sind 42 lykische Münzen registriert, M. PRICE / N. WAGGONER, The «Asyut» Hoard, 1975.

[58] Die frühe Elektron-Prägung kannte auch kleine bis sehr kleine Teilwerte. Später kommen fast nur Statere und Hekten, also Sechstel-Statere, vor. Zwölftel-Statere sind dann äußerst selten.

[59] Kyzikenoi oder Kyzikener ist die gängige Bezeichnung für die Elektron-Statere. Der Schreibende benutzt Kyzikener für Stater und Hekte.

[60] Übersichtlich dargestellt von F. KIECHLE, Literaturüberblicke der griechischen Numismatik: Mysien, Troas, Aiolis, Lesbos, JNG 10 (1959-1960) 96-98. 121-128.

behandelte die metallurgische Zusammensetzung, die Wertverhältnisse zwischen den Kyzikenern und anderen Münzen[62], sowie Herkunft und Aussage der Bilder[63]. Auch die Erwähnung in antiken Quellen wurde vermerkt[64]. Man stellte aber diese wichtigen Einzeluntersuchungen an, ohne einige wesentliche Voraussetzungen und Zusammenhänge aufzuzeigen. War diese einzigartige Münzschöpfung nun griechisch oder persisch oder kyzikenisch? Wer war in persischer Zeit Herr in Kyzikos, der Großkönig, der Satrap des nordwestlichen Kleinasiens oder der Stadtmagistrat? Wer war Inhaber des Münzregals? Inwieweit war Kyzikos im 5.Jahrhundert von Athen oder Sparta abhängig?

Schon um 560-550 v.Chr. hat die Elektronprägung in Kyzikos begonnen, also vor der Eroberung des Nordwestens durch die Generäle von Kyros II[65]. Von etwa 540-535 an bis zum Eintritt der Stadt in den attischen Seebund um 445 war Kyzikos persisch, ebenso nach dem Antalkidas-Frieden von 387 bis auf Alexander, also insgesamt während etwa 150 Jahren von den ungefähr 220 Jahren der gesamten Münzprägung von Kyzikos[66]. Trotzdem ist von persischer Einflußnahme auf die Münzprägung nicht das Geringste zu bemerken. Andererseits zeigten sich auch die für die Ausmünzung Verantwortlichen vom persischen Umfeld nicht beeindruckt.

Zur Zeit der athenischen Vorherrschaft in den griechischen Städten Kleinasiens muß sich Kyzikos – trotz Tributzahlungen an Athen – einer weitgehenden Unabhängigkeit erfreut haben. Sonst ist das Einverständnis Athens mit der städtischen Elektron- und Silberproduktion gar nicht zu verstehen; hatten die Athener doch in anderen Städten die Münzprägung zugunsten ihrer Eulen rigoros eingeschränkt[67].

[61] Die korpusartige Behandlung durch H. VON FRITZE, Die Elektronprägung von Kyzikos, Nomisma 7 (1912) 1-38 ist immer noch grundlegend. Siehe auch K. REGLING, Der griechische Goldschatz von Prinkopo, ZfN 41 (1931) 1-46 und neuerdings insbesondere G.K. JENKINS / M. CASTRO HIPOLITO, A catalogue of the Calouste Gulbenkian collection of Greek coins II, 1989, 61-72.
[62] F. KIECHLE, JNG 10 (1959-1960) Nrn. 74. 79. 80 und 87.
[63] F. KIECHLE, JNG 10 (1959-1960) Nrn 103. 110. 114. 121 und 130. Siehe auch G.K. JENKINS, Ancient Greek coins, 1972, 96-97.
[64] G.K. JENKINS, Ancient Greek coins, 1972, 96; F. KIECHLE, JNG 10 (1959-1960) Nr. 139; M. LALOUX, RBN 2 (1971) 31-69.
[65] Im Jahre 546 hatte Kyros II. Sardis erobert und Kroisos besiegt. Dann überließ er seinen medischen Generalen Mazaros und Harpagos die Befriedung des kleinasiatischen Nordwestens, der unter Darius I. mit der Bezeichnung «Die Männer am Meer» erscheint. Kyzikos dürfte kaum vor 540 persisch geworden sein.
[66] Wie oben im Text dargelegt, war auch die Portraitprägung des Granden Pharnabazos in Kyzikos Lokalgeld. Das gleiche gilt für die von der Stadt ausgebrachte Münze in der Gemeinschaftsemission mit anderen Städten der Ägäis um 394-390 v.Chr., die auf der allen städtischen Ausgaben gemeinsamen Vorderseite Herakles als Kind mit den Schlangen zeigt (Tf. VIII 68 ). Auffällig ist, daß diese Gemeinschaftsprägungen dem persischen Gewichtsstandard folgen, und zu beachten, daß die von Kyzikos dafür eingesetzte Rückseite mit dem großen Löwenkopf über dem Thunfisch auch auf der ersten Serie der umfangreichen Prägung der Stadt im 4.Jh. von Tetradrachmen in rhodischem Gewicht erscheint. – S. KARWIESE, NC 1980, 1-27 datiert die Gemeinschaftsprägung 405-404, was für Kyzikos bedeuten würde, daß der Löwenkopf erst nach Jahrzehnten wieder erschiene.
[67] Seit über hundert Jahren beschäftigt sich die Forschung mit der Datierung des Athener Münzdekrets. Historiker, Epigraphiker und Numismatiker haben sich noch immer nicht

Die Gründe für diese Ausnahmebehandlung sind offensichtlich die wirtschaftliche Stärke der Stadt und ihre geographische Lage hinter dem Hellespont. Gute Beziehungen zu Kyzikos lagen im ureigensten Interesse Athens, selbst in Zeiten von dessen größter Machtentfaltung.

Die entscheidende, aber zu wenig beachtete Tatsache der Duldung der Kyzikener durch den Großkönig hat hingegen einen ganz anderen Grund. In der Forschung spricht man von einem Münzmonopol der achämenidischen Herrscher[68]. Nichts könnte falscher sein. Sie hätten die Produktion der Kyzikener kurzerhand abstellen können, wenn sie es gewollt hätten. Warum folgten die späteren Großkönige nicht dem monopolistischen Vorbild, das die Athener in der zweiten Hälfte des 5.Jahrhunderts gegeben hatten? Zwar verfügten sie über das von Darius I. eingeführte wichtige, ja unerläßliche Reichsgeld der Dareiken und Sigloi[69], aber die wirtschaftlich notwendige Ergänzung durch das Lokalgeld vom hochwertigen Elektron- und Goldstater herunter bis zum winzigen Tetartemorion in Silber ließen sie bewußt zu. Auf der Prägung des Reichsgeldes und der Duldung des vielgestaltigen Lokalgeldes beruhte die Münzpolitik der Achämeniden.

Gewiß ist die Münze in dem von den Griechen besiedelten westlichen Kleinasien entstanden, und es schließen die ersten Elektronmünzen von Kyzikos an dieses früheste Elektrongeld an (Tf. I 1-5). Es ist auch offensichtlich, daß die späteren Kyzikener durch ihre Bilder mit dem griechischen Westen verbunden sind. Aber Kyzikos war sehr lange eine Stadt im Perserreich, und die Kyzikener erfreuten sich des Wohlwollens der Oberherren. Aber genauso wesentlich ist, daß es das

---

darüber einigen können, ob es um 449 oder 425 v.Chr. erlassen wurde. Nur einige neuere Arbeiten seien genannt: E.S.G. ROBINSON, The Athenian currency decree and the coinages of the allies, Hesperia 8 (1949) 324-340; C.G. STARR, Athenian coinage 480-449 B.C. (1970) 68-72; Th.R. MARTIN, Sovereignty and coinage in classical Greece, 1985, 203-204; D.M. LEWIS, The Athenian coinage decree, in: I. CARRADICE (ed.), The regal coinage of the Persian empire (BAR.IS 343), 1987, 53-63; H.B. MATTINGLY, The Athenian coinage decree and the assertion of empire, id. 65-71. – In unserem Zusammenhang ist wesentlich, daß die Anordnung der Athener zwar nicht völlig und überall durchgesetzt werden konnte, aber doch meistens ihre Wirkung zeitigte, so in Lampsakos und Knidos, wie hier unten im Text erwähnt. Ganz außer Frage steht, daß das Münzdekret, wann immer es erlassen wurde, eine eminent politische, monopolistische Maßnahme war; so M.I. FINLEY, The Ancient Economy, Berkeley/CA - Los Angeles/CA 1973, 168: «... Athenian coins alone were to be current for all purposes in the Athenian empire ...»; H.B. MATTINGLY, in: I. CARRADICE (ed.), The regal coinage of the Persian empire, 1987, 65: «... a political and imperial manifesto ...»; C.M. KRAAY, Archaic and Classical Greek Coins, 1976, 71: «... it was a frankly imperial measure ...». Der Gegensatz zur Münzpolitik der Achämeniden könnte nicht größer sein.

[68] Vgl. F. KIECHLE, JNG 10 (1959-1960) 98f.

[69] Siehe oben im Text «1. Das Reichsgeld» [S. 3f[. R.N. FRYE, The history of ancient Iran, 1984, 116 betont: «It is not too much to suggest that the spread of money economy played an important role in the stability of the Achaemenid empire and continuing allegiance to it». Dies war allerdings erst möglich nach der Einführung von Dareike und Siglos, die anderthalb Jahrhunderte nach der Erfindung des gemünzten Goldes erfolgte. Wenn FRYE ebendort von der «introduction of payments, indeed coinage itself» als ein «Achaemenid phaenomenon» spricht, so kann man ihm nur folgen, wenn er die Wirkung von Siglos und Dareike nach 500 im Auge hatte.

Elektrongeld von Kyzikos schon geraume Zeit vor der persischen Eroberung gab und daß es seine außergewöhnliche Stellung der Voraussicht und der Tüchtigkeit der städtischen Autoritäten verdankt. In dieser Sicht sind also die Kyzikener griechisch, persisch und kyzikenisch. Aber festzuhalten gilt, daß eine solch hochwertige, unabhängige und aus der Münzstätte einer einzigen Stadt stammende Traditionsprägung, also Lokalgeld par excellence, nur im Perserreich verwirklicht werden konnte.

Die Hafenstadt Lampsakos in Mysien prägte Goldstatere im Gewicht der persischen Dareike[70] in der 1.Hälfte des 4. Jahrhunderts (Tf. VIII 72-76), also zu einer Zeit, als nach dem Antalkidas-Frieden die persische Herrschaft über den Westen Kleinasiens völlig gesichert war. Wie die Kyzikener waren die goldenen Lampsakener in dieser absehbaren Zeitspanne eine internationale Währung, und wie die langlebigen Elektronmünzen der nördlichen Hafenstadt waren sie Meisterwerke der Münzkunst[71]. Ja sie bilden eine noch prachtvollere und in sich geschlossene Serie, weil Bilder statt des quadratum incusum auf der Rückseite erscheinen[72] und man auf Teilwerte verzichtete. Eine goldene, völlig unabhängige Prachtprägung, selbstbewußt neben der offiziellen Golddareike des damals mächtigen Großreiches gestellt, erscheint uns Heutigen als eine solche Zumutung, daß man versteht, daß sie nur als eine privilegierte Ausdehnung der persischen Gold-Reichsprägung aufgefaßt wurde[73]. Dies ist aber eine Wertung aus heutiger Sicht, die außerdem den Extremfall gesondert betrachtet. Von einem Privileg nur für Lampsakos kann nicht die Rede sein. Die Achämeniden waren keine Kaiser oder Päpste, die einzelne Münzprivilegien als Geschenk oder Verkauf mit Brief und Siegel bekundeten. Sie kannten weder Monopol noch Prestige, ja sie ließen die Herren und Städte im Reich gewähren und sicherten so den Geldumlauf, was sich im Falle von Lampsakos in besonders eklatanter Weise zeigt. Wenn dies nicht oder zu wenig beachtet wird, bleibt das Münzwesen im Reich der Achämeniden unverständlich.

Die Ausprägung von Elektron-Sechstelstateren von Phokaia (Tf. VIII 77-78) und Mytilene (Tf. VIII 79-80) war von kürzerer Dauer[74]. Sie folgte den gleichen Normen wie in Kyzikos und diente dem Außenhandel im Nordwesten Kleinasiens. Eine

---

[70] Bereits der kyzikenische Elektron-Stater hatte der Dareike grosso modo im Wert entsprochen, vgl. F. KIECHLE, JNG 10 (1959-1960) 97, Anm. 12 mit Literatur. Es hat jedenfalls die achämenidische Verwaltung nicht gestört, daß die lokale Goldprägung von Lampsakos im gleichen Gewicht ausgebracht wurde wie die Leitmünze der Reichswährung, die Dareike.

[71] Man beachte die Monographie von A. BALDWIN, Lampsakos: The Gold Staters, Silver and Bronze Coinages, AJN 53 (1924) 1-76.

[72] Ein auf einer Vorderseite erscheinender Kopf in der Tiara herkömmlicher Art wird meistens als Portrait des Satrapen Orontas aufgefaßt, obwohl keine Namensnennung dies bezeugt. Selbst wenn Orontas feststünde, wäre dies nur ein Portrait unter vielen Bildern. Von einem wesentlichen Einfluß des persischen Umfeldes kann nicht die Rede sein, von irgendwelcher Anordnung aus Susa schon gar nicht. Zu Kleinmünzen von Kisthene und «Adramytheon» in Silber und Bronze, bisweilen mit OPONTA auf der Rückseite, siehe H.A. TROXELL, SNR 60 (1981) 27ff. Sie bezweifelt die Zuschreibung des Lampsakener Goldstaters an Orontas.

[73] C.M. KRAAY, Archaic and Classical Greek Coins, 1976, 249.

[74] F. BODENSTEDT, Die Elektronmünzen von Phokaia und Mytilene, Tübingen 1981.

Besonderheit liegt darin, daß die beiden Münzstätten alternativ prägten und sich so die Produktion teilten. Gewiß bot das achämenidische Commonwealth die Möglichkeit, daß sich die in Erscheinung und Wirkung bedeutende lokale Elektron- und Goldprägung entwickeln konnte, aber die Münzherren von Kyzikos, Lampsakos, Phokaia und Mytilene verdankten ihre unangefochtene Stellung auch ihrer eigenen Vision und ihrem Durchsetzungsvermögen. In Kyzikos hatte man frühzeitig die Möglichkeiten erkannt, die eine eigene hochwertige Münzprägung bot. Die anderen Städte folgten zu ihrer Zeit. Alle brachten es fertig, die laufende Nachfrage in vorbildlicher Weise zu befriedigen.

## 5.4. Das Silbergeld der Städte (Tf. IX 81 - XI 103)

Kyzikos kannte auch eine gewichtige Tetradrachmen-Prägung eindeutig lokaler Art im 4. Jahrhundert (Tf. VIII 69)[75], während Lampsakos erst später dazukam[76]. Hier soll nicht eine Beschreibung der Städteprägung in Kleinasien und anderen Reichsteilen gegeben werden. Uns beschäftigt die Bedeutung der lokalen Silberprägung im Geldwesen[77]. Die Städte prägten Geld, wann immer sie es benötigten, in der passenden Stückelung und mit eigenen Bildern und Legenden. Und die persischen Oberherren ließen auch dies zu, ganz im Gegensatz zu Athen, das in dem wohl kurz nach 450 v.Chr. erlassenen Münzdekret jedes nicht-attische Geld auf dem Gebiet des Seebundes verbot[78]. Die numismatische Forschung bietet einen Überblick über die Münzprägung der an der kleinasiatischen Küste und deren Randgebieten gelegenen Städte[79]. Neben dem Silbergeld der Städte gibt es bisweilen Bronzemünzen, die aber spät und selten sind. Die kleinasiatischen Münzen der Städte sind in Metall, Standard, Herstellungsart, Bilderwahl, Stempelschnitt und meist auch Schrift so griechisch, daß man sie mit Recht in der griechischen Münzkunde behandelt. Aber es ist unbegreiflich und unstatthaft, daß man oft nicht einmal erwähnt, daß sie so nur im Reich der Achämeniden überhaupt entstehen konnten. Man denke nur

---

[75] Im englischen Sprachgebrauch auch «civic» oder «municipal», im französischen «monnayage local».

[76] Zu Anfang des zweiten Jahrhunderts wurden lokale Tetradrachmen geprägt, vorher Alexander-Tetradrachmen, und schon in der ersten Hälfte des 5. Jh.s hatte es eine beachtliche Elektron- und Silberprägung gegeben. Auch hier in diesem Zusammenhang ist festzuhalten, daß in Lampsakos jede Münzschöpfung mit dem athenischen Münzdekret aussetzte.

[77] I. CARRADICE, The regal coinage of the Persian empire, 1987, 93 betont die gesteigerte Produktion lokalen Silbergeldes im Perserreich nach ca. 400. Vgl. oben Anm. 51.

[78] Siehe oben Anm. 67 und unten Anm. 80.

[79] Unersetzlich ist immer noch B.V. HEAD, Historia Numorum, ²1911 und E. BABELON, Traité des monnaies grecques et romaines. 2$^e$ partie, 1910-1912. C.M. KRAAY, Archaic and Classical Greek Coins, 1976, hat dem Perserreich ein größeres Kapitel gewidmet. SNG VON AULOCK für ganz Kleinasien und SNG Levante für Kilikien sind bewundernswerte Leistungen zweier Sammler und bieten fast unerschöpfliche Möglichkeiten für die interdisziplinäre Forschung.

an ein Beispiel, das karische Knidos ganz im Südwesten[80]. Um 530 v.Chr., also mit der Konsolidierung der persischen Herrschaft nach den Feldzügen von Kyros II. und seinen Generälen, setzte die Prägung von Drachmen (Tf. IX 81-82) und Halbobolen ein, wird auch nach der Unterdrückung des Ionischen Aufstandes von 499 v.Chr. und nach der Niederlage der Perser in der Seeschlacht bei Mykale von 479 v.Chr. weitergeführt, setzt aber schlagartig mit der Durchsetzung des athenischen Münzdekrets aus. Kennzeichnenderweise beginnt die Münzschöpfung von Didrachmen und Tetradrachmen (Tf. IX 83-85) mit den alten knidischen Bildern bald nach dem Friedensschluß unter Antalkidas 387 v.Chr. wieder und gedeiht unter dessen «Königsfrieden» jahrzehntelang.

Ähnlich ist die Entwicklung der Münzprägung in den großen ionischen Städte Ephesus und Milet sowie in Klazomenai. Die jüngsten riesigen Münzfunde bekunden eine erstaunliche Blütezeit von Wirtschaft und Kunst an der kleinasiatischen Westküste und auf den Inseln vom Königsfrieden bis zum Alexandersturm[81]. Man betont meist die Schwächung des Perserreiches durch den Satrapenaufstand um 375 v.Chr., vergißt dabei aber die erstaunliche, wiedergewonnene Stärke um die Mitte des Jahrhunderts, wofür auch die reiche und umfassende Münzversorgung in dieser Zeit spricht.

Aus der Fülle der Stadtprägungen im Osten Kleinasiens sei hier eine herausgegriffen, weil auch sie einen Extremfall darstellt, nämlich die Statere und Kleinmünzen von Nagidos an der kilikischen Küste (Tf. IX 86-87). Sie setzten erst um 400 v.Chr. ein, dauerten ohne sichtliche Unterbrechung bis in die Alexanderzeit, und sind in Bildwahl, Stempelschnitt und Legendenschrift durch und durch griechisch. In diesen Details unterscheidet sich also die Münzprägung dieser Küstenstadt grundlegend von derjenigen von Tarsos. Hat die achämenidische Verwaltung Nagidos eine besondere Münzproduktion in einer Nischenposition zugestanden? Vom Zugriff der persischen Granden scheint die Stadt und ihre Münzstätte fast ganz verschont geblieben zu sein, denn bisher kennt man nur ein Stempelpaar mit dem aramäisch geschriebenen Namen des mächtigen Granden Pharnabazos (Tf. IX 86)[82]. Jedenfalls haben sich die städtischen Münzherren vom persischen Umfeld nicht beeinflussen lassen. Nur den

---

[80] Siehe H.A. CAHN, Knidos – die Münzen des sechsten und fünften Jahrhunderts v.Chr. (AMUGS 4), 1970, 15-17 und zum «attischen Münzdekret» grundlegend 162-166.

[81] Dies gilt auch besonders für Kyzikos und Rhodos. Nur einige Funde wurden bisher verzeichnet: IGCH 1204, 1209-1210, 1212-1218 sowie Coin Hoards 1, 1975, 29 sowie 5, 1979, 24. --Für Milet ist bei B. DEPPERT-LIPPITZ, Die Münzprägung Milets vom 4. bis 1. Jahrhundert vor Christus (Typos 5), 1984 im Katalog ein Teil des Fundmaterials verzeichnet.

[82] SNG Paris, Cilicie (1993; Bearbeitung durch E. LEVANTE), 23 = BMC Cilicia XL. 10 = B.V. HEAD, Historia Numorum, ²1911, 726 = C.M. KRAAY, Archaic and Classical Greek Coins, 1976, No. 1013. – PH. LEDERER, Die Staterprägung der Stadt Nagidos, ZfN 41 (1932) Nr. 20, schließt vom Unikum («1 Vs.-, 1 Rs.-Stempel, 1 Stempelpaar, 1 Münze») auf «eine kurze Periode der Satrapenherrschaft» (S. 39. 42) in Nagidos, als ob es ansonsten unter eigener oder nichtpersischer Herrschaft gestanden hätte, etwa wie eine souveräne Enklave im Perserreich. Tatsächlich hat sich der Grande Pharnabazos der Münzstätte Nagidos bedient, wie er es auch in Kyzikos und Kilikien tat. Die beträchtliche Stadtprägung bleibt bei aller Sonderstellung lokales Geld, geduldet vom Großkönig, wie die vielen anderen örtlichen Prägungen.

persischen Münzfuß haben sie angewandt, um den Umlauf ihrer Münzen zu fördern[83].

Das Silberstadtgeld des kleinen Nagidos war einheitlich und in sich geschlossen, das des großen Tarsos etwas weiter östlich an der kilikischen Küste vielfältig und auf den Außenhandel sowie die Verwendung im Westen und Osten ausgerichtet, wofür die Münzfunde zeugen. Die Ausmünzung im persischen Tarsos dauerte hundert Jahre, war gegliedert vom Stater bis zum Obol und seinen Teilen, zeigte lokale, griechische und östliche Bilder sowie aramäische und griechische Legenden, kannte mehrere Auftraggeber und diente verschiedenen Zwecken. Die Voraussetzung für diesen großen und vielgestaltigen Münzausstoß war die schon im letzten Viertel des 5. Jahrhunderts tätige, technisch wohlausgerüstete städtische Münzstätte. Der Name der Stadt wird besonders betont, auch in Verbindung mit dem Namen von Gottheiten wie Nergal Tars[84] und Baaltars. Es war also lokales Stadtgeld[85], das die Münzstätte verließ unabhängig davon, wer die Auftraggeber waren: zuerst die städtischen Autoritäten (Tf. X 88-89)[86], dann die durchziehenden oder ansässigen persischen Granden (Tf. X 90 - XI 96.98) und sogar noch die ersten makedonischen Funktionäre (Tf. XI 97). Es wäre also nicht verwunderlich, wenn die tarsischen Bilder Alexanders Reichsprägung beeinflußt hätten[87]. Bedeutungsvoll ist jedenfalls, daß die Münzstätte von Tarsos sehr bald nach Alexanders Ankunft im Jahre 333 v.Chr. mit der Prägung seiner neuen Tetradrachmen begann und dafür dieselben Stempelschneider eingesetzt wurden, die in der Perserzeit dort gearbeitet hatten! Wichtig war die Tätigkeit der tarsischen Münzstätte für die Finanzierung der Militäraktionen der persischen Granden im 4. Jahrhundert gewesen. Begünstigt wurde diese Funktion durch die strategisch zentrale Lage der Stadt als Etappenort zwischen dem persischen Hochland

---

[83] Das Durchschnittsgewicht kommt dem von 2 persischen Sigloi nahe. Der Stater wird deshalb auch als «double siglos» bezeichnet.

[84] Siehe L. MILDENBERG, Nergal in Tarsos, in: FS H. Bloesch (AK Bh. 9), Bern 1972, 78-80 [hier S. 31-34].

[85] Obwohl bisweilen der Name *klk* oder *ḥlk* vorkommt, bedeutet dies nicht, daß es sich um eine «Satrapenprägung» handelt. Die Bilder sind tarsisch, nicht satrapisch. Außerdem können die häufigen Prägungsaufträge der persischen Granden an die Münzstätte Tarsos schon deshalb keine Emissionen der Satrapie Kilikien schaffen, weil einige von ihnen überhaupt nicht oder nur zeitweilig als kilikische Satrapen fungierten. Das einmalige Erscheinen eines sitzenden persischen Kriegers, in dem man vielleicht einen persischen Satrapen sehen könnte, unter Datames oder die auch nur einmal vorkommende, umschriebene Satrapenlegende gegen Ende von Mazaios' langem Wirken in Tarsos ändern an dieser Sachlage nichts.

[86] Für die unter dem Namen oder Titel Syennis laufenden kilikischen «Dynasten» soll das Vorderseitenbild eines Reiters stehen. Auf der Rückseite steht jedoch der Name der Stadt Tars oder Nergal Tars in aramäischer Schrift, was für lokales Stadtgeld spricht. Vgl. C.M. KRAAY, Archaic and Classical Greek Coins, 1976, 280.

[87] Für M.J. PRICE, The coinage in the name of Alexander the Great and Philip Arrhidaeus I-II, Zürich - London 1991, 27-29, ist die Tetradrachmen-Weltwährung noch im makedonischen «Amphipolis» um 336 entstanden. Für Tarsos gegen Ende 333 sprachen sich aus: O.H. ZERVOS, in: FS M. Thompson, 1979, 295-305 und NC 1982, 166-179; F. DE CALLATAY, RBN 1982, 5-25 und H.A. TROXELL, in: FS N. Waggoner, 1991, 49-61. Der Schreibende hat sich zu dieser Kontroverse in seinem Mazday-Artikel, INJ 2 (1990-1991) 8, Anm. 7 und 17, Anm. 42 geäußert [hier S. 45; 47].

und der kleinasiatischen Westküste, durch das fruchtbare Hinterland und eben durch die Verfügbarkeit eines hervorragenden Münzateliers[88]. Für die Bedeutung der tarsischen Münzproduktion und deren Ausstrahlung spricht auch die erstaunliche Tatsache, daß der persische Grande Mazaios, einst Herr über Kilikien und Transeuphratesien, den Baaltars noch in Babylon um 330 v.Chr. auf seine «Löwen»-Tetradrachmen (Tf. XI 99) setzt, nachdem ihn Alexander dort als Verwalter installiert hatte[89].

Die persischen Großkönige ließen es zu, daß in der phönikischen Hafenstadt Sidon[90] die «wichtigste Münzprägung in diesem Teil der Welt bis auf Alexander» entstehen konnte (Tf. XI 100-103)[91]: eine Produktion, ebenfalls während 100 Jahren, eine ungewöhnlich reiche Stückelung von sehr schweren bis zu sehr leichten Stücken, eine Arbeitsteilung mit Tyros[92], der zweiten großen Stadt am Meer[93], prägnante Bilder, eine umfangreiche Geldschöpfung für den städtischen Geldumlauf und insbesondere den Fernhandel auch in entlegene Gebiete[94]. In schroffem Gegensatz zu diesen eindeutigen Aussagen einer der wichtigsten Stadtgeldprägung im Perserreich stehen die rätselhaften Abkürzungen auf sidonischen Münzen. Die volle Bedeutung dieser phönizischen Buchstabengruppen und der Grund für diese seltsame Praxis bedürfen der Klärung. Der eindeutige Charakter dieser Emissionen als Stadtgeld wird besonders deutlich durch die Prägetätigkeit des erwähnten Granden Mazaios in Sidon. Wo vorher ein bis zwei Buchstaben im Münzrund standen, die als Abkürzungen von Königsnamen[95] gedeutet werden, steht jetzt der volle Name des Granden *mzdy*. Alles andere behält er in seiner Münzprägung bei, selbst nach der Niederschlagung der Tennes-Revolte[96]. Viel Tinte ist letztlich geflossen über die

---

[88] C.M. HARRISON, The Coinage of the Persian Satraps, 321 betont, daß jedenfalls Pharnabazos sich auf Kilikien für logistische Hilfe stützte und daß seine tarsischen Münzen einen Teil dieses Beitrages darstellten.

[89] Siehe im Text hier oben unter 2.

[90] Siehe J. ELAYI, Sidon – Cité autonome de l'empire Perse, Paris [2]1990, bes. 214 und 218.

[91] Dies das Urteil von B.V. HEAD, Historia Nummorum, [2]1911, 794.

[92] C.M. KRAAY, Archaic and Classical Greek Coins, 1976, 288.

[93] Die bedeutende, Jahrhunderte dauernde Münzprägung in Tyros begann bereits um 450.

[94] Die höheren Nominale gelangten nach Medien und Persien sowie in großem Ausmaße nach Ägypten: IGCH 1252. 1256. 1504. 1510. 1636. 1639. 1650. 1651. 1653. 1790. 1792. – Ungewöhnlich ist, daß die beträchtliche Kleinmünzprägung nicht nur in Sidon und Umgebung zirkulierte, sondern ihren Weg fand bis ins nördliche Phönizien sowie nach Syrien und Palästina, wobei ihr Anteil am Fund von Nablus besonders zu vermerken ist: IGCH 1483. 1485. 1486. 1488-1493. 1504 (Nablus). 1506.

[95] Jedenfalls wurde ein allfälliges Veto der persischen Verwaltung gegen die Nennung des vollen Namens eines Stadtkönigs der allgemeinen Münzpolitik der Achämeniden zuwiderlaufen. Ein solches Veto darf schon deshalb nicht angenommen werden, weil es eine Münzgruppe, aber mit abweichendem Gewicht, aus der sidonischen Münzstätte oder einer Nebenmünzstätte gibt, auf welcher der Name des Stadtkönigs Baana ausgeschrieben und abgekürzt gesetzt ist. Siehe L. MILDENBERG, Baana, ErIs 19 (1987) 29*-35* [hier S. 35-42].

[96] Hierzu D. BARAG, The effects of the Tennes rebellion on Palestine, BASOR 183 (1966) 6-12.

Zuordnung der Bilder, wobei der persische Einfluß besonders betont wurde[97]. Gewiß trifft dies für den bogenschießenden König und den «königlichen Helden» im Kampf mit dem Löwen zu, aber die sidonische Galeere und die Stadtmauer mit den Türmen sind eindeutig lokale Bilder. Diese Zusammenstellung entspricht durchaus der Bedeutung der Stadt mit ihrem besonderen Status wie gleichermaßen der pragmatischen Haltung der Achämeniden.

Schließlich eine Betrachtung der Münzprägung von Gaza[98], lokales Stadtgeld in Silber par excellence. Es findet sich dort auch nicht die Spur einer Einzelherrschaft. Weder gibt es einen Hinweis auf einen örtlichen Machthaber, noch auf eine fremde Dominanz. Gewiß führte die Weihrauchstraße nach Gaza als Endstation[99], und hat es dort wohl auch ein arabisches Handelskontor gegeben, aber arabisch war weder die Stadtbehörde noch die Münzprägung. Auch phönizische Präsenz ist anzunehmen, mehr nicht. Gewiß gehörte Gaza zu Transeuphratesien und damit zum persischen Reich. Dafür spricht nicht nur die Tatsache des zwei Monate dauernden Widerstandes gegen Alexander, sondern auch die strategisch wichtige Lage der Stadt an den Straßen zu Wasser und zu Land, nicht nur während der persischen Herrschaft über Ägypten. Die Münzprägung ist von langer Dauer und hat einen beträchtlichen Umfang, eine beachtliche Stückelung, eigene und fremde Bilder und insbesondere den allgegenwärtigen Stadtnamen in semitischen Buchstaben und die Bezeichnung des Stadtgottes Marnas durch den ersten Buchstaben M (*mēm*). Es ist eine eigenständige Geldschöpfung einer blühenden, international geprägten Hafenstadt für den internen Gebrauch und den Außenhandel. Münzherren waren die Stadtväter. Nicht nur in den Küstenstädten des Nordens Arados, Byblos. Tyros und Sidon, sondern auch im Süden in Aschdod, Askalon[100] und Gaza gab es von 450 bis 331 v.Chr. lokales Silbergeld in einem wichtigen Gebiet des Perserreiches. Die Großkönige waren mit ihrer Münzpolitik erfolgreich. Dabei zeigt die Struktur des Münzwesens, daß die Organe der Provinzen und lokalen Körperschaften die wichtigsten Verwaltungseinheiten waren, die Landschaften und Städte auch im Achämenidenreich noch das tragende Gerüst bildeten[101]. Demgegenüber waren die Bereiche und Funktionen der Satrapien nie so eindeutig bestimmt, wie man früher nach Herodots Nomoi-Konstruktion angenommen hatte[102].

---

[97] J. ELAYI / J. SAPIN, Nouveaux regards sur la Transeuphratène (1991) 14 sprechen von einer «iconographie d'inspiration perse».

[98] Siehe zum Folgenden L. MILDENBERG, Transeuphratène 2 (1990) 137-145 [hier S. 79-87]; ders., in: Akten des XIII. Internationalen Kongresses für Klass. Archäologie, 1990, 431-432 [hier S. 77-78], beides mit Abb.

[99] Vgl. L. MILDENBERG, Akten Berlin 1988, 1990, Karte: Abb. 1 auf S. 432 [hier Tf. XXIV].

[100] Es gibt auch eine nennenswerte, in die Region und ihr Münzwesen passende Münzserie mit der Legende *'āleph - nūn*, was als der erste und letzte Buchstabe des Stadtnamens Askalon aufgefaßt wird.

[101] E. LIPINSKI, Transeuphratène 3 (1990) 97: «Les provinces d'une satrapie correspondaient à des entités géographiques, ethniques et linguistiques, voire à des structures politiques héréditées du passé».

[102] Zu jüngeren, kritischen Betrachtungen von Herodots Liste der Nomoi siehe insbesondere P. CALMEYER, Transeuphratène 3 (1990) 113. 123 sowie T.C. YOUNG, Cambridge

## 6. Das späte Königsgeld (Tf. XII 104 - XIV 124)

### 6.1. Die Gruppe mit dem Königstitel (Tf. XII 104-106)

Mit einer kleinen Münzserie hat sich die Forschung seit anderthalb Jahrhunderten besonders eingehend beschäftigt[103]. Bilderwahl, Gestaltung, Gewicht und Funddaten weisen auf Kleinasien und 410-390 v. Chr. hin. Auf der Vorderseite der drei bisher bekannt gewordenen Tetradrachmen erscheinen bärtige Köpfe, bedeckt mit der Tiara, in hervorragendem Stempelschnitt. Zu den Tetradrachmen gehören Teilstücke: Drachmen, Halbdrachmen und Kleinbronzen. Es ist noch nicht möglich, die Köpfe zu benennen, ja selbst sie auch nur als gesicherte Portraits aufzufassen; denn es fehlt – im Gegensatz zu anderen vereinzelten Prägungen – die entscheidende Nennung der Namen. Die Rückseiten der drei bisher bekannt gewordenen Exemplare sind verschieden: Leier, Eule in Athener Manier, Großkönig im Knielaufschritt mit sidonischer Galeere als Beizeichen. Die Rückseitenlegenden hingegen sind einheitlich (*BAΣ*, *BAΣIΛ* und *BAΣIΛE*), was sich nur auf den Großkönig beziehen kann, der ja auch auf einer Rückseite erscheint. Durch seine ausdrückliche Nennung erweist sich die Gruppe als Reichsgeld, selbst wenn sie ein persischer Funktionär herstellen ließ. Es ist begreiflich, daß es für die Forschung verlockend ist, in diesen Tiaraköpfen die Portraits der mächtigen persischen Granden um die Jahrhundertwende wie Tissaphernes, Tiribazos und Pharnabazos zu suchen; nur bringt auch die verlockendste Theorie noch keine Gewißheit. Man sollte von dem einzigen Bildnis ausgehen, das eindeutig benannt ist, dem des Pharnabazos auf der oben beschriebenen Kyzikos-Emission (Tf. II 22-23; XII 107). Nun hat man den Kopf mit der Tetradrachme mit der König-Rückseite ebenfalls als das Bildnis des Pharnabazos gedeutet, obwohl die Gesichtszüge völlig verschieden sind. Es kann kein Zufall sein, daß die anderen Tiara-Köpfe nicht benannt sind. Der Grund ist in der zeremoniellen Darstellung des Königs und der Betonung seines Titels zu suchen[104]. Um 400 v.Chr. konnte selbst der mächtigste Grande gewiß seinen eigenen Namen nicht neben das als solches bezeichnete Königsbild setzen[105] und erst recht nicht seinen eigenen Kopf mitsamt

---

Ancient History 4, Nachdruck ²1992, 90 und E. LIPINSKI, Transeuphratène 3 (1990) 106.

[103] Grundlegend ist E.S.G. ROBINSON, NC 1948, 48-56.

[104] Es ist anzumerken, daß M.C. ROOT, The king and kingship in Achaemenid Art, 1979, 17, keinen Grund sieht, warum sich der Großkönig durch das Erscheinen eines Satrapenportraits bedroht fühlen sollte. Selbst wenn man voraussetzt, daß die Tiaraköpfe wirklich Portraits eines bestimmten Satrapen, also weder konventionelle Bilder noch solche anderer Funktionäre, darstellen, muß doch festgehalten werden, daß ein solches Satrapenportrait zusätzlich zum Bild und zum Titel des Großkönigs auf derselben Münze kaum denkbar ist.

[105] In der augenfälligen Betonung des Bildes und Titels des Großkönigs ist die vom Schreibenden gewählte Bezeichnung «Das späte Königsgeld» als Reichsgeld begründet. Daß der Königstitel in griechischen Abkürzungen gegeben ist, besagt nur, daß die Emission für Griechisch sprechende Benutzer gedacht war. Die bisher bekannt gewordenen drei Unikate haben ganz verschiedene Rückseitenbilder, von denen das mit der Eule

seinem Namen. Etwas ganz anderes ist die genannte Prägung in Kyzikos, die besagt, daß der dargestellte und benannte Pharnabazos die lokale Münzstätte benützt und lokale und unverbindliche Bilder verwendet, um Geld für die Soldzahlungen zu schaffen[106].

Die Faszination der Suche nach den frühen Portraits, die durch die Tiaraköpfe erleichtert wird, sollte aber nicht den Blick für die münzpolitische Bedeutung dieser Incerta verschließen, worüber bisher nichts zu lesen ist. Wenn es sich um Reichsgeld handelt, was der Schreibende vorschlägt, so wäre nach einer Unterbrechung von 100 Jahren wieder eine königliche Prägung eingeführt worden. Die persische Münzpolitik müßte man dann als so elastisch ansehen, daß neben den importierten Münzen und dem vielgestaltigen, fast flächendeckenden lokalen Geld durchaus die Möglichkeit gegeben war, für einen besonderen Zweck auch Reichsgeld zu schaffen, sofern sich dies als nötig erwies.

## 6.2. Die Gruppe mit dem König als Bogenschützen (Tf. XII 108-111; XIII 112)

Um 340 v.Chr. dürfte eine größere kompakte, aber auch enigmatische Serie von Tetradrachmen entstanden sein[107], Vorderseite: Großkönig mit Lanze und Bogen in Dareike- / Siglos-Manier im Knielaufschritt; Rückseite: Voluten auf granuliertem Grund. Auf einem Stück findet sich die ionische Legende *ΠΥΘΑΓΟΡΗΣ*[108], was als Beamtennamen auch in Ephesus vorkommt. Gewichtsstandard, Herstellungsart und einige wenige, wenn auch nicht völlig gesicherte Fundangaben weisen ebenfalls auf diese große Stadt hin. Nur ist durch den Großkönig auf der Vorderseite die Emission eindeutig als achämenidisch gekennzeichnet, und zwar wiederum als Reichsgeld. Von einer Satrapenprägung kann nicht die Rede sein; denn Namen oder gar Portrait, ja selbst der konventionelle bärtige Kopf mit der Tiara, fehlen. Bleibt die Lokalprägung; aber hier erscheint weder die Biene von Ephesus noch das Wappen oder Emblem irgendeiner anderen ionischen Stadt. Was bedeutet aber die rätselhafte Rückseite? Ist es die Landkarte von Mittel-Ionien mit der bogenförmigen Bergkette zwischen den Tälern des Hermos und Meander mit Ephesos an der Küste im Westen, und zwar in völlig vertikaler Sicht? In der beträchtlichen Ausmünzung mit breiter Streuung bis nach Medien und in die Sogdiana findet sich keine Legende außer dem

---

gegengestempelt ist. Dies spricht für eine kurzlebige Emission, vielleicht eine Probeprägung. Siehe dazu jüngst D. BELLINGER, der auf «problematische Zuschreibungen» an Tissaphernes hinweist, in: Die Bank 5 (1993) 308.

[106] Siehe oben Anm. 66.

[107] Behandelt von A.E.M. JOHNSTON, The earliest preserved Greek map: a new Ionian coin type, JHS 87 (1967) 66-94, Pl. 11, 1-6 mit ergänzenden Bronze-Kleinmünzen mit denselben Bildern.

[108] BMC Ionia, Pl. 31,12 = E. BABELON, Traité des monnaies grecques et romaines. 2ᵉ partie, 1910-1912, Pl. 89,6; weitere Exemplare ohne diese Legende ders., Traité, Pl. 89,7-12. – Bronzemünzen mit den gleichen Bildern (id., Traité, Pl. 89, 13) wurden in Ionien gefunden, die Tetradrachmen aber auch weiter im Osten (IGCH 1790 Malayer bei Ekbatana und 1822 am Oxus in Sogdanien).

genannten Personennamen Pythagores, auch wenig Beizeichen oder Abkürzungen. Dies hat dazu geführt, daß man die ganze Gruppe in der großen ionischen Stadt lokalisierte und annahm, der Condottiere Memnon der Rhodier hätte sie angeordnet[109]. Im Jahre 338 v.Chr. hatte sich Ephesus erhoben und Philip II. von Mazedonien zu Hilfe gerufen. Ein persisches Heer unter Memnon eroberte Ephesos zurück. Er hielt die Stadt bis zum Eintreffen Alexanders und mag die Prägung in der Zeit des *drôle de guerre*, also vor der Schlacht am Granikos, angeordnet haben. Allerdings sprechen die vielen sehr verschiedenen Stempel für Vorder- und Rückseite für eine länger andauernde und auch frühere Produktion. Als wesentliche Konstante bleibt das Bild des achämenidischen Herrschers in der deutlichen Zackenkrone mit Lanze und Bogen, womit die Ausmünzung als spätes Königsgeld zu verstehen ist.

### 6.3. Die Gruppe mit König und Reiter (Tf. XIII 114 - XIV 123)

Eine dritte späte Emission von Tetradrachmen ebenfalls im rhodischen Gewicht, begleitet von Kleinmünzen in Silber und Bronze, zeigt auf der Vorderseite den bogenschießenden Großkönig mit Köcher im Knielaufschritt in Dareike- / Siglos-Manier, bekleidet mit Krone und Mantel. Auf der Rückseite sprengt ein Krieger in persischer Tracht mit Tiara oder auch runder Kappe auf einem Schlachtroß im Galopp nach rechts, die Lanze schwingend[110]. In den Feldern finden sich Beizeichen sowie griechische und aramäische Buchstaben, vor allem aber auf der Königsseite die Legende *BA* für *ΒΑΣΙΛΕΩΣ* (Tf. XIV 121-123). Daß es sich auch hier um Reichsgeld handelt, ist deshalb offensichtlich, selbst dann, wenn man den Reiter als Satrapen auffaßt. Bei der chronologischen Einordnung dieser dritten königlichen Prägung[111] sollte man nicht nur die Tetradrachme mit dem karischen Zeus-Labrandeus (Tf. XII 108) und dem stehenden bogenschießenden Großkönig beachten[112], sondern

---

[109] Die von E.E.M. JOHNSTONE, JHS 87 (1967) 89 geäußerte Meinung, ein persischer General würde eher das Bild des persischen Großkönigs auf die Münzvorderseite setzen als ein Satrap es täte, beachtet die Tatsache nicht, daß die persischen Granden eben sowohl Satrapen als auch Heerführer waren. Sofern Memnon diese Münzen prägen ließ, so emittiert er als persischer Funktionär Soldgeld, wie vor ihm die Granden Tiribazos, Pharnabazos, Datames und Mazaios es getan hatten. – M. MITCHINER, Indo-Greek and Indo-Scythian Coinage I, London 1975, 18, Typ 17, legt die Prägungen unserer Gruppe 2 provisorisch nach Babylonien.

[110] Man vermerke ROOTS Vergleich, in: Achaemenid History 7 (1991) Anm. 8, Abb. 6 und 8 der Reiterseite mit Darstellungen auf Siegeln und ebenso ihre Kritik an der Kennzeichnung dieser Szene als ein Produkt griechischer Stempelschneider. Letzteres ist wohl die Folge des «hellénocentrisme», so J. ELAYI / J. SAPIN, Nouveaux regards sur la Transeuphratène (1991) 30, in der Interpretation eines einzelnen Münzbildnisses.

[111] Anepigraphische Münzserien bleiben für den Schreibenden Incerta, selbst wenn Zuschreibungen wahrscheinlich sind. Die numismatische Evidenz ist entscheidend, vgl. L. MILDENBERG, HSCP 91 (1987) 381-395 [hier S.253-262]. Hier im Textzusammenhang bezeichnet die Inschrift *BA* Königsgeld, eine Prägung des Reichs. Mehr kann nicht ausgesagt werden.

[112] E. BABELON, Traité des monnaies grecques et romaines. 2e partie, 1910-1912, Pl. 81,6 und BMC Ionia Pl. 31,1.

insbesondere eine breite Tetradrachme mit dem Großkönig, Bogen und Speer haltend wie auf der Vorderseite der vorigen «Landkarten»-Emission, aber mit der Rückseite des reitenden Persers (Tf. XIII 116)[113]. Diese letztere Prägung leitet also von den bisher besprochen beiden Gruppen zu der hier erörterten dritten Gruppe des Königsgeldes über, was bisher kaum vermerkt worden ist[114]. Man hat betont, daß das Königsbild in unserer dritten späten Gruppe auf der Vorderseite der Darstellung der Doppeldareiken unter Alexander sehr nahe kommt[115]. Beide Prägungen liegen allerdings nicht weit auseinander, aber bei der großen dritten Gruppe handelt es sich um spätes Königsgeld vor Alexander. Dafür sprechen Technik, Metall, Gewicht, Bilder und die Legende, die den persischen König bezeichnet.

## 6.4. Die Gruppe der Eulen-Tetradrachmen des Artaxerxes III. als Pharao
### (Tf. XIV 124)

Aufschlußreich ist eine vierte Emission: Das Königsgeld von Artaxerxes III. Im Jahre 1954 wurde die erste östliche Eulentetradrachme mit einer demotischen Legende bekannt gemacht. Die zweite wurde 1973 veröffentlicht. Neuerdings tauchten noch drei weitere Exemplare in Auktionskatalogen auf. Und schließlich fanden sich 8 weitere in einer jüngsten Fundpublikation[116]. Dies alles zeigt schon, daß wir es mit einer relevanten ägyptischen Großgeld-Emission zu tun haben, die um so bemerkenswerter ist, als die Legende «Artaxerxes Pharao»[117] lautet und als Münzstätte Memphis angenommen werden kann. Der Rückeroberer des Nillandes Artaxerxes III. Ochos hat also nach 343 v.Chr. als persischer Großkönig und ägyptischer Pharao sein Reichsgeld für die wiedergewonnene Satrapie geprägt. Artaxerxes Memnon II. kann der Münzherr nicht gewesen sein, denn er selbst hatte Ägypten zu Anfang seiner Regierungszeit verloren. Es wäre aus vielen Gründen auch nicht zu zweifeln gewesen, daß diese Eulen in die 2.Hälfte des 4. Jahrhunderts gehören, wenn überhaupt kein Name darauf gestanden hätte[118]. Man hat diese erstaunliche Emission mit der Notwendigkeit zu erklären versucht, Söldner für die Rückeroberung zu bezahlen. Das würde voraussetzen, daß man Demotisch verstehende Truppen im syrisch-palästinischen Aufmarschgebiet hätte anwerben können, was nicht möglich gewesen wäre. Hätte Ochos für Soldzahlungen an Griechen geprägt, so hätte er seinen griechischen

---

[113] Die Stempelkoppelung, veröffentlicht von F. IMHOOF-BLUMER, aus seiner Sammlung, in: Kleinasiatische Münzen, 1901-1902, Tf. 19, 23; auch ders., SNR 1906, 266, Nr. 12, und E. BABELON, Traité, 162, Nr. 117 («Euagoras II»).

[114] Die Ausnahme dürfte eben F. IMHOOF-BLUMER, Kleinasiatische Münzen, 518f (Anm.) sein.

[115] D. SCHLUMBERGER, L'argent grec dans l'empire achéménide, 1953, 58-62.

[116] M.J PRICE, More from Memphis and the Syria 1989 Hoard, in: FS R. Carson – K. Jenkins, London 1993, 31-35 (mit Lit.) und Pl. IX-X.

[117] A.F. SHORE, The demotic inscription of a coin of Artaxerxes, NC 1974, 5-8.

[118] Die von M. PRICE, in: FS R. Carson – K. Jenkins, 1993, 31-35 aufgezeigte Fundevidenz ist eindeutig. Dazu kommen die Bilder eben der demotischen Tetradrachmen und die Tatsache der Fortsetzung der Artaxerxes III.-Serie durch die Prägungen der letzten persischen Satrapen in Ägypten, Sabakes und Mazakes (siehe unten Anm. 123).

Königstitel verwendet. Außerdem dachte man an Donationen an ägyptische Würdentrager nach der Rückeroberung[119]. Im letzteren Falle würde das in Memphis geprägte persische Reichsgeld also doch für politische Zwecke innerhalb der Satrapie eingesetzt worden sein. Dies gilt auch dann, wenn man die Prägung als eine unmittelbare Machtdemonstration des neuen Pharao auffaßt[120]. Jedenfalls ist nicht einzusehen, warum die Prägungen nicht auch der allgemeinen Verwaltung und der Wirtschaftsentwicklung hätten dienen können. Wenn man letzteres verneint, gibt die Verwendung des Demotischen keinen Sinn. Wenn man es – wie der Schreibende – eindeutig bejaht, zeigt sich auch hier der praktische Sinn und die Elastizität der achämenidischen Münzpolitik. Während 150 Jahren stand nie der Name eines Großkönigs auf dem Reichsgeld, weil man es als solches ohnehin erkannte. Jetzt, nachdem man Ägypten zurückerobert hatte, in dem nur die athenischen Eulen gängig waren[121], ließ der Großkönig sie eben prägen und seinen Namen auf Demotisch daraufsetzen und nicht in Aramäisch, der Sprache der Reichskanzlei, damit der Benutzer leicht erkennen konnte, wer das alt-neue Geld herstellen ließ. Tatsache, Legende und Erscheinungsbild dieser Emission ergänzen andere Sachquellen, die ein «normales Leben»[122] unter Ochos aufzeigen, und widerlegen schon allein die negativen Berichte über ihn in Ägypten, wie sie die antiken Historiker überliefern[123].

---

[119] M. PRICE, in: FS R. Carson --K. Jenkins, 1993, 31.

[120] A.S. WALKER, in: Leu 52 (1991) 91, Nr. 125.

[121] IGCH 1644 Asyut, Vergrabung um 475, mit 127 Athener Tetradrachmen; 1649 Tell el-Maskhouta, Vergrabung um 400, mit bis zu 7000 Athener Tetradrachmen des 5.Jh.s; 1663 Tell el-Athrib, Vergrabung im 4.Jh., 109 Athener Tetradrachmen und 130 Athener Tetradrachmen-Imitationen. – T.V. BUTTREY, Akten des 9. Internationalen Numismatischen Kongresses, Louvain-La-Neuve / Luxembourg 1982, 130 schließt auf eine planmäßige und kontrollierte Münzprägung von Athener Eulen im späten pharaonischen Königreich im 4.Jh. vor der Rückeroberung durch Ochos.

[122] Siehe E. BRESCIANI, CHI 2 (1985) 526: «The Lille demotic papyrus 27 on the other hand depicts Egypt during the time of Artaxerxes as enjoying a normal life, with temple possessions remaining untouched».

[123] Auch der von Ochos eingesetzte Satrap Sabakes prägte für Ägypten Athener Eulen, die seinen Namen auf Aramäisch tragen ṣwyk (ṣādē, wāw, yōd, kaf). Als Münzstätte gilt seit E.T. NEWELL, Numismatic Notes and Monographs 82 (1938) 72-75. 82-88 Memphis. Der Satrap fiel bei Issus. Die Ausmünzung dürfte zwischen 335 und November 333 erfolgt sein. Auf ihn folgte Mazakes mzdk, der die Eulenprägung für Ägypten bis zu seiner Kapitulation vor Alexander (Arrian, Anabasis 3,1,2) fortsetzte. Man nimmt auch an, da später unter ihm Eulen in Babylonien geprägt wurden, siehe O. MØRKHOLM, Early Hellenistic Coinage (1991) 57. Ganz am Ende des Reichs kommt es also doch noch zu einer wirklichen, relevanten Prägung für eine Satrapie. Der höchste Würdenträger prägte mit seinem Namen für den ägyptischen Geldumlauf Großsilber-Münzen, die auch für Soldzahlungen verwendet werden konnten. Um eine lokale Emission kann es sich nicht handeln: das wichtige, begleitende Kleingeld fehlt; die Bilder sind attisch, nicht lokal; kein Stadtnamen oder Wappen erscheint; eine städtische Silber-Münzstätte wie etwa in Tarsos gab es nicht, da die einheimischen Pharaonen nur Gold, und auch dies nur gelegentlich und mit geringem Ausstoß, herausgaben. Von Provinzialgeld kann auch nicht die Rede sein, da Sabakes und Mazakes Satrapen und keine Gouverneure waren und Ägypten immer eine große Satrapie, keine Provinz. Ochos' Eulen erweisen sich andererseits durch die Nennung seines Pharaotitels eindeutig als Königsgeld. Zum Obigen siehe neben M.J. PRICE, in: FS R. Carson – K. Jenkins, 1993, 31-35 und ders., FS N. Waggoner, 1991, 66-

## Zusammenfassung

Unsere Strukturanalyse zeigt eine vielfältige und gut funktionierende Münzschöpfung von Darius I. bis Alexander. Die Großkönige haben mit der Prägung ihres Reichsgeldes achämenidischer Art sehr wohl von ihrem Prärogativ Gebrauch gemacht, wenn es notwendig war, aber auch gleichzeitig mit der Zulassung des Münzimportes, der Schaffung von Silberkleingeld durch die Provinzgouverneure[124] und vor allem durch die Duldung der allgegenwärtigen Lokalprägungen verschiedenster Art eine gute Geldversorgung ermöglicht. Dies geschah in einem Großreich zu Zeiten, als die Athener, oft erfolgreiche Gegner der Achämeniden, ein Münzmonopol in ihrem Herrschaftsgebiet strikt durchsetzten, und im Westen durch den Münzexport und die virtuose Handhabung des Zwangsumtausches und der Abwertungen die Kassen gefüllt wurden[125]. Die persische Münzpolitik als Schwäche auszulegen, wäre ebenso unstatthaft wie die Vermutung zu äußern, man habe dort die Regeln des Geldwesens nicht begriffen oder vernachlässigt. Man hat vielmehr bewußt entschieden, wichtige, ergänzende Funktionen den lokalen Körperschaften zu überlassen. Man hat bewußt den freien Handel gefördert[126]. Dies war kein Unwissen, sondern Klarsicht, keine Schwäche, sondern Stärke des in vielem bewundernswerten persischen Reiches.

---

69 auch G. LE RIDER, SM 85 (1972) 3 sowie H. NICOLET-PIERRE, in: FS M. Thompson, 1979, 221-230, Pl. 25-26.

[124] In dem Nablus-Hort (IGCH 1504, Vergrabung um 332) fand sich ein Viertelobol (Y. MESHORER / S. QEDAR, The coinage of Samaria, 1991, No. 57) mit den Bildern aus der – in der Sicht des Schreibenden – dritten, wichtigen Gruppe des Königsgeldes. Dieser Viertelobol ist in mehrfacher Hinsicht bemerkenswert. Die winzige Münze folgt den gleichartigen Königstetradrachmen, ist also später. Die großen Stücke dürfen wiederum wegen ihrer im Text erwähnten Ähnlichkeit mit den Alexander-Doppeldareiken nicht zu früh angesetzt werden. Es gibt ferner in Samaria den Großkönig in den verschiedensten Münzbildern, als Bogenschützen aber bisher nur in zwei Stempeln; mit dem lanzenschwingenden Reiter nur in dem erwähnten einzigen Stempelpaar. Nirgends in der gesamten, vielgestaltigen Prägung findet sich aber der Königstitel, weder ausgeschrieben noch abgekürzt, was den entscheidenden Unterschied zwischen Provinzial- und Königsgeld ausmacht. Der Provinzgouverneur hatte freie Hand in der Wahl seiner Bilder, die Verwendung des Königstitels hatte er zu unterlassen.

[125] Der Münzexport der Griechen ins Perserreich im 5. und 4. Jh. muß für die Lieferanten lukrativ gewesen sein, sonst ist Umfang und Dauer nicht verständlich. Das hier im Text und in den Anmerkungen besprochene athenische Münzdekret ist eine eindeutige Zwangsmaßnahme, und die Produktion des minderwertigen Geldes in Athen nach dem Peloponnesischen Krieg ein frühes Beispiel einer Abwertung zu Lasten der Bevölkerung.

[126] Für Knidos siehe hierzu H.A. CAHN, Knidos – die Münzen des sechsten und fünften Jahrhunderts v.Chr., 1970, 15 mit der Feststellung: «Die Blüte der Stadt wurde durch die Perser nicht geknickt».

# Nergal in Tarsos. Ein numismatischer Beitrag

## (Tf. XIV)[1]

Über die Erscheinungsformen des altbabylonischen Gottes Nergal in der phönizischen und graeco-römischen Kultur ist ausführlich von berufener Seite gehandelt worden[2]. Nergal ist in Tyros als Melqart, also als der Baal der Stadt, aufgefaßt worden, und Melqart wiederum hat sich dem griechischen Herakles angeglichen. Alle drei Gottheiten haben wenigstens zwei Eigenschaften gemeinsam: einmal symbolisieren sie das Werden und Vergehen, und zum andern sind sie die Beschützer der Menschen gegen wilde Tiere, insbesondere Bezwinger der Löwen[3]. Nun ist das Kultbild des Nergal bisher mit einiger Sicherheit nur in der Gravur eines Siegelzylinders erkannt worden. Der Gott steht hier, bewaffnet mit Schwert und Doppelkeule, über einem auf einer Bergkuppe liegenden menschlichen Körper. Je eine Darstellung in Terrakotta und Stein hat man auf Nergal gedeutet[4]. Nicht befaßt hat man sich bisher mit der numismatischen Evidenz. Wo aber wären Münzen zu suchen, die das Kultbild eines semitischen Gottes zeigen würden? Doch wohl in den Städten und Gebieten, in denen aramäische Münzinschriften starken Einfluß aus dem vorderen Orient verraten, also in den Handelsplätzen und den Küstenebenen des nordöstlichen Mittelmeeres[5]. Dort haben sich um die Mitte des ersten vorchristlichen Jahrtausends lokale autochthone Lebensformen mit westlichen und östlichen Kulturen vermischt.

In der Tat verraten die Silbermünzen des kilikischen Hauptortes Tarsos am Kydnos aus der zweiten Hälfte des fünften Jahrhunderts nicht nur den Namen des Nergal, sondern gleichzeitig auch sein Bild. Schon E. BABELON hat zuerst 1893[6]

---

[1] Wertvolle Hinweise erhielt ich von G. Kenneth Jenkins. Ihm und einem Tessiner Sammler bin ich für die Erlaubnis verbunden, hier wichtige Stücke erstmalig zu veröffentlichen. Zu danken habe ich H. von Aulock für die Erlaubnis, eine seiner Münzen abzubilden. Die Photographien wurden hergestellt von Silvia Hurter und in den Ateliers des Britischen Museums sowie der Staatlichen Münzsammlung München und des Schweizerischen Landesmuseums Zürich. G. Le Rider erlaubte die Publikation des Pariser Stückes Tf. XIV 1.

[2] H. SEYRIG, Antiquités syriennes, Syria 24 (1944-1945) 62-80. Wir verdanken dieser grundlegenden Studie wichtige Anregungen und Hinweise.

[3] H. SEYRIG, Syria 24 (1944-1945) 71ff.

[4] H. SEYRIG, Syria 24 (1944-1945) 74,1.

[5] Man denke an Issos, Mallos, Nagidos, Soli und Tarsos in Kilikien, dann an Kition und Lapethos auf Zypern (nicht Salamis: die Buchstaben auf den Kleinmünzen BMC Cyprus, 1904, XCIXf sind nicht semitisch), ferner an Hieropolis-Bambyce in der Cyrrhestica.

[6] E. BABELON, Les Perses achéménides, Paris 1893, 18, Pl. 3,6.

und dann 1910[7] einen tarsischen Drittelstater mit einem halben Flügelpferde und einer stehenden Figur beschrieben und dessen aramäische Legenden als *trz* = TaRZ = Tarsos lesen wollen (Tf. XIV 1). H. VON AULOCK erkannte 1966[8], daß die Inschrift aus vier, nicht aus drei Buchstaben bestand. Er las sie zwar von unten nach oben, fand aber trotzdem die fast richtige Wiedergabe als *lgrnr* Da ihm der Sinn nicht klar war, setzte er ein Fragezeichen hinter seine Lesung (Tf. XIV 2). Wenn man aber die Legende von oben nach unten und von innen her liest, erkennt man leicht: *nrgl* = NeRGaL, also unseren Nergal. Dieser Name als Bezeichnung findet sich neben einer stehenden bärtigen Gestalt, die einen langen Mantel trägt und einen Bogen in der Linken, sowie einen aufgestützten Stab in der Rechten hält. Im Britischen Museum wird seit 1806 ein ähnliches, meines Wissens unpubliziertes Stück aufbewahrt (Tf. XIV 3). Es zeigt die Protome eines gehörnten Greifen und die gleiche stehende Figur. Auffällig an der Kleidung ist hier nur der große mittlere Gewandzipfel. Die Legende ist wiederum klar: *lnrgl* = LeNeRGaL = Dem Nergal.

Glücklicherweise erwarb das Britische Museum auch die tarsische Münze, die nun den entscheidenden ikonographischen und epigraphischen Beitrag zu unserem Thema leistet (Tf. XI 88). Es handelt sich um einen bisher unpublizierten Stater[9]. Die Vorderseite zeigt einen bärtigen bekleideten Reiter[10], der eine Blume hält. Auf der Rückseite steht nun die uns schon bekannte bärtige Gestalt von vorn, in den Mantel mit dem charakteristischen Zipfel gehüllt. Wiederum hält sie in der Linken den Bogen und in der Rechten den langen Stab. Hier aber hat sie sich nun auf einen nach rechts kauernden Löwen gestellt. Links im Feld ein Baum, der Blüten oder Früchte trägt. Alle diese Attribute weisen auf Nergal, den Gott des Krieges und der Jagd[11], den Bändiger der Löwen und im gleichen Maße den Gott der Fluren[12]. Rechts im Felde steht in prachtvoller aramäischer Kursive geschrieben, was wir sehen: *nrgl* = Nergal.

Unter diesem Namen steht nun aber erstmals auch derjenige der Stadt: *trz* = TaRZ = Tarsos. Die numismatische Evidenz bezeugt also Ende des fünften Jahrhunderts[13] einen Nergalatars, einen Nergal von Tarsos, bevor in den siebziger

---

[7] E. BABELON, Traité des monnaies grecques et romaines 2,2, 1910, 525, Pl. 106,5.

[8] Bei der Veröffentlichung seines Exemplars: SNG H. VON AULOCK 13 (1966) No. 5910.

[9] Publikation durch G.K. JENKINS im British Museum Quarterly in Vorbereitung.

[10] Den gleichen Reiter, aber nach links gewandt, zeigen die Statere E. BABELON, Traité des monnaies grecques et romaines 2,2, 1910, Pl. 106,1 = G. MACDONALD, Catalogue of Greek Coins in the Hunterian Collection 2, 1901, Pl. 60,7, sowie E. BABELON, Traité, Pl. 106,3 (Paris) und Pl. 106,6 = G. MACDONALD, op.cit., Pl. 60,6. Das letztere Stück bringt den aramäischen Stadtnamen von Tarsos.

[11] Der Kult des vielgeschichtigen Gottes Nergal kam von Zweistromland über Syrien und das nördliche Palästina nach Tarsos; H. SEYRIG, Syria 24 (1944-1945) 70,4 bringt dafür eine Fülle von Belegen, darunter auch die Bibelstelle 2.Kön. 17,30.

[12] Sehr gut zu diesen Eigenschaften des Nergal und in die frühe autochtone Münzprägung von Tarsos würden die Incerta G. MACDONALD, Catalogue of Greek Coins in the Hunterian Collection 3, 1905, Pl. 77,15/16 passen – nach Gewicht und Typen: Löwenbändiger mit Keule (Herakles ?), aber mit der Bogentasche, mit welcher der Held hier nichts anfangen könnte, und Kuh, ihr Kälbchen säugend.

[13] Grundlegend für die Chronologie der frühen Prägungen von Tarsos C.M. KRAAY, The Celenderis Hoard, NumChron 1962, 1ff. – KRAAY datiert die uns interessierende homo-

Jahren des vierten Jahrhunderts der Baaltars, der Baal von Tarsos, auf den Silbermünzen der persischen Satrapen erscheint. Der Olymp der Stadt bevölkert sich später noch mit anderen Gottheiten, deren Gestalten und Namen uns die Münzen verraten, so mit Ana[14] und Sandan[15]. Die drei Silbermünzen, die wir bisher besprachen, zeigen uns also den gleichen Gott in Namen und Gestalt. Sie bilden zudem eine in Gewicht, Stil und Typen homogene Gruppe, deren Zuschreibung an Tarsos nun gesichert ist.

In jüngster Zeit ist nun eine weitere, ebenfalls unpublizierte Großsilberprägung aufgetaucht, durch die das bisher gewonnene einheitliche Ergebnis gewandelt und bereichert wird. Sie dürfte zwei bis drei Jahrzehnte später entstanden sein als der soeben besprochene Stater. Es darf uns bei der Erscheinung des Nergal von Tarsos nicht wundern, wenn wir auf eine veränderte Darstellung des Gottes stoßen. Von den tarsischen Münzen mit solchen Bildern kurz vor und nach der Wende vom fünften zum vierten Jahrhundert kennen wir bisher nur die wenigen aufgeführten Beispiele. Deshalb müssen diese Serien aber keinesfalls klein und unbedeutend gewesen sein. Gewiß sind aber bei der elektischen Stadtkultur von Tarsos vielgestaltige Bilder des gleichen Gottes innerhalb der bestimmten Zeitperiode von einigen Jahrzehnten durchaus zu erwarten. Dazu mögen andere und verschiedene Kultbilder in den benachbarten Zentren gekommen sein. Die Münzbeamten und Stempelschneider sind von dieser Vielfalt sicher nicht unbeeinflußt gewesen.

Der zweite neue Stater von Tarsos (Tf. XIV 5), heute in einer Privatsammlung, ist in der Tat von ganz anderer Art als die bisher behandelten Stücke. Er hat einen

---

gene Gruppe E. BABELON, Traité des monnaies grecques et romaines 2,2, 1910, Pl. 106, 1-7 und 10 (nicht: 8/9 mit ihrem runden Incusum) nach den Stateren mit der grossen Ähre, die für ihn die frühesten Prägungen von Tarsos und um 410 entstanden sind. Als ein Argument für diesen Ansatz nennt er unseren Reiter, der auf den späteren Stateren mit dem Hopliten wieder auftaucht. Die beiden Reiterdarstellungen sind aber grundverschieden. – Wir möchten das Fehlen unserer Gruppe im Funde von Kelenderis damit erklären, daß sie eben etwas früher anzusetzen ist als die Ähren-Statere. Dafür spricht nicht nur die Tatsache, daß die grosse Ähre später in der Hopliten-Gruppe wieder erscheint, sondern vor allem der dicke Schrötling, der Stil und eben auch die Vorderseite mit unserem Reiter. Da er ohne Tiara ist und eine Blume hält, handelt es sich um den lokalen Herrscher von Tarsos, einen noch selbständigen Vasallen des persischen Grossreiches.

[14] SNG H. VON AULOCK, Nos. 5947-5950; BMC Cilicia, 1900, LXXX, Pl. 29,14-15.

[15] Die allgemein als Sandan beschriebene Gottheit auf den tarsischen Bronzemünzen der frühen Kaiserzeit (SNG Sammlung von Aulock Nrn. 5968-5970) erinnert stark an unser Nergal-Bildnis, das ein halbes Jahrtausend zurückliegt: wiederum hält der Gott Bogen und Doppelaxt sowie zwei Ähren. Er steht frei auf einem Löwen, der jetzt gehörnt ist. – Diese Münzen sind durch die gemeinsame Vorderseite (Stadtgöttin mit Schleier und Mauerkrone) mit Bronzeprägungen verbunden, die aber das Monument des Sandan in Tarsos (SNG H. VON AULOCK Nos. 5971-5972) zeigen und so wiederum an die tarsischen Tetradrachmen der Seleukiden von Antiochios VII. bis Antiochios IX. anknüpfen. Das Kultbild des Gottes befindet sich hier in einem architektonischen Aufbau und steht auf einem Fabelwesen: Körper eines Ziegenbockes mit Stummelschwanz, bisweilen Kopf eines doppeltgehörnten Tieres (Löwe ?), bisweilen Menschenkopf mit hohem Schmuck (siehe Katalog Naville 10, 1925, Nos. 1305-1306. 1358. 1370. 1444-1449. 1487-1491). Auf den seleukidischen Drachmen von Tarsos steht Sandan frei im Raum, ohne den architektonischen Rahmen. – Zum Ganzen vergleiche man H. SEYRIG, Deux reliquaires, Syria 36 (1959) 47f.

breiten, dünneren Flan und ein flacheres Quadratum incusum. Sein Stil ist wesentlich feiner. Die Vorderseite zeigt den nackten Bellerophon auf dem fliegenden Pegasos, mit der Lanze nach unten stechend. In der Münzprägung taucht der korinthische Heros erst nach der Jahrhundertwende auf. Von Lykien, wohin er einst aus Tiryns gekommen war, bis Tarsos ist kein weiter Weg. Bemerkenswert ist aber, daß diese im Typus neue und im Stempelschnitt feine und schwungvolle Vorderseite mit einer Rückseite verbunden ist, die wohl nicht aus der gleichen Hand stammt und auch mit dem Sagenthema nichts zu tun hat, das auf der Vorderseite angeschlagen wird. Zu unserer Überraschung lesen wir aber auf der Rückseite oben rechts und links wiederum: *nrgl trz* = NeRGaL TaRZ = Nergal von Tarsos. Dieses spätere Bildnis zeigt den Gott zwischen einer breiten Staude und einer großen, schmalen Ähre nach links stehend. Auch hat er den gewohnten Bogen geschultert. Gekleidet ist er jedoch schon in persischer Tracht mit Kidaris und Kandys. In der Rechten hält er die Doppelaxt, die Labrys, die wohl hier vertretend für die ursprüngliche Keule mit dem doppelten Katzenkopf steht, die wir von dem alten Kultbild auf der Siegelgravur her schon kennen[16]. Während uns die Rückseite mit dem Löwen verrät, in welcher Gestalt Nergal Ende des fünften Jahrhunderts in Kilikien verehrt wurde, zeigt uns nun die Rückseite mit der Doppelaxt, wie man sich Nergal anfangs des vierten Jahrhunderts vorzustellen hat.

Mit dem Bellerophon-Nergal-Stater verbunden ist ein Teilstück, ein Drittelstater, mit Bellerophon auf beiden Seiten, ohne Legende; G.F. HILL hatte schon 1923 vorgeschlagen, diese Prägung nach Tarsos zu legen[17]. Das neue Ganzstück mit dem Bellerophon, Nergal und dem Namen von Tarsos beweist nun, daß HILL recht hatte. Eine solche Feststellung wird den Archäologen und Numismatiker, dem der vorliegende Beitrag gewidmet ist, gewiß freuen.

[16] H. SEYRIG, Syria 24 (1944-1945) 74,1.
[17] NumChr 1923, Pl. 10,42.

# Baana.
# Preliminary Studies of the Local Coinage in the Fifth Persian Satrapy, Part 2

## (Tf. XV - XVI)

MICHAEL AVI-YONAH was well aware of the interconnection of numismatics with epigraphy and archaeology as primary historical sources. More often than not, numismatics provided the major part. In the case of the Baana coin series, however, epigraphy has redressed the balance in a spectacular way.

## 1. Coinage Policy in the Fifth Satrapy

The fifth satrapy of the Persian Empire comprised the provinces west of the Euphrates river, *'eber nahᵃrā* : the whole of Syria, Phoenicia, Palestine and Cyprus. The satrap, with his administrative center in the North, enjoyed a great deal of independence[1], but he had to share his power with local kingdoms and self-governing city-states within his realm[2]. The Persian kings tolerated local customs and beliefs.

---

[1] For Part 1, see L. MILDENBERG, Yehud: A Preliminary Study of the Provincial Coinage of Judaea, in: FS M. Thompson, Wetteren 1979, 183-196 [hier S. 67-76]. Photographs, information and other assistance were gratefully received from M. Amandry, D. Bateson, C. Caflish, Th. Fischer, H. Gabelmann, M. Hengel, S. Hurter, M. Price, M. Rizack, W. Röllig, R. Stucky, N. Waggoner, A. Walker and J. Zahle.

In the course of the 4th century BCE, some western satraps became hereditary rulers. BABELON, Traité, cols. 3-16, asserts that the satraps had the right to strike their own silver coins only in time of war, acting as lieutenants for the Great King. The coinage issued by several satraps was, however, prolific, of long duration and of quite autocratic aspect. The heads of the satraps Tissaphernes (ca. 411 BCE and ca. 410 BCE), Pharnabazos (ca. 395 BCE) and Orontas (leading the great revolt, ca. 360 BCE) are the first real portraits in ancient coinage. See the fundamental articles by E.S.G. ROBINSON, NC 1948, 48-56, and ANSMN 9 (1960) 4-5. Cp. G.K. JENKINS, Ancient Greek Coins, London 1972, 103, Nos. 218-219; C.M. KRAAY, Archaic and Classical Greek Coins, London 1976, Nos. 206. 949-951; A. BALDWIN, Lampsakos: the Goldstaters, New York 1924, no. 21 and Pl. 2:15- 17; W. SCHWABACHER, Satrapenbildnisse, in: FS für E. Langlotz, Bonn 1957, 27-32, Pl. IV.

[2] See E. STERN, Material Culture of the Land of the Bible in the Persian Period 538-332 B.C., Warminster - Jerusalem 1982, VIII; and E.T. MULLEN, A New Royal Sidonian Inscription, BASOR 216 (1974) 26, who stresses «a satrapal system in which Sidon was a vasal kingdom». Cp. H.J. KATZENSTEIN, Tyre in the Early Persian Period, BA 42 (1979) 32, on Herodotus's account (3,91-92) and on the fact that in Phoenicia there were «no subordinate governors as in Samaria and Jerusalem». This privileged status of Sidon, but

Their liberal system of interior administration was based, however, on the vital, centralized services[3] of garrisons, roads, communications and taxes, as on the monopoly of foreign policy.

The money circulation truly reflects this kind of government. The Persian kings fully exercised their regal prerogative to strike gold coins[4]. The denomination, purity, fabric and types of their gold darics remained exactly the same for two centuries. The darics had conquered the ancient world[5] before Alexander introduced his gold staters. The silver coinage was, however, neither centralized nor uniformed. Hoard evidence demonstrates in a striking way that imported Greek silver coins were used as high denominations widely and for a long time. During extended periods, some satraps in the West, the kings of Sidon, Byblos, the Cypriote city-states[6] and the great commercial centers at Tyre[7], Gaza[8] and Arados issued large, medium and small silver coins which supplemented the imported supply from Greece. The silver sigloi with Persian types[9] served as money of medium size mainly in Asia Minor[10], while the

---

also of Tyre, Byblus and Aradus, is confirmed by the mere fact that these Phoenician cities struck their own large silver coins.

[3] In this respect, the use of the Aramaic language as *lingua franca* , together with the Aramaic script, can hardly be overestimated. See H.J. KATZENSTEIN, BA 42 (1979) 30.

[4] The Persians adopted the monetary system of the Lydians, and towards the end of the 6th century BCE began striking gold darics of ca. 8 gr. and silver sigloi of ca. 5.5 gr. See D. SCHLUMBERGER, L'Argent Grec dans l'Empire Achéménide, Paris 1953, 12.

[5] Persian darics are found from Sicily (IGCH, 2122 and 2124) to the Oxus river (IGCH, 1822). Because of the regal prerogative, the great economical importance and the long tradition, it is out of the question that the darics were struck by any other authority than the Great King.

[6] Their right to strike silver coins was never disputed by the Persian government (see above, n. 4). Some Cypriote and Carian rulers even issued gold coins, but on a small scale, in low denominations and with local types only.

[7] The silver coinage of this important trade city, the «Mistress of the Sea», is a *res sui generis*. It lasted – with short interruptions – for five hundred years, conserved Tyre's own monetary types during this whole period, defied the insignia of all overlords, from the Persian Great Kings to the Roman Emperors, and distinguished itself by clear marks of denomination and date. The prestige and quality of the Tyrian commercial money was so eminent that the Jews were bound to pay their duties to the Temple in Jerusalem in Tyrian and no other silver coins. Compare the tempting theory that the Tyrian and Sidonian coins «were conceived in conjunction and were intended to compliment each other», C.M. KRAAY, Archaic and Classical Greek Coins, 1976, 288.

[8] Gaza was not only the final coastal destination of important trade roads, but also the capital of a Persian province (see E. STERN, Material Culture of the Land of the Bible in the Persian Period, 1982, 7. 237). Its coin production of medium and small silver, especially prolific around 400 BCE, served the foreign commerce and the needs of the city and its hinterland.

[9] Though the siglos never became the main silver currency in the Persian Empire, one has to keep in mind that it had been conceived as Achaemenian money. Darics and sigloi do not essentially differ in types and fabric.

[10] The sigloi occur in great quantities among Asia Minor finds (IGCH: 18 hoards), in smaller numbers in Egyptian deposits (Asyut: M. PRICE / N. WAGGONER, Archaic Greek Silver Coinage. The «Asyut» Hoard, London 1975: 17 pieces) and in a very few specimens in hoards unearthed in the Levant and the territories further east. Thus, in IGCH not

small and very small silver coins used in daily life[11] were struck by local authorities[12].

## 2. The Baana[13] Series

In 1905, G. MACDONALD (Cat. of Greek Coins in the Hunterian Collection III, Glasgow) published three enigmatic silver staters (Tf. XV 2. 5. 7) which obviously belonged together and presumably were found at a single site some decades before. At about the same time, three pieces from the same issue had entered the Paris Cabinet (Tf. XV 3. 4. 8). Two third-staters, also belonging to the group, are known from the Philipsen and de Nanteuil collections. As late as 1986, a stater from the same dies as the first Hunter piece (Tf. XV 2) turned up and was published in an auction catalogue (Tf. XV 1).

MACDONALD considered his three staters in the Hunter collection to be «Uncertain of Phoenicia 500-450 B.C.», whereas J.P. SIX in 1884 had ascribed them to Cilicia. BABELON had succinctly stated «dynast vers 430» in 1893, but in 1907 ventured a date «vers 475 avant J.C.» and an attribution to Tripolis or Ake. G.F. HILL, in his BMC Phoenicia of 1910, thought of some Phoenician ruler or city in Cyprus about the middle of the 5th century BCE. Finally, the compiler of the 1986 sale catalogue convincingly stated «Phönizischer Raum, 5.Jh.»[14].

The Baana coins follow the Persian standard of about 11 gr. for the stater - and not the Attic, Phoenician or Rhodian standard, all known in the Empire. This fact already hints at Syria-Phoenicia-Palestine, and not to 5th-century Cyprus and Cilicia, which then used a heavier standard. Southern Phoenicia and Palestine have to be excluded, too, because the highest denomination struck there was then by and large the drachm of ca. 4 gr.

As to the Baana types, the hero struggling with the small lion is the Phoenician Melqart, as later coins of Tyre and Carthage indicate. He is not a Cypriote Herakles, who always carries a bow in his outstretched hand[15]. The head of Herakles occurs on

one single siglos is registered for Palestine, and one specimen only in each single hoard in Syria (IGCH 1481), Phoenicia (IGCH 1483) and Transjordan (IGCH 1482). D. SCHLUMBERGER, L'Argent Grec dans l'Empire Achéménide, 1953, 6-12, and Asyut, 97-98.

[11] These minute silver coins are either provincial money issued by the governors of Judaea (see L. MILDENBERG, Yehud: A Preliminary Study of the Provincial Coinage of Judaea, in: FS M. Thompson, Wetteren 1979, 183-196 [hier S. 67-76]) or Samaria (see Y. MESHORER, Ancient Jewish Coinage I, Dix Hills/NY 1982, Pl. 56:2-3; and A. SPAER, IEJ 29 (1979), Pl. 25 A-B), or local money struck by dynasts and cities in the southern territories of the fifth satrapy – the so-called «Philisto-Arabian» coins.

[12] In the fifth satrapy, bronze coinage slowly appeared towards the middle of the 4th century BCE. Some bronzes were then issued at Aradus, Byblus and Sidon, but very few at Tyre and Cyprus, and none in Judaea and Samaria.

[13] *b'n'*, rendered Baana.

[14] S. HURTER : «König Baana?».

[15] BMC Cyprus, 8-9, Nos. 2-6; and 10-11, Nos. 10-35, Citium (see here Tf. XVI 16); E.S.G. ROBINSON, NC 1948, Pl. 5:2; and G.K. JENKINS, Ancient Greek Coins, 1972, Nos. 326-327 (Lapethos). Cp. E.T. NEWELL, Miscellanea Numismatica: Cyrene to India,

a few Cilician coins, but not the fighting hero[16]. The Persian Great King stabbing the large lion with his dagger, also appearing on the Sidonian city coinage[17] (Tf. XV 12; XVI 13. 15), is a type perfectly fitting a Phoenician mint. Finally, the unusual cow with or without the suckling calf is a general Graeco-Persian image, popular from Illyria to the Euphrates[18] (Tf. XVI 17. 20. 21).

As to the chronology of the Baana group, the distinct incuse square on the first stater had suggested a high date to early scholars. Certainly, this piece can not be placed in the 4th century BCE. Coinage in the East, however, followed examples of continental Greece with a considerable delay. In addition, the dotted incuse square on all other Baana pieces hints at a date late in the 5th century BCE.

The inscriptions, finally, present the clue for the understanding of the whole series. In the third group of the Baana series (Tf. XV 7. 8), the legend *bēt - ʿayin - nūn - ʾālef* appears: thus «Baana». The corresponding third-stater (Tf. XV 9) has the abbreviation of the word: *bēt - ʿayin* , the two first letters. The second stater (Tf. XV 4. 5) shows a not very successful monogram, with only the *bēt* quite clear. Baana is known neither as a locality nor as a value or date. It is the name of a person. But who was this Baana?

---

ANSNNM 82 (1938), Nos. 5-8. A near parallel to the Baana-Melqart, however, is found on an engraved gem (Tf. XVI 19).

[16] SNG H. VON AULOCK, Nos. 5716 (Mallos), 5733 (Nagidos) and 5862-5863 (Soloi).

[17] H. SEYRIG's, Syria 36 (1959) 52-60 interpretation of the dignitaries in and behind the chariot on the heavy Sidonian coins as the Phoenician Baal and the king of Sidon has been widely accepted, cf. C.M. KRAAY / M. HIRMER, Greek Coins, London 1966, 366, Nos. 683-684; G.K. JENKINS, Ancient Greek Coins, 1972, 42 and 136 with No. 333; D. HARDEN, The Phoenicians, New York 1962, 233, n. 172. However, the bearded man in the Persian cape (the *kandys* ) riding in the chariot or about to stab the lion, does not wear the pointed bonnet (see J. BORCHARDT, Die Dependenz des Grosskönigs von Sidon vom persischen Grosskönig, in: FS für K. Bittel, Mainz 1983, 107, and n. 37), but a distinctive crown (the *kidaris* ), as seen on the Persepolis reliefs (R. GHIRSHMAN, Iran: Protoiranier, Meder, Achämeniden, München 1964, 233, 241, 246, 248 and especially 250-254) and cylinder seals (A. FURTWÄNGLER, Die antiken Gemmen I-III, Leipzig - Berlin 1900, Pl. 1:11.13.14 [here Tf. XVI 18] and 16; E. PORADA , P. Aforgan Collection, Washington 1948, 826). Compare Darius the Great wearing the ragged circlet crown on the Bisutun relief (GHIRSHMAN, Iran, 1964, 284). It is, therefore, preferable to retain the time-honoured interpretation of the type as the Persian Great King, as pointed out by I. KLEEMANN, Der Satrapen-Sarkophag aus Sidon, IstForsch 20 (1958) 164; and J.W. BETLYON, The Coinage and Mints of Phoenicia, Chico/CA 1982, 25-26, nn. 17-19. In this respect, it is noteworthy that the Great King in his Persian attire is also found on a rare Tarsus stater of Persian standard; there, the Achaemenian ruler has already stabbed the lion (Hunter II, Pl. 50:5).

[18] Greek and Graeco-Persian 5th century BCE gemstones (A. FURTWÄNGLER, Die antiken Gemmen I-III, 1900, Pl. 8:46 [here Tf. XVI 20]; Cat. L. Mildenberg Coll., Mainz 1983, No. 130 bis) and Greek coins, struck ca. 400 BCE in Apollonia. Dyrrhachion (here Ill. 17), Karystos, Korkyra, Lycia and Tarsus. The type seems to originate, however, from the East; see the ivories from Arslan Tash on the Euphrates, ca. 800 BCE, H.T. BOSSERT, Altsyrien, Tübingen 1951, No. 678; Cat. E. Borowski Coll., Mainz 1981, Nos. 245-248; Cat. N. Schimmel Coll., Mainz 1978, No. 144 (here Tf. XVI 21).

## 3. The Eshmun Inscription

BABELON's early assumption of a «dynaste Baana» was, indeed, proven right by another French scholar in 1965, when M. DUNAND published an inscription found on the base of a votive statue of a boy, which had come to light on the site of the Eshmun temple near Sidon[19]. It reads as follows: *hsml z 'š ytn b'lšlm bn mlk b'n' mlk ṣdnm bn mlk 'bd'(š)mn mlk ṣdnm bn mlk b'lšlm mlk ṣdnm l'dny l'šmn b'n ydl ybrk* - «This is the image which Ba'alšallim, son of king Ba'ana', king of the Sidonians, son of king 'Abd'ešmun, king of the Sidonians, son of king Ba'alšallim, king of the Sidonians, gave to his lord, to 'Ešmun, at the spring Yidal. May he (the son represented by the statue) be blessed»[20].

The epigraphic evidence of this primary source tells us, now, that Baana was «King of the Sidonians» when the inscription was carved. There is no reason to doubt that this is the Baana of our coin series[21]. Though the coin script is basically different in its ductus from the lapidary script on the stone, the similarity of the Phoenician letter forms is striking[22]. As noted above, the standard and the types of our coins are quite appropriate for a Sidonian royal issue. The Eshmun inscription establishes a new Sidonian dynasty. The new kings must be inserted between ca. 460 and ca. 380 BCE[23]. In any event, Baana must be placed in the late 5th century BCE,

---

[19] For the first publication and further literature, see Select Bibliography.

[20] Transcription and English translation by E.T. MULLEN, BASOR 216 (1974) 25, who amended DURAND's version by reading: 'Abd'ešmun for 'Abdamon, Yidal for Yidlal, and «May be blessed» for «Qu'il bénisse». J. TEIXIDOR, Bulletin d'épigraphie sémitique 6, Syria 49 (1972) 432 was allowed to publish a good photograph of the inscription and also reads *ydl* and «Qu'il le bénisse» (p. 432. No. 115), but not: 'Abd'ešmun.

[21] After the publication of the Eshmun inscription, A. VANEL, Le septième ostracon phénicien, MUSJ 45 (1965) 353, tentatively read *B'N'* on an ostracon and (in his n. 3) proposed two rulers for our Baana coin series, one with the full name and the other with the abbreviated name *B'*. The whole Baana series – presented in this paper for the first time – is, however, homogenous in standard, fabric (compact flans), types and lettering. J.W. BETLYON, The Coinage and Mints of Phoenicia, 1982, 29, n. 32. states that our Baana coins «are not related to Sidon in any way. This is a different Ba'na' from the king of Sidon». The type of the Great King about to stab the lion is, however, Sidonian (see above, n. 18). Further, it seems incomprehensible that the abbreviations *bēt* and *bēt - 'ayin* should indicate the Sidonian king Baana (BETLYON, The Coinage and Mints of Phoenicia, 1982, Nos. 15-16), whereas the full name Baana, on one of our coins and in the Sidonian Eshmun inscription, should mean a different king. Until a primary source proves the name, date and reign of this different king, BETLYON's assumption cannot be accepted.

[22] Especially the *bēt* and *nūn* (compare MULLEN's paleographic chart, line 5).

[23] See W. RÖLLIG, Beiträge zur nordsemitischen Epigraphik, 3. Eine neue Dynastie in Sidon, WO 5 (1965) 123 («ca. 460 bis 400 v.Chr.»); E.T. MULLEN, BASOR 216 (1974) 28 («Ba'na' ca. 400-389»); M. DUNAND, Nouvelles inscriptions Phéniciennes du temple d'Echmoun à Bostan ech-Cheikh, près Sidon, BMB 18 (1965) 105-109 («V^e siècle: la dynastie de Ba'alchillem à Ba'ana...»); id., La statuaire de la favissa du temple d'Echmoun à Sidon, in: FS für K. Galling, Tübingen 1970, 61-67, Pl. 1a («Ba'ana aurait régné vers 420 d'après le style de ses flans monétaires»).

the approximate date already ? arrived at by numismatic evidence. In addition, recent archaeological research attributes the Lykian sarcophagus in Sidon to Baana and dates it around 400 BCE[24].

# 4. Conclusion

As we read in the Eshmun inscription, the first Baalshillem was King of the Sidonians and Baana's grandfather. The second Baalshillem was Baana's son. We do not know, however, whether the second, in fact, became king. It is not even certain whether he was heir to the throne or simply one of Baana's sons. Under these circumstances, one would hope that the numismatic evidence could allow us to identify which Sidonian coins - especially the heavy silver galley/chariot pieces and their quarters with the king stabbing the lion - are to be attributed to Baana and which, if any, to the second Baalshillem[25]. Unfortunately, the so-called abbreviations in this period - many *bēt* s[26], some *'ayin* s, a few *mēm* s and other single letters, all differently placed - can at best serve as hints, not as numismatic evidence. Nevertheless, our coin series was definitely struck late in the 5th centuy by Baana[27], King of the Sidonians, as the epigraphic, archaeological and numismatic evidence has proven. The Sidonian city coins with *bēt* , *'ayin* - *bēt* and *bēt* - *mēm* have, however, nothing to do with Baana, whereas the very few isolated city coins with *bēt* - *'ayin* (?)[28] may have been struck under his reign[29]. One might be tempted to ascribe the

---

[24] H. GABELMANN, Die Inhaber des Lykischen und des Satrapensarkophages, AA 1982, 494.

[25] A desideratum expressed by MULLEN, BASOR 216 (1974) 28. Here one has to keep in mind that *'ayin* - *bēt* can not be read as *bēt* - *'ayin* (so BMC Phoenicia, XC-XCII). Moreover, it seems hazardous to understand the bet as an abbreviation of a name. See next note below.

[26] The *bēt* often also occurs on the so-called «Philisto-Arabian» coins of different origin (see SNG. ANS II, No. 80162; BABELON, Traité, Nos. 1050. 1055 and 1058; Leu 2, 297; Leu 13, 315). It must, therefore, have a meaning understood throughout the entire fifth satrapy. A form of guaranty for good metal and correct weight comes to mind.

[27] As to the name Baana, MULLEN, BASOR 216 (1974) 25 states that «*B'n'* is no doubt an abbreviated hypocoristic name». One is, indeed, induced to such an assumption if one understands the letters on the Sidonian city coins as secured abbreviations of royal names. It is, however, difficult to conceive that the name of the king reigning in the time of the dedication of the inscribed statue to Eshmun would be rendered in a diminutive form, whereas the names of the preceding kings and that of Baana's son are all solemnly written in full.

[28] Only very few specimens may exist. In any case, the reading *bēt* - *'ayin* on the octadrachm BMC Phoenicia, 141,8, is quite uncertain because of heavy corrosion. The two letters on the didrachm in the ANS (here Tf. XV 12) have been read by BETLYON, The Coinage and Mints of Phoenicia, 1982, 9, No. 16, as *bēt* - *'ayin* , as has been alread noted by NEWELL (information from N. WAGGONER). P. NASTER, Le developement des monnayages phéniciennes avant Alexandre, d'après les trésors, in: International Numismatic Convention, Proceedings, Tel Aviv - Jerusalem 1967, 21, mentions one didrachm with *bēt* - *'ayin* in the Beni-Hasan hoard, but this specimen has not been illustrated and could not be retrieved.

few pieces with *bēt - mēm* to the second Baalshillem, but an abbreviation of the first and last letters is unlikely.

Our Baana series and the general Sidonian city coins should not, however, be lumped together. The standard is different and neither the fighting Melqart nor the cow appear in the uniform, longlasting and prolific city coinage. All this implies a specific use for our Baana issue. It might have been produced for a special purpose or on a special occasion. One can only hope that further evidence from a primary source will enlighten us in the future.

## Select Bibliography

1. General:

BETLYON J.W., The Coinage and Mints of Phoenicia (HSM 26), Chico/CA 1982.

FURTWÄNGLER A., Die antiken Gemmen I-III, Leipzig-Berlin 1900.

GHIRSHMAN R., Iran: Protoiranier, Meder, Achämeniden, München 1964.

HARDEN D., The Phoenicians, New York 1962.

JENKINS G.K., Ancient Greek Coins, London 1972.

KATZENSTEIN H.J., Tyre in the Early Persian Period, BA 42 (1979) 23-34.

KLEEMANN I., Der Satrapen-Sarkophag aus Sidon, IstForsch 20 (1958) 160-165.

KRAAY C.M., Archaic and Classical Greek Coins, London 1976.

KRAAY C.M. / Hirmer M., Greek Coins, London 1966.

MESHORER Y., Ancient Jewish Coinage I-II, Dix Hills/NY 1982.

MILDENBERG L., Yehud: A Preliminary Study of the Provincial Coinage of Judaea, in: FS M. Thompson, Wetteren 1979, 183-196 [hier S. 67-76].

NASTER P., Le suivant du char royal sur les doubles statères de Sidon, RBN 103 (1957) 1-20.

NASTER P., Le developement des monnayages phéniciennes avant Alexandre, d'après les trésors, in: International Numismatic Convention, Proceedings, Tel Aviv - Jerusalem 1967, 3-24.

NEWELL E.T., Miscellanea Numismatica: Cyrene to India, ANSNNM 82 (1938).

PECKHAM J.B., The Development of the Late Phoenician Script, Cambridge/MA 1968.

ROUVIER J., Numismatique des villes de la Phénicie, Sidon, JIAN 5 (1902) 99-116.

SCHLUMBERGER D., L'Argent Grec dans l'Empire Achéménide, Paris 1953.

STERN E., Material Culture of the Land of the Bible in the Persian Period 538-332 B.C., Warminster - Jerusalem 1982.

VANEL A., Le septième ostracon phénicien, MUSJ 45 (1965) 352-353.

---

[29] Our Baana series seems, in fact, to offer the only valuable hint that the «abbreviations» of letters on the city coins of Sidon may indicate the names of city kings: a monogram formed by *bēt* and probably *ʿayin* and *nūn* , then the two first letters *bēt* and *ʿayin* in correct order, and finally the full name *bēt - ʿayin - nūn - ʾālef* all three occur in the same homogenous series.

## 2. The Baana Series:

BABELON E., Les Perses AchÈmÈnides, Paris 1893, 44-47, Pl. 8:1-2.
BABELON E., Traité, cols. 497-502, Pl. 116:1-3.
HILL J.F., BMC Phoenica, Introduction, pp. CXXIV-CXXV.
HURTER S., Leu 38 (1986) 155.
MACDONALD G., Cat. of Greek Coins in the Hunterian Collection III, Glasgow 1905, 272-273, Pl. 77:15-17.
SIX J.P., NC 1884, 152-153, Nos. 2-4, Pl. 5:1-2.

## 3. The Eshmun Inscription:

DUNAND M., Nouvelles inscriptions phéniciennes du temple d'Echmoun à Bostan ech-Cheikh, près Sidon, BMB 18 (1965) 105-109.
DUNAND M., La statuaire de la favissa du temple d'Echmoun à Sidon, in: FS für K. Galling, Tübingen 1970, 61-67, Pl. 1a.
DUNAND M., Statuette offerte par Ba'alchillem, vers 420. Trouvée dans la favissa, BMB 26 (1973) 8-25, Pl. 10:1.
DUNAND M., Les rois de Sidon au temps des Perses, MUSJ 49 (1975-1976) 491-499.
BORCHARDT J., Die Dependenz des Grosskönigs von Sidon vom persischen Grosskönig, in: FS für K. Bittel, Mainz 1983, 105-120.
GABELMANN H., Die Inhaber des Lykischen und des Satrapensarkophages, AA 1982, 493-495.
MULLEN E.T., A New Royal Sidonian Inscription, BASOR 216 (1974) 25-30.
NASTER P., Le suivant du char royal sur les doubles statères de Sidon, RBN 103 (1957) 1-20.
RÖLLIG W., Beiträge zur nordsemitischen Epigraphik, 3. Eine neue Dynastie in Sidon, WO 5 (1965) 121-124.
TEIXIDOR J., Bulletin d'épigraphie sémitique 6, Syria 49 (1972) 432-433.

# Notes on the Coin Issues of Mazday[*]

## (Tf. XVII - XVIII )

Around 361 B.C. Artaxerxes II appointed the Persian nobleman Mazday (Mazaeus – Mazaios)[1] as satrap[2] of Cilicia, and by 345 he had been appointed ruler over the huge satrapy of Transeuphratesia as well[3]. Mazaeus remained in power till the battle of Gaugamela around 1st October 331[4]. Commanding the Persian right wing he

---

[*] The writer is grateful for help to D. Barag, Sh. Qedar, G. Le Rider and W. Röllig. He is especially indebted to M.J. Price and A.S. Walker. For help with photographs the writer is indebted to M. Amandry, C. Arnold-Bucchi, R. Freeman, D. Gorny, S. Hurter, M. Metcalf, Z. Radovan and M.J. Price.

[1] On Mazaeus see H. BERVE, Das Alexanderreich auf prosopographischer Grundlage 2: Prosopographie, München 1926, 243-244, No. 484 and especially J.P. SIX, Le satrape Mazaios, NC 3rd ser. 4 (1884) 97-159.

[2] The title satrap (Khšatrapâvan in Old Persian, satrapēs in Greek and in translation hyparchos is not found on coins which is a noteworthy conspicuous fact (see below, n. 25). The second highest Persian dignitary, the governor, however, appears as phh on the small silver coins of the province of Yehud-Judaea in the fourth century B.C. See L. MILDENBERG, Yehud: A Preliminary Study of the Provincial Coinage of Judaea, in: Greek Numismatics and Archaeology. Essays in Honor of M. Thompson, Wetteren, 1979, 183-196 [hier S. 67-76], and id., Yehud-Münzen, in: H. WEIPPERT, Palästina in vorhellenistischer Zeit (HdA, Vorderasien II,1), München 1988, 719-728; Y. MESHORER, Ancient Jewish Coinage I, Dix Hills/NY 1982, 13-34, and D. BARAG, A Silver Coin of Yoḥanan the High Priest, INJ 9 (1986-1987) 4-21.

[3] Transeuphratesia = Ebīr Nāri in Akkadian, identical with Aššur used in cuneiform writing [P. CALMEYER, Die sogenannte fünfte Satrapie und die achaimenidischen Documente, Transeuphratène 3 (1990) 118, n. 58], = ᶜabar nahᵃrā in Aramaic and ʿEber ha-nāhār in Hebrew, was originally a part of the Dahyāus Athuriya [CALMEYER, Transeuphratène 3 (1990) 111. 123], then was separated from remaining Babylonia in the 20th regnal year of Darius I [E. LIPINSKI, Géographie linguistique de la Transeuphratène à l'époque achéménide, Transeuphratène 3 (1990) 98] or 36th year [F. JOANNES, Pouvoirs locaux et organisations du territoire en Babylonie achéménide, Transeuphratène 3 (1990) 178, n. 17, quoting M. STOLPER] and finally governed together with Cilicia by Mazaeus after the Tennes revolt was crushed. On the unreliability of the ancient traditions (especially Herodotus, 2,91) and the limited value of the Achaemenid sources on the territory of Transeuphratesia, the «so called fifth satrapy», see CALMEYER, Transeuphratène 3 (1990) 111-112, and LIPINSKI, Transeuphratène 3 (1990) 98. 102. Compare n. 40 below.

[4] H. BERVE, Das Alexanderreich 2, 1926, 244, concludes from Mazaeus' command at Gaugamela that he was not ruling Cilicia at that time, but was then responsible for «Syrien und Mesopotamien». E. BABELON, Traité col. 444 seems to understand Arsames' command of the cavalry in the battle at Granicus in the spring of 334 in the same manner. J.D. BING, Reattribution of the «Myriandrus» Alexanders. The case for Issus, AJN 2nd ser. 1 (1989) 17-24, reached a similar conclusion from a thorough survey of the literary

«almost defeated Alexander»[5]. After Darius III had fled the battle field, Mazaeus succeeded in withdrawing to Babylon. He surrendered the great city to Alexander[6] and was appointed satrap of Babylonia during the same month. Mazaeus died in 328 after having served three Persian kings and the Macedonian conqueror for more than three decades of an astonishing career. The following notes may prove that his coin issues were no less extraordinary.

# 1. Tarsus

For nearly a century the prolific mint of Tarsus had struck for the indigenous local dynasts and the Persian dignitaries who succeeded them. Until ca. 380 B.C., in the time of Tiribazus, one of several ubiquitous Achaemenid commanders of long standing, the coinage of Tarsus was bilingual, bearing Aramaic and Greek legends. However, the legends of the subsequent issues of Pharnabazus at Tarsus (378-374 B.C.) were only in Aramaic (Tf. XVII 1). He named the Cilician territory in Aramaic, ḥlk or klk , and introduced the coin type of the Baʿal of Tarsus, bʿltrz (usually termed Baaltars). That latter coin type dominated the emissions of Tarsus for the following half a century, appearing on all staters, tetradrachms and fractions at several mints of Mazaeus and finally also on Alexander's local silver coinage at

---

sources. There is, however, no clear evidence for Mazaeus' function and whereabouts from spring 334 till autumn 333 (see below, n. 32). Be that as it may, as the satrap of both Cilicia and Transeuphratesia before the Granicus and certainly of Transeuphratesia during Alexander's campaign in Phoenicia, Palestine and Egypt in 333-331, Mazaeus had to bear the brunt of fighting against Alexander between the battles of Issus and Gaugamela» (R.N. FRYE, The History of Ancient Iran, München 1984, 139). It is unlikely that Mazaeus was ever satrap of Babylonia or Mesopotamia in Persian times. His prominent rôle at Gaugamela and his following retreat to Babylon should not be understood in this manner. P. HÖGEMANN, Alexander der Grosse und Arabien (Zetemata 82), München 1985, 31, quoting O. LEUZE (Die Satrapieneinteilung in Syrien und im Zweistromland von 520-320 v.Chr., Weimar 1935), and A. SCHALIT, Scripta Hierosolymitana 1 (1954) 64-77, points out that the 5th satrapy under Mazaeus comprised no Mesopotamian territories.

[5] R.N. FRYE, The History of Ancient Iran, 1984, 139.

[6] There is a hostile tendency in the judgements on Mazaeus by Diodorus, Curtius Rufus and probably already by Cleitarchus (see especially H. BERVE, Das Alexanderreich 2, 1926, 244). Did the historians consider him as a traitor, as E. BABELON, Traité, col. 445, does? For R.N. FRYE, The History of Ancient Iran, 1984, 139, following A.R. BELLINGER, Essays on the Coinage of Alexander the Great (ANSNS 11), New York 1963, 61-64, the fact of Mazaeus' Babylonian coinage (see here below, section 5) under Alexander seems to hint at «an agreement between Mazaios and Alexander involving the surrender of Babylon to the latter». Mazaeus was certainly a powerful man in the years of the decline of the Persian Empire, but was he in a position to negotiate with Alexander after the disaster of Gaugamela? E. BADIAN, Alexander in Iran, in: The Cambridge History of Iran, 2, Cambridge 1985, 438, notes that the grandee might have had Babylonian family connections. The untimely flight of Darius III from the battlefield at Gaugamela, Mazaeus' own insight into the hopeless situation and his awareness of Alexander's terrible actions after Tyre's and Gaza's resistance explain his endeavors to save the great city and its inhabitants.

Tarsus[7]. Pharnabazus and his contemporary, Datames[8], enriched the repertoire of the mint of Tarsus not only with Levantine, but also with Achaemenid and Greek types (Tf. XVII 2-3)[9], yet maintained Baaltars in varying guises. Thus, obviously, the Persian grandees, whenever and for whatever purpose they struck coins at Tarsus[10], did not issue orders that their coins had to appear as imperial or satrapal issues. They needed a good and well-known currency and received it in the style of Tarsus from that great local mint. Tiribazus, Pharnabazus and Datames were powerful Persian generals and at the same time high dignitaries who held, during their careers, different offices in various western parts of the Achaemenid empire. Their presence at Tarsus was temporary. Mazaeus, however, did not come from another office, in a distant satrapy, when he was installed at Tarsus after the collapse of the revolt of the satraps. He became the first and last regular Cilician satrap whose capital was Tarsus, for at least 27 years, as is vindicated by his distinctive and rich coinage (Tf. XVII 4-9)[11]. All his coins have the figure of Baaltars and the Aramaic legend *b ʿltrz* on the obverse. The inscription on the reverses is inevitably *mzdy* – Mazday in a

---

[7] The date and mint of Alexander's first imperial tetradrachms is disputed: «Amphipolis» around 336 [M.J. PRICE, The Coinage in the Name of Alexander the Great and Philip Arrhidaeus, Zürich - London 1991, 27-29] or Tarsus 333-332 [cf. O.H. ZERVOS, On the Earliest Coins of Alexander the Great, NC 142 (1982) 166-179; M. WEIGELT, Der sitzende Zeus auf den Alexander-Tetradrachmen der Münzstätte Tarsos, SM 132 (1983) 77-80, and H.A. TROXELL, Alexander's Earliest Macedonian Silver, in: Mnemata, Papers in Memory of N.M. Waggoner, ed. by W.E. METCALF, New York 1991, 4-61, Pl. 10-14, throughout]. The interpretation of the reverse image is decisive. It was ZERVOS who recognized the influence of the Baal of Tarsus on the seated Zeus. According to PRICE there were other models, not on coins. Did, however, Alexander have Phidias' seated Olympic Zeus in mind? As there seems to be no similar and popular model on any relevant Greek coinage before 336, the Tarsus Baaltars should not be excluded *a priori* , as TROXELL, ibid., 56 argues. The longlasting and abundant Baaltars issues, certainly used for mercenary pay, could have been known in Macedonia. When reaching Tarsus the Macedonian conquerors saw the local issues with Baaltars and accepted them as close to their own concept of Zeus. It seems unlikely that Alexander needed and conceived an entirely new coinage at the very early stage of his reign in Macedonia, see below n. 42.

[8] On the origin of Datames' name see A. LEMAIRE, Recherches d'épigraphie araméenne en Asie Mineure et en Egypte et le problème d'acculturation, in: Achaemenid History VI, Leiden 1991, 203-205, reading convincingly *trkmw* .

[9] Especially the presentation scene of the god Ana and the conventional image of a satrap in Persian attire accompanied by the winged solar disk. For Greek images see e.g. the facing female head in the manner of the die-engraver Kimon of Syracuse, the frequent helmeted warrior heads interpreted by KRAAY, quoting O. MØRKHOLM, as «probably idealized heads of generals representing the source of military pay» (C.M. KRAAY, Archaic and Classical Greek Coins, London 1976, 282).

[10] C.M. KRAAY, Archaic and Classical Greek Coins, 1976, 83 suggests that the *mmt* of Tarsus may have produced money for the satraps «who were simply using the area as a base of operations». A. LEMAIRE / H. LOZACHMEUR, La Cilicie à l'époque perse. Recherches sur les pouvoirs locaux et l'organisation du territoire, Transeuphratène 3 (1990) 148: «ce monnayage "satrapique" est, en fait, un monnayage militaire».

[11] See E. BABELON, Traité, cols. 443-461; C.M. KRAAY, Archaic and Classical Greek Coins, 1976, Nos. 1042-1045; M. ALRAM, Nomina propria Iranica in nummis, Wien 1986, 113-114.

strikingly uniform ductus, a real personal badge. On the fractions only the first two letters of his name appear, *mēm* and *zayin* . The types are lion vanquishing a stag (Tf. XVII4), lion over a bull (Tf. XVII 5) and, finally, again the lion attacking the bull, but now placed over two parallel rows of fortifications (Tf. XVII 7-9).

The inscription of the group with the fortifications is unique and significant: *mzdy zy ʿl ʿbrnhrʾ wḥlk* «Mazaeus who is over Transeuphratesia and Cilicia» (S. 53 Nr. 5). It means that he was at that time ruling the huge satrapy of Transeuphratesia, named first, as well as Cilicia. Thus, after having been the only real local satrap of Cilicia, he became the first and only Persian grandee who kept his original satrapy and was additionally nominated to rule another, more important and larger territory. From the suppression of the Phoenician revolt, in ca. 345 B.C. till at least the eve of Alexander's conquest in 334, Mazaeus was, in fact, the viceroy of the greater part of the Levant. Furthermore the numismatist encounters here the unique case in which the title of a Persian satrap appears on a coin. The keyword for the understanding is *zy* (*zayin* - *yōd* ), «who is», the Aramaic relative pronoun[12]. Its meaning was already clearly stated by HALEVY and LIDZBARSKI a century ago. The reverse type is perfectly fitting as it depicts the Pylae Ciliciae, the Cilician Gates, an important transit pass fortified on both ends of the road from Cilicia to Transeuphratesia[13].

## 2. «Myriandrus» and «Issus»: Recte Tarsus

In 1920 E.T. NEWELL attributed the so-called «lion» staters, in Persic weight, with Baaltars and the legend *bʿltrz* on the obverse and the striding lion and the legend *mzdy* - Mazaeus on the reverse, to the north-Syrian maritime city Myriandrus (Tf. XVII 1-12; XVIII 13-14). Since then this has remained the opinio communis. In the SNG E. Levante of 1986, however, this attribution was only accepted with reservation: «No corroborating evidence had so far turned up and probably part of these coins were minted at Tarsus». In 1991 M. PRICE wrote: «The identification of this mint was one of Newell's most daring attributions» and warned «The attribution to Myriandrus should be accepted with caution»[14]. This writer holds that this group too was struck by Mazaeus in Tarsus and represents his last issue in that city.

It cannot be stressed enough that the satraps of Transeuphratesia refrained from producing coinage because the local money supply was amply sufficient. Neither did

---

[12] M. LIDZBARSKI, Handbuch der Nordsemitischen Epigraphik I, Weimar 1898, 267: «Partikel der Beziehung zwischen Nomen und Satz (Relativpartikel): Mazdaimünzen...»; J. HALEVY, in: E. MEYER, Geschichte des Altertums VI (ed. Cotta), 1952-1958, 46 n.: «Mazdai, der über ʿAbar Naharah und Kilikien gesetzt ist».

[13] The fortifications are depicted as parallel rows and, therefore, cannot be the walls of Tarsus, as HILL, 82 had stated. Their meaning has already been recognized by J.P. SIX, NC 3rd ser. 4 (1884) 137 (Xenophon, Anabasis 1,4,4).

[14] SNG E. Levante, Cilicia, Bern 1986, n. at No. 181; M.J. PRICE, The Coinage in the Name of Alexander the Great and Philip Arrhidaeus, 1991, 401. J.D. BING, AJN 2nd ser. 1 (1989) 2, n. 4 records that C.M. HARRISON in her dissertation of 1982 (not seen by this writer) «refuted Newell's Myriandrian thesis».

Mazaeus produce any satrapal issues there. Rather, he only appears with his name, or its abbreviation, on strictly local issues. He carefully maintained the local standard, fabric and types which testifies to his empirical approach, respecting the Achaemenid monetary policy even in the final stage of that empire. This approach would be contradicted by the establishment of a new mint at Myriandrus.

After 350 B.C. the two satrapies formed one territory and not two separate entities with different mints striking exclusively for either Cilicia or Transeuphratesia. With local money production centers of long standing at hand like Tarsus and Sidon, there was no need whatsoever to create new mint installations in a minor town situated between these two great cities.

On the coins which NEWELL attributed to Myriandrus the same legends are found as on the undisputed coins of Tarsus with Baaltars and Mazday, not merely Baaltars or Mazday alone. All these legends are written in the standardized Aramaic coin script of Tarsus - neither in Phoenician nor in a mixed script. The letter forms are uniform to such a degree that they betray their origin from the mint of Tarsus. The weight standard and fabric are the same in both groups. NEWELL's main argument against the attribution of the «lion» staters to Tarsus is his firm statement that «from the issues under Datames to the last ones under Alexander» the wheat ear and the bunch of grapes «constantly occur». This, however, is incorrect[15]. Furthermore, his comparison of Baaltars' appearance in other Eastern mints, of later times, with those of the Tyrian Melqart-Herakles in Mediterranaean issues is inappropriate. A corresponding coin legend which would read *mlqrt ṣr*, «Melqart of Tyre» is unknown, and Tyre was the mother city of several Phoenician colonies, whereas Tarsus was not. Finally, there is no hoard evidence supporting the attribution to Myriandrus[16]. The same considerationss outlined above are sufficient to reject also a recent attribution of Mazaeus Persic «lion» staters to Issus[17]. A further specific argument against Issus is striking: the last coins of Issus were struck around 380 B.C. with the ethnikon *EEIKON* and the Aramaic *trybṣw* for Tribazus. The reinstallation of a mint after almost half a century so near to the permanent and prolific production center of Tarsus, which also struck coins for other Cilician cities, is unlikely whether Issus belonged to Cilicia or Transeuphratesia. Anyway, the alleged separation of the two satrapies, based on the literary reports of Alexander's conquest, is far from certain. The numismatic facts do not support it: the names of Mazday and Alexander's appointee Balacrus (Tf. XVII 10) appear on the coins and not that of Arsames, a Persian commander at both the battle on the Granicus and in the battle of

---

[15] See SNG Levante, Cilicia, 1986, Nos. 100-101 and M. ALRAM, Nomina propria Iranica in nummis, 1986, 144, No. 355 n.

[16] IGCH 1748, Warka in Babylonia 1929: «Myriandrus. Mazaeus: 1 st». There is only this «Myriandrus» stater listed and it occured together with a stater of Pharnabazus from Tarsus and another of Mazaeus as well as a siglos! This composition clearly hints at an origin of the deposit from Asia Minor and not from Syria. It is likely that the stater listed as Myriandrus comes from Tarsus.

[17] J.D. BING, AJN 2nd ser. 1 (1989) 10-15, deals also with Mazaeus' «lion» staters.

Issus, whom the historians report as the last authority in Tarsus before the Macedonian approach[18].

The lion attacking the bull placed above the Cilician Gates was a new reverse type introduced by Mazaeus. The striding lion was his last innovation. It is noteworthy that test cuts occur neither on the coins struck by the former Persian grandees in Tarsus nor on Mazaeus' early issues. They begin to appear on Mazaeus' last issues and are then frequently found on Balacrus' coinage of Tarsus. Test cuts hint at troubled times. The «lion» staters, with and without Mazaeus' name[19], might have been struck in the wake of the Macedonian threat, for a special purpose, probably to pay the mercenaries even outside Tarsus, but they do come from the mint of Tarsus.

# 3. Sidon

The monetary production of Sidon[20] is the prime example of a great autonomous coinage[21] which was possible only in the Persian commonwealth: a mint tradition of a century; a well structured issue ranging from very large denominations down to tiny fractions; the prevailing of distinctively local images and the exclusiveness of Phoenician lettering. Thus, this coinage, which was based on a strong political and economic position[22], is different from the imperial issues[23], the provincial coinages[24] or the ephemeral «satrapal» emissions[25]. Mazaeus' Sidonian coinage differs

---

[18] Diodorus 17,19,4. See J.D. BING, AJN 2nd ser. 1 (1989) 13, nn. 42-43.

[19] The production of the anonymous «lion» staters may have occured under Arsames as *locum tenens* for Mazaeus in Tarsus. M.A. DANDAMAEV, A Political History of the Achaemenid Empire, Leiden 1989, 322 calls Arsames «the governor of Cilicia».

[20] See J. ELAYI, Sidon, Cité autonome de l'Empire Perse, Paris 1989, 214. 218, throughout, especially the discussion of the royal and civic components of the Sidonian coinage.

[21] «The most important coinage of this part of the world down to the time of Alexander the Great» (B.V. HEAD, Historia numorum, 794).

[22] The Phoenician cities, providing the Persian fleet, ranked high in the Achaemenid power structure. As guardians of the coast and the transit roads they were irreplaceable. This essential factor is one reason why they recovered soon after the total defeat of their revolt in 351/350 B.C. The other reason is their new satrap Mazaeus' lenient rule, as his monetary policy indicates. See text below.

[23] The gold daric created by Darius I around 500 B.C. and the roughly contemporary silver siglos with the same or similar images that were struck in Asia Minor and served mainly as pay for the mercenary forces.

[24] See below section 4: Samaria; see also A Survey of Numismatic Research 1985-1990, Vol. I, Brussels 1991, 103-104 [hier S. 55-56], for the publications of the Yehud coins.

[25] Though the Hekatomnid rulers were generally complying with their satrapal duties [P. FREI, Zentralgewalt und Lokalautonomie im achämenidischen Kleinasien, Transeuphratène 3 (1990) 168], their great Carian silver coinage was local and autonomous, not satrapal. The kings of Cyprus were local rulers in their own right within the Persian commonwealth, their varied and longlasting coinage has no features whatsoever of a satrapal coinage. The prolific issues of Tarsus minted by the Persian grandees from the time of Tiribazus through most of Mazaeus' rule were local issues. Even Pharnabazus' Cyzicus tetradrachm with his name in Greek and his portrait in Persian attire is basically a local issue, as the reverse image with the tunny badge indicates. Thus, where and when did a relevant, distinctly satrapal coinage came into being?

from the previous issues only by bearing his name in the left field of the reverse, above the chariot, and by the date marked on the obverse (Tf. XVIII 15). On Sidonian coins he thus appeared only as the ruler of the city and not as the viceroy of the Levant[26]. It is noteworthy that in this way Mazaeus respected the civic prerogative of coin production in every respect even a short time after the revolt led by Sidon had been crushed. Of equal interest is Mazaeus' long minting authority in Sidon, testifying to the Persian grandee's unrivalled exercise of power in the Levant for thirty years[27].

## 4. Samaria

Recently two important hoards of small silver coins came to light. Both hoards consisted mainly of coins from the Persian province of Samaria, part of the satrapy of Transeuphratesia under Mazaeus' jurisdiction. As the publication of 1991 has documented, not only did the names of both the province and several local dignitaries appear on the coins, but also the name of Mazaeus, abbreviated by the first two letters *mēm* and *zayin* (Tf. XVIII 16-17)[28]. This is the usual abbreviation, as minted on the small fractions of Tarsus and Sidon. However, it does not mean that «Mazaeus' name does not have any independent significance»[29]. On the contrary, it is out of the question that the provincial governor would have used the name of his superior, that of the most powerful satrap, without the latter's permission. It is a decisive fact that the name of the province, *šmryn* , is marked on the obverse and that of the satrap, *mz* , is marked on the reverse of a coin emitted during Mazaeus' rule[30]. That means that Mazaeus is the superior minting authority also in the province of Samaria as he was in Tarsus and Sidon.

## 5. Babylon

After his gallant and nearly successful struggle against Alexander at Gaugamela[31], Mazaeus had finally to withdraw to Babylon, where he surrendered on the approach of

---

[26] Only one name is written in full, that of Mazaeus, C.M. KRAAY, Archaic and Classical Greek Coins, 1976, 290. The fractions, however, display the first two letters *mēm* and *zayin* which unequivocally indicate Mazaeus. The same is true for the name of the Sidonian king Baana (*bʿnʾ* in full and *bʿ*) on an issue attributed to a Sidonian mint, cf. L. MILDENBERG, Baana, ErIs 18 (1987) 29 [hier S. 35 - 42].

[27] The riddle of the dates on Mazaeus' Sidonian coins seems to be solved by the Samaria and the Nablus hoards, the first ending with year 13, the second beginning with year 14 (Samaria, 50, 66 and 77). The regnal years of Artaxerxes III are thus marked on the Sidonian coins, as A. LEMAIRE, in: A Survey of Numismatic Research 1985-1990, Vol. I, Brussels 1991, 98, n. 19 had suggested. See J. ELAYI, Sidon, 1989, 118-119.

[28] Samaria, Introduction, 8.

[29] Ibid., 17.

[30] Ibid., 47, No. 16; cf. 47, No. 15, 48, No. 21 and 53, No. 48.

[31] See above, nn. 4 and 5.

the Macedonians in 331 B.C.[32]. In October of the same year Alexander was pro-claimed king of Babylon, and, for whatever reasons[33], the conqueror abandoned his former practice of replacing Persian dignitaries by his Greek officials and installed Mazaeus as his representative in Babylon[34]. This is remarkable enough, but the real surprise is the fact that he allowed this formidable Persian soldier and experienced administrator to strike coins and even to put his name in Aramaic, not in Greek, on these issues (Tf. XVIII 18-19). Mazaeus' signature *mzdy* -Mazday, his badge, created decades ago in Tarsus under Persian rule, now appeared again under Alexander in dis-tant Babylon. This seems to have happened at about the same time[35] as the intro-duction in the mint of Babylon of Alexander's own imperial tetradrachms, the new international currency. It is thus easily understandable that historians doubted whe-ther Mazaeus' «lion» tetradrachms were struck with Alexander's permission and sought for «hoards and more firm evidence to substantiate a presumed policy of Alexander in granting such a right»[36]. As for hoards, there was already in 1953 the evidence of the Hillah deposit[37], from the immediate neighborhood of Babylon, with its five Mazaeus «lion» tetradrachms. This was followed by the two 1973 Babylon

---

[32] According to the ancient historians describing Alexander's conquest, Mazaeus was not present at the battles of Granicus and Issus. Provided that their attitude was unbiased (see above, n. 6) and in appreciation of his prominent part in the battle of Gaugamela, one can reasonably assume that his activity from 333 till 332 was concentrated on the defense of northern Syria. That does not mean that he lost his position in Cilicia or Phoenicia (see his continuous coinage production in Sidon). BING's observation, AJN 2nd ser. 1 (1989) 12, that Arsames may have functioned as Mazaeus' «subordinate in command of the de-fense in Cilicia» may well be to the point. A. LEMAIRE / H. LOZACHMEUR, Transeuphratène 3 (1990) 148 state: «... Arsamès ... pourrait n'avoir être qu'un subordonné de Mazdaï qui pourrait être resté satrape de Transeuphratène et de Cilicie jusqu'en 332...». Whether Mazaeus formally had power over northern Syria just before Gaugamela, is not of decisive importance. The factual power in the city of Babylon was his when the Macedonian army advanced. Curtius 4,16 says that Mazaeus marched to Babylon, with part of his army, after Gaugamela; see above, n. 4, and below, n. 40.

[33] See above, n. 6.

[34] E. BADIAN, in: The Cambridge History of Iran, 2, 1985, 434: «Alexander appointed Mazaeus satrap». That does not seem to mean that the Persian grandee was in direct com-mand of the Macedonian troops there. Mazaeus administrated Babylonia with the city of Babylon as its center, not the whole of Mesopotamia, see F. JOANNES, Transeuphratène 3 (1990) 182.

[35] «It looks, therefore, possible that the Mazaeus issues and the imperial issues were struck in parallel, but it is impossible to say with certainty that one group was slightly earlier than the other» (M.J. PRICE's letter to the writer, 21 April 1991).

[36] R.N. FRYE, The History of Ancient Iran, München 1984, 139-140; E. BADIAN, in: The Cambridge History of Iran, 2, 1985, 438, n. 1, tends, however, to accept the mint at Babylon: «The coins of Mazaeus seem certain». M.J. PRICE, The Coinage in the Name of Alexander the Great and Philip Arrhidaeus, 1991, 451, stresses: «These latter issues can safely be placed at Babylon».

[37] G. LE RIDER, Tetradrachmes «au lion» et imitations d'Athènes en Babylonie, SM 85 (1972) 1-7, especially 4 (description of the tetradrachms).

hoards[38]. Further firm evidence is furnished by the change of the Persic weight of the «lion» staters to the Attic weight of the tetradrachms[39]. One has to remember also that the production of Mazaeus' «lion» tetradrachms and the imperial tetradrachms was presumably parallel and, finally, that the sequence which started with Mazaeus' Tarsus staters with lions on the Persic standard was followed at Babylon by his Attic weight «lion» tetradrachms[40]. It is also a significant fact that the «lion» tetradrachms struck by the Persian grandee were followed by the anonymous «lion» tetradrachms in Mazaeus' manner, produced with differing symbols in several eastern mints, into the twenties of the fourth century B.C., long after Mazaeus' death in 328.

The «lion» tetradrachms initiated by Mazaeus are a remarkable creation. The flans are thick. The borders show bulges and hammer blows[41]. Their legends and images, which came from the West, were new for the East, thus making the frequently found test cuts understandable. In fact, they constitute a new currency that bridges the gap between the many eastern Athenian owl imitations and other local coins produced in the 340s and 330s in the Persian realm and Alexander's new imperial money. It would not be surprising, therefore, to assume that the Macedonian administration de-

---

[38] CH 1 (1975) No. 38 and CH 3 (1977) No. 22, and recently J.M. PRICE, Circulation at Babylon in 323 B.C., in: Mnemata. Papers in Memory of N.M. Waggoner, ed. by W.E. METCALF, 1991, throughout, especially 67. 69.

[39] The weight is, in fact, a little lighter than the Attic norms and equals two Babylonian shekels. As the Tyrian example shows, a coin issue in the Attic standard before Alexander's conquest is not impossible in Phoenicia [see A. LEMAIRE, Le monnayage de Tyr et celui dit d'Acco dans la deuxième moitie du IVe siècle av. J.C., RN 6e sér. 18 (1976) 11 -24 throughout], but the production of Mazaeus' «lion» tetradrachms in Tarsus just before or just after Issus is unlikely, though the types and the lettering of the heavy tetradrachms and the preceding lighter staters are conspicuously similar. Until now, «lion» tetradrachms seem not to occur in hoards unearthed outside Babylonia [G. LE RIDER, SM 85 (1972) 6]. Did Mazaeus evacuate some mint craftsmen to the East, as had already been suspected by J.P. SIX, NC 3rd ser. 4 (1884) 138: «Je voudrais même aller plus loin avec eux jusqu'à Babylon, où Mazaeus est chargé du gouvernement par Alexandre»?

[40] There is another coinage, in the Attic standard, in the area controlled by Mazaeus: the didrachms struck in Hierapolis-Bambyce Cyrrhesticae near the western band of the Euphrates (Tf. XVIII 21-24). The striding and crouching lions on the didrachms of Hierapolis may have been influenced by Mazaeus' Tarsus issues and thus indicate a beginning of the coinage before Alexander reached the city. It is, however, inconceivable that the astonishing emission displaying the conqueror's name, ’lksndr , could have come into being before the summer of 331 B.C. See A Survey of Numismatic Research 1985-1990, Vol. I, Brussels 1991, 99, n. 31 with references. The lack of information on Mazaeus' whereabouts and functions between the battles of the Granicus and Gaugamela is worsened by the fact that the frontiers of Abar Nahara do not seem to have been clearly defined even in this late time. See P. CALMEYER, Transeuphratène 3 (1990) 111-112. 123, and E. LIPINSKI, Transeuphratène 3 (1990) 88. 102.

[41] Surprisingly, similar peculiarities can be seen on the thick shekels of the Bellum Iudaicum, A.D. 66-70, which are also a newly created, distinct coinage, see L. MILDENBERG, Schekel-Fragen, in: FS Herbert A. Cahn, Basel 1985, 83-88 [hier S. 170-175].

cided to present the seated figure of Zeus on the reverse of the imperial silver coins having been inspired by the image of the Baal of Tarsus[42].

Mazaeus was the only Persian grandee who served three Achaemenid Great Kings[43]. He was the only administrator of two important satrapies at one and the same time proudly stating this exceptional rank on his coins, and he produced money in three different Persian mints. He was one of the prominent survivors of earlier times, holding a high position under Alexander after having fought against him. In this capacity he again struck his own coins, displaying his name and his own types besides the new international currency in Alexander's name. All these coins formed an escort for his long career throughout the Levant; and he had them inscribed only in Semitic script, an action which is no less noteworthy than all his other extraordinary achievements.

## Supplementary Select Bibliography

AULOCK H. VON, Die Prägung des Balakros in Kilikien, JNG 14 (1964) 79-82

BETLYON J.W., The Coinage and Mints of Phoenicia, the pre-Alexandrine Period, Chico/CA 1982

ERZEN A., Kilikien bis zum Ende der Perserherrschaft, Leipzig 1940

HOWORTH H.H., A Note on Some Coins Generally Attributed to Mazaios the Satrap of Cilicia and Syria, NC, 4th ser. 3 (1903) 81-87

LUYNES H.DE, Essai sur la numismatique des Satrapies de la Phénicie, Paris 1846.

ex de Luynes: Catalogue de la collection de Luynes, Paris 1924

MESHORER Y. / QEDAR SH., The Coinage of Samaria in the Fourth Century BCE, Jerusalem - Los Angeles 1991

MØRKHOLM O., Early Hellenistic Coinage from the Accession of Alexander to the Peace of Apamaea, Cambridge 1991

MOYSEY R.A., The Silver Stater Issues of Pharnabazos and Datames from the Mint of Tarsus in Cilicia, MN 31 (1986) 7-61

NASTER P., Le dévelopement des monnayages phéniciens avant Alexandre d'après les trésors, Proceedings of the International Numismatic Convention Jerusalem 1963, Tel Aviv, 1967, 3-24

NEWELL E.T., Tarsos under Alexander, AJN 52 (1918) 69-115

NEWELL E.T., Myriandros-Alexandria Kat'Isson, AJN 53 (1919) 1-42, Pl. 1-3

---

[42] See above n. 7 and H.A. TROXELL, ibid., 58, who convincingly argues «that Alexanders from Tarsus must have made their way to Macedon before the introduction of the Alexander coinage there».

[43] Without counting the Achaemenid prince Arses who, nominally, became king in 338 B.C. The power, however, was in the hands of the court eunuch Bagoas who first poisoned Artaxerxes III, then put Arses on the throne and finally poisoned him in 336, after the prince's unsuccessful attempt to rid himself of the dangerous eunuch.

SCHULTZ S., Literaturüberblicke der griechischen Numismatik, Kilikien, Chiron 18
    (1988) 115-121
SEIBERT J., Alexander der Grosse, Darmstadt 1981
SNG H. VON AULOCK, Asia Minor, Berlin 1957-1968.

## Legends of the coins illustrated on Plates XVII - XVIII

1.  *b ʿltrz*
2.  *prnbzw klk*
3.  *trkmw*
4.  *mzdy*
5.  *mzdy zy ʿl ʿbr nhrʾ wḥlk*
6.  *mzdy*
7.  *mz*
8.  *šn*
9.  *b ʿldgn*
10. *ʿtr ʿth*
11. *ʾlksndr*

# Palästina in der persischen Zeit

## 1. Das Umfeld

Über die persischen Verwaltungseinheiten in Palästina berichtet neuerdings E. STERN[1]. Die dort stationierten Garnisonen wurden durch C. TUPLIN behandelt[2]. Über die nicht-numismatischen Sachquellen unterrichtet man sich durch die kurze Synopsis der Inschriften auf Stein, Ostraka, Papyri, Keilschrifttafeln, Siegel, Bullen, Metallgegenständen und Tongefässen bei H. WEIPPERT[3].

## 2. Der Münzumlauf

Einen wichtigen Beitrag zur Erfassung des Münzumlaufs im Palästina der persischen Zeit erbringen erstmalig J. ELAYI und A. LEMAIRE mit ihrem *Bulletin d'information sur la Syrie-Palestine* in der neuen Zeitschrift *Transeuphratène* [4]. Das Reichsgeld hat in unserem Gebiet keine Rolle gespielt; denn weder die goldenen Dareiken noch die in und für Kleinasien geprägten silbernen Sigloi werden hier gefunden[5]. Eigenes Geld der 5. Satrapie Abar Nahara hat es gar nicht gegeben, also konnte es auch nicht in der südlichen Levante zirkuliert haben[6], wie L. MILDENBERG betonte[7]. Der Satrap brauchte nicht zu prägen, denn vor etwa 450 v.

---

[1] E. STERN, New Evidence on the Administrative Division of Palestine in the Persian Period, in: Achaemenid History IV. Proceedings of the Groningen 1986 Achaemenid History Workshop, Leiden 1990, 221-226.

[2] C. TUPLIN, Xenophon and the Garrisons of the Achaemenid Empire, AMI 20 (1987) 167-245, insbesondere 238.

[3] H. WEIPPERT, Palästina in vorhellenistischer Zeit (HdA Vorderasien II,1), München 1988, 693-697.

[4] J. ELAYI / A. LEMAIRE, Numismatique, Transeuphratène 1 (1989) 159-163: 11. Les monnaies «philisto-arabes».

[5] Nach Transeuphratène 1 (1989) 163 wäre die in einer Grabung von Samaria-Sebaste gefundene Dareike die einzige Ausnahme. Diese Münze ist also im Norden Palästinas gefunden worden und dürfte eine nachpersische Prägung sein.

[6] Die Emissionen mit dem Namen Mazdai-Mazaeus sind rein lokale, sidonische Prägungen, die in jeder Hinsicht den vorhergehenden Serien folgen. Mazdai schafft also für Sidon Geld als Herrscher der Stadt und Nachfolger der sidonischen Könige, keinesfalls als Satrap von Abar Nahara, als Münzherr dieser 5.Satrapie.

[7] L. MILDENBERG, The Philisto-Arabian Coins. A Preview, in: T. HACKENS / GH. MOUCHARTE (ed.), Numismatique et histoire économique phéniciennes et puniques. Actes

Chr. genügte das Hacksilber[8]. Dann beginnt die reiche Silberprägung der phönizischen Städte, die das Angebot der importierten griechischen Silbermünzen ergänzt.

Im Süden beginnt die eigene lokale Geldversorgung um die Jahrhundertwende, zuerst mit Drachmen und deren Teilen nach attischem Muster; später setzen sich dann eigene Bilder durch.

Für die Provinzen Samaria und Judaea prägten deren Statthalter Silber-Kleingeld für den täglichen Gebrauch mit einem beträchtlichen Ausstoß um die Mitte des 4. Jahrhunderts. Neuerdings hat P. MACHINIST die früheren Publikationen dieser Provinzialprägungen gesichtet und unternommen, sie historisch zu deuten[9].

# 3. Samaria

Erst durch den Münzfund aus dem Gebiet von *Nablus* im Jahre 1968[10] ist völlig klar geworden, daß es eine Prägung der persischen Provinz Samaria im 4.Jahrhundert gegeben hat und nicht eine solche einer Stadt oder einer Münzhoheit; denn der Name der Provinz erscheint in Hebräisch und Aramäisch auf diesem für den täglichen Bedarf bestimmten Silber-Kleingeld. Einzelne dieser Fundstücke erschienen inzwischen auch in Auktionskatalogen unserer Berichtsperiode[11]. Eine Gesamt-Fundpublikation, die vorrangig ist, steht noch aus. Jüngst tauchten neben Streufunden zwei weitere Horte auf, deren Lokalisierung und Zusammensetzung als gesichert angegeben wird. Sie enthielten nur Silberkleinmünzen, also wohl ausschließlich Provinzialgeld. Neuerdings wurden die hier beschriebenen Münzen der Provinz Samaria nur vergleichsweise behandelt[12]. Eine Gesamtdarstellung der Prägungen von Samaria durch MESHORER und QEDAR ist in Vorbereitung [s. jetzt Y. MESHORER / SH. QEDAR, The Coinage of Samaria in the Fourth Century BCE, Jerusalem – Los Angeles 1991 ]. Sie wird sich auf die erwähnten Horte stützen und die Textfunde vom *Wādī ed-Dāliyeh* ergänzen, eine Perspektive, auf die soeben STERN hingewiesen hat[13].

---

du Colloque tenu à Louvain-la-Neuve 1987 (Num.Lov. 9; Stud.Phoen. 9), Louvain 1992, 33-40 [hier S. 88-94].

[8] C.M. KRAAY / P.R.S. MOOREY, Two Fifth Century Hoards from the Near East, RN 6e série, 10 (1968) 181-235.

[9] P. MACHINIST, The First Coins of Judah and Samaria, Numismatics and History in the Achaemenid and Early Hellenistic Periods, Tenth Achaemenid History Workshop, Ann Arbor/MI 1990, 1-12 (Vorveröffentlichung).

[10] IGCH 1504: «burial c.332 B.C. (Spaer)».

[11] Vgl. Leu 28 (1986) Nrn. 157-158; Leu 45 (1988) Nr. 279 [mit der Lesung *mēm-* ʿ*ayin* für Mazdai-Mazaeus um 340]; F. Sternberg, Katalog 22 (1989) Nrn. 140-144.

[12] L. MILDENBERG, Numismatic Evidence, HSCP 91 (1987) 389 [hier S. 253-262].

[13] E. STERN, in: Achaemenid History IV, Leiden 1990, 225.

## 4. Judaea

Das silberne Provinz-Kleingeld Samarias ist keine Einzelerscheinung. Die ab 1966 im Laufe eines Jahrzehnts zu Tage getretenen Yehud-Münzen, Obole sowie deren Teilstücke, tragen den Namen der Provinz zuerst auf Aramäisch *yhd*, dann auf Hebräisch *yhdh*, aber immer in palaeohebräischer Schrift. Zuerst erscheint zusätzlich der Name des jüdischen Statthalters mitsamt seinem persischen Titel *Yḥzqyh hpḥh*, Yehezqiyah, der Pascha, später der Name allein. Zwar beginnt die Prägung gleichzeitig mit der Samarias in der 1. Hälfte des 4.Jahrhunderts, aber sie endet erst in der ptolemäischen Zeit anfangs des 3.Jahrhunderts, was durch MILDENBERG wiederum betont wurde[14]. Neue wesentliche Evidenz wurde in dem in diesem Survey behandelten Zeitabschnitt aufgezeigt: D. BARAG las eine verwilderte palaeohebräische Münzlegende als *Ywḥnn hkwhn*, Yoḥanan, der Priester, und datierte sie ans Ende der persischen Zeit[15]. A. SPAER beschrieb eine vermutlich 1985 bei Hebron gefundene Kleinmünze mit dem Namen *ydwˁ*, Jaddua, in aramäischer Kursive und datierte sie ins zweite Viertel des 4.Jahrhunderts[16]. Yoḥanan und Jaddua sind Namen, die jüdische Hohepriester trugen. – Anzumerken ist noch der Vorschlag von J.W. BETLYON, die Yehud-Münzen analog der phönizischen Münzprägung zu datieren[17].

## 5. Die Küstenstädte

Ashdod hat Drachmen und Kleinmünzen geprägt, auf denen teils der ausgeschriebene Name der Stadt *ʾālef-šīn-dālet-dālet* steht, teils die Abkürzung durch die zwei ersten Buchstaben. Dazu kommt eine Gruppe ohne jede Inschrift, die durch Stempelkoppelungen mit der Hauptserie verbunden ist. MESHORER ist die Erstpublikation zu verdanken, ebenso ein soeben erschienener Abriss[18], in den auch Prägungen aufgenommen wurden, die ähnliche Bilder, aber keine Stempelverbindungen aufweisen. LEMAIRE vermutet die volle Legende Ashdod in Buchstabenspuren auf einem Obol in dem *Abū Šūše* -Material[19]. Im Laufe des letz-

---

[14] L. MILDENBERG, Über das Kleingeld in der persischen Provinz Judaea, in: H. WEIPPERT, Palästina in vorhellenistischer Zeit, 1988, 179-728. Vgl. J.C. GREENFIELD, Decouvertes épigraphiques récentes au service de l'histoire du retour de l'exil à Bar-Kokhba, in: E.M. LAPERROUSAS (ed.), Archéologie, Art et Histoire de la Palestine, Paris 1988, 45-46.

[15] Die letzte, zusammenfassende Darstellung ist D. BARAG, A Silver Coin of Yohanan the High Priest and the Coinage of Judea in the Fourth Century B.C., INJ 9 (1986-1987) 4-21.

[16] A. SPAER, Jaddua the High Priest?, INJ 9 (1986-1987) 1-3.

[17] J.W. BETLYON, The Provincial Government of Persian Period Judea and the Yehud Coins, JBL 105 (1986) 633-642.

[18] Y. MESHORER, The Mints of Ashdod and Ascalon during the Late Persian Period, ErIsr 20 [Y. Yadin Memorial Volume] (1989) 287-291 (hebr.; Engl. Summary 305*).

[19] A. LEMAIRE, Le trésor d'Abou Shousheh et le monnayage d'Ashdod avant Alexandre, RN 6e série, 32 (1990) 257-263. Vgl. C. LAMBERT, Egypto-Arabian, Phoenician and Other Coins of the Fourth Century B.C. found in Palestine, QDAP 2 (1933) 1-10 und M.C.

ten Jahrzehnts ist es jedenfalls gelungen, eine neue, beträchtliche Münzprägung darzustellen, die sich in Ashdod eindeutig als eine lokale, autonome Stadtprägung erweist und nicht als die Emission eines Satrapen oder Statthalters oder Einzelherrschers.

Askalon (?): In einer ebenfalls deutlich abgrenzbaren Gruppe finden sich die zwei Buchstaben ʼālef ' und nūn, also a - n . Sie könnten für den ersten und letzten Buchstaben des Namens ʼālef-šīn-qōf-lāmed-nūn stehen, was MESHORER annimmt[20]. In der südlichen Münzprägung kommt diese Art der Abkürzung allerdings nicht vor. Auch die Überlegung, daß man durch a-n eine Verwechslung mit Ashdod vermeiden wollte (beide Namen beginnen mit ʼālef-šīn ), dürfte nicht weiterführen; denn mindestens für den dritten Buchstaben wäre Platz im Münzfeld vorhanden gewesen.

Gaza: Die längst bekannte Prägung von Drachmen und Kleinmünzen zeigt den vollen oder abgekürzten Stadtnamen oder das mēm für den Stadtgott Marnas, eine bis in die spätrömische Kaiserzeit gebräuchliche Marke. Erst in unserer Berichtperiode hat sich gezeigt, daß auch die Tetradrachmen-Emission der Gaza-Eulen nicht unbeträchtlich ist. Dauer, Umfang, Standard, Bilder und Inschriften des Gesamtausstoßes sprechen für eine eigenständige, autonome Stadtprägung. Nur die zeitraubende Erfassung des gesamten Materials kann auch hier weiterführen. Einige Vorarbeiten durch MILDENBERG sind erschienen[21]. In dem jüngst erschienenen Abriss der Geschichte Gazas in persischer Zeit von KATZENSTEIN wird auch auf die Münzprägung hingewiesen[22].

# 6. Der Süden

In den letzten Jahren hat sich ebenfalls herausgestellt, daß auch im Süden die Münzprägung in der persischen Zeit umfangreich und vielgestaltig war. RIZACK hat durch die Veröffentlichung einer Kleinsilbermünze mit dem aramäisch geschriebenen Namen eines Herrschers als Münzherrn von Liḥyān neben der üblichen Eule gezeigt, daß die südlichen Münzen bis tief nach Nordarabien geprägt wurden[23]. Eine genaue Bestimmung der nördlichen Grenzlinie steht noch aus; denn wir wissen nicht genau,

---

KRAAY, Some Notes on the Abu Shusheh Hoard, IEJ 28 (1978) 190-192 sowie IGCH 1507.

[20] Y. MESHORER, ErIs 20 (1989) 287-291 (hebr.; Engl. Summary 305*).

[21] L. MILDENBERG, Gaza von 420 bis 332 nach den Sachquellen, Akten des XIII. Internationalen Kongresses für Klassische Archäologie Berlin 1988, Mainz 1990, 431f [hier S. 77-78], sowie id., Gaza Mint Authorities in Persian Time. Preliminary Studies in the Local Coinage in the Fifth Persian Satrapy, Part 4, Transeuphratène 2 (1990) 137-146 [hier S. 79-87].

[22] H.J. KATZENSTEIN, Gaza in the Persian Period, Transeuphratène 1 (1989) 67-86, Münzen 78 und 84 mit Anm. 138.

[23] M.A. RIZACK, A Coin with the Aramic Legend ŠHRW, a King-Governor of Liḥyan, ANSMN 29 (1984) 25-28.

wie weit herab die persische Provinz Judaea gereicht hat[24]. Daß die Küstenebene nicht zu Judaea gehört hat, ist sicher. Das Hauptgebiet der südlichen Prägungen war das Hinterland östlich und südlich von Gaza mit dem oberen Negev und damit dem Endstück der Weihrauchstraße. Über dieses arabische Land orientiert man sich durch die jüngeren Arbeiten von EPHʿAL, KNAUF und GRAF[25]. Im Süden wurden wiederum Drachmen und deren Teilstücke geprägt, zuerst Nachahmungen der attischen Typen, später Münzen mit vielen eigenständigen, bisweilen bizarren Bildern. Es finden sich nur wenige Inschriften, die oft zwar gelesen, aber nicht verstanden werden können. Ein sprechendes Beispiel ist die Legende *mnpt* auf dem *Abū Šūše* - Obol Nr. 4[26], dessen erstaunliche Forschungsgeschichte neulich von ELAYI und LEMAIRE skizziert wurde[27]. Nach manchen Irrwegen steht die Lesung fest, aber der sprachlich überzeugende Hinweis auf das ägyptische Memphis durch LIPINSKI[28] stößt auf die Schwierigkeit, daß nie auch nur eine einzige Münze dieser Art in Ägypten gefunden wurde. Auch die Deutung der Bilder ist schwierig. Ist etwa der Kamelreiter auf den stempelgleichen Drachmen im Britischen Museum[29] und der Bibliothèque Nationale[30] nach KNAUF der nordarabische Kriegsgott Ruḍā[31] oder nur ein arabischer Speerschleuderer auf dem *šadād*-Kampfsattel[32]? In Stückelung, Metall, Fabrik, Schrift, Bildern und Prägedauer, die nur bis auf Alexander reicht, entspricht die südliche Prägung der von Gaza in solchem Maße, daß eine Lohnmünzstätte für fremde Rechnung neben dem betriebsamen städtischen Atelier denkbar erscheint, worauf MILDENBERG in Vorberichten hingewiesen hat[33].

---

[24] Zur Situation im 5.Jahrhundert v. Chr. siehe Z. KALLAI, The Southern Border of the Land of Israel – Pattern and Application, VT 37 (1987) 438-445.

[25] I. EPHʿAL, The Ancient Arabs, Jerusalem – Leiden 1982, und E.A. KNAUF, Ismael – Untersuchung zur Geschichte Palästinas und Nordarabiens im 1.Jahrtausend v. Chr., Wiesbaden [2]1989, sowie D.F. GRAF, Arabia during Achaemenid Times, in: Achaemenid History IV, 1990, 131-148.

[26] Siehe C. LAMBERT, QDAP 2 (1933) 1-10 und C.M. KRAAY, IEJ 28 (1978) 190-192 sowie IGCH 1507 mit weiterer Literatur, Angabe der Fund- und Vergrabungszeit: «c. 330 B.C. (Naster)».

[27] J. ELAYI / A. LEMAIRE, Transeuphratène 1 (1989) 161.

[28] E. LIPINSKI, Aramaic Coins from the Fifth and Fourth Centuries B.C., Studia P. Naster Oblata 1 (Numismatica Antiqua, OrLovA 12), Leuven 1982, 23-32, insbesondere 30.

[29] BMC Palestine, Pl. 19:25.

[30] E. BABELON, Traité, No. 1068.

[31] Mit dem Cognomen Shaiʿ al-Qaum nach E.A. KNAUF, Dushara and Shaiʿ al-Qaum, in: Lectio difficilior probabilior? Mélanges offerts à F. Smyth-Florentin, ed. TH. RÖMER (BDBAT 12), Heidelberg 1991, 19-29.

[32] Zu dieser wichtigen technischen Entwicklung siehe E.A. KNAUF, Ismael, [2]1989, 61. 109, Anm. 25.

[33] L. MILDENBERG, in: Akten des XIII. Internationalen Kongresses für Klassische Archäologie, 1990, 431f [hier S. 77f], sowie id., Transeuphratène 2 (1990) 137-146 [hier S. 79-87].

# On the Money Circulation in Palestine from Artaxerxes II till Ptolemy I.
## Preliminary Studies of the Local Coinage in the Fifth Persian Satrapy. Part 5*

(Tf. XIX - XX)

Résumé : De 404 à 332, ni la monnaie impériale perse ni les monnaies «satrapiques» n'ont circulé en Palestine. Le numéraire quotidien dans les provinces de Judée et de Samarie était assuré au IV$^e$ siècle par leurs gouverneurs sous forme de monnaies divisionnaires en argent, les monnaies provinciales. Quelques monnaies grecques importées circulaient encore, s'ajoutant aux nombreux tétradrachmes pseudo-athéniens. La masse monétaire était cependant constituée par les frappes locales, produisant des drachmes en argent et des divisionnaires pour les cités maritimes et des monnaies philisto-arabes pour les autorités émettrices arabes. Il faut surtout souligner l'originalité du monnayage provincial de la Judée qui continua à être frappé après la période perse, sous la domination macédonienne et ptolémaïque.

## Introduction

Coinage and currency in any part of the Persian Empire and at any time cannot be understood if their scope and structure have not been clarified. It is therefore necessary to examine the money circulation in the decades before Artaxerxes II came to power in 404 and to compare it with the situation in the ninety odd years till the death of Ptolemy I in 282.

In the last quarter of the fifth century, silver metal was still the main mean of payment under the Achaemenids. How this worked is demonstrated by a scene portrayed true to life in a marriage contract of a former slave girl in 420 from the archive of the Aramaean speaking Jews serving in the Persian garrison of Elephantine: «If, on the other hand, Yehoyishma should divorce her husband, she shall became

---

* Part 1: Yehud: A Preliminary Study of the Provincial Coinage of Judaea, in: FS M. Thompson, Wetteren 1979, 183-196 [hier S. 67-76];   Part 2: Baana: Preliminary Studies of the Local Coinage in the Fifth Persian Satrapy, ErIs [M. Avi-Yonah Vol.] 19 (1987) 29-35 [hier S. 35 - 42];   Part 3: The Philisto-Arabian Coins – A Preview. Preliminary Studies of the Local Coinage in the Fifth Persian Satrapy, in: Actes du colloque tenu à Louvain-la-Neuve, 13-16 mai 1987 (Stud. Phoen. 9), Louvain 1992, 33-40 [hier S. 88-94];   Part 4: Gaza Mint Authorities in Persian Time, Transeuphratène 2 (1990) 137-146 [hier S. 79-87].

liable for divorce money. She shall sit by the scales and weigh out to her husband Ananiah 7 shekels and 2 quarters»[1].

In addition to silver metal, imported Greek silver coins were available, as the hoards and the local imitations show, often cut into small pieces to be used in the manner of Yehoyishma[2]. The imperial money, the silver siglos and the gold daric, was created around 500, as is proved by the coin used as a seal which was published by M.C. ROOT[3]. The much discussed, but still not clearly defined, satrap coins appeared around 400[4]. From about 360 on, the provincial coinage came into being, because the province governors cared now for the supply of the daily cash in the form of small silver coins. The last main group of money is represented by the longlasting, colourful and often substantial local coinages which in the Western Levant began just after 450. The mint authorities of these local issues were kings, dynasts or other rulers and city officials within the Persian realm. This fact attests the practical, pragmatic money policy of the Achaemenid administration[5] which contrasts sharply with all kinds of centralized, monopolized currencies in Antiquity. Suffice it to mention the closed, uniformed system conceived for Egypt by the followers of Ptolemy I and carried through well into the fourth century A.D.

# 1. The imperial coinage

As to the situation in Palestine, we dispose here of a most valuable tool for any study, the Inventory of Greek Coin Hoards, published in 1973 and supplemented by annual news collected by M. PRICE. Not to be disdained are indications received

---

[1] ANET[3] 549 = E.G. KRAELING, The Brooklyn Museum Aramaic Papyri, New Haven/CT 1953, Papyrus 7; B. PORTEN / J.C. GREENFIELD, Jews of Elephantine and Aramaeans of Syene, Jerusalem 1984, 54, however, translate I. 26: «She shall place upon the balance-scale and give her husband Ananiah silver, 7 shekels, 2 quarters».

[2] C.M. KRAAY / P.R.S. MOOREY, Two Fifth Century Hoards from the Near East, RN 10 (1968) 181-235.

[3] M.C. ROOT, Evidence from Persepolis for the Dating of Persian and Archaic Greek Coinage, NC 148 (1988) 1-12.

[4] See L. MILDENBERG, Gaza Mint Authorities in Persian Time, Transeuphratène 2 (1990) 139, n. 10 [hier S. 81].

[5] The first local coins appear around 450 in Tyros. Their output lasts till 332, thus not only in periods of decline of the Empire. The Achaemenid money policy is in accordance with the general principle of the administration to grant autonomy to the local authorities on lower level. The government in Susa did not mind at all that the names of the governors of small provinces, whether Persian or not, appeared, with or without their titles, on the small silver coins serving for the daily cash. There are, however, monetary issues by high officials which come close to real sovereign coinages. In the distant West, the Carian rulers of the Hekatomnid dynasty did never cease to act as Persian satraps, see especially the trilingual inscription in the Letoon at Lycian Xanthos, S. HORNBLOWER, Mausolus, Oxford 1982, 366-367 and P. FREI, Zentralgewalt und Lokalautonomie im achämenidischen Kleinasien, Transeuphratène 3 (1990) no. 26, p. 168, with n. 34. However, their longlasting and prolific money production of high silver nominals and even some gold coins display their own names and their Carian types from the beginning of the fourth century till the time of Alexander's conquest.

from local officials, collectors and dealers. Here is a short survey: some Greek silver coins from archaic and early classical issues have been found in Palestine, but we do not know of any substantial hoard of the sixth and fifth centuries. Most surprising is the result that no imperial silver sigloi have been unearthed in Palestine and only one late gold daric was found in Samaria-Sebaste[6]. More astonishing even is the Abarnahara satrap's abstention from striking coins, as I have stressed before[7]. Mazdai's name does appear indeed, on coins of Sidon, but I insist here again that he simply continued the local coinage as Sidon's ruler after the Persian reconquest of the rebellious city. He acts, too, as a local mint authority putting his name or initials on few tiny coins from the Nablus hoard[8]. Tarsus is first of all a city, but the famous group of Tarsian silver staters with the names of Mazdai and of Transeuphratesia and Cilicia is a satrapal issue and, thus, entirely different from the pieces just discussed, in fact a distinct maior emission of a satrap[9].

## 2. The provincial coinage

My Yehud study in the Festschrift M. Thompson has found considerable attention as far as it dealt with the small silver coins, surprisingly displaying the names of the Persian province Judaea, its governor and even his title. No attention, however, has been paid, so far as I know, to the unusual and essential fact, duly stressed by me, that the Yehud coinage did continue well into the third century. This continuation is highly significant in the context of our colloquium. These tiny silver coins have, indeed, teared down the political and economical frontiers of the time. They survived Alexander and existed till the death of Ptolemy I[10].

It has been argued against me that the Yehud coinage lasted even much longer, showing the portrait not of Ptolemy I, but of Ptolemy II, who «unlike his father was very generous to the Jews»[11]. In a survey following the Festschrift M. Thompson article and recently published, I have stressed that the daily cash under

---

[6] J. ELAYI / A. LEMAIRE, Numismatique, Transeuphratène 1 (1989) 163.

[7] L. MILDENBERG, Transeuphratène 2 (1990) 138 [hier S. 2f].

[8] Y. MESHORER / SH. QEDAR, The Coinage of Samaria in the Fourth Century, Jerusalem - Los Angeles 1991, nos. 14, 16, 21, 28, (name always abbreviated by the first two letters: *MZ* ).

[9] The great coinage of Tarsus always displays the name of the city in Greek and Aramaic which testifies for a loval municipal coinage, but sometimes also the name of Cilicia. The first Persian satraps added their names in Aramaic, nothing more. It is only after the defeat of the Phoenician rebel cities in 343 that Mazaeus-Mazdai governed Transeuphratesia, the Fifth Satrapy, and Cilicia as a satrap, stating his double function by his name and power: *MZDY ZY 'L 'BR NHR' WḤLK*, «Mazaeus who is over Transeuphratesia and Cilicia».

[10] M. HENGEL, in: CHJud II, 55: «In the areas under Ptolemaic rule there was a strict monopoly of coinage which had ist own standard, which was quite different from the usual attic one». This is certainly to the point for the later Ptolemies, but under Ptolemy I the Yehud silver coins with his portrait and those in small size of him and his queen Berenice I were still struck in the attic weight.

[11] Y. MESHORER, Ancient Jewish Coinage I, Dix Hills/NY 1982, 184.

Ptolemy II was copper and that, therefore, small silver coins had simply no *raison d'être* anymore[12]. Further, the reestablishment of such a Judaean silver cash coinage after an interruption of half a century seems highly hazardous to me. Finally, there is new evidence which reinforces my chronology: triobols (or hemidrachms) with a most characteristic head of Ptolemy I[13]. The denomination, however, is new and surprising. The output of the last Yehud group, which had emerged so suddenly on the market in the seventies, might be more varied and substantial than we ever thought. There is other significant evidence, obviously neglected by recent scholarship, historians and art historians alike: I had emphasized the importance of the first real portrait of a living queen, Berenike I. This was, as the press slogan nowadays goes, neither «confirmed nor rejected».

In the course of the last decades another revelation did occur: the coinage of the Palestinian province of Samaria in Persian times emerged in the so-called Nablus hoard of 1968. Few other stray and hoard finds followed. Y. MESHORER and SH. QEDAR have just published a comprehensive study of these materials[14]. Hopefully, S. HURTER and A. SPAER will still care for a full publication of the Nablus hoard, an exhaustive *Fundbericht*, illustrating all specimens. Meanwhile, I can only stress in our context that this money issued in the province Samaria has been buried during the troubled years from the Persian reconquest of Egypt, thus about 344, till the Alexander storm of 332, in contrast to the Yehud hoard which was hidden around 280. On the issues of the province of Samaria we find, in fact, the same metal, denomination and script as on the coins of the province of Iudaea. The full name of the province does appear in two forms, *Šōmrōn* and *Šāmrayin*, but not the full name and not the title of a governor, as on several Yehud coins. Two letters only can be detected, *sāmekh - nūn*, which may be an abbreviation of Sanballat, the name of several governors of Samaria, but full evidence is still lacking.

There is another difference to be noted: for Judaea, we have only one specimen of a higher denomination - the unique Yehud drachm in the British Museum. In the Nablus hoard, there were several drachms and obols of the same types. It is sure that these drachms and obols come from the same Nablus hoard, but are they both a Samarian production? There are many non-Samarian issues in this mixed hoard. The significance in our context is obvious: the Persian administration of two Palestinian provinces produced their own coins for the money circulation in their territory during the fourth century until Alexander.

---

[12] L. MILDENBERG, in: H. WEIPPERT, Palästina in vorhellenistischer Zeit (HdA Vorderasien II/1), München 1988, 727.

[13] Y. MESHORER, Ancient Jewish Coinage I, 1982, 184, ill. 2.

[14] Y. MESHORER / SH. QEDAR, The Coinage of Samaria, 1991.

# 3. The local coinage

This is, as mentioned before, our largest and most diversified group. First of all, we have to deal shortly with the Eastern silver tetradrachms produced in the Athenian manner. It is certain that they all have been made in the vast territory from the Nile to the Oxus from about 410 till Alexander's money reform. But nobody can tell till this day what has been struck, when, where and by whom if the issues are anepigraphic; I mean full evidence, not assumptions. After over 40 years of experience, I personally would not dare to pretend that I can discern always and with certainty between Athenian originals and their Eastern imitations (Tf. XIX 1-4). And I doubt, whether the essayer, installed for that purpose on the Athenian Agora, about 400, was always able to do so[15]. The hoard evidence, so far as it is known, may give some indications, but no certainty at all, as these coins circulated widely as a sort of *moneta franca* .

## A. The cities by the sea

First of all: Gaza. I shall certainly not repeat what I have said in several papers dealing with this great city[16]. But in our context of today, I have to stress that the coinage is obviously the major reliable source and that it testifies to its status which is unique in the South: autonomy, city-State administration («Cité-Etat du type polis» in the wording of the invitation to this colloquium), economic power, interconnection on land and sea (being the terminus of the frankincense road), cosmopolitan life. May I stress again only one fact: there is not the slightest hint in the coinage to a king or dynast or satrap or governor or local ruler of any kind, but much similarity to Tyre with the exception that old Gaza was not the same anymore after Alexander had burnt it to the ground, whereas Tyre recovered soon. The Gaza coinage lasted from about 420/410 till 332. It is abundant and varied, displaying tetradrachms of Athenian type (Tf. XIX 5-8), drachms with Athenian and local types and fractions with different images (Tf. XIX 9-12). This coinage proves the importance of Gaza as the main port and road junction in the South, whereas literary sources before Alexander's conquest are silent and systematic excavations in the city and the port have not been undertaken.

Then Ashdod: there is now new and indisputable evidence for the coinage of Ashdod, another city by the sea, open for influence from many directions[17], the full

---

[15] See T.R. MARTIN, Silver Coins and Public Slaves in the Athenian Law of 375/4 B.C., in: Mnemata. Papers in Memory of N.M. Waggoner, New York 1991, 21-47.

[16] L. MILDENBERG, Gaza von 420 bis 332 nach den Sachquellen, in Akten des XIII. Internationalen Kongresses für Klassische Archäologie, Berlin 1988, Mainz 1990, 431-432 [hier S. 77-78], and id., Transeuphratène 2 (1990) 137-146 [hier S. 79-87].

[17] See Y. MESHORER, The Mints of Ashdod and Ascalon during the Late Persian Period, ErIs 20 (1989) 287-291 (in Hebrew with English summary p. 205), also Y. MESHORER / SH. QEDAR, The Coinage of Samaria, 1991, 9, ill., and A. LEMAIRE's reading proposal

name of the city written in four letters and the abbreviation by the two first letters, drachms and fractions with distinct types in Attic weight (Tf. XX 13-15) as in Gaza, revealing even some die links. The output must, however, been much less important than that of the great city in the South.

Further Ascalon: there is an impressive homogenous group which, too, must belong to a mint in southern Palestine because of provenance, metal, denomination, fabric, type and lettering. Again, no evidence for a ruler as the minting authority. This is the third, clearly municipal coinage at the southern coast (Tf. XX 16-20). For once, all coins are inscribed, which is noteworthy: two letters, *ʾāleph* and *nūn* . Anthedon is too closely situated to the port of Gaza and too small a locality to produce a considerable coinage. It is all doubtful whether this city already existed in the 4th century. Most scholars seem to vote for *ʾAšqəlōn* -Ascalon because of the first and last letters. Such an abbreviation is assumed for some Phoenician seals and few Punic inscriptions. On small Byblos coins[18] abbreviations occur by the first two letters and by the first and last letter. There is, indeed, convincing evidence on small coins of Samaria[19]. In the southern coinage, however, the last letter is never used in this way. Surely, Ascalon is, too, a city by the sea, situated between Gaza and Ashdod, and would, therefore, be an appropriate candidate. But as long as convincing evidence from the South is lacking, a cautious numismatist would not dare a definite attribution.

## B. The coinage at the southern border

This second main group of the so-called Philisto-Arabian coins displays the same metal, standard, fabric and script as the coins struck in the cities by the sea. The types are very similar (Tf. XX 21-24). Have they all been struck in Gaza in the municipal or parallel mint[20]? Could these for the most part sophisticated coins have been conceived and produced in a tent? Until now, scholarship has revealed small desert fortresses and caravanserais only, no real urban settlements. But the coins are here and do come from the region.

---

*ʾŠDD* on a small silver coin in the so-called Abu Shusheh hoard, published by C. LAMBERT, Egypto-Arabian, Phoenician, and other Coins of the Fourth Century B.C. Found in Palestine, QDAP 2 (1932) 1-10, Pl. 2:59; M. THOMPSON et al., IGCH, New York 1973; cf. A. LEMAIRE, Le trésor d'Abou Shousheh et le monnayage d'Ashdod avant Alexandre, RN 6e série 32 (1990) 257-263.

[18] J. ELAYI, Les monnaies de Byblos au sphinx et au faucon, RSF 11 (1983) 5-17, esp. 9; J. ELAYI / A. LEMAIRE, Les petites monnaies de Tyr au dauphin avec inscription, NAC 19 (1990) 112.

[19] That means evidence for an abbreviation by the first and the last letter: on a small silver coin, the full name of the province Samaria *ŠMRYN* appears right of a seated Persian king, whereas on another piece with the same obverse image the abbreviation *ŠN* is seen left to the seated king: Y. MESHORER / SH. QEDAR, The Coinage of Samaria, 1991, nos. 18 and 21 and p. 48.

[20] Compare L. MILDENBERG, Transeuphratène 2 (1990) 141 [hier S. 5-7].

But does this southern border region still belong to Palestine and to the Persian Empire? And who are the minting authorities? In my view, the Great King did never rule the desert. Before him, Nabonid had tried to accomplish the impossible and had failed. Nehemia's «Geshem the Arab» and Herodotus' «King of the Arabs» of the mid-fifth century remain pale figures, as recent studies have shown. When and where did they rule? Was their main occupation to collect tribute for the Achaemenid Great King? We are on somewhat safer ground as to «Qainu, son of Gesem, King of Qedar», inscribed on one of the Brooklyn silver bowls from Tell el-Maskhūṭa in the Delta[21] which had an Arab garrison in the second part of the fifth century, thus well before the Persians lost Egypt in 404. Our period is, however, the fourth century and our region is the land between the brook of Egypt, the creek of the Araba and the Ramon crater, thus the territories of the frankincense road with the still flourishing spice trade. Were the Arabs dwelling there: Qedarites, Idumaeans or early Nabataeans? Anyway, their rulers were our minting authorities, not the Persian administration. The frankincense trade was then only feasible, if these Arab rulers, the Persian officials at the *via maris*, the spice transporters and the operators at the terminus, the port of Gaza, worked together, as I have stressed before[22].

Collectors and dealers confirm that our Philisto-Arabian coins are found together with those of the coastal cities, not only around Gaza, but also in the Hebron neighbourhood. They represent, therefore, a part of the money circulation in Palestine and had to be discussed here.

## 4. The money circulation from 332 till 282

We have already seen that the Yehud coins continue through the Macedonian period well into Ptolemaic times. One would be prepared to encounter silver tetradrachms and their fractions struck by these new governments often in the hoards or on the market as well. But here the hoard evidence is rather scanty: 2 hoards from Galilaea with tetradrachms of Alexander III and his successors: IGCH 1510 Kinneret with 40 Alexanders from different mints and 64 double shekels of Sidon down to Mazaeus – a significant mixture – and IGCH 152 Tarchiha with 111 Alexander tetradrachms, mainly from his Ake-Ptolemais mint. Ptolemy I issues have been unearthed rarely and in Samaria only by the Shechem excavations: 1. 1956 (IGCH 1584) 15 bronzes, which strengthens again my argument that the introduction of the bronze coinage (a fiduciary currency – «monnaie fiduciaire») for the daily cash occurred under Ptolemy I already and became dominant under Ptolemy II, excluding late tiny silver coins; 2. 1966 (IGCH 1588) a pot hoard of 35 tetradrachms from Ptolemy I (4 specimens) to Ptolemy V, thus a group assembled at the beginning of the second century and, therefore, not essential in our context. As to Gaza after 332, the city and its mint did

---

[21] I. Rabinowitz, Aramaic Inscriptions from the Fifth Century B.C.E. from a North Arab Shrine in Egypt, JNES 15 (1956) 1-10 and W.J. Dumbrell, The Tell el-Maskhuṭa Bowls and the Kingdom of Qedar in the Persian Period, BASOR 203 (1971) 33-34.

[22] See L. Mildenberg, Transeuphratène 2 (1990) 146 [hier S. 86f].

not recover for a long time, whereas Antigonos Monophtalmos reopened the mint of Tyre in 307. Ptolemy I used it at some time between 294 and 286, an astounding resurrection of the island city – in striking contrast to the southern port.

## Conclusion

In Palestine, from 404 till 332, neither Persian imperial money nor satrapal coins did circulate. The daily cash for the provinces of Judaea and Samaria in the 4th century was secured by their governours in form of the small silver coins, the provincial money. Some imported Greek silver coins did still circulate in addition to substantial quantities of local Athenian tetradrachm imitations. The bulk of the money supply, however, came from local mints, producing silver drachms and fractions for the cities by the sea and for the minting authorities issuing the southern Philisto-Arabian coins. For this entire local coinages, the metal was silver exclusively, the standard Athenian, the denominations medium and small, the legends Semitic and the types colourful, partly borrowed, partly original. Relevant in our context is the emergence of two truly great coinages, that of the city-states by the sea and that of the Arab minting authorities.

Especially noteworthy today is the up to now unique fact of the overlapping production of the Yehud coins, the provincial money of Judaea from Persian over Macedonian to Ptolemaic rule. Before I conclude, I have to rectify a former statement. The present text has been conceived in spring 1991. One may have noticed before that I deplored that two of the essential propositions of my Yehud-study of 1979 have «neither been confirmed nor rejected». This cannot be said anymore. The late O. MØRKHOLM had, indeed, agreed with me in 1982, as it is shown in his «Early Hellenistic Coinage», published posthumously in summer 1991[23]. As for Berenike I, he accepts now «the earliest strictly contemporary portrait» of a queen. As for the Ptolemaic royal monopoly in monetary matters, he, too, regards the overlapping Yehud coinage «a surprising exception for which no satisfactory explanation has been offered». I do certainly not pretend to offer this explanation which the great numismatist and historian could not give, but the evidence itself hints to a still pragmatic policy under Ptolemy I who allowed the old cash supply to be continued in a small border province. That with the reign of Ptolemy II the monopoly in Egypt was tightened is another matter of fact.

---

[23] O. MØRKHOLM, Early Hellenistic Coinage, ed. P. GRIERSON and U. WESTERMARK, Cambridge 1991, 70.

# Yehud: A Preliminary Study of the Provincial Coinage of Judaea[*]

(Tf. XXI - XXII)

## 1. The Yehud Drachm with the God on the Winged Wheel (Tf. XXI 1)

### 1.1. The Legend

The drachm BMC Palestine Pl. 19,29, «the unique and much discussed piece in the British Museum»[1], has an inscription with three Aramaic letters *yhd*. Early scholars read the third letter as *w* and the legend therefore as *yhw*, the name of the Jewish God. The third letter, however, can also be a *d*, a fact long known[2]. In this case the word would be *yhd* (spelled here Yehud), the Aramaic name of the province of Judaea. This second reading was definitely accepted after the appearance of the minute silver coins[3] and the stamped seals, bullae and jar impressions[4] which where of different types, but showed the Yehud inscription. In recent years this evidence has become overwhelming. There can no longer be any doubt: the inscription on the BM drachm is *yhd* and means Judaea in Aramaic.

---

[*] For discussion I am indebted to A. Spaer; for photographs to A. Bromberg, S. Hurter, G. K. Jenkins, D. Jeselsohn, Y. Meshorer, M.J. Price, A. Spaer and S. Qedar; for revision of the English text to P.K. Erhart and G.M. Bendall.

[1] B. Kanael, Altjüdische Münzen, JNG 17 (1967) 164-165; Y. Meshorer, Jewish Coins of the Second Temple Period, Jerusalem 1967, 36-38; M.J. Price, Coins and the Bible, London 1975, 10-11; H. Kienle, Der Gott auf dem Flügelrad. Zu den ungelösten Fragen der synkretistischen Münze BMC Palestine S. 181, Nr. 291 (GOF 6,7), Wiesbaden 1975, with survey of major literature.

[2] M. Lidzbarski, Handbuch der nordsemitischen Epigraphik, Weimar 1898, Pl. 45; E.L. Sukenik, Paralipomena Palaestinensia, JPOS 14 (1934) 178-182; id., More About the Oldest Coins ot Judaea, JPOS 15 (1935) 341-343; F.M. Cross, Judaean Stamps, ErIs 9 (1969) 24-26.

[3] Y. Meshorer, Jewish Coins of the Second Temple Period, 1967, 35-40; L.Y. Rahmani, Silver Coins of the fourth Century BC from Tel Gamma, IEJ 21 (1971) 158-160; A. Kindler, Silver Coins Bearing the Name of Judaea from the Early Hellenistic Period, IEJ 24 (1974) 73-76; D. Jeselsohn, A New Coin Type with Hebrew Inscription, IEJ 24 (1974) 77-78; A. Spaer, Some More Yehud Coins, IEJ 27 (1977) 200-203.

[4] N. Avigad, Bullae and Seals from a Post-Exilic Judaean Archive (Qedem 4), Jerusalem 1976.

## 1.2. The Types

Both the obverse and the reverse types of the BM drachm have an «undoubted pagan character»[5], which seems unsuitable for the Jewish population of Judaea[6]. The obverse displays the bearded head of a man in a Corinthian helmet[7]; the reverse the bearded figure of a deity seated on a winged wheel. The deity wears a long himation and holds a large Egyptian falcon in his outstretched left hand. The figure is observed from the lower right by a huge head of the Egyptian demi-god Bes facing left. At the top is the Yehud legend which is in Aramaic, the official language of the Persian Empire, and is written in the Palaeo-Aramaic script. The figure on the winged wheel obviousiy does not represent the God of the Jews[8], or even a Greek or Persian deity, but instead appears to be a composite creature, a highly syncretistic image formed from most heterogeneous elements. That which is depicted is not a specific god, but a general conception of deity easily comprehensible to many people in the western part of the Persian Empire[9].

## 1.3. Mint, Minting Authority, Standard, Date

The BM drachm was certainly struck for Judaea as the legend indicates. The Persian Empire was anything but a centralized state in the fourth century, with the result that some satrapies, provinces and cities[10] minted their own local coins[11]. Therefore, it is

---

[5] Y. MESHORER, Jewish Coins of the Second Temple Period, 1967, 37.

[6] The design is indeed offensive to the eyes of today's Jews. This may not bave been the case in Judaea during the later period of Persian rule.

[7] The Corinthian helmet is a Greek feature, and bearded and helmeted heads of gods, heroes and warriors occur in Greek coinage of the fourth century from Sicily to Cilicia. A comparison of our obverse with the head, profile left, of the Syrian-Sicilian god Hadranus of the third century – cf. M. Särström, A Study in the Coinage of the Mamartines, Lund 1940, Pl. 18,137-146 – is indeed «fortuitous», as G.F. HILL put it (BMC Palestine, LXXXVII). For the syncretistic nature of the Philisto-Arabian drachms and small silver, cf. E. BABELON, Traité 2, 640.

[8] M. PRICE, Coins and the Bible, 1975, 10: «...for there can be no doubt that the bearded figure seated on a winged wheel is a deity and thus the God of the Jews»; Y. MESHORER, Jewish Coins of the Second Temple Period, 1967, 37: «... a representation of God as the Persians pictured Him ..., a customary procedure of theirs». – The syncretistic nature of the type, however, a priori precludes its identification with the God of the Jews, be it Jewish or Persian in manner. Furthermore, the coinage in the western part of the Persian Empire is of a local character, cf. L. MILDENBERG, Nergal in Tarsos, in: Festschrift für H. Bloesch (AK.B 9), 1973, 78-80 [hier S. 31 - 34]: on Cilician coins the Babylonian god Nergal is rendered in the manner of Tarsus and so labelled «Nergal Tars».

[9] BMC Palestine, LXXXVIII: «The characteristic of all this group of coins is that they represent types likely to attract the people among whom they circulated». Cf. H. KIENLE, Der Gott auf dem Flügelrad, 1975, 26.

[10] The minting authority under which coins were issued by both satraps and provincial governors was ultimately the Persian Empire. After 395, however, the satraps of Asia Minor put their own names and local types on silver and gold money. This holds true for

most likely that this unique coin was issued by the provincial governor of Judaea and produced in a local Judaean mint, possibly Jerusalem. It has recently been pointed out[12] that no larger silver coins of the Persian period and only «two coins of the early Yehud series were found in controlled excavations in Jerusalem»[13]. As early as 1914 G.F. HILL in BMC Palestine had separated our drachm and a second coin of similar fabric, style, weight and type[14] from all of the other so-called «Philisto-Arabian» drachms of Attic weight in the British Museum. The earlier Philisto-Arabian pieces, in fact, weigh around 3.8 g The heaviest coin in the BM weights 4.21 g, the lightest 3.35 g. Several pieces appeared in recent auction sales: highest weight 4.17 g, lowest 3.37 g[15], and the unique drachm only 3.29 g. This difference in weight is one of the reasons why the large series of usual Philisto-Arabian coins[16] is earlier than the smaller group with the unique piece. The smaller group cannot, however, be placed at the end of the Persian domination just before

---

the local rulers of some Cyprian city-states as well. The «kings» of the major cities on the Phoenician coast were less independent but, nevertheless, struck their own silver coins. For the special status of a «metropolis» of Berytus and Sidon, cf. BMC Phoenicia, 1. CVI. For Gaza as «metropolis» and the local prince or dynast *'bd'l* (Ebedel or Abdiel) cf. Y. MESHORER, Three Gaza Coins from the Persian Period, IMN 12 (1977) 78-79.

[11] Cf. D. SCHLUMBERGER, L'argent grec dans l'Empire Achéménide, Paris 1953, especially 30: «Jusqu'à la conquête macédonienne, la circulation de la monnaie d'argent dans l'empire perse reste dans une large mesure archaïque et dépendante du monde grec». The issues described in n. 11 above, however, are neither archaic nor dependent upon the Greek world; they are personal and local, although in general the satraps and local authorities employed some Greek types and perhaps even die engravers from Greece. – In Palestine the small silver denominations must have been essential for the local economy; hoards with such small silver so far known are large: see the Nablus hoard with many obols of Cilician and Phoenician type (IGCH 1504) and the Bethlehem hoard of minute Yehud silver, cf. A. SPAER, IEJ 27 (1977) 203.

[12] A. SPAER, IEJ 27 (1977) 203, n. 7.

[13] Cf. M. BROSHI, Excavations on Mount Zion, 1971-1972, IEJ 26 (1977) 83 and n. 6 (reference to a coin found in a Jerusalem dig 1969).

[14] Pl. 19,28. Some other pieces of this second group of lower weight: E. BABELON, Traité, Pl. 124,12-13.18; H. BLOESCH, Das Winterthurer Münzkabinett 1948-1958, SNR 1958, n. 83 and Hess-Leu 31, 6-7 Dec. 1966, 531; Bank Leu 2, 25 April 1972, 297, obverse illustrated M. PRICE, Coins and the Bible, 1975, fig. 11; Cahn 71, 14 April 1931, 575, attributed to Ascalon or Ashdod by E.T. NEWELL, Miscellanea Numismatica: Cyrene to India (ANSNNM 82), New York 1938, 20. The weights ot these coins oscillate between 3.32 g and 2.81 g. They all have an incuse square with a border of large dots or a cable pattern.

[15] The heaviest coin in the BM weights 4.21 g, the lightest 3.35 g. Several pieces appeared in recent auction sales: highest weight 4.17 g, lowest 3.37 g.

[16] For the entire series of «Philisto-Arabian» and «Egypto-Arabian» coins see E. BABELON, Traité, pls. 123,10-25 and 124,1-28; also BMC Palestine, Pl. 19; cf. E.T. NEWELL, Miscellanea Numismatica, 1938, 20-32 and A. KINDLER, The Greco-Phoenician Coins Struck in Palestine in the Time of the Persian Empire, INJ 1 (1963) 2-6; 2 (1963) 25-27.

Alexander's conquest of Judaea[17] for several reasons. To begin with, by that time the minute silver coins with the Yehud legend prevailed. Furthermore, the smaller group obviously belongs to the series of Philisto-Arabian drachms and, therefore, cannot be some 50 years later than the larger and earlier group. On the other hand, the unique drachm must be earlier than the Yehud minute silver coins because its Yehud legend is written in Palaeo-Aramaic script[18] while those of all other Yehud coins are written in Palaeo-Hebrew letters. The style of the unique drachm may also be of some help in dating the coin, for the head of the bearded warrior on the obverse is rendered not in profile, but instead with a «face three-quarter r.»[19], as was fashionable in the eastern part of the Mediterranean during the first half of the fourth century.

A preliminary chronological scheme would, therefore, place the larger group of Philisto-Arabian coins around 400-380[20], and the smaller group with the unique drachm around 380-360.

## 2. The Yehud Minute Siver Coins[21]

### 2.1. Under Persian Rule

#### 2.1.1. Group One (Tf. XXI 2-9)

During the fifth and fourth centuries the coinage of the western provinces of the Persian Empire was strongly influenced by Greek types, particularly those of Athens. This is true not only for the two consecutive groups of Philisto-Arabian drachms just discussed but also for the earliest Yehud minute coins. Most follow the usual Athenian pattern with the head of Pallas Athene on the obverse and her owl[22] on the reverse. Because of their similarity to both groups of Philisto-Arabian drachms, the tiny «Athenian» pieces must be placed near the two heavier issues. The epigraphical style of this first group of Yehud minimae is notorious for its poor script-forms, retrograde writing and irregular placement of letters. The head of Pallas Athene and the owl are often coarsely rendered as well. It seems clear, therefore, that at the introduction of this local coinage the die engravers had little experience and skill.

---

[17] Y. MESHORER, Jewish Coins of the Second Temple Period, 1967, 38: «all these coins were struck during a period commencing not earlier than 350 BCE». N. AVIGAD, Bullae and Seals, 1976, 28 seems to accept a date even «towards the end of Persian rule over Judah».

[18] F.M. CROSS, ErIs 9 (1969) 23 indeed attributed our unique drachm to the fifth century because of the early script forms of the legend.

[19] BMC Palestine, 181, no. 29.

[20] The early Philisto-Arabian coins imitate several popular issues of early and mid-fifth-century Greek mints, especially Athens and Lampsacus, and, therefore, should not be dated as late as the mid-fourth century.

[21] For literature see n. 4 above.

[22] The bird on the reverse of our nos. 2 and 3 appears to be walking rather than standing. Y. MESHORER, Jewish Coins of the Second Temple Period, 1967, no. 3 called it an owl. This writer thinks of a daylight bird of prey, probably a falcon.

## 2.1.2. Group Two (Tf. XXI 10-13)

The first extremely small coin of the second group retains the owl of the previous group on the reverse, but now the bird is very carefully executed, as is characteristic of Group Two. The obverse, however, reveals a quite new type, the lily[23]. The following coin which is somewhat larger, repeats the lily on the obverse but displays on its reverse a type already known to us from the unique drachm in the BM – namely, the Egyptian falcon, which appears here with extended wings in fine style and workmanship. The form of the accompanying Yehud inscription is excellent: yhd. Finally, the third piece, once again very small, repeats the falcon and the flawless legend seen on the previous reverse. The obverse, however, has a new type, an impressive head of the Persian Great King in the kidaris, which resembles those already known to us on darics and other Persian coins. Obviously, this second group of Yehud minute coins represents a clearly defined and well-designed issue on the Persian pattern minted in Judaea by the provincial governor during peaceful times.

## 2.1.3. Group Three (Tf. XXII 14-18)

This is a special and extraordinary series. The obverse now exhibits a facing head, one of the most popular Greek designs, a type created about 406 by the Syracusan engraver Kimon and widely copied in Sicily, Magna Graecia, continental Greece, Asia Minor and Syria-Palestine around the turn of the fifth and throughout the fourth century[24]. The reverse, however, represents the Athenian owl once again. Both the obverse and the reverse types are carelessly executed and of coarse style. In addition to the facing head on the obverse, this group includes a second innovation which is highly significant. On the reverse instead of Yehud we read *yhzqyh hphh* [25], that is, «Yehezqiyah the Governour»[26]. As all the coins of this third group were found ex-

---

[23] On the lily as «a flower of the ancient land of Israel» cf. Y. MESHORER, op.cit., 1967, 38.

[24] L. O. TUDEER, Die Tetradrachmenprägung von Syrakus in der Periode der signierenden Künstler, Berlin 1913, nos. 78-81. For die links, date and influence (also on male heads) see L. MILDENBERG, Kimon in the manner of Segesta, in: Actes du 8ème CIN, New York - Washington, septembre 1973, Paris - Basel 1976, 113-21 [hier S. 110-115]. Cf. the facing female head BMC Palestine, Pl. 20,1-3. The coiffure on our tiny coins is clearly female.

[25] For the title *hphh* (Hebrew and Palaeo-Hebrew script) = «The Governour», see N. AVIGAD, Bullae and Seals, 1976, 6-7. For a list of the provincial governors of Judaea cf. id., op.cit., 35: «Yehezqiyah ca. 330 BCE».

[26] The first coin of this type was found in Beth-Zur and showed the name only, the title being off the flan: O.R. SELLERS, The Citadel of Beth Zur, Philadelphia/PN 1933, n. 9. W.F. ALBRIGHT suggested (see SELLERS, op. cit., n. 5) that Yehezqiyah may be identical with the High Priest of this name mentioned by Josephus, Ap. 187-189 and that the right to strike coins was granted to him by Ptolemy I. The first part of ALBRIGHT's suggestion cannot be excluded a priori, but the second one must be abandoned for two reasons. The

clusively in Judaea and together with the minute coins employing the Yehud legend, we can fairly assume that Yeḥezqiyah was a governor of Judaea. Before this time the minting authority was simply Yehud, the Persian province of Judaea, and the official in charge was anonymous. Now for the first time a specific man makes his appearance on the coins, a governor identified by his name and rank[27]. Yeḥezqiyah styles himself neither priest nor prince but governour, which underlines the fact that he is not issuing these coins in his own right but instead acting for an overlord – obviously a Persian, as Yeḥezqiyah uses a Persian title. We may assume, therefore, that Yeḥezqiyah struck these coins during the last years of Persian rule before Alexander's conquest.

## 2.2. During the Macedonian Occupation (Tf. XXII 19-20)

A small group of Yehud minute coins shows on the obverse a youthful head turned to the left and on the reverse a protome of a feline (apparently a lynx) turned either to l. or r. with curved or straight wings. Below this protome the name of Yeḥezqiyah again appears, but, to our surprise, Yeḥezqiyah has now dropped his title of governor, which had a distinct Persian meaning. This is significant as it seems to indicate that he no longer depended upon the Persian satrap who resided at Damascus[28] but upon a new overlord, namely, Alexander the Great or his representative. There is another purely numismatic argument for this hypothesis: the lynx protome is also found on the early Ptolemaic minute coins of Judaea[29], but it soon disappears. The lynx protome thus links the Macedonian group of Yeḥezqiyah's

---

minute coins with Yeḥezqiyah's name and title as well as those with his name but no title still belong to the fourth century. Furthermore, the personal name of an official would not appear on a silver issue of the centralized Ptolemaic coinage where legends are the prerogative of the kings and queens. Even the exceptional mention of a province here – and this in a language other than Greek – is unusual. Cf. the Yehudah minute silver coins described here no. 24.

[27] The coins of Yeḥezqiyah - with or without his title - belong with the other minute Yehud issues. All the pieces which appeared recently have the same metallurgical appearance and the same dark silver patina. All these tiny pieces form a homogeneous whole (see summary of this chapter). KIENLE's assumption (Der Gott auf dem Flügelrad, 1975, 11, n. 1) that the Yeḥezqiyah coins should be eliminated from the Yehud series because they lack the characteristic legend «Yehud» is, therefore, unconvincing.

[28] N. AVIGAD, Bullae and Seals, 1976, 35, gives a list of the Jewish governours of Persian Judaea, our Yeḥezqiyah being the last Jew to hold this office and very likely the last Persian governor of the province. Despite the long file ot Jewish governours, the Yehud coins are not autonomous Jewish issues. The governor of Judaea – whether Jew or not – depended upon the satrap of the Fifth Satrapy and certainly had neither the power and status of the satraps of Asia Minor nor the privilege of striking coins as did the Cyprian «Kings» and the Phoenician cities (n. 11). There is no evidence for the «autonomous Jewish authority» which Y. MESHORER, Jewish Coins of the Second Temple Period, 1967, 36, is inclined to accept.

[29] The bronze coin published by A. KINDLER, IEJ 24 (1974) 75, Pl. 11, O-P should belong to Judaea rather than to Tyre. The head is similar to the heads depicted on some Yehud minute coins, and the protome on the reverse resembles our lynx, not a hippocamp.

coins with the entire series of Ptolemaic Yehud coins. Obviously, the coins of Yehezqiyah with the lynx protome reverse and without the governor title are earlier than the Ptolemaic series but later than his minute coins from the Persian period with this name and title on the owl reverse. We may, therefore, presume, that Yehezqiyah's lynx coins were minted during or at the end of the Macedonian period in Judaea.

## 2.3. In the Ptolemaic Kingdom

It is a surprising and undeniable fact that the new and abundant series of Yehud minute coins contained many pieces with portraits of Ptolemy I wearing the royal diadem and of his consort Berenike I. Well-centered coins from this Ptolemaic Yehud series inform us that the legend is now given in the Hebrew form *yhdh* = «Yehudah» instead of the earlier Aramaic form *yhd* = «Yehud». At first glance we are able to recognize that after a few transitional pieces there follows a new group of quite normal, regular Ptolemaic coins with the usual obverse and reverse types. Thus the Yehud coinage ultimately ends with a uniform Hellenistic issue designed and rigorously controlled by the central government of the Ptolemaic state in Alexandria. This presents a striking contrast to all earlier Yehud coins which display a multitude of borrowed or local types, sometimes combined with the name and title of a local official.

### 2.3.1. Group One (Tf. XXII 21-22)

The transition from the earlier local and provincial coinage to the centralized Ptolemaic coinage did not occur all of a sudden. The youthful male head of the Macedonian period was initially retained for the obverse while the Ptolemaic eagle appears now for the first time on the reverse. The legend continues to be formed by only three letters (*yhd* ).

### 2.3.2. Group Two (Tf. XXII 23-25)

The head of Ptolemy I Soter now enters on the obverse while on the very first issue of this group the lynx reappears on the reverse. The head of the king seems to be bare initially. Later pieces observe the Ptolemaic canon of diademed portrait on the obverse and eagle standing on a fulmen on the reverse. The legend is now in Hebrew and written in four letters: *yhdh* = «Yehudah».

### 2.3.3. Group Three (Tf. XXII 26-28)

To the great surprise of the numismatist and the historian alike, the head of the King[30] on the obverse is now joined by a portrait of an elderly lady - obviously Queen Berenike I - on the reverse[31]. The fact that the name of the recently conquered province of Judaea is written in Hebrew (and not in Aramaic or Greek) beside the Ptolemaic eagle and even beside Berenike's head proves that these tiny silver pieces were struck for, and probably in, Judaea in the otherwise traditional pattern of Ptolemaic coinage.

### 2.3.4. Summary: Mint, Minting Authority, Chronology

The Yehud minute silver coins in Persian, Macedonian and Ptolemaic times form a homogeneous whole. All are very small, all were found in Judaea, and all employ Palaeo-Aramaic and Palaeo-Hebrew legends exclusively. The legends indicate either the name of the province of Judaea or the name and title of its governor. Moreover, all these tiny pieces were struck within a fairly determinable period.

Can we establish the mint and the minting authorities for all these small coins? The bulk was discovered recently and seems to come from the area south of Jerusalem, more precisely from the Bethlehem district both east and west of the main road to Hebron[32]. This does not mean, however, that all the minute coins were struck there. The production spanned at least half a century and saw three consecutive

---

[30] The principal portrait coinage of Ptolemy I as king (proclamation 305/304) was issued during his later years around 300-285. Judaea fell into the hands of Ptolemy I after the battle of Ipsus in 301; therefore, the Yehud coins with his portrait alone may have been struck in the first decade of the third century. The pieces with portraits of both Ptolemy and his consort may fall into the second decade, as Berenike I was proclaimed queen only in 290 B.C.

[31] Our tiny coins, in fact, illustrate the only certain contemporary coin portrait of Berenike I and, therefore, provide an extraordinary enrichment of our knowledge. Prior to this only *posthumous* coin portraits of Berenike I were known: either in profile behind the head of her husband on the large dynastic gold issues with *Theeōn Adelphōn* , struck by the successors of Ptolemy I Soter; or alone on drachms and bronzes of the same size of Ptolemaic Cyrene with the monogram of Magas, her son from her first marriage, governor after 298 and independent king about 270-250 B.C., the father of Berenike II. E.S.G. ROBINSON in BMC Cyrenaica, CLII and 75, has with good reason attributed the latter pieces to «Magas in revolt 277-261 B C. (?)», and «in the name of his divinized stepfather and mother». ROBINSON was mistaken, however, when he went on to state: «Berenice had no official position and to find her treated on a par with Ptolemy would be most surprising». The Yehud coins with Berenike's portrait brought forth just this surprise whether they were struck during the lifetime of Ptolemy I or – after 283/282, but before Berenike's death (about 279) by their son Ptolemy II Philadelphus. Our tiny coins may even exhibit the only contemporary portrait of the first Ptolemaic queen in existence. Cf. H. KYRIELEIS, Bildnisse der Ptolemäer, Berlin 1975, 2: «Bildnisse der Berenike I sind nur auf den Theon-Adelphon-Münzen und auf dem Kameo-Abguss in Alexandria, nicht aber in der Rundplastik faßbar».

[32] A. SPAER, IEJ 27 (1977) 203.

governements. For traditional and cultural as well as demographic and topographic reasons, we cannot exclude Jerusalem as the administrative center of the provincial authorities during all three periods. If so, Jerusalem may have been the mint, but this has not yet been established. There seems no doubt, however, that during all three periods the local governor of the province of Judaea issued the final order to strike the minute coins. Under Persian rule he must have received his authorization from the satrap residing in Damascus and not directly from the Great King himself. Toward the end of the Persian period and during the Macedonian domination, the governor may have acted without formal authorization but never in his own right[33]. Under Ptolemaic rule, the strategos must have received authorization – and perhaps even detailed instructions as to the coin types – directly from Alexandria.

As to the chronological framework, the transition between the first and second half of the fourth century may be assumed the terminus post quem and the death of Ptolemy I in winter 283-282 the terminus ante quem[34]. For the internal chronology, preliminary and approximate dates may be assigned as follows: Persian rule, Group One 360-350, Group Two 350-340, Group Three 340-331; Macedonian rule 330-312; Ptolemaic rule 300-283/282.

## 3. The Yehud Coins and the Coins of the Jews

The unique BM drachm and all of the minute coins just discussed are local issues struck in and for Judaea by consecutive provincial administrations. The sovereign right to strike these silver coins belonged to the foreign overlord who exercised this right either directly or through official representatives. It is, therefore, clear that all Yehud coins were Judaean provincial issues and not coins of the Jews although they were used by the Jewish population. The Jews had no coinage of their own before the end of the second century. The Hasmonaeans of the second generation were the first Jewish rulers to exercise the right to strike bronze coins which had been granted to their ancestors by Antiochus VII. They were thus privileged to start a local, Jewish autonomous coinage by a special act of their sovereign, the Seleucid King.

---

[33] The governor was subordinate to the satrap. E. BABELON, Les Perses Achéménides, Paris 1893, Introduction 23, deals with the question ot whether or not the satraps themselves were independent and had the right to strike coins: «A ces questions multiples, nous répondrons: Les satrapes de l'Empire perse n'ont jamais eu le droit de frapper monnaie en tant que satrapes». See also n. 11 above.

[34] Coins with the portrait of Ptolemy I and the Ptolemaic eagle were also struck by his successors till Roman times, but D. JESELSOHN, IEJ 24 (1974) 77-78, has already pointed to the «affinity» between the Ptolemaic Yehud Coins and the earlier Yehud issues. As stressed in n. 28 above, the Yehud portrait coins have indeed been found with other Yehud pieces, and together they form a homogeneous group. For these reasons, the gap between the last Yehezqiyah coins and the first Ptolemaic pieces must have been rather short, probably only ten to twenty years. The last Ptolemaic Yehud coins are no later than about 279 BC, cp. n. 31.

The only sovereign-coinage of the Jews in antiquity was, in fact, the silver and bronze money issued by the Jews in revolt during the *Bellum Iudaicum* and the Bar Kochba War.

# Gaza von 420 bis 332 nach den Sachquellen

## (Tf. XXIII)

Gaza hat Alexander zwei Monate widerstanden, obwohl es eine Stadt am Meer und ohne natürlichen Schutz war. Herodot verglich Gaza in seiner Bedeutung mit Sardis. Die Stadt war immer ein wichtiger Hafen und Verkehrsknotenpunkt, aber es gab außer den topographischen Gegebenheiten noch andere Faktoren, welche die bedeutende Stellung in der persischen Zeit bestimmten, worauf die Sachquellen hinweisen.

## 1. Die Weihrauchstraße

Gaza lag genau an der Stelle, an der die kürzestmögliche Wüstenpiste von der südarabischen Küste das Mittelmeer erreicht (Abb. S.310). Dies ist durch die uns heute bekannt gewordenen Kastelle und Karawansereien belegt. Von Gaza fächern dann die Straßen aus, auf denen zur See Griechenland, zu Lande Phönikien und Syrien sowie auf der Wüstenstraße und durch die Küstenschiffahrt das Nildelta erreicht werden konnten.

## 2. Der Sonderstatus von Gaza

Man konnte die Luxusgüter aus den fernen Gebieten auf der Weihrauchstraße nur nach Gaza ziehen lassen, wenn die Stadt den Karawanen immer offenstand und dort optimale Voraussetzungen für den Weitertransport gegeben waren. All dies bedingte eine enge Interessengemeinschaft zwischen den Eigentümern, Transporteuren und Verladern der wertvollen Waren. Wie ein Schlaglicht erhellt eine Sachquelle diese Zusammenarbeit, nämlich die Inschrift auf den Stelen im minäischen Staatstempel von Qarnāwu um 300 v. Chr. mit den Namen von 72 dem Heiligtum gewidmeten oder dort verzeichneten fremden Frauen. Gaza erscheint dort als Herkunftsort von nicht weniger als 29 «Hierodulen», während Dedan, auch an der nördlichen Weihrauchstraße gelegen, mit neun Namen an zweiter Stelle steht. Eine rege und dauernde Verbindung bestand also zwischen dem Minäer-Reich und der Stadt am Mittelmeer. Gaza war im letzten Viertel des 5. Jahrhunderts die führende Wirtschaftsmetropole im Süden der 5. persischen Satrapie Abarnahara und nahe der 6. Satrapie Ägypten. In den Jahren der Unabhängigkeit Ägyptens von der Jahrhundertwende bis 343 wurde die Stadt zur Grenzfeste am Meer, wohin die Handelsströme von Süden, Osten und Norden noch immer ungehindert gelangen konnten. In der ganzen Periode von 420 bis 332 hat sich Gaza einer priviligierten, autonomen Stellung erfreut, ja einen Sonderstatus wie Sidon und Tyros genossen. Die Achämeniden müssen eine Garnison in oder nahe bei Gaza gehalten haben, sonst wäre die Verbindung zwischen den beiden Satrapien nicht gesichert gewesen und der starke Widerstand gegen Alexander unerklärlich. Persischer Einfluß in Nordarabien war beträchtlich, wofür die Ostraka von Eilat und der aramäische Titel *pehā,* der nur einen persischen Statthalter bezeichnen kann, auf einer lihyanischen Inschrift aus der 2. Hälfte des 5. Jahrhunderts sprechen. Entscheidend war aber, daß die persische Diplomatie einen stabilen *modus vivendi* mit den Arabern – Qedrener oder Idumäer oder frühe Nabatäer – sichern konnte, was später nur Hadrian gelingen sollte. Schon Herodot war sich dessen bewußt. Im ägyptischen Tell el-Mashūta lag kurz vor 400 eine persische Garnison arabischer Söldner, was die dort gefundene Silberschale mit der Widmung in reichsaramäischer Schrift «Qainu bar Geshem, König von Qedar» und der dort gehobene Riesenfund von Tetradrachmen athenischen Typus bezeugen. Persern und Arabern lag daran, daß die Spezereien aus dem Süden sicher nach Gaza gelangen und dort weiterversandt werden konnten. Dies ermöglichte die Sonderstellung der Stadt.

## 3. Die numismatische Evidenz

Die Tatsache von Gaza's autonomem Status wird durch eine weitere, entscheidende Sachquelle erwiesen, die um 420 einsetzende und bis kurz vor Alexander dauernde reiche Münzprägung der Stadt mit der Nennung ihres Namens in aramäischer Schrift. Diese Silberprägung ist fein gegliedert und deckte ebenso den Bedarf an lokalem Kleingeld wie den des Außenhandels; denn dieses Gaza-Geld wird auch außerhalb des Einflußgebietes der Stadt gefunden. Neben der städtischen Münzstätte war in Gaza auch eine betriebsame Lohnmünzstätte aktiv, die für Städte, Dynasten und Scheichs der Region prägte (Tf. XXIII 2). In Juda und Samaria schufen die persischen Gouverneure zur gleichen Zeit Silberkleingeld für ihre Provinzen, während der mächtige Satrap, der im Norden residierte, sich jeder Prägetätigkeit enthielt, dies in erstaunlichem Gegensatz zu seinen Kollegen in Kleinasien. Es zeigt sich auch in der Geldschöpfung die vielfältige staats- und verwaltungsrechtliche Struktur des späteren Achämenidenreiches in seiner Anpassungsfähigkeit und Elastizität, von der Gaza in hohem Maße Nutzen zog.

# Gaza Mint Authorities in Persian Times.
# Preliminary Studies of the Local Coinage in the Fifth
# Persian Satrapy. Part 4[*]

## (Tf. XXIV - XXVII)

Résumé: Gaza n'a jamais été fouillée, mais on peut imaginer son importance d'après sa position privilégiée comme terminus de la route de l'encens et comme principale station de la *via maris*, ainsi que d'après son port, draînant le trafic maritime vers l'Égypte, la Phénicie, Chypre et la Grèce. Les témoignages principaux sur l'importance de la cité sont les lignes d'Hérodote qui la comparait avec Sardes, les deux groupes d'inscriptions minéennes témoignant d'une connexion unique avec l'Arabie et surtout ses deux grands monnayages des années 420 à 332, les séries municipales ainsi que les émissions frappées pour les autorités arabes. Dans le «Commomwealth achéménide», Gaza a pu se développer comme ville autonome et internationale; mais sa fin était proche car Alexandre la détruisit impitoyablement.

## 1. Introduction

In your June 1987 circular for this colloquium, the magic word «l'approche pluridisciplinaire» appears. At the last international congresses and symposia, a lot was said about the importance of interdisciplinary research, but all what we realized in turn was the fact that numismatic study was considered as the indispensable, but despised handmaid, the classical *ancilla*, but not as the essential discipline which it is for, e.g., the byzantinist H. HUNGER[1]: «eine Grundlagen- und keine Hilfswissenschaft».

In the *Cambridge History of Iran*, published in 1985, A.D.H. BIVAR holds that «The satrapies of Lydia and Transeuphratesia... issued coinage for much of their period of Persian rule»[2]. The imperial siglos was, indeed, issued by the satrap of Lydia, presumably in Sardis, on order of the Great King. However, the superior ad-

---

[*] Cf. Part 1: Yehud: A Preliminary Study of the Provincial Coinage of Judaea, in: FS M. Thompson, Wetteren 1979, 183-196 [hier S. 67- 76]; Part 2: Baana: Preliminary Studies of the Local Coinage in the Fifth Persian Satrapy, ErIs 19 (1987; M. Avi-Yonah Volume) 29-35 [hier S. 35 - 42]; Part 3: The Philisto-Arabian coins - a Preview, in: Numismatique et histoire économique phéniciennes et puniques. Actes du Colloque tenu à Louvain-la-Neuve, 1987, ed. T. HACKENS - GH. MOUCHARTE (Num.Lov. 9; Stud.Phoen. 9), Louvain 1992, 33-40 [hier S. 88-94].

[1] H. HUNGER, XI. Internationaler Byzantinistenkongress, Akten II/I, JbÖByz 32 (1982) 162.

[2] A.D.H. BIVAR, Achaemenid Coins, Weights and Measures, in: Cambridge History of Iran, London 1985, 620.

ministrator[3] in huge Abar Nahara did not strike one single coin for his satrapy, because there was money enough in his realm without his own issues. When Mazaeus put his name on Sidonian money, he did so as the regent of the city, and not at all as the satrap of Abar Nahara[4]. The renowned Iranist M.A. DANDAMAEV stated in 1974: «Als Hauptzahlungsmittel diente der Silberschekel, der 5,6 g wog»[5]. Presumably, his Russian text was incorrectly translated, because he meant the siglos and not the shekel which is a silver weight of 8,4 g. But DANDAMAEV was basically wrong, because silver bullion and imported Greek silver coins were the main means of payment[6]. The siglos did not circulate at all in Abar Nahara, as the hoards prove[7].

We have to say a word about the design and structure of the coinage in the Persian Empire, as Transeuphratesia-Aba Nahara was an important part of it and Gaza was situated within Abar Nahara. First, the imperial money[8]: the gold daric of 8.4 g, first struck around 500 B.C.[9], and the silver siglos with exactly the same image and an

---

[3] Usually called «satrap», thus the Persian official, responsible for the largest administrative unit. The term «governour» is used here exclusively for the Persian official of lower rank, administrating a province which is a smaller administrative unit. *'Abar Nah$^a$rā* = *'Eber han-Nahar* in Hebrew = The Land West of the River (Euphrates) is the satrapy, Judaea (*Yəhūd* ) and Samaria (*Šāmərayin* ) are provinces (*mədīnōt* ); see H. WEIPPERT, Palästina in vorhellenistischer Zeit, München 1988, 687.

[4] Mazaeus put his name, not his title, on the very spot in the coin field where the Sidonian kings had indicated their names. He scrupulously followed their examples in the metal, weight standard, denominations, types and script. - Mazaeus' name only also appears occasionally with images of Persian flavour on small silver coins of the Nablus hoard (ICCH 1504, Samaria, 1968, burial ca. 332 B.C.), thus on local cash, and not at all on provincial or even satrapical money.

[5] Beiträge zur Achämenidengeschichte, ed. G. WALSER (Historia, Einzelschriften H. 18), 1972, 45.

[6] «It cannot be too much stressed that to a very large degree the empire ran not only not on coinage but not even on precious metal», C.J. TUPLIN, The Administration of the Achaemenid Empire (British Archaeological Reports 343), 1987, 109-166. On silver scrap («Hacksilber»), see D. SCHLUMBERGER, L 'Argent Grec dans l'Empire Achéménide, Paris 1953, 17, and the Plates XX-XXI, XXV in C.M. KRAAY / P.R.S. MOOREY, Two Fifth Century Hoards from the Near East, RN 10 (1968) 181-235. For the poor acceptance of the introduction of coinage by Darius I, see R.N. FRYE, The History of Ancient Iran, München 1984, 116.

[7] A recent listing is given by I. CARRADICE, The «Regal» Coinage of the Persian Empire (British Archaeological Reports 343), 1987, 79, Table A. His hoard no. 12, Antilebanon, Syria 1978 is unauthenticated, as he himself marked it with a question mark. His hoard no. 24, Lebanon 1983 (not registered in ICCH or Coin Hoards, London) seems uncertain, too, as it is said to come from Beyrout, also a major marketplace for coins found in South-Eastern Turkey. See D. SCHLUMBERGER, ibid., 12.

[8] Usually called «regal» coinage, a term also used by CARRADICE. «Imperial» coinage seems more appropriate, as the Great Kings ruled one of the largest and longest lasting empires in antiquity. For the daric and the siglos, see E.S.G. ROBINSON, The Beginnings of Achaemenid Coinage, NC 1958, 187-193, and I. CARRADICE, ibid., 75-93.

[9] There is now important factual evidence for the date, see M. COOK ROOT, Evidence from Persepolis for the Dating of Persian and Archaic Greek Coinage, NC 148 (1988) 1-12 with conclusion p. 11: «The Archer coin used as Seal 1393 on Persepolis Fortification Tablet 1495 proves that by 500 BC at the latest (by the 22$^{nd}$ year of Darius I) the shooting Archer type has been minted and put into circulation».

average weight of 5.45 g, emitted for the first time in Western Asia Minor also about 500, and mainly used for mercenary wages. Second the provincial coinage: small silver cash issued in the fourth century B.C. by the governors of the provinces of Judaea and Samaria in the hinterland. And third, the manifold local coinages to which the so called satrapical issues also belong[10]. Much attention is paid to these few portrait coins by recent scholarship, whereas the ubiquitous small silver issues, the essential daily cash, are unduly neglected[11].

## 2. Gaza at the sea and on the roads

For simple topographical reasons, Gaza with its port nearby became the terminus of the main desert route from Southern Arabia to the Mediterranean[12]. The frankincense road ended in Gaza and not in Elath or at the Phoenician coast in the North. Gaza's strong position as junction, fortress and port is proven by late fourth century Ma'īn inscriptions[13], first by the reference to «Egypt, Gaza and Ashur» as major powers of the Levant, and, second, by the list of hierodules on the temple stelae in Qarnāwu, the capital of the Minaeans in Southern Arabia. The origin of 72 ladies is recorded there. None comes from Ma'īn itself, 8 from Egypt, 9 from the Arabian desert center Dedan, but no less than 29 from Gaza!

---

[10] A true, early «satrapical» coin with a real portrait and the name in Greek script of the man depicted on it seems to be Pharnabazus' local issue for Cyzicus. Mazaeus' name and full title as the superior administrator of Abar Nahara and Cilicia appear in Aramaic letters on definitely local coins of Tarsus. Tiribazus' name only is found on the city coins of Soli, Mallus, Tarsus and Issus. The great coinages of the Hekatomnids in Caria, the dynasts of Lycia and the rulers on Cyprus were, indeed, struck within the Empire, but are local, not Persian issues.

[11] «Ces petits chefs-d'oeuvre du monnayage dont nous savons si peu de chose et qui ont servi d'instrument de l'économie quotidienne...», D. BEREND, Reflexions sur les fractions du monnayage grec, in: FS L. Mildenberg, Wetteren 1984, 7.

[12] On the three routes branching off from Yathrib-Medina to the North, see I. EPHʿAL, The Ancient Arabs. Nomads on the Borders of the Fertile Crescent 9th-6th Centuries BCE, Jerusalem - Leiden 1982, 14-15, who also stresses the dominating position of the three trade centers: Gaza, Tyre and Damascus. The North-Western route from Medina via Dedan to Gaza is, however, the shortest and most convenient access to the Mediterranean, avoiding the edges of the Nafud and Syrian deserts, and has become, therefore, the classical frankincense road. On the importance of the trade in spices and the domestication of the camel see EPHʿAL, ibid., 4. On the introduction of the shadâd saddle, see E.A. KNAUF, Ismael. Untersuchungen zur Geschichte Palästinas und Nordarabiens im 1.Jahrtausend v.Chr., Wiesbaden ²1989, 40-41, with footnote 182.

[13] For the reference «to the political geography of the Levant as "Egypt, Gaza and Ashur"», see D.F. GRAF, Greek Tyrants and Achaemenid Politics, in: FS Ch.G. Starr, University Press of America 1985, no. 40, 111. For the hierodules, see H. VON WISSMANN, Die Geschichte des Sabäerreiches und der Feldzug des Aelius Gallus, in: ANRW II,9,1 (1976) 408-411; id., PRE Suppl. 12 (1970) 956-960. Qarnāwu was founded ca. 380, the great temple ca. 305. K. MLAKER, Die Hierodulenlisten von Maʿin nebst Untersuchungen zur altsüdarabischen Rechtsgeschichte und Chronologie, Leipzig 1943, thinks that the stelae are somewhat later. It is unlikely that the ladies left Gaza as children and not conceivable that this happened just after 332.

Whether this astonishing fact hints at a mid-fourth century Minaean office or settlement within the precincts of Gaza or not, the strong position of the city in the profitable frankincense trade cannot be doubted and should not be underestimated. This was the basis of the city's fame and power which explains Alexander's difficulties in 332. As S. HORNBLOWER states: «it is striking that some of the best resistance to Alexander west of Iran came from those cities - Halikarnassos, Gaza, Tyre - where there was a long tradition of mediatized rule»[14].

## 3. Gaza's legal status

The Minaean connection does not, however, prove that Gaza was an Arab city[15]. Herodotus describes the coast ahead and behind Gaza and not the city itself[16]. He records Arab ἐμπόρια thus commerce centers-comptoirs, not cities or fortresses and certainly not territories. Also, Gaza did not belong to Sidon or Tyre. Phoenician territory stretched down to Ascalon, not further South[17]. Was Gaza simply Persian: a garrison fortress or even a provincial capital? The strategical position near the Egyptian gate had to be indeed held by a Persian garrison, but this unit may have been located inside or outside the city. The events at Alexander's siege of Gaza confirm a strong garrison with a commander of high rank at that time[18]. Recent ex-

---

[14] S. HORNBLOWER, Mausolus, Oxford 1982, 152.

[15] Here, «Arab» indicates the tribes dwelling East and South of Gaza. The region in the East is understood by Diodorus (19,52,2 and 88,1) during early Hellenistic times as the Idumaean eparchy. The Nabatean realm, mainly on the former Edomite territory and on the desert further South, is of later date. In the fifth century and presumably in the first half of the fourth century, the Arab tribe, dominating this vast territory and other desert land, was Qedar. The whole region was, however, neither an organized state, though kings and queens of Arabia and of Qedar occur since the eighth century, nor a definite Persian satrapy or «other administratively uniform organization»: I. EPHᶜAL, The Ancient Arabs, 1982, 193. «Indirect rule» (P. HÖGEMANN, Alexander der Grosse und Arabien, München 1985, 202-203) only seems conceivable in the Western Arab desert; a sort of «Association to the Achaemenid Empire» may be another form of a modus vivendi: E.A. KNAUF, Ismael, ²1989, 77. In any case, as E. STERN, Material Culture of the Land of the Bible in the Persian Period 538-332 B.C., Westminster - Jerusalem 1982, 239, stresses: «Persian rule was interested to preserve the good will of the Arab tribes».

[16] Herodotus describes the coast in his own time in *Histories* 3,5, whereas in 3,4, he reports the story of Phanes as desert scout during the campaign of Cambyses against Egypt which occurred a century previously. The «King of the Arabs» is mentioned in 3,4 only. There seems to be no agreement between 3,5 and 3,4. On Herodotus' reports see J. WIESEHÖFER, Die «Freunde» und «Wohltäter» des Großkönigs, Studia Iranica 9 (1986) 7-21.

[17] A. LEMAIRE, Les Phéniciens et le commerce entre la Mer Rouge et la Mer Méditerranée, in: Stud. Phoen. V, Leuven 1987, 56.

[18] We know very little of Batis, the commander. Was he a Persian or an Arab? See P. HÖGEMANN, Alexander der Grosse und Arabien, 1985, 47. It is not surprising that he is told to have hired Arabian mercenaries for the defence. Arabs had already served in the Persian Tell el-Maskhuta garrison in the Eastern Nile delta in the last decade of the fifth century. Batis could not have succeeded in holding Gaza against Alexander for two months without these reinforcements. The permanent garrison in the fourth century might have

cavations have unearthed traces of several fortified caravansaries South of Gaza. There is, however, no evidence that Gaza was a provincial capital. There were governors in the Judaean and Samarian hinterland, but none in Phoenicia at the coast. Some scholars seem to assume Persian provinces in the South, for instance Dor and Ashdod[19]. The newly discovered coins of Ashdod, however, are clearly local and not provincial issues. A garrison near or in Gaza does not mean that the city was a capital of a province and ruled by its governor. The Qarnāwu lists, Herodots' note and especially the local Gaza coinage, to be described here, indicate a different legal status within the Persian realm. Some scholars go so far as to think of Gaza as a sort of a freeport in Persian times[20]. It was an autonomous city, surely, and a cosmopolitan center, similar – *cum grano salis* – to Sidon and Tyre. In his paper for this colloqium, P. FREI stresses that major cities were responsible local administrative units, «Lokalkörperschaften», reached directly by the Great King.

## 4. The coinage of the city of Gaza

In his admirable British Museum Catalogue of the Greek Coins of Palestine, published in 1914, G.F. HILL did not accept any Gaza coins before ca. 150 B.C., but subsumed them and others under a group with «a more general title»[21]. He then proposed the heading «Philisto-Arabian» and «Egypto-Arabian». Some later cataloguers went to the other extreme, simply attributing all the enigmatic coins which are said to come from the South to the city of Gaza. Both concepts do not meet the evidence.

The attribution of a prolific and organized coinage to the city of Gaza proper is backed by several facts. First, the inscriptions: *ʿzh* , the full name of Gaza in three letters, then the version of the first two letters *ʿz / zʿ* and finally the first letter *ʿ* only. This is the name of a city, like *gbl* for Byblos and *ṣr* for Tyre, and not that of a satrapy or province, like *klk-ḥlk* [22] for Cilicia, *ʿbr nhrʾ* for Transeuphratesia or

---

been smaller. See C.J. TUPLIN, Xenophon and the Garrisons of the Achaemenid Empire, AMI 20 (1987) 167-245, and compare id., Persian Garrison in Xenophon and Other Sources, in: Achaemenid History III, Leiden 1988, 67-70. On the «brutal capture» and «unnecessarily cruel destruction» of Gaza by Alexander, see P. HÖGEMANN, Alexander der Grosse und Arabien, 1985, 48. Gaza's city coinage ceased for 200 years.

[19] E. STERN, Material Culture of the Land of the Bible in the Persian Period, 1982, 229; cp. H. WEIPPERT, Palästina in vorhellenistischer Zeit, 1988, 687.

[20] S. MITTMANN, Die Küste Palästinas bei Herodot, ZDPV 99 (1983) 138: «Gaza selbst (kam) damit offenbar in den Genuß eines zollfreien Handels». P. HÖGEMANN, Alexander d.Gr. und Arabien, 1985, 48: «...mit Gaza als eine Art Freihandelshafen». There seems to be no immediate evidence of such a far reaching conclusion, but it is obvious that Gaza must have enjoyed an extensive autonomy for the benefit of the city, the Arab traders and the Great King. For local autonomy see D.F. GRAF, loc. cit. (n. 13), 96: «Extant signs of Persian involvement in provincial or municipal governments suggest only efforts to preserve the existing regimes of local dynasts or rulers, not to install appointees».

[21] BMC Palestine, LXXXIV.

[22] See P. NASTER, Toponymes en caractères araméens sur les monnaies anatoliennes (5e-4e s. av. J.-C.), RBN 1988, 7-17, Pl. I.

*yhd* for Judaea, *šmryn* for Samaria. Further, we realize that the letter *mēm* for Marnas, the City God, appears on the coins. The unequivocal sign stands for Gaza from ca. 400 B.C. till the end of the ancient coinage of the city under Gordian III ca. 240 A.D. The second fact is the weight standard: in sharp contrast to the abundant issues of the great cities at the Phoenician coast, Gaza struck her coins exclusively on the Attic standard[23] which fits the needs of an active trading port and emphasizes the independence from Sidon and Tyre with their Phoenician standard. Third, the denomination: a marked preference for the drachm. Fourth, the types: the dominant image, the forepart of a horse, appears in Gaza only. Finally, we have the hoard evidence: the bulk of the inscribed coins of the city of Gaza comes from the immediate area; very few scattered pieces come from the region somewhat further North and not one secured and untouched specimen from Phoenicia, Syria or Egypt[24].

## 5. Coin production in Gaza by order of external authorities

The intriguing, varied issues, called Philisto-Arabian by HILL and, less successfully, Graeco-Phoenician[25], Graeco-Palestinian[26] or even Graeco-Persian[27] by others, are in fact the local coins from the Southern borders of Abar Nahara, thus from the vast territories around Gaza. They are found in the same area as the Gaza municipal coins. They have always been offered together and on the same market place[28], namely Jerusalem[29]. Both groups have the same fabric, weight standard and denomination

---

[23] There is new inscriptional evidence for the use of the Athenian weight standard in the Judaean hinterland in the fourth century. In a record of loans, the amounts due are given in *šiqlīn* (shekels), *ribʿīn* (quarters) and *maʿat* (sixths). There can be no doubt that these denominations correspond to the internationally dominating Athenian currency system of tetradrachms, drachms and obols. The document was found in a cave on a ridge situated «one kilometer west of ancient Jericho», S.H. ESHEL / H. MISGAV, A Fourth Century B.C.E. Document from Ketef Yeriḥo, IEJ 38 (1988) 158-176, Pl. 26.

[24] The Gaza drachm registered in ICCH 1482 «may be intrusive», as C.M. KRAAY / P.R.S. MOOREY, RN 10 (1968) 191-192, no. 89 say. The coin is worn and cannot, therefore, have been buried before 400 B.C., whereas the burial of the hoard has to be dated ca. 445. ICCH 1651 registers a Gaza fragment in the hoard of Beni-Hasan (250 km south of Cairo), buried ca. 360 B.C., unearthed in 1903. A fragment may serve as silver bullion and is expected, therefore, to travel far. H. SEYRIG noted on all but one of the labels of his drachms and fractions, now in BN, Cab. des Medailles, Paris: «trouvée à Gaza» or «apportée à Gaza». On the label of one piece, reg. no. 277, the remark «trouvée à Byblos» appears.

[25] A. KINDLER, The Graeco-Phoenician Coins Struck in Palestine in the Time of the Persian Empire, INJ 1 (1963) 2; J. ELAYI, Pénétration grecque en Phénicie sous l'Empire Perse, Nancy 1988, 45: «Retenons provisoirement le terme "gréco-phéniciennes", bien qu'inadéquat».

[26] Y. MESHORER, in: SNG ANS 6, 1981, note preceeding no. 1.

[27] Y. MESHORER, Graeco-Persian Coins of Palestine, INB 1 (1962) 18-19.

[28] Beyrout and Cairo, two important market plases, do not seem to have made any substantial contribution to our field. H. SEYRIG, who carefully noted pedigrees, did not report such coin purchases in Beyrout, nor did B.Y. BERRY in Cairo.

[29] The two major private collections of Gaza and Philisto-Arabian coins were formed in Jerusalem after World War II.

and are very similar in types and engraving. Thus, they must be contemporary and certainly come from the same milieu. It is most likely that both groups originate from the same place, from Gaza; either from the city mint or from another work-shop, situated in the precincts of Gaza, whose equipment was hired by external min-ting authorities.

## 6. Chronology

In Byblos and Tyre, the very first coins were struck around 450 B.C.[30]; Aradus and Sidon followed around 420 with sizeable emissions[31]. For Gaza, the dominant city on the Southern coast, the political and economic situation in the second half of the fifth century could not have been much different from that in the North. In any case, the fading out of the handy money supply from Athens in the last 15 years of the Peloponnesian War[32] did affect all trading centers on the coast, Gaza no less than Sidon and Tyre. For this reason alone, the beginning of the Gaza municipal coinage ca. 420-410 seems likely. Unfortunately, overstrikes and hoard evidence do not allow us to ascertain an exact date. No Gaza specimen overstruck on a foreign coin with a certain date seems to be known. The recorded hoard evidence, often decisive, is scanty and questionable here[33]. But other elements of the numismatic evidence[34] are helpful: the first local imitations of Athenian tetradrachms were struck in the Levant around 410[35]. The Gaza municipal mint seems to have been prone to experiment.

---

[30] The group of silver staters with a reclining sphinx and a kind of double lotus, all struck from the same dies, has been attributed to Byblos because of the hoard evidence; five of the six pieces known to this writer are said to come from Byblos. Large denominations, valuable coins, are often transported over long distances. H. SEYRIG has, however, recorded that some of his fractions displaying a sphinx have, indeed, been found on the beach of Byblos. The small fractions are local cash which usually does not travel. Thus, the sphinx-staters may, indeed, also belong to Byblos. The fabric is clearly mid-fifth century and similar to the fabric of the first Tyros staters which are dated ca. 450 by a fresh specimen in the Jordanian hoard: IGCH 1482, burial ca. 445: C.M. KRAAY / P.R.S. MOOREY, RN 10 (1968) 191, no. 88; C.M. KRAAY, Archaic and Classical Greek Coins, London 1976, 287-288.

[31] See the rich material gathered by J. ROUVIER, Numismatique des villes de la Phénicie, JIAN 3 (1900) 125-168. 237-312; 4 (1901) 35-66. 125-152. 193-232; 5, 1902, 99-134. 229-284; 6 (1903) 17-46, 209-232; 7 (1904) 65-108, the survey by J.W. BETLYON, The Coinage and Mints of Phoenicia - The Pre-Alexandrine Period, Chico/CA 1980, whose datings differ considerably from those given here and in J. ELAYI, Pénétration grecque en Phénicie, 1988, 39-60.

[32] See C.M. KRAAY, Archaic and Classical Greek Coins, 1976, 287; E.S.G. ROBINSON, Some Problems in the Later Fifth Century Coinage of Athens, ANSMN 9 (1960) 1-15, es-pecially 8: «... it is, significantly, just in these years (413-407 B.C.: this writer) that the direct imitation of Athenian tetradrachms begins in the Levant».

[33] See supra, footnotes 7 and 24.

[34] For an appreciation, see L. MILDENBERG, Numismatic Evidence, HSCP 91 (1987) 381-395 [hier S. 253-262].

[35] For the later Egyptian tetradrachm-imitations bearing the name of the Persian satraps Sabakes and Mazakes in aramaic script, see H. NICOLET-PIERRE, Monnaies des deux der-

Tetradrachms were produced, closely copying the Athenian models, sometimes adding the Marnas *mēm* to the usual owl in profile, sometimes putting the city's name to the facing owl between olive branches. Even when the mint authorities decided to create their own drachms with the name of Gaza, they did not only apply the Athenian standard, but used also the Athenian owls for the reverse. On the obverse, however, the Gaza officials imitated the mid-fifth century Janus head[36] of Tenedus. Considering the necessary lapse of time for the travel of the Tenedus drachms to the Levant and their acceptance in Gaza, we again reach a period of ca. 420-410.

In addition to the message of the imitations, we have the fact of the stable procedures of coin production, the technology. The deep incuse square, the quadratum incusum proper, with straight, deep bordering, is certainly earlier than the dotted and banded square within a shallow quadratum incusum. The deep incuse square belongs to the fifth century and to the beginning of the fourth. If we again consider the slow development in the East, 420-410 is a plausible assumption for the first coins of the city of Gaza which show the deep incuse square clearly.

## 7. The two minting authorities in Gaza

a) The City. All details of the coinage confirm that it is neither the Persian central administration nor the satrap of Abar Nahara nor a provincial governor who is responsible for these issues. This is local money. The minting authority is he city[37]. There is ample inscriptional, numismatic and literary evidence for kings as rulers within the Achaemenid Empire in the cities of the Phoenician coast and of Cyprus. But there is none for Gaza from the end of the fifth century till Alexander. All we know is that Batis defended Gaza against Alexander for two months. He is a garrison commander, not a king or an administrator. Analogy is guesswork, not fact. As we do not know of any local king, dynast or ruler, we can neither exclude a priori that there existed one nor exclude a priori that Gaza was governed by a city council. The coinage, the road junction, the evidence of the two Maʿīn inscriptions, the port activity, the use of imported Greek ware[38], Herodotus' description of Gaza's topographi-

---

niers satrapes d'Égypte avant Alexandre, in: FS M. Thompson, Wetteren 1979, 221-239, Pl. 25-26.

[36] Generally, the mid-fifth century issues of Lampsacus are considered as the originals which have been copied in Gaza. Both faces on the Lampsacus Janus-heads are, however, clearly female. The Tenedus type shows a bearded male head and a female head, as depicted on the first coins of the city of Gaza.

[37] As P. HÖGEMANN, Alexander d.Gr. und Arabien, 1985, 47 n. 3, has stressed, the ancient historians take Gaza either as a Persian or an Arab or a Persian-Arab city. It was, indeed, none of these. The trade and port activity must have brought Greeks and Phoenicians to Gaza, probably other people, too. The extraction of the inhabitants, however, does not determine the status of the city. For strategic reasons alone, the Great Kings could not allow Arab sovereignty over Gaza. They either had to make it a Persian city or tolerate an autonomous system, as they did on Cyprus and the Phoenician coast. Obviously, the local Gaza city coins prove this autonomy.

[38] See J. ELAYI, Pénétration grecque en Phénicie, 1988, maps VIII, X, XIV, XVII, XXVIII, and tables I-II.

cal position and his view that the city in his time was not much smaller than Sardis - $\Sigma\alpha\rho\delta\iota\omega\nu$ $o\dot{\upsilon}$ $\pi o\lambda\lambda\tilde{\omega}$ $\dot{\epsilon}\lambda\dot{\alpha}\sigma\sigma o\nu o\varsigma$[39] characterize Gaza as an international center which could well have been administrated by a municipal council of autocratic or even democratic nature. This council was the mint authority for Gaza's municipal coinage which was much larger and varied than it was assumed previously and did influence other issues at the coast.

b) The Arab Authorities. There is Arab country East and South of Gaza; desert land with local rulers. The vast area from Gaza to the Dead Sea and till Petra and further South was their territory[40]. The Great King did not reign over the desert, certainly not from the end of the fifth century on, as the whole area under consideration here did not become «part of the realm of Alexander the Great and his successors»[41]. The Minean traders transported valuable goods to and from Gaza in a steady flow. This could only have been possible if a mutual agreement existed between the Arab[42] and Persian authorities and between them and the city of Gaza. Then it is easily conceivable that the Arab rulers used the Gaza craftsmen of the city mint or their own atelier on the spot as soon as they needed their own money for the development of their desert trade. Thus, the Gaza craftsmen worked on order for the Arab authorities. Until recent times, the territory of this first Arab coinage has been assumed to stretch from Gaza East till Beer Sheba and South to Petra at the furthest. One little silver coin has broadened our horizon considerably and, at the same time, drastically demonstrated how limited our materials and our knowledge still are[43].

---

[39] See supra, footnote 16.

[40] As to the region East and South-East of Gaza, I. EPH<sup>c</sup>AL, The Ancient Arabs, 1982, 200, no. 679, stresses that «in the mid-4th century... the Edomite-Arab penetration into Southern Palestine was complete». This is supported by the local Arab coins described here, as they have been struck in Gaza from ca. 400 till 332, are often found in that area and are entirely different from the provincial issues of Judaea.

[41] I. EPH<sup>c</sup>AL, The Ancient Arabs, 1982, 205.

[42] On the most prominent Arab tribe, see supra, no. 14, and E.A. KNAUF, Ismael, ²1989, 103-108 («Geschichte der Qedar in persischer und hellenistischer Zeit»).

[43] See M.A. RIZACK, A Coin with the Aramaic Legend Šhrw, a King Governor of Lihyān, ANSMN 29 (1984) 25-28.

# The Philisto-Arabian Coins - A Preview.
## Preliminary Studies of the Local Coinage in the Fifth Persian Satrapy. Part 3[*]

### (Tf. XXVIII - XXX)

### 1. The Coinage Policy of the Persian Empire

It was the prerogative of the Great Kings to strike gold coins[1]. For two hundred years, their gold darics were the most prestigious coins of the ancient world[2]. It is highly significant that these darics remained the only substantial imperial money in the Persian realm[3]. Whereas the centralized states kept the entire money supply under strict control, the Achaemenid rulers not only allowed a considerable import of silver money[4], but also tolerated the silver coinages of their satraps and governors; even

---

[*]   Part 1: Yehud: A Preliminary Study of the Provincial Coinage of Judaea, in: FS in Honour of M. Thompson, Wetteren, 1979, 183-196, Pl. 21-22 [hier S. 67-76; Part 2: Baana: Preliminary Studies of the Local Coinage in the Fifth Persian Satrapy, ErIs 19 (M. Avi-Yonah Memorial Vol.) (1987) 28*-35* [hier S. 35-42]. – For help and advice, the author is indebted to M. Amandry, P. Frei, Y. Meshorer, M. Price, M. Rizack, W. Röllig, M. Sherabani, A. Spaer, N. Waggoner, R. Wenning and J. Wiesehöfer. [Die hier eingearbeiteten Addenda & Corrigenda wurden von L. MILDENBERG 1993 mit dem Sonderdruck verteilt. Die Hrsg.]

[1] The prerogative to strike gold coins was, however, not as exclusive as in Hellenistic and Roman times. In the 4th century, the Carian satraps could issue gold coins as did the Cypriote city kings, presumably even not only in the years of their open revolt against Persia (Caria: E. BABELON, Traité des monnaies grecques et romaines, Paris 1901-1933, Pl. 90:14 (= Traité) and Cyprus: Traité, Pl. 127: 22-25; 5-8:25-27; 129:8).

[2] Purity, types and fabric remained unchanged. Darics appear in many hoards from Sicily (IGCH 2122, 2124) to the Oxus river (IGCH 1822).

[3] Cf. infra n. 18 for the sigloi. The 4th century tetradrachms with the Great King in *kidaris* and *kandys* on one side and different types on the other side are coins issued by Western satraps for their territories and not by the Great King for the Empire.

[4] Large silver denominations from Athens, but also from other Greek mints, served as current means of payment in the East, especially in the 5th century. In many hoards chisel cut coins and untouched pieces appear at the same time. Cf. M. PRICE / N. WAGGONER, Archaic Greek Silver Coinage: The Asyut Hoard, London 1975 (= Asyut) and D. SCHLUMBERGER, L'argent grec dans l'empire achéménide, Paris 1953, entire.   [The increasing number of Egyptian owl tetradrachms of Athenian type, but with the Demotic inscription *Artaxerxes Pharao*, struck ca. 340 (see M. PRICE, More from Memphis and the Syria 1989 Hoard, FS Carson-Jenkins, London 1993, 31-35, pls. IV - X) hint at a Persian imperial coinage in the 4th century, not a satrapal one. The tetradrachms depicting the Great King with bow and spear, or shooting, may indeed have been struck in Western Asia

the money issued by local authorities, kings, dynasts, self governing cities and probably even chiefs of nomadic tribes[5] of very different kind and standing was permitted. The Persian imperial gold coinage was conceived as a centralized, uniform international issue. The silver coinage struck within the empire was autonomous and varied. The permission to strike these local silver coins could be explicit or implied. It could be granted directly by the imperial court or indirectly by the satrap or it could be simply tolerated by both[6].

The Achaemenids fostered autonomy in local institutions, cults and customs and at the same time strictly supervised the central and vital functions of foreign policy, defence and taxation. In this respect the Persian Empire was organized in a manner similar to the confederated states of our time[7]. Modern terms as «liberal» or «tolerant»[8] may be misleading in this context, but even those historians who view the Achaemenid history through greek-tinted glasses do admit that the subjugated nationalities did not loose their identity in the Persian Empire[9].

## 2. The Circulation of Money in the Fifth Satrapy

We know little of the political, economic and cultural situation in the huge satrapy Abar Nahara (Beyond the River), situated west of the Euphrates, which comprised the whole of Syria, Phoenicia, Palestine and Cyprus[10]. Modern scholarship has been unable to establish the residence of the satrap: it might have been Damascus, Sidon or elsewhere[11]. It seems, too, that another anomaly has escaped the full attention of numismatists and historians alike: why did the satrap not strike coins[12] as did his

---

Minor, but they clearly belong to the late imperial coinage of the Achaemenid Empire. This attribution is strengthened by the Greek title of the Great King – BASILEōS, BASI, BAS, BA.]

[5] Note the type of a striding camel (BMC Pl. 19:25; Traité Pl. 124:17) and cf. infra n. 25.

[6] Cf. P. FREI, Zentralgewalt und Lokalautonomie im Achämenidenreich, in: Reichsidee und Reichsorganisation im Perserreich (OBO 55), Fribourg - Göttingen 1984, entire, especially p. 13 with n. 17 and p. 26, on the institution of imperial authorization (Reichsautorisation) on the base of the Letoon Trilingue of Xanthos, and compare the incorporation of Egyptian law into the Persian Codex by Darius I and also the aramaic archives of the Jewish military colony in Elephantine and some texts in the biblical books of Esra, Nehemiah and Esther.

[7] Cf. K. KOCH, Weltordnung und Reichsidee im alten Iran, in: P. FREI / id., Reichsidee und Reichsorganisation im Perserreich (OBO 55), Fribourg - Göttingen 1984, 63.

[8] CAH IV, ed. by J.B. BURY / S.A. COOK et al., Cambridge 1923, 187: «The Persian was a tolerant government».

[9] K. KOCH, in: Reichsidee und Reichsorganisation, 1984, 49-54, especially 53.

[10] CAH IV, 194-198: «The Twenty Satrapies» with map.

[11] Cf. recently R. STUCKY, Ras Shamra-Leukos Limen, Paris 1983, 164: «Die Lage des Satrapensitzes, die man nach Aleppo, Damaskus, Tripolis und Sidon lokalisieren wollte, ist unbekannt». [Cf. now P. CALMEYER, Die sogenannte fünfte Satrapie und die achaimenidischen Dokumente, Transeuphratène 3 (1990), 109-129; E. LIPINSKI, Géographie linguistique de la Transeuphratène à l'époque achéménide, ibid., 96-107].

[12] Some tetradrachms with the Great King in kidaris and kandys (cf. supra n. 4) have been

colleagues Tissaphernes, Pharnabazos, Tiribazos, Orontas, Datames, Mazaios and the Carians Hekatomnos, Maussollos, Idrieos and Pixodaros? One could argue that the Hekatomnid satraps reigning in distant Caria were, in fact, independent, hereditary rulers, but should not forget that they remained active Persian officials nevertheless[13]. The satrap of Cilicia, however, was nearby[14] and his coins circulated, indeed, in the territory of the fifth satrapy[15]. Furthermore, the satrap of the Fifth did not hold a lower or less important position than his colleagues who established mints.

The hoards provide a good reason why the satrap may have refrained from issuing coins. The silver money supply was astonishingly rich and varied without the satrap's own coinage. There was a large inflow from the mint of Athens and other Greek cities, Cilician small cash, money struck by the Phoenician cities on the coast, provincial small silver provided by the Palestinian governors and finally the drachms, hemidrachms and fractions created by cities and rulers in the South. These latter silver issues are the so called «Philisto-Arabians».

But where is the Persian imperial money? Actually it does not circulate in the South. The high denomination of the gold daric does not appear in the hoards[16]. The same is true for the silver siglos[17], as this issue is struck in and for Asia Minor only

---

tentatively attributed to Phoenicia, but hoard evidence, denomination, types and style clearly indicate issues by Western satraps.

[13] This is proven by the Carian satrap Pixodaros' additional function as satrap of Lycia, recorded in the Letoon trilingue of Xanthos. Cf. P. FREI, in: Reichsidee und Reichsorganisation, 1984, 12.

[14] Mazaios, the powerful satrap, active from about 361 till about 334, for a certain period governed Cilicia and the Fifth Satrapy acoording to his title on some coins of Tarsos *mzdy zy 'l 'br nhr' whlk* «Mazaios who (is) over Abar Nahara and Cilicia». He did also strike coins with his name *MZDY* (probably pronounced Mazdai) in the Fifth Satrapy, but definitely not as its satrap, but as the ruler of Sidon, meticulously keeping the city's denominations and types - a highly important feature. Cf. J.W. BETLYON, The Coinage and Mints of Phoenica. The Pre-Alexandrine Period (HSM 26), Chico/CA 1980, 15. [On Mazaios see now supra, S. 43-53].

[15] Abu Shusheh and Nablus hoards (IGCH 1507 and 1504 with literature). [The satraps used local mints, especially in Transit Cilicia, for the production of their general monetray needs, not for the currency of a specific satrapy or province. «The overall picture of coins minted on behalf of Persians does not warrant the assumption that Persian commanders brought to the mint, along with their bullion, demands that special designs be used for their coins, much less that their images be used as types»: C.M. HARRISON, Coins of the Persian Satraps, Ann Arbor 1992, 445 (Diss. Univ. of Pennsylvania 1982)].

[16] This can not be a mere «coincidence» (E. STERN, Material Culture of the Land of the Bible in the Persian Period 538-332 B.C., Warminster - Jerusalem, 1982, 227), but is an important matter of record. The negative numismatic evidence is irrefutable, but not final. It is valid until positive evidence emerges, - in this case a substantial and secured hoard of darics unearthed in the South. Cf. L. MILDENBERG, The Numismatic Evidence, HSCP 91 (1987) 381-395 [hier S. 253-262]. STERN, Material Culture, 223 in another context admits the significance of the negative numismatic evidence.

[17] Even in Syria and Northern Phoenicia the sigloi appear very rarely in hoards (one siglos in IGCH 1481 and another in IGCH 1483). Further South one siglos only was found near Bostra in the Hauran (IGCH 1482). Cf. D. SCHLUMBERGER, L'argent grec dans l'empire

and serves mainly for paying the Greek mercenaries there. These findings, surprising at the first glance, are strengthened by current experience on the Jerusalem coin market. Darics and sigloi very rarely appear there, but Greek, Cilician and Phoenician silver coins occur from time to time. The bulk of the Philisto-Arabian coins has been offered just in Jerusalem in the course of the last 50 years[18].


## 3. The Coins Struck in the Southern Provinces

«Philisto-Arabians» and «Egypto-Arabians» were preliminary and auxiliary terms used by G.F. HILL in 1914[19]. He was well aware that he could not be more specific, as very little was known then. Meanwhile, some new evidence was obtained which would allow us to call these intriguing issues the autonomous, local coins of the Southern Persian Provinces. The north of the satrapy was, obviously, a territory for the plentiful, longlasting coinage of the great cities at the sea: Arados, Byblos, Sidon, Tyros. The central area remained a large empty spot on the numismatic map until the finds of the thirties and early seventies appeared and suddenly unveiled an abundant provincial coinage of small silver struck by the Persian governors of Samaria[20] and Judaea[21]. Not only the names of these two provinces appear on these tiny coins, but also the names of governors, one with this title (Tf. XXVIII 1)[22]. In the Southern foothills of Judaea and near Ashdod in the plain the country of the «Philisto-Arabians» begins. But how far to the South does it go? One coin found and published lately[23] indicates the northern Hedjaz as the Southern border[24].

---

achéménide, 1953, 6-12, and Asyut p. 97-98. The Hoard referred to by I. CARRADICE, The «Regal» Coinage of the Persian Empire (BAR.IS 343), Oxford 1987, as No. 24 (p. 79), shown in London 1983, is said to come from Lebanon. South-Eastern Turkey is more likely. [See I. CARRADICE, Regal Coinage in the Persian Empire, in: Coinage and Administration in the Athenian and Persian Empires (BAR IS 343; Oxford 1987), 77-93, pls. X - XV.]

[18] The largest and most important private collections of Philisto-Arabian coins have been formed in the City of Jerusalem.

[19] BMC p. LXXXIII-LXXXIX and 176-183. HILL himself stated p. LXXXIII: «Under these not very satisfactory headings are here catalogued certain groups of silver coins».

[20] The Nablus hoard of 1968 (IGCH 1504) with fractions bearing the name of the province Samaria šmryn . Cf. SNG ANS nos. 18, 19, 22, 23, 26; Y. MESHORER, Ancient Jewish Coinage I, Dix Hills/NY 1982, 98, 160; Oxford, Ashmolean, Report of the Visitors 1970, Pl. 12, cf. also A. SPAER, A Coin of Jeroboam, IEJ 29 (1979) 218 (presumably from a stray find near Nablus).

[21] The finds in Jerusalem and South of Jerusalem. Cf. L. MILDENBERG, Yehud, supra n. 1 with literature and E. STERN, Material Culture of the Land of the Bible in the Persian Period, 1982, 224 with n. 35 and 36. [For the coins issued by the governors of the Persian province of Samaria, see now Y. MESHORER - S. QEDAR, The Coins of Samaria in the Fourth Century BCE. Los Angeles 1991].

[22] In Phoenicia, there were no governors in an intermediary position between the satrap of the Fifth and the great city states, whereas the provincial governors of Samaria and Judaea did depend directly upon the satrap residing in the North.

[23] M.A. RIZACK, A Coin with the Aramaic Legend ŠHRW , a King Governor of LIḤYÂN, ANSMN 29 (1984) 25-28.

Admittedly, the boundaries can still not be drawn with any certainty, but we can guess today where this money was issued. The question of why this coinage came into being can be more easily answered. People in the South needed cash to serve their local and distant trade purposes.

## 4. The Date of the Southern Issues

The second major question is when. This is a preliminary survey, a preview far from being the last word. Early scholars had based their dates on comparison of styles which is a risky procedure. Another part of the numismatic evidence, however, is helpful. Many types of the early Philisto-Arabians are imitations of mid-fifth century Greek silver coins. Here, one has to consider that a long interval may have occured between the prototype and the copy. About thirty years passed by before Kimon's facing Arethusa reached Tarsos and about fifty before it became Philisto Arabian (Tf. XXVIII 2). But Syracuse is far. Thirty years may be a safer guess between the Lampsakos'Janus-head and the earliest Gaza copy (Tf. XXVIII 3); thus 460/450 and 430/420 are likely. The dating of 430/420 for the earliest Gaza drachms is supported by another comparison: At that time, Sidon and Tyros had developed their main coinages, the heavy denominations[25]. Gaza is their counterpart, being the best of ports in the South. Her importance as the final destination of the desert routes and the major junction of the coastal roads can hardly be overestimated (Tf. XXVIII 4). Similar strategic and economic needs may have caused the issue of simultaneous coinages in these port cities.

HILL clearly distinguished between a large early and a small later group of Philisto-Arabian drachms, the first having the weight of about 4 g, the second of about 3 g. This is a good argument sustained by the evidence of types and imitations[26]. The first group may be dated about 420-370 and the second about 370-330. To give an exact final date is risky. Alexander's conquest did not change the legal, economic and cultural institutions overnight and everywhere; not even the entire coinage, which certainly was one of his pet interests. The provincial silver issues of Judaea, for instance, go down till around 280: the same standard, similar types, fabric and legends under Persian, Macedonian and Ptolemaic rule (Tf. XXIX 5)[27].

---

[24] Arabia «was long ago abandoned as a tribute-paying satrapy» (A.T. OLMSTEAD, History of the Persian Empire, Chicago [6]1970, 293), but the Liḥyān coin (preceding note) with the ruler's name in Aramaic script, with the same denomination and types as most of the Yehud coins attests to close connections between Northern Arabia and the Southern territories of the Fifth Satrapy. Obviously, the able diplomats of the Persian court did secure efficient cooperation with the Arab chiefs.

[25] J.W. BETLYON, The Coinage and Mints of Phoenica, 1980, Pl. 1:3 (435-420); C.M. KRAAY, Archaic and Classival Greek Coins, London 1976, 288-1054 (about 430); G.K. JENKINS, Ancient Greek Coins, Fribourg 1972, 136 stresses the unmistakeably «Achaemenid flavour» of these coins. Did the Sidonian city-kings issue in lieu of the Persian administration?

[26] BMC, p. LXXXV.

[27] L. MILDENBERG, Yehud: A Preliminary Study of the Provincial Coinage of Judaea, in: FS

## 5. The Minting Authorities

It is, unfortunately, premature to give a final answer to the most difficult question of the «Philisto-Arabians». The cities of Ashdod and Gaza put their names on their issues. Some groups may be connected with Gaza, though they are anepigraphic; the decisive die link, however, still escapes us. There are some letters or letter combinations the meaning of which eludes the cautious observer. That ʾālef - nūn (Tf. XXIX 6) means Ascalon by indicating the first and the last letter, is by no means proven[28]. The name of a ruler in distant Liḥyān, mentioned before, is an important contribution and reminds us how little we know in this field. Most of the Southern coins do not reveal any inscription and their types, weights and flan forms do not give obvious indications of the mint. A few issues display single words which we can read[29], but still not understand (Tf. XXIX 7 and XXX :8)[30]. Definite hoard evidence would be of great importance, but – alas – does not exist.

The silver obols and their subdivisions were certainly the cash of every day life, thus local money. Some mints, however, struck drachms and hemidrachms, first and mainly of Athenian standard, which could be easily used in foreign trade. These issues were created as money for this trade by the cities, rulers and chiefs along the caravan routes and roads in the South.

---

in Honour of M. Thompson, Wetteren, 1979, 183-196 [hier S. 67-76].

[28] SNG ANS, 25 and 31, and Y. MESHORER, Ancient Jewish Coinage I, 1982: Ascalon. E. LIPINSKI, Egyptian Aramaic Coins from the Fifth and Fourth Centuries B.C., in: Studia P. Naster Oblata I (Numismatica Antiqua, OrLovA 12), Leuven 1982, 31: Heliopolis.

[29] Sometimes, however, even the reading is difficult. The reasonable proposition to read *Tadanmu*, the Satrap Datames' aramaic name, on small silver coins from Abū Shūsheh (SNG ANS, 24) is not entirely convincing, because the essential last letter *wāw* is missing in the legend. Further, the Abū Shūsheh find seems to be more an accumulation than a hoard. If the coin has, indeed, been struck, by Datames, Tarsos could have been the mint. E. LIPINSKI, in: Studia P. Naster Oblata I, 1982, 30, reads the legend, however, *mnpt* for Memphis in Egypt.

[30] Two examples have been published lately, Y. MESHORER, Three Gaza Coins from the Persian Period, IMN 12 (1977) 78-79, n. 2-3. The reading *bēt - ʾālef - mēm* on a drachm with unmistakable Athenian images seems plausible, though the first letter may be understood otherwise. The translation «in the territory» and the tentative attribution of the coin to Gaza, however, is disputable. The comparison with a legend on bronze coins of Sidon and Berytos from the second century B.C. might still have some significance (BMC Phoenicia, 155-156, n. 87-91 and p. 52, 5), but the word ʾm - metropolis -has to be rendered literally, as Hill does, thus ʾm = mother and within the entire legend as mother city: «(to) Sidon, mother city of Carthage, Hippo, Citium, Tyros». On the new drachm, names of the offspring of Sidon do not appear. Moreover, no colonies founded by Gaza are known or even probable. On the other drachm, also displaying Athenian types, the reading of the name ʿbdʾl (Ebedel or Abdiel) is incontestable, but does not give any clear indication of the mint. Gaza is not impossible, but far from being proven.

## 6. The Types of the Southern Coins

After: where, why, when and by whom, finally the question: what is illustrated on the coins? The general picture is multiform. Within the money circulation of the fifth Satrapy, already varied in its general aspect – as stressed before –, the Southern issues form a specific, extremely colourful group (Tf. XXX 9). Local taste[31] and necessities of trade prevail. Greek types and especially Athenian images were popular, but eclectic representations, too, pleased the Southerners and their visitors. Influence from Greece in the north was stronger than from Egypt in the South. Some types might have been especially created for the Arab camel riders of the caravans (Tf. XXX 10). The extreme diversity of the images must have been caused by the *raison d'être* of this coinage and not by the intention to indicate magistrates or mint overseers, as has been argued lately[32]. Anyway, this kind of money could only come into being in that distant Southern area of transit under the astonishing rule of the late Persian Great Kings who had delegated power and guaranteed ethnical and religious freedom and local autonomy to their citizen.

## 7. Further Research

Any progress in this field depends upon close observation of the market place, registration of find spots, archaeological findings, scholarly cooperation and finally gathering and interpretation of all available material in the frame of a corpus. Only the first steps have been made. Hopefully, the next generation will do the rest.

---

[31] In his survey of the Eastern coinages from about 425 till about 340, D. SCHLUMBERGER, L'argent grec dans l'empire achéménide, 1953, 24 ranges the Philisto-Arabians among the «monnaies complémentaires» and grades some of them as «moins douées" («certaines philisto-arabes et surtout les pseudo-Athéniennes»). It seems, how-ever, that in the South the Philisto-Arabians were the principal coins. Many of them are more or less Athenian imitations and quite a few are of equal or even better workmanship than the Athenian models which themselves become «uniform to the point of monotony - an uninspired repetition of the old formulas, and often carelessly executed at that», E.S.G. ROBINSON, Some Problems in the Later Fifth Century Coinage of Athens, ANSMN 9 (1960) Pl. 1. [For the Sidonian Coinage, cf. J. ELAYI, Sidon, cité autonome de l'empire Perse (Paris 1989), 197-233].

[32] E. STERN, Material Culture of the Land of the Bible in the Persian Period, 1982, 223-224.

# Bes on Philisto-Arabian Coins

(Tf. XXXI)

## 1. The Term «Philisto-Arabian». A Clarification

The term *Philisto-Arabian* was first used by HILL in his *BMC Palestine* published in 1914[1]. Recently, several other names have been proposed: *Graeco-Phoenician* [2], *Graeco-Palestinian* and *Graeco-Persian* [3]. The origin of coinage has, indeed, been located in Greek Western Anatolia in the 7th century B.C.; and the weight standard of the Philisto-Arabian coinage, though much oscillating, is basically Attic, as the Athenian owls served as prototypes. But the dies were, obviously, cut by local craftsmen who created indigenous works, not by Greek engravers producing Greek art. Finally the *images* (I avoid the ambiguous term *type* and do not rely on the subjective concept of *style* ) are of very different origin, the models coming from a vast area, stretching from Sicilian Syracuse (Tf. XXXI 14-15) to the Arabian desert (Tf. XXXI 13). Greek images are frequent around 400, but fade during the course of the 4th century; Phoenician and Persian influences exist, but are certainly not strong. We have to do with an eclectic coinage, stimulated by influences from many directions, but at the same time displaying autochthonous features (Tf. XXXI 1. 3. 10. 17. 18)[4]. All that is characteristic for a coinage emerging in a region which was the crossroads of the Levant, where the routes from the Euphrates to the Nile and from the Mediterranean to the desert all met[5]. Thus, all three new names are unacceptable. They are based on misleading stylistic considerations and, in the end, on pro-Hellenic prejudice. Especially inappropriate is the term *Graeco-Palestinian* . It is inaccurate if *Palestinian* is meant to indicate the territory, because in the greater part of Palestine no Philisto-Arabian coins were produced. And it is void, if

---

[1] G.F. HILL, BMC Palestine, London 1914, LXXXIII-LXXXIV.

[2] First stated by A. KINDLER in 1963: see L. MILDENBERG, Gaza mint authorities in Persian time, Transeuphratène 2 (1990) 143, n. 25 [hier S. 84].

[3] Y. MESHORER, Greco-Persian Coins of Palestine, INB 1 (1962) 18-19; id. in 1981, however, «Graeco-Palestinian coins», title preceding no. 1 in SNG ANS, Part 6, Palestine-South Arabia; Y. MESHORER / S. QEDAR, The coinage of Samaria in the fourth century BCE, Jerusalem 1991, use finally HILL's term: «the so-called Philisto-Arabian coinage».

[4] A striking image is the bearded head of a sheikh on the observe and an arab camel rider on the reverse of the drachm BMC Palestine, Pl. XIX,25. Tf. XXXI 1 may be Cypriote.

[5] See L. MILDENBERG, Transeuphratène 2 (1990) 139-140 with n. 12 [hier S. 81]; id., Gaza von 420 bis 332 nach den Sachquellen, in: Akten des XIII. Internationalen Kongresses für Klassische Archäologie Berlin 1988, Mainz 1990, 430-431, with map [hier S. 77-78].

Palestinian models are meant, because they simply do not exist. We are, in fact, dealing with the monetary production of the southern cities on the shore of the Mediterranean and of the rulers of the territory at the border of the desert. As this description is rather too long to be a title, we can, indeed, retain HILLs time-honoured name, *Philisto-Arabian*, as being soundly based on geographic criteria: the cities on the sea have always been part of the Philistine region, and the realm of the sheikhs – Arab land.

## 2. The So-Called Egypto-Arabians

In a recent article, I have asked: *Where and when did a relevant, distinctly satrapal coinage come into being?* [6]. Today I have to ask, *were there any Egypto-Arabian coins?* I have to stress that, in fact, there were none. In my modest view, Sir GEORGE FRANCIS HILL is the greatest numismatist of modern times (he is one of the three scholars to whom I have dared to dedicate my *Bar Kokhba* book), but for once he was wrong, coining the term *Egypto-Arabian* on the basis of the Bes heads occuring on our coinage[7]. Not one Philisto-Arabian coin, so far as is known from published hoard evidence, has ever been found in Egypt, not even along its eastern borders. It can also not be maintained that «the head of Bes is due to *direct* Egyptian influence», as HILL wrote[8]. The guardian-genius Bes was popular in the Levant before the 4th century[9]. Local artifacts from the north depicting Bes in various materials are more likely to have influenced our engravers. In any event, an incuse depiction of Bes is found on 5th century coins of Sidon[10]; and a large Bes head facing left is on the famous Yehud drachm, with the reverse of a seated man on the winged chair, struck in the first part of the 4th century[11].

In the Persian province of Samaria, Bes must have been a current image around 350, the time of the Philisto-Arabian Bes coins, as the local, minute, Samarian coins clearly demonstrate[12]. Finally, there are many different Bes images on our coinage (full figure Tf. XXXI 16. 18; half figure ibid. 1; heads facing ibid 2.5-9.11; and in profile ibid 19), heads combined with those of men, animals and monsters (Tf. XXXI 3-4. 10. 12), not only the facing head (combined with the facing

---

[6] Id., Notes on the coin issues of Mazday, INJ 11 (1990-1991) 14, n. 25 [hier S. 46].

[7] BMC Palestine, Pl. XX,1-4. 7 and Tf. XXXI 14.15.19, are now given to Cilicia.

[8] BMC Palestine, p. LXXXIX.

[9] See the standing bronze Bes from the 8th-7th centuries B. C. found in Nimrud, Fort Salmanassar, locus C 6 (M.E.L. MALLOWAN, Nimrud and its Remains, London 1966, fig. 361), illustrated in: Sumer, Assur, Babylon. 7000 Jahre Kunst und Kultur an Euphrat und Tigris, ed. E. STROMMENGER, Mainz 1979, no. 143.

[10] J.W. BETLYON, The Coinage and Mints of Phoenicia. The Pre-Alexandrine Period, Chico/CA 1982, Pl. 1. 4 and 10.

[11] BMC Palestine, Pl. XIX,29; H. KIENLE, Der Gott auf dem Flügelrad (GOF VI,7), Wiesbaden 1975, entire; L. MILDENBERG, Yehud: A preliminary Study of the provincial Coinage of Judaea, in: FS M. Thompson, Wetteren 1979, 183-186, Pl. 21,1 [hier S. 67-70; Tf. XXI].

[12] MESHORER - QEDAR, The coinage of Samaria, 1991, Ill. 27. 43. 72-75.

Arethusa head) on which HILL's *Egypto* -attribution was mainly based (Tf. XXXI 14-15). In 1914, *only* a small part of the Bes material was known, and even less was represented in the trays of the British Museum. It has to be stressed that the Bes issues form an organic, indivisible part of the entire series and can, therefore, *not* be described under a separate heading. As to Bes representation on Philisto-Arabian coins, there does not seem to be any direct influence from Egypt in the 4th century; but the beloved creature, ultimately originating in Egypt, had, by that time, come to play an important part in the iconography of the Levant in general and, no less noteworthy, on that of the Philisto-Arabian coinage in particular.

P.S.: New hoards indicate that the facing Arethusa head / facing Bes head coins (Tf. XXXI 14-15), described by HILL as «Egypto-Arabian», belong to Cilicia. This is confirmed by the fact that they never occur on the Jerusalem market.

# II.

## Griechische, kleinasiatische und punische Münzprägungen

# Von der Kunst der griechischen Kleinmünzen

## (Tf. XXXII - XXXIII)

In den letzten Jahren hat sich die Gunst der Sammler einem Gebiete zugewandt, das sie bisher vernachlässigt hatten, den sehr kleinen Silbermünzen der griechischen Antike. In der numismatischen Literatur sind diesen winzigen Prägungen aber auch in neuester Zeit nur wenige Einzelstudien gewidmet worden. Deshalb mag vielleicht dem Jubilar und manchem Leser willkommen sein, was hier in der gebotenen Kürze in Wort und Bild aufzuzeigen versucht wurde[*].

Zuerst ein paar Worte über das Silber als das bevorzugte Münzmetall der griechischen Prägungen. Es ist weit häufiger als jedes andere Metall. Die Fächerung in Silber ist ganz erstaunlich, und zwar in den meisten Währungsgebieten. Man denke nur an den attischen Münzfuß und die Stückelung in Athen, die vom Zehndrachmenstück, das über 40 g wog, bis zum winzigen Achtelobol reicht, der ungefähr 0,09 g hielt. Die reiche Geldskala, für die heute Papier, Silber, Nickel und Kupfer benötigt werden, bestand in Athen allein in Silber. Die Gründe dafür sind naheliegend: reichliches Silbervorkommen und eine hochentwickelte Import- und Exportwirtschaft, deren Träger die anerkannte athenische Silberwährung war.

In Kleinasien, Sizilien und der Kyrenaika gab es eine stärker gegliederte Münzprägung auch in Elektron oder Gold, und zwar erfolgte diese Prägung in den seltereren Metallen in allen drei Perioden der griechischen Kunst – der archaischen, klassischen und hellenistischen. Die Bronzeprägung setzte später ein und hatte eine weniger reiche Gliederung aufzuweisen als die der anderen Metalle. Für unser heutiges Thema kommen die Prägungen in Elektron und Gold nicht in Betracht. Eine kleinformatige Elektron- oder Goldmünze ist wertmäßig kein kleines Geldstück mehr, und das meiste griechische Bronzegeld ist großformatig und daher schon gar nicht mehr als Kleingeld anzusprechen.

Nach dem Metall nun einige Angaben über Gewicht und Durchmesser. Die Grundeinheit der Drachme im attischen Münzfuß von ungefähr 4,1 g teilt sich in 6 Obole, so daß ein Obol knapp 0,7 g wiegt. Etwas schwerer ist die einem anderen System angehörende und in Sizilien und Großgriechenland heimische Litra, ein Zehntelstater von ungefähr 0,86 g. Was eine griechische Kleinmünze ist, darüber gibt es wohl noch keine akzeptierte Lehrmeinung. Die kleinsten Einheiten sind Litra und Obol sowie deren Unterteilungen, z. B. die Obolengruppe mit Halb-, Viertel-

---

[*] Der vorliegende Essay ist die erweiterte Textfassung eines 1962 auf der Fifth Israel Numismatic Convention gehaltenen Vortrages, von dem eine gekürzte englische Zusammenfassung in INB 2 (1962) 35-389 erschienen ist.

und Achtelobolen. Die hier behandelte Skala reicht, in Millimetern ausgedrückt, von ungefähr 12 bis 2 mm herab, also – um einen Vergleich zu wagen – von einer Pille bis zu einem Streichholzkopf. Von den Münzen, die auf den Tafeln gezeigt werden, wiegt die schwerste 0,98 g, die leichteste 0,68 g.

Man wird sich gewiß fragen, wie sind solche sehr kleinen Maße und Gewichte überhaupt möglich? Wie konnten solch kleine Stempel geschnitten werden, derart winzige Silbermünzen geprägt werden, wie ist dieser Geldumlauf denkbar?

Auf diese technischen Fragen können wohl noch keine bündigen Antworten gegeben werden. Man hat noch keinen Kleinmünzenstempel gefunden, wohl auch nicht die typischen, äußerst feinen Instrumente für den Stempelschnitt oder besonders zierliche Prägeinstrumente. Aber unsere Verwunderung über die Tatsache dieser winzigen Münzen darf uns nicht dazu verführen, von den heutigen Verhältnissen einfach auf die der Antike zu schließen.

Daß wir heute die Kleinmünzen mit der Lupe betrachten und insbesondere in der Vergrößerung bewundern, besagt noch nicht, daß es in der Antike gleich oder auch nur ähnlich war. Der große Reichtum der Kleinmünzenprägung in Silber beweist doch, daß diese Emissionen einen festen Sitz im Leben der damaligen Zeit gehabt haben müssen, auch wenn dies uns heute erstaunlich erscheinen mag. Aus der Wirtschaft muß sich also ein Bedürfnis für dieses Kleingeld ergeben haben. Die damaligen Künstler waren in der Lage, klare und den ästhetischen Anforderungen der Zeit entsprechende Typen und Legenden auf dem eng begrenzten Flan zu schneiden. Die Münzstätten brachten die Prägungen der winzigen und oft dünnen Münzen tatsächlich zustande. Für die Aufbewahrung diente wohl nicht nur der Mund, wie die literarischen Quellen bezeugen, sondern auch der Geldbeutel.

Aus diesem kurz skizzierten technischen Komplex verdienen zwei Beobachtungen besonderes Interesse, weil sie für unser Urteil über die künstlerische Qualität der Kleinmünzen von Bedeutung sind. Zuerst: Die Stempelschneider verfügten über die klassischen Instrumente des Gemmen- und Münzstempelschnitts, Stichel, Rundperl und Bohrer, aber niemals über die Hilfsmittel unserer Zeit: die Brillen, Lupen, Storchschnäbel und dergleichen. Wenn von Nero berichtet wird, daß er einen Kristall ins Auge geklemmt haben soll, so ist damit noch nicht gesagt, daß die griechischen Stempelschneider optische Hilfsmittel hatten oder auch nur brauchten. Die Geschichte der Optik ist ja noch keine tausend Jahre alt. Selbst die einfachen Hilfsmittel der Fixierung des Zentrums durch einen Punkt, Vorzeichnung sowie Skizzierung einer mit dem Rande konzentrisch laufenden Kreislinie – alles bisweilen auf den größeren Prägungen vorkommende Details – lassen sich auf Kleinmünzen nicht feststellen. Es ist wohl schon so, daß die Künstler jener Zeit ebenso wie die Benützer der Münzen starke und unverbrauchte Augen hatten. Die Stempelschneider haben mit den einfachsten Instrumenten und in einem spontanen schöpferischen Akt ihre von uns bewunderten Bilder geschaffen.

Das zweite: In der Großsilberprägung steht bekanntlich der qualitativ hochstehende Stempelschnitt bisweilen im Kontrast zu der unsorgfältigen Ausprägung: Doppelschläge, eingerissene Ränder, flaue Ausprägung des Münzzentrums und vor allem krasse Dezentrierung ließen oft Einzelstücke entstehen, die heute einen Liebhaber enttäuschen. Bei den Kleinmünzen sind diese schweren Mängel viel seltener. Die kleineren Maße und Gewichte verlangten einfach mehr Sorgfalt und Kontrolle in der Münzstätte. Das Ergebnis ist ein im allgemeinen sehr befriedigender Aspekt der Kleinmünzprägung.

Bei der Betrachtung der Kleinmünze als Kunstwerk mag man zuerst geneigt sein, die erstaunlichen Leistungen der Stempelschneider zu überschätzen. Gewiß, es bedurfte für die Gravur dieser winzigen Stempel hervorragender Augen, einer ruhigen Hand und besonderer Geschicklichkeit, aber alle diese Voraussetzungen machen noch nicht das Kunstwerk aus. Kunst wird weder in Metern noch in Millimetern gemessen. Rembrandts Nachtwache ist nicht ein Kunstwerk, weil es viele Quadratmeter umspannt, und ein kleines Blatt Dürers nicht deshalb bewundernswert und kostbar, weil es eine Miniatur ist. Die originelle Idee, Auge und Hand des Meisters, die Tiefe seines Blicks und die strenge Disziplin – mit der Beschränkung auf das Wesentliche und dem Verzicht auf den Effekt – bleiben entscheidend. Reine Bravourstücke in riesigen oder winzigen Maßstäben vermögen nicht zu fesseln.

Wenn wir soeben von der beim Werk der Meister der Kleinmünzen nötigen Beschränkung auf das Wesentliche sprachen, so führt uns dies zu einer wichtigen Erkenntnis. Wir fragen zuerst: Sind die Obolen einfach entsprechende Verkleinerungen der Tetradrachmen aus derselben Zeit und die Litren solche der Statere? Ergeben die maßstäblichen Verkleinerungen automatiseh das Dessin? Nein, denn zuerst einmal ist festzustellen, daß solche maßstäbliche Verkleinerungen oder Vergrößerungen der Antike fremd waren. Wo genau dieselben Typen für Vorder- und Rückseite verlangt wurden, wie bei den großen Währungen, zum Beispiel Aegina, Athen und anderen, wurden neue Stempel mit denselben Darstellungen für das Kleingeld geschnitten, ein sklavisches Kopieren ist nicht festzustellen. Sonst entstehen aber meist ganz neue, besondere Typen für das Kleingeld, was bei dem Ideenreichtum und der Vielseitigkeit der Künstler gar nicht verwundert. Diese neuen Typen sind dann besonders ansprechend, wenn der Stempelschneider sich auf eine einfache, klare Darstellung beschränkte. In der archaischen und frühklassischen Zeit ist dies in der Groß- und Kleinmünzenprägung ohnehin üblich, in den späteren Perioden bringt die Großmünzenprägung oft viel besser entwickelte Bilder, während die Stempelschneider der Kleinmünzen sich auch dann noch in glücklicher Weise auf einen Gegenstand konzentrierten. Nur einige Beispiele aus Großgriechenland und Sizilien: Die ungeheuer reiche Kleinmünzenprägung von Tarent zeigt viele Beispiele für die glänzende Herausarbeitung eigener markanter Typen, zum Beispiel den schwimmenden Delphin ohne seinen Reiter, einzelne Gefäße, einen Kranz, zwei Halbmonde, eine Muschel. OSCAR RAVEL schrieb im Vorwort zu seinem Katalog der Sammlung Vlasto der Münzen von Tarent: «The part of the small denominations, which owing to their small size have always been ignored by the collectors, shows such a sequence of small works of art and is so complete, that every museum would be pleased to have it in its cabinet. For many numismatists some of these tiny pieces will be a real revelation».

In Messana gibt es winzige Kleinmünzen vom üblichen Typ, dem springenden Hasen, aber auch solche, die – pars pro toto – nur den Vorderteil oder den Kopf des Tieres mit den langen, lustigen Ohren zeigen. Auf dem Revers erscheinen aber statt des Maultiergespanns ein einzelner Delphin oder nur die drei Buchstaben MEΣ. Im

Rhegium der klassischen Zeit geht die Löwenmaske *en face* vom Tetradrachmon durch bis zum Bruchteil des Obols, aber statt des Kopfes des Apollon steht auf dem Avers der Kleinmünzen symbolisch der Ölzweig zusammen mit den Buchstaben *PH*.

Das Kleinsilber von Athen hat einen anderen Aspekt. Durch die Jahrhunderte hindurch erscheinen aus wirtschaftspolitischen Erwägungen auf den Groß- und Kleinmünzen stets die gleichen Typen, der Kopf der Pallas Athene auf der Vorderseite, die Eule auf der Rückseite. Die Göttin und der ihr heilige Vogel wurden so zu Symbolen der immer gleichbleibenden Güte des Geldes, der Stabilität der Weltwährung.

Aber überall in der griechischen Antike wollten Groß- und Kleinmünzen nichts anderes sein als Geld. Erst in der Periode der signierenden Künstler – insbesondere im letzten Viertel des 5. Jahrhunderts und im ersten Viertel des 4. Jahrhunderts vor Christus – wollte die Münze auch als Kunstwerk gelten, denn der signierende Meister war sich seiner Kunst bewußt und dokumentierte dies der Öffentlichkeit durch seine Signatur. Ob seine Schöpfung aber in Tat und Wahrheit ein Kunstwerk war, darüber entschied erst die Nachwelt bis auf unsere Tage. Gewiß gibt es viele unsignierte Meisterleistungen, aber auch manche signierten Stücke von eher bescheidener Qualität. Jedenfalls finden wir in der Periode der signierenden Künstler hervorragende Werke mit voller Signatur auch auf relativ kleinen Münzen. Man denke nur an die von Euainetos und Choirion gezeichneten Drachmen in Catana. Signierte Obolen oder Litren sind selten, und die Signatur erfolgte nur durch den Anfangsbuchstaben des Künstlernamens, zum Beispiel mit einem *Π* für Prokles, den hervorragenden Meister der klassischen Prägung in Naxos auf Sizilien. Ähnliches gilt wohl auch für das *E* des Euainetos, der in Catana und in Syrakus gewirkt hat. Allerdings gab es in Syrakus auch Kleinmünzen mit dem Buchstaben *E*, die ihres Stiles wegen Euainetos wohl kaum mehr zugeschrieben werden dürfen. Hier haben Nachahmer das Signum benutzt. Euainetos bleibt mit Kimon der signierende Meister der repräsentativen Zehndrachmenprägung und der kostbaren Hundertlitrenstücke in Gold. Prokles und Euainetos wollten auch ihre Kleinmünzen als Kunstwerke gelten lassen, sonst hätten sie sie nicht signiert. Die Stempelschneider vor und nach ihnen signierten ihre Kleinmünzen nicht, und viele von ihnen waren trotzdem wahre Meister.

Wir müssen abschließend sicher festhalten, daß die Kleinmünzenprägung in Silber eine Reihe von Kunstwerken eigener Art aufzuweisen hat. Wir haben in der griechischen Münzprägung viele orginelle Meisterwerke, eine große Menge von Durchschnittsstücken von oft hoher Qualität und schlechtere Erzeugnisse in allen Metallen und Größen. Der geringe Wert des Silberkleingeldes bedingt durchaus nicht eine geringere Ausführung. In diesem Sinne dürfen wir die Kleinmünzen keinesfalls unterschätzen, wie es ebenso unberechtigt wäre, den Stempelschnitt auf kleinstem Flan seiner technischen Fertigkeit wegen künstlerisch zu überschätzen. Als Ganzes bleibt die griechische Münzglyptik gewiß unerreicht, die Kleinmünzen in Silber tragen zu diesem Ruhme im gleichen Maße bei wie die großen Stücke.

# Mithrapata und Perikles

(Tf. XXXIV - XXXVI)

Im Jahre 1957 machten Hirten im Abzugsgraben des Sees von Podalia, dem heutigen Elmali, einen Münzfund, der uns durch seine zum größten Teil bisher unbekannten, faszinierenden Prägungen eine vertiefte Erkenntnis des lykischen Münzwesens der ersten Hälfte des vierten vorchristlichen Jahrhunderts und damit zugleich eine erneuerte und bereicherte Vorstellung vom Leben in den kleinen Fürstentümern im südlichen Kleinasien erschlossen hat.

OLÇAY hat im «Istanbuler Bulletin» 1958-1959 kurz mitgeteilt, daß 514 Stücke aus dem Funde von Podalia in das dortige Nationalmuseum gelangt sind. Wir wissen noch nicht, wieviel davon lykische Prägungen sind. JENKINS, MØRKHOLM und LE RIDER haben inzwischen hervorragende lykische Einzelstücke veröffentlicht oder angezeigt. In öffentlichen und privaten Sammlungen und im Handel habe ich bisher 150 sicher aus Podalia stammende lykische Stücke registrieren können, davon 61 des Mithrapata und 55 des Perikles. Sie ersehen bereits aus diesen Zahlen, daß die Publikation der in Istanbul liegenden großen Gruppe abgewartet werden muß, bevor endgültige Schlüsse gezogen werden können. Unser Römer Kongreß bietet aber gewiß das geeignetste Forum für einen vorläufigen informativen Überblick, wenigstens über die zwei wichtigsten Gruppen des Fundes, die Münzen der Dynasten Mithrapata und Perikles.

Vermerken Sie aber bitte zuerst, welche Prägungen überhaupt als aus dem Funde stammend angegeben werden: nur Silber, und zwar Einzelstücke von Tarsus, Drachmen von Aspendus des Reiter- / Wildschwein-Typus vom Ende des 5. Jahrhunderts sowie Statere des Rinder- / Schleuder-Typus mit dem sitzenden Adler als Beizeichen von der Mitte des 4. Jahrhunderts, beides in größeren Mengen, und schließlich die lykischen Statere, Tetrobole und Diobole mit den Namen:

*Mithrapata*
*Zämu*
*Trebenimus*
*Aruvatiyäsi*
*Väd*
*Zag*
*Zät*
*Vakhssärä*
*Zakhaba*
*Zäru*
*Perikles*

Was mir an Stempelverbindungen von Mithrapata und Perikles bekannt geworden ist, sehen Sie auf den beiden Tafeln (XXXIV und XXXV). Es wäre mir unmöglich gewesen, Ihnen diese 32 Stempelverbindungen mit ihren 19 Vorder- und 27 Rückseiten im Lichtbild einzeln so deutlich vorzustellen. Da die einzelnen Stempel aber auch noch sehr variieren und alles andere als ein monotones Bild zeigen, so mußte ich ihre eingehende Beschreibung schon aus Zeitmangel schriftlich geben.

Gestatten Sie, daß ich an Hand der Tafeln kursorisch nur die wichtigsten Probleme kurz bespreche:

## 1. Die Münzstätten

Die sonst gut bekannten lykischen Inschriften für Xanthus und Telmessus fanden sich im Funde bisher nirgends. Wo Mithrapata geprägt hat, können wir heute noch nicht sagen. Eines haben Sie aber gewiß auf den ersten Blick erkannt: alle die bisher gänzlich unbekannt gewesenen Stücke mit dem bärtigen Kopf im Profil wurden in *einer* Münzstätte geprägt. JENKINS hat 1959 bereits drei Stempelkoppelungen erkannt und vorausgesagt: «It seems amply clear that if the whole material were available, the entire series would prove to be closely linked together by dies form beginning to end». Nun, wir haben heute 9 Stempelkoppelungen und nur noch, wie Sie sehen, Lücken an zwei Stellen (nach No. 4 und nach No. 9), aber beide Male sind die nicht verbundenen Stempel fast zum Verwechseln ähnlich. Die Statere des Mithrapata mit der großen Triskelis haben das gleiche klare Quadratum Incusum und eine ähnliche Schrift, vor allem auch einen sehr ähnlichen metallurgischen Befund und sind gleich schlecht geprägt. Die Löwenmaske jedoch ist eckiger, und der allgemeine Aspekt ein durchaus anderer. Solange wir keine Stempelkoppelung unter den Löwenmasken der beiden Gruppen finden, muß die Frage, ob gleiche oder andere Münzstätte, noch offen bleiben.

Bei Perikles konnte bisher bei den 3 Gruppen mit den verschiedenen Köpfen eine Koppelung untereinander nicht festgestellt werden. Die erste Gruppe nennt den Namen *Periklä* und die Ortsbezeichnung *Vähntäzä*, deren Identität mit Antiphellus feststeht. Die 3 Gruppen haben aber die gleichen sehr ähnlichen Köpfe, auf die wir sofort noch zu sprechen kommen. Daher dürften alle diese Stücke in Antiphellus geprägt sein. Alle mir bekannt gewordenen Diobole mit der Syrakusaner Vorder- und der Akanthus-Rückseite sind aus demselben Stempelpaar geprägt. Außer dem Namen des Dynasten bringen auch sie eine neue Inschrift *Vädäviä*, für die ich eine eindeutige Erklärung noch nicht geben kann. Das erste *V* mag «von» bedeuten, die Endung des Wortes mag ein Genitiv sein. Möglich sind nur Patronym, Personen- oder Ortsnamen. Die Ähnlichkeit in Konzeption und Stil mit den Stateren ist allerdings auffallend, trotzdem kann über die Münzstätte noch nichts Endgültiges ausgesagt werden.

Die wenigen Tetrobole mit der großen Triskelis sind von beiden anderen Gruppen gänzlich verschieden. Sie wurden von anderen Stempelschneidern und Münzmeistern an einem anderen Ort und wohl auch nicht zur gleichen Zeit gefertigt.

## 2. Götterbild oder Portrait

Der Kopf des Mithrapata trägt keinen Kranz. Der erste schmale Kopf hat die Haare hochgenommen und in 2 Wellen gelegt, was aussieht wie ein Kranz, aber keiner ist. Trotzdem lehnt sich dieser Kopf bezeichnenderweise noch an ein Götterbildnis an. Aber der Name Mithrapata wird klar angezeigt. Die dann folgende Reihe bringt eindeutige Portraits, deren erstaunlich weite Skala von der mehr oder minder idealisierenden bis zur stark veristischen Auffassung, ja fast bis zur leichten Karikatur reicht. Die große Vielfalt und die starke Kraft dieser Portraits sollten uns nicht verwundern, wenn wir an die Bildnisse der persischen Satrapen Pharnabazes und Tissaphernes denken, die bereits einige Jahrzehnte vorher in Kleinasien entstanden sind.

Der Kopf des bärtigen Perikles *en face* hat zuerst einen Lorbeerkranz. Allerdings sieht man deutlich nur den Teil über der linken Stirnhälfte. Die zwei Büschel oben links und rechts weichen zudem sehr von der üblichen Bekränzung ab. Der breite, zweite Kopf hat ein eigenartiges Gebilde, das man am besten als Quasi-Kranz bezeichnet. Nur die obere Reihe existiert, die untere Reihe des Kranzes soll durch Haarlocken vorgetäuscht werden. Bei dritten Kopf hat man sich gänzlich von der Tradition befreit: Der Kranz ist verschwunden, die Haare flattern locker als Umrahmung, der Blick des Beschauers ist ganz auf das schmale, individuelle Antlitz gerichtet, auf das sich alles konzentriert. Der Durchbruch zum Portrait ist erfolgt, und zwar auf der Vorderseite, während der Name wie bei Mithrapata auf der Rückseite stehenbleibt. Zu beachten ist, daß man die Portraitzüge auf dem Revers erkennen kann. Der bärtige Krieger ist Perikles.

## 3. Chronologie

Zuerst ist festzustellen, daß die Portrait- und Triskelisstücke Mithrapatas mit Gewißheit aus dem einen Fund von Podalia stammen, sodaß es sich um ein- und denselben Dynasten handeln muß. Für Mithrapata galt aber bisher der Ansatz von ungefähr 390 v.Chr., während Perikles für 372 inschriftlich belegt ist und Lykien in den Satrapenaufstand 362-360 hineingezogen haben soll. Nun zeigen merkliche Gebrauchsspuren nur die frühen Drachmen mit dem Wildschwein von Aspendus. In der ganzen Mithrapata-Gruppe finden sich nur einige Stücke mit leichten Gebrauchsspuren, während die Prägungen des Perikles zwar großenteils schlecht geprägt und teils überprägt, aber doch frisch sind. Die beiden Dynasten sind also fast gleichzeitig anzusetzen, was bei den lykischen Dynastenstaaten durchaus möglich ist. Die Prägungen des Mithrapata mögen vielleicht etwas früher entstanden sein.

Die Statere von Aspendus vom Ringertyp mit dem Adler als Beizeichen sind alle stempelfrisch. Ihr Ansatz ist üblicherweise 370 oder wohl auch etwas später. Man kann für die Mithrapata-Prägung daher ungefähr 380-370, für die des Perikles vielleicht 375-365 ansetzen. Der Hort mag also durchaus in den Jahren des Satrapenaufstandes vor 360 am See von Podalia vergraben worden sein.

## 4. Stil und Charakter der Prägungen

Zuerst fällt der ganz erstaunliche Reichtum und die große Varietät auf. Dies ist nur ein kleiner Teil des Geldes, das in einem kleinen lykischen Dynastenstaat geprägt worden ist. Nicht nur die Portrait-Auffassungen sind sehr verschieden, sondern auch die portraitlosen Triskelisstücke sind durch eine Fülle von Beizeichen unterschieden. Dies alles ist nur zu verstehen, wenn wir ein reiches pulsierende Leben in einem kleinen, aber blühenden Staatswesen annehmen, das dieses schöne, verschiedenartige Geld prägen ließ.

Daher ist es wohl abwegig, eigene lokale Kräfte abzustreiten, von denen die Portraits geschaffen wurden. Diese Bildnisse sind durchaus originell, ob sie nun von Lykiern oder in Lykien ansässigen griechischen Künstlern geschnitten sind.

Stark ist aber die Beeinflussung durch die griechische Münzprägung, die in Lykien sehr gut bekannt gewesen sein muß: In der Prägung des Mithrapata erinnern Maske und Vorderteil des Löwen an die Prägungen von Samos sowie Knidus und Lindus. Der Kopf des jungen Herakles von vorn ist von den Obolen von Tarent bekannt. Der Kopf des Hermes von vorn ist dem von Ainos sehr ähnlich, nur die Flügel auf dem Petasus sind neu. – Noch viel stärker beeinflußt ist die Prägung des Perikles. Das Meisterwerk des Eukleidas von Syrakus mit dem heute so seltenen schmalen Kopf mit dem Stempelriß steht auf der Rückseite der Diobolen. An Stelle der Signatur finden wir nur die Protome einer Harpie, was uns an das Harpienmonument von Xanthus denken läßt. Einer der allerbesten Stempel von Akanthus steht auf der Vorderseite dieses kleinen und doch großartigen Stückes. – Der bärtige Krieger sieht aus wie der Ajax von Locri Opuntii oder der Leukaspis von Syrakus, die beide ungefähr gleichzeitig sind. Das Portrait des Perikles mit den wehenden Haaren steht unter dem starken Einfluß von Kimons Meisterwerk, der Syrakusaner Arethusa en face.

Ganz in der Nähe wurden um diese Zeit auch Münzen mit semitischen Inschriften, aber von griechischem Stil geschlagen. Es war *eine* reiche Mittelmeerwelt, in der Ideen, Menschen und Dinge frei gewandert sind – trotz Sklaverei und Krieg. In diesem Sinne wollen Sie meinen heutigen Beitrag zu unserem Kongreßthema aufnehmen: *numismatica mediterranea.*

## Stempelkopplungen der Statere des Mithrapata mit Portrait

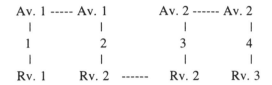

```
Av. 1 ----- Av. 1          Av. 2 ------ Av. 2
  |           |              |           |
  1           2              3           4
  |           |              |           |
Rv. 1       Rv. 2  ------  Rv. 2       Rv. 3


Av. 3 ----- Av. 3       Av. 4 ------  Av. 4      Av. 5
  |           |           |            |          |
  5           6           7            8          9
  |           |           |            |          |
Rv. 4       Rv. 5 ------ Rv. 5       Rv. 6 ------ Rv. 6


       Av. 6 ------   Av. 6 ------  Av. 7
         |              |            |
         10             11           12
         |              |            |
       Rv. 7          Rv. 8 ------  Rv. 8
```

# Kimon in the manner of Segesta[*]

## (Tf. XXXVII - XXXVIII)

## 1. Segesta's survival in 409

The last decade of the 5th century changed the face of Greek Sicily. The Carthaginians marched East and destroyed Selinus and Himera in 409. By 405 Akragas and Gela did not exist any more, Camarina was evacuated in the same year. The Sikelians stood aside. One important city was literally between the frontier lines: Segesta. As the remains of the magnificent temple and theatre and the legends and types of the coinage show, the culture of Segesta was Greek, but the inhabitants were not. They were not Punic either, though their coinage had considerable influence on the Punic cities of Panormos, Motya and Eryx. The foreign policy of Segesta was to keep its independence: she resisted the pressure of her Selinuntine neighbours. She is said to have caused the invasion of the Athenians in 414 and also that of the Carthaginians in 409. If it is true that Segesta and the Carthaginians worked to a certain extent in unison, why then did she not survive the Punic invasion of 409? Thus, the destruction of southern Selinus, Segesta's eternal enemy, does not mean that the great northern city had the same fate. In any case, Diodoros mentions Segesta as still existing in his chronicle of the year 397, the year of Motya's destruction. He states specifically that Hamilcar arrived in time to save the Segestans from the second siege laid by Dionysios of Syracuse[1].

## 2. The new coin

It is generally agreed that Kimon engraved his signed Syracuse tetradrachms with the female head *en face* in the last decade of the 5th century, presumably shortly before 405. Now, if we assume that Segesta lost her independence c. 409 – as some writers do[2] – there could not have existed any coins struck there showing «Kimon in the

---

[*] I am grateful to G.K. Jenkins for valuable advice. I am also indebted to S. Hurter and the owner of the new Segestan coin. Photographs by The British Museum, London (1-2, 11-12); Cabinet des Médailles, Paris (6); M. Hirmer, Munich (8, 20-21); S. Hurter, Zürich (3, 5, 7, 9, 13, 16, 18-19, 22); P. Strauss, Basel (4). – Reproduced photographs from G.E. Rizzo, Sicilia, plate VII, 11 (10) and Ph. Lederer, Segesta, plate (14-15, 17, 23-26).

[1] Diodoros XIV,35.

[2] Ph. Lederer, Die Tetradrachmenprägung von Segesta, 1910, 14; J.F. Healy, Artists, engravers and style in Greek coinage, Bulletin of the John Rylands Library 54 (1971) 161

manner of Segesta», because the Kimonian example could not possibly have reached the Segestan copyist. But there is a new unique coin: On the obverse the hunter with two Laconian hounds, the inscription *ΕΓΕΣΤΑΙΩΝ*. The reverse shows indeed a Segestan version of a facing head in the style and type of Kimon. The legend in tiny letters, on the lower left side of the field, reads *ΣΕΓΕΣΤΑΖΙΒ Segestassie, vulgo Segestazib* . The border shows some signs of advanced crystallisation (Tf. XXXVII 13; XXXVIII 19).

The question arises, of course, as to which of the two facing Kimonian heads was imitated by the Segestan engraver? A comparison of the new Segestan type with the two Kimon dies makes clear that the fuller head with the thicker hairlocks (Tf. XXXVII 6) has served this purpose. The Segestan artist has engraved his head with Kimon's type directly before his eyes, as he saw it. The result was that his new head turns slightly to the right, whereas on the Kimonian example it looks slightly to the left. We also remark that the Kimonian head is the obverse of the Syracusan coin, whilst the head of the Segestan copy forms the reverse. This latter is a bad position for striking, as TUDEER put it: «Dem Kimon also gebührt der Fortschritt, über Eukleidas (Tf. XXXVII 5) hinaus für einen Kopf von vorn die Vorderseite als den richtigen Platz erkannt zu haben»[3].

## 3. Kimon's prototype

Kimon engraved two dies with facing heads. We know already that the die with the fuller head was imitated in Segesta. Is the fuller head now the first or the second creation by Kimon? In order to answer this vital question, we have to study the whole group (Tf. XXXVII 6-9): We have two obverse dies, both signed Kimon on the *ampyx* and inscribed *ΑΡΕΘΟΣΑ* above the head and two reverse dies, one is signed by Kimon between the two exergue lines, the other is unsigned. The die flaws prove that the chronological order given here is correct: The fourth die-combination (Tf. XXXVII 9) has obviously been struck after the third (Tf. XXXVII 8), because several flaws between Arethusa's lips do not exist on the obverse of the third die-couple. The fourth was struck also after the second (XXXVII 7), because a long horizontal thorn-like flaw over the wheel of the chariot cannot be seen on the second die-combination. The third coin (Tf. XXXVII 8) must come after the first (XXXVII 6), because the flaw above the arm of the auriga, still tiny on the first die-combination, has increased in size considerably on the third. Finally, the second couple of dies (Tf. XXXVII 7) come after the first (XXXVII 6), because the first does still not show the wedge-like flaw under the chin of Arethusa. We must, therefore,

---

(«Segesta fell in 410 BC» - *sic* !); E.S.G. ROBINSON, A Catalogue of the C. Gulbenkian Collection of Greek Coins, 1971, 80; G.H. JENKINS, SNR 50 (1971) 32 has expressed the contrary view which is shared in this paper.

[3] L.TH. TUDEER, Die Tetradrachmenprägung in der Periode der signierenden Künstler, 1913, 183. Hence, TUDEER saw clearly that it was Phrygillos – with the die signed *PhRY* on the *ampyx* – who first had put Arethusa's head on the obverse of a Syracusan coin (148, no. 49: obverse 16).

conclude that the die-combination with the full head and the signed reverse must have been struck first[4]. That this is indeed the prototype is also sustained by the existence of a close copy of this die on one of the last didrachms of Camarina (Tf. XXXVII 10) and by an observation by TUDEER: on the first head, left in the field, there are two clearly visible letters, a Sigma and an Omega[5]. Kimon wanted to write the Ethnikon $\Sigma YPAKO\Sigma I\Omega N$ in the usual manner on the obverse, then changed his mind and connected the two engraved letters with the tips of the locks – thus hiding his initial blunder.

## 4. The Ancestor Aigestes

As we have seen, the numismatic evidence shows that the Segestan die-cutter imitated Kimon's prototype, a fact which is essential for the chronology of the Segestan group in question (Tf. XXXVIII 19-22). The one central hunter-obverse we know already is combined with four different reverse-heads, all in deep circular die-marks. We notice immediately that this obverse is litterally covered with die-flaws all slightly increasing in size in the course of use. Evidently, all four die-combinations known were struck within a short period of time. On the other hand, there is not a single coin known which shows this obverse in fresh or less worn state: its former and larger production is still hidden in the soil.

The obverse die must have heen of great importance to the Segestan mint-authorities, even to that point that they finally took a slightly older didrachm-die and combined it with our hunter obverse. There are several die flaws below the neck of the small female head on the tetradrachms which still do not exist on the didrachms. – Why was this hunter-die so popular in Segesta? Is it a picture of a cult image? Style and execution of the die indicate certainly an excellent artist whose work was expensive and who surpassed the man who cut the two known earlier hunter dies used on the reverses of the first Segestan tetradrachms with the conventional Sicilian slow quadriga on the obverse (Tf. XXXVIII 14-16). But this cannot be the only reason why the Segestans used it again and again and combined it as an obverse with four different female heads of Syracusan flavour, three of which are of outstanding workmanship. Could the main reason of the whole remarkable group be a demonstration of political independence, even after the new Syracusan ruler Dionysios concluded a peave treaty with the Carthaginians in 404?

The hunting youth standing near the terminal figure is neither Pan (the horn is missing), nor the river god Krimisos (the two dogs and spears exclude this assumption), but the legendary ancestor-founder of the city: Aigestes[6]. The legend says

---

[4] In fact, our first two die-couples (and not the last two) occurred in mint condition in the Ognina find, buried c. 403, according to C. BOEHRINGER's hoard report, rendered to the 1973 Congress just before this paper was read.

[5] L.TH. TUDEER, Die Tetradrachmenprägung, 1913, note 3, reads four letters: *SIōN*; E.S.G. ROBINSON, A Catalogue of the C. Gulbenkian Collection, 1971, 35, no. 95, recognises on the Locker Lampson specimen, also four: *OSIō*.

[6] Segesta's legendary tradition supports the identification of the hunter with the ancestor

clearly *ΕΓΕΣΤΑΙΩΝ* without the first *Σ*. E.S. G. ROBINSON[7] describes the type: «The context is the war between Segesta and Selinus which led to the intervention of Athens. In dramatic symbolism the founder of the city is on the watch for Selinuntine invaders and his alerted hounds seem already to have picked them up». He dates our group c. 415-412 whereas KRAAY[8] says c. 405 and JENKINS[9] assumes cautiously 405 to 400 for the hunter series and the Kimonian facing tetradrachms. The new facing head in Segesta and a Segestan didrachm (of our type) struck over a very late didrachm of Camarina[10] to be dated towards the middle of the decade hint to a date of c. 405-400[11], leaving still the period of time of some few years for the last tetradrachms with the fast quadriga. Was the meaning of the popular Segestan hunter-obverse a proclamation that Aigestes still stands strong protecting his Segesta when the other cities around fall and perish?

## 5. Aigeste / Segesta - ancestress of the city

It has been generally agreed that the head of the ancestress Aigeste[12] is depicted on the coins. Strange legends are often found around her head: *ΣΕΓΕΣΤΑ‡ΙΒΕΜΙ*, *ΣΕΓΕΣΤΑ‡ΙΒ*, *ΣΕΓΕΣΤΑ‡ΙΑ*, *ΣΕΓΕΣΤΑ‡ΙΕ*.

Our new head *de face* is inscribed *ΣΕΓΕΣΤΑ‡ΙΒ*. What does this mean? This most difficult question has been discussed again and again by historians, linguists and numismatists. In the discussion following my paper on Punic inscriptions on the Paris 1953[13] Congress H.A. CAHN asked my opinion on *ΣΕΓΕΣΤΑ‡ΙΒ*. All I could answer was that this is not a problem of Semitic, but of Greek philology. According to the newest philological studies on *ΣΕΓΕΣΤΑ‡ΙΒ* it appears that I might have been right.

Segesta's strategic position was just between the frontiers of Greek and Carthaginian dominations. Segesta's coinage was under strong Greek influence, but there is not a single Segestan coin of purely Greek style. The Segestans were, as just mentioned, neither Greeks nor Carthaginians. We have to stress that they were not Sikels either. Following Greek and Roman authors, especially Thukydides and Virgil, some modern writers have called them Elymians, but it is not clear where

---

Aigestes and of the girl's head with the head of the ancestress Aigeste and also of the dog with the local river god Krimisos: Sale Catalogue Bank Leu AG - MMAG, 25th May 1974, Kunstfreund 144, no. 100. Cp. L. LACROIX, Monnaies et Colonisation dans l'Occident Grec, 1965, 56ss. Against our interpretation: K. ZIEGLER, art. Segesta, PRE, col. 1068.

[7] E.S.G. ROBINSON, A Catalogue of the C. Gulbenkian Collection, 1971, 81.

[8] C.M. KRAAY / M. HIRMER, Greek Coins, 1966, 300, nos. 203-204.

[9] G.K. JENKINS, Ancient Greek Coins, 1972, nos. 418-419, 430-431.

[10] PH. LEDERER, Berliner Münzblätter 40 (1919) 407, Pl. 85: 4; G.E. RIZZO, Monete Greche della Sicilia, 1946, 287, fig. 90.

[11] Our late date 405-400 for the central hunter group has been supported by the Ognina hoard buried c. 403 (see above n. 4), where a considerable number of late Segestan didrachms were found, but not one Segestan tetradrachm.

[12] See note 6 above.

[13] Actes, 1957, 149ss [hier S. 136-137].

these Elymians come from[14]. Recently, the students of the Greek dialects seem to have found the solution for our legend and the origin of the Elymians: They came from the West Coast of Asia Minor and were either Ionians from Phokaia or – more likely – Aeolians. In 1888 already, KINCH demonstrated that in the oldest Corinthian-Megarian texts B and E mean both E. Later, MEISTER and LARFELD found that I has assumed the value of SS. ARENA gives the final conclusion «Leggerei dunque IIB = *ssié* . Quest'ultima forma, come aveva già rilevato il Kinch, deve essere esplizativa del viso rappresentato: mi pare quindi che l'unica possibile interpretazione sia quella di θεή, cosí come IIOM (*ssios* ) corrisponderebbe a θεός»[15].

Obviously, these findings fit with a frequent phenomenon of Greek coinage. The legend indicates the head or figure represented: Zeus, Hera, Apollon, Poseidon, Hygieia, Eirene and many others. In our connection: ΣΕΓΕΣΤΑ IIB EMI = Segesta – *ssié – emi* = Segesta-goddess – I am = I am the goddess Segesta.

## 6. The position of the new die in the coinage of Segesta

The new Segestan head *de face* is not an unexpected and isolated curiosity, but is only one case in a long series of Segestan imitations of coins of Syracuse. Here are some examples only: An exquisite head within a circular border in the manner of the Demareteion on the reverse die of a didrachmon (JAMESON 707); the two splendid profile heads in the middle of our group (nos. 20-21) have been strongly influenced by a distinct group of large Syracuse heads, turned left and right, to be dated c. 410/ 405 (TUDEER reverses nos. 41, 46 and 47). These two Segestan profile heads do not go back to Kimon, Euainetos, Eukleidas or Parmenides who all have been suggested, but to this «master of the large head».

It is noteworthy that all these Segestan imitations of Syracuse coins, including our new facing head, are impressive works. Most of them come even near to the Greek example, but it remains always a distinct Segestan touch, partitularly in the expression of the eyes and mouth. It seems that these excellent engravers were «hellenized» local artists.

The new head *de face* is not the only facing «Kimonian» head in the coinage of the north western Sicilian cities towards the end of the century. The latest Motya didrachms (Tf. XXXVII 11) and litrae (Tf. XXXVIII 12) show another very near copy of Kimon's Arethusa and have, therefore, been dated c. 400[16]. Further, our new reverse is not the first and only facing head at Segesta. In the middle of the 5th century the city had struck litrae with Aigeste's fully facing head (LLOYD 1191) and c. 425 those with the head slightly turned to the left, surrounded by two olive twigs (Tf. XXXVII 1).

---

[14] L. LACROIX, Monnaies et Colonisation dans l'Occident Grec, 1965, note 56ss., especially 66: «Par ailleurs, les Elymes restent pour nous une population mystérieuse».

[15] R. ARENA, SEGESTA‡∀IB, Archivio Glottologico Italiano 44, 1, 17-25 with bibliography. I am indebted to R. ARENA for this detailed, elucidatory article.

[16] G.K. JENKINS, SNR 50 (1971) 31-32.

Finally, facing heads are found on Greek coins from the beginning of the 5th century till Kimon's time[17]. The representation of the human face in three-quarters view was certainly not invented by him. Earlier heads of fine style of this type occur in Amphipolis, Kyzikos, Syracuse, a crude one in Gela (Tf. XXXVII 2-5). Kimon's masterpiece of the Arethusa *de face* is the last stage of this long development; at the same time it is the beginning of a new perception of the facing head which was to last for centuries.

## 7. The revised chronology of the tetradrachms of Segesta

In his famous study «Die Tetradrachmenprägung von Segesta», 1910, LEDERER dated the whole series from 454/453 till 409. The single groups were dated as follows: nos. 1-4 from 454/453 till 426; nos. 5-6 from 425/424 till 417; nos. 7-8: 416-415, and nos. 9-11 from 415 till 409.

But, as we have seen, all pieces with our hunter obverse and the female head on the reverse form a homogeneous group of coins (Tf. XXXVIII 19-22) struck within a short period of time: 405-400. Therefore, the tetradrachms with the didrachm obverse cannot be isolated from the three others. Further, the tetradrachm with the hunter type turned left shows a female head of late, clearly Punic style (no. 26) and cannot possibly be dated before 400, certainly not 416/415. Finally, the unique Paris tetradrachm of fine classical style with horned hunter on the obverse and standing nymph sacrifying (Tf. XXXVIII 17) imitates the very last coin of Himera with the rectangular altar. Therefore, it has to be dated c. 410. It is evidently a sort of a trial piece launched just before the Carthaginian invasion and abandoned after the fall of Himera in 409.

To conclude, here is the revised chronology: first group c. 415, the second central series – our hunter group – 405-400, the third and last group 400-398, the unique «trial piece» c. 410 and the coarse «Punic» head 398/397. I hope to have shown you that our new piece *de face* has considerably enriched this picture.

---

[17] K. REGLING, Münze als Kunstwerk, 1924, 83; G.K. JENKINS, The Coinage of Gela, 1970, 84-85.

# Über Kimon und Euainetos im Funde von Naro

## (Tf. XXXIX - XL)

## Literatur im Überblick 1891-1985[1]

1891    A.J. EVANS, Syracusan «Medaillons» and Their Engravers,
        in: NC, 205-375.

1892    Spink & Son, Some Syracusan Medaillons from the Sta. Maria Hoard,
        London.

1908    A.C. HEADLAM, Some Notes on Sicilian Coins, in: NC, 4-9.

1913    L.O.TH. TUDEER, Die Tetradrachmenprägung von Syrakus in der Periode
        der signierenden Künstler, Berlin.

1914    K. REGLING, Dekadrachmen des Kimon, Amtliche Berichte der Königlichen
        Kunstsammlungen, Berlin.

1930    A. GALLATIN, Syracusan Dekadrachms of the Euainetos Type,
        Cambridge - Harvard.

1941    J.H. JONGKEES, The Kimonian Decadrachms, Utrecht.

1941    J. LIEGLE, Euainetos (101. Winkelmannsprogramm), Berlin.

1946    G.E. RIZZO, Monete Greche della Sicilia I-II, Roma.

1948    C.T. SELTMANN, The Engravers of the Akragantine Decadrachms,
        in: NC, 1-10.

1961    G.K. JENKINS, Dionysios I of Syracuse and His Coinage,
        in: Bull. 8 of the Inst. of Classical Studies, London University.

1966    C.M. KRAAY and M. HIRMER, Greek Coins, London.

1966    G.K. JENKINS, Coins of Greek Sicily, British Mus., Oxford - London.

1970    G.K. JENKINS, The Coinage of Gela (AMUGS 2), Berlin.

1971    E.S.G. ROBINSON, A Cat. of the Calouste Gulbenkian Coll., Lisbon.

1972    G.K. JENKINS, Ancient Greek Coins, London.

1975    R.R. HOLLOWAY, La struttura delle emissione di Siracusa nel periodo
        dei «signierende Künstler», in: AIIN 21-22 (1974-1975) 41-48.

1976    L. MILDENBERG, Kimon in the Manner of Segesta, in: Actes du 8ème
        CIN, New York - Washington 1973, Paris - Basel [hier S. 110-115].

1976    C.M. KRAAY, Archaic and Classical Greek Coins, London.

1976    M.R. ALFÖLDI, Dekadrachmon, Wiesbaden.

1978    C. BOEHRINGER, Rekonstruktion des Schatzfundes von Ognina 1923,
        in: SNR 57, 102-143.

1979    C. BOEHRINGER, Zur Finanzpolitik und Münzprägung des Dionysios,
        in: Essays M. Thompson, Wetteren 1979, 9-32.

1980    U. WESTERMARK / G.K. JENKINS, The Coinage of Kamarina, London.

1985    The A. S. Dewing Collection of Greek Coins, ed. L. MILDENBERG and
        S. HURTER (ACNAC 6), cols. 55-59, nos. 868-924 (C. BOEHRINGER).

---

[1] Über den Fund von Naro und seine Bedeutung für die Datierung der Syrakusaner Dekadrachmen hat der Schreibende seit 1960 in Vorträgen mehrfach berichtet.

## 1. Die Naro-Gipse im Britischen Museum[2]

Im Gegensatz zu anderen Münzhändlern seiner Generation[3] hat Jacob Hirsch keine wissenschaftlichen Arbeiten hinterlassen. Man verdankt ihm aber zwei Serien von Auktionskatalogen meist antiker Münzen[4], die noch heute hochgeschätzt werden und seinen Ruf mitbegründet haben[5]. Daß er nicht zur Feder gegriffen hat, bedeutet aber keinesfalls, daß ihm die numismatische Forschung gleichgültig gewesen sei. Der Publikationsfonds der Schweizerischen Numismatischen Gesellschaft ist ihm zu verdanken[6]. Wenig bekannt dürfte sein großes Interesse an Münzfunden sein, deren Bedeutung er aber frühzeitig erkannt haben muß; denn er ließ immer Gipse von ganzen Münzfunden oder bedeutenderen, aus Funden stammenden Komplexen herstellen, bald nachdem sie in seine Hände gelangt waren. Diese Materialien blieben aber nicht in seinen Büroschränken liegen[7], sondern wurden größeren Münzkabinetten übergeben[8]. Den hinterlassenen Papieren Jacob Hirsch's und Auskünften seines lebenslangen Kollegen Tom Virzi[9] entnahm der Schreibende, dass Jacob Hirsch Gipse von den 21 Naro-Dekadrachmen[10], die er *en bloc* 1924[11] erworben hatte, im Britischen Museum deponierte[12].

---

[2] In Hirsch's Geschäftspapieren steht überall *Canicatti*. ROBINSON 1971 versteht darunter *Canicattini*, das ungefähr 20 km westlich von Syrakus liegt. Es gibt jedoch sehr wohl einen grösseren Flecken, der *Canicatti* heisst und der etwa 25 km nordöstlich von Agrigent liegt. *Naro* ist etwa 20 km östlich Agrigent gelegen. *Canicatti* und *Naro* sind also Nachbarorte, in deren Umgebung der Hort ans Licht kam. An der Zuverlässigkeit von Hirsch's Angaben ist deshalb nicht zu zweifeln.
[3] Man denke an J. Cahn, L. Forrer sen., L. Naville, O. Ravel und A. Sambon.
[4] Über 50 Jahre lang war J. Hirsch auch ein führender Experte und Händler auf dem Gebiet der Kunst der Antike.
[5] J. Hirsch, München, 1-135 in den Jahren 1898 bis 1914 und L. Naville - Ars Classica, Genf-Luzern, 1-18 von 1921 bis 1938. Sorgfalt in der Beschreibung und der Illustration sowie eine aussergewöhnliche Materialfülle machen diese Auktionskataloge zu wichtigen Arbeitsmitteln von bleibendem Wert.
[6] Die Gesellschaft verwendet seit Jahren die ihr testamentarisch überlassenen Mittel zur Mitfinanzierung ihrer Publikationen (SNR, SM, Schweizer Münzkataloge, Typos-Monographien zur Antiken Numismatik).
[7] Durch die Zeitläufe bedingt führte Hirsch's Weg von München über Genf und Paris nach New York.
[8] H.-D. Schulz berichtet in einer brieflichen Mitteilung über den Fund von *Sakha*, einen Fund römischer Goldmünzen, von denen die Gipse von Hirsch dem Berliner Kabinett anvertraut worden waren. Über F. Imhoof-Blumer und dessen Nachfolger gelangten ebenfalls Materialien aus Hirsch's Beständen in die Winterthurer Gipssammlung.
[9] Sammler von Bronzemünzen und figürlichen Terrakotten Großgriechenlands und Siziliens.
[10] In Hirsch's Papieren, soweit sie dem Schreibenden zugänglich waren, fand sich kein Hinweis, daß er auch die 60 in IGCH 2118 als *fdc* (sic!) bezeichneten Tetradrachmen erworben hat. Während von den 23 Syrakusaner Dekadrachmen insgesamt 8 schliesslich in Hirsch's Luzerner Auktionen 13 und 17 gelangten, wie der hier unten zusammengestellte Katalog zeigt, findet sich von den erwähnten Tetradrachmen auch in seinen

## 2. Zur Zuschreibung und Datierung

C. M. KRAAY hat nicht nur eine einleuchtende Gliederung für die letzten Syrakusaner Tetradrachmenprägungen des 5. Jahrhunderts vorgeschlagen, sondern auch gewichtige Argumente für die Zuweisung der Dekadrachmen vom Kimon- und Euainetos-Typ an Dionysios I. (405-367) vorgebracht[13]. Zwar dürfte die von ihm herangezogene Kimon-Tetradrachme[14], die gewiss um die Jahrhundertwende entstand, nicht aus der Hand des Meisters selbst stammen[15], aber unter dem starken Einfluss der Dekadrachmenserie vom kimonischen Typ steht sie jedenfalls. Wären die Dekadrachmen als Siegesprägungen, als «Medaillons», um 413 entstanden, was die frühere Forschung meinte und bisweilen auch heute noch angenommen wird[16], so würden etwa 15 Jahre zwischen dem Dekadrachmen-Vorbild und der so ähnlichen kimonischen Tetradrachmen-Kopie liegen, und dies in Syrakus selbst. Eine höchst unwahrscheinliche Annahme! Wie G. KENNETH JENKINS[17] und der Schreibende[18] betonten, wurden Kimon's Werke in Segesta und insbesondere in Motya kopiert, das von Dionysios I. um 398 zerstört wurde. Kimon's Tetradrachmen *de face* und seine Dekadrachmen sind als die Vorbilder früher anzusetzen als die Nachahmungen und deshalb vor 398-397 geprägt. Der *terminus ante quem* steht also fest. Ein so eindeutiger *terminus post quem* war bisher nicht auszumachen. Es ist aber unwahrscheinlich, daß auch diese Originale und Kopien zeitlich weit auseinander liegen. Ein Zeitraum von etwa fünf Jahren scheint plausibel[19], zehn Jahre aber unwahrschein-

---

Handkatalogen keine Spur.

[11] Aus Hirsch's Notizen geht hervor, dass C.S. Gulbenkian die Agrigentiner Dekadrachme und die sechs Syrakusaner Dekadrachmen aus dem Funde von Naro schon Mitte Februar 1925 erworben hat. Es ist deshalb wahrscheinlicher, dass der Fund in der zweiten Hälfte des Jahres 1924 gehoben worden ist.

[12] Diese Tatsache wurde erst von ROBINSON 1971 festgehalten. Warum GALLATIN 1930 diese Materialien nicht berücksichtigte, obwohl er sich im Vorwort bei Hirsch für vielseitige Hilfe bedankte, war nicht mehr auszumachen. Auch JONGKEES 1941 kennt das Depositum nicht, was auf die Kriegszeit zurückzuführen sein mag. – Der Dank des Schreibenden geht an G.K. Jenkins für die Erlaubnis, die Gipse 1960 photographieren zu dürfen.

[13] KRAAY 1966, 288; id. 1976, 220-224.

[14] TUDEER, 105 (Vs. 36, Rs. 72). Der Vorderseitenstempel ist eine späte Schöpfung vom Beginn des 4.Jahrhunderts, der Kopf auf dem Rückseitenstempel eine gleichzeitige minutiöse, aber kunstlose Kopie eines Werkes aus dem Umkreis Kimon's, nämlich der sogenannten Punierin, JONGKEES, 13, Tf. II M.

[15] Kein Stempelschneider der Antike hat größeren Wert auf seine Signatur gelegt als Kimon, und dies in seinem gesamten Œuvre. Einen Kopfstempel seiner Dekadrachmen (hier Tf. XXXIX 4-6) hat er gar zweimal gezeichnet. Es sollten deshalb nur signierte Stempel als Werke dieses Meisters angesehen werden.

[16] Zur Forschungsgeschichte siehe oben Literatur 1891-1985 und insbesondere M.R. ALFÖLDI, 1976, 117-127 (Sonderdruck 39-49). Vgl. C. BOEHRINGER, 1979, 12-14.

[17] G.K. JENKINS, 1961, 86; id., 1966, 237-28.

[18] L. MILDENBERG, 1976, 113-115.

[19] Nach KRAAY, 1976, 228 können Syrakusaner Tetradrachmen aus den Jahren 414-413 in

lich, fünfzehn Jahre gewiß zu lang. Zudem ist hier zu vermerken, daß Kimon's Arethusa *de face* in der Gruppe mit der Ähre im Abschnitt[20] und der sehr bewegten Quadriga steht[21], deshalb erst ins letzte Jahrzehnt des 5. Jahrhunderts gehört[22].

Dionysios I. brauchte, wie jüngst wieder betont wurde[23], das hochwertige Edelmetallgeld zur Vorbereitung und Durchführung seiner Kriegszüge gegen das karthagische Reich. Die Mittel dazu verschaffte er sich durch die Ausplünderung der eigenen und der unterworfenen Bevölkerung mittels Steuern und Tribute. Raubzüge verschmähte er ebenso wenig wie die subtile Maßnahme der Emittierung von minderwertigen Scheidemünzen für den internen Zahlungsverkehr, wodurch er letztlich die sizilische Wirtschaft ruinierte und Syrakus' Untergang vorbereitete. Die großen

---

Panormus 410-409 nachgeahmt worden sein.

[20] R.R. HOLLOWAY, 1975, 43: «L''atelier' della spiga di grano ... sarebbe contemporanea a quella del 'atelier' del delfino». Es mag möglich sein, daß für die große und reiche Syrakusanerprägung in den letzten zwei Jahrzehnten des 5. Jahrhunderts mehr als ein Münztisch tätig war und manche Gruppen parallel laufen. Aber es gibt neben den zwei gegeneinander schwimmenden Delphinen, der Ähre und dem einen Delphin noch eine Reihe anderer Abschnittgestaltungen und Beizeichen, deren Einordnung in HOLLOWAY's Schema schwierig ist. Es ist zudem unbestreitbar, dass die zwei Delphine die früheste Gruppe (etwa 420 bis 412), der eine Delphin aber die späteste (etwa 400 bis 380) kennzeichnen. Die Ähre ist von etwa 410 bis 400 vorherrschend. Aufschlußreich ist die Verteilung nach TUDEER's Material: zwei Delphine 7 Stempel, Ähre 21, ein Delphin 4 und andere 4! Gestützt wird die hier vertretene Gliederung durch Parallelen aus anderen sizilischen Münzstätten der Zeit: Messana mit den zwei Delphinen in identischer Gestaltung (etwa 420 bis 410) und der Abwandlung des Ährenmotivs im Feld (etwa 410 bis 405); Gela mit der Ähre im Abschnitt (etwa 410 bis 405)! Selinunt mit der grossen Ähre unter der n.r. sprengenden Quadriga auf der letzten Tetradrachme der Stadt (kurz vor 409) und Segesta mit den Nachahmungen der Ährenmotive von Syrakus und Messana (Didrachme etwa 410, Tetradrachme etwa 405 bis 400).

[21] R.R. HOLLOWAY, 1975, 45-46 weist im Sinne von JONGKEES Kimon's Dekadrachmen dem Ähren-«Atelier», die des Euainetos dem Delphin-«Atelier» zu. Solange keine Stempelverbindung zwischen den beiden Dekadrachmen-Serien gefunden wird, kann man annehmen, daß sie an getrennten Tischen geprägt wurden, nicht mehr. Die Wiederaufnahme der Grossilber-Prägung nach einem Unterbruch von mehr als einem halben Jahrhundert macht es eher wahrscheinlich, daß dafür in der Münzstätte besondere Vorkehrungen getroffen wurden.

[22] In dem bis 397 karthagischen Westen der Insel wurden Kimon's signierte Tetradrachmen und Dekadrachmen kopiert. Und dies dürfte einige Jahre vor bis einige Jahre nach der Jahrhundertwende geschehen sein. Wenn man sich an die plausible Spanne von etwa fünf Jahren hält (s.o. Anm. 19), käme man für den ersten kimonischen *de face* -Stempel (L. MILDENBERG, 1976; L.O.TH. TUDEER, 80-81, aber dort nicht 1. Stempel) auf frühestens etwa 407. In L. MILDENBERG, 1976, 119 steht der Ansatz 406 (nicht 405, wie WESTERMARK - JENKINS, 1980, Anm. 354 zitieren). Es ist hier festzuhalten, daß der erste Kopf in der sehr kleinen Drachmen-Serie von Kamarina (WESTERMARK - JENKINS, 1980, 167) eine nahe Kopie von Kimon's erstem Arethusa-Stempel ist, wobei der Kamarina-Kopf auf der Rückseite erscheint. Und Kamarina ging 405 unter. Der erste Stempel von Kimon's Arethusa *de face* -Serie kann also nicht später als etwa 406 entstanden sein. War es vielleicht so, daß Dionysios I. von Kimon's signierter Arethusa beeindruckt war und ihm deshalb den Auftrag für die ersten Dekadrachmenstempel erteilte, als er 405 zur Macht kam?

[23] JENKINS, 1961, 86; BOEHRINGER, 1979, 10-13; ALFÖLDI, 1976, 129-130 (Sonderdruck S. 51-52).

Nominale in Gold und Silber waren nicht nur sehr geeignet für die Entlöhnung der unentbehrlichen Söldner, sondern kündeten auch als die besten Medien der Zeit von der Macht des Tyrannen und der Größe Syrakus'. Beides erklärt die erstaunliche Verdünnung der einst so reichen Tetradrachmenprägung nach 405.

Den Entscheid zugunsten der Spätdatierung der großen Nominale erbrachten aber die Horte, in denen unsignierte Dekadrachmen vom Euainetos-Typ in großen Mengen gemeinsam mit Prägungen des 4. Jahrhunderts vorkommen[24]. Dabei sind die dort gefundenen Dekadrachmen keinesfalls abgeschliffen, haben also nicht lange zirkuliert. Ein Ansatz von 413 für die signierten Euainetos-Stücke würde deshalb bedingen, daß zwischen diesen und den unsignierten ein Unterbruch von mindestens fünfzehn Jahren liegt, was nicht möglich ist. Ob nun die grosse Serie der Euainetos-Dekadrachmen nach der kleineren Kimon-Gruppe einsetzt oder ob sie anfangs parallel laufen[25], in die Zeit des Dionysios I. gehören beide.

Ähnliches gilt für die Goldprägung. Ob sie nach der Großsilberprägung kommt oder wiederum anfangs parallel läuft[26], ein Beginn vor 405 ist nach der Fundevidenz von Avola 1888 sehr unwahrscheinlich[27]. Schließlich muß noch angemerkt werden,

---

[24] Contessa 1888 (IGCH 2119) nach JENKINS 1961, S. 86: «not before c. 390-385»; Canicattine 1896 (IGCH 2125) nach C.M. KRAAY: «burial 400-350»; S. Maria di Licodia 1890 (IGCH 2123) nach G.K. JENKINS: «burial c. 370»; Messina 1948 (IGCH 2126) nach C.M. KRAAY: «burial 400-350»; Manfria 1948 (IGCH 2121) nach G.K. JENKINS: «burial 390-380»; Sicily 1962 (IGCH 2128) nach C.M. KRAAY: «burial 400-350»; Gela environs (Coin Hoards, V, p. 11, no. 28): «310 BC». – Nach glaubwürdigen Mitteilungen wurde der letzte dieser Funde (Gela 1977) in Wirklichkeit Ende Januar 1978 gehoben. Es handelt sich dabei um eine große Ansammlung von sizilischen Münzen aus dem 5. und 4. Jahrhundert, möglicherweise um einen von mehreren Generationen gehorteten Familienbesitz. Es müssen auch etwa 80 bis 100 Syrakusaner Dekadrachmen darin gewesen sein, zum größten Teil unsignierte Stücke vom Euainetos-Typ. Jedenfalls berichtet man von nur etwa 10 signierten Euainetos-Exemplaren und 10 bis 15 Stücken vom kimonischen Typ, signiert und unsigniert, was die zu erwartende Zusammensetzung ergäbe.

[25] In KRAAY - HIRMER 1966, 288 unten wird die gesamte Prägung der Kimon-Dekadrachmen ums Jahr 405 angesetzt und die der Euainetos-Dekadrachmen von etwa 395 bis etwa 370 angenommen. Die Fundevidenz, insbesondere die von Naro, dürfte aber eher für die Jahre 405 bis 400 bei Kimon und etwa 403 bis etwa 385 bei Euainetos sprechen. Die signierten Stücke stehen bei beiden am Anfang. Auch bei diesen etwas anderen Ansätzen behält KRAAY's Hinweis, daß das populäre Arethusa-Modell der Euainetos-Dekadrachmen auf Sizilien und in der griechischen Welt erst im Laufe des 4. Jahrhunderts nachgeahmt wurde, seine volle Gültigkeit.

[26] JENKINS 1961, 68 datiert die 100- und 50-Litren in Gold etwa 385 bis 370 und meint, sie würden die früheren Dekadrachmen ersetzen. Da die Goldemission nicht unerheblich ist und eine Reihe von durch Kimon und Euainetos signierten Stempel aufweist, mag sie um 400 oder kurz vorher eingesetzt haben. Jedenfalls tragen Kimon's Silber- und Goldstempel ganz ähnliche Signaturen und stammen vom Meister selbst. Daß Kimon noch um 385 in Syrakus tätig war, ist unwahrscheinlich. Starb er früh? Es ist auch unwahrscheinlich, daß die Groß-Goldprägung erst einsetzt, als die Groß-Silberprägung aufhört. Dionysios I. brauchte wohl beide und besaß auch das dafür notwendige Edelmetall.

[27] IGCH 2124: «burial c. 360 B.C. (Baldwin)». Vgl. JENKINS 1961, 86 unten, der betont, daß viele der Syrakusanischen Goldmünzen recht frisch waren und bei Goldstateren von Lampsakos aus der Mitte des 4.Jahrhunderts lagen.

daß in dem neuerdings überzeugend rekonstruierten Fund von Ognina[28], der gegen Ende des 5. Jahrhunderts vergraben worden sein muß, sich je eine Tetradrachme aus den zwei ersten Stempelkoppelungen von Kimon's Arethusa-Gruppe *de face* [29] in frischer Erhaltung fand, aber keine einzige Dekadrachme[30]. Wiederum: Ob man die Kimon-Tetradrachmen vor den Kimon-Dekadrachmen ansetzt oder ob man beide anfangs als gleichzeitig versteht, die traditionelle Frühdatierung von Kimon's œuvre und der Dekadrachmenprägung läßt sich nicht halten.

## 3. Die Fundevidenz von Naro[31]

### 3.1. Das Material

Die meisten sizilischen Funde von Silbermünzen aus der Zeit um die Jahrhundertwende sind gemischt. Sie enthalten Dekadrachmen, sizilische und frühe sikulopunische Tetradrachmen sowie Statere von Korinth und dessen Kolonien, die «Pegasi»[32]. Im Ognina-Hort fanden sich keine Dekadrachmen, in einem Fund von 1962 sollen nur Dekadrachmen vertreten sein[33]. Beides ist unüblich. Wie oben betont[34], bleibt ungeklärt, ob der Fund von Naro auch kleinere Nominale enthielt oder nicht. Gewiß ist, daß die Agrigent-Dekadrachme SNG Lloyd 817 sowie die auf den Tf. 1 und 2 gezeichneten 24 Dekadrachmen (1 Agrigent und 23 Syrakus) aus Naro stammen. Mit an Sicherheit grenzender Wahrscheinlichkeit ist anzunehmen, daß damals dem führenden Händler Jacob Hirsch keine Syrakusaner Dekadrachmen entgingen, also das ganze Material hier vorliegt, soweit es die großen Stücke betrifft.

---

[28] C. BOEHRINGER 1978, 102-143.

[29] TUDEER 1913, 80 und 81; L. MILDENBERG 1976, 6 und 7.

[30] Diese negative Fundevidenz ist zwar nicht schlüssig für die Prägeabfolge in der Münzstätte von Syrakus, aber als ein Argument unter anderen muß sie beachtet werden. Die großen Nominale wurden unter Dionysios I. geprägt, also können sie nicht vor 405 begonnen haben. Andererseits wird Kimon's erster Arethusa-Stempel *de face*, wie hier oben Anm. 22 betont, gewiß vor 405 entstanden sein.

[31] Über den Ort siehe oben Anm. 2, über die Zeit Anm. 11.

[32] Zuverlässige Angaben über Münzfunde im Mittelmeerraum sind schwer zu erhalten. Dies gilt insbesondere für griechische Münzen Siziliens. Völlige Gewißheit über Ort, Zeit, Fundumstände und Fundzusammensetzung ist nur durch Zusammenarbeit von Behörden, Archäologen und Numismatikern bei offiziellen Grabungen zu gewinnen.

[33] IGCH 2128 Sicily, 1962.

[34] Anm. 10.

## 3.2. Die Stempel

*Agrigent* : Die Gruppe ist sehr klein[35]; bekannt geworden sind zwei Vorderseiten und drei Rückseiten, vier Stempelverbindungen. Die zwei Naro-Stücke zeigen je einen der beiden Vorderseitenstempel, kommen aber aus dem gleichen Rückseitenstempel.

*Syrakus, Kimon* : 10 Exemplare; alle 3 bekannten Vorderseiten mit der Quadriga sind in Naro vertreten, von den 14 bekannten Rückseiten mit dem weiblichen Kopf finden sich fünf. Dabei ist festzuhalten, daß von den 6 signierten Rückseiten drei von den 4 ersten vorkommen, während der zweite Stempel fehlt[36].

*Syrakus, Euainetos* : 13 Exemplare; 3 Quadriga-Vorderserseiten und 5 Kopf-Rückseiten, die letzteren sämtliche unter dem Halsabschnitt signiert. Von den 5 Rückseitenstempeln zeigen die ersten 3 weder einen Buchstaben noch ein Beizeichen, die letzteren 2 ein Delta.

## 3.3. Die Prägeabfolge

Von den beiden Agrigentiner Naro-Dekadrachmen ist das Gulbenkian-Exemplar (Tf. XXXIX 1) vor dem Lloyd-Exemplar (SNG 817) geprägt, wie die etwas stärkere Verrostung der gleichen Rückseite bei dem letzteren zeigt.

Bei den Kimon-Dekadrachmen wird die Prägeabfolge der ersten sechs Exemplare (Tf. XXXIX 2-7) durch die immer stärker werdende Verrostung des auf der Bodenlinie signierten, ersten Vorderseitenstempels eindeutig festgestellt[37]. Noch wichtiger ist, daß selbst in dem begrenzten Naro-Material drei Exemplare aus dem koppelnden, KI signierten Kopfstempel vorkommen, wobei die Stempelabnützung zweifelsfrei die Reihenfolge 7-8-9 ergibt. Das Exemplar 7 stammt aus dem ersten Vorderseitenstempel in stark verrostetem Zustand, die Exemplare 8-9 hingegen sind schon aus dem zweiten Vorderseitenstempel geprägt.

Die Prägeabfolge der einzelnen Naro-Exemplare innerhalb der drei Gruppen der signierten Euainetos-Dekadrachmen ist durch die fortschreitende Abnutzung der Vorder- und Rückseitenstempel gesichert. Jedoch sind die drei Gruppen nicht stempelverbunden.

---

[35] SELTMAN 1948, 3 verzeichnet 6 Stücke, die beiden Naro-Exemplaren eingeschlossen. Dazu kommt das HUNT-Stück, Wealth of the Ancient World, Beverly Hills/CA 1983, no. 77 aus dem gleichen Stempelpaar wie das Naro-Exemplar SNG Lloyd 817 sowie die Münze Schweizerischer Bankverein Zürich, 27.10.1977, 37.

[36] JONGKEES 1941, 2; Leu-MMAG 28.05.1974 Kunstfreund, 126.

[37] Die unterliegenden Vorderseitenstempel beider Syrakusaner Dekadrachmenserien wurden intensiv genutzt. Trotzdem zeigt nur ein Euainetos-Quadrigastempel stärkere Stempelrisse (GALLATIN Quadriga 4, Naro hier Tf. 2,13). Dagegen rosteten diese eisernen Quadrigen-Stempel so schnell und stark, dass sie mit der Zeit ersetzt werden mußten, wie der Übergang von Exemplar 7 zu Exemplar 8 des Naro-Fundes zeigt.

## 3.4. Der Befund

Die beiden Agrigentiner Dekadrachmen sind abgeschliffen[38]. Auch auf den beiden signierten Kimon-Dekadrachmen vom 1. Typ (Tf. XXXIX 2-3) sind Gebrauchsspuren zu erkennen, aber sie sind weniger auffällig. Auch wenn man diese Details nicht überbetont, wird doch deutlich, daß die Agrigentiner Groß-Silberprägung vor der kimonischen Dekadrachmen-Serie liegt. Agrigent wurde 406 zerstört. Allgemein wird angenommen, daß die großen Stücke dort nicht vor 411 geprägt wurden. Dabei suchte die frühere Forschung nach besonderen Anlässen für Dekadrachmen-Prägungen, während wirtschaftliche Notwendigkeiten unbeachtet blieben. Für Agrigent dachte man an den Sieg eines Bürgers der Stadt namens Euainetos bei den Olympischen Spielen von 412. Ob man sich mit dieser Annahme befreunden kann oder nicht, jedenfalls deuten der *terminus ante quem* von 406, die Erhaltung der beiden Agrigentiner Naro-Dekadrachmen und deren bewegte Quadriga auf eine Entstehungszeit um 410-408. Damit wird deutlich, daß Kimon's erste Dekadrachmenstempel und damit der Beginn der Syrakusaner Großsilber-Prägung in den Beginn der Herrschaft des Dionysios I. und also in die Jahre 405-404 gehören; denn nach der numismatischen Evidenz von Naro müssen einige Jahre zwischen der Prägung der Dekadrachmen von Agrigent und Syrakus liegen.

Die obigen Feststellungen waren davon ausgegangen, daß die signierten Dekadrachmen-Stempel des Kimon vor den unsignierten kommen. Aber ist dies sicher? Die Prägeabfolge der Naro-Stücke 2-9, alle signiert, ist nach Stempelkoppelung und Stempelzustand eindeutig. Auch innerhalb der kleinen Gruppe von unsignierten Naro-Stücken ist die Reihenfolge 10-11 durch die Entwicklung der Stempelbrüche auf dem gemeinsamen Vorderseitenstempel gegeben. Der Unterschied in der Erhaltung zwischen den signierten und unsignierten Naro-Gruppen ist jedoch klein. Wie JONGKEES gesehen hat, sind aber zwei nicht in Naro vorkommende unsignierte Kopfstempel[39] durch den zweiten Quadrigastempel mit der gesamten signierten Gruppe verbunden. Dieser Quadrigastempel war aber schon merklich verrostet, als aus den zwei unsignierten Kopfstempeln geprägt wurde, was beweist, daß die unsignierte Gruppe nach der signierten kommt.

JONGKEES hatte nur den auf der Bodenseite signierten Quadrigastempel sowie den einen mit ihm verbundenen Kopfstempel mit dem flachen Relief und dem unter dem Halsabschnitt nach rechts hervorschwimmenden Delphin sowie der Signatur *KIIM* (Tf. XXXIX 2-3) Kimon zugeschrieben und als Prototyp angesehen. Alle anderen Stempelkoppelungen, signiert oder unsigniert, waren für ihn aus stilistischen Gründen nur Schöpfungen des «Pseudo-Kimon» und anderer Epigonen. Wie Naro zeigt, steht die eine, von JONGKEES anerkannte Koppelung allerdings am Anfang,

---

[38] Die hohen Stellen der Quadriga-Vorderseite haben keine Zeichnung mehr. Auch die Brustfedern des vorderen Adlers sind nicht mehr zu sehen. Man könnte an eine flaue Prägung im Zentrum des inkusen Münzbildes denken, wenn nicht auch die höchste Stelle des linken, vorderen Flügels des hinteren, flügelschlagenden Adlers merklich abgeschliffen wäre.

[39] JONGKEES 8 (mit den Stempelverletzungen etwas stärker als üblich) und JONGKEES 9 (mit dem Ethnikon in winzigen Lettern).

aber einen signierenden «Pseudo-Kimon» kann es nicht gegeben haben. Die anderen, fast gleichzeitigen Naro-Exemplare (Tf. XXXIX 4-7) sind nämlich kaum weniger frisch und kommen ebenfalls aus dem signierten Vorderseitenstempel und nur aus signierten Rückseitenstempeln. Eine Koppelung (Tf. XXXIX 4-6) ist gar dreimal signiert (*KIMΩN* auf der Leiste, *KIMΩN* auf dem unteren Delphin und *K* auf dem Ampyx), ein einmaliges, aber für diesen signaturbesessenen Meister kennzeichnendes Detail. Ausserdem ist auszuschließen, daß man sich in Syrakus für ein so offensichtliches Täuschungsmanöver hergegeben hätte. Und schließlich ist ein Axiom unserer Disziplin, daß stimmt, was auf den Münzen steht: was Kimon mit *KIIM*, *KIMΩN*, *K* und *KI* signiert hat, stammt von ihm. Aus den gleichen Gründen können wir an Kimon mit völliger Gewißheit nur das geben, was er signiert hat. Als Werk dieses Meisters sollte kein unsignierter Stempel bezeichnet werden, weder in Syrakus noch anderswo, so kimonisch er auch manchem Betrachter vorkommen mag. Was die unsignierten Dekadrachmen-Stempel betrifft, so mögen sie aus Kimon's Umkreis stammen, vielleicht aus seinem «Atelier». Daß er sie selbst geschnitten hat, kann nicht bewiesen werden, ja ist unwahrscheinlich.

Die dreizehn Euianetos-Dekadrachmen im Funde von Naro sind sämtliche etwas weniger abgeschliffen als die zehn Kimon-Dekadrachmen. Dabei ist offensichtlich, dass die Gruppe der acht Exemplare mit dem Delta noch etwas frischer ist als die der sechs ohne diesen Buchstaben. Alle acht Delta-Stücke kommen aus demselben Quadriga-Stempel, sieben aus dem gleichen Rückseitenstempel. Dies ist die häufig festzustellende «Verdichtung» der zeitlich letzten Exemplare in einem Fund, also mehr späte als frühe Stücke. Das Naro-Exemplar, Tf. XL 17, kommt vor den stempelgleichen Stücken 18-24, deren Reihenfolge wiederum feststeht. Die fortschreitende Verrostung des Vorderseitenstempels sichert beides. Ob die Gruppe 12-13 vor oder nach der Gruppe 14-16 kommt, kann auf Grund des Naro-Materials nicht entschieden werden, da die drei Gruppen unverbunden sind[40].

Einen weiteren wichtigen Beitrag zur Gesamtbeurteilung der Dekadrachmenprägung erbringt der Fund von Naro dadurch, daß sich keine unsignierten Euainetos-Dekadrachmen darin befanden. Diese Tatsache ist ebenso unüblich wie die erhebliche Anzahl von Kimon-Stücken im Vergleich zu den Euainetos-Stücken[41]. Beides bezeugt, daß das Naro-Material aus einer frühen Periode der Syrakusaner Dekadrachmenprägung kommt.

## 4. Zusammenfassung

Die numismatische Evidenz des Fundes von Naro spricht gegen die Frühdatierung der Syrakusaner Dekadrachmen und für deren Zuweisung an die Zeit von Dionysios I.

Kimon's Schaffen beginnt mit den Tetradrachmen *de face*, die um 406 anzusetzen sind. Sein erstes Dekadrachmen-Werk mit dem signierten Quadrigastempel und dem

---

[40] Die Gliederung des Naro-Materials auf den Tafeln folgt bei diesem Sachverhalt in etwa der von GALLATIN aufgestellten Ordnung, wobei der erste Kopfstempel C7 zuerst steht.

[41] Das Verhältnis bei Naro ist 10 zu 13, bei anderen Funden etwa 1 zu 10.

signierten Kopfstempel in flachem Relief dürfte um 405-404 entstanden sein. Die anderen signierten Kopfstempel folgten bald nach. Die späteren unsignierten Stempel gehören zur Kimon-Serie, stammen aber nicht aus seiner Hand. Um die Jahrhundertwende oder kurz danach dürfte auch die Prägung aus den unsignierten Stempeln aussetzen.

Die ersten signierten Euainetos-Dekadrachmen setzen kurz nach den ersten signierten Kimon-Dekadrachmen ein, etwa um 404-403. Sie dürften wohl während eines knappen Jahrzehnts ausgebracht worden sein, also einige Jahre lang gleichzeitig mit den signierten und unsignierten Stücken vom Kimon-Typ. Die Prägung der unsignierten Euainetos-Dekadrachmen dürfte wohl um 395 beginnen und wurde bis etwa 385 fortgesetzt[42]. Die Goldprägung mag fünf bis zehn Jahre länger gedauert haben.

Die Agrigentiner Dekadrachmen sind einige Jahre vor dem Untergang der Stadt 406 entstanden, also wohl um 410-408.

Sämtliche Syrakusaner Dekadrachmen aus dem Fund von Naro wurden um 400 geprägt und kamen wenige Jahre nach der Jahrhundertwende unter die Erde. Gehörten die 25 Naro-Dekadrachmen zur Kriegskasse eines Söldnertrupps oder in die Schatulle eines Söldnerführers auf einem ums Jahr 398 erfolgten Marsch durch den Süden Siziliens gegen Motya und Segesta, die beide bald darauf von Dionysios I. genommen wurden? Diese beträchtliche Summe könnte bei einem Scharmützel mit karthagischen Truppen in der Gegend von Naro dem Boden anvertraut worden sein.

---

[42] Daß G.E. RIZZO anderthalb Jahrzehnte nach dem Erscheinen von GALLATINs Stempelstudie die unsignierten Euainetos-Dekadrachmen aus stilistischen Gründen vor die signierten setzt, ist heute schwer verständlich.

## Katalog

| Lfde. Nr. gleiche Vs./Rs. | Signatur Vs./Rs. | Gewicht | Stempel-Stellung | Literatur | Standort |
|---|---|---|---|---|---|
| 1 | – | 43.50 | ↓ | Seltman 10a (dies Ex.) | Gulbenkian 168 |
| 2 | KIMΩN/KIM | 43.19 | ↖ | Jongkees 1i (dies Ex.) | SNG Lloyd 1409 |
| 3 | » | 43.30 | ↙ | Jongkees 1f (dies Ex.) | Gulbenkian 301 |
| 4 | KIMΩN/K/KIMΩN | 43.36 | ? | Jongkees 3 | AC 17, 236 |
| 5 | » | 43.17 | ↘ | Jongkees 3 | Gulbenkian 303 |
| 6 | » | 43.17 | ? | Jongkees 3t (dies Ex.) | AC 13, 335 |
| 7 | KIMΩN/KI | 43.34 | ↑ | Jongkees 6d (dies Ex.) | Dewing 870 ex Gallatin coll. |
| 8 | KI | 43.35 | ? | Jongkees 7k (dies Ex.) | AC 17, 766 ex AC 13, 336 |
| 9 | KI | 42.99 | ↘ | Jongkees 7f (dies Ex.) | SNG Lloyd 1410 |
| 10 | – | 43.04 | ↖ | Jongkees 10 | Gulbenkian 306 |
| 11 | – | 42.86 | ↘ | Jongkees 11 | Gulbenkian 307 |
| 12 | -/EY AINE | 43.16 | ← | Gallatin Vs. 4/Rs. C7 : 5 (dies Ex.) | SNG Lloyd 1412 |
| 13 | » | 43.26 | ↗ | Gallatin Vs. 4/Rs. C9 : 1 (dies Ex.) | Dewing 884 ex Gallatin coll. ex AC 13, 34 |
| 14 | » | 43.05 | ↙ | Gallatin Vs. 2/Rs. C8 : 1 (dies Ex.) | Dewing 875 ex Gallatin coll. |
| 15 | » | 43.17 | ↘ | Gallatin Vs. 2/Rs. C8 : 2 (dies Ex.) | Gulbenkian 311 |
| 16 | » | ? | ? | Gallatin Vs. 2/Rs. C8 | ? |
| 17 | -/Δ EY AINE | 43.17 | ↗ | Gallatin Vs. 9/Rs. D1 : 1 (dies Ex.) | Gulbenkian 314 |
| 18 | -/Δ EY AINE | ? | ? | Gallatin Vs. 9/Rs. D2 | ? |
| 19 | » | ? | ? | Gallatin Vs. 9/Rs. D2 | ? |
| 20 | » | 43.37 | ↗ | Gallatin Vs. 9/Rs. D2 : 1 (dies Ex.) | SNG Lloyd 1413 |
| 21 | » | 43.19 | ? | Gallatin Vs. 9/Rs. D2 | AC 13, 340 |
| 22 | » | 43.29 | ? | Gallatin Vs. 9/Rs. D2 | AC 13, 342 |
| 23 | » | 43.33 | ? | Gallatin Vs. 9/Rs. D2 | AC 13, 341 |
| 24 | » | 43.30 | ? | Gallatin Vs. 9/Rs. D2 | AC 13, 343 |

# The Cyzicenes: A Reappraisal

(Tf. XLI - XLII)

Early in this century B.V. HEAD remarked that the «Cyzicene mint possessed a practical monopoly of coining[1]» the electrum staters, Cyzicenes, that circulated along the Ionian and Caspian Seas. In 1931 K. REGLING called this electrum coinage of Cyzicus «die interessanteste Münzreihe aller Zeiten und Länder»[2]. It is no wonder, then, that early scholarship dealt so extensively with the material[3]. In particular, there were studies of the metallurgical findings, as well as of the exchange rate against other currencies[4]. Further studies dealt with the chronology[5], the iconogra-

---

[1] B.V. HEAD, Historia Numorum, Oxford 1911, 522.

[2] K. REGLING, Der griechische Goldschatz von Prinkipo, ZfN 41 (1931) 3.

[3] H. v. FRITZE's corpus-like study of 1912, Die Elektronprägung von Kyzikos, Nomisma 7 (1912) 1-38, based on the observation of the development of the *quadratum incusum*, is still the basis of today's scholarship. Significant additions have been REGLING's Prinkipo hoard publication of 1931; M. LALOUX's survey of the sources in M. LALOUX, La circulation des monnaies d'électrum de Cyzique, RBN 11 (1971) 31-69; and the die study in G.K. JENKINS and M.C. CASTRO HIPOLITO, A Catalogue of the Calouste Gulbenkian Collection of Greek Coins, Part 2, Lisbon 1989, 62, showing one reverse linked with six obverses. M.R. KAISER-RAISS is preparing a corpus of the electrum coinage of Cyzicus using the materials collected by the late F. BODENSTEDT.

[4] See R. BOGAERT, Le cours du statère de Cyzique aux Vème et IVème siècles avant J.C., AC 32 (1963) 85-119; id., Encore le cours du statère de Cyzique aux Vème et IVème siècles avant J.C., AC 34 (1965) 121-28; M.S.K. EDDY, The Value of the Cyzicene Stater at Athens in the Fifth Century, ANSMN 16 (1970) 13-22; J. GUÉPIN, Le cours de Cyzicène, AC 34 (1965) 199-203; J.F. HEALEY, Greek White and Gold Electrum, in: Metallurgy in Numismatics 1, ed. D.M. METCALF and W.A. ODDY, London 1980, 194-215; D. ROUVIER, Notes techniques sur les statères de Cyzique, SNR 38 (1957) 11-20, with figs. 1-13 on Pl. 2-5; W.E. THOMPSON, The Value of the Kyzicene Stater, NC 1963, 1-4, and H.T. WADE-GERRY, The Ratio of Silver to Gold during the Peloponnesian War: IG I 301, NC 1930, 16-38 (a commentary to the British Museum stone inscription 24).

[5] According to H. v. FRITZE, Die Elektronprägung von Kyzikos, Nomisma 7 (1912) 1-38, the electrum coinage of Cyzicus began as early as the last decade of the seventh century B.C. His chronology has been widely accepted. It must be recognized, however, that the *quadratum incusum* of the very early anonymous electrum coins and that on the early Cyzicus specimens differ considerably. Furthermore, the inclusion of the earliest tunny-head pieces in the first series of the Cyzicenes indicates that the coinage cannot have been initiated much earlier than 550 B.C. This author suggests 570 B.C. as the earliest date for the coinage. The production of the Cyzicenes, but not their circulation, came to an end during the reign of Alexander, not later than 330 B.C.

phy[6], the circulation[7], and the occurrence of the Cyzicenes in ancient sources[8]. Some essential questions, however, have neither been asked nor answered.

## 1. An Extraordinary Coinage

The Cyzicenes are at once extraordinary and unique. There is no other ancient municipal coinage in precious metal which was produced without interruption for over 220 years. The great and long-lasting money production was Cyzicus' own achievement: it was never prohibited or disturbed by her powerful overlords, the great-kings of Persia and the Athenians[9]. Cyzicus was a small city on a peninsula with two harbors in a favorable, sheltered position between the Hellespont and Thracian Bosporos. It was neither a major power nor an independent state. Yet even at Athens the Cyzicenes became a popular currency, a position which no other foreign coinage ever attained there.

The defining characteristics of the Cyzicenes are at once monumental in their constancy and in their variety: the denominations (staters and one sixth staters)[10] are

---

[6] The diversity and beauty of the full range of 240 different obverse images have fascinated scholars although some have over-emphasized the influence of Greek models. There are a few obvious direct imitations, such as the Gela river god protome [Tf XLI 14; H. v. FRITZE, Nomisma 7 (1912) 174]. Others are ingenious modifications, such as the Tarentum dolphin rider holding a tunny with a second tunny below [Tf. XLI 11, H. v. FRITZE, Nomisma 7 (1912) 110]. The majority of the images, however, were created in Cyzicus itself with a preference first for animals and monsters and later for statuary representations and human images.

[7] Hoard distribution shows an intense circulation at the Propontis (ICGH 1239: K. REGLING, ZfN 41 (1931) 1-46, Pl. 1-4]; Thracia, the lower Danube, and Dnjestr region (ICGH 689, 714, 726, 734, 1002); and the Tauric Chersonese and lower Don region (ICGH 1011, 1012, 1013). See below for the importance of the Cyzicenes in the Athenian economy. On single finds from the western and northern shores of the Black Sea, see S.A. BULATOVICH, Klad Kizikinov iz Orlovki [A hoard of Cyzicus staters from Orlovka], Vestnik Drevnei Istorii 2 (1970) 73-86; G.H. POENAYRU-BORDEA, Les régions balkaniques et le littoral septentrional du Pont-Euxin, in: A Survey of Numismatic Research, 1978-1984, London 1986, 87-116; D.B. SHELOV, Coinage on the Bosphorus VI-II centuries B.C., trans. H.B. WELLS (BAR.IS 46), Oxford 1977; and A.N. ZOGRAPH, Monnaies antiques trouvées au Caucase, Travaux du Dept. Numismatique 1, Leningrad 1945, 29-85 (Russian text, French summary). See also, Coin Hoards 1,20; 2,1.1, 2.4 and 2.7.

[8] For proof of frequent transactions in Cyzicenes between Greece and the Black Sea region, see the sources cited in K. REGLING, ZfN 41 (1931) 44-45, and M. LALOUX, La circulation des monnaies d'électrum de Cyzique, RBN 11 (1971) 45-49.

[9] This impressive fact was mentioned in 1913 by P. GARDNER, Coinage of the Athenian Empire, JHS 33 (1913) 147-88, and stressed by L. MILDENBERG, Über das Münzwesen im Reich der Achämeniden, AMI 26 (1993) 55-79 [hier S. 3-30]. See also LALOUX's remark, RBN 11 (1971) 34, «Les Perses auraient même favorisé le monnayage de Cyzique».

[10] The Cyzicene electrum coinage is mainly comprised of the stater and its sixth, the hecte. Only a few one-twelfth staters, or hemihectes, were struck, mostly in the sixth century. Even fewer one-twenty-fourth staters are known (G.K. JENKINS and M.C. CASTRO

constant; the *quadratum incusum* as reverse is immutable; and there is a multiplicity of obverse images that changed allegedly year after year[11]. The metallic content and thus the color of each specimen may differ, but the weight, established *al pezzo*, remains always the same, at 16 g[12]. The whole electrum is anepigraphic: neither the full nor the abbreviated name of the city is found on the Cyzicenes[13]. The electrum coinage and Cyzicus's prolific silver coinage (obols and their divisions in the sixth and fifth centuries, tetradrachms of Rhodian standard in the fourth) run side-by-side, but remain strictly separated and basically different from each other.

## 2. The Trade Coinage

Cyzicus's electrum money has been found near the Bosporus and Dardanelles, in Thrace, the Tauric Chersonese, and Colchis, as well as in western Asia Minor and northern Greece[14]. The Cyzicenes were a generally accepted means of payment, indispensable along the grain routes on land and sea. There are no indications that Cyzicus had direct access to precious metals. There are rivers to the south which may have carried alluvial gold nuggets or sand, but their embankments were hardly owned by citizens of Cyzicus. Nearby, to the south, at Daskyleion, resided the Persian satrap of northwestern Asia Minor. The salting and exporting of fish[15], presumably tunny, could not have been profitable enough to pay for the substantial import of precious metal required for the Cyzicus mint. Why and how did it happen then that such a highly important trade coinage came into being and endured for centuries in a small city? It would seem to be due to the vision, industry, political, and technical

---

HIPOLITO, A Catalogue of the C. Gulbenkan Collection of Greek Coins, Part 2, 1989, 645, with lyre, an exceptional motif).

[11] G.K. JENKINS and M.C. CASTRO HIPOLITO, A Catalogue of the C. Gulbenkan Collection of Greek Coins, Part 2, 1989, 61: «It seems extremely tempting to think that such a number of types might be of a more or less annual nature». But, see below, pp. 7-8 for this author's viewpoint.

[12] This weight corresponds to roughly two Persian darics. It is noteworthy that both the imperial gold daric and the Cyzicene kept their full weight until the end of production. Obviously, the Cyzicus mint personnel successfully mixed alloys of quite different metallic composition and value, but nevertheless properly fixed the weight of each single flan before striking. For the high technical level of the work in the mint at Cyzicus see above, n. 4, especially D. ROUVIER, SNR 38 (1957) 18, fig. V, who holds that the required weight was calibrated by filing.

[13]There exists only one inscription, the word *ELEUThERIA* in two lines on six late staters and one twelfth-stater [H. v. FRITZE, Nomisma 7 (1912) 215; K. REGLING, Der griechische Goldschatz von Prinkipo, ZfN 41 (1931) 129-134]. This is, however, a mere description of the image and a sort of homage to «freedom», rather than an allusion to a historical event or a reproduction in small scale of a statue.

[14] See above, n. 7.

[15] See M. LALOUX, RBN 11 (1971) 33 with n. 5, and C.M. KRAAY / M. HIRMER, Greek Coins, London 1966, 368.

skill of the Cyzicus administrative and minting authority along with the tolerance of their overlords.

## 3. The Conventional Coinage

The color of the individual Cyzicus specimens differed considerably. Thus, it is obvious that the real value in precious metal of all Cyzicenes was not equal. Yet, their general acceptance must have been undisputed. «It seems even very unlikely that such a stater or hecte had ever been put on a scale, as it was well known that their weight itself did not change», as KRAAY put it[16]. It sufficed that the customer always saw the tunny badge and the incuse square. Thus, we are dealing with a purely conventional coinage[17]. Buyer and seller agreed from the beginning that the business would be conducted in Cyzicus's electrum money in the simplest possible way. The Cyzicenes could even be changed at a fixed rate against local silver coins, as the Olbia decree clearly demonstrates: one Cyzicene was to be firmly equal to eleven Olbia silver staters with the same buying and selling rate. All other monetary exchange rates were to be negotiated between the dealers involved[18].

The Cyzicenes were widely used in both local and international credit businesses by the Athenian public and by institutional and private contractors. At the beginning of the fourth century, the treasury of the Pallas Athena temple granted a loan to the city of Athens payable in silver and in Cyzicus' electrum staters[19]. The temple and state officials knew that the Cyzicenes were a stable, generally accepted currency. Likewise, a refund of a personal credit in the year 327, mentioned by Demosthenes, *Against Phormion* 23, is especially noteworthy, as it shows the importance of the Cyzicenes in international trade, even after Cyzicus was forced to cease its own money production[20].

It did not matter that the single specimens differed in color (golden, reddish, or pale) as it was a practice of long standing in Athens that the Cyzicenes, and they alone, had been excluded from the usual control procedure which all other foreign

---

[16] C.M. KRAAY, Archaic and Classical Greek Coins, London 1976, 261.

[17] G.K. JENKINS and M.C. CASTRO HIPOLITO, A Catalogue of the C. Gulbenkan Collection of Greek Coins, Part 2, 1989, 62: «It is clear that some degree of conventionality must have entered into the question of the value of the Cyzicenes», but it must be stressed that full convertibility by convention was the precondition for the factual monopoly of the Cyzicenes as an international trade currency.

[18] W. DITTENBERGER, Sylloge Inscriptionum Graecarum, Leipzig 1915-1917, n. 218.

[19] M. LALOUX, RBN 11 (1971) 46-49.

[20] «Vers 327 un marchand aurait remboursé un prêt de 2000 drachmes contracté à Athènes pour le voyage allée-retour au Pont. Au lieu de remettre la somme de 2600 drachmes à Athènes même, comme convenu, il aurait payé 120 statères de Cyzique au Bosphore» [M. LALOUX, RBN 11 (1971) 64]. This was a bad rate for the merchant, as he got less than 22 Athenian drachms for one Cyzicus electrum stater, whereas at Athens he would have received at least 24 drachms (see next note).

coins had to undergo[21]. In the vast territories where it circulated, the receiver of a Cyzicene knew by experience that the next merchant would take it at full rate, even if it sometimes looked rather suspicious. Without such a stable, smoothly functioning convention the receiver would have been forced to ask for full metallic value which would have been established by a trial cut or other test. No Cyzicenes with trial cuts are known, not even on those that look very pale.

## 4. The International Coinage

As no inscriptions were put on the coinage, it obviously means that they were not needed. One can understand that the Cyzicenes were well known without explanatory legends in the Marmara Sea region, but they are also found in large parts of the ancient world. Further, all documents known, especially the Athenian and Olbian texts, prove their undisputed strong position in the international trade. The gold darics of the Persian Empire, the Athenian silver tetradrachms, and Alexander's imperial gold and silver issues are certainly leading international coinages issued by great powers. But what stood behind the Cyzicus electrum? Certainly there was neither a decisive political strength nor a considerable economic one. A comparable city was Tyre, an island in a good topographical situation with a busy port, favored too by Persia, but with its ship-building industry in a far stronger economic position. The great city of Tyre, however, created a silver coinage only beginning around 450, with a restricted area of circulation[22]. The city of Cyzicus, however, in spite of all its limitations, succeeded in transforming its time-honored local electrum into an international trade coinage which had no equal in antiquity.

## 5. The Plethora of Images

The Persian gold daric and silver siglos displayed only one image, the armed great king with the spiked crown, in Persian attire, from Darius I until Alexander. For centuries, the Athenian silver tetradrachms, introduced around 525 BC., always sho-

---

[21] The fixed relation in accounting at Athens seems to have been 1 Cyzicene equalled 24 Athenian drachms, or 6 «owl» tetradrachms. M.S.K. EDDY, The Value of the Cyzicene Stater at Athens in the Fifth Century, ANSMN 16 (1970) 13-16, nn. 11-13 surveys the proposals of several scholars and concludes (pp. 21-22) that the Athenians accepted the Cyzicenes at the rate of 24 drachms, but asked 24 drachms and 5 obols when they dispersed them. Thus, the difference between the buying and selling rates was 5 obols. In this way Athenian bankers earned 5 obols selling the valuable Cyzicenes, «a very important international currency» (EDDY, p. 21), but at the same time acknowledged the general acceptance of the Cyzicenes by abstaining from checking them for weight and/or fineness.
[22] It is doubtful whether prehellenistic Tyrian coins circulated outside Phoenicia. IGCH lists only three hoards (1252, 1256, 1259) from southeastern Anatolia with one or two isolated Tyrian pieces. But none of these three hoards is undisputed and even the find places are not certain (e.g., 1252: «Asia Minor or Egypt»).

wed one image for the obverse, the helmeted profile head of Pallas Athena facing right, and one image for the reverse, the seated owl with the letters $A\Theta E$. This uniformity and monumentality together with the high metallic quality were forceful factors in the creation and the success of these world currencies.

In other great coinage of the Greek world one image for obverse and reverse likewise prevailed, but the die engravers had a free hand to vary the representations. Thus, while at Syracuse a magnificent, diversified coinage arose, the obverse always showed a female head surrounded by four dolphins and the reverse always showed a chariot, either slow or fast moving. In Thracian Abdera one obverse image, the griffin, was retained, while the reverse image changed regularly, although this occurred over a limited time span in the second half of the fifth and the first quarter of the fourth centuries[23].

On the Cyzicenes the obverse images are constantly changed during the whole period of production, from about 550 to 330 B.C., amounting «to around 240 different types»[24]. Why was there this plethora of images on the electrum coinage of Cyzicus? The basic conceptional difference between local city silver money and electrum trade coinage has been noted, and KRAAY stresses that «it is unlikely that official transactions at Cyzicus were conducted in electrum rather than in the silver which bore the city's name and its types...»[25]. But this gives no explanation for the impressive variety of images.

The idea that the plethora of images was caused by the necessity to prepare one design for each annual production of the Cyzicenes has to be dismissed. This assumption has been too readily adopted, especially by scholars who stressed that the approximate number of images should be increased from 220 to about 240[26]. The entire time span of the production of the Cyzicenes is 220 years, 240 at the most. If the annual theory were accepted, then we would already know all the images ever used and there would not be any additional unknown images. Can we really claim omniscience and conclude that no new images are hidden in the earth of the vast territories where the Cyzicenes circulated[27]? In addition, in a business transaction, the payer and the recipient of Cyzicenes did not care whether these coins were produced

---

[23] J.M.F. MAY, The Coinage of Abdera, 540-345 B.C., London 1966, 187-461 (mainly periods 5-8, 445-375 B.C.). Furthermore, changing images on the Abdera reverses occur only in connection with the changing inscriptions of the magistrates' names. On the magistrates and other mint officials, see A. FURTWÄNGLER, Griechische Vieltypenprägung und Münzbeamte, SNR 61 (1982) 5-25, and on Abdera, ibid. 16-18.

[24] G.K. JENKINS and M.C. CASTRO HIPOLITO, A Catalogue of the C. Gulbenkan Collection of Greek Coins, Part 2, 1989, 61.

[25] C.M. KRAAY, Archaic and Classical Greek Coins, 1976, 261. See C.M. KRAAY / M. HIRMER, Greek Coins, 1966, 368, stating that the Cyzicenes were a «trade currency, comparable to the Maria Theresia Taler».

[26] See also H.A. CAHN, in: Griechische Münzen. Aus der Sammlung eines Kunstfreundes. Bank Leu and Münzen und Medaillen, Zürich, 218, May 1974, 12.

[27] Only a few images are known for the early Cyzicenes. The wealth of designs begins with v. FRITZE's group IIa which is dated around 520 B.C. by recent scholarship. The number of different images must be considerably higher than the number of years of production.

annually or at irregular intervals. All that mattered for them was that the Cyzicenes were available and the recipient could be sure that they were unquestionably acceptable.

It has also been proposed to understand the varying images on the Cyzicenes as the signatures of the changing magistrates responsible for the electrum coinage. This is not a convincing alternative. The names of magistrates occur on late classical and hellenistic coinage, not in the sixth and fifth centuries. There is no evidence to date for such a specialized office in Cyzicus[28]. The appointment of new magistrates annually, or for shorter or longer periods of time, would demand at least 240 different civil servants. This practice would have been detrimental to a smoothly functioning, continuous mint activity. Not individual short-term officials, but the municipality as a whole was responsible for the planning, production, and marketing of the Cyzicenes.

Is there then quite another explanation for the ever growing number of images? Surely the authorities of Cyzicus made a virtue out of necessity. For technical reasons the reverse dies with the incuse square had to be put into the anvil[29], whereas usually the obverse die is embedded in this sheltered position. As it was the die with the image that had to endure the blow of the striking hammer, many more image dies than incuse square dies were needed.

In Cyzicus one could have ordered, of course, one new die after the other of a constant, never-changing motif, as the minting authorities of the darics and the Athenian owl tetradrachms did. Obviously, the Cyzicus municipality considered the eternal incuse squares and tunny badges[30] sufficient to establish the stability of their international trade currency[31]. At the same time they succeeded in making the Cyzicenes appealing to many different peoples by the beauty, diversity, and numbers of their changing images[32]. It seems obvious that in Cyzicus the municipal autho-

---

[28] See A. FURTWÄNGLER, SNR 61 (1982) 16.

[29] Clearly demonstrated by D. ROUVIER, SNR 38 (1957) 16 and fig. 8-10. This is also shown by the die study in G.K. JENKINS and M.C. CASTRO HIPOLITO, A Catalogue of the C. Gulbenkan Collection of Greek Coins, Part 2, 1989, 62.

[30] During the entire long coinage period of the Cyzicenes, the tunny fish appears as clearly recognizable, in rather large size, and in a prominent place, often supporting the varying obverse images. It cannot be maintained that on late archaic Cyzicenes the tunny badge was reduced to a small symbol. See literature quoted by A. FURTWÄNGLER, SNR 61 (1982) 97 with nn. 9-20.

[31] It has been stressed that the primary identification sign of the electrum coinage of Cyzicus, Mytilene, and Phocaea was the combination of flan shape and metal and types, «die 'Einheit' Schrötlingform – Metall – Typenwechsel» [A. FURTWÄNGLER, SNR 61 (1982) 23]. At Cyzicus, however, there are varying flan forms. There are other characteristics that distinguish the Cyzicenes. In particular, there was the remarkable retention of the incuse square until the very end of the production, while elsewhere it was long out of fashion. Also noteworthy was the permanent, obvious appearance of the tunny badge. Equally important was the unwavering full weight and the continuing use of electrum. Also significant was the intentional altering and embellishment of the obverse designs.

[32] For a plausible explanation of how the municipal authority procured the motifs and selected the best, see A. FURTWÄNGLER, SNR 61 (1982) 20, n. 96. For the iconography and its general interpretation, see above, n. 6.

rity, the city council, was well aware of the farreaching effect of the altered images on the unwavering popularity of their international, conventional trade coinage. They adopted beautiful and interesting motifs wherever they could get them, at home and abroad. They depicted gods, human beings, and animals in addition to statues, everyday scenes, and monsters. Inanimate objects were rarely chosen as they may have been considered uninteresting. The lyre [v. FRITZE, Nomisma 7 (1912) 181] could at least be played, and thus awakened to life. Most of the many images are beautifully engraved, and Cyzicus' commercial money was art *par excellence* .

## 6. The Cyzicenes and the Great Powers

It seems incredulous that it has not been asked why the great kings of Persia did not simply take over the Cyzicene mint. It produced a well established, successful trade coinage for a small city situated within their realm and even in close proximity to their main administrative center. Was not the Cyzicene a strong formidable competitor with their gold daric? No, it was not. It has been said that the Archaemenids possessed a monopoly on gold coinage[33]. They did not even think of such a prerogative. They relied on their own imperial coinage, the gold daric and the silver siglos, and permitted local monetary production[34]. Throughout their empire they fostered not only local autonomy in political, economic, and cultural matters[35], but also in money production. Their coinage policy cannot be understood in the categories of law and administration of the later centralist states. The electrum coinage of Cyzicus hat begun well before Cyrus' generals conquered northwest Asia Minor in the late forties of the sixth century, but it could never have been continued and extended without the explicit or tacit permission of the Achaemenids.

For about 150 years during the city's long coinage period of at least 220 years, Cyzicus was Persian – from about 540 until 445 B.C., and again from 387 up to the end of the empire[36]. During the Athenian hegemony in the intermediate period of about 60 years, the production of the Cyzicenes continued as usual. This is an as-

---

[33] F. KIECHLE, Mysien-Troas-Aiolis-Lesbos, Literaturüberblicke der griechischen Numismatik, JNG 10 (1960) 99. He states explicitly «daß im 4. Jahrhundert der Grosskönig sein Monopol der Goldprägung gegenüber den griechischen Poleis Kleinasiens nicht mehr aufrecht zu erhalten vermochte». There was, however, no such monopoly. Furthermore, it must be emphasized that after the «King's Peace» of 387 the powerful great kings Artaxerxes II and Artaxerxes III could have easily stopped any local coinage, if they had chosen to do so.

[34] Stressed by L. MILDENBERG, AMI 26 (1993) 62-70 [hier S. 12-24].

[35] See E.A. KNAUF, Die Umwelt des Alten Testaments, Stuttgart 1994, 171-72: «Um Vielfalt und Eigenleben der ihnen anvertrauten Städte und Stämme und Völker zu pflegen, gewährten die persischen Großkönige ihnen juristische, religiöse und kulturelle Autonomie, soweit sie mit den Interessen des Gesamtreiches vereinbar war».

[36] Cyzicus was not sheltered from the effects of the wars in whichs Persia, Athens, Sparta, and the Greek cities of Asia Minor were involved. There were, however, long decades of peace in which Cyzicus was a quiet and flourishing Persian city, as well as other shorter periods when Cyzicus was either tolerated or favored by Athens.

tounding fact. Whereas Athens enforced its coinage monopoly by law in the territories of the members of the Delian League[37], she did not ban the production of the Cyzicenes, even though Cyzicus was a member of the League with a yearly tribute of nine talents[38]. In the mid-fifth century, Athens certainly could have forbidden the striking of Cyzicenes, but this was not in her best interest. In fact, for the Athenians, the Cyzicenes were a valuable means of payment, a sort of clearing instrument. The Persians did not think to stop the Cyzicenes; the Athenians did not want to do so.

---

[37] See L. MILDENBERG, AMI 26 (1993) 65 n. 67 [hier S. 17], on the Athenian Coinage Decree.

[38] The frontiers between the spheres of Persian and Greek influence were fluid, and often Cyzicus hat to manœuver. However, no warlord laid hands on the mint of the Cyzicenes. Around 400 B.C., silver coins were struck im Cyzicus stating the name of the powerful Persian grandee Pharnabazos, but they conformed to the framework for the city's local silver coinage [see L. MILDENBERG, AMI 26 (1993) 58-60 (hier S. 7-10), and pls. 6,32-33 (hier Tf. III), and 13,107 (hier Tf. XII)].

# Les inscriptions des monnaies Carthaginoises

Il y a soixante ans que le fameux numismate danois, L. MÜLLER, a consacré de nombreuses et importantes études à la vaste série des monnaies carthaginoises. De nos jours, le monnayage de Carthage est l'objet des efforts de M. ROBINSON, qui prépare le catalogue du Musée Britannique pour la Zeugitane. Mon intérêt pour cette série a été provoqué par mes modestes travaux dans le domaine des monnaies juives anciennes. Les pièces carthaginoises et juives, ainsi que les monnaies de Sidon, Tyr, Tarse, Chypre, etc., ont des inscriptions en écriture cursive du vieux sémitique du Nord, auquel appartiennent le phénicien ou punique, l'hébraïque, l'araméen, etc. Cette écriture, qui ne correspond à celle d'aucune des langues sémitiques ultérieures, a toutefois eu longue vie. On la trouve dans tout le I$^{er}$ millénaire avant notre ère – sur la stèle du roi Méša de Moab au Louvre, dans les inscriptions phéniciennes et hébraïques, et finalement, pendant la renaissance remarquable au temps des deux guerres juives contre Néron et Hadrien.

Comme vous le savez, les sources de l'histoire du grand empire carthaginois sont très insuffisantes. Les fouilles exécutées sur le site de Carthage par DÖRPFELD ont eu très peu de résultats. Les grandes guerres puniques ne sont connues que du point de vue romain. En comparant notre connaissance du monde grec, hellénistiques et romain avec les résultats des études historiques sur Carthage, on constate facilement que l'examen et l'interprétation du monnayage de Carthage sont d'une grande importance. Les inscriptions, les types originaux et imités, le style des pièces et surtout le particularités des trouvailles doivent donc donner des indications importantes. Récemment, on a fait une grande trouvaille des didrachmes libyens surfrappés sur des didrachmes carthaginois de la fin du III$^e$ siècle. Ces pièces sont généralement d'un argent d'assez bonne qualité, quoiqu'un certain nombre des didrachmes carthaginois de cette trouvaille soient de mauvais aloi. L'inflation s'est donc développée à Carthage dans une période assez courte. J'aimerais bien recevoir des information additionelles concernant cette trouvaille.

En général, les inscriptions des monnaies antiques donnent un nom de personne ou de divinité ou d'état, mais les légendes de la série carthaginoise sont tout autres.

Les inscription ne donnent pas des noms, mais des indications. Il faut comparer ces inscriptions avec les légendes des monnaies grecques contemporaines pour bien saisir la différence fondamentale. Je n'en discuterai ici qu'un seul exemple important. Alors que les pièces grecques de Sicile portent les noms des Syracusains, des Catanéens, etc., l'inscription des triples statères d'électrum de Carthage enseigne simplement que cette monnaie a été frappé «dans le pays» – BEARZAT (b'rṣt). On peut facilement conclure de ce fait qu'il doit exister encore un monnayage *hors* du pays, c'est-à-dire, dans les colonies carthaginoises de la Méditerranée. On a voulu lire cette inscription remarquable BYRSAT, et y voir le nom de la forteresse de Carthage BYRSA, mais, dans ce cas, l'inscription devrait être Bebyrsa, et non Bearzat. Cette interprétation est donc exclue pour des raisons philologiques très simples.

J'ai essayé de classer toutes les inscription en trois groupes. Cette classification n'est qu'une hypothèse préliminaire, car il me semble prématuré de présenter une classification définitive ou une table chronologique exacte.

Au premier groupe, vous trouvez des noms: ERECH pour ERYX, et HAMATUA pour MOTYA. ZIZ doit correspondre à Panormus, parce que nous possédons une petite monnaie bilingue: d'un côté Sche Baal ZIZ ($\check{s}b\,^{\lsquo}l\ zz$) et de l'autre côté $\Pi ANOPMI T\Omega N$, RESCHMELKART ($r\check{s}mlqrt$) veut dire la tête de Melqart, ce qui correspond exactement à *Cephaloedium* et *Heraclea Minoa*. Le fait qu'on trouve ces noms sur les monnaies est significatif: ces villes ont été sous la domination carthaginoise, mais elles ont eu une certaine autonomie.

Les inscription du deuxième groupe sont des explications. L'interprétation de la première légende est difficile: *Karat Chadaschat* ($qrt\ \dot{h}d\check{s}t$) signifie «ville neuve». Depuis longtemps, l'opinion commune est que le mot romain Carthago et le nom grec Karchedon sont dérivés de ces deux mots puniques. Bien sûr, la capitale a été une ville neuve pour les anciens colonisateurs tyriens; mais pour les conquérants postérieurs de la Sicile occidentale, la capitale de leur administration (probablement Panorme) était aussi une ville neuve quand on la comparait avec la métropole africaine. Sur beaucoup de pièces est écrit, en toutes lettres ou en anbrégé, le mot *Mechaschbim* ($m\dot{h}\check{s}bm$), qu'on traduira au mieux par «quaestores» ou fonctionnaires des finances. Ainsi est donc nommé un organe important de l'administration carthaginoise. Une autre inscription est encore plus significative: *Am Machanat* ($^{\lsquo}m\ m\dot{h}nt$), peuple du camp et *Scheam Machanat* ($\check{s}^{\lsquo}m\ m\dot{h}nt$), au peuple du camp. Une seule interprétation me semble possible: ce sont là des pièces frappées par l'administration militaire carthaginoise dans le pays occupés.

Dans la troisiéme groupe on ne connaît qu'une seule légende BEARZAT ($b\,^{\rsquo}r\dot{s}t$), que nous venons d'expliquer.

# Punic Coinage on the Eve of the First War against Rome. A Reconsideration

(Tf. XLIII - XLV)

## 1. The Structure of the Coinage

The scope of this paper is to clarify the structure of Punic coinage in Sicily and Africa from the fifth century till the First War against Rome[1]. I shall not rely on stylistic[2] arguments, but on the basic facts of the numismatic evidence[3] only: metals, denominations, details of fabric, legends, types, overstrikes, imitations and hoards.

Primarily, three main categories of coinage emerge, clearly separated from each other: local, provincial and metropolitan, – an obvious division which, however, has not been sufficiently emphasized before.

### 1.1. The Local Coinage in Sicily[4]

The major Western Sicilian cities within the Carthaginian realm, Segesta[5], Panormos, Eryx, Thermai and Solunt, struck first silver and later bronze coins from the second quarter of the fifth century on with Greek and Punic legends. The main silver denominations were the drachm and the litra, but larger and smaller silver

---

[1]  See H.A. CAHN - L. MILDENBERG - R. RUSSO - H. VOEGTLI, Griechische Münzen aus Großgriechenland und Sizilien, Basel 1988, 153-157, Nos. 556-571, the description of the Siculo-Punic coins by the present writer, and id., Sikulo-punische Münzlegenden, SNR 72 (1993) 5-21 [hier S. 150-160].

[2]  The specific usefulness of stylistic comparison should not be minimized, but its significance for chronological research must not be overstated.

[3]  L. MILDENBERG, Numismatic Evidence, HSCP 91 (1987) 381-395 [hier S. 253-262].

[4]  A. HOLM, Geschichte des sicilischen Münzwesens bis zur Zeit des Augustus, Leipzig 1898, considered all the coins struck on the island of Sicily as municipal issues and divided them into three clearly separated groups.

[5] The coinage of Segesta displaying own types with Greek and Graeco-Elymian legends was not abolished when the city lost its independence by seeking shelter under the Carthaginian protection. The rich silver money production lasted from mid-fifth century till 397 B.C., when Dionysius I of Syracuse conquered and destroyed the city. See L.-M. HANS, Karthago und Sizilien, Hildesheim - Zürich - New York 1983, 13; L. MILDENBERG, Kimon in the Manner of Segesta, in: The Eighth CIN, 1973. Proceedings, 1976, 113-121 [hier S. 110-115].

coins, too, were issued. These cities, and not at all the Carthaginian administration, produced the cash for every day needs, the small silver litra, the commun local money[6]. One has to keep in mind here that the names of the cities appear currently on this local money; the fabric is Sicilian, the influence of the Greek mints in Eastern Sicily is predominant and all the city coins are found in Sicily.

## 1.2. The Provincial Coinage in Sicily

This mass coinage, beginning about 410, ending with the First War against Rome, was registered and explained by G. KENNETH JENKINS in his monumental corpus, published by instalments in the SNR 1971-1978[7]. For this special series an examination of the single components of the numismatic evidence seems particularly appropriate. Metals: mainly silver, electrum – some few struck in about 265 only – , gold – an enigma to be discussed here later. Denominations: from 410 till 265 tetradrachms only. Fabric: striking from loose dies and marked protuberances – both highly important and much neglected findings (Tf. XLIII 1). Legends: the issuing Carthaginian provincial institutions are explicitly named on the coins in good Punic lettering. Types: the Sicilian Kore-Persephone and the Carthaginian horse are predominant. Overstrikes occur very rarely. The early beginning of the series was established to c. 410. Imitations: strong influence on the female head and the quadriga in Syracuse, under Dionysios I (405-367). Finally hoards: a highly significant fact is that hoards appear in Sicily only and that no Sicilian provincial-institutional coins in silver have ever been found in North Africa[8].

It has to be noted that JENKINS' sharp eyes have established the beginning of the tetradrachm coinage to c. 410 B.C. without a shadow of a doubt, but he hold at the same time that the mint was Carthage proper[9]. Though the latter statement was, too, universally accepted, it is certainly wrong: 1) he reads the obverse legend *qrtḥdšt*, «New City», in isolation instead of reading it jointly with the reverse legend *mḥnt*, «army» rather than «camp». Both together simply mean «Carthaginian Military Administration». 2) Even if one insists that the reverse legend has nothing to do with the obverse legend, one has to acknowledge that there are also New Cities on Cyprus and in Spain. Seen from Carthage in North Africa, *Carthago Nova* in Spain is, for instance, a new city, too. 3) Coin production from loose dies and protuberances[10] do only occur in Sicily. 4) Not one specimen from this first tetradrachm

---

[6] In the past, the small Sicilian silver coins were often neglected by numismatic scholarship. Only recently, currency, technology, and art of these essential emissions, the daily cash, were fully treated within the corpora and single studies.

[7] G.K. JENKINS, Coins of Punic Sicily I-IV, RSN 50 (1971) 25-78; 53 (1974) 23-41; 56 (1977) 5-65; 57 (1978) 5-68.

[8] Check IGCH 2259-2308, where gold and electrum coins from the «Carthage Mint» are registered. Large hoards of late bronze coins are found on the African continent.

[9] G.K. JENKINS, RSN 53 (1974) 26.

[10] Distinct protuberances are ubiquitous during the fifth century on the island. The technology seems to be the same for the silver and the bronze coins. Marked protuberances are also found on some *Magna Graecia* silver coins of this period, which hints to the

series comes from a registered African hoard or is reported to have ever been found there. I have presented other facts for this proposed reconsideration in another context[11], but the arguments outlined above certainly suffice to prove that the Punic coinage begins in Sicily.

There are other major institutions of the Carthaginian administration in Sicily mentioned on the coins: ʿm (h)mḥnt, «people (assembly) of the army», thus military authority; mḥšbm, «paymasters», thus high officials of the finance administration; bʾrṣt, «in the countries», and finally r(ʾ)š mlqrt : as I have already stressed in the description of specimen 558 in the Basel Antikenmuseum catalogue of Greek Coins of Magna Graecia and Sicily of 1988, the communis opinio, ruling for more than 100 years and stating that this is the name of a Sicilian city[12], has to be abandoned. The derivative sense of the legend can be «Melqart's Cape», but literally it simply means «Melqart's Head»[13] which, indeed, is the first type appearing in this series (Tf. XLIII 2). Further, this cannot be a city coinage for the simple reason that there are no existing fractions with this legend, only tetradrachms as in other provincial-institutional issues. Thus, another component of the numismatic evidence is decisive – that of the exclusive denomination. This is the second major reconsideration which I propose.

### 1.3. The Metropolitan Coinage

No coins have been issued in Carthage proper earlier than around the turn from the fourth to the third century. Curiously enough, they start in precious metal and not in silver, just the opposite of the development in Sicily. The fabric of the coins is also entirely different: firmly fixed dies at vertical axes were used on the electrum staters, not the loose ones of the Sicilian mint[14]. Further, the metropolitan coins are anepigraphic, with no legends whatsoever. Finally, they have clear mintmarks in the form of one or several dots, which is not the case in Carthaginian Sicily. Find spots of this first gold and electrum coins are located mainly in Sardinia and Sicily, occasio-

---

works of Sicilian craftsmen, not only of Sicilian die engravers, in Southern Italy.

[11] See L. MILDENBERG et al., Griechische Münzen aus Großgriechenland und Sizilien, 1988, 153-157, Nos. 556-571, and id., SNR 72 (1993) 5-21 [hier S. 150-160].

[12] R. STUART POOLE, BMC Sicily, London 1876, 251. See L. MILDENBERG, in: H.A. CAHN et al., Griechische Münzen aus Großgriechenland und Sizilien, 1988, and cp. E. ACQUARO, Le monete, in: I Fenici, ed. S. MOSCATI, Milano 1988, 464-473 (see 469), where rš mlqrt is translated «gli eletti di Melqart», in the sense of «the officials of Melqart». This is far from the literal sense of the legend, but does not exclude the present writer's interpretation. Officials of the army unit «Melqart's Head» may, indeed, have been the minting authority of the issue.

[13] C. BONNET, Melqart (Stud. Phoen. 8), Leuven - Namur 1988, 267-269.

[14] For the «criterion of the die-axis» see G.K. JENKINS, RSN 57 (1978) 38. – The careful registration of the die position, introduced by G.F. HILL using arrows in his BMC Phoenicia, London 1910, is – inter alia – an essential tool in discerning coins from modern forgeries; see L. MILDENBERG, «Those ridiculous arrows». On the meaning of the die Position, Nomismatika Chronika 8 (1989) 23-27 [hier S. 263-264].

nally in Tunis. The only similarity between the provincial and metropolitan coinages is the marked preference for Kore-Persephone for the obverse type[15] and the horse images[16] for the reverse type.

At this point, we have to investigate the gold staters with an average weight of 8.45 g. The technical tools of the numismatic evidence described here in the introduction enlighten us in many respects, but they are no magic wands which open all doors. For the time being, we cannot ascertain where these gold staters were struck. At one hand, they have mintmarks and are anepigraphic, as the somewhat later electrum staters. At the other hand, these gold staters are struck from the loose «Sicilian» dies, whereas the electrum staters and all subsequent metropolitan coins in different metals (gold, electrum, silver, billion, bronze) are struck from firmly fixed dies (Tf. XLIV)! Under these circumstances one might think that the types might be helpful, but gold and electrum staters have identical images. And the hoard evidence? Again a failure, because the areas of the find spots for the gold and electrum staters are the same as mentioned above. I have never understood that this impass does not exist for the *communis opinio* , taking for granted that the gold coins were struck in Carthage. For me, it is inconceivable that the basic techniques of coin production in a mint are changed from one day to the other and that a mint official suddenly decides to fix the hitherto loose dies. The only unproven explanation I have to offer is that gold staters were struck in Carthaginian Sicily in the first period of the War against Agathocles, whereas electrum staters were issued in Carthage in the second period, after the Syracusan king had landed on the African coast[17].

## 2. The War Coinage of the Years 265-250 B.C.

This issue is a *res sui generis* . War money par excellence, it has to be clearly differentiated from the preceding and the following Punic coinages. The concentration of all economic resources just before and during the early years of the First Punic War necessitated the simultaneous production of high denominations in precious metals in Sicily and in the Metropolis, which had never happened before! The output was large and condensed. It lasted about 10 years, 15 at the most. It is again clearly determined by the evidence of metal, denomination, legends, details of fabric and hoards, as shown by the following synopsis (Tf. XLV):

---

[15] The female head wearing a Phrygian cap appears on a special and limited issue. See G.K. JENKINS, RSN 56 (1977) 24-31; L. MILDENBERG, in: H.A. CAHN et al., Griechische Münzen aus Grossgriechenland und Sizilien, 1988, 155, nos. 561-562. Cp. L.-M. HANS, Die Göttin mit der Tiara, RSN 66 (1987) 47-58.

[16] The pegasus and the lion are secondary images. The palm tree is not a main type, but mostly a companion of the horse in its different representations.

[17] In any case, hoards evidence and identity of type and diameter hint to a production of gold and electrum within a decade.

| Carthage<br>(Fixed dies) | | | Sicily<br>(Loose   dies) | | |
|---|---|---|---|---|---|
| Gold Trihemistaters | 12.45 g | c.260 | Silver Dodecadrachms | 44,15 g | c.265 |
| Electrum Trihemistaters | 10.85 g | c.250 | Silver Hexadrachms | 21,95 g | c.265 |
| Gold Tristaters? | 4.90 g | c.260 | Silver Decadrachms[18] | 37,90 g | c.260 |
| | | | Electrum Tristaters | 21,85 g | c.260 |

Here, the simultaneous production is clearly demonstrated. The homogeneity of the Carthaginian group is obvious. The same is true for the Sicilian group. The chronological framework is not based on stylistic arguments, but on the evidence of hoard-composition, metals and denominations. These coins are all valuable money: precious metal only, large pieces only. These are the means of payment to finance a war, to pay the mercenaries. Every effort has been made to issue these high denominations in a short period of time. The bulk has been emitted within five years.

Finally, we have to sum up the main facts of the numismatic evidence which definitely decide, where the coins have been struck. Carthage: fixed dies, mintmarks, no legends. Sicily: loose dies, protuberances, institutional legends. As to the major hoards: all known gold trihemistaters come from two Tunis finds, the first made in 1948 with up to 60 specimens[19], the second in 1985 with about 40 pieces. A reliable insider assured me that a «few» gold tristaters came with these about 40 gold trihemistaters. As the reverse type was quite unusual and the engraving of the date-palm differing in style from the convention, the authenticity was doubted in some quarters. One piece appeared in a recent Munich auction sale, another was shown in the British Museum, where the die position was carefully checked: 12 h, correct for the mint of Carthage! Though I have learnt in the last 40 years not to underrate the knowledge of the master-counterfeiter, I do not think that he knew what I have stressed here. In addition, the weights of both pieces are perfect: 24.93 and 24.82 g. I assume, therefore, that these new tristaters are genuine, unless an examination of the gold composition, the strikinglines and the border will prove me wrong. Under the assumption that these new gold tristaters are genuine, they demonstrate that very high denominations, very valuable money, were mobilized in the capital to finance the war.

As to the silver, it certainly came from Sicily. The by far largest silver decadrachms find has been made near Palermo in 1958[20]. The silver dodecadrachms, de-

---

[18] The splendid pegasus on the reverse of the decadrachms is influenced by the staters of Corinth and her colonies, which served as the main means of payment in the fourth century on the island. They were even issued in Greece for export to Sicily until Timoleon began to strike his own Syracusan pegasi in the Corinthian manner. See H.A. CAHN et al., Griechische Münzen aus Grossgriechenland und Sizilien, 1988, 86. 141; C.M. KRAAY, Timoleon and Corinthian Coinage in Sicily, in: The Eighth CIN, 1973. Proceedings, 1976, 95-105; R.J.A. TALBERT, Timoleon and the Revival of Greek Sicily 344-317, Cambridge 1974, 161-178; W. HUSS, Geschichte der Karthager, München 1985, 492, n. 26.

[19] IGCH 2271.

[20] IGCH 2008.

cadrachms and hexadrachms, as the electrum tristaters, come from Sicily. Not one has ever been found in North Africa.

In the treaties between Carthage and Rome, Sardinia was indicated as a forbidden zone, Sicily was not[21]. «It seems uncertain how much we can deduce from this», JENKINS stressed[22]. Anyway, without the Sicilian money of the sixties the First War against Rome could not be waged.

---

[21] C. MAREK, Die Bestimmungen des zweiten römisch-punischen Vertrages über die Grenzen der karthagischen Hoheitsgewässer, Chiron 7 (1977) 1-7 (see 2).
[22] G.K. JENKINS, RSN 57 (1978) 39, n. 41.

# The Mint of the First Carthaginian Coins

## (Tf. XLVI - XLVII)

The Carthaginians issued tetradrachms in Western Sicily during the whole 4th century. In G.K. JENKINS' monumental «Coins of Punic Sicily», part I, 1971[1], «the tacit assumption was that it probably began only after the destruction of Motya (397 B.C.)»[2]. In Bank Leu Auction 2 of 1972, however, an Akragas tetradrachm appeared, which was overstruck, as it `was duly noted. JENKINS himself recognized the underlying issue[3], an early Carthaginian coin. As Akragas was destroyed in 406, the original Carthaginian coin must have been struck some time before that date. JENKINS has convincingly proposed the years 410/409 when money was needed for the campaign led by Hannibal son of Gisgo. The first series might, indeed, have begun as «purely military coinage»[4], but it goes down from 410/409 till around 390, the military legend *mḥnt* («camp») finally disappears and the output is considerable. Economic considerations should, therefore, not be excluded *a priori* [5].

JENKINS' sharp eyes enabled him to unearth an undisputable, essential and farreaching fact, but the conclusions he drew from this discovery were erroneous, though widely accepted[6]. He stated «... the mint, as well as the minting authorities, for the first tetradrachm series was at Carthage itself»[7], but the mint was, in fact, Sicilian and the minting authority the Carthaginian administration on the island. Following are the specific elements of numismatic evidence[8] which for once prove our friend wrong.

---

[1] SNR 50 (1971) 26-78.

[2] SNR 53 (1974) 23.

[3] G.K. JENKINS, SNR 53 (1974) 24, Pl. 6-7.

[4] JENKINS, SNR 53 (1974) 25.

[5] As L.-M. HANS, Karthago und Sizilien, Hildesheim 1983, 231, n. 62, commenting JENKINS' view based on J.M. KEYNES, has already stated.

[6] Contra: L. MILDENBERG, Punic coinage on the eve of the first war against Rome, a reconsideration, in: Punic Wars (Stud. Phoen. 10; OrLovA 33), Leuven 1989, 6 [hier S. 139]. For L.-M. HANS, Karthago und Sizilien, 1983, 129 the Carthage mint assumption is unlikely. W. HUSS, Geschichte der Karthager, München 1985, following HANS, holds that in all probability the coins of the first series were struck in a Sicilian city.

[7] G.K. JENKINS, SNR 53 (1974) 26.

[8] See L. MILDENBERG, Numismatic Evidence, HSCP 91 (1987) 381-395 [hier S. 253-262].

# 1. The Hoards

The Siculo-Punic tetradrachms are found on the island. Not one has ever been found in Africa[9]. This writer has stressed in the past that negative evidence alone cannot be conclusive, as we cannot know what is still hidden in the earth[10]. However, unless a substantial hoard of Siculo-Punic tetradrachms is found in Tunis or the neighbouring countries, the Sicilian hoard evidence remains valid and rejects the Carthage mint thesis.

# 2. The Protuberances

Marked thornlike protuberances[11] are visible on coins struck in Sicily, Greek and Carthaginian issues, whereas the money produced in Carthage proper is round.

These protuberances are remainders from the typical Sicilian casting process of the flans which had been made in a row of moulds. They occur in the Carthaginian West as in the Greek East around 410.

# 3. The Die Axis

The coins struck in Carthage were made with fixed dies, those produced in Sicily from loose dies. This is another finding of the numismatic evidence which has not been duly considered[12]. One could perhaps argue that the die engravers might have moved from Sicily to Carthage, but it is inconceivable that the whole mint with its elaborate technique was transported overseas during the turbulent years of 410/409.

# 4. The Exclusive Denomination

The Carthaginian coinage in Sicily began with tetradrachms only. This Siculo-Punic tetradrachm issue lasted a full hundred years. There are no didrachms, drachms or fractions. This exclusive denomination, another important element of numismatic evidence, indicates an abundant, uniform and prestigious money supply. Such a coinage was a demonstration of power directed at the Greek cities on the island, especially Syracuse, with their great silver tetradrachm series. But at the same time it was an economic move putting forward a strong and lasting currency. The highest representative of the Carthaginian state acted as the minting authority working through his

---

[9] L. MILDENBERG, in: Punic Wars, 1989, 6, n. 8 [hier S.139].

[10] L. MILDENBERG, A Bar Kokhba didrachm, INJ 8 (1984-1985) 33 [hier S. 208].

[11] L.-M. HANS, Karthago und Sizilien, 1983, 129 and n. 109, following an information by H.R. BALDUS, refers to the «Gußnaht», but does not arrive at a definite conclusion.

[12] It is only in the presentation of series 6 in part IV, SNR 57 (1978) (5-68) 38 that JENKINS indicates the die axis and stresses its importance.

main administrative agencies[13], all specified on the coins which testifies to a purely institutional coinage: *Qrtḥdšt, mḥnt, mḥšbm, b'rṣt,* and *ršmlqrt* [14]. Such a coinage is basically different from the local city money[15] produced within the Carthaginian realm in Segesta, Eryx, Solus, Panormus, Motya and, of course, from the later metropolitan issues of Carthage proper. The first series of 410/409 to 390 is an integral part of this entire institutional coinage: same denomination and same metal, flan production and striking process, die engraving, Punic legends and matching images. To remove it from its Sicilian institutional context and to put it into a then not existing metropolitan mint, is not conceivable.

The first Siculo-Punic tetradrachms, and thus the first Carthaginian coins at all, were struck in Sicily. One has to face the fact and its far-reaching consequences.

---

[13] *Qrtḥdšt* = New City, *mḥnt* = Camp, *mḥšbm* = Quaestores, *b'rṣt* = In the Territories, *ršmlqrt* = Melqart's Head.

[14] *Ršmlqrt* is not a Sicilian city, as unanimously stated in scholarship since 1876, but a Carthaginian institution. See L. MILDENBERG, in: Punic Wars, 1989, 8 [hier S. 140].

[15] This is a distinct autonomous coinage on permission of the Carthaginian authorities producing the small silver denominations for the daily cash, also some tetradrachm issues in addition to bronze coins struck in the Second half of the 4th century.

# Ršmlqrt

It seems rather surprising to express an opinion disagreeing with KENNETH JENKINS in a *Festschrift* in his honour, especially if this comes from the editor of his monumental «Coins of Punic Sicily»[1]. He was, however, always willing to discuss a problem and, hopefully, will accept this short note as a token of friendship and esteem.

For more than a century, general opinion has understood *ršmlqrt* and *r'šmlqrt* to be the name of a city in Sicily[2]. Few timid doubts have been cast on this assertion, but no decisive alternative has been proposed[3]. In part I of his corpus, JENKINS reviewed the possible candidates and tentatively voted for the city of Selinus-Selinunte[4]. As my interpretation of the inscription contradicts early and recent scholarship, I dealt with the matter in a detailed article «Sikulo-punische Münzlegenden» (SNR 72, 1993, 5-21 [hier S. 150-160]). In the short description of specimen 558 in the Basel Antikenmuseum catalogue of a collection exhibited there[5], I mentioned my disagreement with the *opinio communis*. It seems, however, appropriate to summarise my view here.

*Ršmlqrt - r'šmlqrt* is not a name of a city or location, but of a Carthaginian provincial institution in Western Sicily[6]. As JENKINS has demonstrated, silver tetradrachms with these legends were struck in the second part of the fourth century on

---

[1] G.K. JENKINS, Coins of Punic Sicily I-IV, SNR 50 (1971) 25-78; 53 (1974) 23-41; 56 (1977) 5-65; 57 (1978) 5-68.

[2] R. STUART POOLE, BMC Sicily, London 1876, 251.

[3] C.M. KRAAY, in: C.M. KRAAY and M. HIRMER, Greek Coins, London 1966, 291 translates «Headland of Melcarth» and stresses the «head» element in the legend. L.-M. HANS, Karthago und Sizilien, Hildesheim 1983, 131 says «Kap/Kopf des Herakles» and states: «Grundsätzlich ist aber einzuwenden, daß die Übersetzung von *ršmlqrt* kein stichhaltiges Argument für die Lokalisierung darstellt». L.I. MANFREDI, Ršmlqrt: Nota sulla Numismatica Punica di Sicilia, RIN 87 (1985) 3-8 indicates: «moneta emessa della zecca di Melqart», but also: «moneta emessa sotto l'autorità della communità del tempio di Melqart». There are no epigraphic or other sources in favour of a temple coinage in Sicily. The minting authority ist the Carthaginian state acting through its provincial administration. A further delegation to a temple community seems unlikely. E. ACQUARO, Le Monete, in: I Fenici, ed. S. MOSCATI, Milano 1988, translates the coin inscription «gli eletti di Melqart», which ist far from the literal meaning.

[4] K. JENKINS, SNR 50 (1971) 53-5.

[5] H.A. CAHN et al., Antikenmuseum Basel und Sammlung Ludwig, Griechische Münzen aus Großgriechenland und Sizilien, Basel 1988, 154.

[6] Cp. L. MILDENBERG, Punic Coinage on the eve of the first war against Rome. A reconsideration, in: Punic Wars, ed. H. Devijver - E. Lipinski (OrLovA 33; Stud. Phoen. 10), Leuven 1989, 8 [hier S. 140].

the island, which is proved by hoards, die positions, protuberances and imitations. In the common series, only tetradrachms appear (fig. 1), no didrachms and drachms, no small silver fractions and no bronzes, as JENKINS has also stressed. But this exclusive tetradrachm denomination is an indisputable element of the numismatic evidence. It is as decisive for the four series marked *qrthdšt*, *ʿm mhnt, mhšbm* and *b'rst* as it is for the fifth *ršmlqrt* [7]. All these are provincial, institutional issues, neither local, municipal nor metropolitan coins. Cities produce small denominations for the daily needs of the people and mark it with their names. Many litrae and their divisions struck by Western Sicilian cities are known, but none displaying the legends of any of the five institutional groups[8]. Obviously, the Carthaginian administration in the West aimed at a prestigious production of large denominations as an economic counterpoise to the great heavy silver issues of the Greek East. That this move was successful is proved by the many mixed hoards unearthed in all parts of Sicily.

Even if the conception of an institutional coinage could be refuted or had not been proposed, the attribution to any city would, nevertheless, be unsubstantiated. The second part of the inscription indicates the Phoenician-Punic god Melqart[9]. The literal translation of the first part means simply head or peak. There is a secondary meaning, namely cape or promontory, as *rú-šá-qad-š*, Holy Cape near Akko in Northern Palestine, later called *Rās en-Nāqūra*. Similar later names are known in the Eastern Mediterranean, but none from Sicily[10].

If the secondary meaning were attractive, the search for a suitable location on the island would, nevertheless, be a lost cause. Kephaloidion, Panormos and Eryx are topographically possible, but they have their own coins and have to be excluded together with Herakleia Minoa, Lilybaion, Solus, Thermai and Drepana, as JENKINS has demonstrated. The Akropolis of Selinus stands, indeed, on a small ledge between two rivulets, but the elevation is low to the point that JENKINS himself considers it

---

[7] *Qrthdšt* means, indeed, «New City», but it occurs together with *mhnt* – «Camp», thus in the sense of »Carthaginian Military Administration». *Mhšbm* are high finance officials. *B'rst* means «In the Territories». These four series are essentially connected with the fifth, *Ršmlqrt*.. There is no reason to isolate the latter and to understand it as the name of a city.

[8] Cf. K. JENKINS, SNR 57 (1978) 58, Pl. 24, E-F, a litra of uncertain attribution with the remark: «The head seems to resemble that of Ršmlqrt 26». The head, however, is conceived in the manner of the Syracusan masters Eumenes and Eukleidas, the horse protome is different from that on the Siculo-punic pieces. Moreover, the indispensable punic inscription or, at least, its abbreviation is missing.

[9] Cf. C. BONNEt, Melqart (Stud. Phoen. 8), Leiden 1988, 267-269.

[10] See M. SZNYCZER L'assamblée du peuple dans les cités puniques d'après les témoignages épigraphiques, Semitica 25 (1975) 44-68 with the inscription on 52-63 *b'm qrthdšt* (literally «In the people of New City»), *b'm ybšm* («In the poeple of Ibiza»), *b'm lkš* («In the people of Lyxus»), and *b'm 'lpky* («In the people of Lepcis-Leptis Magna»). All these names have equivalents in ancient and modern languages, the coin legends *mhnt, mhšbm, b'rst* and *ršmlqrt* have none, neither in Sicily nor elsewhere. This is also true for CIS 264 with *š b'm ršmlqrt* and CIS 3707 with *š b'm r'šmlqrt* (an essential parallel to the coin inscriptions *ʿm mhnt, ʿm hmhnt* and *š ʿm mhnt* ) which means «Belonging to the people of Melqart's Head».

«an insignificant feature of the landscape»[11]. It is, however, significant that the prototype of the *ršmlqrt* series shows a bearded head of Melqart; a Rēš Melqart, indeed (Tf. XLVI Fig. 4:8; XL 27).

For all these reasons, the translation «Melqart's Cape» for the coin legend has to be abondoned and the literal meaning «Melqart's Head» accepted. It might have been the name of an army unit, but it indicates, in fact, a Carthaginian provincial institution, not a Sicilian city.

---

[11] K. Jenkins, SNR 50 (1971) 54.

# Sikulo-punische Münzlegenden

## (Tf. XLVIII - L)

«On revient toujours à ses premiers amours». Beim CIN in Paris 1953 hatte der Schreibende einen ganz vorläufigen Bericht vorgelegt, den die Herausgeber der *Actes* gar «Les Inscriptions des Monnaies Carthaginoises» nannten[1]. Manches war stichhaltig, anderes weniger. Die scharfe Trennung zwischen den punischen Namen[2] für Städte wie Eryx, Motya, Solus, Thermai sowie Panormos einerseits[3] und den blossen Bezeichnungen («indications», «explications») anderseits hat sich als angebracht erwiesen. Nur sollte man die letzteren besser als Institutionen bezeichnen. Mit den Hauptlegenden dieser institutionellen Emissionen beschäftigt sich der vorliegende Beitrag.

Inzwischen ist das Schrifttum gewachsen, insbesondere mit den Arbeiten der spanischen und italienischen Schule. Sehr viel ist G. KENNETH JENKINS zu verdanken,

---

[1] CIN 1953: Actes, Paris 1957, 149-151 [hier S. 136-137]. Wertvolle Hinweise werden verdankt C. Bonnet, S. Hurter, D. Jeselsohn, E. Lipinski und insbesondere W. Röllig. Der hier vorliegende Beitrag ist eine neue, erweiterte Fassung eines 1987 für eine Veröffentlichung konzipierten Artikels, die bisher [1993] nicht erschienen ist [jetzt: Zu einigen sikulo-phönizischen Münzlegenden, in: Italiam fato profugi Hesperinaque venerunt litora. Numismatic Studies dedicated to Vladimir and Elvira Eliza Clain-Stefanelli (Numismatica Lovaniensia 12; Louvain-la-Neuve 1996), 259-272 mit einer nicht zugehörigen Abb. auf S. 271]. JENKINS I-IV = G.K. JENKINS, Coins of Punic Sicily, Parts I-IV, SNR 50 (1971) 25-78; SNR 53 (1974) 23-41; SNR 56 (1977) 5- 65; SNR 57 (1978) 5-68.
[2] Die Legenden 'rk, mṭw', kfr' für Eryx, Motya und Solus. Der punische Name für Thermai, dessen Tetradrachmen besonders ausgeprägt sikulo-punische Züge haben können, ist jedoch nicht gesichert.
[3] Die elymäische Stadt Segesta prägte Münzen von ca. 480 bis ca. 397. Diese Emissionen wurden zwar vom Geld der griechischen Städte Siziliens beeinflusst, zeigten aber auch eigenständige Bilder. Obwohl Segesta von ca. 409 bis ca. 397 zum Gebiet der Karthager gehörte, haben diese keinerlei Einfluss auf die Münzprägung genommen, welche meist syrakusanische Köpfe, aber nur selten Gespannseiten abbildet. Die Segesta zugestandene Münzautonomie ging in dessen letzten Prägeperioden noch weiter als bei den meisten andern Städten im Westen (Zugeständnis eigenständiger Legenden), weshalb eigentlich nicht von sikulo-punischen Münzen aus Segesta gesprochen werden kann. Vergleiche P. LEDERER, Die Tetradrachmenprägung von Segesta, München 1910, und C.M. KRAAY, in: KRAAY - HIRMER, Greek Coins, London 1972, 170-171 sowie L. MILDENBERG, Kimon in the Manner of Segesta, CIN 1973, Proceedings, Paris - Basel 1976, 113-121 [hier S. 110-115].

dessen «Coins of Punic Sicily» der gesicherten Stempelabfolge wegen die Grundlage für jede weitere Forschung bilden[4].

Der Ruf nach interdisziplinären Studien wird immer lauter. Historiker, Philologen und Epigraphiker nehmen aber noch immer nicht die volle numismatische Evidenz zur Kenntnis, so daß ihre Argumente bisweilen im leeren Raum verpuffen. Dabei sind die faktischen Aussagen, nicht deren Interpretationen, von Währung, Legenden (insbesondere Bilinguen), Fabrik (Rand mit Protuberanzen und Stempelstellung), metallurgischem Befund, Überprägungen, Funden und Stempelabfolgen unwiderleg-bar[5].

## 1. Einiges zur numismatischen Evidenz

### 1.1. Elementares

Die Währung ist attisch, die Fabrik sizilisch, das Erscheinungsbild einheitlich und für eine Reichsprägung charakteristisch (einerseits die Bilder von Kore-Persephone[6] sowie Tanit[7] und andererseits die Typen Pferd, Pferdprotome, Pegasus, Quadriga sowie Löwe und Palme), die Schrift meist ein schöner und reiner punischer Duktus, die starke Vorherrschaft vollgewichtiger Tetradrachmen ungewöhnlich.

### 1.2. Stadt- und Provinzialgeld

Die karthagische Verwaltung beliess den wichtigeren Orten in ihrem Machtbereich eine weitgehende Münzautonomie. Sie prägten mit ihren eigenen Münzbildern und der Nennung ihrer Namen auf Punisch und Griechisch Silbergeld in mittleren und kleinen Sorten. Auf diese Weise stellten sie die lokale Geldversorgung für das tägliche Leben sicher (Tf. XLIX 14-17). Zusätzlich kommen aus Motya eine kleine Emission von Tetradrachmen, die meist Typen von Agrigent und bisweilen von Syrakus imitierten (Tf. XLIX 16.18), aus Thermai eine noch kleinere Serie von Tetradrachmen nach Syrakusaner Vorbildern (Tf. XLIX 20) und aus Eryx wenige

---

[4] JENKINS I-IV; die vier Artikel bilden einen Corpus der sikulo-punischen Münzen.

[5] Für interdisziplinäre Forschung siehe insbesondere E. ACQUARO, Problematica e per-spettive degli studi di numismatica punica, NACQT 4 (1975) 97-108. – Zu den faktischen Aussagen siehe L. MILDENBERG, The Numismatic Evidence, HSCP 91 (1987) 381-395 [hier S. 253-262].

[6] Kornblätter und Ähren bezeichnen den häufigsten weiblichen Kopf auf sikulo-punischen Münzen als Kore-Persephone, einer offensichtlich auf ganz Sizilien populären Gottheit, für die es nicht notwendigerweise eine karthagische Entsprechung gegeben haben muß.

[7] Im Gegensatz zu Kore-Persephone gelangt der Frauenkopf in der phrygischen Tiara von außen in den sizilischen Westen. Man hat ihn als Venus, Dido, Astarte oder als Personifikation von Karthago gedeutet. Auf einer phönizischen Stele der hellenistischen Zeit wird der Name ʿbdtnt («Knecht der Tanit») mit Artemidoros wiedergegeben, weshalb JENKINS III, 29, unsere Gottheit als Tanit-Artemis versteht. Vgl. L.-M. HANS, Die Göttin mit der Tiara, SNR 66 (1987) 47-58, die an die Göttin von Eryx denkt.

Stücke (Tf. XLIX 21). Weit größer, wenn auch noch immer nicht sehr umfangreich, ist die Tetradrachmenprägung von Panormos (Tf. L 23), die nur am Anfang unter dem Einfluß von Selinunt, dann aber ganz eindeutig unter dem von Syrakus steht. Von dem lokalen Stadtgeld grundsätzlich verschieden ist das Provinzialgeld. Es handelt sich hier um eine sehr umfangreiche, vielseitige und lange Zeit ausgebrachte Großsilberprägung der verschiedenen karthagischen Provinzinstitutionen. Da sie keine mittleren und kleinen Sorten, sondern hauptsächlich Tetradrachmen[8] neben einer begrenzten Serie von Dekadrachmen prägten und jeweils an den Haupttypen festhielten, müssen diese bedeutenden institutionellen Emissionen überregionalen und regionalen sowie militärischen Zwecken gedient haben, wofür eben auch die hier zu behandelnden Münzlegenden sprechen.

## 1.3. Fremdes und Eigenes

Die Grenzen zwischen dem Gebiet der Griechen im Osten und dem der Karthager im Westen waren durchlässig. Nur so konnte der starke Einfluß der Münzprägung der griechischen Siedlungen auf das Geldwesen der karthagischen Institutionen und der abhängigen Städte wirksam werden. Dabei musste jede Form von Prestigedenken den karthagischen Verwaltern fremd gewesen sein; denn nur wenige eigene Bilder tauchen auf, nämlich Pferdedarstellungen, die Palme und bisweilen der Kopf einer Göttin mit Haube[9], die nicht in das griechische Pantheon gehört (Tf. XLVIII 5-6). Alle anderen Münztypen sind entlehnt. Dabei ist die Ausrichtung auf Syrakus bei den institutionellen Emissionen besonders auffällig. Einige sikulo-punische Stempel stammen gar aus der Hand griechischer Meister (Tf. L 24), wobei daraus aber nicht hervorgeht, daß sie sich auch im Westen niedergelassen haben. Vieles ist blosse Kopie durch örtliche Handwerker. Manche Entwürfe aber sind eigenständig und von beeindruckender Kraft.

## 1.4. Funde

Horte und Streufunde sind auch für die Deutung der Legenden von entscheidender Bedeutung. Sie belegen ausnahmslos die «total disparity»[10] zwischen Gold und Silber. Das Großsilber, die schweren Stücke wie die Tetradrachmen, werden in Sizilien gefunden, keinesfalls in Nordafrika[11], während die Prägungen in Gold und

---

[8] In sehr großen Mengen wurden Tetradrachmen von den verschiedenen karthagischen Provinzinstitutionen geprägt. Die letzteren sind auch verantwortlich für eine ansehnliche Dekadrachmenprägung mit der Legende *b'rṣt* und eine begrenzte Prägung von anepigraphischen Dodekadrachmen und Hexadrachmen. In Elektron waren die Emissionen der Institutionen noch geringer; von den Tristateren mit *b'rṣt* sind nur wenige Exemplare bekannt. – Zur Ausmünzung der karthagischen Provinzinstitutionen siehe L. MILDENBERG, Punic Coinage on the Eve of the First War against Rome: a reconsideration, in: Stud. Phoen. 10, Leuwen 1989, 5- 14 [hier S. 138-143].

[9] Siehe oben Anm. 7.

[10] JENKINS III, 11.

[11] IGCH 1910-2266 erwähnt 2 Horte aus Süditalien und 28 auf Sizilien, die sikulo-pu-

Elektron hauptsächlich von dem afrikanischen Kontinentn aber auch von der Insel stammen[12]. Jeder informierte Händler wird bestätigen, daß seit Jahren große Mengen sikulo-punischer Tetradrachmen aus Sizilien kommen, während Tunesien als Umschlagplatz für den neuesten und den etwas weiter zurückliegenden Hort von goldenen Trihemistateren (Tf. L 32) feststeht[13].

## 2. Die Legenden

### 2.1. *Qrtḥdšt* und *mḥnt* (Tf. XLVIII 1-2)[14]

Dies sind die Inschriften auf den frühesten sikulo-punischen Tetradrachmen; denn aufgrund der Überprägung eines Tetradrachmons von Akragas (Tf. XLIX 13) auf einen dieser frühesten Typen (Tf. XLVIII 1) gelangte JENKINS 1972 in logischer Weise zu einem Ansatz von etwa 410. Die wörtliche Übersetzung ist eindeutig: «Neustadt» auf der Vorderseite, «Lager» auf der Rückseite. Aber der Sinn der Worte? JENKINS votierte für die Stadt Karthago. «Neustadt» ist jedoch zweideutig: von Phönizien aus gesehen war es Karthago, aus der Perspektive von Karthago kann es ein Ort auf Sizilien gewesen sein. Aber selbst wenn man *qrtḥdšt* als Karthago auffaßt, ist damit nicht bewiesen, daß die Metropole selbst gemeint war. Ebenso kann die Legende für die karthagische Herrschaft stehen. Liest man beide Inschriften

---

nische Münzen enthielten, aber keinen einzigen aus Nordafrika oder von anderen Inseln als Malta und Sardinien! Die neuesten Daten bestätigen dies: Coin Hoards III (1972, 12,20-21; IV (1978, 28) und VI (1981, 21). Zwar kann eine negative Evidenz keine völlige Gewißheit bringen, aber bis zum Auftauchen eines gesicherten, substantiellen Silberfundes in Nordafrika bleibt sie ein nicht wegzudeutender Hinweis. JENKINS II, 23, betont selbst, daß Stücke aus der ersten sikulo-punischen Serie, die er nach Karthago legt, im Fund von Vito Superiore bei Reggio di Calabria (IGCH 1910) vorkamen, vermerkt aber nicht, daß solche bisher in Nordafrika nicht gefunden wurden. Selbst wenn man die Herstellung der frühesten Gruppen der ersten Serie in Karthago und einen Transport dieses Geldes auf die Insel annimmt, kommt man aber über die anderen Fakten der numismatischen Evidenz nicht hinweg, denn, daß man in der Metropole auf sizilische Art und Weise geprägt hätte, kann man doch wohl nicht behaupten. – Hierzu siehe neuerdings L. MILDENBERG, The Mint of the First Carthaginian Coins, Florilegium Numismaticum, Studia in honorem U. Westermark edita, Stockholm 1992, 289-293 [hier S. 144-146].

[12] Die großen Elektronstücke mit der Legende *b'rṣt* stammen von der Insel; die einfachen Elektronstatere werden zwar auf Sizilien gefunden, aber Fabrik und Typen sprechen eher für eine Prägung auf dem afrikanischen Kontinent. Siehe L. MILDENBERG, Punic Coinage on the Eve of the First War against Rome, in: Stud. Phoen. 10, Leuwen 1989, 5-14 [hier S. 138-143].

[13] Zum Schatzfund von Tunis (IGCH 2271) von 1948 kommt nun ein neuerer Hort, ebenfalls aus Tunesien, aus dem rund 30 Stücke 1986 auf dem Markt erschienen. Beide Funde enthielten fast nur stempelfrische Stücke, was für das von H.-R. BALDUS, Unbekannte Reflexe der römischen Nordafrika-Expedition von 265/255 v.Chr. in der karthagischen Münzprägung, Chiron 12 (1982) 163-190 vorgeschlagene Prägedatum, nämlich das Kriegsjahr 255 spricht. Die Stempelstellung ist ausnahmslos 12 h, was eine Prägung aus fixierten Stempeln und die Herkunft aus der Münzstätte Karthago bedeutet.

[14] Siehe unten die Faksimile-Wiedergabe der einzelnen, hier besprochenen Legenden.

zusammen, kommt man wörtlich zu «Karthago – Militärverwaltung» und sinngemäß zu «Karthagische Militärverwaltung»[15]. Wo ist dieselbe nun zu lokalisieren? Einige der oben genannten Faktoren der numismatischen Evidenz sind zu befragen: die Funde, wie betont, sprechen für Sizilien, die wenigen Überprägungen, die wir kennen, desgleichen. Entscheidend ist die Technik der Prägung; denn wir treffen überall auf die nur auf der Insel vorkommenden gegenständigen Protuberanzen und die für Sizilien typischen unregelmäßigen Stempelstellungen. Aber selbst die Evidenz der Legendenfolge und der Münztypen bestätigt dieses Ergebnis: im Laufe der Prägung wechseln in der ersten Gruppe die Legenden oder erscheinen nur auf einer Seite, um dann gänzlich zu verschwinden. Ein solches Vorgehen wäre bei einer in der Metropole erfolgten Reichsprägung, die auf Tradition und Einheitlichkeit angewiesen ist, gänzlich unangebracht. Bei den Münzbildern wird gegen Ende der Prägung die gezäumte Pferdeprotome vom freien Pferd abgelöst, also dem siegreichen karthagischen Wappentier, eine Münzpropaganda, die nur auf der umkämpften Insel sinnvoll erscheint. Die Prägung der frühesten sikulo-punischen Tetradrachmen begann um 409 im Zusammenhang mit der Landung des grossen Expeditionsheeres auf Sizilien, wurde auf der Insel verwirklicht und anfänglich und hauptsächlich wohl für Soldzahlungen verwendet. JENKINS' Gedanken müssen schon in diese Richtung gegangen sein, bevor er sich fur die Münzstätte Karthago entschied; denn er behält sich vor: «... it remains just possible that perhaps the last issue of the first series, nos. 38 48, where the free type replaces the horse forepart, might signify a move of the mint to Sicily»[16].

## 2.2. ʿmmḫnt – ʿmhmḫnt – šʿmmḫnt (Tf. XLVIII 5-7.9)

Die erste Legende bedeutet wörtlich «Volk des Lagers», also Heer. Bei der zweiten ist der Artikel als dritter Buchstabe eingeschoben. Die Übersetzung lautet desgleichen «Volk des Lagers». Bei der dritten Legende steht das Relativum š vor dem ersten Wort ʿm , so daß sich die Übersetzung «das (Geld) des Volkes des Lagers» ergibt[17]. Das Heer – oder auch die Militärverwaltung – schaffen also Geld in ihrer Eigenschaft

---

[15] Gewiß ist «Karthago – Militärverwaltung» nicht das Gleiche wie «Karthagische Militärverwaltung», was mḫnt-qrtḫdšt heißen müßte. Die sprachliche Folge aber ergibt sich für den Benützer der Münze, je nachdem, ob er die Vorderseite oder die Rückseite zuerst zu Gesicht bekommt und liest. Deshalb ist die sinngemäße Übersetzung «Karthagische Militärverwaltung» statthaft, was nicht der Fall wäre, wenn die beiden Wörter fortlaufend auf einer Münzseite oder in einer Linie eines Textes stünden.

[16] Wie oben im Text und in Anm. 11 betont, ist die ganze erste Serie und die gesamte sikulo-punische Edelmetallprägung auf Sizilien entstanden, wobei JENKINS' früher Ansatz für die erste Serie unbestreitbar ist. Bronzen haben die Karthager in der zweiten Hälfte des 4. Jahrhunderts und später nicht nur in Nordafrika, sondern auch auf Sardinien und Sizilien geprägt.

[17] Die von E. ACQUARO, Note di epigrafia monetale punica I, RIN 74 (1974) 77-81, vorgeschlagene Deutung von ʿm als eine Art Volksversammlung («una qualche assemblea») schließt die Heeresemission nicht aus, ist aber für das Verständnis der Legendengruppe nicht wesentlich. Vgl. M. SZNYCER, L'assemblé du peuple dans les cités puniques d'après les témoignages épigraphiques, Semitica 25 (1975) 47-68.

als wichtige Institution der karthagischen Exekutive auf der Insel, die mit dem Oberkommando identisch gewesen sein kann, aber nicht muß.

## 2.3. *mḥšbm – mm* (Tf. XLVIII 8.10)

Die vollständige Legende *mḥšbm* heisst wörtlich «Rechnungsführer». In der Hauptstadt Karthago waren dies Funktionäre der zivilen Finanzadministration, auf Sizilien aber wohl hohe Beamte der karthagischen Zentralverwaltung, die für die Wirtschaft und die Tresorerie verantwortlich waren, also nicht nur und ausschließlich untergeordnete Heereszahlmeister. – Diese Annahme eines hohen und selbständigen Amtes der *mḥšbm* würde die Deutung der abgekürzten Legende *mm* als *m(ḥšbm)* - *m(ḥnt)* , also «Lagerzahlmeister», ausschließen. Ferner ist diese früher verfochtene These mit den Tatsachen nicht vereinbar, daß *mḥšbm* und *mḥnt* gar nicht zusammen auf einer Münze vorkommen, was bei *qrtḥdšt* und *mḥnt* der Fall war, und daß es in dieser späten Serie immer *ʿmmḥnt* und nie *mḥnt* heißt! Und schließlich ist zu betonen, daß es zwei klar getrennte, aufeinander folgende Serien mit dem Herakleskopf gibt, die erstere mit *ʿmmḥnt* und die zweite mit *mḥšbm* [18]. Aber was bedeutet dann *mm* ? Ein Name, der mit *mm* beginnt, ist kaum vorstellbar. Ist es eine Abkürzung? Nun bilden Abkürzungen schon auf phönizischen, insbesondere sidonischen Münzen eine wirkliche *crux* der numismatischen Forschung. Das Gleiche gilt für die Abkürzung auf sikulo-punischen Münzen. Bis heute gibt es jedenfalls noch keine plausible Erklärung für das eine *m* , und die zwei Buchstaben *ḥb* (Tf. L 25)[19]. Nun ist im Phönizisch-Punischen eine Abkürzung durch die ersten und letzten Buchstaben eines Wortes nicht unmöglich, so daß wir für *mm* wieder bei *m(ḥšb)m* wären. Diese mit allem Vorbehalt vorgebrachte Deutung[20] begegnet allerdings der Schwierigkeit, dass die Abkürzung *mm* in der früheren Serie mit dem Kopf der Kore-Persephone vorkommt (Tf. XLVIII 8), während das ausgeschriebene Wort *mḥšbm* erst in der zweiten und letzten Gruppe der späteren Serie mit dem Herakleskopf erscheint (Tf. XLVIII 10).

---

[18] «If it were otherwise there seems little point in the distinction of the two kinds of legend on the coins», JENKINS IV, 8.

[19] JENKINS III, 36, Anm. 229; 36, Nr. 230F; 34, Nrn. 91-100. Auf der Münze Nr. 100 stehen auf der Rückseite unten die zwei punischen Buchstaben *ḥb* und oben die zwei griechischen Buchstaben *Sō*. Es dürfte sich um Abkürzungen für Namen oder Begriffe handeln. Im letzteren Fall könnte man *ḥb* zu *ḥbr* (Kollegium) und *Sō* zu *sōma* (Gesamtheit, Korporation) ergänzen und mit allem Vorbehalt wieder an eine Verwaltungsinstitution denken. Die Anomalie, daß nur auf diesem einen Stempel Abkürzungen in zwei Sprachen vorkommen, ließe sich vielleicht damit erklären, daß es sich um einen einmaligen Versuch, eine Art Münzprobe, handeln könnte. Bei allem bleiben die von A.M. BISI, Monete con leggenda punica e neopunica del Museo Nazionale di Napoli, AIIN 16-17 (1969-1970) 85, geäußerten Zweifel an der Erklärungsmöglichkeit dieser Kurzschrift bestehen.

[20] Zu den Abkürzungen auf den Münzen der 5. persischen Satrapie siehe L. MILDENBERG, Baana, ErIs 19 (1987) 33, Anm. 29 [hier S. 41], sowie J. ELAYI - A.G. ELAYI, Abbreviations and Numbers on Phoenician pre-Alexandrine Coinages: The Sidonian Example, NACQT 17 (1988) 27-36.

## 2.4. *b'rṣt* (Tf. XLIX 11; L 28)

Auch hier muß man sich an die ganz wörtliche Übersetzung halten, die «in den Ländern» lautet. Die Übersetzung «in dem Reich» geht zu weit, womit die These unwahrscheinlich wird, *b'rṣt* könne als Hinweis darauf verstanden werden, dass diese Münzen auch in Nordafrika umlaufen durften[21]. JENKINS hat schon 1966 im Sinne der wörtlichen Übersetzung argumentiert: «BeARZat meaning 'in the land' clearly implies that the mint was not at Carthage. The evidence of hoards supplies the clue. The whole group of electrum and silver must have been minted in Sicily»[22]. In dem abschließenden, vierten SNR-Artikel betont JENKINS nochmals die Fundevidenz ebenso wie die für Sizilien typische, variable Stempelstellung und übersetzt jetzt *b'rṣt* mit «in the territory»[23]. Daß das westliche Sizilien ein wichtiges karthagisches Territorium war, ist einleuchtend. Da die *b'rṣt* -Münzen ausschließlich auf Sizilien gefunden wurden und wegen ihrer Fabrik nur dort geprägt sein können, geht es jedoch nicht an, daß man den Plural «in den Ländern» überinterpretiert und etwa eine Prägung oder einen Vermerk der Umlaufgültigkeit auch für Sardinien oder das punische Spanien annimmt. Es dürften eher Regionen gemeint gewesen sein, in die das karthagische Sizilien aufgeteilt war.

## 2.5. *ršmlqrt* und *r'šmlqrt* (Tf. XLVIII 3-4; L 27)

Silbermünzen mit dieser Legende wurden in der zweiten Hälfte des 4.Jahrhunderts auf Sizilien geprägt. Dies ist durch die Evidenz der Funde, Stempelstellungen, Protuberanzen und nachgeahmten Typen erwiesen. Aber was bedeutet diese Inschrift? Sie besteht aus zwei Wörtern. Das zweite ist der Name des phönizisch-punischen Gottes Melqart. Für das erste ist die wörtliche und naheliegendste Übersetzung «Kopf, Haupt, Spitze». Man ist in unserem Zusammenhang wiederum gut beraten, sich daran zu halten. Für *rš* und *r'š* ist jedoch die Bedeutung «Kap» ebenfalls belegt. So heißt die Landzunge bei Akko seit altersher *rú-ša-qad-š* , also «heiliges Kap»[24] oder auch *ba-'a-li-ra-'a-ši* , also «Baals-Kap»[25]. Spätere Belege gibt es auch

---

[21] H.-R. BALDUS, Chiron 12 (1982) 178: «(gültig / umlaufsfähig) im (ganzen) Lande / Reich». Die Gleichsetzung Land / Reich ist nicht möglich. Auch mit den adjektivischen Ergänzungen geht diese Interpretation zu weit. Ferner bleibt die negative Fundevidenz so lange wesentlich, bis sie nicht widerlegt ist (siehe oben Anm. 11). Daß das «Fehlen von Nachrichten über Funde ... auf nordafrikanischem Boden nichts zu besagen habe» (BALDUS, 179), müßte bewiesen werden. Auf die Anfälligkeit von BALDUS' These, die *b'rṣt* -Münzen seien auf Sizilien geprägt, nach Nordafrika transportiert und von dort wieder auf die Insel zurückgebracht worden, hat U. WESTERMARK, International Numismatic Congress 1986, Survey, London 1986, 24 hingewiesen.

[22] G.K. JENKINS - R.B. LEWIS, Carthaginian Gold and Electrum Coins, London 1966, 35.

[23] JENKINS IV, 36-39.

[24] Das Rãs en-Nãqũra, identifiziert von M. NOTH, Die Wege der Pharaonenheere in Palästina und Syrien IV: Ramses II. in Syrien, ZDPV 64 (1941) 62, Anm. 4.

aus dem westlichen Mittelmeer, jedoch bezeichnenderweise nicht aus Sizilien. Bis vor kurzem[26] hatte die gesamte Forschung *rš* und *r'š* nur als Kap verstanden und einen passenden Platz dafür gesucht. Dafür käme aber ausschließlich eine wichtige, eindeutig innerhalb des karthagischen Gebietes und an einem ausgesprochenen Vorgebirge liegende Stadt in Frage, für welche die *ršmlqrt* - Prägung wahrscheinlich gemacht werden könnte. Alle diese Bedingungen erfüllt aber keiner der bisher vorgeschlagenen Orte (Kephaloidion, Heraklea Minoa, Lilibayon, Panormos und Selinunt). Dies kann auch nicht der Fall sein für irgendeinen anderen Platz, den man noch aufspüren sollte; denn die Münzprägung spricht gegen jede lokale Deutung. Die von den karthagischen Institutionen emittierten Münzgruppen mit den Legenden *qrthdšt* – *mhšbm* und *b'rṣt* bestehen ausschließlich aus Großsilber und zu allermeist aus Tetradrachmen, kennen jedenfalls keinerlei Kleingeld[27]. Die gesamte, umfangreiche *ršmlqrt*- Prägung besteht desgleichen nur aus Tetradrachmen. Dies ist die entscheidende numismatische Evidenz der ausschließlichen Denomination; *ršmlqrt* ist also kein Ort, sondern die Bezeichnung einer weiteren prägenden Institution. Es mag sich um eine große Heeresmünzstätte handeln, die durchaus nicht an einen Ort gebunden sein muß, oder um das Atelier einer bestimmten Heereseinheit, die sich stolz «Haupt des Melqart» nennt[28]. Vergessen wir auch nicht, dass die *ršmlqrt*- Serie

---

[25] [Wörtlich «Baal des Vorgebirges.] Ebenfalls das Rās en-Nāqūra. Siehe dazu E. LIPINSKI, Note de topographie historique: Ba'li-Ra'ši et Ra'šu Qudšu, RB 78 (1971) 84f.

[26] C.M. KRAAY, in: KRAAY - HIRMER, Greek Coins, 1972, 299, hält fest: «Neither of these identifications is really convincing». Er dürfte der erste gewesen, dem bei der Deutung *rš* = Kap nicht wohl war, denn er übersetzt ebendort: «headland of Melcart». Von einer Stadt war er also bereits abgekommen. Das «head» trifft zu, das «land» ist eine zu weitgehende Interpretation. – L.-M. HANS, Karthago und Sizilien, Hildesheim 1983, 131, gibt «Kap/Kopf des Herakles», ohne sich zu entscheiden, als Übersetzung und sieht die Schwierigkeit im zweiten Teil der Legende: «Grundsätzlich ist aber einzuwenden, daß die Übersetzung von *ršmlqrt* kein stichhaltiges Argument für eine Lokalisierung darstellt, zumal aufgrund ihrer geographischen Lage und ihrer Beziehung zum Herakleskult einige weitere Orte in Frage kämen, z.B. Selinunt». Trotz der bestechenden, grundsätzlichen Feststellung ist man also hier wieder bei der lokalen These. – Neuerdings gibt L.I. MANFREDI, *Ršmlqrt, r'šmlqrt* : Nota sulla numismatica punica di Sicilia, RIN 87 (1985) 3-8, nicht mehr einen Ort an, sondern schlägt eine Tempelemission vor: «moneta emessa della zecca di Malqart», «moneta emessa sotto l'autorità della comunità del tempio di Melqart». Der hier wörtlich angeführte Text überzeugt völlig in seinem ersten Teil, wiederum aber durchaus nicht im zweiten: die epigraphischen Daten sind unsicher und eine Tempelprägung ist nirgends auf Sizilien nachgewiesen. Alle Parallelemissionen stammen von Institutionen der karthagischen Verwaltung und nicht aus einem Heiligtum.

[27] In den Addenda JENKINS IV, 58, und Tf. 24, E und F wird eine Litra mit weiblichem Kopf nach links und einer Pferdeprotome vorgestellt und aufgrund eines stilistischen Vergleichs mit dem Kopf eines *ršmlqrt*- Tetradrachmons mit allem Vorbehalt dieser Gruppe zugeordnet. Der Kopf ist jedoch ganz in der Art der signierenden Meister in Syrakus (Eumenes, Eukleidas) gestaltet, und auch die Pferdeprotome ist in Auffassung und Details keinesfalls sikulo-punisch. JENKINS' Hypothese scheitert auch am Fehlen jeglicher Legende, während sämtliche *ršmlqrt*- Tetradrachmen die punische Inschrift tragen.

[28] «La dimension 'politique' du culte de Melqart» wird betont von C. BONNET, Le culte de Melqart à Carthage: Un cas de conservatisme religieux, in: Stud. Phoen. 4, Namur 1986, 222, Anm. 47. Ebendort weitere Lit.

tatsächlich mit einem Melqartkopf (Tf. L 27), also buchstäblich mit dem «Haupt des Melqart», beginnt[29].

## 2.6. ṣyṣ [30]

Die Münzlegenden der meisten punischen Städte auf Sizilien sind unumstritten. Viel Tinte ist jedoch geflossen über die Inschrift ṣyṣ [31]. Dabei ist JENKINS' Darlegungen[32] wenig hinzuzufügen. Es wurde aber allgemein der Tatsache nicht Rechnung getragen, daß bereits die unbestreitbare Stempelabfolge der frühesten Didrachmen von Motya, ṣyṣ und Segesta eine lokale Parallelprägung der drei Städte sichert[33]. Die

---

[29] Die unbegründete Annahme, ršmlqrt sei Heraclea Minoa, ist über hundert Jahre alt (R. STUART POOLE, BMC Sicily, 1876, 251), zitiert von M. SZNYCER, Semitica 25 (1975) 60, Anm. 12. Von allen Kandidaten ist es der unwahrscheinlichste: es liegt östlich des Halykos, der eigentlichen Grenze der Machtbereiche, wenn es auch bisweilen karthagisch beherrscht war. Selbst ohne die oben dargelegte numismatische Evidenz muß nicht nur Heraclea Minoa, sondern die ganze lokale Theorie aufgegeben werden: 1) ršmlqrt kommt auf keiner sizilischen Steininschrift vor; 2) CIS 264 hat ʿm ršmlqrt und CIS 3707 ʿm rʾšmlqrt, also wörtlich «Volk des Haupts des Melqart». Dies ist eine wesentliche und bisher nicht beachtete Parallele zu den sikulo-punischen Münzlegenden ʿm mḥnt und š ʿm mḥnt, wie sie oben besprochen wurden. – Allerdings bezeichnen die in Karthago gefundenen Stelen jeweils einen Spender aus einem andern Ort als der Hauptstadt (M. SZNYCER, 59.62.65), aber kein einziger gesicherter sizilischer Ort ist darunter, dagegen mehrere sardische. 3) Die Inschriften (M. SZNYCER, 52. 63) bʿm qrtḥdšt («im Volk von Karthago», ob nun das große oder eines der späteren kleinen gemeint ist), bʿm ybšm («im Volk von Ibiza»), bʿm lkš («im Volk von Lixus»), bʿm lpky («im Volk von Lepcis», Leptis Magna) u.a. haben jedenfalls ihre Entsprechung in alten und neuen Sprachen. Die Münzlegenden ršmlqrt und rʾšmlqrt haben keinerlei solche Entsprechungen, können es auch nicht, da sie Institutionen bezeichnen. Das ʿm in CIS 264 und in CIS 3707 ist also «zugehörig zum Volk (oder zur Volksversammlung) der (Heereseinheit) 'Haupt des Melqart'» aufzufassen, wenn die Spender der karthagischen Stelen aus Sizilien stammen. Es ist jedoch a priori nicht auszuschließen daß «es einen Ort beziehungsweise einen vermutlich als Vorgebirge am Meer liegenden Landstrich gab, dessen Bewohner, wie diejenigen von Ibiza und Lixus, sich nach ihm nennen konnten. Es gibt keinen Hinweis darauf, daß dieses ršmlqrt , beziehungsweise rʾšmlqrt , in Sizilien lag» (Mitteilung von W. Röllig). – Zu Obigem siehe neuerdings auch L. MILDENBERG, Ršmlqrt, in: Studies in Honour of R. Carson and K. Jenkins, London 1993, 7-8 [hier S. 147-149].

[30] Die früheste ṣyṣ--Legende auf der Panormos-Drachme mit Hahn und Krabbe sowie Delphin um 430 (JENKINS I, Tf. 6 A) ist also lange vor der großen karthagischen Invasion von 410/409 entstanden.

[31] Zur früheren Forschung siehe die Zusammenfassung durch U. WESTERMARK, CIN 1986, Survey, London 1986, 24, und L.I. MANFREDI, Sys Coin Legend: a proposal of interpretation, RBN 138 (1992) 25-31.

[32] JENKINS I, 27-31.

[33] JENKINS I, Tf. 1-2: 14,15,16,17, Z 1, Z 2, Z 3,A. Die sechs erstgenannten und die zwei letztgenannten haben jeweils den gleichen Vorderseitenstempel. – Zu den Lokalprägungen im westlichen Sizilien siehe L. MILDENBERG, Punic Coinage on the Eve of the First War against Rome: a reconsideration, in: Stud. Phoen. 10, Leuwen 1989, 5-6 [hier S. 138-140] sowie MILDENBERG, Ršmlqrt, in: Studies in Honour of R. Carson and K. Jenkins, 1993, 7-8 [hier S. 147-149].

Münzlegende ṣyṣ kann also hier keinesfalls den Namen einer Institution oder irgend etwas anderes bedeuten. Vielmehr ist sie der Name eines Ortes. Dieser Befund wird noch erhärtet durch die Inschrift šbʿlṣyṣ , einer Konstruktion mit dem punischen Relativpronomen š, die wörtlich «des Baal von ṣyṣ» heißt und der Bezeichnung «Baal von Tarsos» u.a. entspricht. Daraus hat JENKINS längst die nicht zu widerlegende Folgerung gezogen: «in the legend šbʿlṣyṣ the element ṣyṣ must designate the name of the city»[34]. Um welchen Ort handelt es sich nun bei ṣyṣ ? Hier sind wiederum Hinweise aus der frühen Prägung unbeachtet geblieben: das frühe Bild des schnüffelnden, rennenden Hundes, in Motya und Segesta bereits heimisch, leitet von Kopf-Rückseiten mit der Inschrift ṣyṣ (Tf. XLIX 12) unmittelbar zu einer solchen mit der Legende ΠΑΝΟΡΜΙΤΙΚΟΝ über, worauf in der Folge die Legende ΠΑΝΟΡΜΟΣ über dem stehenden Hund folgt[35]. Wir wußten also bereits, daß ṣyṣ gleich ΠΑΝΟΡΜΟΣ ist, wenn es nicht zusätzlich die eklatante numismatische Evidenz der bilinguen Litra ṣyṣ auf der Vorderseite und ΠΑΝΟΡΜΟΣ auf der Rückseite (Tf. XLIX 14) gäbe[36]. Es ist nicht einzusehen, warum auf der Rückseite einer Münze, dazu noch kleinen Formats, ein Stadtname auf Griechisch und auf der Vorderseite irgendetwas anderes auf Punisch stehen sollte, wie man annahm[37]. Wie in anderen bilinguen und trilinguen Sachquellen der Antike, soll den verschiedensprachigen Benutzern der Münze gesagt werden, wo sie emittiert wurde. Die Verschiedenheit von Sprache und Schrift ist keine Ausnahme; denn auch bei Solus gibt es zwei verschiedene Namen, das griechische ΣΟΛΟΝΤΙΝΟΝ und kfrʾ , während Motya und Eryx auf Griechisch und Punisch entsprechende, fast gleichlautende Namen führen. Zu betonen bleibt noch, daß nach der Erweiterung und Stärkung der punischen Herrschaft über Westsizilien in den Jahren nach 409 die beachtliche Prägung von Tetradrachmen in der Stadt begreiflicherweise den punischen Namen ṣyṣ zeigt. Wie beim umfangreicheren und vielgestaltigeren Münzausstoss der karthagischen Provinzinstitutionen auf der Insel nach 409[38], sind auch die ṣyṣ- Tetradrachmen des 4. Jahrhunderts stark von Syrakus beeinflußt. Durch die konstante Beibehaltung des seit spätestens 430[39] gängigen punischen Namens ṣyṣ für Panomos wird aber die eigenständige städtische Prägung betont[40], wie dies auch im späten Motya mit

---

[34] JENKINS I, S. 31-32 mit Tf. 24,12.

[35] Siehe JENKINS I, Tf. 2 und 6.

[36] L.I. MANFREDI, RBN 138 (1992) 25-26, sagt irrtümlicherweise: «... the Greek *PANORMOS* and the Punic ṣyṣ ... form a single legend on the reserve of a silver litra ...». In Wirklichkeit steht ṣyṣ auf der Vorderseite und *PANORMOS* auf der Rückseite der Litra JENKINS Tf. 24, 6 = Tf. 2, Y, also in der Art inschriftlicher Bilinguen. Zu beachten ist, daß auf der Litra mit gleichen Bildern, JENKINS Tf. 24, 5 = Tf. 2, X nur ṣyṣ erscheint, und zwar auf der Rückseite.

[37] A.M. BISI, AIIN 16-17 (1969-1970) 85.

[38] Siehe dazu L. MILDENBERG, Punic Coinage on the Eve of the First War against Rome: a reconsideration, in: Stud. Phoen. 10, Leuwen 1989, 5-8 [hier S. 138-140].

[39] Siehe oben Anm. 30.

[40] Damit ist noch keinesfalls gesagt, daß in der Serie mit den ṣyṣ- Legenden «coins of different cities were adapted and conformed by means of the sys legend», wie es L.I. MANFREDI, RBN 138 (1992) 31, scheinen will. Die numismatische Evidenz spricht jedenfalls in der Gruppe der ṣyṣ- Tetradrachmen für eine in Gewicht, Fabrik und Bildern homo-

eigenen Bildern und dem punischen Namen *mṭw'* der Fall ist. Wie schliesslich *ṣyṣ* (nordsemitische Wurzel für «glitzernd, schimmernd, glänzend») als Name am besten wiederzugeben sei[41], steht auf einem anderen Blatt. Das Eigenschaftswort paßt jedenfalls für die so schön gelegene Stadt am Meer und Kap.

Die Legenden und ihre Transkription

| | | |
|---|---|---|
| 1. | ⲭW△Ηⲭ△Φ | *qrtḥdšt* |
| 2. | ⲭꓵΗꟿ | *mḥnt* |
| 3. | ⲭꓵΗꟿꟿO | *'m mḥnt* |
| 4. | ⲭꓵΗꟿ⅄ꟿO | *'m hmḥnt* |
| 5. | ⲭꓵΗꟿꟿOW | *š'mmḥnt* |
| 6. | ꟿ⅃WΗꟿ | *mḥšbm* |
| 7. | ꟿꟿ | *mm* |
| 8. | ⲭ┌△ⲕ⅃ | *b'rṣt* |
| 9. | ⲭ△ΦⳐꟿW△ | *ršmlqrt* |
| 10. | ⲭ△ΦⳐꟿWⲕ△ | *r'šmlqrt* |
| 11. | ┌⅄┌ | *ṣyṣ* |
| 12. | ⲕⲩ⊗ꟿ | *mṭw'* |
| 13. | ⅃Η | *ḫb* |

---

gene Serie, in der durchaus nicht der Einfluß verschiedener Städte auszumachen ist.
[41] Vgl. hierzu die Erläuterungen in L.I. MANFREDI, RBN 138 (1992) (27-29) 31 und ihre mit Vorbehalt geäußerte Gleichsetzung von *ṣyṣ* als Schmuck oder Ornament mit *hormos* als Halskette. Das griechische Wort hat aber eine zweite Bedeutung, nämlich Ankerplatz, Hafen. Ein Wortspiel wäre nicht unmöglich und würde die Gleichsetzung *ṣyṣ* = *PANORMOS* stützen.

# III.

## Münzen der jüdischen Aufstände gegen die Römer

# Rebel Coinage in the Roman Empire
## (Tf. LI)

The minting of gold and silver coins was the prerogative of the *princeps* , and his portrait, name and titles had to appear upon them[1]. The privilege also extended to members of his family, but only with his permission. A gold or silver issue which did not meet these preconditions was *ipso facto* illegal.

From the time of Augustus[2] through the first five «happy» years of Nero's reign, non-imperial coinage in precious metals was simply inconceivable in areas under direct Roman control[3]. During the last three months of Nero's life, from mid-March until the 9t[h] of June, 68[4], coins appeared from Gallia-Hispania and Africa exclusively, minted by the opposition[5] in the *Bellum Civile* . This minting was commonly referred to as the coinage of Vindex and Clodius Macer. Although Tacitus, Suetonius, Pliny the Elder and Pliny the Younger, Cluvius, Josephus, Juvenal, Philostratos and Dio Cassius provide detailed reports on the major events of the times, these sources tell us little about Vindex and Clodius Macer and even less about the origin, purpose and circulation of their coinage.

## 1. Vindex

C. Julius Vindex, the brave Roman *adsertor ille a Nerone libertatis* [6] rose up against Nero, not against Rome. His only desire was to replace him with a good emperor, in

---

[1]  In 27 BCE the Senate bestowed the honorary title of Augustus, «the Illustrous», on Octavianus, the adopted son of Gaius Julius Caesar. From then on, the full title of the Roman *princeps* became *Imperator Caesar Augustus,* a highly important and strictly observed form.

[2]  By his monetary reform, Augustus unified the coinage and at the same time firmly established the *princeps* ' exclusive right to issue money. The assumption that the *SC* on the imperial bronze coinage indicates the right of the Senate to strike these issues is erroneous. See M.R. ALFÖLDI, Antike Numismatik 1, Mainz 1978, 186-187.

[3]  Even the secondary, so called «autonomous» bronze coinage, struck mainly by cities in the Eastern provinces, could only come into being by the *princeps* ' explicit permission, granted as a special favor.

[4]  By and large, this money was issued as silver denarii. The gold aurei were very rare. No bronze coinage seems to be known.

[5]  «Monnayage d'opposition» instead of «monnayage d'état». See E.D. NICOLAS, De Néron à Vespasian 2, Paris 1979, 1303-1387.

[6]  Pliny the Elder, nat. hist. 20, 57, 160. The full wording reads: *Iulium vindicem adsertorem illum a Nerone libertatis*, «Vindex and adsertor are equivalents in meaning», C.M.

the manner of Augustus and Claudius; but he found himself with no other choice than the aged senator Galba, then governor of Spain. Vindex vainly hoped for the support of the powerful army of *Germania Superior* , commanded by L. Verginius Rufus (whose epitaph, written in the year 96, reads *Hic situs est Rufus, pulso qui vindice quondam / imperium adseruit non sibi sed patriae* )[7], but the troops from Upper Germany marched south and defeated Vindex in May 68 at the battle of Vesontio (Besançon). The immediate causes and the course of this battle are among the enigmas of Roman history[8].

Though there is no conclusive hoard evidence, we do have specimens of the so-called Vindex coins. The die links prove that these issues come from one mint, or at least from mints employing the same personnel[9]. All the coins struck in the spring of 68, presumably by people in the entourage of Galba who had remained as governor after Vindex' rebellion against Nero had been crushed, clearly refer to Augustus, not to the Republic. They stress the importance of good government and the independence of the provinces. They bear no portraits, names or titles of living persons.

---

KRAAY, NC 1949, 139. C. Julius Vindex, *Propraetor Galliae Lugdunensis* , had no legion at his disposal, but had to rely entirely on auxiliary forces and new levies. He must have hoped for backing from his powerful neighbor, L. Virginius Rufus, *legatus Germaniae Superioris* , and the old influential senator S. Sulpicius Galba, then *proconsul Hispaniae Tarraconensis.* But the cautious Galba did not move from his distant province after Vindex had started the rebellion, whereas a rather small detachment of the army from Upper Germany massacred Vindex's inexperienced troops at Vesontio and forced him to commit suicide. For the part of L. Verginius Rufus in this sad event, see below, n. 8.

[7] Pliny the Younger, ep. 6,10.

[8] The attitude of L. Verginius Rufus should not only be judged by his epitaph, composed almost thirty years after Vesontio, in which he praises his conception of, and stand for, the «legitimate imperium», as stressed by C.H.V. SUTHERLAND, The Concepts *Adsertor* and *Salus* as Used by Vindex and Galba, NC 1984, 30-32. It has not been proved that Rufus ordered the attack against Vindex at Vesontio. SUTHERLAND's view (id., 31), that Rufus wanted to protect «the integrity of Rome's northern frontiers» by eliminating Vindex seems unconvincing. A battle between the armies of two neighboring provinces obviously would not strengthen Roman rule, especially as Gallic soldiers were serving in both armies. The mere fact that Rufus survived the Civil War and the reign of the Flavian emperors clearly shows that he was not considered to have acted in Nero's name. He must have succeeded in gaining an unchallengeable personal position, not only because he had declined three times to become emperor, but also because he must have exercised extreme prudence and clear foresight in the spring and summer of 68. A. GARZETTI, From Tiberius to the Antonines, London 1974, 187, hints at Rufus' *modus operandi* in 68, later also used skillfully by Galba, but clumsily by Clodius Macer: «Verginius Rufus declared himself at the disposal of the Senate, that is, he refused obedience to the Princeps». See P.H. MARTIN, Die anonymen Münzen des Jahres 68 nach Christus, Mainz 1974, 64-68; E.D. NICOLAS, De Néron à Vespasian 1, 1979, 309-321; SUTHERLAND, Royal Imperial Coinage, London rev. ed. 1984, 199, with n. 6.

[9] This has been shown by P.H. MARTIN, Die anonymen Münzen des Jahres 68, 1974, 87. Where the coins were struck, however, is a matter of controversy. MARTIN contends that the entire coinage was produced by the entourage of Galba in Spain. NICOLAS, De Néron à Vespasian 2, 1979, 1303-1387 following H. MATTINGLY, BMCRE, intr. 189-202, and SUTHERLAND (RIC, 197-200 and NC, 31), stresses that they originated in Spain, Gaul and Africa. Future hoard evidence in addition to further die studies will, hopefully, help to identify the mints and their operators.

What we have here is no more than provisional, anonymous Civil War coinage issued over a short period of time by the Roman opposition to Nero for the provinces of Gallia and Hispania. It remains Roman coinage.

## 2. Clodius Macer

L. Clodius Macer was no Vindex. The goal of the *legatus Augusti pro praetore exercitus Africae* , who commanded the *Legio III Augusta* , was not to depose Nero in order to replace him with a good emperor, but to capture the throne for himself. Like Vindex, he took advantage of Nero's rapidly declining power in 68, during the Jewish Revolt. One should not place too much faith in the retrospective reports by historians about Macer's liaison with Nero's mistress Calvia Crispinilla, but should carefully examine his coins instead. Their wording is moderate at the beginning, but becomes shrill towards the end. Macer's first coins are similar to the Gallo-Hispanic silver coins described above. The symbols are *libertas* , *victoria* and *Roma* . After Macer's levy of the new legion, *I Macriana* , and the consolidation of his position in the city of Carthage, his coins boldly display the *Legio Liberatrix* and the personification of Africa with its lion. He even dared to use the symbol of Sicilia, thus stressing his temporary control of the straits between the continent and the island which could enable him to block the vital transport of grain from Africa to Rome. Finally – in striking contrast to the so-called Vindex coinage – Macer's portrait, name and title appear on his money. However, curiously enough, he did not dare to take the final step: he refers to himself only as Propraetor, not as Caesar or Augustus[10]. Furthermore, the letters *SC* (*senatus consulto* ) appear on all of his coins, thus substantiating his claim to be acting as a delegate of the Senate in minting money. In actual fact, the Senate's authority to mint even bronze coins was clearly limited in imperial times by the emperor's wishes[11]. It will suffice to look at the *sestertii* of Trajan, and even more so, of Hadrian, every detail of which was determined by the *princeps*, who thus created what are perhaps the grandest issues in all of Roman coinage. In any event, Macer's intention to apply to the Senate during Nero's agony did not help his cause. His head and name on the African coins were reason enough for Galba to have his competitor murdered immediately after the old senator's proclamation as emperor[12]. It must be stressed, however, that, like Nero's other opponents in Gaul and Spain, Clodius Macer, the Roman general in Africa, issued Roman money as a Roman pretender, not as a foreign rebel.

---

[10] Macer lacked experience, foresight and determination. His cause, therefore, was lost from the beginning, whereas most of the other pretenders in the Civil War were cast different mold and achieved their goal, if only for a short period of time.

[11] Above, n. 2. At the beginning of the Civil War, the Senate must nevertheless have been an influential body, as demonstrated by the formal deference shown by Macer, Rufus and Galba to this republican institution.

[12] The fact that Galba's procurator, Trebonius Caritianus, succeeded in having Macer killed in his own African province in the fall of 68 proves that the legate was unable to retain any real power in Africa.

## 3. Vabalathus and Zenobia

From Nero's point of view, the coinage of both Vindex and Macer was illegal. Nearly two hundred years were to pass before the advent of other such illegal coinage, i.e. during the troubled times of the emperors of the dynasties of Valerian I and Claudius II, who were engaged in a desperate struggle against external enemies: the Sassanian Empire and the Germanic tribes. After Shapur I's crushing victory over Valerian at Edessa (c. 260) and the emperor's terrible death, Septimius Odenathus [Udainat], the Romanized Semitic king of Tadmor-Palmyrene, became the chief defender of the Roman East and succeeded both in removing the usurper Quietus and in recapturing much of the territory lost to the Persians. In 263, Gallienus granted him the title *dux Romanorum* . After Odenathus' second successful campaign, during which he reached the outskirts of Ktesiphon in 267, Gallienus bestowed upon him the prestigious military title of *imperator* [13]. Odenathus was not to enjoy this honor for long as he was murdered in the same year by his kinsmen. This was the «hour of destiny» for Odenathusí second queen, Septimia Zenobia (Bat Zabbai), who reigned in lieu of her young son Vabalathus (Wahb'allāt), otherwise known by his Hellenized name of Athenodorus. During the next two years, Zenobia consolidated her personal power and Palmyra's position. What happened next, following the death of Claudius II Gothicus and of his brother Quintillus in March 270, made Zenobia one of the great queens of antiquity. In an unprecedented campaign during the summer and fall of 270, the Palmyrene armies conquered the entire territory lying between the Persian border to the East, the Black Sea to the North and the Nile Delta to the South, including, of course, Syria-Palestine. The new emperor, the Pannonian Aurelian, was totally occupied at the time fighting the Sarmatii along the Danube and the Alemanni in the Alps; consequently, in December 270, the Palmyrenes dared to strike coins in Syria and Egypt, very cautiously at first, as Zenobia was well aware of the implication of such action. On the *antoniniani* struck in Syria, Vabalathus is called *Vir Consularis Rex Imperator Dux Romanorum* , titles which his father, Odenathus, had already received[14]. In this instance, *Imperator* means «High Commander», not «Emperor»; neither *Caesar* nor *Augustus* appears on these coins. Furthermore, Vabalathus head is not only laureate, but also diademed, thereby stressing his position as king. Numismatic research in languages other than German has sadly neglected this important detail, although DELBRÜCK described it long

---

[13] The assumption of A. BALDINI, Corsa di Cultura Sull'Arte Ravennate e Bizantine 23, 1976, that Odenathus may have received the title Augustus in 267, because Vabalathus and Zenobia were later called Augustus and Augusta, is mistaken. Odenathus had never been Augustus and never struck coins. On his coins of 270, Vabalathus used only titles to which his father Odenathus had full rights.

[14] In the abbreviated legend, only the interpretation of the *C* is in question. *Vir Clarissimus* has been proposed, because it occurs on a papyrus. Certainly, Vabalathus and his father Odenathus were never Roman *consules* , but V. PICOZZi, Numismatica, Settembre-Decembre 1961, 126, convincingly recommended the reading *Consularis* , on the basis of the numismatic and papyrological evidence in its entirety.

ago[15]. Last but not least, Aurelian appears as Augustus only on the reverse of the Vabalathus issues, and not on the obverse, a numismatic detail which was certainly not to the liking of the emperor[16] who – unfortunately for the Palmyrenes – proved to be one of the most powerful rulers in Roman history. In the mint of Alexandria in Egypt, billon tetradrachms of Vabalathus and Aurelian bear the dates $\Delta$ and $E$ for the king and $A$ and $B$ for the emperor, from December 270 until March 272. Several papyri testify that this joint issue with the respective titles of Vabalathus and Aurelian was regarded as legal coinage[17]. Then, in the spring of 272, a dramatic and decisive change occurred, the reasons for which are difficult to establish and are beyond the scope of this paper: Vabalathus and Zenobia suddenly appear on the coins as $\Sigma EBA\Sigma TO\Sigma$ and $\Sigma EBA\Sigma TH$ in Alexandria, and as *Augustus* and *Augusta* in Syria[18]! Aurelian now had either to accept the coins and their implication, as a *fait accompli* – as Maximianus was to do some decades later in Britain in the case of Carausius – or to remove these dangerous Palmyrene competitors once and for all[19]. He chose the second alternative and destroyed Zenobia's shortlived, but extensive, realm.

The last coins issued by the Palmyrenes show their imperial portraits, names and titles as self-declared Roman rulers; these coins were illegal from Aurelian's point of view, as there had been no proclamation, not even by a Roman army unit. They remain, however, entirely Roman in symbol, legend, language and spirit, rather than Palmyrene, for which the symbols should have been those of the city, the legends those of the kingdom, the language Semitic and the spirit Oriental. The Palmyrenes did not seek freedom from Rome; they aspired to become Roman emperors or co-emperors themselves. Their coinage reflects this attitude but, as in the case of the Vindex and Macer issues, lacks any sign whatsoever of rebellion.

---

[15] R. Delbrück, Die Münzbildnisse von Maximus bis Carinus, Berlin 1940, 161.

[16] It is noteworthy that the Queen met her match in Aurelian not only in the military, but also in the monetary field. The Pannonian emperor was well aware of the political and economic implications of the monetary system; hence his reform of the imperial coinage; see W.E. METCALF, in: A Survey of Numismatic Research, 1972-1977, Berne 1979, 128-186. For Aurelian's personality, see DELBRÜCK, op.cit., 51-53.

[17] The types and legends of the early coins of Vabalathus point, in fact, to the same legal position which the king occupies in the Egyptian papyri (see V. PICOZZI, Numismatica, Settembre-Decembre 1961, 125-216). By no means can the early coins have been considered illegal.

[18] Through their last coins, the Palmyrenes declared their pretention openly, announcing that they were the rulers of the Roman East. Obviously, they underrated Aurelian and overestimated their own power.

[19] Aurelian may have already planned his campaign against the Palmyrenes in the course of 271. He may have massed his troops toward the end of that year. Was it that move to the East by the emperor, victorious on the northern frontiers, which caused Zenobia to abandon her «compromise political solution» (see R.A.G. CARSON, QTir 7, 1948, 222) and to embark upon open confrontation? At any rate, the Queen must have missed the opportunity to seek a sound and lasting *modus vivendi* with the powerful Pannonian.

## 4. The Jewish Revolt

That the coins of the years 68 and 270-272 were not really rebel coinage is demonstrated by the fact that they were neither withdrawn from circulation and melted down nor even overstruck, as is clearly proved by the mixed hoards that have come to light. Obviously, they continued to be legal tender in the succeeding years. Was there then any *real* rebel coinage in the Roman Empire?

Under the early emperors, Iudaea was governed by Roman procurators. Jewish settlements, Jerusalem and the Temple were intact. The Temple tax had to be paid by half a Tyrian «shekel»[20], but the currency of daily life was Roman gold and silver, with Latin and Greek legends, and the local small bronze coins with Greek legends issued on behalf of the emperors by their procurators. After the outbreak of the war in 66, this situation changed almost overnight in a drastic and significant way: on the new coins, a Jewish Temple chalice replaced the Roman emperor's head, «Shekel of Israel» replaced the emperor's title, and the legend was in Palaeo-Hebrew[21] instead of Latin or Greek. But even more significant was the *ʾālef* whose meaning was immediately understood: the first year of the re-established sovereign Jewish state with its own currency. Not only were the Jewish symbols and the proclamatory Palaeo-Hebrew legends new and revolutionary; even the shape of the coins was entirely different[22]. In retrospect, it is quite clear that in antiquity the minting of such an issue was the most obvious declaration of independence. We also know that in terms of type, denomination, inscription, fabric and style there was nothing comparable in ancient times. From the Roman point of view, the new Jewish issues were rebel money, in fact the first real rebel coinage within the Roman Empire, created by a foreign people in its own way and on its own land liberated from Roman domination.

## 5. Bar Kokhba

The Jewish money circulated in Iudaea for five years; with the loss of independence and the destruction of the Temple, Roman money came back into circulation. The Jewish peasants, however, remained on their land. For the Empire, the troubled times were over; significantly enough, Vespasian, the victor in the Jewish war, secured the throne and the peace for himself and for his sons Titus and Domitian.

---

[20] The conventional term «shekel» for the Tyrian tetradrachms is arbitrary and anachronistic. The word «shekel» appeared for the first time as a denomination on the large silver of the Jewish Revolt; later it was only used by Josephus who, of course, knew the legends on the coins of the Jewish Revolt; see L. MILDENBERG, Schekel-Fragen, in: FS H.A. Cahn, Basel 1985, 83-84 and nn. 6-8 [hier S. 170-175].

[21] On the significant use of the Palaeo-Hebrew script instead of the «square script» of the time, and on the monumental form of the Palaeo-Hebrew letters on the shekels, see id., 87.

[22] See id., 87-88.

Nerva proved to be an excellent administrator. Trajan, the *optimus princeps* , extended Roman rule beyond the Danube and in the east. Hadrian consolidated Roman power, creating the golden age of the *Pax Romana* . Rejecting the idea of any further conquest, he protected the northern frontier against the Britons by ordering the construction of a major defensive wall. In the first, peaceful half of Hadrian's reign, he did not show any hostile attitude towards the Jews or other groups in his vast empire. During his grand tour (c. 130), however, Hadrian must have changed his mind, as he ordered a new city to be built on the site of Jerusalem, which he called *Aelia Capitolina* . Soon after, he declared circumcision equal to castration, in order to amalgamate the Jews into his Graeco-Roman *Oikoumene.* The Jewish peasants did not comply.

With the outbreak of the second and last revolt in Iudaea, a new, large local silver coin appeared once again, with the image of the great Temple of Jerusalem in place of the Roman emperor's head, and another «Declaration of Independence» in Palaeo-Hebrew letters: «Year One of the Redemption of Israel». But this time the rebels no longer had at their disposal the temple treasury with its silver supply. Thus, one could detect traces of Trajan's or Hadrian's head as it appeared on the underlying Roman coin, which Shimeon bar Kosiba and his men had overstruck. In this respect, Bar Kokhba's money is an even more classic example of rebel coinage than that issued during the Jewish war[23].

In the context of a symposium devoted to «Greece and Rome in Eretz Israel», it cannot be stressed too strongly that the only true rebel coinage ever produced in the Roman Empire originated here. Twice the Jews created an independent state and twice they produced sovereign coinage on the territory of the Roman province of Iudaea, within the boundaries of the Roman Empire.

---

[23] See L. MILDENBERG, The Coinage of the Bar Kokhba War, Aarau u.a. 1984.

# Schekel-Fragen

Seit Jahrhunderten beschäftigt sich die Forschung mit den jüdischen Schekeln[1]. Ging diese Faszination von der Erkenntnis aus, daß es sich um die erste souveräne Prägung der Juden überhaupt handelt[2], oder aber – wie ich meine – von den Geheimnissen, welche diese Silbermünzen des *Bellum Iudaicum* noch immer umgeben?

## 1. Schekel Israels

Warum stehen gerade diese Worte auf der Vorderseite der Schekel? Eigenartigerweise scheint diese Frage bisher nie gestellt worden zu sein. Dabei sind Währungs- und Münzbezeichnungen in der ganzen Antike auf den Prägungen selbst doch ungebräuchlich[3]. Im ersten Jahrhundert nach der Zeitenwende kommen sie jedenfalls sehr selten und nur auf wenigen Bronzen vor[4]. Daß wir das Geld der Aufständischen vor uns haben, ist durch eine Fülle typischer Münzfunde inner- und außerhalb Jerusalems bewiesen[5]. Aber der Schekel war ursprünglich keine Münzsorte. Das aus *šīn*, *qōf* und *lāmed* gebildete semitische Verbum bedeutet «abwiegen». Schekel (babylon. *šiqlu*) als Gewicht ist schon im 2.Jahrtausend nachgewiesen und kommt als solches in der Bibel vor. Daß aus der uralten Gewichtseinheit schließlich eine Münzsorte im *Bellum Iudaicum* wurde[6], ist darauf zurückzuführen, daß jeder Jude gehalten war,

---

[1] Das umfangreiche Schrifttum von 1180 (Mosche ben Maimon – «Maimonides») bis 1959 ist von L. KADMAN, The Coins of the Jewish War, 1960, 155-176 zusammengestellt. Vgl. B. KANAEL, Literaturüberblick Altjüdische Münzen, JNG 17 (1967) 182-184. 249-255.

[2] Die früheren Kleinmünzen in Silber waren eindeutig Emissionen der persischen, makedonischen und ptolemäischen Oberherrn für ihre Provinz «Yehud» oder «Yehuda», also Judäas; L. MILDENBERG, in: Essays M. Thompson, 1979, 183-196 [hier S. 67-76]. Die Bronzen der Herodianer waren autonome Scheidemünzen, also Kleingeld, geprägt mit Erlaubnis des seleukidischen und römischen Reiches.

[3] Anfangsbuchstaben von Nominalen und Wertzeichen wie Kugeln und Kreuze kommen auf Kleinsilber- und Bronzemünzen vor, aber selbst sie sind selten. Nirgend jedoch findet sich vor den jüdischen Schekeln von 66-70 das Wort «Siglos» oder «Schekel» auf den Münzen verzeichnet.

[4] Man denke an die Oboloi, Assaria und Chalki auf Chios und das bronzene Didrachmon auf Rhodos.

[5] Siehe die neueste Zusammenstellung bei Y. MESHORER, Ancient Jewish Coinage II, 1982, sub «Finds», 126f. Zu den Ausgrabungen von Masada und Jerusalem s. 96.

[6] Zur Gewichtseinheit siehe neuerdings SH. QEDAR, Gewichte aus drei Jahrtausenden. Auktionskatalog Münz-Zentrum Köln 32 (1978) 7f. 10f. 15f und 37 (1979) 11-32, wobei die Werte in Gramm sehr verschieden sind. – Zum Siglos-Schekel als Rechnungseinheit

eine Steuer an den Tempel von Jerusalem zu entrichten. Daß diese Steuer einen Halb-Schekel betrug, wissen wir aus der jüdischen Tradition, die sich ausführlich damit beschäftigt[7] und dabei Josephus bestätigt[8]. Wir können dies auch aus der römischen Judensteuer schließen, die Vespasian einführte, indem er die alte Tempelabgabe im Betrag beibehielt, aber nun in die Reichskasse abführte, worüber noch Dio Cassius um 200 berichtet[9]. Das Tetradrachmon der syrischen Provinzialprägung wog etwas über 14 g, das «Didrachmon», das von nun an die Juden zu zahlen hatten, also gut 7 g, genau das Gewicht der Halbschekel des *Bellum Iudaicum*. Auf dem Wege über die Steuereinheit der letzten Jahrhunderte vor dem Ausbruch des Krieges entstand also die Geldeinheit der Juden von 66-70, die nachher wieder zur Steuereinheit für die Römer wurde. Daß die Geldeinheit nun aber auf den jüdischen Münzen selbst betont wurde, ist kennzeichnend für die proklamatorische Prägung der Aufstände gegen Rom. Wenn dem so ist, war es dann noch nötig, auf der Münze anzugeben, um was für einen Schekel es sich handelt? Warum mußte man den Schekel Israels deklarieren? Auch hier führt der Weg zum Verständnis über die alte Tempelsteuer und den Willen zur Proklamation. Es steht fest, daß in den zweihundert Jahren vor dem Ausbruch des Krieges die Tempelabgabe mit dem «Silber von Tyros», und nur mit ihm, geleistet werden mußte[10]. Der Grund ist offensichtlich: die tyrischen Tetradrachmen[11] und Didrachmen bildeten die einzige stabile, verfügbare und neutrale Großsilberwährung, weil den Hasmonäern und Herodianern von den seleukidischen und römischen Oberherrn nur das Recht zur Prägung bronzener Scheidemünzen eingeräumt worden war. Daß man für den jüdischen Tempel das tyrische Silbergeld gesucht hatte, obwohl es den Kopf des Melqart-Herakles samt seiner Keule und den ptolemäisch-seleukidischen Adler auf der *prora* der Hafenstadt zeigte, mag nur uns heutige verwundern[12]. Vor dem *Bellum Iudaicum* galten ökonomische Gesetze, von

---

siehe P. FREI, Die Trilingue vom Letoon, SNR 56 (1977) 70-72 und 74-76. – Zum persischen Siglos von ungefähr 5,5 g als Münzeinheit siehe die attischen Schatzlisten (K. REGLING, Wörterbuch der Münzkunde, 1930, 632). – Der Schekel des *Bellum Iudaicum* entspricht als Münzeinheit mit seinem Durchschnittsgewicht von 14,30 g jedoch den in Phönizien, Syrien und Palästina seit Jahrhunderten gängigen reduzierten Tetradrachmen. Gewichte in diesem Wert und möglicherweise aus der Zeit des *Bellum Iudaicum* scheinen bisher nur in einem Exemplar bekannt geworden zu sein, sofern die Wertzahl richtig gelesen ist: QEDAR, Gewichte aus drei Jahrtausenden, 14, Nr. 51, Blei 14,32 g.

[7] Im eigenen Traktat «Scheqalim» in Mischna und Talmud.
[8] Siehe unten Anm. 13.
[9] Loeb Classical Library 176, 271: Epitome aus Cassius Dio 65.7.2.
[10] Tosephta Bechorot 8,7; vgl. Tosephta Ketubot 12,1 und 13,20.
[11] Die späthellenistischen Tyros-Tetradrachmen (BMC Phoenicia, 233-249, Nos. 44-212!) ebenso wie das etwa zeitgleiche Großsilber von Seleucia Pieria (BMC Galatia etc., 270f, Nos. 16-23), Aradus (BMC Phoenicia, 23-35, Nos. 178-291!) und Sidon (BMC Phoenicia, 158f, Nos. 100-110) folgen im Gewicht und teils auch in den Typen der Rückseite den seleukidischen und ptolemäischen Tetradrachmen der Zeit. Die seltenen Tetradrachmen von Ascalon (BMC Palestine, 107f, Nos. 18-20) hingegen sind leicht und zeigen – im Gegensatz zu den anderen Städteprägungen – das Bild eines Ptolemäers und der Kleopatra VII.
[12] Viele neuere archäologische Funde machen deutlich, daß man sich in der jüdischen Kunst der hellenistischen und römischen Zeit oft über das biblische Bilderverbot hinweg-

ideologischen Skrupeln war man weit entfernt. Mit dem Beginn des Krieges jedoch kam der Umschwung: es war von entscheidender Bedeutung für die Aufständischen, daß sie ihr eigenes Silbergeld schufen, das wichtigste Medium für die Unabhängigkeitserklärung in jener Zeit. Die Wortverbindung «Schekel Israels» war der dafür passende Slogan, die zündende Proklamation.

## 2. Ära

Das tyrische Silbergeld ist datiert. Das jüdische Aufstandsgeld ist es auch. An eine Ära jedoch kann es nicht anschließen; denn zwischen dem uralten Staat der Könige und der neugewonnene Souveränität liegt die Kluft von Jahrhunderten. Nichts ist eindrücklicher, ja bedeutsamer als der eine lapidare Buchstabe ʾālef , also der erste Buchstabe des nordsemitischen Alphabets. Er dokumentiert das erste Jahr der neuen Prägung, der neuen Ära und der neuen Zeit. Das ganze Münzbild der Vorderseite deklariert so auf engem Raum die Staatshoheit (Israel), die Währung (Schekel)[13] und das Prägejahr (ʾālef). Die Jahre 2, 3, 4 und 5 folgen, bis zur Eroberung Jerusalems und Zerstörung des Tempels im fünften Jahr, dem Jahre 70 nach der Zeitenwende.

## 3. Das heilige Jerusalem

Warum erklärt man «Jerusalem ist heilig» und «Das heilige Jerusalem» auf der Rückseite? Dies geschah keinesfalls aus ideologischen Gründen; denn die Geltung Jerusalems für die Juden mußte doch nicht betont werden, solange es jüdisch war und blieb. Dies steht ganz im Gegensatz zum Bar-Kochba-Krieg von 132-135, in dem man vermittels der Münzen zur Wiedergewinnung der Stadt aufrief. Auf den heute sogenannten tyrischen «Schekeln»[14] war zu lesen gewesen, daß sie aus dem «Heiligen Tyros» stammen. Auf den wirklichen Schekeln des *Bellum Iudaicum* stellte man deshalb fest, daß sie aus dem «Heiligen Jerusalem» kommen – ein schla-

---

setzte.

[13] Joseph., ant. 3,8,2 (§ 195) nennt das tyrische Tetradrachmon tatsächlich *siglos* , weil ihm seine Verwendung durch die Juden als Tempelschekel sehr wohl vertraut war, spricht aber im Bell. Iud. 2,21,2 (§ 592) nur von tyrischem Geld. Die Nennung der Münzbezeichnung Schekel auf den jüdischen Stücken ist einzigartig.

[14] G.F. HILL nennt das städtische Großsilber von Sidon und Tyros «Schekel», nicht aber das von Seleucia Pieria, Aradus und Ascalon, was nicht einzusehen ist. Das tyrische Tetradrachmon heute als «Schekel» zu bezeichnen, wäre nur statthaft, wenn es damals in der Stadt oder in zeitgenössischen Quellen so genannt worden wäre, wofür es keinen Anhaltspunkt gibt. Auf dem tyrischen Großsilber vom Anfang des 5. Jahrhunderts findet sich zwar die Wertzahl «Ein Dreissigstel» (Leu - MMAG 28.05.1974, Kunstfreund 170) und auf den kleineren Stücken steht «Halb-Silber», aber keinesfalls, wie E. BABELON, Traité 981, falsch übersetzt, «demi sicle d'argent». Von der Münzbezeichnung «Schekel» ist nun wirklich nicht die Rede.

gendes Argument für das neue jüdische Geld, das für Tempel und Wirtschaft[15] geschaffen worden war.

## 4. Die Tempelsteuer

Die Teilstücke der tyrischen Schekel sind heute wenig zu sehen. Die Halben sind sehr selten, die Viertel äußerst selten. Nun betrug die jüdische Tempelsteuer nur einen halben tyrischen «Schekel». Sind die tyrischen Halbstücke so meist in den Tempelschatz von Jerusalem gewandert und deshalb heute so selten geworden? Oder wurde in Wirklichkeit die Tempelsteuer pro Familie oder Gemeinde abgeliefert und in ganzen tyrischen «Schekeln» nach Jerusalem transportiert? Gab es gar Zahlung durch Verrechnung zugunsten der Tempelkasse, die doch wohl die Funktion eines zentralen Geldinstitutes gehabt haben könnte? Wir wissen es nicht. Es ist jedoch verständlich, daß die Aufständischen neben den ganzen auch halbe Schekel prägten. Die Bevölkerung erhielt mit dem Halbstück den eigenen handlichen Steuerbatzen und gleichzeitig eine praktische Münze, die sich zwischen dem höchsten Silberwert und dem größten Bronze-Nominal einordnen ließ.

## 5. Die Typen

Warum wählte man neue Münzbilder? Das Gefäß auf der Vorderseite[16] und der Granatapfel-Zweig[17] auf der Rückseite haben keine Vorgänger und keine Nachfolger. Mit der Feststellung, es handle sich um eindeutig jüdische Symbole, um Bilder, die «dem nationalen und religiösen Stolz der Bevölkerung entgegenkommen»[18], ist wenig gesagt. Warum griff man denn dann nicht auf die naheliegende Tempel-Menorah, den siebenarmigen Leuchter, auf den Kleinbronzen des letzten Hasmonäers Antigonos Mattathias zurück? Sind die drei Kornähren auf den Bronzemünzen von Agrippa I., dem Enkel von Herodes I., nicht wichtigere Früchte des Landes als Granatäpfel-Zweige? Ein Blick auf die Münzbilder der späteren Erhebung, des Bar-Kochba-Krieges, erhellt, warum die Männer des ersten Aufstandes für ihre Schekel auf die

---

[15] Die tyrischen Stadtprägungen Melqart-Herakles / Adler dauern von ungefähr 126 vor der Zeitenwende bis in Neros letzte Regierungsjahre. Aber schon unter Augustus setzt die syrische Provinzialprägung ums Jahr 20 in Antiochia ein, in Tyros erst unter Nero. Die römischen Tetradrachmen folgen im Gewicht ihren Vorgängern (Durchschnittsgewicht unter Nero 14,64 g nach W. WRUCK, Die syrische Provinzialprägung, 1931, 172), sind aber geringhaltig. Die Schekel und Halbschekel des *Bellum Iudaicum* mußten, da sie auch für die Tempelsteuer verwendet wurden, wiederum ein Gewicht von 14,00 bis 14,50 g haben, aber vollwertig sein.

[16] Y. MESHORER, Ancient Jewish Coinage II, 1982, 126f hat darauf hingewiesen, daß das Gefäss auf den Münzen des *Bellum Iudaicum* dem Kelch mit kurzem Fuß und runder Wölbung gleicht, der auf dem Schaubrottisch des Titus-Bogen in Rom steht.

[17] Man hat auch schon an Mohnkapseln und Hagebutten gedacht, also an andere in Judäa heimische Früchte und damit jüdische Bilder.

[18] Y. MESHORER, Ancient Jewish Coinage II, 1982, 106.

Münzbilder der Vergangenheit verzichteten. Eminent jüdische Bilder, der Tempel mit Tempelgeräten und Früchten des Landes, beherrschen die Prägungen der letzten Erhebung. Aber wie konnte Bar Kochbas Administration die jüdischen Tempelschekel kopieren, wenn es keinen Tempel mehr gab und der römische *Fiscus Iudaicus* das Feld beherrschte? Die Bilder der silbernen Schekel und Halbschekel mußten sich, weil sie als neues, jüdisches Geld und als neuer, eigener Steuerbatzen gebraucht wurden, eindeutig in ihren Bildern und Legenden von den tyrischen Stücken und den bronzenen Scheidemünzen der Hasmonäer und Herodianer abheben. Deshalb fiel die Wahl im Jahre 66 auf neue, frische und unverbrauchte Typen, die jedem Juden im Lande und jedem Tempelbesucher vertraut waren.

# 6. Die Schekel-Schrift

Mehr noch als das Münzbild spricht die Münzschrift für die staatliche und kulturelle Renaissance im *Bellum Iudaicum* . Die Legenden der Hasmonäer-Bronzen sind in paläo-hebräischer Kursive geschrieben, einer ausgesprochenen Schreibschrift. Dann folgten während eines Jahrhunderts die griechischen Legenden der Herodianer-Bronzen und der Kleinbronzen der römischen Prokuratoren. Mit dem *Bellum Iudaicum* erscheint nach dem langen Unterbruch wieder die paläo-hebräische Schrift, aber auf den Silbermünzen von einer ganz anderen Fraktur, wie es sie wiederum nicht vorher und nachher gegeben hat, die Schekel-Schrift. In erstaunlichem Gegensatz zu der Schrift auf den Bronzemünzen des Krieges, die im wesentlichen kursiv bleibt, sehen wir nun auf dem Silber monumentale, gerade stehende, einheitliche paläo-hebräische Buchstaben, wie sie auf Steininschriften vorkommen, nicht in geschriebenen Briefen und Dokumenten auf Papyrus und ähnlichen Materialien[19]. Wie ist so etwas möglich – in einer Zeit, in der, wie die Dokumentenfunde aus der judäischen Wüste zeigen, sich im täglichen Leben die neue jüdische Quadratschrift schon durchgesetzt hatte[20]? Die Administration der Aufständischen muß von einem im wahrsten Sinne des Wortes der alten Schrift kundigen Experten beraten worden sein, vielleicht des Verwalters des Tempelarchivs. In der monumentalen Kunstschrift dieses Mannes – oder seines Kreises – ist die uralte Schrift bewußt wiedererweckt und später folgerichtig von den Stempelschneidern der Schekelprägung der nachfolgenden Jahre verwendet worden.

---

[19] Die Unterschiede in Form und Duktus der Schrift auf den Schekeln sind gering. Vom Jahr 2 an hat sich jedenfalls die monumentale Kunstschrift eindeutig durchgesetzt.

[20] In den Dokumenten von der judäischen Wüste wird nur der Gottesname in paläo-hebräischen Lettern geschrieben, alles Andere in der neuen jüdischen Quadratschrift, die sich erstaunlicherweise aus der aramäischen Schreibung entwickelt hat.

## 7. Der Sinn der dicken Schekel

Früheren Forschern war es sehr wohl aufgefallen, daß die jüdischen Schekel einen ungewöhnlich dicken Schrötling aufweisen[21], während neuere Arbeiten unverständlicherweise darüber kein Wort verlieren oder gar die unbestreitbare Tatsache *expressis verbis* leugnen[22], daß es seit der archaischen Zeit so etwas noch gegeben habe[23]. Dabei mag die Herstellung der dicken Schrötlinge keine großen Schwierigkeiten bereitet haben, aber deren Prägung sehr wohl. Dies beweist die Randbearbeitung; denn Prägerisse wurden immer mit dem Hammer geglättet, wobei eine zugespitzte Randform entstand. Warum mußten die Arbeiter in der Münzstätte diese zusätzliche Arbeit auf sich nehmen? Warum mußten die jüdischen Schekel unbedingt dick sein? Nun, sie sollten den tyrischen Stücken in Gewicht und Feinheit gleichen, aber keinesfalls, wie wir gesehen haben, in den Bildern, den Legenden und der Schrift und schon gar nicht, wie jetzt klar wird, in der Form. Die Tyrer waren groß und dünn, deshalb sollten die jüdischen Schekel klein und dick ausgebracht werden. Es war den Aufständischen offensichtlich daran gelegen, daß ihr Silbergeld, welches die wiedergewonnene Souveränität verkündete, sein eigenes unverwechselbares Aussehen hatte. So viele Fragen, wird sich der Jubilar[24] sagen, aber wohl mit dem Schreibenden einig gehen, daß es nie genug sein können und schlüssige Antworten auf manche Probleme nur durch ein Schekel-Corpus gegeben werden können.

---

[21] Man denke nur an C.N. MEYER, Die Zuteilung der dicken silbernen Schekel und Halbschekel ... (1919) und H.J. STEIN, Why the thick Shekels belong to the First Revolt ..., The Numismatist 63 (1950).

[22] L. KADMAN, The Coins of the Jewish War, 1960, 61: «... the Jewish shekels are exactly of the same weight, size and thickness as the Tyrian shekels of the first century CE ...». Tatsächlich ist das Verhältnis von Dicke zu Durchmesser bei den jüdischen Stücken 1 zu 4, bei den tyrischen 1 zu 8. Die wirklichen Schekel sind also doppelt so dick wie die tyrischen «Schekel».

[23] Man mag an die persischen «Löwenstatere» des ausgehenden 4. Jahrhunderts denken, die einen verhältnismäßig massiven Schrötling aufweisen. Legt man sie aber neben die jüdischen Schekel, so wird klar, daß die letzteren wesentlich dicker sind und dies trotz niedrigerem Gewicht. Die «Löwenstatere» wiegen etwas über 15 g, ihr Durchmesser ist größer als der der jüdischen Schekel.

[24] Herbert A. Cahn.

# Numismatische Evidenz zur Chronologie der Bar Kochba-Erhebung*

(Tf. LII)

Über den letzten Freiheitskrieg, den die Juden unter dem Oberbefehl Bar Kochbas gegen das Römische Reich führten[1], geben die literarischen Quellen nur geringen Aufschluß[2]. Um so wesentlicher sind die Anhaltspunkte, die aus den Monu-

---

* Verf. ist Prof. F.M. Heichelheim, University of Toronto, Dr. H.A. Cahn, Basel, und Mr. H.B. Mattingly, Cambridge, für wertvolle Hinweise und vielen Persönlichkeiten für die Überlassung von Materialien verpflichtet. Über den Gegenstand der vorliegenden Studie hat Verf. im Dezember 1947 in der Freien Vereinigung Zürcherischer Numismatiker berichtet.

[1] Man hat diesem bedeutenden Ereignis in alten und neuen Sprachen verschiedenartige Namen beigelegt («Der Krieg des Ben Kosiba», «Der letzte Kampf», «Der Krieg der Juden», «Der zweite Aufstand», «Die Bar-Kochba-Erhebung», «Der zweite Jüdische Unabhängigkeitskrieg» u.a.). Daß sich keine prägnante und einheitliche Bezeichnung durchgesetzt hat, wird nach einer Prüfung des literarischen Befundes verständlich. Die jüdische Tradition spricht lediglich von dem Heerführer Ben Kosiba, erst Eusebius, der Vater der Kirchengeschichte, nennt ihn *Barchōchebas*. Daß dieser Mann mit dem Simeon auf den Münzen der Aufständischen identisch wäre, ist keinesfalls bewiesen [vgl. jetzt aber unten S. 235]. – Jedenfalls handelt es sich um den dritten und letzten Waffengang, da man nach dem *Bellum Iudaicum* (66-70) gegen die Flavier gewiß auch den heftigen Kampf der Juden gegen Trajan (115-117) während seiner parthischen Expedition rechnen muß, der insbesondere in Aegypten, in der Cyrenaika und auf Cypern geführt wurde.

[2] Die römischen, jüdischen und christlichen Überlieferungen sind spärlich, nicht eben zuverlässig und gewiß nicht unvoreingenommen. So verdunkelt die jüdische Tradition ganz bewußt das Bild des Heerführers. Eusebius' (hist. eccl. 4,6,1) Zugang ist auch hier apologetisch, und Dio Cassius' (69,12-14) in anekdotenhaftem Zusammenhange stehender Bericht ist nur in den Epitomen des griechischen Mönches Johannes Xiphilinus aus dem 11.Jahrhundert erhalten. Wertvoll sind die eher unbeabsichtigten Hinweise der literarischen Berichte: So zeugen die jüdischen Traditionen jedenfalls für eine Kriegsdauer von 3 1/2 Jahren, den denkwürdigen Schlußkampf um die Festung Bethar, die Bedeutung des Heerführers und des maßgebenden Schriftgelehrten Rabbi Akiba sowie für die Tatsache der Münzprägung. Dio, der amtliche römische Quellen aus der Zeit Hadrians benutzt, gibt wohl den äußeren Rahmen, die Schwere des Kampfes und die römische Strategie zutreffend wieder. (Auch die Rolle des von Britannien herangezogenen Feldherrn Sextus Minucius Julius Severus wird klar, obwohl Dio ihn verwechselt!) Die von ihm ganz genau genannten Zahlen der jüdischen Verluste sind aber wohl, obwohl sie nach Mommsens Vorgang allgemein wiedergegeben werden, ebensolche maßlose Übertreibungen wie manche talmudischen Berichte vom Wüten Ben Kosibas in Bethar. Der kundige Eusebius, der gewiß auch die jüdischen Überlieferungen gekannt hat, gibt einige zuverlässige Daten und Namen. Die *Vita Hadriani* des Spartian (14-2, ed. HOHL 1927, 15) und Fronto in seinen

mentalquellen – und unter ihnen nicht zuletzt den numismatischen – gewonnen werden können. Da nun auch die römische Reichsprägung nur einige wenige Hinweise[3] gestattet, so wird die Wichtigkeit der umfangreichen jüdischen Aufstandsprägungen offensichtlich. Und als ein Beitrag zu deren dringender Gesamtdarstellung möge auch die vorliegende Mitteilung zur Chronologie jenes bedeutenden Ereignisses gegen Ende der Regierung des Kaisers Hadrian dienen.

Daß die Münzen der Bar Kochba-Erhebung auf ältere, fremde Stücke überprägt sind, daß es sich also um *Überprägungen* handelt, ist sehr früh erkannt worden. Längst hat man auch daran gedacht, daß Spuren von Typen und Legenden der «Unterliegenden», fremden Münzen es ermöglichen könnten, die jüdischen Prägungen – und damit die Erhebung – zu *datieren*, nachdem ja die letzteren selbst nicht nach einer bekannten Aera bezeichnet sind[4]. Die bisherigen Untersuchungen waren zu einer *Früh*- Datierung (etwa 10 Jahre früher als der übliche Ansatz von etwa 131/132 bis 135 unserer Zeitrechnung) gelangt, weil sie sich auf wenige unterliegende Stücke und nur auf Denare beschränken mußten, deren Datierung zudem nicht gelingen konnte. Allerdings finden sich die Spuren der unterliegenden Gepräge auf den Silbermünzen der Aufständischen viel häufiger und deutlicher sichtbar als auf den Bronzen. Aber aus ihnen ließen sich bisher keine eindeutigen Kriterien ableiten, weil bei den Hadrian-Denaren des Ateliers von Rom und der östlichen Prägestätten nun einmal die sonst übliche Datierung auf Grund der Titulatur der Kaiser gar nicht möglich ist[5], und die häufig erkennbaren, unterliegenden Tetradrachmen von Tyros[6] und Antiochia ad Orontem eben keine Prägungen Hadrians, sondern seiner Vorgänger Nero bis Trajan sind.

---

Briefen über den parthischen Krieg (ed. NABER, 218) streifen den Krieg nur kurz.
[3]   Nach P.L. STRACK, Untersuchungen zur römischen Reichsprägung II, 1933, 135, spricht das Erscheinen eines Kriegsschiffes und die Legende FELICITATI AUG auf den Münzen für eine Seereise Hadrians auf den Kriegsschauplatz und zurück in den Jahren 134-135. Ferner bezögen sich sehr späte Siegesmünzen auf die Beendigung des Krieges 135 (p.137). Hadians Seereise erscheint auch auf Festmünzen von Elis. Vgl. C.T. SELTMANN, Greek Sculpture and Some Festival Coins, Hesperia 17 (1948) 78f. – Zu inschriftlichen Quellen vgl. M. AVI-YONAH, Tombstone of P. Aelius Capito, QDAP 8 (1938) 57f, n. 19.
[4]   Über die Prägeperioden v. im Text infra sub 2. - Vgl. L. MILDENBERG, The Eleazar Coins of the Bar Kochba Rebellion, Hist. Jud. 11 (1949) 99f, n. 41 [hier S. 199].
[5]   Hadrian nennt sich in der Reichsprägung COS III von 119 an bis zu seinem Tode 138! Der Vermerk des Konsulatsjahres an sich gestattet also Schlüsse für die Chonologie nur von 117 bis 119. Es gibt aber andere Kriterien für die Datierung der Reichsprägung und außerdem abweichende autonome Prägungen. Daran dachte L. HAMBURGER, Die Münzprägungen während des letzten Aufstandes der Israeliten gegen Rom, 1892, noch nicht und ließ sich auch von der Tatsache, daß er nur 3 – unzweifelhaft sehr frühe – Hadriandenare kannte, irreleiten. Zumal er auch den Quellenwert der literarischen Überlieferung überschätzte, so gelangte er zu einem «Beginn der Belagerung der Feste Bethar um das Jahr 120 d.chr.Zeitr» (ZfN 18, 332)! Neuerdings hat M. AUERBACH, Zur politischen Geschichte der Juden unter Kaiser Hadrian, Berlin - Wien 1924, 325 die Frühdatierung entschieden verfochten.
[6]   Vgl. L. MILDENBERG, Eine Überprägung des 2.Aufstandes der Juden gegen Rom, SNR 33 (1947-1948) 17-24.

In den letzten Jahrzehnten haben jedoch die Meister der römischen Münzkunde «wenige, jetzt gesicherte Kriterien der Chronologie»[7] herausgearbeitet, so daß man nun einige Hoffnung hegen konnte, an Hand der so häufigen Spuren auf den jüdischen Denaren endlich zum Ziele zu gelangen. Es tauchen nämlich *erst nach 128* zusätzliche, typenerklärende Inschriften auf dem Revers gemeinsam mit der Lapidarlegende *HADRIANUS AUGUSTUS* und dem Vermerk *PP* (zuerst auf dem Avers, dann einige Jahre später auf dem Revers) auf. Jetzt ließ also der Kaiser die Prinzipien, Ziele und denkwürdigen Ereignisse seiner Herrschaft auf den über Länder und Meere gelangenden Münzen proklamieren und sich schließlich auf ihnen «Pater Patriae» nennen.

Es wird verständlich, daß die eine *Früh*-Datierung vertretende These schon erschüttert würde, wenn man klare Spuren entweder einer typenerklärenden Legende oder des *PP* auf einer jüdischen Münze entdeckte. Als die unterliegende römische Münze geschlagen wurde, wäre dann nach der Frühdatierung der Freiheitskrieg der Juden schon einige Jahre beendet gewesen! Nun ist der Schreibende schon vor einiger Zeit auf einen jüdischen Denar gestoßen, der einst Colonel Allotte de la Fuye gehörte, und der in aller Deutlichkeit den Namen *HADRIANUS* und die typenerklärende Legende *IUSTITIA* erhalten hat (Tf. LII 1). Solche Bezeichnungen kommen nur zusammen mit dem Vermerk *PP* vor. Ob nun *PP* auf dem Avers oder Revers stand, könnte allein die völlig eindeutige Identifizierung eines der römischen Stempel zeigen, was trotz umfangreicher Vergleiche bei der Fülle der Varianten noch nicht gelingen konnte. Jedenfalls aber zeugen die ganz deutlichen Spuren für einen *nach* 128 erfolgten Stempelschnitt. Vielleicht gehört der Hadriandenar in die Prägeperiode von 128-132. Es ist jedoch auch die Möglichkeit nicht von vornherein auszuschließen, daß er aus der darauffolgenden Prägeperiode (etwa 132 bis etwa 135/36) stammt, wie das sehr ähnliche daneben abgebildete Stück (Tf. LII 2).

Nachdem nun die Versuche, mit Hilfe der Denare zu einer Datierung zu kommen, zu diesem vorläufigen Ergebnis geführt hatten, bestand kein Grund, sich auch weiterhin auf diesen Weg zu beschränken. Es blieb zu untersuchen, ob nicht doch die spärlichen Spuren auf den viel häufigeren Bronzen der Bar Kochba-Erhebung zum gewünschten Ziele führten. Nachdem als Schrötlinge hier die verschiedenartigsten fremden Bronzen[8] dienten, so schien es durchaus denkbar, daß auch die Erzeugnisse der dem Aufstandsgebiet am nächsten liegenden *autonomen* Prägestätten – etwa Ascalon[9] und Gaza – auftauchten. Insbesondere waren da die *Mittelbronzen Hadrians*

[7] So P.L. STRACK, Untersuchungen zur römischen Reichsprägung II, 1933, 133. – H.B. MATTINGLY, Coins of the Roman Empire in the British Museum, Vol. III, 1936, CXIV: «The chronology of the reign is extremely difficult ... The acceptance by Hadrian of the title 'Pater Patriae' early in AD 128 gives an important dividing line in the long period from AD 119 to 138».

[8] E. ROGERS, A handy guide to Jewish coins, 1914, Pl. 7,4 hat eine Mittelbronze mit ganz deutlichen Spuren der unterliegenden Ptolemäerprägung veröffentlicht!

[9] Die Bronzeprägung Ascalons von Nero bis Hadrian ist viel umfangreicher als die Gazas und hat gewiß den aufständischen Juden unterliegende Münzen geliefert. Spuren der Ascalon-Gepräge finden sich häufig. Ein solches deutliches Stück ist von A. REIFENBERG, Ancient Jewish Coins, ²1947, No. 200a publiziert worden. Da es Hadrian-Bronzen von Ascalon noch in den dreißiger Jahren gibt, und dieselben nach der Aera der Stadt datiert

*von Gaza* aus den ersten Jahren des 3. Jahrzehnts zu beachten, da diese ja *doppelt* datiert sind! Und tatsächlich hat schon MADDEN ein solches Stück in einem Holzschnitt (Tf. LII 8) abgebildet und es allerdings Trajan zugeschrieben[10]. Auch ROGERS besaß eine solche Bronze und publizierte sie vor einem Vierteljahrhundert in einer ausgezeichneten Photographie als ein Beispiel für eine besonders deutliche Überprägung. Auch er sah in seiner Münze eine Prägung Trajans[11]! In Wirklichkeit handelt es sich wieder um eine jener doppelt datierten Mittelbronzen Hadrians von Gaza (Tf. LII 5). Und diesmal sind die Spuren auf Avers und Revers ganz eindeutig und in unserem Zusammenhange von entscheidender Wichtigkeit. Ein drittes Stück (Tf. LII 7) befindet sich im Britischen Museum. Es ist mit seinem deutlichen *EΠI* sicher nach Gaza zu weisen, obwohl die Vermutung HILLs in seinem BMC Palestine in ganz andere Richtung ging[12]. Vermutlich gehört auch noch eine zweite Münze des Britischen Museums (Tf. LII :9) in diese Serie. Daß es noch manch andere gibt, ist sehr wahrscheinlich.

## 1. Die unterliegenden Gaza-Bronzen Hadrians

Ende der zwanziger Jahre des 2. nachchristlichen Jahrhunderts war Hadrian auf seiner großen Orientreise auch nach Gaza gekommen. Zu Ehren seines Besuches anläßlich dieser Rundreise, der ἐπιδημία, wurden die Prägungen dieser Stadt von jenem Jahr 129-130 an datiert[13]. Es wird nun auf dem Revers, der die Stadtgöttin und den Stadtnamen zeigt, stets verzeichnet: *A·EΠI, ·B·EΠI, ·Γ·EΠI*, also erstes Jahr (seit) der Rundreise, zweites Jahr, drittes Jahr usw. Außerdem aber steht das laufende Jahr der alten Aera von Gaza weiterhin im Münzrund: *YP, AYP, BYP* = Jahr 190, Jahr 191, Jahr 192, usw. Aber nur bei der Serie des Jahres mit den Datenvermerken *Γ·EΠI* und *BYP* (192) wird das letztere Datum auf den kleinen, freien Raum zwischen dem Stadtnamen und dem senkrecht aufgestützten Speer der Stadtgöttin vermerkt. (Auf dem Avers aller dieser Prägungen lesen wir stets *AYTOKAITPA · AΔPIANOΣ* um die nach rechts gestellte, lorbeergeschmückte und bekleidete Büste Hadrians). Wenn man also auf einer jüdischen Bronze der Aufständischen mit ungefähr demselben Durchmesser und Gewicht[14] einen dieser beiden eindeutigen Vermerke des Datums

---

sind, so bestünde auch hier die theoretische Möglichkeit, daß aus solchen datierbaren Spuren Rückschlüsse auf die Chronologie der Bar Kochba-Erhebung gezogen werden könnten.

[10] F.W. MADDEN, Coins of the Jews, 1881, 240, No. 22: "struck on a coin of Trajan».

[11] E. ROGERS, A handy guide to Jewish coins, 1914, 91, No. 3: «overstruck on AE of Trajan at Gaza. The Tyche of Trajan's coin quite clear».

[12] G.F. HILL, BMC Palestine, 1914, 312, n. 81: «Struck on a coin of Caesarea (?) such as BMC, Galatia, 47, no. 18».

[13] Vgl. BMC Palestine, 1914, LXXIIIf.

[14] Genaue Übereinstimmung ist nicht zu erwarten; denn einerseits variieren die fremden Serien in Größe und Gewicht und andererseits vergrößert sich der Durchmesser durch das Aushämmern der alten Gepräge und verkleinert sich das Gewicht durch das nachherige Abfeilen stehengebliebener Reste.

entdecken könnte, so stünde fest, daß die unterliegende Münze im Prägejahr 131-132 in Gaza geprägt worden ist.

## 2. Die jüdischen Münzen

Die häufigsten Mittelbronzen der Bar Kochba-Erhebung zeigten auf dem Avers ein großes Weinblatt mit einer Ranke am Stiel hängend und auf dem Revers eine Dattelpalme mit zwei Früchtebündeln. Die Inschrift um das Weinblatt lautet je nach der Prägeperiode «Jahr Eins der Erlösung Israels», «Jahr 2 der Freiheit Israels» und «Der Freiheit Jerusalems». Unter der Palme steht stets der Name Simeon, entweder mit dem Zusatz «Fürstpatriarch Israels» oder nur ausgeschrieben in fünf Buchstaben und schließlich abgekürzt durch die drei ersten Buchstaben.

In diese umfangreichste Serie der Gesamtprägung gehören eben auch die vier vorliegenden Münzen, auf denen sich Teile von Typen und Legenden der Prägung von Gaza erhalten haben. Alle vier stammen aus der dritten und letzten Prägeperiode, die durch die Inschrift «Der Freiheit Jerusalems» gekennzeichnet ist. Das wichtigste ROGERsche Exemplar (Tf. LII 6) hat den Namen Simeon in fünf Buchstaben, obwohl nur drei (der erste, zweite und fünfte) deutlich zu erkennen sind. Diese jüdische Münze ist – ebenso wie die von MADDEN im Holzschnitt publizierte und das eine Stück des Britischen Museums – eine späte Prägung, jedoch kein Erzeugnis der allerletzten Zeit, keine Notprägung. Sowohl Stempelschnitt wie Ausprägung dürften in einem Zeitpunkt erfolgt sein, als die Organisation der Aufständischen, und damit auch ihre Münzwerkstätte, noch alle ihre Funktionen voll ausübte[15]. Nicht der Fall ist dies bei dem zweiten Exemplar des Britischen Museums, in dem wir eine unterliegende Gaza-Bronze vermuten (Tf. LII 9). Hier ist der Stempelschnitt offensichtlich von unkundiger Hand, in der Hast und Not der Auflösung, erfolgt; denn die Legende unter der Palme ist nicht nur spiegelverkehrt (retrograd), sondern auch noch die mechanische (positive) Übertragung einer schon sehr späten irregulären und flüchtigen Inschrift.

## 3. Die Überprägung

Die Münzen von Gaza sind stets seitwendig («direct die-position»), diese[16] jüdischen Mittelbronzen jedoch kopfwendig («revers die-position») geprägt. Das von MADDEN

---

[15] Die Feststellung eines einzigen, geschlossenen Systems von Stempelverbindungen, das alle Kleinbronzen gemeinsam mit allen Silberdenaren sämtlicher drei Prägeperioden umfaßt, spricht für das Bestehen einer zentralen, die Staatsgewalt ausübenden Organisation, welche dieses eigene Geld in einer einzigen Münzstätte schuf. Vgl. L. MILDENBERG, Hist. Jud. 11 (1949) 99ff, appendix [hier Tf. LIII - LIV].

[16] Die ganze Serie mit den Typen Weinblatt und Dattelbaum wendet kopfwendig, ebenso sämtliche Kleinbronzen. Seitwendig ist die Stempelsetzung dagegen bei den Großbronzen und der Leier-Serie der Mittelbronzen ebenso wie bei den Tetradrachmen. Daß aus dieser Tatsache jedoch nicht weitgehende Schlüsse gezogen werden dürfen, darauf weist schon allein der Umstand hin, daß die gewiß geschlossene Denar-Reihe doppelte Stempelstellung

abgebildete Stück ist so entstanden, daß der jüdische Münzmeister als Schrötling die Prägung von Gaza mit deren Revers nach oben – und zwar ohne jede Verschiebung ganz senkrecht – in sein Gerät einlegte und dann mit seinem eigenen Reversstempel überprägte. Die senkrecht mit der Spitze nach oben stehende Palme verdeckt also hier die senkrecht mit dem Kopf nach oben stehende Stadtgöttin völlig, da ja beide genau in der Münzmitte dargestellt sind. Auch das Weinblatt des jüdischen Avers-Stempels kommt also genau auf die Kaiserbüste des Avers der Gazaprägung zu liegen – nur mit dem Stiel nach unten, da die beiden Prägungen ja nicht im selben Sinne wenden! Der überprägenden Hand ist jedoch der Hammerschlag zwar wuchtig genug geraten, aber etwas nach links abgerutscht, so daß am rechten Rande des Revers neben der Palme sich von der fremden Legende die Buchstaben *EΠ* des Gaza-Revers an der «richtigen» Stelle erhalten haben. Genau darunter auf dem Avers blieb der ganze erste Teil der Legende *A ΥΤΚΑΙ ΤΡΑ* nebst Schleife und Enden des Stirnbandes stehen.

Bei der im heutigen Zusammenhange besonders interessierenden Münze ROGERS' wurde wieder Revers auf Revers geprägt, jedoch die als Unterlage dienende Gaza-Bronze um 90° im entgegengesetzten Uhrzeigersinne verschoben, so daß der Palmenstamm und die Stadtgöttin mit ihrem langen Speer sich gegenseitig durchschneiden, der obere Teil des Weinblattes mit dem Stiel aber das Profil Hadrians zudeckt. Bei dem sicher nach Gaza gehörenden Exemplar des Britischen Museums mit *EΠΙ* liegt nochmals Revers auf Revers, der «Schrötling» ist jedoch um 90° im Uhrzeigersinne verschoben. Auch bei der vierten abgebildeten Überprägung, jener späten jüdischen Münze, liegt Revers auf Revers, was neben dem höchst charakteristischen Profil und dem Gewicht (vgl. Anm. 14) auf ein Erzeugnis von Gaza schließen läßt. Jedenfalls ließen sich also vorerst drei mit Sicherheit nach Gaza zu weisende Mittelbronzen und eine weitere, mit großer Wahrscheinlichkeit hierher gehörende Münze feststellen.

Von diesen Stücken ist das Exemplar aus der Sammlung ROGERS (Tf. Nr. 6) nicht nur deshalb besonders bemerkenswert, weil auf ihm beidseitig große Teile der unterliegenden Typen deutlich erhalten geblieben sind. Seine Bedeutung liegt besonders darin, daß links von dem die Palme ganz sichtbar durchschneidenden Speer beträchtliche, desgleichen teilweise durch den Stamm gehende Reste des Datumvermerkes 192 der Aera von Gaza (= 3. Jahr der Rundreise = 131/132 unserer Zeitrechnung) zu erkennen sind. Dies ist entscheidend; denn würde die unterliegende Gaza-Bronze aus irgendeinem anderen Prägejahr vor oder nach 131/132 stammen so hätten keinesfalls gleich links neben dem Speer im Münzzentrum irgendwelche Spuren entdeckt werden können. Auf den Gaza-Bronzen aller anderen Prägejahre ist nämlich dieser Datumvermerk an einer ganz anderen Stelle (rechts unten am Rande nach dem *EΠΙ* und nicht mitten im Feld) angebracht, und links vom Speer ist nur leerer Raum zu finden. Zu allem kann man aber eben diesen abweichenden Datumsvermerk von 192 der Aera von Gaza auf dem ROGERschen Exemplar mit völlig genügender Deutlichkeit erkennen. Glücklicherweise kann die Untersuchung also hier zu einer eindeutigen Datierung gelangen, die im Grunde dem zu schwachen Hammerschlag des überprägenden Münzmeisters der Aufständischen zu danken ist.

---

und außerdem noch Verschiebungen kennt.

Auf solche Weise erhielten sich hartnäckig fast auf der ganzen Fläche Teile der Gaza-Stempel. Den Lorbeer des vergöttlichten Kaisers und das Füllhorn der Stadtgöttin tilgten die Juden schließlich mit der Feile! Aber in die Münzmitte konnten sie mit diesem Instrument nicht gelangen, weshalb wir noch heute die Umrisse der Tyche mit ihrem Speer und beträchtliche Teile des Datumvermerks erkennen können.

*

Aus diesem Befunde ist nun der zwingende Schluß zu ziehen, daß der Vorgang der Überprägung bei dem ROGERschen Exemplar nur nach der Entstehung der Gaza-Bronze, also nach 131/132 erfolgt sein kann. Damit ist der *terminus post quem* für diese Münze des letzten Krieges der Juden gegen die Römer gewonnen, und der Versuch zu dessen Frühdatierung an der numismatischen Evidenz gescheitert. Unter keinen Umständen kann im Augenblick der Überprägung der Kampf schon zu Ende gewesen sein. Als *terminus ante quem* für den Zusammenbruch der Bar Kochba-Erhebung, also den Fall der letzten jüdischen Bergfeste Bethar, hat man mit guten Gründen die zweite Akklamation Hadrians *IMP(erator) II* in den ersten Herbstmonaten 135 angenommen[17]. Sie muß ja nach einem großen Ereignis, einem bedeutenden Siege erfolgt sein. Da nun lateinische und griechische Inschriften, die besseren literarischen Überlieferungen[18] und einige Hinweise der römischen Reichsprägung und der Prägung von Olympia-Elis für den bisher oft angezweifelten Ansatz von 132-135 sprechen, so ist dieser durch die nun in Gestalt der Über-prägungen aufgezeigte numismatische Evidenz zur Gewißheit geworden. Diese Auf-hellung der Chronologie der Bar Kochba-Erhebung dürfte der römischen wie jüdischen Geschichtsforschung willkommen sein.

---

[17] H.B. MATTINGLY, Coins of the Roman Empire in the British Museum, Vol. III, 1936, CXf (Zeittafel); P.L. STRACK, Untersuchungen zur römischen Reichsprägung II, 1933, 136.

[18] In CIL XII,82, einem lateinischen Militärdiplom von Wroxeter, führt Hadrian im April 135 noch nicht den Titel *IMP II*. In diesem Zeitpunkt dürfte also die Niederlage der Juden noch nicht besiegelt gewesen sein. Dagegen haben griechische und lateinische Inschriften vom Herbst und Winter 135 den neuen Titel. Vgl. F.M. HEICHELHEIM, New Light on the End of Bar Kochba's War, JQR 34 (1943), 61; C.T. SELTMANN, Hesperia 17 (1948) 85.

# The Eleazar Coins of the Bar Kochba Rebellion[*]

## (Tf. LIII - LIV)

> «De quelque côté que l'on se tourne, les contradictions abondent et les difficultés se multiplient. C'est en recherchant les pièces nouvelles, en les publiant à mesure qu'elles se présentent, en accumulant les rapprochements et les hypothèses, que l'on pourra trouver la clef de tous ces mystères et sortir de l'incertitude dans laquelle je suis contraint de demeurer. J'ai tâché de donner l'exemple, c'est ma seule excuse» (Le Comte M. DE VOGÜÉ, Monnaies Juives, Eleasar, RN 1860, 290).

## Introductory Remarks[1]

In these notable words MELCHIOR DE VOGÜÉ, a pioneer in Semitic epigraphy, summed up the task of Jewish numismatics, namely, a comprehensive, careful assembly and publication of the scattered material as well as an examination and comparison of the various interpretations. This task is still as urgent today as it was almost a century ago.

In recent decades, the paths of north-Semitic epigraphy and Jewish numismatics seem to have crossed all too rarely, which is especially regrettable since Jewish numismatics is in need of a basic discussion of the epigraphical problems, for the coin-inscriptions are late derivatives from old, timehonored script-characters, which were revived once more and played their part in history in the heroic wars of the Jews against Rome.

The last Jewish rebellion against the *Imperium Romanum* (132-135 C.E.) produced the last independent coinage of the Jews, which in its range and significance far surpasses the earlier productions. The choice of the ancient script and traditional symbols, the proclamations conveyed by the inscriptions, and the incessant recoining of an astonishing quantity of foreign silver and bronzes are highly significant for the spirit and aims of the rebels. The indications which we may thus gain from the study of this coinage for the history of the rebellion are all the more important

---

[*] This study is dedicated to the cherished memory of the author's mother, Mrs. Jenny Loeb Mildenberg, born May 6, 1887, in Wohnbach near Frankfort on-the-Main, who died at an unknown date in one of the eastern extermination camps as a victim of Nazi barbarism.
[1] The writer wishes to express his gratitude to all the authors, museum curators, coin dealers, and collectors, who were kind enough to supply materials or to make suggestions for the present study. He is specially indebted to Dr. H.A. Cahn of Basel.

because only few other archaeological sources are available and the scanty literary tradition is not of a high value.

The present study is concerned with that particular series of the rebellion coinage the inscription of which is very hard to decipher, namely, the words *ʾlʿzr hkhn* , «Eleazar the Priest», occurring in a great variety of forms. The other name found with a title in a coin inscription, *Šmʿwn nśyʾ Yśrʾl* «Simon, Nasi ('Patriarch') of Israel», has at any rate a familiar ring and permits some explanations. In contrast to this, the title «The Priest» (compare the titulature of the Maccabean coinage, «The High Priest») is surprising. No one knows the reason why the «Eleazar» inscription appears in so irregular a manner on the coins, what caused the minting of this series, or who this Eleazar really was.

For this reason the author will attempt to take stock of all the Eleazar coins known to him, to clarify their singular epigraphical character, as well as their position and importance in the rebels' coinage, and finally to explain the meaning of the name and title. This will lead to a provisional survey of that coinage as a whole.

# 1. The Inscriptions and Types of the Eleazar Coins

## 1.1. The Legends

The over-all picture which we obtain of the Hebrew inscriptions on Jewish coins from the period of the Maccabees to that of Bar Kochba is unique.

A conscious revival of a language no longer spoken in daily life took place. It was an emphatic reinstatement of what was old, venerable and sanctified by law[2]. During the whole period the spoken language was Aramaic; but for the legends of the coins Hebrew was used.

These legends were written in the so-called «coin-script», which in itself is an intentional revival of the old Hebraic cursive-script of the first half of the first millennium BCE. The script in general use during these later centuries was the Aramaic in square forms. The revived old script as used for the inscriptions by unskilful craftsmen no longer obeys its original laws, for there had been no continuity of survival or development up to the time of the striking of the Eleazar coins. Their script cannot be compared with the contemporary script that was then in general use[3]. It was

---

[2] It was rooted in the very nature of the Maccabaean community (after the victory of the Orthodox over the Hellenists; cf. E. BICKERMANN, Der Gott der Makkabäer, Berlin 1937, 137), as well as in that of both rebellions against Rome (recovery of political sovereignty and of religious as well as cultural independence).

[3] For this reason alone, one should not rely solely on purely epigraphic argumentation; for a long time it misled the advocates of the early dating of the thick shekels and the alleged bronzes of Simon Maccabaeus, until finally the question was decided against them by archaeological, numismatic, and historical evidence. This threefold evidence offers proof against the latest, and occasionally suggestive, attempt at early dating, W. WIRGIN, The Problem of the Shekels, Seaby's Coin and Medals Bulletin 366 (Nov. 1948) 495-499.

merely a readoption of an obsolete script for the single and important purpose of serving as the official script for the coinage[4].

The fact of such a revival may cause a great variety of opinions and errors[5]. It is possible that several old models with differing characters were employed. There is considerable divergence in the training and general approach of the die-engravers. Moreover, the conditions caused by years of bitter war against the Roman Empire make themselves felt at every point. Far more important than a careful execution or flawless inscribing of the legends became the mere fact that the Jews' own national symbols and their own timehonored characters appear on the coins to proclaim the reestablishment of Jewish sovereignty. All these considerations explain the many irregular features of the coin-script most typically represented by the inscription «Eleazar the Priest»[6].

## 1.2. The Eleazar Legends

The two words «Eleazar the Priest» never occur on the coins of the Bar Kochba Rebellion in regular normal writing. The letters are grouped on the bronzes under the palm and on the denars around the jug in so many perplexing ways that generations of students had to make all kinds of efforts to decipher this legend. At first they thought even of some secret code, in fact, a deliberate mystification. It was only at the beginning of this century that one could finally break the vicious circle of

---

[4] The script on the ossuaries of the time has quite another character. It is clearly square in form, even though it has a rather cursive appearance; cf. E. SUKENIK, in: Samuel Krauss Anniversary Volume, Jerusalem 1936, 87-93. The same applies to the script of the Nash Papyrus, W.F. ALBRIGHT, The Nash Papyrus: A Biblical Fragment from the Maccabean Age, JBL 56 (1947) 145-176. Even if one should assume a dating 100-200 years later, cf. F. ROSENTHAL, Die aramaistische Forschung seit Th. Nöldekes Veröffentlichungen, Leiden 1939, 373, this still is a Hebraic papyrus from the time of the coinage under consideration and in a script far removed from the ancient Hebrew writing (the Nash Papyrus includes such fundamental items as the Decalogue and the «Shema» prayer).

[5] In this connection, D. DIRINGER, Le Iscrizioni Antico-Ebraiche Palestinesi, Firenze 1934, 329, n. 1, Appendice II, writes: «Non è del resto escluso che, ... cosi accanto alla scrittura quadrata possa essere rimasta sempre in uso la scrittura antica ...». This view, however, is contradicted by the archaeological findings (see above), the historical development of the script (the square Hebraic script developed by way of the Aramaic, which served as the official script of the Persian Empire, and not directly from the ancient Hebrew cursive script; cf. also the script of the Elephantine papyri), and the numismatic evidence (the abundance of irregular forms from the various periods of coinage shows that even the die-engravers – not to speak of the public – were not fully acquainted with the Old Hebraic script).

[6] Strange letter-order, omissions, transpositions, abbreviations, parts of legends reversed, and whole inscriptions written in «retrograde» direction, distorted forms, and meaningless surface-scratched characters. Even such complete series as the tetradrachms of the Bar Kochba Rebellion and the «thick» silver shekels of the Jewish War are not free from several of these features. The latter, however, remain in spite of this fact an exceptional phenomenon, because of the perfect minting, their uniform symbolism, and monumental script. This phenomenon still awaits explanation.

strange misreadings and explain the recurrence of the two words in varying forms[7]. Since then, however, no effort has been made to identify every single letter of this irregular legend on the basis of the material which became available in ever increasing quantities. Hence, even now the alphabet used in the Eleazar inscription is not quite clear and correct as given in the standard script-tables[8], and misreadings have obstinately perpetuated themselves up to today[9]. For this reason the presentation in words and pictures on Pl. LIV of the epigraphical findings in the Eleazar legends may well prove useful.

E 1: AE. 'Retrograde' inscription on both sides of the trunk of the palm, in two horizontal lines. The *lāmed* is set half a row lower.

E 2: AE. 'Retrograde' like E 1, only the two letters, *zayin* and *rēsh*, are set about half a row above the others, on the right.

---

[7] It was M. DE VOGÜE who first paved the way for the understanding of these legends (Monnaies Juives, Eleasar, RN 1860, 290), shortly after F. DE SAULCY had published Eleazar coins in woodcuts (Recherches sur la numismatique judaïque, Paris 1854). Two years after the publication of DE VOGÜE's study, M.A. LEVY, Geschichte der jüdischen Münzen, Leipzig 1862, 99, allowed himself one of the worst misreadings in the history of this deciphering. An important advance was marked by F.W. MADDEN with his Hebraic alphabet-table (Coins of the Jews, London 1881). F.W. MADDEN, however, still attributed the Eleazar coins to the first rebellion, the Jewish War, whereas TH. REINACH, Les Monnaies Juives, Paris 1888, on purely numismatic grounds ascribed them to the second, the Bar Kochba Rebellion. L. HAMBURGER, Die Münzprägungen während des letzten Aufstandes der Israeliten gegen Rom, ZfN 18 (1892) 241-348, discussed the personality of Eleazar and gave attention to the overstrikes; but they induced him to a dating which is ten years too early. In the standard epigraphical works there are some brief but valuable suggestions (cf. M. LIDZBARSKI, Handbuch der nordsemitischen Epigraphik, Weimar 1898, 184-185; G.A. COOKE, A Textbook of North-Semitic Inscriptions, Oxford 1903, 352-359, Pl. X). E. SCHÜRER, Geschichte des jüdischen Volkes I, Leipzig, 1901, appendix 769, drew too far-reaching conclusions from the fact that no Eleazar issues from the second and third coinage periods were known. G.F. HILL, BMC Palestine, London 1914, presented the then state of secure knowledge which is even today basic. In the same year, E. ROGERS, A Handy Guide to Jewish Coins, London 1914, 56, n. 1, Pl. 5:2) published the first Eleazar coins of the third coinage period. The only specimen known from the second period was first described and illustrated in 1931 by C. LAMBERT, Coins in the Palestine Museum, QDAP 1 (1931) 71, Pl. XXXVII, No. 8; see infra Appendix, Explanations to Plate, No. 5). More recently, M. NARKISS, Coins of Palestine I, Jerusalem 1936 (in Hebrew) reviewed the Eleazar bronzes, and A. REIFENBERG, Ancient Jewish Coins, Jerusalem 21947, dealt with all the Eleazar issues.

[8] HILL's alphabet-table does not list the normal form of the letter *zayin*, which had been discovered by DE VOGÜE and COOKE and is today well known from the inscriptions, particularly from the seals of the royal period. HILL faithfully reproduced the correct form on p. 302, under No. 1. The form of the *kāf* is also not rendered correctly. All the retrograde forms are found among the normal characters. It may be noted that the British Museum has apparently no specimen with the die E 3; nor does it possess any Eleazar denarius (according to information received from Mr. E.H.G. Robinson).

[9] M. NARKISS, Coins of Palestine I, 1936, 122, misread three *hē*'s and also 10 letters instead of 9. He did not list E 3 and E 5.

E 3: AE. Inscription with normally formed characters and no inversions; every single letter – read in the customary script-direction – can be clearly identified. The nine letters, however, are not arranged in lines, but scattered fortuitously on the free flan under the date palm.

E 4: AE. Inscription in three horizontal rows – normal letter-forms in normal script-direction. Only the last letter of the second word, the *nūn*, has fallen out of line. The die-engraver, finding at the end that he had no more room for this letter, put it in where there was a space – in the middle. The last letter is to the right of the trunk, in the second row after the *zayin* .

E 5: AR. The Eleazar Legend on the denars. It can be read (with the normal form of the letters) in the regular direction, but two letters, *zayin* and *lāmed* , are inverted, and the *kāf* and *rēsh* have a form somewhat modified by the engraver. The second word is written in full with *wāw*, so that there are ten letters.

According to this, E 3, E 4 and, with the two exceptions mentioned, E 5 as well, offer the correct letter-forms for the «Eleazar» legend in the normal script-direction. The lettering of legends E 1 and E 2 in the retrograde script-direction allow us to test the findings from a concrete example: seen in a mirror, they correspond completely to the normal forms. In fact, the very reason for the existence of these 'retrograde' inscriptions is that the inexperienced die-sinker adopted with great exactitude the lettering of this model (positive, of course) for his die, without knowing the basic rule of his trade. Hence, it is clear that only the normal forms should be introduced from the Eleazar alphabet into the tabulation of the Jewish coin-script: these forms are shown on Pl. LIV by the letter E.

### 1.3. The Other Legends on the Eleazar Coins

The above exposition of the epigraphical findings has shown a large number of remarkable and characteristically irregular forms in the Eleazar legends which are arranged around the palm or the jug[10]. What is the picture when one turns to the legends[11] around the grape-cluster on the other side of the Eleazar coins? There we do not find a single retrograde or misplaced letter, let alone retrograde legends or any arbitrary scattering of the inscription[12]. Whoever engraved this die, knew the fundamental rules of his craft. Fully understanding how it was to be achieved, he set out to produce legible, comprehensible inscriptions. Here is a typical phenomenon: the

---

[10] The Eleazar inscriptions are still more irregular than the legends on other series, so that it is not surprising that scholars could think of an intentional mystification or of a secret code. The reason for these irregular features may be found in the fact that the Eleazar dies of the bronzes of the first year had been sunk at a very early date.

[11] With the exception of the so-called «hybrid» denars, which show on the obverse the first three letters of the name Simon in a wreath.

[12] E 3; cf. supra note 10.

dies of the obverse and reverse of the coins of this series must be the work of more than one hand[13]. The man who finally struck the Eleazar coins thus combined the productions of several engravers. It will become clear in the course of the present inquiry that the minter even employed dies from different periods for a single coin; he did not cast in preparation any blank of his own, but «overstruck» a foreign, already current coin.

The inscriptions, all easily legible, even if occasionally rather abbreviated, which accompany the Eleazar legends, are also found on the other issues of the Bar Kochba Rebellion. The epigraphical picture which they present – so far as the material at present available permits – may here be summarized as follows.

G: The Legends around the Grapes

G 1: «Year One of the Redemption of Israel» *šnt ʾḥt lgʾlt Yśr(ʾl)*.
The die is a gem of Jewish engraving art. The epigraphically flawless inscription fits elegantly into the flan around the grape cluster. These small bronze pieces – their size was predetermined, the denomination being very common in the East – offered little room for the 16 letters of this, the longest legend of the «Bar-Kochba» coinage. Even the engravers of the tetradrachms which were twice as large failed to find so happy a solution for the problem of how to use the available space. Our artist saw that, even if quite small, 16 letters would not fit into the space on the coin. He contented himself with rendering 14 letters with delicate conciseness, correctly, clearly, and in a satisfying aesthetic form, and resolutely omitted the last two – *ʾālef* and *lāmed* . The example of his abbreviation, which was in no way overdone, and perfectly understandable, was followed in the later issues.

G 2: «Y(ear) Two of the Fr(eedom) of Israel» *š(nt) b lḥr(wt) Yśr(ʾl)*.
This inscription has no less than three abbreviations which, however, are not confusing. The form of the letters is clumsy. The vinestem and the point of the grape cluster arbitrarily divide two words. Yet, there is no really irregular feature observable.

G 3: «To the Freedom of Jerusalem» *lḥrwt Yršl(m)*.
Here a letter is omitted only in the second word, namely, the last *mēm*, whereas the first word is unabbreviated and indeed written out in full with the *wāw* , and between the second and third letters of this word there is an empty, unused space. The letters are very shallowly cut, which is also the case in general on the coins of this period, especially on the later specimens. Epigraphically, the form of the letters is still flawless. One gets the impression that the engraving of this die

---

[13] A feature which can be proved also for the earliest tetradrachms; cf. L. Mildenberg, Eine Überprägung des 2. Aufstandes der Juden gegen Rom, SNR 33 (1947) 17-24.

was executed in haste, though not yet in the desperate conditions of the break-down that prevailed during the final phase of the Rebellion[14].

Only on some of the small silver coins – «overstruck» denars – which bear the legend «Eleazar the Priest», a triangular legend composed of three letters is found alongside the G legends (the only ones on the small bronze): *šīn*, *mēm*, and *'ayin*. These letters are beautifully and correctly engraved and, in the writer's opinion, represent yet another abbreviation, one of a quite unmistakable nature for the rebels, even though less obvious to the beholder today: the first three of the five letters of the word Simon (*Šm'wn* )[15]. The five letters of this name occur very frequently on the coins of the Rebellion, especially in the second and third periods of coinage. The denars with the wreath show them constantly, often in the abbreviated form.

### 1.4. The Symbols

The symbolism of the coin series under consideration is as simple and clear as the epigraphical picture is perplexing and disorderly, thanks to the irregular Eleazar legends[16]. All the bronzes show on one side the palm tree, on the other the cluster of grapes. All the denars, so far known, show on the one side the jug together with the Eleazar legend, on the reverse, the grapes or the wreath. This uniform symbolism in no way deviates from the types generally employed. All the types of this series are taken from the flora of the land and from the life of the people: the grapes and the vine had already become the favorite symbols for Israel herself. References to them abound in the Bible, while the Prophets employ them for purposes of parable. Moreover, they abound in ancient Jewish art.

In the Maccabean and Herodian coinages (with the exception of the small bronzes with the seven-branched candle stick of Mattathias Antigonus and of a series of Herod Archelaus with vine branch, grapes, and vine leaf) borrowed symbols slightly offensive to the Jews predominate through-out, and distinguish these as only autonomous and not sovereign coinages, whereas already on the coins of the procurators the indigenous plants – palm and vine – appear. A delicately-chased vine-leaf graces the small bronze of the First Rebellion, and on the Eleazar bronze and the great series of medium bronzes of the second Rebellion, these two important products of the land are set forth quite emphatically as symbolic representations. On the victory coin age of the Flavians, after the suppression of the first Jewish Rebellion, there appeared the palm tree, which already in earlier times was regarded as a symbol for Judaea. Now, under that same date palm with its characteristic bunches of fruit, the rebels

---

[14] These emergency issues, which are usually – but not very happily – designated as «barbarous», quite clearly stand out among the other pieces as the very last coins. They deserve special attention.

[15] Cf. infra, at note 24.

[16] Cf., besides M. NARKISS, Coins of Palestine I, 1936, and A. REIFENBERG, Ancient Jewish Coins, 21947, especially P. ROMANOFF, Jewish Symbols on Ancient Jewish Coins, Philadelphia 1944.

replace the *ΙΟΥΔΑΙΑΣ ΕΑΛΩΚΙΑΣ* inscription (on the «Judaea Capta» coins struck in Palestine) with SIMON (Nasi Israel) and ELEAZAR THE PRIEST. Finally, by the olive wreath, the third important cultivated plant of the country, otherwise strangely neglected, is represented. The one-handled, narrow-necked jug with the fine lip was the favorite vessel for wine and water in daily life, while the two-handled amphora with the wide mouth was used for the heavier, thick-flowing oil.

The choice of these symbols becomes clear and significant only when one considers what the rebels did not want to see on their coins, namely, borrowed types[17], human figures or faces, animals or celestial bodies[18]; for these were portrayed on the foreign coins, which had circulated in the country and which were now «overstruck» by the rebels. They wanted to get rid of these hated objects. For this purpose they used the minter's tools, and even the file[19]. They replaced them with the objects close to their hearts and pure in their eyes. One can imagine what it meant to a Jew to see a bunch of grapes on a coin instead of the idolized portrait of the emperor and the various «numina», and to find around the grapes neither a Latin nor a Greek inscription, but a significant legend in his own ancient script[20]. And this in the year 132 CE, when the Romans had developed to perfection the methods of proclaiming their political program on the coins, whereas the Jews, who clearly understood what this implied, could not forget their two mighty, but unsuccessful uprisings.

## 1.5. The Style

Among the die-sinkers of the Eleazar series there were many real artists. Two dies, in particular, from one period are among the finest work that Jewish coin-engraving has to show. They are G 1 and E 5. Framed by the delicate, flawless inscription of 14 letters a ripe cluster of grapes is hanging from a beautifully poised vine-branch. The individual berries stand out with plastic clarity. A small jagged leaf unobtru-sively finds a place on the coin-flan. The legend begins near the leaf and ends at the stem,

---

[17] In this respect the far less consequential autonomous coinage of the Maccabees could not be a model for the rebels. One may only consider the cornucopiae, poppy-head, anchor, and wheel with eight ray-like spokes.

[18] This consideration alone makes the unique appearance of a star on some tetradrachms (and that above the Temple) most unlikely. Actually letters, rosettes, crosses, or wavy lines are found there; cf. L. MILDENBERG, SNR 33 (1947) 18, n. 5.

[19] The furrows on many coins of the Bar Kochba Rebellion are patently traces left by the file. They are found precisely where traces of the underlying type or legend still remained after overstriking.

[20] The exclusive use of the old Hebraic script, revived solely for coins, has been observed on three occasions. The early Maccabean coinage begins with ancient Hebrew inscriptions, but Alexander Jannaeus and Mattathias Antigonus struck already coins with ancient Hebraic legends on the obverse and Greek legends on the reverse. The Herodian dynasty issued no coins with the ancient or any other Hebrew script; the ancient characters appear for the second time in the Jewish War (66-70 CE). A generation later, the old Hebraic script was readopted for the third time on the coins of the second Jewish war of independence, the Bar Kochba Rebellion.

to which the last letter clings closely. This well-balanced composition shows indeed a sublime harmony. Such perfection is lacking in the handsome Eleazar-die of the denars E 5. Here, the two retrograde letters form a disturbing element in the legend. Its cramped appearance (*kwhn* written in full instead of *khn* ) suggests a later correction. The palm branch straggles of the flan. In contrast to this, the one-handled, narrow-necked jug is beautifully formed, and the contours, especially at the top, are drawn by a master's hand. This jug recurs constantly on the denars of the other minting periods, but always in cruder forms.

The other dies of the Eleazar series are of medium quality only. Yet among them not a single examlple of the later dies can be discovered, which crop up in most of the other series and whose makers must have had hardly any idea how to engrave a die.

## 2. Description and Interpretation of the Eleazar Coinage

### 2.1. The Range of the Coinage

So far the small bronzes and denars with the legend «Eleazar the Priest» have been treated here. Already in his time, DE VOGÜÉ had identified a genuine Eleazar denar[21], namely, the perforated and cracked specimen that is today in the Bibliothèque Nationale in Paris. It has the legend «Eleazar the Priest» around the jug and «Year One of the Redemption of Israel» around the grapes. This badly damaged piece remained for long decades the only known specimen. Many scholars listed it in their catalogues[22], while others did not take notice of it[23], and this even in the books which have become standard works.

After DE VOGÜÉ's discovery, a few other denars came to light, which had been struck from the same Eleazar die (E 5), but showed on the other side the first three of the five letters of the name Simon (*Šm'wn* ) in the wreath (die S). This was taken — and with good reason – as an abbreviation for Simon, by far the most common name in the whole coinage. Thus, as a result, these specimens were considered to be «hybrid» coins. The late Professor BEHREND PICK read these three letters, however, as a complete, unabbreviated word, and, thinking of the Shema-Prayer, translated it as «Hear!»[24]. Of course, if that were so, he had found a very remarkable Eleazar de-

---

[21] See Pl. LIII 8.

[22] So TH. REINACH, Les Monnaies Juives, 1888, 63, fig. 26; L. HAMBURGER, ZfN 18 (1892) 254; A. REIFENBERG, Ancient Jewish Coins, [2]1947, 61, No. 170.

[23] So G.F. HILL, BMC Palestine (and many others before and after him), as the British Museum possesses no Eleazar denar.

[24] Contributions to Palestinian Numismatics, Numismatic Review 2 (1945) 5-11. These Simon-Eleazar denars are certainly «freaks»; for the Rebellion coinage is distinguished by the fact that a name (Simon, Eleazar, Jerusalem) appears on one side of the coin, while on the other the coinsge period is indicated. They are accidental, not regular issues, as the coins with two coinage-period inscriptions. For both groups of coins, however, the terrn «hybrid» is inadequate, as all these inscriptions are more proclamations than real statements of the minting-authorities or of the dates.

nar. Unfortunately, PICK did not devote much research to Jewish coins. He ignored the undeniable facts that abbreviations are common on the coinage of the Bar Kochba Rebellion, that the name Simon in this very same olive wreath, with its nine divisions, appears everywhere written in full, and that for so bold a conclusion one must procure stronger supporting evidence from the general findings and the essential nature of the Jewish coinage.

For decades DE VOGÜÉ's Eleazar denar was not given the attention which it deserves. Because it was known only from a woodcut, the fact was overlooked that it has its die in common with the Eleazar bronze, namely, G 1[25]. It further escaped notice that in an auction catalogue a second Eleazar denar was published, with the same dies for both sides as DE VOGÜÉ's specimen[26]. Finally, this writer obtained a plaster cast of an unpublished specimen in the Vatican, which is a third Eleazar denar. Moreover, this piece – and here lies its special importance – is splendidly preserved, quite clearly overstruck, and has only the reverse die in common with the two others[27]. Its die with the grape cluster – similar to G 1, but not in any way identical – connects the small series of Eleazar denars with the long series of Simon denars.

Our preliminary spade work has thus produced the following findings: So far we know of Eleazar bronzes from the first, second, and third periods of coinage and of Eleazar denars only from the first period[28].

### 2.2. The Personality of «Eleazar the Priest»

This central problem of the coinage of the Bar Kochba Rebellion can merely be illuminated, not solved from the narrow point of view of the present investigation, which deals only with the small series of Eleazar coins. Numismatic research alone cannot give the last word. It must be suplplemented by a careful analysis of the other sources.

It was demonstrated above that there could have been no intention of emphasizing the words «Eleazar the Priest», since not a single legend is clear and free from mis-

---

[25] That this die, G 1, appears also on one of the so-called «hybrid» denars (BMC Palestine, 289, No. 5, Pl. XXXIII, 8 = Plate, No. 13), did not escape the attention of BEHREND PICK. The assumption that it is also found on the other «hybrid» denar of the British Museum («both have as obverse silver offstrikes of a copper coin of Eleazar») is, however, not proved. That die (G 1a) is certainly very similar to, but not identical with, the usual one.

[26] L. HAMBURGER, Catalogue, Dec. 16, 1907, No. 544. Dr. H.A. Cahn of Basel directed the writers attention to the coins illustrated there.

[27] To the left, above the grape cluster, there appears the outline of a head with the bow of the head-band (presumably Vespasian's) and above that, five letters of the legend. The specimen is in the Vatican and illustrated on Pl. LIII as No. 7. The author wishes to thank Marchese Camillo Serafini, Governor of the Vatican State and Director of the Coin Collection, for his kindness in placing plastercasts of the Jewish coins at his disposal and in describing them carefully. The «Feu Grégoire» Collection in the Vatican has patently great importance for Jewish numismatics.

[28] Cf. infra note 41.

takes. Moreover, Eleazar cannot be said to have had his own clearly distinguishing symbols. Whoever had these dies engraved and used for minting, obviously had not the faintest intention of this kind. It might help to consider the other «issuing authorities» named on the coins: Simon (written out, abbreviated, or appearing as «Simon Nasi of Israel») and «Jerusalem». It goes without saying that the city of Jerusalem did not authorize the coinage. Rather, this was a significant word inscribed as a symbol in letters (on the tetradrachms the pictorial symbol of the city, namely, the inner layout of the Temple as imagined by the rebels was added to the word)[29]. JERUSALEM was a proclamation, a program. Does this not permit us to draw certain conclusions about the nature and importance of the two other «authorities»?

It is also significant that, in complete contrast to the other contemporaneous coinages, the name of the «issuing authorities» on the Rebellion coinage under consideration appears by no means exclusively on the obverse[30]. The name Simon appears on obverse and reverse, «Eleazar the Priest» is always found on the reverse. Nothing else but the types decided which die should lie on top, which underneath in minting. So we find the grapes constantly on the obverse, while the palm and jug keep firmly to the reverse. The minter himself did not take the legends as guide. Furthermore, the «issuing authority», Eleazar, was certainly not concerned to see that his name and title appeared flawlessly and legibly on the coins, nor that he had his own symbols, nor either, that on his coins the inflexible rule of the coinage of the outer world was observed, and the «issuing authority» be named on the obverse.

Therefore, there is every reason to believe that one may not apply the concepts and methods of, for instance, Greek and Roman numismatic research to the study of this Jewish Rebellion coinage. Not only the coin-inscriptions, but also the Jewish coinage itself in this war of independence was based, in form and spirit, on laws of its own. To establish these laws – is the task of Jewish numismatics.

In this connection, one can say nothing more on the difficult question of the «issuing authorities» of the Eleazar series than what was indicated above: the issuing authority was the rebel organization itself[31]. The mint-masters were themselves rebels. On the coins appear the names and titles (or else the names employed symboli-

---

[29] On the tetradrachms, to which the author intends to devote a separate study. Beside archaeological and numismatic arguments, the strongest evidence against the assumption by prominent scholars of a synagogue is the close connection of this inscription with this building around which it appears. For the rebels the association of the word «Jerusalem» with the Temple was more obvious than that with a synagogue and its Torah-shrine. If such a synagogue in Jerusalem is taken into consideration, however, the question inevitably arises, when and how this synagogue could have been built there, cf. L. MILDENBERG, SNR 33 (1947) 22, n. 23.

[30] The problem, which side of the coins is to be regarded as the obverse and which as the reverse, can be solved by a numerical comparison of the dies. By the hammer-blow minting-technique far more demands were made on the reverse-die, which lay always in the upper frame, than on the protected, underlying obverse. In this way, the die, G 1, lasted so long that is was combined with seven different reverse-dies in the bronze and silver coinage. G 1 is thus an obverse.

[31] The fact of the coinage and its essential character are, indeed, evidence for the activity of such an independent, governmental organization.

cally alone[32]) of the authorities generally recognized as legitimate in the Jewish world of the time, that is, the politically important officials; not the military commander Ben Kosiba (Bar Kochba) and not the spiritual leader Rabbi Akiba ben Joseph, who, indeed, was neither Nasi (Patriarch, President of the Sanhedrin) nor Kohen (Priest). The rebels were thinking above all of the prominent first[33] patriarchs with the name Simon, whose rightful claims they may well have respected, and whose reputation would vouch for the legitimacy of the rebellion [s. jetzt aber u. S. 219 Anm. 3]. After all, what else could they have opposed to the idolized portrait of the emperor, which they hated and sought to abolish, than the name and the title of their own legitimate leader? Bar Kochba himself may well have given the order for the coinage, but we cannot justifiably assume that he desired to put his own first name on the coins, particularly as there is not the slightest indication that his name was actually Simon[34]. Whatever claims this man, whose deeds have thrilled later ages, may have made even in those years, he would surely not have described himself as «Nasi», since this was the title of a house of scribes who succeeded each other in the presidency of the Sanhedrin. With the legend «Eleazar the Priest», again, the rebels very likely had in mind the designation «High Priest» on the autonomous bronze of the Maccabees[35]. The office of High Priest was abolished with the destruction of the Temple. Yet there may well have been a representative personality from a recognized priestly family whose name and descent had symbolic significance on the coins. This personality was Eleazar. Whether this Eleazar is or is not identical with one or another of the rabbis of this name who are known in Jewish tradition, can at present be only a matter of conjecture. The hypothesis of the prominent numismatist, L. HAMBURGER, identfiying «Eleazar the Priest» with Rabbi Eleazar

---

[32] The parallelism of the legends «Simon» and «Eleazar» with «Jerusalem», their appearance on the obverse and reverse, and their combination with the other «proclamatory» legends («Redemption» and «Freedom» of Israel, and «To the Freedom of Jerusalem») speak for the existence of a definite intention: the two first names (with and without the qualifying titles) as well as the word «Jerusalem», were declarations of a program that was intended to vouch effectively for the legitimacy and justice of the rebels' cause (cf. P. ROMANOFF, Jewish Symbols on Ancient Jewish Coins, 1944, 37: «propaganda coins»).

[33] In the first third of the second century CE there were patriarchs who bore this name.

[34] Thus it seems improbable that «Simon» of the coins can be identified with Bar Kochba and Bar Kochba be regarded as the authority for the coinage. The way in which Bar Kochba was deliberately obscured in the literary sources of the subsequent centuries is proof enough of the importance of the man. If mention of the «coins of Ben Kosiba» is found in the later tradition (cf. A. REIFENBERG, Ancient Jewish Coins, [2]1947, 34, n. 4), thereby the fact received unintentional recognition that the Jewish military commander left an indelible mark on the last rebellion against Rome (see tMa'aser Sheni 1,5; jMa'aser Sheni 1,2; bBaba Qamma 97b). The identity of Ben Kosiba (not Bar Kochba; for Eusebius, hist. eccl. IV,6,1, is the first in the fourth century to give this form: Barchochebas) with Simon and Ben Kosiba's minting authority, is not proved, however, by these traditions. It seems that Eusebius knew the comment by Rabbi Akiba ben Joseph on Num. 24,17, cf. jTa'anit 4,8 (68d). This comment is probably the origin of the identification, Ben Kosiba = Bar Kochba («son of a star») = Simon on the coins.

[35] «Jehochanan, the High Priest, and the Community of the Jews», etc.

ben Asaria[36], has not yet been proved. However, it has not so far been refuted. In any event, the unanimous tradition that Rabbi Eleazar ben Asaria came from a priestly family lends support to this view.


## 2.3. The Mint

The problem of the mint, important from the numismatic and also from the historical point of view, can be solved on the basis of the materials available. The assumption must be eliminated that some of the coins were struck at a mint within the territory first seized by the rebels, others at a mint in Jerusalem after its capture by the Jews, and the remaining coins at a provisional mint, perhaps in the fortress of Bethar, in the last phase of the long and cruel war. Without exception, all Eleazar coins, silver as well as bronze, were issued by one and the same, possibly travelling mint; for a single interlinking dies system can be established, since the several dies were combined by the minter to produce many kinds of coins[37]. Once more it is clear that a uniform, traditional, and artistically finished coinage, such as is met elsewhere, could not have been intended and is not to be expected. That the coins were overstruck was important; that the Jews' own ancient script and their own symbols were thus displayed, was still more important; but the really vital point was that it was possible to mint at all, and that the rebels' own coinage was in circulation. As long as coins were struck, the Jews' recovered sovereignty was a living reality. Thereby proof was given that the rebels' cause was not yet lost. Considered from this aspect, the vast production of coins in these years of war becomes comprehensible.

---

[36] L. HAMBURGER, ZfN 18 (1892) 304-325; E. SCHÜRER, Geschichte des jüdischen Volkes I, 3rd and 4th ed., Leipzig 1907, 684, rejects HAMBURGER's thesis. SCHÜREr's assumption that Eleazar played a leading role in the Revolt and was later substituted by Bar Kochba, rests on conclusions drawn from the few Eleazar coins then published, which unfortunately included no example of the not very rare Eleazar bronzes of the third (Pl. LIII 6) and none of the second coinage period. Due to the publications of C. LAMBERT, QDAP 1 (1931) 71, and A. REIFENBERG, PEQ 1935, 83-84), SCHÜRER's hypothesis has been abandoned.

[37] This well-established interlinking die system is very long and includes the comprehensive series of the denars (with the sole exception of very few, characteristically doubtful specimens) and the common small bronzes. Only the most important first branches and main links are shown on the accompanying plate.

## 2.4. The Chronology of the Coinage

That the minter combined separate dies of the Eleazar series with each other and also with dies from other series of roughly the same diameter, that one die is thus linked with another, creating the aforementioned «system» of dies, is clearly demonstrated on Pl. LIII. The limited scope of the present study and the material available do not permit the precise establishing of the order of coinage on correct numismatic, epigraphic, and stylistic lines. The provisional results may, however, be set forth as follows.

This writer first investigated the obverse die G 1, with its delicate balance of pictorial design and script, and came across a remarkable set of facts, which may be made clear through the following sketch, the accompanying Pl. LIII, and the illustration on Pl. LIV.

a) This die, G 1, belongs to by far the greatest number of all *Eleazar* coins. Indeed, it is their distinguishing mark (Pl. LIII Nos. 1-4, 8, 9).

b) On the Eleazar bronzes it is combined with no less than four different reverse dies, the epigraphically so irregular E 1, E 2, E 3, and E 4.

c) At the same time, however, the die could also serve for the *Jerusalem* bronze coinage (Pl. LIII 15), and this clearly was not very early the case (cf. the die-condition of G 1 on the few pieces known so far). This assumption is also supported by the fact that the reverse die, with which G 1 is here combined, was further used for the «Jerusalem» bronze coinage of the *second* coinage period (Pl. LIII 16). In fact, the minter had all these dies at hand and combined them in all possible ways, without much concern for the inscriptions (dates and «issuing authorities»), whereby the symbols gave him the main guidance in his work.

d) The die G 1 was also employed for the Eleazar denars and this at a time (with the advanced wearing-out of the die) when it had already become a veteran of the bronze coinage (Pl. LIII 8, 9). The Eleazar series was thus begun by the rebels not in silver, but in bronze. At this later time, towards the end of the first period of coinage, and for the small silver coins, the die G 1 had finally to be eliminated. It was replaced by a very similar and still quite pleasing successor (G 1a), which is, however, unmistakably an inferior copy: the grape-cluster is clumsier and of cruder design, the leaf (smaller, and now with three points) hardly looks like a vine-leaf any longer, and the vine-stem is flat and no longer joined to the border of dots. In the inscription, the *lāmed* is striking with its sharp point, and so is the last letter, the *rēsh* , the top of which is half cut off by the stem of the vine. This copy, now, seems to have been used only in the silver coinage. One can see it as the obverse of the bestpreserved Eleazar denar (Pl. LIII 7), and of the strange, so-called hybrid coin (Pl. LIII 14), with its *two* «date inscriptions», which in any other ancient coinage would be incompatible with each other: «Year One of the Redemption of Israel» and «Year 2 of the Freedom of Israel». If one considers, however, how manifold the die combinations of the Jewish rebellion coinage are in general, that the term «year» must have comprehended even as much as a whole main coinage-period, and that such temporary overlapping is to be taken for granted, then one may readily understand the existence of such coins. One need not then resort to postulating purely accidental «hybrid» mintings, which in fact are by no means so unusual.

e) This is further confirmed by the fact that the die G 1, at the end of its long service, was combined with a «date» inscription for the second coinage period (Pl. LIII 13). This was probably the last case in which G 1 was employed. It would not be surprising if it were found elsewhere, just as it cannot be excluded that Eleazar denars of the other coinage-periods may still appear.

Since all four existing reverse dies of the bronzes, with their epigraphically sharply differentiated legends, have solely the die G 1 as obverse, useful indications for establishing the sequence of minting should be obtained from observing the gradual changes in the condition of these dies. One might thus expect the obvious result that in each case a new die was sunk for the reverse and employed only when its predecessor, owing to the disproportionately larger demands made on it in the course of minting – compared with the obverse die – became first unsightly and then unusable. But our findings run contrary to this expectation: it was not the case that E 1 was engraved and used in striking right at the beginning of the first period of the coinage, and E 4 appeared at the very end of this «Year One of the Redemption of Israel». Rather, after careful comparison of the available material, the writer considers the assumption justified, that all four dies for the bronzes E 1, E 2, E 3, E 4 were produced at the beginning of the Eleazar rebellion coinage and, moreover, in close succession to each other. Indeed, it must have been inexperienced die-sinkers, by no means fully acquainted with the old Hebraic script, who early engraved these dies with the long and difficult legends as a series of trial pieces.

This explanation is supported not only by the astonishing frequency of irregular phenomena in the E dies, but also by the fact that the most regular and legible die, E 4, was the one most often used up to the latest possible moment. In fact, the only Eleazar bronze so far known from the second coinage speriod (Pl. LIII 5) was struck from this same die, which then was already much worn. It is just this, namely, the most regular die, E 4, which in the third and last main coinage period, was copied quite closely, although superficially (Pl. LIII 6), when Eleazar coins had to be struck. One has only to investigate the condition of the opposite die, G 3 (see Pl. LIII 6, 18, 19), to know that this occurred very late indeed.

Let us return, however, for a short while to the first period of coinage. How and when the E dies were engraved, has been established to some degree. What was, however, the order of minting of the Eleazar coins? The «interlinking die system» and observation of the wearing-out of the dies clearly show that, as far as the bronzes are concerned, the issues of the last period «To the Freedom of Jerusalem» followed those of the «Year 2 of the Freedom of Israel», and these in turn followed the first period «Year One of the Redemption of Israel».

The Eleazar denars were struck after these four groups of the bronzes from the «Year One». The mint, however, employed the four Eleazar dies simultaneously for a certain time in the middle of the first period of coinage. The very first coins were perhaps struck from the die with the «scattered» inscription, E 3, very shortly after that minting was begun from E 1, also; then a little later E 2 was employed as well.

But individual pieces were also struck from die E 4 quite early. The last-mentioned, the clearest of the dies, finally held the field up to the end of the first coinage period.

The scanty material available will hardly permit any decisive judgment on the order of minting (the relative chronology) for the Eleazar denars. All one can say now is that the piece shown as No. 8 on Pl. LIII is an early issue.

## 2.5. The Date of the Rebellion

The early dating of the Bar Kochba Rebellion has been derived from numismatic[38] as well as literary[39] evidence. This erroneous assumption of some scholars might have been avoided by a more precise analysis of the historical context, a far more comprehensive investigation of the overstrikes, and a more critical attitude toward the literary tradition. In any case, the existence of so many undoubtedly *late* coins of Hadrian, overstruck by the Jewish rebels, establishes the more usual late dating, 132-135 CE, as highly probable. The writer has been able to identify several of such late «underlying», i.e., overstruck, coins of Hadrian, and hopes to publish an essay on overstrikes, giving the definitive date 132 C.E. as the *terminus post quem* [hier S. 176-182]. On the Eleazar series it was so far not possible to establish with certainty any such clear traces. Yet new material may bring forth some evidence on this point, too.

## 2.6. The Technique of Minting

The rebels' mint did not cast blanks of its own, but prepared foreign coins of diameters varying within certain limits as the basis of its coinage. Thus the Eleazar coins outwardly do not give the impression of a uniform and finished coinage. It is not surprising, therefore, that the flan is often of a wider diameter than the usual standard-size die. There are also several badly centered pieces known. The «basic» coins of the Eleazar coinage were, however, carefully worked over beforehand, and the striking itself was executed with equal care. Just as in the case of the die-engraving, so also the whole process of minting was not hastily carried out as became finally unavoidable at the end of the rebellion coinage in the desperate conditions of the collapse.

---

[38] Thus, quite decidedly, L. HAMBURGER, ZfN 18 (1892) 258-303, on the basis of the few early Hadrianic denars then known to him.

[39] See also M. AUERBACH, Zur politischen Geschichte der Juden unter Kaiser Hadrian, Berlin - Vienna 1924, 325; cf. PAUL L. STRACK, Untersuchungen zur römiscben Reichsprägung II, Stuttgart 1933, 132, n. 293.

# 3. Conclusions

## 3.1. Sovereign Coinage

The coinage of the Maccabees and the Herods had been an autonomous coinage[40]; they never struck in silver. A silver coinage by virtue of their own right was carried out by the Jews only in the two short periods in which they were truly independent and fully sovereign, namely, during the first and second Jewish wars of independence. The coinage itself was on both occasions the most conspicuous expression of national existence, and was intended as such.

In the Bar Kochba Rebellion, the rebel organization created one comprehensive and yet unified silver and bronze coinage. This coinage was in two respects threefold: there is a «Jerusalem», a «Simon», and an «Eleazar» coinage; all three have issues in both metals, as has been demonstrated above regarding the Eleazar denars. It is, however, not a question of «issuing authorities» in the usual sense, and far-reaching conclusions from the names alone may contradict the numismatic evidence. Eleazar was probably a legitimate authority of the time, not, however, a leader in the Rebellion next, or in opposition, to Bar Kochba. His name and title of «Priest» would, then, have merely a symbolic significance for the cause of the rebels.

The coinage as a whole is subdivided into three main coinage periods, the «Year One of the Redemption of Israel», «Year 2 of the Freedom of Israel», and «To the Freedom of Jerusalem». In all three periods «Jerusalem», «Simon», and «Eleazar» coins were issued[41]. The «interlinking die system» and the appearance of many emergency issues only in the third period confirm the assumption that the three periods roughly succeed each other in time[42].

---

[40] [1] Macc. 15:2-9. Antiochus VII Sidetes had to grant Simon Maccabaeus autonomy of local coinage, which subsequently included only coins of Simon Maccabaeus' successors in bronze. This right of coinage was a derivative and restricted right. The rebels' coinage in silver and bronze was produced by virtue of a sovereign right of their own.

[41] There should then be in each coinage, silver and bronze, three times three, that is, nine, or, altogether, eighteen groups. More groups can be counted if one refuses to identify «Simon, Nasi of Israel», «Simon» and «SiME(on)». The multiplicity would be even greater, if one should think of a gold coinage. The rebels would not have shrunk from overstriking foreign gold coins, as far as they had any or did not need them for more important purposes than as currency. According to the material available to the author, specimens for 14 of these 18 groups can be identified with certainty. New numismatic evidence may well make this picture still more complete. At present the coinage in its entirety allows to make the following subdivisions (Abbreviations: T = Tetradrachme, D = denarius, LB = Large Bronze, MB = Middle Bronze, SB = Small Bronze) [s. Tabelle auf S. 201].

[42] Particularly instructive for establishing the precise order of minting is the comparison of the respective condition of the dies of the so-called «hybrid» specimens which are no rarities.

## 3.2. Rebellion Coinage

The whole coinage could come into being only as a result of the rising of the Jews against the *Imperium Romanum*. It is to be understood in the light of this fundamental consideration.

For the production of blanks of their own two preconditions would have been necessary: sufficient time and the execution of a complete technical process. But why should the rebels have taken so much trouble upon themselves when long-current foreign, especially Roman[43], coins were at hand or had been captured as booty? These could be easily overstruck. This very overstriking was also deliberately adopted.

The interlinking die system shows that all Eleazar coins, as well as the other, closely-connected «Jerusalem» and «Simon» series, must have been produced by one and the same mint. The minting must have taken place wherever the rebel organization, which exercised the authority to mint coins, happened to be at any time. And the very fact of this single interlinking die system makes it likely that the coinage was managed by an organization, in fact the governmental organization of the rebels, which throughout all three periods had the power to coin.

The conditions during the Bar Kochba Rebellion and its nature explain not only the vast quantity of overstrikes, but also the many epigraphic irregularities, the most typical being the «Eleazar the Priest» legend. The Eleazar bronzes of the first coinage period came into existence very early, certainly before the Eleazar denars. In this beginning of their coinage, which probably coincided roughly with the early days of the uprising, the rebels already wanted to see the old Hebraic script on their coins. But for this script at most only a few copies or examples were at hand, and it had not yet been mastered by the die-engravers of the Eleazar coins, who were mere beginners in the trade.

## 3.3. Coinage as Proclamation

The Jewish rebels must have realized to what a mighty instrument of policy the ancient coinage of the Romans had by then developed. They turned this instrument in their own way against the Roman Empire, from whose iron fetters they hoped to free themselves. Quite deliberately, they *erased* the pattern on the original Roman coins by hammering[44], by overstriking, and often by the removal by file of any traces which had still remained. This practice resulted from technical, religious, and above all, political considerations. On the products of their own characteristically plentiful

---

[43] Clear traces can be found of restrikes of products of the mint of Rome, of the provincial mints, of smaller autonomous mints, and even of Hellenistic coins.

[44] The edges of the coins offer eloquent testimony to this work. Most impressive is the denarius published by G.F. HILL, BMC Palestine, 288, No. 1, Pl. XXX:4, which was hammered into the right condition, but not yet overstruck. – In the spring of 1947, the author started anew collecting material of the above described kinds. He would greatly appreciate receiving casts and photographs of specimens unknown to him.

and manifold coinage they announced their recovered national existence through the forceful language of their symbols and through the ancient script, as well as the meaning of their legends.

For the men of the Bar Kochba Rebellion their coins were a solemn proclamation of their endeavors. This is the meaning of all their coinage, not least of the noteworthy Eleazar coins.

| Metal: | Silver (AR) | | | Bronze (AE) | | | total |
|---|---|---|---|---|---|---|---|
| Periods of coinage: | I | II | III | I | II | III | |
| «JERUSALEM» | T | T | | LB | LB | | |
| | | | | LB | LB | | 5 |
| «SIMEON» | | | | LB | | | |
| + «Nasi of Israel» | | | | MB | MB | | |
| 5 letters | | | | LB | | | |
| | | T | T | MB | MB | MB | |
| | | D | D | | SB | | |
| 3 letters | | D | | MB | MB | MB | 5 |
| «ELEAZAR THE PRIEST» | D | | | SB | SB | SB | 4 |
| | | | | | | | 14 |

# The Monetary System of the Bar Kokhba Coinage

## (Tf. LV - LVI)

## 1. The Monetary Character

Historians of the past have often deplored the fact that there was no Josephus to record the Bar Kokhba war and that only few scattered fragments of Roman, Christian and Jewish literary sources exist. These historians mentioned that the rebels struck coins, but they failed to study and understand this coinage. On the other hand, numismatists – from ECKHEL to recent times – were fascinated by the abundance of the authochthonic types and the proclamatory legends, but they remained entangled in the many enigmas of the whole coinage and therefore did not stress duly that these silver and bronze coins were in the first line and essentially – money. Both historians and numismatists have to learn their lesson now from the new papyri – the general theme of this convention being the numismatist's special «memento».

### 1.1. Territory

The first postulate of a sovereign coinage is full control of a certain territory. This does not need to be large, as proved by many siege coinages issued by small and unimportant cities and fortresses since the Renaissance. The rebels conquered and administered a large part of Judaea. The papyri tell us that they reigned in the east as far as the shore of the Dead Sea. They went down to the south-west where the 22nd Roman legion, the *Deiotariana* , was defeated. The whole pattern of the coinage clearly shows that Jerusalem was conquered and remained in the rebels' hands for a certain length of time [vgl. aber unten S. 212-216]. But we do not know with full certainty of any hoard of Bar Kokhba coins found outside Judaea, for instance in Galilea. On the base of numismatic evidence we can only assume that the rebels controlled a large part of the South during a certain length of time, which enabled them to issue an abundant and varied coinage.

### 1.2. Authority

To mint silver coins of one's own, to usurp the right of silver coinage in a Roman province was tantamount to high treason. There were no autonomous silver coins in Hadrian's empire. Until the new evidence provided by the papyri found in the Judaean

Desert it was generally believed that the rebels' administration assumed the assignation of the Roman emperor and herewith one of his main prerogatives: the minting of a sovereign coinage. The papyri, however, give decisive proof that Shimon Bar Koseba, the man called Bar Kokhba since the time of the Mishna, took over the land from the Roman emperor and leased it to the peasants. This is a new fact that cannot be underlined too strongly. We have to take literally what we read on the coins: Shimon was the «Prince of Israel», the man who had the whole power and made full use of it. We can therefore safely assume that he was also the minting authority. This in spite of the fact that the name of Eleazar the Priest appears on coins mainly at the beginning of the war, as well as the name of Jerusalem during the whole period of the coinage which is *in nuce* rightly called after Bar Kokhba.

### 1.3. Exclusivity

The money which Shimon Bar Koseba struck during the time of the insurrection was the exclusive legal tender in Judaea. No other currency was allowed and accepted; the state's mint monopoly was total. The general character of the rebels' coinage, the overstriking in particular, made numismatists presume such an exclusivity, but it took the Dead Sea papyri to prove it. They mention the *sela‘* and the *sūs* , our Bar Kokhba tetradrachm and denarius, as the only currency used on the Jewish territory during the war.

## 2. The Rebellion Coinage

### 2.1. Limited validity

The validity of the coins of the Bar Kokhba war was, needless to say, strictly limited in time: not less than three years, not more than four. It was also locally restricted. It is unlikely that Bar Kokhba's coins were accepted outside the rebels' territory and moreover it is most improbable that the few survivors of the war who remained scattered in the north could use this kind of money. A bronze coin with a countermark stamped after the final defeat is known, but it remained legal tender on account of its official countermark and not because it was a Bar Kokhba coin.

### 2.2. The rebels means and needs

To start an insurrection against the Roman empire and its garrisons – the new documents mention legionary detachments even in small settlements – needed not only leadership, manpower and organization, but also money. It has been repeated over and over that the rebels took the money of the defeated Roman legions and garrisons as booty, which was certainly the case. On the other hand, Bar Kokhba was a war leader *par excellence* who would have succeeded in raising a war loan from his own people in order to increase the funds of the rebel organization for internal and external purposes. And what kind of money could the people of Judaea give but the currency of the period: tetradrachms of the Roman provincial mints of Antiochia and Tyros, drachms of Caesarea and bronze coins of the autonomous mints in Palestine. Even coins no longer in circulation, such as Ptolemaic bronzes were supplied and subsequently overstruck. The cash Bar Kokhba could get from the legions and garrisons probably consisted also of Roman imperial denarii, some dupondii and asses, and of coins struck in the Eastern mints.

Now we come to a fundamental question which, to my knowledge, has not been raised by students so far, and which must be discussed here. Why did Bar Kokhba not issue any gold coins? We can safely assume that he had gold coins at his disposal. Roman imperial *aurei* from Augustus to Hadrian are found often and even quite recently in Egypt, in Turkey and in most other countries of the Near East. Moreover, would a high Roman official or officer, a private person, Jewish or not Jewish, living in Judaea or travelling through the country, not carry some aurei? The rebels did not need gold coins for their internal circulation; silver and bronze were sufficient for local purposes. Bar Kokhba kept the gold in his treasury to satisfy the rebels' most urgent needs on which their survival depended: to buy weapons and food or even, may be, benevolent neutrality from their neighbours – the Nabateans in the East, for instance.

### 2.3. Overstriking – extent and significance

In my opinion, it was Shimon Bar Kokhba's intention to create his own sovereign coinage bearing typical Jewish types and proclamatory legends by mere overstriking of foreign coins, without casting his own planchets. It is not that the rebels' organization and the technical skill were so poor that they were unable to cast regular planchets. The good craftsmanship of the die-cutters, apart from the final period of the war, proves the contrary. The question is whether they had to prepare their own planchets. The author hopes to show later in this communication that there was only one mint and that this mint was located inside the rebel headquarters. In contrast to the Jewish War, the headquarter was most probably not situated always in the same place throughout the insurrection which was essentially a long and cruel guerrilla war in a mountainous country. It is not impossible that one of the rather carelessly overstruck *cistophori* of Hadrian which were issued in the east shortly before the outbreak of the war gave the rebels the idea that there was an easy and simple way to issue a rich coinage immediately: overstriking the available coins! This policy of overstriking, and nothing else, had manifold and far-reaching results: there was no clearly defined pattern and no homogenity of the coinage as in the Jewish War. The coins of the Bar Kokhba War show most divergent fabrics, which are due to the various foreign mint-systems which supplied the coins to be overstruck. There are also great differences in weight. In the bronze coinage the weights were simply and carelessly adjusted by filing.

As there was no proper standard, it is evident that no denominations could be written on the coins, as it was the case in the Jewish War where we note the values SHEKEL [of] ISRAEL, HALF SHEKEL and QUARTER SHEKEL on the obverse of the silver and HALF and QUARTER on the reverse of the large bronze pieces.
Finally, by overstriking the rebels produced normal, good money and not the bad one in debased metal which is characteristic for the «war and emergency money» as for the issues in the inflationary periods of all times.

## 3. The Monetary Pattern

### 3.1. Denominations

Although the Bar Kokhba overstruck coinage was not based on a clear and exact relation to metals and weights, it nevertheless must have been understood and valuated correctly by the people. Without a marked value and without even a constant, easily controllable exact weight, the man in the street would have been lost, if the denomination was not recognizable by the type.

All big silver coins depict the temple on the obverse and the Lulab and Ethrog on the reverse. Therefore it was clear to everybody that this was the highest silver value which replaced the current tetradrachm of the Syrian provincial coinage. It was logical and reasonable that this big silver coin was called so far tetradrachm by numismatists, before the papyri unveiled us its real name – *sela‹* . On the other hand, the smaller silver coin – called sus in these documents – has many varieties, which picture vessels, musical instruments, plants and fruits. It seems that the mint officials in the rebels organization believed that there was no need to indicate the value by one type as people were supposed to know the relation between the big and the small silver. The texts tell us that these officials were wrong: in a legal document dated in the fourth year of the Redemption of Israel a price of 88 *sūs*, equivalent to 22 *sela‹*, is mentioned. Thus even in the fourth year of the Bar Kokhba War it was still necessary to give the clear and exact relation between the big and the small silver coin – a striking example of the importance of clearly defined denominations in an ancient rebellion coinage.

The monetary system of the Bar Kokhba bronze coinage is more complex. To begin with, it sounds indeed rather surprising that the weight of the large bronzes lies between more than 40 grams and less than 15 grams. This is due to the fact that the rebels overstruck all large bronze coins available which came from very different mints and periods. There is no doubt that all large bronzes had the same value, because all had the amphora on the obverse and the wreath on the reverse. Here the value of the metal itself seems to have lost importance. It would be unreasonable to assume that people calculated and paid using scales in order to establish the right value! Regarding the small bronzes, here again there is a difference in weight, but not as enormous as with the large bronzes. Again there is only one type – bunch of grapes on the obverse and palm-tree on the reverse – which decides the value. Similar to the case of the silver coinage, four small bronzes were probably equivalent to a large one. Although the individual differences in weights are sometimes high, the average weights and the general aspect of the frequency tables seem to indicate this preliminary thesis. The medium bronzes, in contrast to the two other bronze groups, show two types for the obverse and three types for the reverse. The mint officials could use several types without confusing the people because it was obvious that one large bronze equalled two medium or four small coins.

Finally, a few words regarding the interesting question of the relation between silver and bronze. It could be assumed that the rebellious Jews followed the general pattern of the roman coinage system, where one Syrian tetradrachm of 14 grams equalled 32 Syrian *dupondii* of 14 grams or one *denarius* equalled roughly four *sestertii*. But I would not like to develop a final theory before studies on the weights are ready and before the exact texts of the papyri are available.

### 3.2. Die-sequences and dating

Mainly students of ancient Greek coins have so far developed the method of die-comparison. They succeeded in collecting enough material on one specific coinage to trace a whole chain of interlinking dies and to establish the exact die-sequences. The author has shown in 1949 in a paper on the Eleazar coins of the Bar Kokhba rebellion that all the small Eleazar bronzes (of year one, the second year and the undated group) not only form a chain of interlinking dies between themselves, but also are connected with a group of silver *denarii*, mainly of year one, as well as with all the other small bronzes of the three periods [hier S. 183-201]. While compiling the Corpus of the Bar Kokhba coins, the author has established the die-sequences of the silver tetradrachms. Also in this important group the dies are interlinked from the beginning to the end – as shown on plates at the end of this paper.

As for the problem of the dating, those students of the Bar Kokhba coinage who, since LEOPOLD HAMBURGER and Sir GEORGE FRANCIS HILL, put the undated series at the end, were proved right by the papyri. As far as we can judge from the information so far available, the dates «year 3 of the freedom of Israel» and «fourth year of the redemption of Israel» are reported. In fact, the simple wording of the dating legends on the coins and the existence of several hybrids which link pieces of year one with year two and year two with the undated issue, must lead to the conclusion HAMBURGER and HILL already came to.

These clearly established die-sequences prove the inner chronology beyond any doubt. The author stated in 1949 «the interlinking die system and the observation of the wearing out of dies clearly show that, as far as bronzes are concerned, the issues of the last period 'to the freedom of Jerusalem' followed those of 'Year 2 of the Freedom of Israel' and these in turn followed the first period 'Year one of the redemption of Israel'».

In connection with the problem of the dating, a further point has to be noted. The numeral output differs considerably in the 3 periods. Only a limited number of silver coins were struck in the first year, considerably more in the second year, but the bulk of silver coins came from the undated period. The following proportion can tentatively be assumed: 5% : 30% : 65%. In the bronze coinage, however, years one and two are far more frequent, covering approximately half of the whole output. Evidently, much more bronze coins were at hand at the beginning of the war than silver which came later as booty, enforced or voluntary contributions, or perhaps even from the tenant-farmers' rent.

The proportional numbers given above fit well with the new facts discovered in the papyri, particularly with the newly secured dates of year 3 and 4.

### 3.3. The mint

The die-sequences established by the author for the Eleazar and related coins and recently those for the tetradrachms prove that either of these series was struck in one mint only. It is moreover very likely that the small bronzes and the denarii of all the 3 periods are connected by one chain of interlinking dies. The few large bronzes existing form one coherent group and the same goes for the large group of the medium bronzes with its particularly uniform appearance. The author ventures therefore to assume that all the coins of the Bar Kokhba War were struck in one mint.

There are other arguments in favour of this theory. The overstriking, for instance, indicates that the rebels wanted to get quickly their own money. What reason should they have had to set up more than one mint, with new craftsmen who had to have a good knowledge of the ancient Hebrew script? And why should they have undertaken the dangerous transport of the foreign coins to another place far away from the headquarter!

The papyri that have so far been published show the extraordinary importance of Bar Kokhba. He was the prince of Israel and the coins bear his name proudly. He was the military leader of the rebellion, its heart and brain. On him depended the crucial decisions in this struggle for life and death. Coinage was certainly one important achievement of the rebels. There is absolutely no reason why the mint should be separated from the central administration, all the more if we consider the personal interest Bar Kokhba seems to have taken in the coinage. There was only one mint, operating in his headquarters, which produced his money, the Bar Kokhba coinage.

*

Finally very few words on coins and papyri. The papyri relate facts, simple mere facts which enable us to understand the Bar Kokhba coinage better. They prove that most of the students of the Jewish coins were right in their main statements. Not in one important detail coins and papyri seem to contradict. But the papyri brought single new facts none of the numismatists of the past or the present could have imagined.

As objective historical sources, however, the Bar Kokhba coins essentially remain of the highest importance. The numismatists' interpretation may be doubted, but the coins themselves, their values, legends and types, their diebreaks and die-sequences, are again simple, mere facts. This International Numismatic Convention is working in the coins' and papyri's own country. It is our duty here to let the great facts of the Bar Kokhba coins speak.

# A Bar Kokhba Didrachm

## (Tf. LVII)

## 1. A lesson on numismatic evidence

«Numismatic evidence is irrefutable, but not final»[1]. Certainly, we can trust the types and legends which appear on an ancient coin, but we can never know all that is hidden in the ground. For centuries, Bar Kokhba silver tetradrachms, denarii-drachms and large, medium and small bronzes have been known, illustrated and described. This writer has devoted long years to the study of the coinage and finally published its corpus in 1984[2]. In May 1985 a knowledgeable friend showed him a heavily incrustated silver coin, obviously a Bar Kokhba didrachm (Tf. LVII 1).

In the corpus, the fact had been stressed that tridrachms of Caesarea Cappadociae occasionally occur in Bar Kokhba hoards, but that they were not overstruck by the Jewish mint. Tridrachms did not fit into the contemporary monetary system in Syria-Phoenicia and therefore not into the structure of the Bar Kokhba coinage[3]. Didrachms, however, would. But not one foreign didrachm, either untouched or hammered flat for overstriking, had been found together with Bar Kokhba coins in any hoard up to 1984[4]. There was no reason, therefore, to assume that Bar Kokhba didrachms had been struck, though some Syrian-Phoenician didrachms which could have served for overstriking have indeed been recorded[5]. A recent mixed hoard from the neighbourhood of Hebron did contain just such a Syrian-Phoenician didrachm together with five similar tetradrachms and some bronze city coins, in the midst of Bar Kokhba silver and bronze issues[6]. However, the argument based in the hitherto enti-

---

[1] In an unpublished paper read by the writer on the 16th of May, 1985, in Jerusalem [s. hier S. 253-262]. The writer is grateful to the owner of the coin for permission to publish it here.

[2] L. MILDENBERG, The Coinage of the Bar Kokhba War (Typos 6), Aarau u.a. 1984.

[3] L. MILDENBERG, The Coinage of the Bar Kokhba War, 1984, 88.

[4] Foreign coins, some already hammered flat for overstriking, are frequently found together with Bar Kokhba coins. See L. MILDENBERG, The Coinage of the Bar Kokhba War, 1984, 54-57, Hoards 5, 12, 13, 14, 19, 21, 24, 29, and Y. MESHORER, IMJ Spring (1985) 43-50, coin no. 5.

[5] E.A. SYDENHAM, Caesarea in Cappadocia, London, 1953, no. 181; BMC, Galatia, etc., no. 58; W. WRUCK, Die syrische Provinzialprägung von Augustus bis Trajan, Stuttgart 1931, no. 145; D.R. WALKER, The Metrology of the Roman Silver Coinage II (BAR Suppl.Series 22), London 1977, 93.

[6] Y. MESHORER, IMJ Spring (1985) 43-50, coin no. 5.

rely negative hoard-evidence became null and void as soon as the incrustated Bar
Kokhba didrachm appeared.

## 2. The underlying coin

The weight of the new Bar Kokhba didrachm was 7.85 g. before cleaning and is now
7.62 g. after the heavy greyish layer covering the metal had been carefully removed
(Tf. LVII 2,3).

Now, the outline of Trajan's head and the letters ...*AIΣ NEP TPA*... of the original obverse legend are clearly visible when the Jewish obverse is turned upside down.
On the reverse, above the lulav, the letters ..*ΠΑΤ*.. (from *ΥΠΑΤΟΣ*) can be seen and
the feathered right leg of an eagle can be recognized in the globular central part of the
lulav. Thus, the weight and the remaining traces of the underlying types and legends
clearly indicate what coin was overstruck.

There is a rather limited issue of Trajanic didrachms dated *COS II* from Caesarea
Cappadociae, displaying different reverse types. They all, are, however, too light to
fit as planchets for our coin[7]. However, there is a small group of Trajanic didrachms
of *COS III* , thus of the year 100, with an eagle and a club on the reverse, issued in
Syria-Phoenicia (Tf. LVII 4,5). They have the right weight, are different from the
Caesarea issues in style and fabric and are, indeed, found in Judaea[8]. One of these
pieces is the underlying coin of the new Bar Kokhba didrachm.

## 3. The types

Obviously, the temple facade was intended to be shown on the didrachm obverse, but
it was conceived differently from the depiction on the tetradrachms, as now only two
columns appear instead of four. This is a clear program: four columns indicate four
drachms, two columns two drachms. The two columns stand on three steps and support a double architrave. The usual ornament found above the architrave on the tetra-

---

[7] D.R. WALKER, Metrology, 1977, 72. In Trajanic times Nabatean silver coins were
overstruck in Roman mints. Nabatean didrachms are, however, lighter than our new didrachm.

[8] D.R. WALKER, Metrology, 1977, 101. – The new mixed Hebron hoard [MESHORER, IMJ
Spring (1985) 43-50, coin no. 5] and our new Bar Kokhba didrachm also found in Bar
Kokhba territory lend further support to the probability that the Trajanic eagle didrachms
come from a mint in Syria-Phoenicia as WALKER had stressed and not from Caesarea
Cappadociae as WROTH and SYDENHAM assumed. WRUCK ascribed all coins with a club
from the Syrian provincial coinage to the mint of Tyre (Die syrische Provinzialprägung,
1931, no. 145). The club, however, also appears on coins of Caesarea (BMC, Galatia,
etc., nos. 81-84). Coins bearing the club as subsidiary type to the head of Melqart-
Herakles and the eagle, however, point to the important autonomous silver coinage of the
city of Tyre issued from the end of the second century B.C. till the first century A.D.

drachms is missing here[9]. Between the columns stands a low chest on two feet. The chest itself, which entirely lacks three-dimensionality, was meant to be without lid, as the upper border is rendered by a single concave line and not by the convex double line which is the way the chest on the tetradrachms is depicted.

The reverse type is a rather clumsy version of the lulav on the tetradrachms. The etrog is missing as on a few tetradrachm dies.

## 4. The legends

As on the tetradrachms, the obverse inscription reads Shim'on in five letters; thus Shim'on bar Kosiba, commonly called Bar Kokhba. The letter-forms are clear and well drawn with three letters to the right and two to the left. This differs from the arrangements on the tetradrachms where we see two letters to the right and three to the left.

The legend on the reverse indicates the third and last coinage period «For the Freedom of Jerusalem». In strong contrast to the writing on the obverse, the letter-forms here are entirely irregular: the two *rēsh* 's are retrograde and even different from each other, the *yōd* is rendered in mirror script, the *mēm* is misunderstood and while the two *wāw* 's have the correct Hasmonean form, they are also in mirror image.

## 5. The denomination

Given the position of the coinage in the daily life of the years 132-135, the production of an additional denomination in the form of a silver didrachm was certainly not a must, as two single denarii-drachms, of which there was an ample supply, made up the same amount. However, a two drachms-coin was a handy, easily acceptable piece. It is noteworthy in this context that the new denomination was manufactured like all other Bar Kokhba coins: the edge is vertically cut and the reverse is concave and deeply struck. The vertical die position at 12 h of the new coin is the most frequently used. The flan is rather thin and large and the striking not well centered, but both defects occur occasionally on other Bar Kokhba issues[10].

---

[9] For these quite different ornaments see MILDENBERG, The Coinage of the Bar Kokhba War, 1984, fig. 11. The new didrachm with its two columns is an additional and decisive argument against the interpretation and the dating of the tetrastyle facade by A. MUEHSAM, Coin and Temple, Leeds - Leiden 1966.

[10] Obviously, the otherwise customary protecting ring guard has not been used here which hints at a very late production; see infra and MILDENBERG, The Coinage of the Bar Kokhba War, 1984, 27. 58.

## 6. Trial piece or necessity coin?

Our coin is the first example of this denomination to come to light. The distyle temple is otherwise unknown in this coinage. The marked difference in the scripts of the obverse and reverse is unusual and betrays that two engravers cut the dies. For this reason one could think that the coin is a sort of a trial piece or pattern, struck in a few specimens only. But a specific detail of the numismatic evidence precludes this explanation: on the obverse a long and thick horizontal diebreak runs from the first lower stroke of the *shīn* through the pearl border to the edge of the flan. Obviously, the new didrachm is not an early, but a late product of this die. The output must have been considerable, though for the time being we only know of this unique specimen.

The unskillful engraving of the temple and the lulav, the rather poor striking and especially the quite irregular lettering of the reverse legend support the attribution of the new coin to the small irregular coinage rather than to the large regular one. The conclusion is unambigous: the personnel of the small irregular mint must have come into the possession of a number of Trajanic Syrian-Phoenician didrachms at a time when the supply of foreign tetradrachms and denarii-drachms for overstriking had become more and more limited. Presumably the mint-offcial in charge decided to have dies cut for the production of Jewish didrachms. He was obliged to make do with the work of unskilled engravers and mintmasters. Therefore, the new Bar Kokhba didrachm is not a trial piece, but a necessity striking produced under difficult circumstances in a probably isolated workshop quite at the end of the last desperate struggle of the Jews against the Roman Empire.

# Bar Kochba in Jerusalem?[*]

(Tf. LVIII)

Über die Bedeutung der Legende «Jerusalem» auf den Münzen des Bar-Kochba-
Krieges (132-135) ist sich die gesamte moderne Geschichtsschreibung[1] mit der heu-
tigen Numismatik[2] einig: Jerusalem wurde von den Aufständischen am Anfang der
Erhebung erobert und erst im dritten Jahr des Krieges wieder an die Römer verloren.
Wenn der Name der Stadt auf der Vorderseite der Tempeltetradrachmen des «Jahres
Eins der Befreiung Israels» in aller Deutlichkeit steht (Tf. LVIII Abb. 1), so sei
Jerusalem eben Prägestätte und Prägeherrin zugleich.

   Der Name «Jerusalem» findet sich aber auch auf den früheren
Tempeltetradrachmen des Jahres 2 (Tf. LVIII Abb. 2-3), wird aber dann von dem
Namen «Simon» auf den gleichen Tetradrachmen des gleichen Jahres 2 ersetzt, die
etwas später im Jahre geprägt wurden (Tf. LVIII Abb. 4). Diese unbestrittene
Tatsache widerspricht der Jerusalem-These, die ja mindestens volle zwei Jahre
annimmt. Schlimmer noch, ihre Verfechter haben die umfangreiche Bronzeprägung
gänzlich unberücksichtigt gelassen: in der dritten und letzten, der undatierten
Prägeperiode gibt es die häufigen Kleinbronzen gerade mit der Inschrift «Jerusalem»
(sic!) unter der Palme (Tf. LVIII Abb. 9). Und ganz beiseite geschoben haben sie
auch die reiche Bronzeprägung mit der gleichen ersten Datierungsinschrift wie die der
Tempeltetradrachmen, aber mit den Legenden «Eleazar der Priester» und «Simon
Fürst Israels» (Tf. LVIII Abb. 6. 10-12). Sie haben auch nicht berücksichtigt, daß es
einen Vorderseitenstempel gibt, der die gesamte Denarprägung mit der

---

[*]   Aus einem am 30.November 1976 in Zürich gehaltenen Vortrag.
[1]   Y. YADIN, Bar Kochba, 1971, 18. E. SCHÜRER [- G.VERMES], The History of the Jewish
People ..., Revised edition, Edinburgh 1973, 545. 550; M. GRANT, The Jews in the
Roman World, 1973, 250ff; M. AVI-YONAH, Palaestina, PRE Suppl. 13 (1974) 402; E.M.
SMALLWOOD, The Jews under Roman Rule, 1976, 44ff.
[2]   A. REIFENBERG, Ancient Jewish Coins, 21947, 35; B. KANAEL, JNG 17 (1967) 258; Y.
MESHORER, Jewish Coins, 1967, 93f; A. KINDLER, Catalogue Collection Bank Israel,
1974, 60f, aber Zweifel auf S.58; W. KELLNER, Auktionskatalog F. Sternberg, Zürich
25.Nov. 1976, 53f: «Autonome Prägung für Jerusalem».

Kleinbronzengruppe[3] verbindet (Tf. LVIII Abb. 5-8), und daß die gesamte Bar-Kochba-Prägung aus einer einzigen Münzstätte stammt, die wohl im Hauptquartier zu lokalisieren ist[4]. Damit scheidet Jerusalem als Prägestätte aus.

Die Verfechter der Jerusalem-These unter den Numismatikern standen auch deshalb auf verlorenem Posten, weil sie einer fundamentalen Verkennung der Bedeutung der für den Bar-Kochba-Krieg typischen Legenden unterlagen. Das Prägerecht ist von Anfang an in den Händen der Rebellenorganisation. Jerusalem kann also niemals Prägeherrin gewesen sein. Die Legenden sind rein proklamatorischer Natur. Einerseits verkünden sie, daß das Jahr «Eins der Befreiung Israels» angebrochen ist, dem das «Jahr 2 der Freiheit Israels» folgt. Andererseits stehen sie zuerst für ihre beiden Führer und dann nur noch für den weltlichen Herrn ein, auch für «Jerusalem», und am Schluß «für die Freiheit Jerusalems», die immer noch nicht erreicht ist.

Wenn die Jerusalem-These in der numismatischen Evidenz also keine Stütze findet, so steht es mit den Aussagen der nicht-jüdischen literarischen Quellen etwas anders. Appianos, ein Zeitgenosse der Hauptakteure des Dramas, hat in seiner Römischen Geschichte[5] eine kurze, aber prägnante Schilderung des Schicksals der Stadt Jerusalem von den Zeiten des Pompejus bis zu denen des Hadrian hinterlassen[6]. Er beschreibt die Zerstörung Jerusalems, darunter die letzte durch Hadrian, die in seinen eigenen Tagen erfolgt sei.

Nun wurde mit Recht darauf hingewiesen, daß Hadrian keinen Grund gehabt hätte, Jerusalem zu zerstören, wenn es in römischer Hand geblieben wäre[7]. Aber es muß doch festgehalten werden, daß Appianos keinesfalls sagt, Bar Kochba hätte Jerusalem erobert, und Hadrian hätte es ihm dann wieder abgenommen.

Die Zerstörung der Stadt durch Hadrian wird lediglich als drittes und letztes Glied einer Kette von Verwüstungen Jerusalems genannt. Der Terminus «Zerstörung» steht hier allgemein für die endgültige Etablierung der römischen Herrschaft nach der Vernichtung des jüdischen Widerstandswillens. Ein weiterer Zeitgenosse, Justinos Martys, spricht in seinem nach 150 geschriebenen Dialog mit dem Juden Tryphon gar von der «Eroberung» der Stadt[8]. Aber auch diese «Eroberung» der Stadt kann durchaus für die Beendigung des ganzen Krieges stehen. Die späteren christlichen Überlieferungen des Eusebios und Hieronymus, die ebenfalls von einer Belagerung oder Zerstörung Jerusalems durch Hadrian berichten, kommen aus zweiter Hand.

---

[3] L. MILDENBERG, The Eleazar Coins of the Bar Kochba Rebellion, Historia Judaica 11 (1949) Tf. 2 [hier Tf. LIV].

[4] L. MILDENBERG, Hist. Jud. 11 (1949) 101 [hier S. 195]; ders., Jerusalem International Numismatic Convention Proceedings, 1963, Jerusalem 1967, 46f [hier S. 207].

[5] *Rhōmaïkē*, um 160 geschrieben. Die Text-Tradition ist schlecht: «Die 24 Bücher ... sind zum Teil nur in byzantinischen Auszügen erhalten und einzeln oder in Gruppen verschieden überliefert ...», H. HUNGER et al., Die Textüberlieferung der antiken Literatur und der Bibel, 1975, 585.

[6] Kapitel Syr. 50/252. Vgl. E. SCHÜRER [- G. VERMES], The History of the Jewish People, 1973, 550, Anm. 160.

[7] E.M. SMALLWOOD, The Jews under Roman Rule, 1976, 444, aber auch dort: «There is no explicit literary reference to the Jewish recovery of Jerusalem».

[8] Dialogus cum Tryphone 108,3.

Festzuhalten ist, daß die jüdischen literarischen Quellen die Aussage des Appianos und Justinos nicht stützen. Bar Kochba tritt im Felde und hauptsächlich in Bethar auf. Jerusalems Schicksal wird allerdings an einer Stelle erwähnt, auf die sich AVI-YONAH beruft: «Es blieb dem Statthalter Quintus Tineius Rufus nichts anderes übrig, als die X. Legion und die römische Zivilbevölkerung aus Jerusalem zurückzuziehen, ein Ereignis, das in der Megi[l]lat Ta[ʻa]nit für den 17.Elul (Juli/August) verzeichnet ist. In Jerusalem wurde eine geordnete Verwaltung eingerichtet»[9]. In dem meist herangezogenen Text der «Fastenrolle»[10] heißt es allerdings: «So verließen die Römer Jerusalem». Aber in zwei Handschriften steht etwas anderes: «So wurden die Römer herausgetrieben aus Judaea und Jerusalem». AVI-YONAH berücksichtigt nur die erstgenannte Fassung. Die Textüberlieferung ist demnach völlig unsicher, und die Meinungen über deren Sinn sind geteilt, weil die Fastenrolle nichts darüber verrät, wann dies geschah. Niemand kann also mit Gewißheit sagen, ob es sich hier um einen Hinweis auf das *Bellum Iudaicum* (66-73) oder den Bar-Kochba-Krieg (132-135) oder gar die Hasmonäer-Erhebung (166-152 v.Chr.) handelt, wobei das Scholion zur Fastenrolle von der Zeit der «Könige der Griechen» spricht, also von den Seleukiden. Letzteres würde nur für die Hasmonäer-Zeit gelten[11].

Wie steht es aber mit den Rollenfunden vom Toten Meer? Sie nennen uns eine ganze Reihe wichtiger Orte in Judäa, die in den Händen der Aufständischen waren, aber nicht Jerusalem. Nur in einem einzigen Datierungsfragment glaubt J.T. MILIK den Namen Jerusalem lesen zu können. Er fügt aber hinzu, daß dieses kleine Stück Papyrus aus einem Rattenloch stammt und sehr wohl auf das Bellum Iudaicum Bezug haben kann[12]. Wir haben also hier eine negative Evidenz, nicht eine einzige gesicherte Belegstelle für Jerusalem in den Rollenfunden, und dies wiegt schwer.

Entscheidend ist aber eine zweite negative Evidenz, und sie ist numismatischer Art. Wie die Untersuchung der Münzfunde zeigt, war das Territorium der Aufständischen das judäische Hochland unter Ausschluß Jerusalems. Dieses ist ein eindeutiges Ergebnis, das von den Rollenfunden bestätigt wird. Es ist auch festzuhalten, daß es in den letzten 100 Jahren keine einzige zuverlässige Nachricht von einem Bar-Kochba-Münzfund gegeben hat, der in Jerusalem selbst gemacht worden wäre. N. AVIGAD hat jüngst große Teile des direkt beim Tempelberg liegenden Jerusalemer «Jewish Quarter» in der Oberstadt systematisch ausgegraben. Er fand Münzen von der persischen Periode durch alle Besiedlungsschichten hindurch bis in die neuere Zeit, darunter Prägungen der Hasmonäer, Herodianer und eine bedeutende Gruppe des Bellum Iudaicum, aber kein einziges Bar-Kochba-Stück[13]. Die gleiche Erfahrung wie

[9] AVI-YONAH, PRE Suppl. 13 (1974) 402.
[10] Edition H. LICHTENSTEIN, Die Fastenrolle ..., HUCA 8-9 (1931-1932) 257-351; J.A. FITZMYER - D.J. HARRINGTON, A Manual of Palestinian Aramaic Texts, 1978, 186 Nr. 150:6].
[11] Hinweis D. Jeselsohn, Jerusalem.
[12] Discoveries in the Judaean Desert II, Oxford 1961, 134f. Der Schriftduktus ist früh.
[13] Archaeological Discoveries in the Jewish Quarter of Jerusalem, IMJ 1976, 24f: «coins».

N. Avigad in Jerusalem machte Y. Yadin auf Masada. Unter den 5000 Münzen, die er dort fand, stammte nicht eine einzige aus dem Bar-Kochba-Krieg[14].
Im Jahre 132 residierte der Konsular Q. Tineius Rufus als Legat für Judäa in Cäsarea ad Mare. Die Legio VI Ferrata lag nordöstlich seiner Residenz auf der Straße nach Samaria und Galiläa in Capercotna, das später «Legio» genannt wurde. Die Legio X Fretensis befand sich im Lager in Jerusalem[15]. Wie wir aus den Rollenfunden wissen, gab es einzelne, kleinere römische Garnisonen in ganz Judäa.
Unter diesen Umständen konnte der Kampf weder im Gebiet von Cäsarea noch in Jerusalem selbst begonnen haben, sondern irgendwo im judäischen Hochland – und zwar als Guerillakrieg. Bar Kochba hat also dort losgeschlagen, wo er Aussicht auf den wichtigen Anfangserfolg hatte. An dem Felsen von Masada hätte er sich festgerannt. Die Eroberung der Hügelstellungen in Jerusalem mit der dort seit 60 Jahren installierten Legion wäre für ihn zu verlustreich gewesen. Er zog es offensichtlich vor, sein Herrschaftsgebiet in den judäischen Bergen zu konsolidieren und den Angriff der Römer in einem für ihn günstigen Gelände zu erwarten. Andererseits ist es durchaus möglich, daß der Statthalter die volle Gefahr nicht erkannte und den Gegner falsch einschätzte, als er die 6. Legion nach Süden in Marsch setzte und die 10. gar aus dem sicheren Jerusalem abzog und in die Wüste Juda beorderte. Bar Kochba muß beiden schwere Verluste beigebracht und sie zum Rückzug gezwungen haben. Es muß ihm auch gelungen sein, die aus den benachbarten Provinzen herbeigeeilten römischen Hilfstruppen zu besiegen. Daß er die aus Ägypten herbeiziehende Legio XXII Deiotariana abgefangen und wohl fast gänzlich aufgerieben hat, ist wahrscheinlich[16].
Nur so sind die bedeutenden Anfangserfolge zu erklären. Aus ihnen ergibt sich eine dreieinhalb Jahre lang andauernde Herrschaft über das schwer zugängliche judäische Hochland und eine ungestörte Administration dieses nicht kleinen Gebietes[17]. Dann lief die Kampagne des Severus an. Stück für Stück des Bar Kochba-Territoriums wurde, wohl von Süden her[18], zurückerobert. Für einen solchen

---

[14] YADIN, Bar Kochba, 1971, 188. Zu YADINs Gedanken, IEJ 15 (1965) 119, für die Aufständischen wäre Masada zu einer Falle geworden, siehe SMALLWOOD, The Jews under Roman Rule, 1976, 443, Anm. 62 (Vergleich mit Herodion).

[15] Zu dem Legaten und den beiden Legionen vgl. SCHÜRER [-VERMES], The History of the Jewish People, 1973, 547ff, Anm. 150; AVI-YONAH, PRE Suppl. 13 (1974) 400 (mit Belegen in CIL III, 6814-6816 und A. ECK, Vestigia 13, 1970, 17, Anm. 84) sowie SMALLWOOD, The Jews under Roman Rule, 1976, 436f und besonders G.W. BOWERSOCK, JRS 65 (1975) 184 (Besprechung der revidierten Edition von Schürer).

[16] Die 22. Legion wird zum letzten Male im Jahre 119 erwähnt und kommt in der Gesamtliste der Legionen von 145 nicht mehr vor. Allerdings wissen wir nichts über die Deiotariana von 119 bis 132. Siehe hierzu besonders: SMALLWOOD, The Jews under Roman Rule, 1976, 447, n. 72; SCHÜRER[-VERMES], The History of the Jewish People, 1973, 548, n. 150 (6) unten; AVI-YONAH, PRE Suppl. 13 (1974) 403; A. KINDLER, in: Numismatic Studies and Researches II, 1958, 68.

[17] Hierfür zeugen nicht nur die ungewöhnlich große Kriegsmacht, die Hadrian aufbot (wohl 4, wenn nicht 5 Legionen, viele Hilfstruppen und die syrische Flotte: SCHÜRER[-VERMES], The History of the Jewish People, 1973, Anm. 150,1-7), sondern auch die sprechenden Details der Urkunden vom Toten Meer und die Bar-Kochba-Münzen.

[18] Hinweis Sh. Qedar, Jerusalem.

Verlauf des Krieges sprechen für einmal auch Dios Angaben[19], vor allem aber die Rollenfunde vom Toten Meer, die römischen Sachquellen und schließlich auch die numismatische Evidenz.

Daß die Eroberung Jerusalems und der Wiederaufbau des Tempels ein Hauptziel Bar Kochba's war, das künden die Münzen in ganz unmißverständlicher Weise. Unsere Quellenanalyse hat aber keinen Beweis dafür ergeben, daß es ihm auch gelungen ist, Jerusalem wirklich zu erobern und zu halten.

---

[19] Cassius Dion Cocceianus, *Rhōmaïka*, wohl um 220 verfaßt, besonders 69,13-2 (nur in den byzantinischen Auszügen des 11.Jahrhunderts durch Xiphilinos erhalten).

# Bar Kokhba Coins and Documents[*]

## (Tf. LIX - LXI)

In April 1949 I published an article on the Eleazar coins of the Bar Kokhba rebellion, introducing the die-comparison methodology into Jewish numismatics[1]. At the same time, «decisive steps toward the greatest manuscript find of modern times»[2] were being made in the systematic search of Qumran cave I, undertaken by HARDING and DE VAUX. Today, thirty years later, the Bar Kokhba coins and documents are being used together to clarify the history and significance of the Bar Kokhba war of A.D. 132-135 within Jewish life and within the Roman Empire at large. Numismatists are able to understand the Bar Kokhba coins better knowing the Bar Kokhba documents just as historians are able to make better use of the documents knowing the coins. But do we really know all the documents[3] and coins found? The Dead Sea finds from the sites of Qumran, Murabbaʻat and the Naḥal Ḥever have not, in fact, joined – as they should have – the Bar Kokhba coins as one of the primary sources for the history of the Bar Kokhba war; for neither the Jordanian nor the Israeli scrolls, documents and letters have been published *in toto* [4].

As for the coins, a large body of important material remains unavailable since I still have not published my Corpus of the Bar Kokhba coinage commenced in the late forties. There is, however, a good reason for this delay: between 1965 and 1978 several huge hoards of Bar Kokhba coins, mainly in silver, have come to light, and new coins have therefore been reaching the compiler of the corpus constantly since 1965. The Bar Kokhba texts, on the other hand, have been available to the editors for decades. The recent coin hoards will certainly change the picture of Bar Kokhba coinage for they account for roughly two thirds of all Bar Kokhba coins known – the remaining one third (registered prior to the recent hoard discoveries) being the material known from the time of ECKHEL's «Doctrina Nummorum» (1792-1798) up to the summer of 1965. The evidence of thousands of new coins unearthed only in the

---

[*] This article is the revised text of a James C. Loeb Classical Lecture delivered, with slides, at Harvard University on April 5, 1979. I am indebted to J.T. Milik and Y. Yadin, the editors of the Bar Kokhba papyri, to G. Vermes, E.M. Smallwood, and S. Applebaum for their recent publications and to K. Patricia Erhart for revision of the English text.

[1] Hist. Jud. 11 (1949) 71-108, Pl. 1-2 [hier S. 183-201].

[2] G. VERMES, The Dead Sea Scrolls, London 1977.

[3] J.T. MILIK, Textes hébreux et araméens, in: Discoveries in the Judaean Desert II, Les grottes de Murabbaʻat, Oxford 1961; Y. YADIN, Expedition D to the Judaean Desert, 1960, IEJ 11 (1961) 36ff; id., Expedition D to the Judean Desert, 1961, IEJ 12 (1962) 227ff.

[4] Cf. G. VERMES' bitter statement in The Dead Sea Scrolls, 1977, 23-24.

last decades cannot, of course, be neglected. By the end of 1978, the catalogue part of the Corpus was finally ready when the message came that some hundred silver coins had been found between Bethlehem and Hebron. In early January 1979, I rushed to Bethlehem and saw there 669 silver Bar Kokhba coins, all obviously coming from the same hoard, allegedly found in a locality called el-Fawwār. Permission was granted to register the coins but not to photograph or weigh them. Moreover, fair warning was given at that time that the find must have been larger than the 669 pieces registered; in fact, a figure of around 1500 pieces seems likely.

In the case of the Bar Kokhba war, the unavailability of known evidence such as that provided by the coins and documents is particularly lamentable, for neither the Roman sources in Latin and Greek nor the Jewish and Christian traditions for the so-called Second Jewish Revolt (or Rebellion or War) are of great value. «Aber wie unsäglich dürftig sind überhaupt diese Quellen», the historian EMIL SCHÜRER fittingly exclaimed in 1901 in his brilliant history of the Jewish people in the time of Jesus Christ[5]. Since SCHÜRER the situation has improved, albeit not as much as could be hoped. Even so, the new English edition of SCHÜRER's history[6] and other recent contributions[7] together with the Bar Kokhba documents, letters, and coins undoubtedly offer future historians the opportunity to draw a much more lively and detailed picture of the Bar Kokhba war than their predecessors have been able to do. This article will now, however, merely attempt to survey the new facts and point out the remaining problems.

## 1. The Legend of Bar Kokhba

Fact and fiction intermingle in the legend of Bar Kokhba, the great Jewish war leader of the second century A.D. The Bar Kokhba story begins with a Jewish tradition recorded in the Jerusalem version of the Talmud, namely Ta'anit 4,8-68d on Balaam's prophecy in Numbers 24,17, an eschatological text which is also of key importance for the Qumran community of the Essenes[8]. We must examine closely three passages to understand the conflation which has occurred within our sources for Bar Kokhba. First, the biblical prophecy: «A star shall come out of Jacob ...». Next, from the Talmud, the interpretation which the great rabbi Akiba ben Joseph is reported to have given: «Kosiba came out of Jacob, for when Akiba saw Bar Kosiba, he exclaimed: This is the King Messiah!». And finally, from the Talmud again, Rabbi

---

[5] Geschichte des Jüdischen Volkes im Zeitalter Jesu Christi I, Leipzig 1901, 686.

[6] The new English version: The History of the Jewish People in the Age of Jesus Christ, 175 B.C.-A.D. 135, a new English version, rev. and ed. G. VERMES and F. MILLAR, liter. ed. P. Vermes and organiz. editor M. Black, Edinburgh 1973.

[7] Y. YADIN, Bar Kokhba, London 1971; G. VERMES, The Dead Sea Scrolls, 1977, passim; E.M. SMALLWOOD, The Jews under Roman Rule, Leiden 1976, esp. 428-486; S. APPLEBAUM, Prolegomena to the Study of the Second Jewish Revolt, A.D. 132-135 (BAR Suppl.Series 7), Oxford 1976; B. LIFSHITZ, Jérusalem sous la domination romaine, ANRW II,8 (1977) 444-489.

[8] Cf. G. VERMES, The Dead Sea Scrolls, 1977, 81.

Jochanan ben Torta's retort: «Akiba, grass will grow out of your cheeks and the Son of David will still not have come».

We can easily appreciate what happened. The Hebrew word for star is *kōkhāb*, the Aramaic *kōkhbā*. Rabbi Akiba draws a parallel between the leader of the rebellion, Bar Kosiba, and the long-awaited Messiah by equating the leader's name Kosiba with the word *kōkhbā* or star, a symbol of the Messiah: Bar Kosiba – Bar Kokhba. Thus, the war leader's real name vanished and was replaced by Bar Kokhba until the documents discovered in this century reestablished it. Meanwhile, two versions of the man's name circulated in Jewish tradition. The positive version, accepted also by Eusebius, Jerome, and Justin, identifies the war leader by the Messianic name βαρχοχέβας or «Son of the Star» (Eusebius, in fact, uses simply ἀστήρ, «star»). The negative version is wholly pejorative; it identifies the leader as Bar Koziba changing the *s* (*sāmekh*) to *z* (*zayin*) to make «Son of the Lie»[9].

The messianic name Bar Kokhba is still employed today for the Jewish war leader and this name may prevail in times to come, even though we now know that the man himself never pretended to be the Messiah. The documents discovered 30 years ago give his full name in Hebrew, Aramaic, and Greek: *Shim'ōn ben Kōsibā*, *Shim'ōn bar Kōsibā*, *Nāśī' Yiśrā'ēl* or *Nāśī' 'al Yiśrā'ēl*, which translated means «Simon, son of Kosiba, Prince of (or over) Israel». The title «prince» here does not mean that Bar Kosiba was of princely blood. He simply appropriated this title to legitimize his position as ruler.

In retrospect, it is clear that one should have trusted more fully in the numismatic evidence; for the coins, which have been known and studied for centuries, provide not only the war leader's name Shim'on[10], but also his assumed title *Nāśī' Yiśrā'él*. And one should not have accepted the literary tradition so faithfully. Akiba may have been the brain and even the heart of the revolt, but it does not seem likely that Akiba, in fact, proclaimed the military leader and prince Shim'on Bar Kosiba as the Messiah of the House of David[11].

By the time of the Bar Kokhba rebellion, the heyday of eschatological dreams had been over for nearly a century. The leading Pharisaic rabbis had managed to strengthen their leadership, whereas the priestly Sadducees and the Essene-Chassidic com-

---

[9] Cf. E. SCHÜRER[-G. VERMES], The History of the Jewish People, 1973, 543 and n. 130, see also n. 131.

[10] Along with other scholars, I too hesitated to accept the coins at face value when I stated in 1949: «Bar Kochba himself may well have given the order for the coinage, but we cannot justifiably assume that he desired to put his own first name on the coins as there is not the slightest indication that his name was actually Simon», Hist. Jud. 11 (1949) 92 [hier S. 194]. E. SCHÜRER, Geschichte des Jüdischen Volkes I, 1901, 684, however, was right: «Den eigentlichen Namen des Mannes haben uns die Münzen erhalten».

[11] For the *opinio communis* that Bar Kokhba was identified as the Messiah cf. in particular E. SCHÜRER, Geschichte des Jüdischen Volkes I, 1901, 685; id.[-G. VERMES], The History of the Jewish People, 1973, 544; E.M. SMALLWOOD, The Jews under Roman Rule, 1976, 440; Y. YADIN, Bar Kokhba, 1971, 27; J.T. MILIK, DJD II (1961) 126 ad L.3. For the opposite view see infra and G. ALLON, History, Merḥavia 1955, 36 (Hebrew). Cf. P. SCHÄFER, Studien zur Geschichte und Theologie des Judentums und Urchristentums, Leiden 1978, 90: «Deswegen beinhaltet sie allerdings keineswegs eine feierliche Proklamation Bar Kokhbas zum Messias».

munities had vanished from history with the destruction of the Temple in the *Bellum Iudaicum*. After that Great War of 66-74 and particularly around the year 100, the rabbis at the academy of Jamnia succeeded in forging a new Jewish life centered around the Law without Temple or State. In the first decades of the second century Rabbi Akiba ben Joseph appeared as the undisputed successor of the great Jamnia Pharisaic rabbis Hillel, Jochanan ben Zakkai, and Gamiel II. There was, as we shall see later, a strong reason for Akiba to join forces with the rebellion[12]; nevertheless, the «ordination» of Shim'on ben Kosiba by Rabbi Akiba is a tradition which originated in a misunderstanding of a much later time and, therefore, cannot be considered as historical evidence. Not only does it remain unconfirmed by the Bar Kokhba coins, but it is, in fact, flatly contradicted by the Bar Kokhba letters and documents.

First, the coins. In the past, much emphasis was put on the alleged star[13] seen above the temple on the coins (Tf. LIX 3-9). But for nearly a century numismatists have stressed the fact that the star is actually just a rosette. Other pieces have a wavy line or a cross in the same place, which proves that there is no symbolic value in any of the three designs seen above the temple[14]. Thus, there is absolutely nothing on the second century coins of the Bar Kokhba war to prove the «Son of the Star» tradition of later times.

The evidence of the Bar Kokhba documents is still more striking; it completely excludes an identification of Bar Kokhba as the Messiah. As we have seen, the Jewish military leader did not proclaim himself the King Messiah or the Priest Messiah or the Prophet Messiah[15] but only Prince of Israel. And truly he was a ruler, in both name and deed. Not only did he usurp the emperor's prerogative of striking silver coins, but he also appropriated Roman crown land and leased it for hard cash – his own silver coins – to the Jewish peasants. This fact, which is of the highest importance, is established by the papyri. The most striking document is Murabba'at 24[16], a part of the notarial archives of Beth Guvrin under Bar Kosiba. Yehudah ben Rabba, one of four leaseholders designated by their full names, specifies the location of his allotment and the authority who leases it: «the piece of land which is (now) mine by leasing and which is situated in the town of Naḥash, and which I have leased from Shim'on Prince of Israel». Other documents show us the legendary Bar Kokhba as a pious Jew, a good administrator, and a stern, severe commander. The legend is gone; the man is here to stay.

---

[12] Cf. below, section 8 «The Reason for the War» and cf. G. VERMES, The Dead Sea Scrolls, 1977, 163: «The interest of the Church in the messianic role of Jesus is apt to assign a greater importance to Messianism in Jewish religion than the historical evidence justifies».

[13] Cf. L. HAMBURGER's caustic commentary upon the star thesis in Die Silber-Münzprägung während des letzten Aufstandes der Israeliten gegen Rom, ZfN 18 (1892) 305.

[14] L. MILDENBERG, Hist. Jud. 11 (1949), n. 17 [hier S.190]; id., Eine Überprägung des 2. Aufstandes der Juden gegen Rom, SNR 33 (1947) 18; G. ALLON, History, 1955, 36; Y. MESHORER, in: B. LIFSHITZ, ANRW II,8 (1977) 481 («note additionelle»).

[15] Cf. G. VERMES, The Dead Sea Scrolls, 1977, 182ff.

[16] DJD II (1961) 122-134 and pls. 35-37.

## 2. The Chronology of the Rebellion

Hadrian visited the east in 130 and 131. For once, all the written sources seemed to agree[17]: they all pointed to the year 132 for the outbreak of the war. But still there was no proof. And this time, the Roman Imperial coins, always handy sources of information for historians and archaeologists, did not offer conclusive evidence. There are two reasons for this extraordinary failure. Hadrian dated his coins only at the beginning of his reign, in fact, only during his first three years. On his coins he was successively titled *cos* , *cos II* , and *cos III* , and then he decided – unfortunately for us – to remain *cos III* until his death in 138. Hadrian was accorded tribunician power 22 times, but he neglected to count the *tribunicia potestas* on his coins beyond the first period, something which none of his predecessors or successors neglected to do. As for his additional titles, Hadrian began by designating himself *Imperator Caesar Traianus Hadrianus Optimus Augustus Germanicus Dacicus Parthicus* in the grand manner of Trajan, but he soon reduced all this to a simple but monumental Hadrianus Augustus, to which he later added the conventional *PP* for *Pater Patriae* . This was sufficient for Hadrian and for the Roman citizen of his time.

The second reason for the lack of evidence lies in Hadrian's coinage policy. Hadrian, more than any other emperor, was aware of the tremendous impact that coins had on public opinion. His coinage systematically proclaimed the principles and achievements of his reign and recorded all major events, even down to his arrivals in the different provinces[18]. We might well ask: where are the reflections of the one great war Hadrian fought using all his military might for more than three years? P.L. STRACK has devoted 8 pages to this *Bellum Iudaicum* trying to reconstruct the effects of the Bar Kokhba war on Roman Imperial coinage[19]. There is, however, no evidence. Admittedly, a new *Iudaea Capta* or *Iudaea Devicta* series was impossible because there was no independent Jewish state after 74. A victory coin type such as *De Iudaeis* after the Roman suppression of the Jewish rebellion would, however, have been appropriate, but the emperor's veto must have prevented this. For Hadrian, this τῶν Ἰουδαίων πόλεμος as Dio called it, was a mere revolt, a personal affront to be avenged quickly and erased from memory. Apparently the emperor considered neither the revolt itself nor even an illusion to the subduing of the rebels worthy of mention on his proclamatory coinage.

Does the autonomous bronze coinage in the East in contrast offer any direct chronological indications for the Bar Kokhba rebellion? The answer is unfortunately no. We are, therefore, forced to return to the Bar Kokhba coins. Upon careful investigation, it is apparent that these coins are all overstruck on foreign pieces and very often reveal clear traces of the underlying types and legends. I found an undated Jewish

---

[17] Cf. E. SCHÜRER[-G. VERMES], The History of the Jewish People, 1973, n. 92 and n. 126.

[18] Coins of the Roman Empire in the British Museum III, 339f and 487-496.

[19] Untersuchungen zur Römischen Reichsprägung des zweiten Jahrhunderts, Teil II, Stuttgart 1933, 132-139.

medium bronze[20] in Reverend E. ROGERS' Handy Guide to Jewish Coins published in 1914; the specimen was overstruck on a coin from Gaza which happened to be dated twice, a fact not previously noted. On this interesting piece the two dates 131 and 132 are easily recognized. It is obvious that the Bar Kokhba type must be later than the underlying coin. An irrefutable *terminus post quem* for this Bar Kokhba coin exists.

In 1963 A. KINDLER published another Bar Kokhba-Gaza overstrike, also undated[21]. His coin was issued in Gaza in 132/133, a year later than the one of ROGERS. It therefore seems unlikely that the hostilities could have begun in the spring of 132; the early autumn of 132 seems more probable. Otherwise, KINDLER's bronze could hardly have reached the rebels, as an unrestricted flow of coins from the coast to the Judaean mountains was hardly possible after the outbreak of the war. The Bar Kokhba documents also point to a date in autumn 132. Murabba'at 24, the same lease which revealed Shim'on ben Kosiba as landlord and Prince of Israel, also provides some important evidence for the chronology of the Bar Kokhba rebellion. This contract counts the «year of the Redemption» not only according to the years of the rebels' era but also according to the years of the Sabbatical Cycle. This double dating enables us to establish the year in which the war began because we know how to calculate the sabbatical years. Josephus tells us that the year 68/69 was a sabbatical year. According to the calculations of the editor MILIK, the year 130/131 was just such a sabbatical year. MILIK concluded that the war broke out on the first day of Tishri, a day at the beginning of September in 131[22]. He quoted the writer's article on the overstruck Gaza coin[23] and stated that «cette date s'accorde parfaitement avec les données numismatiques». In fact, MILIK's arithmetic was at fault[24], as was immediately noticed. Making good use of MILIK's own tabulation, one can easily discover that the document Murabba'at 24 places the outbreak of hostilities not in September 131 but in September 132.

A further indication of the date of the war's outbreak appears in the amazing polylingual documents of the Jewish matron Babata. The latest document found in Babata's bundle is dated the nineteenth of August in the year 132. We know that shortly after this Babata fled from Nabataea to the secure Dead Sea settlement of Engedi, a Jewish stronghold. If the war had already started in the spring of 132, Babata would not have had a chance to reach the Engedi area[25] in August or

---

[20] L. MILDENBERG, Numismatische Evidenz zur Chronologie der Bar Kochba-Erhebung, SNR 34 (1948-1949) 19-27, pl. 3 [hier S. 176-182, Tf. LII].

[21] A. KINDLER, Ein Münzpalimpsest aus dem Bar-Kochba-Krieg, SNR 42 (1962-1963) 14-20, pl. 2; M. AVI-YONAH, PRE Suppl. 13 (1974) 401, 60-65, accepts «autumn 132» but stresses that the later Jewish tradition counts the outbreak back to the first Nissan (the New Year during the reign of the Kings) in spring 132; the same counting goes for the *Bellum Iudaicum* (outbreak summer 66, traditional dating first Nissan 66).

[22] DJD II (1961) 125 ad L.1.

[23] Cf. L. MILDENBERG, SNR 34 (1948-1949) 19-27 [hier S. 176-182].

[24] M.R. LEHMANN, Studies in the Murabba'at and Naḥal Ḥever Documents, Revue de Qumran 4 (1963-1964) 56.

[25] Cf. Y. YADIN, IEJ 12 (1962) 248.

September of 132 because the route would have been cut off by the Roman army. Therefore, the war must have broken out in late summer or early autumn of 132.

The Jewish and Roman sources report that the war lasted more than three years[26]. In the coinage, the relatively small issue of the «year one» was followed by a larger output in the «year 2» and by a very large one which was undated. These are the three periods of the Bar Kokhba coinage. The Jews did not date their coins in the third or fourth year of the war, but they continued to date their letters and deeds. The latest date so far known appears in Murabba'at 30[27] in the first line of a bill of sale for a piece of land. The date is the twenty-first of Tishri of the «year four of the Redemption of Israel»; this is the end of September 135. According to Jewish tradition the Bethar stronghold fell on the fatal day of 9 Ab in that year, which means August 135. We know from Roman inscriptions that Hadrian won his acclamation as *imp II* after 134 and probably toward the end of 135[28]. There can be no other reason for the acceptance of this title by the old emperor than his victory over the Jews.

As for the internal chronology and specifically for the course of the war, the coins and documents published so far do not enlighten us. We still do not know whether Bar Kosiba conquered the whole territory by surprise at the outbreak of hostilities or only slowly during the first and second years of the war. The same holds true for the war of reconquest planned by Hadrian's general Iulius Severus after he had arrived from Britain in Judaea. We do not know when it began or how it proceeded.

## 3. The Bar Kokhba Territory

In his critical analysis of the Talmudic sources, BÜCHLER was able to demonstrate as early as 1904 that the rebels' territory was Judaea and not all of Palestine[29]. All the localities mentioned in the Bar Kokhba documents and known to us can be placed within a circle which does not reach the Mediterranean on the West[30], Jerusalem and Jericho on the North, nor Masada on the South (Tf. LX map 1). The same holds true for the major Bar Kokhba coin hoards. They occur in Herodion, Latrūn, Hebron, Idna, Dahariyeh and el-Fawwār, but not in Jerusalem, Jericho, or Masada (Tf. LXI map 2). A synopsis of all the sites evidenced by the Bar Kokhba coins and the do-

---

[26] Cf. above, n. 17; Y. YADIN, Bar Kokhba, 1971, 23; E.M. SMALLWOOD, The Jews under Roman Rule, 1976, 455f; cf. S. APPLEBAUM, Prolegomena to the Study of the Second Jewish Revolt, 1976, 52ff.

[27] DJD II (1961) 124-148.

[28] E. SCHÜRER[-G. VERMES], The History of the Jewish People, 1973, 553, n. 174; A.B. BOSWORTH, Arrian and the Alani, HSCP 81 (1977) 218, n. 5: «Hostilities may have dragged out until the end of the year». I had expressed a similar view, SNR 34 (1948-1949) 26, n. 19 [hier S. 182 Anm. 18].

[29] A. BÜCHLER, JQR 16 (1904) 143ff.

[30] It is unlikely that the rebels ever reached the coast southwest of the Judaean hills as the autonomous Gaza mint struck bronze coins for Hadrian without interruption in the years 131/132 and 132/133 (cf. above, n.20 and n.21), 133/134 and 134/135 (BMC Palestine, 50-52 and 53-55).

cuments uncovered in this century (Tf. LIX map 3) reveals the limits of the Bar Kokhba territory.

As to Jerusalem itself and its situation during the war the following facts were stressed in a recent article by me[31]. Local scholars, dealers, and collectors uniformly agree that Bar Kokhba coin hoards have never been found in the city. N. AVIGAD dug for years in a large area of the Jewish Quarter near the Temple mount. He found coins from as early as the Persian period around 400 B.C. up to the British occupation of this century. For example, shekels and half shekels in silver and many bronzes of the *Bellum Iudaicum* (66-74) were found. There was, in fact only one conspicuous gap in the coin history of Jerusalem: not one single Bar Kokhba coin was found[32]. And this fact is of highest importance. One may say that such an argument *ex silentio* is of little significance. But if the rebels were holding Jerusalem for at least two years, which is the *opinio communis* [33] (and even the view expressed in the new English edition of SCHUERER's history) the greater part of Bar Kokhba coins would obviously have been discovered in Jerusalem. Moreover, we do not know of any Bar Kokhba material found north of Jerusalem, in either Samaria or Galilaea. Nor did YADIN find any Bar Kokhba coins during his excavation of Masada. And why is this the case? Because of simple topographical and strategical reasons. Bar Kosiba wanted to avoid having any of his garrisons fall into the «Masada trap»[34], as had happened with disastrous results in the years 70 to 74. As for Jerusalem, we know for certain that the Roman *Legio Decima Fretensis* had been commanded to hold the city. Bar Kosiba would never have been so foolish as to attack a full Roman legion in a fortified camp such as that of Jerusalem, so easily defensible, situated on the heights[35]. Although it would have been an extremely risky proposition for Bar Kosiba to attack Jerusalem from any direction, it would

---

[31] L. MILDENBERG, Bar Kochba in Jerusalem?, SM 105 (1977) 1-6 [hier S. 212-216].

[32] N. AVIGAD, Archaeological Discoveries in the Jewish Quarter of Jerusalem, Israel Museum, Jerusalem 1976, 24f: «Coins».

[33] Y. YADIN, Bar Kokhba, 1971, 18; B. LIFSHITZ, ANRW II,8 (1977) 482; E.M. SMALLWOOD, The Jews under Roman Rule, 1976, 443; A. GARZETTI, From Tiberius to the Antonines, London 1974, 423. In fact, «There is no explicit literary reference to the Jewish recovery of Jerusalem», as even SMALLWOOD admits (The Jews under Roman Rule, 1976, 444). The generalizing statements in Megillat Ta'anit for 17th Elul and in the Byzantine excerpts of Appian's Rom. Hist. Syr. 50, 252 do not say that the rebels reconquered the city. Even if they indicated such a reconquest it would not be conclusive as it could result from conflation with other dates and events in later epitomes. Appian wrote in the time of the Antonines and may well have had in mind Hadrian's measures after the war.

[34] Y. YADIN, The Excavation of Masada 1963/1964, IEJ 15 (1965) 119. Cf. E.M. SMALLWOOD, The Jews under Roman Rule, 1976, 443, n. 62: a comparison of Masada and Herodion which does not seem convincing to me as the topographical situation of the two fortresses is not the same.

[35] E. SCHÜRER[-G. VERMES], The History of the Jewish People, 1973, 550: «The fortifications were inadequate». I hold that for psychological, topographical, and strategical reasons the Roman administration did not neglect Jerusalem. Cf. G.W. BOWERSOCK in his review of SCHÜRER[-VERMES], The History of the Jewish People, 1973, in: JRS 65 (1975) 145: «The revolt of 115-117 had taught the Romans that a stronger garrison was needed in Judaea».

have been especially dangerous for him to attack the city from the north or north-west, because the Roman garrison in the provincial capital of Caesarea Maritima and the *Legio Sexta Ferrata* at Caparcotna were stationed in his rear. There is irrefutable evidence that Judaea was a consular province with two legions stationed there well before the outbreak of the Bar Kokhba War[36]. As we have seen before, the evidence provided by the coin hoards and the facts given in the documents exclude the possibility that Jerusalem was at any time in the hands of the rebels. There are, however, Bar Kokhba coin inscriptions which seem to prove the contrary. The name Jerusalem is found in all three periods of the Bar Kokhba coinage and the inscription «For the Freedom of Jerusalem» appears on undated coins of the third period. This has led many numismatists and historians to conclude that Jerusalem was in the hands of the rebels during the Bar Kokhba War. The various interpretations suggested may be summarized as follows: first, Jerusalem was reconquered by the rebels at the beginning of the war and remained in their hands for three full years; second, Jerusalem remained in Jewish hands for the first two years only and was then lost again; third, Jerusalem was not only in the hands of the rebels, but the city itself was one of three minting authorities for the rebellion coinage – the two others being the Priest Eleazar, whose name appears on some coins, and Shim'on Bar Kosiba, the legendary Bar Kokhba.

Even if the appearance of the word «Jerusalem» on the Bar Kokhba coinage might suggest that the rebels held the city, such an interpretation could never stand against the weightier evidence of the Bar Kokhba coin hoards and documents. Yet this interpretation remains current, even though it neglects some fundamental facts of the Bar Kokhba coinage stressed by me from 1949 on[37]. There was only one minting authority, the centralized rebel administration. This body employed the name of the Priest Eleazar at the beginning of the revolt to demonstrate the rebels' faithfulness to the Jewish past, just as it employed the name of Shim'on Prince of Israel throughout the revolt to strengthen Bar Kosiba's position as its leader. This same rebel body used the name Jerusalem not as a mint indication, but as a war slogan, a verbal rallying point for the rebel forces. Let me stress here that the Bar Kokhba coinage served the aims of the rebels perfectly. They placed their own Jewish coin types over Roman issues, thereby utilizing money which had previously served the purpose of the Roman Empire. The types of the Bar Kokhba tetradrachms are eloquent: the Temple facade with the slogan «Jerusalem» is meant to replace the portrait and name of the Emperor (Tf. LIX 1-2). On the reverse the palm branch and citrus fruit used during the Feast of the Tabernacles together with date and era are meant to replace the Roman pagan deity and accompanying Latin or Greek inscription.

To conclude our examination of the Jerusalem problem: the thesis that the city was conquered by Bar Kosiba and served as a rebel mint has to be completely abandoned until a substantial hoard of Bar Kokhba coins is found in the city of Jerusalem.

---

[36] B. ISAAC and I. ROLL, ZPE (1979) 145-155 on a new milestone southeast of Acre showing the *Legio II Traiana* in Judaea in A.D. 120 (information G.W. Bowersock).
[37] L. MILDENBERG, Hist. Jud. 11 (1949) 90f [hier S. 195].

## 4. The Rebel State

It was the rebels' aim to create an independent state. Their coinage was a solemn and public declaration of independence. Striking silver coins, the rebels took over one of the Roman emperor's most important prerogatives. With one blow of the hammer they assumed sovereignty and – from the Roman point of view – committed high treason. By overstriking the Roman coins, the rebels kept the Roman monetary standard. Four Bar Kokhba denarii equal one Bar Kokhba tetradrachm, just as four denarii of the imperial mint equal one tetradrachm of the Syrian provincial coinage. This is proven in the Bar Kokhba documents where the rebels' denarius is rendered in Hebrew as *sūs* , the tetradrachm as *sela`* . A legal document dated «24 Tishri of the fourth year of the Redemption of Israel» quotes a price in the following manner: 88 sus (the equivalent of) 22 sela[38].

In the First Revolt of 66-74, the Jewish rebels had controlled a large territory which included the capital Jerusalem, and they had enough silver at their disposal. In the Bar Kokhba revolt, the rebels under Shim`on Bar Kosiba held only a restricted area of Judaea which did not include Jerusalem. They had no silver metal in bars or vessels, but they did have Roman silver coins. Thus it was only by overstriking foreign money that the rebels could create an independent coinage. Perhaps they initially got the idea from carelessly overstruck coins which found their way to Judaea – either from overstruck Hadrianic cistophori issued in Asia Minor shortly before the outbreak of the war or from overstruck Parthian coins of the same period. We have, however, to stress one fact: the exclusive overstriking seen on the Bar Kokhba coinage is not due to a lack of either imagination or skill on the part of the rebels – quite the contrary, as is attested by the craftsmanship of most of the diecutters and of the entire mint personnel.

Where did Bar Kosiba obtain the large amount of Roman imperial and provincial money? Booty is, of course, a likely source. He probably got Roman tetradrachms and drachms from the Syrian provincial mints and imperial denarii, dupondii, and asses, perhaps also some sestertii, from defeated garrisons and small army details. Yet, we must not imagine that Bar Kosiba seized enormous sums of money or even the entire treasury of the 22nd legion, the *Deiotariana* , if he did, after all, succeed in defeating the legion in the southwestern foothills of Judaea on its way from Egypt to the Bar Kokhba territory[39]. A legion on mission would have carried only a restricted amount of money. Moreover, we have no proof that the Jewish rebels ever destroyed the *Deiotariana* .

Furthermore, one wonders whether a Roman soldier serving in a garrison or some other army unit would have carried the small local and autonomous bronze money of Gaza and Ascalon, which eventually made its way into Bar Kosiba's hands and was

---

[38] DJD II (1961) 145, L.21. Cf. Y. YADIN, IEJ 12 (1962) 252 and n. 43.

[39] E. SCHÜRER[-G. VERMES], The History of the Jewish People, 1973, 548, n. 150 (6), a precise exposition of the problem.

overstruck. This is not very probable. Bar Kosiba must have got the bulk of his silver and bronze coins from the Jewish population of Judaea, perhaps some of it as a war levy and some of it as rent from peasants to whom he leased Roman crown land.

We do not know of any Bar Kokhba gold coins, although Roman *aurei* are found throughout the Near East as well as in Israel. Yet, one should not exclude a priori the possibility that Bar Kokhba gold coins existed. The rebels would not have hesitated to start a gold issue, but it seems that they needed Roman and not Jewish gold coins. Where did the rebels get Roman gold from? Roman officials or army officers and private individuals, Jewish or not, who traveled through Judaea or lived in the country certainly carried some aurei. So the rebels must have had some of these gold coins at their disposal. If they did not overstrike them and use them for internal circulation – silver and bronze were, of course, sufficient for this purpose – then the Roman gold must have satisfied larger needs of the insurgents, such as the purchase of weapons or the financing of benevolent neutrality on the Eastern border.

As we have seen, Bar Kosiba had enough time to consolidate the rebel state. He exercised full executive power. He was the possessor of considerable territory and adequate financial means. But did he have enough food, tools, and manpower for the upkeep of the economy and the continuation of the struggle? The size of the Bar Kokhba coinage must have been enormous. I know of up to 100 specimens struck from a single pair of dies and have, for instance, registered more than 200 different die combinations in the denarii issue. The group of medium bronzes is so big that an attempt to reconstruct the system of their interlinking dies within the framework of the corpus now underway has with great reluctance, been abandoned. All this is extraordinary. If Bar Kosiba managed to overcome the technical difficulties involved in issuing such huge quantities of coins of good quality and great variety, then two conclusions are obvious: first, the coinage was a matter of high priority, of great importance for the rebel state; and second, the Jewish population of Judaea in need of this money was numerous. That can only mean that a great part of the Jewish rural population of Judaea had not only survived the disaster of the *Bellum Iudaicum* but still flourished there. The new documents and papyri confirm these conclusions beyond any doubt. Be'ayan, the father of Bar Kosiba's district administrator Jonathan, owned land in the fertile, artificially irrigated territory of Engedi. The Jewish matron Babata and her numerous clan also owned land there. Jewish peasants worked in the Beth Guvrin district on good land. Not only did large Jewish settlements survive but also the legal institutions pertaining to everyday life, the marriage contracts, the bills of divorce, the bonds and the leases. The rebels succeeded in creating an independent Jewish state in the years 132-135, because the conditions were favorable: the rural populahon of Judaea had survived the *Bellum Iudaicum* and prospered there. The Bar Kokhba coins, letters, and documents all reveal this surprising fact.

## 5. Bar Kosiba's Mint

One of the most difficult tasks for young states in our days is to produce their own coinage. They usually prefer to make good use of the services of older established foreign mints. So, how did the rebel administration solve this problem during the Bar Kokhba war? Who gave the order to prepare the Jewish dies and to overstrike the Roman coins? Who struck the coins and where and when did this take place? I have always been convinced that a study of the interlinking dies would answer many of these questions. When I revealed my initial results in 1951 in Jerusalem, the late E.L. SUKENIK commented: «I will not believe one single word of your technical numismatics unless you can produce a dating of the third year». SUKENIK's opinion was that the coinage began with the undated series. But it was SUKENIK's son, YIGAEL YADIN, an archaeologist like his father, working in the caves of the Naḥal Ḥever, who found the document which begins: «On the 28th of Marheshvan in the third year of Shim'on ben Kosiba, Prince of Israel»[40]. Documents of the fourth year are also known now. Why then did the rebels continue to date their deeds and other documents but stop dating their coins after the second year? This apparent discrepancy, admittedly strange at first glance, is the result neither of negligence nor of accident. A date on an official and legal document confirms an obvious fact; the undated Bar Kokhba coin inscriptions, however, have moved beyond the mere confirmation of fact to make an intentional, political declaration, which does not require a date. «For the Freedom of Jerusalem» means: «Let us fight to free Jerusalem».

We already have seen that Bar Kokhba money is extraordinary in design, fabric, volume, and meaning[41]. The same goes for the structure of the coinage. The order given by the rebel administration to the mint personnel was clear: to create a sovereign, proclamatory, and abundant coinage The flans (namely, Roman coins) were at hand, but the dies had to be engraved by diecutters who knew their craft and the Palaeo-Hebrew script. There was no time, no leisure for detailed instructions. The minters were forced to use the dies until they broke. To conserve dies they once even employed the same die for silver and bronze, which is quite unusual[42]. They also used obsolete dies from earlier minting periods, if no others were at hand. Often they combined one obverse die with numerous reverse dies (up to twenty-nine!)[43]. The multitude of interlinking dies is astounding. All these features enable us to clarify – by die study and comparison – the structure of the whole coinage, especially the chronological order of its three periods: «year One of the Redemption of Israel», «year 2 of the Freedom of Israel», and the undated series with the inscription «For the Freedom of Jerusalem» (Tf. LIX). More important still is the fact that such a sequence can only come from one mint[44], probably the rebels' headquarters, whatever

---

[40] Y. YADIN, IEJ 12 (1962) 250.

[41] L. MILDENBERG, Hist. Jud. 11 (1949) 91: «The Jewish coinage itself in this war of independence was based, in form and spirit, on laws of its own».

[42] L. MILDENBERG, Hist. Jud. 11 (1949), die G I on pl. I [hier Tf. LIII].

[43] This long-lived obverse die showing the legend Shim'on within a wreath connects the second coinage period (year 2) with the third (undated, «For the Freedom of Jerusalem»). For illustrations cf. Y. MESHORER, Jewish Coins of the Second Temple Period, Tel Aviv 1967, 184A, 185 (year 2) and 203 (undated) and BMC Palestine, 15,16 (year 2) and 28-34, 55,57 (undated).

[44] In the el-Fawwār hoard of December 1978 there were several irregular «barbarous» denarii. Their dies do not seem to fit into the interlinking system that is characteristic of the whole silver coinage. Unless some die links are found we will have to accept a second,

its location. Finally, the predominance of the name Shim'on on all the issues very soon after the outbreak of the war was surely to indicate that it was Bar Kosiba himself – our legendary Bar Kokhba – who stood behind the coinage.

# 6. The Cultural Renaissance under Bar Kosiba

Was Bar Kosiba nothing but a small-time tyrant and a stern commander? Certainly not. He emerges in the Dead Sea papyri as a devout Jew strictly observing Jewish law. Though he lived in a very troubled time, he still managed to think of the palm branches and fruits needed for the Feast of the Tabernacles and to ask his representative to make sure that the offerings arrived at his headquarters undamaged, as it was prescribed in the Law, that the stem of the citrus fruit should be whole[45]. He became indignant upon discovering that one of his deputies had ill-treated the Galilaeans[46], whoever these Galilaeans were. And he called the soldiers under his command brothers[47].

We already know from the eloquent types and proclamatory legends of his coins that Bar Kosiba fought for an independent Jewish State. And now, we have another decisive piece of numismatic evidence: Bar Kosiba chose an archaic script, a Palaeo-Hebrew letterform, for the Jewish slogans on his coins. This can only mean that Bar Kosiba had a second, even higher goal than simply an independent Jewish State, namely, a cultural renaissance. The scripts on the papyri show how Bar Kosiba's scribes and the people wrote. These letter forms are the square Aramaic characters, first used in the Babylonian exile and developed steadily thereafter. We already know these specific letterforms from stone inscriptions, ossuaries, and other inscribed material, which range in date from about 200 B.C. to A.D. 200. These letterforms are astonishingly similar to modern printed Hebrew and anyone who can read a Hebrew prayerbook should be able to understand them. Yet, this same person would probably be unable to read what is written on the Bar Kokhba coins. There, the letters are not square but cursive. They are, in fact, the characters of the old Palaeo-Hebrew script, with their archaic ductus from the time of the Jewish kings and, therefore, nearly one thousand years old. Palaeo-Hebrew script such as this had already been used on the bronze coins of the Maccabeans around 100 B.C. and on the silver shekels and bronze denominations of the *Bellum Iudaicum* of 66-74; it was also used – and this is significant – for the name of God within some texts of the Dead Sea papyri.

We must not forget that until the year 66 the Jewish people enjoyed virtually unrestricted political independence and total cultural and religious freedom. Under Bar Kosiba the situation was very different. A full 62 years had passed since the destruc-

---

auxiliary mint, active probably toward the end of the war. Even at this late stage the inexperienced engravers and minters in this secondary atelier could have made crude copies of the denarii from the second year without paying attention to the fact that they struck the pieces in the third or fourth year.

45 Y. YADIN, IEJ 11 (1961) 48.
46 DJD II (1961) 159ff.
47 Y. YADIN, IEJ 11 (1961) 44 and 59ff.

tion of the Temple. In taking up the old traditional script – after a long and deep hiatus – Bar Kosiba recalled the glorious days of the great kings before the Babylonian exile. Thirty years ago, I stressed the following point: «The coin-script, which in itself is an intentional revival of the old Hebraic cursive-script ..., was merely a readoption of an obsolete script for the single and important purpose of serving as the official script of the coinage»[48]. In 1949 there was no basis for this rather bold statement other than a careful interpretation of the coins. No wonder numismatists and epigraphers did not share this view but maintained the opinion that the use of the old script never ceased[49]. The old script may, of course, have continued for sacred writings[50] while the everyday script changed. But it seems that the use of this script virtually ceased in the course of the second century for sacred writings as well as for everyday documents. Not only the Dead Sea papyri but also the new private documents and the official letters of Bar Kosiba's reign were written in the new square script, while the coin inscriptions – and only these – were written in the old cursive characters. Under the revolutionary administration the intentional revival of the old script is joined by a preference for Hebrew over Aramaic. As YADIN emphasized, the earlier Bar Kokhba documents were written in Aramaic, the later ones in Hebrew. «Possibly the change was made by a special decree of Bar Kokhba who wanted to restore Hebrew as the official language of the State»[51]. It was indeed the old script, the old language, that Bar Kosiba wanted.

## 7. Bar Kosiba's Failure

For a moment, we have to leave coins and documents in order to touch upon Bar Kosiba's failure. The Jewish state ranged against Hadrian stood no chance. The great emperor, who wanted peace yet did not fear war, had finally achieved a lasting equilibrium on the eastern frontier. The Parthians did not saddle their horses when Bar Kosiba and his rebels rose against Rome, though the moment was favorable. Only as an advance post within a strong eastern power block would Bar Kosiba's rebel state have had a chance of survival. This eastern power block, however, would have had to include Nabataea, which it did not; Nabataea remained a calm and loyal Roman province in the rear of the rebels. Moreover, the Jewish diaspora did not rise

---

[48] L. MILDENBERG, Hist. Jud. 11 (1949) 79.

[49] L. KADMAN, The Hebrew Coin Script, in: Recent Studies and Discoveries on Ancient Jewish and Syrian Coins, Jerusalem 1954, 166ff; D. DIRINGER, Early Hebrew Writing, BA 13 (1950) 86. F.M. CROSS, Jr., The Development of the Jewish Scripts, The Bible and the Ancient Near East, in: Essays in honour of W.F. Albright, New York 1961, 189, n. 5, introduced the term «Early Jewish» for the new script and stated in n. 4 that «in the second century B.C. Palaeo-Hebrew forms, dormant for some four centuries, begin afresh to evolve at a fairly steady pace». I hold that this development did not last up to 132-135 because there is no trace of the Palaeo-Hebrew forms in the legal documents and letters of the Bar Kokhba war. They are all written in the new script.

[50] N. AVIGAD, Bullae and Seals from a Post-Exile Judaean Archive (Qedem 4), Jerusalem 1976, 36, n. 135.

[51] Y. YADIN, Bar Kokhba, 1971, 181.

up in support of Bar Kosiba as might have been hoped for – not in Egypt, not in the Cyrenaica, nor on Cyprus. Its backbone had obviously been crushed during the Jewish revolt of 115. Thus, Bar Kosiba stood in Judaea, a lone warrior for a lost cause.

# 8. The Reason for the War

I am convinced that there is only one major reason for the war despite the fact that a multitude of different causes and combinations of causes have been named in recent studies. As already stated, the Messianic hope cannot be the main reason, nor can it be social unrest that caused the war. In the Jewish tradition we find the *meṣīqīm* (tantalizers) or *ʾannāsīm* (violators) associated with disputes over «land and tenure»[52]. We assume that it was Roman crown land that Bar Kosiba had the audacity to release to the Jewish peasants. We also know of Roman veterans of the *Bellum Iudaicum* who received fertile plots of land[53]. But this does not mean that the entire rural population of Judaea – a rather large body of Jewish peasants – was a weak bunch of day-laborers, an exploited people without land, home, or means! One wonders how those scholars who name rural problems as the chief cause of the rebellion can explain the fact that these poor, dispossessed peasants of Judaea were able to start a revolt and to hold their own against the mighty Roman Empire for at least three full years. No, as said before, the economic conditions were favourable. There was no general «unrest» among the rural population. If there had been, the peasants would never have been able to maintain such a long war as they did.

SMALLWOOD identifies «endemic nationalism»[54] as one of the reasons for the war. A nationalist feeling certainly existed after the *Bellum Iudaicum* and it might well have become epidemic in the course of the Bar Kokhba war. But it seems inconceivable to me that in 132 the Judaean peasants could be led to such a desperate action as open rebellion by nationalistic agitation alone without any provocation from the Romans.

In the first few lines of his report on the Great War, as preserved in Xiphilinus' excerpt, Dio Cassius gives two reasons for the war: the foundation – on the old site of Jerusalem – of Hadrian's own city Aelia Capitolina, and the erection of a temple to Jupiter on the Jewish temple mount[55]. Dio chooses his words carefully, emphasizing that the emperor's forceful action was a personal and deliberate attack upon the Jews. How trustworthy is such a text? Let us consider two things: first, Jerusalem had been a Roman city for 62 years by this time, serving as the camp of the Tenth Legion and housing civilian annexes and Roman shrines; second, the emphasis upon the personal and deliberate character of the emperor's action may be due to Dio-

---

[52] Cf. S. APPLEBAUM, Prolegomena to the Study of the Second Jewish Revolt, 1976, 10ff.
[53] Cf. id., Prolegomena to the Study of the Second Jewish Revolt, 1976, 9; B. LIFSHITZ, ANRW II,8 (1977) 469. 483.
[54] E.M. SMALLWOOD, The Jews under Roman Rule, 1976, 438.
[55] Dio's Rom. Hist. (Loeb Classical Library), Cambridge/MA 1958) 446-447, book LXIX, 12-I.

Xiphilinus and may not, in fact, represent a true picture of the emperor's part in the affair. But the facts reported do fit completely Hadrian's great design of colonization and hellenization for the whole Roman East in the course of his long sojourn there around the year 130. On the other hand, do we have any evidence besides the literary tradition for the two-part action taken by the emperor at Jerusalem? No traces were found of Hadrian's temple[56]. Of course, he might have planned it, even though it was never realized. Only a statue of the emperor seems to have been erected. For the foundation of Aelia Capitolina on the site of Jerusalem, there is, however, strong numismatic evidence. Bronze coins with the legend *Aelia Capitolina* , struck in Jerusalem for Hadrian[57], were found together with Bar Kokhba coins. These Aelia Capitolina coins bear the earliest form of the Latin legend used on Hadrianic coinage, namely, *Imp Caes Traiano Hadriano* , a legend impossible after the Bar Kokhba War at the end of his reign. Finally, there are other Aelia Capitolina coins with the same emperor's bust and the early legend *Imp Caesar Had Aug* but with the head of Sabina and the inscription *Sabina Augusta* (not *Diva Sabina* ) on the reverse[58]. Sabina died and became *Diva* in 136, probably half a year after the end of the war. No historian seems to have grasped the full significance of the legends and types of these Aelia Capitolina coins, yet they do prove that Aelia Capitolina was founded before the war. Obviously, Hadrian did not realize – or did not want to realize – what Jerusalem meant to all Jews when he founded his Greco-Roman city and called it not Hadrianopolis nor Colonia Hadriana but Aelia Capitolina, thereby connecting the city with both his family, the Aelian gens, and with Jupiter Capitolinus[59]! Although this must have been most offensive to the Jews, it would not have been sufficient to seduce them to open rebellion. The real cause must have cut deeper into the heart of the Jews. What was the aim, the goal of this man Shim'on ben Kosiba who organized a revolt against the Roman Empire during one of its most powerful periods and under the rule of one of its greatest emperors? Was he a hero, or a reckless fool who tried the impossible and brought nothing but blood and tears?

In the Scriptores Historiae Augustae, *Vita Hadriani* 14,2 we read: *Moverunt ea tempestate et Iudaei bellum quod vetabantur mutilare genitalia.* After E. MARY SMALLWOOD's Latomus article of 1959, entitled «The Legislation of Hadrian and Antoninus Pius against Circumcision»[60], no one should have doubted that Hadrian's

---

[56] Cf. for the alleged Hadrianic temple and related questions G.W. BOWERSOCK, JRS 65 (1975) 184f sub VIII. The same author in: A Roman Perspectise on the Bar Kochba War, in: Approaches to Ancient Judaism II: Essays in Definition and Historical Description, ed. W. S. GREEN, 1980, stresses that Fronto, De Bello Parthico, ed. M.P.J. VAN DEN HOUT (1954) 2, 206 (... *quantum militum a Iudaeis, quantum ab Britannis caesum?* ) «gives us the Roman perspective». I hold that Fronto, mentioning the casualties, was yet aware of the differences in the nature, duration, course, and strategical importance of the British and Jewish revolts.

[57] Y. MESHORER, Jewish Coins of the Second Temple Period, 1967, 93; id., in: B. LIFSHITZ, ANRW II,8 (1977) 481.

[58] L. KADMAN, The Coins of Aelia Capitolina (CNP I), Jerusalem 1956, n. 7.

[59] E.M. SMALLWOOD, The Jews under Roman Rule, 1976, 434.

[60] Latomus 18 (1959) 334-347 and 20 (1961) 93-96. Cf. E.M. SMALLWOOD, The Jews under Roman Rule, 1976, 426-431, a forceful, up-to-date summary of her pioneer studies.

ban on circumcision was the major cause of the war[61]. Domitian had already banned castration, but Hadrian went much further. He placed circumcision under the Lex Cornelia, which means that he had it classified and prosecuted on the level of murder. He thus made circumcision equal to castration and in doing so he delivered a death blow to Jewish life. And this was the reason why Akiba joined forces with the rebels. Hadrian's decree was intended as an universal ban against a custom which, to his mind, was most objectionable. It was not meant to be a punishment of the Jews after the war, for not only the Jews but many people in the East practiced circumcision. Indeed, we know when circumcision was again permitted to the Jewish people under the reign of Antoninus Pius, it was as an exemption from the universal ban which remained in force for all non-Jews. For Hadrian, circumcision was a barbarous mutilation, for Bar Kosiba it was the essence of Jewish life. Hadrian wanted to extend Greek culture to all parts of his well-organized Empire under the *Pax Romana* . Bar Kosiba wanted to remain a Jew in Judaea. The clash was inevitable. Both had a cause. But what was a matter of policy for the emperor was a question of life or death for the Jew[62].

In conclusion, the Bar Kokhba coins, letters, and documents are valuable historical sources for the history of the rebellion and the nature and deeds of the man who led the Jews through the pain and suffering of these years of war. Yet, many problems remain unsolved. What was the course of the war, the internal chronology? Why is Jerusalem never mentioned in the documents? Who was the Priest Eleazar? Why does the name of the leading rabbi, Akiba ben Joseph, never appear in the Bar Kokhba letters and documents? There is no answer to these questions now, but there remains hope that one or another will find an answer in the not-too-distant future.

---

I join the scholars rejecting the view expressed by H. MANTEL, JQR 18.3 (1968), postscript, that «the Bar-Kokhba revolt was a spontaneous uprising against Roman rule and not a reaction to religious persecution».

[61] G.W. BOWERSOCK, JRS 65 (1975) 185: «principal and immediate cause».

[62] M.D. HERR, The Causes of the Bar Kokhba war, Zion 43.1-2 (Jerusalem 1978) I-ll (Hebrew), accepts circumcision as the «main (or even the sole) cause» (English summary). HERR's essay reached me only in May 1979, thus after my Loeb Lecture on April 5, 1979.

# The Bar Kokhba War in the Light of the Coins and Document Finds 1947-1982

The publication of my book «The Coinage of the Bar Kokhba War» (1984) seems an appropriate occasion to sum-up and reconsider some of the major issues concerning the Bar Kokhba War[1] in the light of the coins and documents discovered between 1947-1982.

## 1. Names

*Shim'on ben Kosiba.* Shim'on, in full or abbreviated, always appeared on the silver and copper coins. The patronym Kosiba was known from the Jewish and Christian tradition. However, only the discovery of documents in 1951/52 and 1960/61[2] has finally established that they form one name. The Greek texts contained the correct pronunciation Kosiba. The traditional misinterpretation of the patronymic in the positive[3] Messianic[4] sense of Kosiba equalling Bar Kokhba may still be today's usage; the correct and true name is, however, Shim'on ben Kosiba.

*Eleazar.* The documents found have not told us who the Eleazar appearing on the silver and bronze coins was. However, they contain a clear warning that one should not rely on any of the traditional candidates. Neither our Eleazar nor Rabbi Akiba ben Joseph is mentioned in the documents. Instead, they refer to a high rabbinical authority not at all mentioned in Jewish tradition, namely Rabbenu Batnava bar Meisa[5].

---

[1] In 1946, S. YEIVIN called his book «The Bar Kokhba War» (I am referring to the 2nd edition, Jerusalem 1957 [Hebrew]). In Jewish numismatic publications the event has been called a war for the first time by A. KINDLER, The Coinage of the Bar Kokhba War, Numismatic Studies and Researches 2, Tel-Aviv - Jerusalem 1958, 62-80, whereas the terms revolt or rebellion, expressing the Roman point of view, prevailed before and are, occasionally, still used today.

[2] J.T. MILIK, Discoveries in the Judaean Desert, II, Oxford 1961; Y. YADIN, Judaean Desert Caves, Survey and Excavations, I-II, IEJ 11 (1961) 3-72; 12 (1962) 167-262.

[3] For the negative equation Kosiba-Koziba (liar), see P. SCHÄFER, Der Bar Kokhba-Aufstand, Tübingen 1981, 51-52.

[4] L. MILDENBERG, Bar Kokhba Coins and Documents, HSCP 84 (1980) 313-315 [hier S. 217-234]; SCHÄFER, Der Bar Kokhba-Aufstand, 1981, 55-62.

[5] Y. YADIN, IEJ 11 (1961) 46; E. SCHÜRER, The History of the Jewish People in the Age of Jesus Christ, I. A New English Version, revised and ed. by G. VERMES / F. MILLAR, Edinburgh 1973, 544, n. 139.

We should hence limit ourselves to the important conclusion that the fighters in this great war recognized leaders whose identity remains hidden to this very day.

*Jerusalem*. For most scholars the appearance of the name Jerusalem on the coins was sufficient to establish the city as the mint and to draw conclusions as to the dates Jerusalem was conquered and lost again by the Jewish troops[6]. On the other hand, several numismatic works stressed that the rebel organization as legal successor to the Roman empire introduced the sovereign coinage[7] and that the words «Jerusalem» and «For the Freedom of Jerusalem» appearing on it did not but constitute proclamatory legends[8]. Indeed in the documents discovered, the city of Jerusalem does not appear among the places in which they were executed or in which letters were written. The only text where one could possibly suspect mention of the name of Jerusalem is dubious[9]. Fatal to the thesis of a mint at Jerusalem[10] is, however, the clear negative evidence of coin finds in the city[11]. Two recently published investigations have reached the same conclusion, namely that Shim'on ben Kosiba «did not succeed in conquering Jerusalem and in holding it»[12].

## 2. Chronology

The literary sources have been unanimous in stating that the rising lasted for three and a half years, but it was only through the numismatic evidence of overstrikes, dealt with in the more modern researches[13], that the date when the war began, na-

---

[6] This is the *opinio communis* . For extensive literature, see P. SCHÄFER, Der Bar Kokhba-Aufstand, 1981, 78, n. 1, and add, B. LIFSCHITZ, Jérusalem sous la domination romaine, ANRW II,8 (1977) 482; M. GRANT, The Jews in the Roman World, New York 1973, 250 «..they seem to have taken Jerusalem»; A. GARZETTI, From Tiberius to the Antonines, London 1974, 423. See S. APPLEBAUM, Prolegomena to the Study of the Second Revolt (British Archaeological Reports, Suppl. series 7), Oxford 1976, 27 who does, however, not commit himself.

[7] L. MILDENBERG, The Eleazar Coins of the Bar Kokhba Rebellion, Hist. Jud. 11 (1949) 92 and n. 31 and 99 [hier S. 194 und 199f].

[8] L. MILDENBERG, Numismatische Evidenz zur Chronologie der Bar Kochba-Erhebung, SNR 34 (1948-1949) 23, n. 16 [hier S. 180 Anm. 15], and id., Hist. Jud. 11 (1949) 99-100 [hier S. 200f].

[9] J.T. MILIK, Discoveries in the Judaean Desert, II, 1961, 135 and Pl. 38. The editor J.T. MILIK, p. 134, seems to hesitate to attribute the papyrus to the Bar Kokhba War.

[10] Several numismatists adhere to the *opinio communis* of the historians: A. REIFENBERG, Ancient Jewish Coins, Jerusalem 21947, 35; B. KANAEL, JNG 17 (1967) 258; W. KELLNER, in: Auction sale catalogue F. Sternberg, Zürich, 25. Nov. 1976, 53-54.

[11] N. AVIGAD, Archaeological Discoveries in the Jewish Quarter of Jerusalem (Israel Museum Publication), Jerusalem 1976, 24-25: Coins.

[12] L. MILDENBERG, Bar Kokhba in Jerusalem?, SM 105 (1977) 1-6 [hier S. 212-216]; P. SCHÄFER, Der Bar Kokhba-Aufstand, 1981, 78-101, rejects the «Jerusalem thesis» by an irrefutable analysis of the classical sources, the Rabbinical literature, the Christian writings and the Bar Kokhha coins.

[13] L. MILDENBERG, SNR 34 (1948-1949) 19-27 [hier S. 176-182]; cf. A. KINDLER, Ein Münzpalimpsest aus dem Bar Kokhba Krieg, SNR 42 (1962-1963) 15-19.

mely the year 132, has been established. This conclusion has been confirmed by a papyrus from Murabba'at, using a double date, and a date in Babata's archive[14]. A late date in the papyri of the archives[15], references in Jewish tradition, and Roman sources, permit a conclusion as to the approximate date when Jewish resistance collapsed, namely in the autumn of A.D. 135[16].

## 3. Territory

It has only recently been shown[17] that the double dated issues of Gaza conclusively prove that Shim'on's troops did not reach the Mediterranean coast in the south-west, since Gaza continued to strike in the name of Hadrian without interruption from A.D. 131/2 till 134/5[18]. Since Jerusalem remained in Roman hands[19], it is unlikely that Shim'on did even temporarily gain territory to the north of the city. The coin finds give clear indications as to the limits of Shim'on's territory. Nothing to the north of Jerusalem, nothing in the Negev, and nothing on the coast, however, a clear concentration in the Judaean heartland from the foothills across the mountains and the desert to the western coast of the Dead Sea[20]. Not only are all the sites where documents have been discovered in this area, but so are also all places mentioned in them, insofar as they have been identified, like Herodion and the oasis of En-Gedi. This evidence was clear even before the latest archaeological discoveries have furnished further proof in the form of hide-outs and subterranean strongpoints which appear to have been the first line of defence of the Jewish troops and which have recently been found in the western foothills on the eastern edge of the coastal plain, the Shefela, along an inland line more or less parallel to the coast[21].

---

[14]  J.T. MILIK, Discoveries in the Judaean Desert, II, 1961, 125, L.1; see L. MILDENBERG L., HSCP 84 (1980) 319 with nn. 24-25 [hier S. 222f].

[15]  J.T. MILIK J.T., Discoveries in the Judaean Desert, II, 1961, 144-148: «21st Tishri of year Four of the Redemption of Israel» = mid September, A.D. 135.

[16]  The evidence for autumn 135 is strong. The same is true for the duration of more than 3 years or even 3 1/2 years. It seems, therefore, more likely that the war began in the spring or early summer rather than in the autumn of A.D. 132. The problem, however, is still not finally solved.

[17]  L. MILDENBERG, HSCP 84 (1980) 320 and n. 30 [hier S. 223].

[18]  BMC Palestine, 146-151, Nos. 14-55.

[19]  See above, n. 12. S. YEIVIN, The Bar Kokhba War, Jerusalem ²1957, 71-74 (Hebrew) still believed that not only Jerusalem, but also Galilee had been reconquered.

[20]  L. MILDENBERG, HSCP 84 (1980) 320-325 [hier S. 223-226]. See L. KADMAN, International Numismatic Convention 1963, Proceedings, Tel Aviv - Jerusalem 1967, 323, Nos. 34-39 and recently D. BARAG, A Note on the Geographical Distribution of Bar Kokhba Coins, INJ 4 (1980) 30-33, and E. DAMATI, Four Bar Kokhha Coins from Khirbet el-'Aqed, INJ 4 (1980) 27-29.

[21]  A. KLONER, Judean Subterranean Hideaways from the Time of Bar-Kokhba, 4-23, The Bar Kokhba Revolt ..., Abstracts of a Symposium, Tel Aviv, March 31 - April 1, 1982, 29-30 (Hebrew); [id., Underground Hiding Complexes from the Bar Kokhba War in the Judean Shephelah, BA 46 (1983), 210-221].

## 4. The Monetary System

Die comparisons and sequence studies since 1949 have shown the following order of issues: «Year One», «Year 2», undated coins[22]. This internal chronology is, however, not identical with the structure of the coinage. The five coin types, large silver, small silver, large bronze, medium bronze and small bronze, constitute five independent groups[23] connected amongst themselves by many die-links all through the three coinage periods and must be dealt with as such. To split these five groups und to try to force them into the chronological outline[24] implies misunderstanding the nature of the coinage.

All Jewish coins struck during the war were overstruck on foreign coins which was first asserted in 1949[25]. That the five Jewish denominations adopted were based on the main types of foreign coins current in Judaea at the time is self-evident by reason of their being struck on these foreign types[26].

The quantities of coins issued in the short period of three and a half years have been found to be very substantial. This may be taken as evidence for a large population[27], a considerable economic potential and a well established governing system, as indeed has been observed by the scholars dealing with the documents and the coins[28].

It has repeatedly been shown that the script, language, content of legends, and choice of symbols on the coins indicate a national and cultural renaissance[29].

---

[22] A. KINDLER, Coins of the Land of Israel. Collection of the Bank of Israel, A Catalogue, Jerusalem 1974, 61. 63. 66. 68 and 70; L. MILDENBERG, Hist. Jud. 11 (1949) Pl. 1 [hier Tf. LIII]; id., The Monetary System of the Bar Kokhba Coinage, International Numismatic Convention 1963, Proceedings, Tel Aviv - Jerusalem, 1967, 41-48 and Pl. VII-VIII [hier S. 202-207].

[23] There is one exception only: one and the same obverse die («Year One of the Redemption of Israel» around hanging grape cluster) is used for the first denarii and the first small bronzes. See L. MILDENBERG, Hist. Jud. 11 (1949) Pls. 1-2 [hier Tf. LIII - LIV].

[24] The method applied by A. KINDLER, Coins of the Land of Israel. Collection of the Bank of Israel, A Catalogue, 1974, and Y. MESHORER, Jewish Coins, 1974 ; id., Ancient Jewish Coins 2, 1982; id., SNG ANS 6, Palestine-South Arabia, New York 1981, but not by G.F. HILL in BMC, Palestine, London 1914, and A. REIFENBERG, Ancient Jewish Coins, [2]1947.

[25] L. MILDENBERG, Hist. Jud. 11 (1949) 98 [hier S. 16]. See A. KINDLER, The Coinage of the Bar Kokhba War, Numismatic Studies and Researches 2, Tel-Aviv - Jerusalem 1958, 78, L.4.

[26] Roman *aurei* are found in Judaea. They were at the disposal of the Jewish administration, but, obviously, used for other purpose than internal circulation. Tridrachms from the mint of Caesarea Cappadociae occur also in Judaean hoards, but they were not overstruck, as they did not fit into the monetary system of the Bar Kokhba coinage.

[27] M. AVI-YONAH, Palaestina, PRE Suppl. 13 (1974) 397; S. APPLEBAUM, Prolegomena to the Study of the Second Revolt, Oxford 1976, 34-35.

[28] J.T. MILIK, Discoveries in the Judaean Desert, II, 1961, 123 and 161; Y. YADIN, IEJ 12 (1962) 257; L. MILDENBERG, HSCP 84 (1980) 325-329 [hier S. 226-228].

[29] Y. YADIN, Bar Kokhba, London 1971, 181; L. MILDENBERG, Hist. Jud. 11 (1949) 102 [hier S. 200f]; id., HSCP 84 (1980) 329-331[hier S. 229-230].

## 5. Cause of the war

One of the attributes above the temple on the tetradrachms, namely the rosette, has been interpreted by several scholars as a star[30] and thus used in support of the Messianic theory[31]. Already in 1892 and again in the forties, this interpretation has been disputed in numismatic publications[32], i.e. already before the documents found in the Judaean Desert have shown Shim'on ben Kosiba to have been not only the army commander but also lay prince without any messianic attributes[33]. The numismatic evidence has only lately established that the foundation of Aelia Capitolina must have taken place prior to 132 A.D.[34]. For Hadrian founding a city in an eastern province must surely have been a matter of routine, though, the provocative choice of name indicates an intentional unilateral demonstration. However, the decisive measure against the Judaean rural population must have been the second intentional and unilateral step taken by the Emperor, namely the *de facto* prohibition of circumcision[35], a prohibition which must be considered to have been the main cause of the war[36]. The legends and depictions on the coins, as also the letters of Shim'on

[30] G.F. HILL, BMC Palestine, 284-285; A. REIFENBERG, Ancient Jewish Coins, ²1947, 60-61; A. KINDLER, Coins of the Land of Israel. Collection of the Bank of Israel, A Catalogue, 1974, 77. 84-85; Y. YADIN, Bar Kokhba, 1971, 25.

[31] P. SCHÄFER, Der Bar Kokhba-Aufstand, 1981, 64-65 reaches a rather negative view on this star-theory and the so-called Messiah-proclamation of Shim'on ben Kosiba by Rabbi Akiba ben Joseph in the rabbinic sources (pp. 55-58). Thirty years ago, these theories were already rejected by G. ALON, A History of the Jews in the Land of Israel, II, Merhavia 1955, 36 (Hebrew).

[32] L. HAMBURGER, ZfN 18 (1892) 305; L. MILDENBERG, SNR 23 (1947) 18 and n. 5 with references to earlier literature.

[33] Quite recently Y. YADIN, Cathedra 26 (1982) 44 announced a hitherto unpublished dating form «Year three of the redemption of Zion through Shim'on bar Kosiba». We know the datings «Year two» and «Year four of the redemption of Israel» from the legal documents J.T. MILIK, Discoveries in the Judaean Desert, II, 1961, 24, 29 and 30, whereas the coins bear the word «redemption» on «Year One» issues only. The legend «Freedom of Zion» is found on the bronzes of the *Bellum Iudaicum* . At the beginning of the Bar Kokhba War the use of «Redemption of Zion» might have had a certain messianic connotation, but not towards the end of the War when the people knew Shim'on already as landlord, ruler and as a commander with the fortunes of war turning against him.

[34] Y. MESHORER, Jewish Coins, 1967 , 93; id. apud B. LIFSCHITZ, ANRW II,8 (1977) 481; L. MILDENBERG, HSCP 84 (1980) 333 [hier S. 232].

[35] In the last decades, the view has gained acceptance that Hadrian's deliberate measures against Jews caused the war; it suffices to mention the view of B.W. HENDERSON, L.W. BARNARD, B. D'ORGEVAL, S.W. BARON, S. YEIVIN, F.M. ABEL, S. PEROWNE, M. GUARDUCCI, R. SYME, the English version of E. SCHÜRER's History, E.M. SMALLWOOD, Y. YADIN, M. GRANT, M. STERN, S. APPLEBAUM, G. BOWERSOCK, M.D. HERR, A.M. RABELLO, Y. MESHORER and L. MILDENBERG. This view is further shared by M.K. THORNTON, Hadrian and his Reign, ANRW II,2 (1975) 456 with literature 464-476.

[36] In the view of a few authors neither the foundation of Aelia Capitolina nor the ban on circumcision was the reason of the war: H. MANTEL, JQR 18 (1959) postscript («spontaneous uprising, not a reaction to religious persecution»); P. SCHÄFER, Der Bar

ben Kosiba, show him and his fighters to have been conscious and God-fearing men unwilling to forego their Jewish heritage.

## 6. Singularity

The extent, structures and objectives of the Jewish coinage during A.D. 132-135 show it to have been a *res sui generis* [37] just as the war was an event of a special nature. When the *Bellum Iudaicum* started in A.D. 66 Jerusalem and its Temple were still standing. In A.D. 132 the *Legio X Fretensis* was stationed in Jerusalem. The place of the High Priest had been taken by the Teacher of the Law. The *Tumultus Iudaicus* of A.D. 115-117 had been a conflict between Greeks and the Jews of the Diaspora in Egypt, Cyrenaica, and Cyprus. The Bar Kokhba War was a conflict between the Roman Empire and the indigenous Jews of Judaea. The wars with the Britons took place in an area lying between Hadrian's Wall and the sea at the northern edge of the old world and outside its frontiers[38]. Shim'on and his warriors withstood the Emperor in a country inside the borders of the Empire situated in an area which had always been of strategic importance. The Parthian Wars had been conflicts between two Empires. The Bar Kokhba War was and remains a special and extraordinary event[39].

---

Kokhba-Aufstand, 1981, 48-50 thinks of a Jewish-Roman conflict which smouldered below the surface and of an internal conflict between Jewish factions; A. GARZETTI, From Tiberius to the Antonines, 1974, even states that the provocation did not come from Hadrian, but from the – Jews (!).

[37] L. MILDENBERG, Hist. Jud. 11 (1949) 91 [hier S. 193].

[38] G. BOWERSOCK, A Roman Perspective on the Bar Kokhba War, in: W.S. GREEN (ed.), Approaches to Ancient Judaism, 2, Ann Arbor/MI 1980, 131-141 concludes from Fronto, De Bello Parthico, ed. M.P.J. VAN DEN HOUT, Leiden, 1954, 2. 206, that to the Romans both wars were of equal importance. For a differing view, see L. MILDENBERG, HSCP 84 (1980) n. 56 [hier S. 232].

[39] L. MILDENBERG, Der Bar Kokhba-Krieg und seine Münzprägung, Geldgeschichtliche Nachrichten 95 (1983) 117-118.

# Der Bar-Kochba-Krieg im Lichte der Münzprägungen[*]

(Tf. LXII - LXVI)

## 1. Über die Bedeutung der Sachquellen

Das Münzrecht ist ein wichtiges Prärogativ souveräner Staaten. Der römische Kaiser konnte es übertragen, teilen und verleihen. Wer es aber ausübte, ohne dazu berechtigt zu sein, erklärte Rom den Krieg. Von allen im Reich lebenden Völkern haben nur die Juden diesen entscheidenden Schritt getan und zwar zweimal – im *Bellum Iudaicum* und im Bar-Kochba-Krieg[1].

Über diese beiden außergewöhnlichen Ereignisse gibt es literarische Überlieferungen aus römischer, jüdischer und christlicher Sicht. Diese Berichte sind sehr verschieden voneinander in Sprache, Umfang, Zuverlässigkeit und Wertung; keiner ist objektiv. Trotzdem wurden die literarischen Quellen von der früheren Forschung bevorzugt, die Sachquellen jedoch vernachlässigt.

Die numismatische Evidenz ist eine Sachquelle *par excellence* . Im Falle des Bar-Kochba-Krieges war die Münzprägung seit Jahrhunderten bekannt (Tf. LXII - LXVI), aber erst jüngst ist ihre Corpus-Bearbeitung vorgelegt worden[2]. Das gleiche gilt für die leider noch immer nicht vollinhaltlich publizierten Dokumentenfunde aus der judäischen Wüste[3]. Unbestreitbare Tatsachen ergeben sich auch aus archäologischen Zusammenhängen und Gesetzestexten. Aufgrund dieser Sachquellen und zuverlässigen literarischen Überlieferungen sollen hier die Probleme behandelt werden, mit denen sich die Erforschung der Geschichte des Bar-Kochba-Krieges beschäftigt.

---

[*] Dieser Text wurde 1986 abgeschlossen. Neuere Literatur konnte nicht mehr berücksichtigt werden.

[1] So war der Aufstand der Zenobia und ihres Sohnes Vabalathus [Wahb'allāt] gegen Kaiser Aurelian im Jahre 270 eine innerrömische Angelegenheit; denn das romanisierte Herrscherhaus von Palmyra diente seit Odenathus, der *Dux Romanorum* und *Imperator* war, als Vorposten des Reiches gegen die Parther. Wenn Zenobia dann als *Augusta* und Vabalathus als *Augustus* auf den Münzen proklamiert werden, erheben sie sich als Römer Anspruch auf die Kaiserwürde. Vgl. L. MILDENBERG, Rebel Coinage in the Roman Empire, in: Greece and Rome in Eretz Israel, ed. A. KASHER et al., Jerusalem 1990, 62-74 [hier S. 163-169].

[2] L. MILDENBERG, The Coinage of the Bar Kokhba War (Typos 6), Aarau u.a. 1984.

[3] Die wichtigsten publizierten Dokumente finden sich in DJD II und Y. YADIN, The Expedition to the Judean Desert, 1960. 1961, IEJ 11 (1961) 36-52; 12 (1962) 226-257.

## 2. Bar Kosiba und Bar-Kochba

Dio nennt den Kampf zwischen dem Römischen Reich und den Juden von Judäa von 132 bis 135 einen Krieg. Jahrhundertelang sprach man aber von Rebellion, Revolte oder Aufstand, was vom römischen Standpunkt aus folgerichtig ist. In Tat und Wahrheit war es ein wirklicher Krieg, dessen Hauptakteure Hadrian und Bar-Kochba waren. Während der Kaiser zu den großen Gestalten der Geschichte zählt, blieb der jüdische Heerführer bis Ende der 40er Jahre unseres Jahrhunderts eine Legende. Bar-Kochba, der Sternensohn, war eine späte Schöpfung der jüdischen Tradition, kein Mensch aus Fleisch und Blut.

Auf den Münzen waren immer sein Vorname und sein Titel zu lesen gewesen: «Šim ͑ōn Fürst Israels» (Tf. LXIV 6-9). Aber war Šim ͑ōn identisch mit Bar-Kochba? Die in den 40er und 60er Jahren entdeckten Rechtsurkunden, Briefe und militärischen Befehle offenbarten endlich die Wahrheit. Der Mann hieß Šim ͑ōn bar Kōsibā und war der Fürst Israels. So sollte er auch genannt werden, während man das Ereignis selbst heute als Bar-Kochba-Krieg auffassen wird.

## 3. Zur Chronologie

Nach Sach- und Schriftquellen hat der Bar-Kochba-Krieg dreieinhalb Jahre gedauert[4]. Das letzte in der judäischen Wüste gefundene Dokument stammt von Ende September 135[5]. Hadrian hat im Laufe des gleichen Jahres den Titel *IMP II* angenommen, wofür es keinen anderen Grund als die Beendigung des Krieges gibt[6]. Rechnet man vom Herbst 135 zurück, so kommt man auf Frühjahr 132 als den Zeitpunkt des Ausbruchs des Kriegs, was wiederum durch Münzüberprägungen (Tf. LXV)[7] und den frühesten Pachtvertrag[8], abgeschlossen zwischen Šim ͑ōn bar Kōsibā[9] als Landeigentümer und jüdischen Bauern, bestätigt wird.

---

[4] Y. YADIN, Bar-Kokhba, London 1971, 23; E. SCHÜRER, The History of the Jewish People in the Age of Jesus Christ (175 B.C.-A.D. 135) Vol. I, New English Version rev. and ed. by G. VERMES and F. MILLAR, Edinburgh 1973, Anm. 92. 126; E.M. SMALLWOOD, The Jews under Roman Rule. From Pompey to Diocletian (StJLA 20), Leiden 1976 and rev. Reprint Leiden 1981, 455-457; P. SCHÄFER, Der Bar Kochba-Aufstand, Studien zum zweiten jüdischen Krieg gegen Rom, Tübingen 1981, 10-22; L. MILDENBERG, Bar Kochba Coins and Documents, HSCP 84 (1980) 315-320 [hier S. 221-223]; id., The Coinage of the Bar Kokhba War, 1984, 82.

[5] Murabba ͑at 30, in: DJD II, 124-148.

[6] L. MILDENBERG, The Coinage of the Bar Kokhba War, 1984, Anm. 224.

[7] L. MILDENBERG, Numismatische Evidenz zur Chronologie der Bar Kochba-Erhebung, SNR 34 (1948-1949) 19-27 [hier S. 176-182]; A. KINDLER, Ein Münzpalimpsest aus dem Bar Kochba-Krieg, SNR 42 (1962-1963) 15-20.

[8] Murabba ͑at 24, in: DJD II, 125.

[9] Dies ist der aramäische Name in den Dokumenten; auf Hebräisch heißt er dort *Šim ͑ōn ben Kōsibā*. Auch auf Griechisch wird der Name gebraucht: *Simōn Chōsiba* (s. YADIN, 44 – Papyrus 6).

## 4. Das Kriegspotential

Dio überliefert unwahrscheinlich hohe Verlustziffern der Juden an Menschen, befestigten Plätzen und Siedlungen[10]. Dies hat dazu geführt, daß in der Forschung bisweilen das Kriegspotential, das die Römer und Juden einsetzten, überschätzt wurde[11]. Jüngst ist dieser maximalistischen Sicht eine minimalistische gegenüber gestellt worden – mit der Annahme, Hadrian hätte nur Spezialtruppen aufmarschieren lassen, auch um deren Effizienz zu testen[12]. Den Vertretern der ersten These ist entgegenzuhalten, daß das hügelige und bergige Gelände die Entfaltung großer Heeresverbände gar nicht zuließ. Gegenüber der zweiten These ist festzustellen, daß ein so langer Krieg auf einem nicht unbeträchtlichen Territorium weder mit einer kleinen römischen Elitetruppe noch mit einer Handvoll jüdischer Guerillas zu führen ist. Jedenfalls stellen die zwei in Jerusalem und in Capercotna – Kəfar ʿOtnay (später Legio) stationierten Legionen bereits eine nicht unerhebliche Streitmacht dar[13]. Für Hadrian war der Ausbruch und der anfängliche Verlauf der Kampfhandlungen ein so unerwartetes und schlimmes Ärgernis, daß er gewiß alles unternahm, um bald damit fertig zu werden. Frontos Registrierung der Verluste[14] und Dios vielsagende Schlußbemerkung, viele Römer seien umgekommen und deshalb habe Hadrian auf die übliche Grußformel an den Senat nach einem gewonnenen Krieg verzichtet[15], weisen auf einen erbitterten und blutigen Krieg hin, der erst durch Julius Severus, den besten Heerführer seiner Zeit, beendigt werden konnte[16]. Ebenso wesentlich für die Beurteilung dieser erstaunlichen Auseinandersetzung ist aber, daß dem großen Aufgebot des römischen Weltreiches mit einem entsprechenden jüdischen Einsatz begegnet wurde. Dafür sprechen nicht nur Dauer und Härte des Krieges, sondern vor allem die Aussage der Sachquellen. Ohne eine zahlreiche und wirtschaftlich starke jüdische Bevölkerung blieben Tatsache, Art und Umfang der

---

[10]  Cassius Dio 69, 12-14. Da uns der Text nur in der Epitome des Johannes Xiphilinus aus dem 11. Jahrhundert bekannt ist, könnten diese Phantasiezahlen von christlichen Autoren des 4. Jahrhunderts stammen, die sie wiederum der jüdischen Tradition entnommen hätten.

[11]  Vgl. S. APPLEBAUM, Prolegomena to the Study of the Second Jewish Revolt (A.D. 132-135) (BAR Suppl. Series 7), Oxford 1976, 44-48.

[12]  M. MOR, in: Greece and Rome in Eretz Israel, ed. A. KASHER et al., 1990.

[13]  Es ist wahrscheinlich, daß die zweite Legion die *Legio VI Ferrata* war und daß sie um das Jahr 123 in Capercotna ihr Lager bezog. Vgl. L. MILDENBERG, The Coinage of the Bar Kokhba War, 1984, Anm. 214.

[14]  Fronto, De Bello Parthico, ein Trostbrief gerichtet an Marcus Aurelius, in: M. Cornelii Frontonis Epistulae, ed. M.P.J. VAN DEN HOUT, Leiden 1954, 2,206. Siehe G.W. BOWERSOCK, A Roman Perspective on the Bar Kochba War, in: Approaches to Ancient Judaism II, ed. W.S. GREEN (Brown Judaic Studies 9), Ann Arbor/MI 1980, 131-141; vgl. MILDENBERG, HSCP 84 (1980) Anm. 56 [hier S. 232]; id., The Coinage of the Bar Kokhba War, 1984, Anm. 185.

[15]  Cassius Dio 69, 14.3.

[16]  Cassius Dio 69, 13.2.

Münzprägung und der Dokumentenfunde unerklärlich[17]. Die jüdische Siedlung in Judäa hatte sich aber nur entwickeln können, weil die Flavier die Bauern auf ihrer angestammten Scholle beließen und die nachfolgenden Kaiser daran nichts änderten[18].

# 5. Das Bar-Kochba-Territorium

Über das von den Juden beherrschte Gebiet machen die literarischen Quellen keine genauen Angaben[19]. Die Sachquellen jedoch lassen uns wiederum nicht im Stich. Stellt man die Orte zusammen, in denen Münzen oder Dokumente gefunden wurden oder die in den Dokumenten erwähnt werden, so erweist sich das Herzland Judäas als das Bar-Kochba-Territorium[20]. Dabei wird deutlich, daß die Küstenebene in der Hand der Römer geblieben war, nicht nur, weil kein einziger Fund von Bar-Kochba-Münzen aus diesem weiten Gebiet stammt, sondern weil in den Küstenstädten von 131/132 bis 136/137 Geld für Hadrian geprägt worden ist[21]. Über Samaria[22] oder gar Galiläa schweigen die Münzen und Dokumente gänzlich, ebenso über Jerusalem. Daß Simʿōn bar Kōsibā Jerusalem wirklich nicht belagert und erobert haben soll, ist überraschend; ebenso, daß die römische Garnison in der hochgelegenen Stadt all die Kriegsjahre hindurch das Gebiet der Rebellen bedroht haben sollte[23]. Aber aufgrund der Tatsache, daß kein einziger Fund von Bar-Kochba-Münzen aus der Stadt kommt[24] und sie in den Dokumenten überhaupt nicht erwähnt wird[25], muß Jerusalem so lange als nicht zum Bar-Kochba-Gebiet gehörend betrachtet werden, bis eine neue unbestreitbare Sachquelle uns eines anderen belehrt[26].

---

[17] L. MILDENBERG, The Coinage of the Bar Kokhba War, 1984, 103.

[18] Mildenberg, op.cit., 1984, 92-94.

[19] In der jüdischen Tradition werden einzelne Orte genannt; deren Lokalisierung ist jedoch umstritten.

[20] MILDENBERG, op.cit., 1984, maps 1-3 [vgl. hier Tf. LIX - LXI]. Vgl. A. BÜCHLER, Die Schauplätze des Bar Kochba-Krieges und die auf diesen bezogenen jüdischen Nachrichten, JQR 16 (1903-1904) 143-205.

[21] G.F. HILL, BMC Palestine, London 1914, 146-151 (Gaza von 131/132 bis 136/137) sowie 129 (Ascalon 132/133).

[22] Eine einzelne, schlecht erhaltene Bar-Kochba-Bronzemünze wurde 15 km nnw von Jericho gefunden. MILDENBERG, op.cit., 1984, Anm. 117.

[23] Daß Simʿōn Jerusalem erobern wollte, dafür sprechen Typen und Legenden der Münzprägung ganz eindeutig. Daß er nicht dazu gekommen ist, zeigt die negative Fundevidenz in der Stadt selbst.

[24] N. Avigad hat in seiner großen Ausgrabung im jüdischen Viertel auch nicht eine einzige Bar-Kochba Münze gefunden. Vgl. L. MILDENBERG, Bar Kochba in Jerusalem?, SM 105 (1977) 1-6 [hier S. 212-216]; id., The Coinage of the Bar Kokhba War, 1984, Anm. 110.

[25] MILDENBERG, The Coinage of the Bar Kokhba War, 1984, Anm. 141.

[26] Unbestreitbar ist nur die positive Fundevidenz, also die Tatsache, daß eine bestimmte Münze oder Münzgruppe an einem bestimmten Ort zu einer bestimmten Zeit gefunden wurde. Die negative Fundevidenz, also die Feststellung, daß bisher an einem bestimmten Ort oder in einem bestimmten Gebiet keine bestimmte Münze oder Münzgruppe gefunden

## 6. Der Staat der Aufständischen

Dreieinhalb Jahre lang war Šim'ōn bar Kōsibā Herr über ein beträchtliches Territorium. Während aufgrund der schriftlichen Überlieferungen sich nur schemenhafte Konturen des Ereignisses ausmachen ließen, beweisen die Münzen und Dokumente eindeutig, daß in Judäa wahrend dieser Zeit Verwaltung, Wirtschaft und Heerwesen voll funktionsfähig waren, es also dort von 132 bis 135 einen Staat der Juden gegeben hat. Schon im Verlauf des «Jahres Eins der Erlösung Israels» hat sich Šim'ōn zum «Fürsten Israels» aufgeschwungen. Er war das Staatsoberhaupt und oberster Kriegsherr in einer Person, dem die «Lagerkommandanten» direkt unterstanden – ebenfalls als leitende zivile und militärische Administratoren zugleich. Sie waren es auch, die für und im Namen des Fürsten Staatsland an die jüdischen Bauern verpachteten[27]. Als allgegenwärtige Zeugen der uneingeschränkten Souveränität und wiedergewonnenen Staatlichkeit kursierten die eigenen Silber- und Bronzemünzen (Tf. LXII), deren Prägung allein schon eine zahlreiche Bevölkerung, größere liquide Mittel und ein organisatorisch und technisch geschultes Beamtenkader voraussetzt (Tf. LXVI).

## 7. Die kulturelle Wiedergeburt

Die Dokumente zeigen Šim'ōn bar Kōsibā als weltlichen Herrscher, Herrn über Grund und Boden, harten Soldaten und gottesfürchtigen Juden. Die Datierungen dieser Dokumente verkünden die Erlösung und Freiheit Israels. Die Münzen stellen dergleichen zuerst die Erlösung und dann die Freiheit Israels fest und rufen schließlich zur Befreiung Jerusalems auf. Das Zeugnis der Sachquellen für die Souveränität und die nationale Erneuerung ist eindeutig. Daß die Juden damals aber auch eine kulturelle Renaissance anstrebten, läßt sich schon aus der Wahl der Bilder und dem Wortlaut der Legenden für die Münzen erahnen (Tf. LXIII). Beweisen läßt sich diese wesentliche Tatsache aber durch ein Detail, das von der frühen Forschung nie beachtet und von den späteren Veröffentlichungen nicht in seiner vollen Tragweite erkannt worden ist: die Umgangssprache der Zeit in Judäa war das Aramäische, das Hebräische wurde allgemein, das Griechische von vielen verstanden. Die Schrift der Zeit war, wie sämtliche Sachquellen aufzeigen, die aus der altaramäischen Schrift entwickelte neue hebräische Quadratschrift, die man die jüdische Schrift genannt hat[28]. Auf den Münzen des Bar-Kochba-Krieges erscheint aber die paläohebräische

---

wurde, ist nicht endgültig. Neufunde können den Stand unseres Wissens erweitern und verändern.

27 Siehe insbesondere die Dokumente Murabba'at 22. 24. 29. 30. 42-45 in DJD II sowie die Dokumente 42-46 bei YADIN, IEJ 12 (1962) 226-257.

28 F.M. CROSS, The Development of the Jewish Scripts, in: The Bible and the Ancient Near East. Essays in Honor of W.F. Albright, New York 1961, 133-202; vgl.

Kursivschrift der Königszeit, die auch schon für die Münzen der Hasmonäer und des *Bellum Iudaicum* verwendet worden war (Tf. LXIV)[29]. Im Bar-Kochba-Krieg erfolgte dies aber zu einer Zeit, als sich die Quadratschrift schon völlig durchgesetzt hatte und seit der Zerstörung des Tempels über 60 Jahre vergangen waren. Der Rückgriff auf die uralte Schrift für die Münzprägung im Jahre 132 ist ein wichtiger Schritt zu einer kulturellen Wiedergeburt, die von den Rebellen bewußt und gezielt angestrebt worden ist[30].

# 8. Der Guerilla-Krieg

Dio schildert einen Guerilla-Krieg in schwierigem Gelände, der durch die römische Strategie der Isolierung und Umzingelung allmählich beendet werden konnte. Seine topographischen Angaben werden durch die neueste archäologische Erforschung der unterirdischen Fluchthöhlen bestätigt[31]. Es liegt auf der Hand, daß Simꜥōn die bestehenden natürlichen Schutzräume und künstlichen unterirdischen Anlagen als ideale Guerilla-Stellungen nutzte. Als letzte Zufluchtsstätten haben gewiß die an den steilen, in die Senke des Toten Meeres abfallenden Bergwänden liegenden Höhlen gedient, wie die Funde in der judäischen Wüste zeigen, und nicht die Bergfestungen wie das Herodeion oder gar das Masada-Plateau[32]. Die Münzfunde beweisen, daß Simꜥōn die inneren Linien im eigentlichen Judäa hielt, was zwar ein gutes Verteidigungsdispositiv ergab, aber auch Julius Severus erlaubte, nach seinem Eintreffen aus Britannien einen Ring um das gesamte Kampfgebiet zu legen und es danach aufzusplittern. Dafür spricht jedenfalls die Tätigkeit einer isolierten zweiten Münzstätte

---

MILDENBERG, op.cit., 1984, Anm. 37 sowie Y. MESHORER, Ancient Jewish Coinage, Vol. II, Dix Hills/NY 1983, 161-163.

[29] Nach E. STERN, The Cambridge History of Judaism. Vol. I: The Persian Period, Cambridge 1984, 85 dürfte die erste Wiederbelebung der archaischen hebräischen Schrift schon bei den Yehud-Münzen der persischen Zeit erfolgt sein, die hier [sc. im «Handbuch der Archäologie»: Vorderasien II/1 (1988)] andernorts [S. 719-728] behandelt werden [vgl. dafür hier S. 67-76].

[30] Vgl. L. MILDENBERG, The Eleazar Coins of the Bar Kochba Rebellion, Historia Judaica 11 (1949) 79 [hier S. 184]; id., HSCP 84 (1980) 329-331 [hier S. 229-230]; id., The Coinage of the Bar Kokhba War, 1984, 67. Erstaunlicherweise wird in den Dokumenten keiner der Rabbinen der Zeit genannt, dagegen aber als hohe rabbinische Autorität Batnaya bar Meisa Rabbenu, der sonst gänzlich unbekannt ist, s. Y. YADIN, IEJ 11 (1961) 46 und E. SCHÜRER [- G. VERMES], The History of the Jewish People Vol. I, 1973, 544, Anm. 139.

[31] L. MILDENBERG, The Coinage of the Bar Kokhba War, 1984, 14.

[32] *Vestigia terrent.* Simꜥōn und seine Kämpfer wollten ein zweites Masada gewiß vermeiden. Ähnliches gilt für das Herodeion, das aber durch Murabbaꜥat 24 B, Zeile 4 als Bar-Kochba-Lokalität im zweiten Kriegsjahr bezeugt ist, ebenso durch den großen Fund von Bar-Kochba Bronzemünzen aller Prägeperioden. Über Masada schweigen begreiflicherweise die Sachquellen: «However, our excavation at Masada from 1963-1965 revealed not one coin of Bar Kochba amongst the five thousand coins discovered there» (Y. YADIN, Bar-Kokhba, 1971, 188). Festzuhalten ist, daß der in der jüdischen Tradition überlieferte Endkampf auf dem Bergrücken von Bethar weder durch Münzfunde noch Dokumente bestätigt wird. Vgl. MILDENBERG, op.cit., 1984, Anm. 180.

der jüdischen Administration im letzten Kriegsjahr[33]. Wenn Šimʿōn bar Kōsibā seine Stellungen in Judäa konsolidierte, aber keine größeren Ausfalloperationen nach Samaria im Norden und an die Küste nach Westen und Südwesten unternahm, was wiederum nach der Verteilung der Münzfunde anzunehmen ist, dann hätten die 10.Legion oder gewisse Abteilungen derselben Jerusalem halten können. Der Aufmarsch der 6.Legion aus dem Lager Capercotna nach Süden wäre dann wohl schon am Anfang des Krieges erfolgt[34]. Der Weg für spätere Verstärkungen war so von der See aus über Caesarea möglich gewesen, ebenso zu Lande aus Ägypten und Syrien. Die östliche Flanke blieb frei. Und nur wenn Šimʿōn von dort die Hilfe der Parther erwartete, war die Strategie der Beherrschung der inneren Linien, also Judäas, sinnvoll. Die Parther kamen nicht. Die Schlinge konnte langsam, aber stetig zugezogen werden.

## 9. Die Ursache des Krieges

Es ist verständlich, daß sich während des Krieges das Nationalgefühl der judäischen Bauern gesteigert hat. Aber haben sie zu den Waffen gegriffen, weil sie ihren eigenen Staat wiedererrichten wollten? War der Bar-Kochba-Krieg der Freiheitskampf eines unterdrückten Volkes? Eine Unterdrückung der jüdischen Bevölkerung in der Provinz Judäa hat es nicht gegeben. Nach dem *Bellum Iudaicum* hatte weder eine allgemeine Versklavung noch Vertreibung stattgefunden. Der *Tumultus Iudaicus* hatte nicht auf Palästina übergegriffen. Von Repressalien Hadrians in Judäa nach der Niederschlagung dieses Aufstandes der jüdischen Diaspora in einigen Teilen des Reichs wissen wir nichts. Das positive Hadrianbild in der jüdischen Tradition[35], das sich nur auf seine Politik von 117 bis etwa 130 beziehen kann, hat also seine Berechtigung. Wenn aber eine nationale Bewegung als die Ursache des Krieges nicht in Frage kommen kann, waren es soziale Mißstände, die zum Kriege führten? Auch dies ist zu verneinen. Von einer ökonomischen Benachteiligung der jüdischen Bauern durch Gesetzgebung und Verwaltung kann nicht die Rede sein. Die schon erwähnte militärische und wirtschaftliche Kraft der Juden wäre nicht zu begreifen, wenn in Judäa Not und Elend geherrscht hätten.

Unbestritten ist, daß es nach dem *Bellum Iudaicum* starke messianische Strömungen gegeben hat. Die jüdische Tradition überliefert zudem die Messias-Ordination Šimʿōn bar Kōsibās als «Bar-Kochba» durch Rabbi Akiba, aber sie ist spät und «in ihrem historischen Wert äußerst zweifelhaft»[36]. Zur Stützung der Messias-These wurde auch die numismatische Evidenz bemüht, indem man in einem der Ornamente über dem Tempel auf den Tetradrachmen einen Stern sehen und diesen

---

[33] MILDENBERG, op.cit., 1984, 51.
[34] S. oben Anm. 13; MILDENBERG, op.cit., 1984, Anm. 214.
[35] M.D. HERR, Persecutions and Martyrdom in Hadrian's Days, ScrH 23 (1972) 93; P. SCHÄFER, Der Bar Kochba-Aufstand, 1981, 237-238. 244. Der entscheidende «Bruch» in Hadrians Wesen und Verhalten geschah um 130, nicht nach 135, wie SCHÄFER annimmt.
[36] P. SCHÄFER, Der Bar Kochba-Aufstand, 1981, 169, Anm. 133, 134; id., Studien zur Geschichte und Theologie des Judentums und Urchristentums, Leiden 1978, 90.

als messianisches «Symbol» deuten wollte. Der Stern ist aber in Wirklichkeit eine Rosette und nur eines von mehreren über dem Tempel stehenden Ornamenten[37]. Überzeugender wäre die messianische Interpretation des Titels *nāśī'* auf den Groß- und einigen Mittelbronzen[38], würde nicht die eindeutige Verwendung eben dieses Titels für den weltlichen Fürsten Šim'ōn bar Kōsibā in zahlreichen Dokumenten aus der judäischen Wüste es ausschließen, daß Šim'ōn sich für den Messias hielt und seine Mitstreiter ihn als solchen anerkannten.

Die Grundlinien von Hadrians *grand dessin*, die eine und friedliche, griechisch-römische Welt zu schaffen, wurden ihm wohl während seiner großen Reise in den Osten deutlich. Zur gleichen Zeit und auch im Osten wurde der Herrscherkult, die Vergöttlichung des Kaisers, in einem Maße propagiert, wie es das Kaiserreich vorher nicht gekannt hatte[39]. Eine römische Stadt auf dem Boden Jerusalems zu gründen, mag für Hadrian auf seiner Reise im Jahre 130 eine Routineangelegenheit gewesen sein, aber daß er sie «Aelia Capitolina» genannt hat, weist schon auf die sich anbahnende Verblendung des bedeutenden Kaisers hin. Für Dio war die Gründung der Kolonie die Ursache des Krieges. Es war dies gewiß eine spektakuläre Maßnahme, die von den Juden als gegen sie gerichtet aufgefaßt werden mußte und sie erbitterte, aber war es eine Sache von Leben und Tod? Die zweite gezielte Maßnahme Hadrians, die wohl Anfang 131 erfolgte, war aber unannehmbar, nämlich die Anwendung des Kastrationsverbotes auf die Beschneidung[40]. Die Befolgung hätte das Ende des jüdischen Lebens bedeutet. Deshalb griffen die Bauern in Judäa zu den Waffen. Ihr Überraschungserfolg weist darauf hin, daß der Kaiser – auch seine *entourage* und die Provinzverwaltung – tatsächlich damit gerechnet hatte, daß die Juden tun würden, was er befahl. Hadrian hatte sich getäuscht und den einzigen großen Krieg seiner Zeit verursacht, der sein Werk damals in Frage stellen und seinen Lebensabend verdüstern sollte.

## 10. Das Ereignis und seine Folgen

Hadrian überlebte das Kriegsende um knapp drei Jahre. Rom hat er nicht mehr verlassen. Auf einen Triumph und die Prägung von Triumphalmünzen, wie die Flavier es nach dem *Bellum Iudaicum* taten, hat er verzichtet. Die Regelung der Nachfolge

---

[37] MILDENBERG, op.cit., 1984, fig. 11; vgl. A. HAMBURGER, Die Silber-Münzprägungen während des letzten Aufstandes der Israeliten gegen Rom, nach einem in der Nähe von Chebron gemachten Münzfunde classificirt, ZfN 18 (1892) 305 (Nachdruck unter dem Titel: Die Münzprägungen während des letzten Aufstandes der Israeliten gegen Rom. Ein Beitrag vom numismatischen Standpunkt zur Geschichte jener Zeit, Berlin 1892).

[38] Über den eschatologischen Sinn des Titels *nāśī'* in Ezechiel 37,24-25 und darnach in den Dokumenten der Gemeinde von Qumran s. G. VERMES, The Dead Sea Scrolls, London 1977, 115 und P. SCHÄFER, Der Bar Kochba-Aufstand, 1981, 67-68.

[39] MILDENBERG, op.cit., 1984, 106-107, Anm. 303 (Kult von Hadrian und Antinous).

[40] Scr.Hist.Aug., Vita Hadriani 14,2; Digesta Iustiniani Augusti 48.8.II.I; A.M. RABELLO, The Legal Condition of the Jews in the Roman Empire, ANRW II, 13 (1980) 700-701.

erwies sich als schwieriger, als er erwartet hatte[41]. Sein Stern war im Verblassen. Selbst die *damnatio memoriae* drohte, wurde aber von seinem Nachfolger Antoninus Pius verhindert. Das Reich aber überwand die Schwächung durch den Bar-Kochba-Krieg und stand bei Hadrians Tod auf der Höhe der Macht. Sein Lebenswerk blieb bestehen.

Ähnliches gilt erstaunlicherweise auch für Šimʿōn bar Kōsibā. Zwar waren die Folgen des Krieges für Judäa verheerend. Die jüdische Siedlung in der Provinz war für lange Zeit zuende. Jerusalem wurde für die Juden zur verbotenen Stadt. Aber das Verbot der Beschneidung wurde kurz nach Hadrians Tod für die Juden aufgehoben. Antoninus Pius und seine Berater hatten eingesehen, daß Hadrians Judenpolitik gescheitert war. Hätten Šimʿōn und seine Männer nicht zu den Waffen gegriffen und hätten sie Hadrian's Verbot befolgt, so hätte es für den neuen, von Hadrian adoptierten Kaiser, der kein Erneuerer, sondern ein Bewahrer war, keinen Grund gegeben, eine fast ein Jahrzehnt lang bestehende rechtliche Regelung zu ändern[42]. Das Gesetz wäre in Kraft geblieben und die jüdische Existenz[43] im Römischen Reich wäre zu Ende gegangen[44]. Der Kampf der Juden war also nicht umsonst gewesen.

---

[41] Hadrian hatte im Sommer 136 seinen alten Schwager Servianus und seinen jungen Großneffen Fuscus ermorden lassen und im Herbst Aelius adoptiert und zum Mitkaiser berufen. Aelius starb am 1.Januar 138.

[42] Gegen die Annahme, Antoninus Pius hätte auch ohne Krieg durch eine Gesandtschaft oder durch andere Umstände dazu bewegt werden können, Hadrians Verbot der Beschneidung aufzuheben, spricht die beharrende Kraft römischer Rechtsnormen und die Politik des bedächtigen Kaisers, der ohne dringenden Zwang zum Handeln sich nicht gegen die Politik seines Adoptivvaters entschieden hätte. Wäre es nicht zum Bruch im Wesen Hadrians und dann zum Bar-Kochba-Krieg gekommen, wäre die Gestalt des großen Friedenskaisers gewiß auch nach seinem Tode übermächtig geblieben.

[43] Wie das Schicksal der Marranen nach der Spanischen Inquisition zeigt, führt der Verzicht auf die Beschneidung und das Verleugnen des Judeseins zum Untergang.

[44] Für die These, daß trotz des Untergangs des jüdischen Lebens im Römischen Reich die jüdische Existenz durch das Weiterbestehen der Gemeinden im Parthischen Reich ohnehin erhalten worden wäre, gibt es keine konkreten Hinweise.

# IV.

## Methodisches

# Numismatic Evidence*
## (Tf. LXVII - LXIX)

Recently ERNST BADIAN stated: «Numismatists' hypotheses are no more inherent in the object themselves, and no less liable to change, than historians': both are attempts to arrange evidence in a pattern»[1]. It is indeed a hypothetical endeavor to establish the date of the Piso-Caepio coinage or the chronology of Roman undated bronze money. The same is true of the attempts to locate a mint of anonymous issues or to estimate the volume of a coinage. Even meticulous weight tables for a coin series can yield only hypothetical data, even if, with the discovery of new hoards, they may prove to be highly probable and most useful.

Numismatic evidence, however, is factual. The coins can yield hard facts in a logical, mathematical, and physical sense. We shall deal here with (1) overstrikes, (2) die links, (3) hoards, (4) types and legends, (5) imitations, and (6) so-called «negative» evidence. We shall avoid «factoids», a word coined by NORMAN MAILER in «Marilyn» and recently defined by FRANZ GEORG MAIER as «mere speculations or guesses which had been repeated so often that they are eventually taken for hard facts»[2].

## 1. Overstrikes

I have pursued the concept of numismatic evidence outlined above for the last forty years. My first identification of a relevant overstrike was entirely due to the unequalled art of printing in the Rev. E. ROGERS' «Handy Guide to Jewish Coins»[3]. In 1947 I came across the plate (fig. 1) which stimulated an article entitled «Numismatische Evidenz zur Chronologie der Bar Kochba-Erhebung»[4]. There I set out my observations on the Rogers coin which has since come, via Virgil Brand and Sotheby (1984), into the holdings of a knowledgeable collector. This bronze, seemingly insignificant at first sight, reveals an underlying coin of Gaza dated twice:

---

*   This article is the revised text of a James C. Loeb Classical Lecture delivered at Harvard University on January 14, 1986. I am grateful to the Editor and M.A. Rizack for revision of the English text. For photographs I am indebted to several friends, especially S. Hurter and Y. Meshorer.
[1]  The Death of Saturninus, Chiron 14 (1984) 101-147.
[2]  Factoids in Ancient History: The Case of Fifth-century Cyprus, JHS 105 (1985) 32-39.
[3]  London 1914.
[4]  SNR 34 (1948-1949) 19-27, Pl. 3 [hier S. 176-182, Tf. LII]. See also HSCP 84 (1980) 311-335 [hier S. 217-234].

the year 192 of the era of Gaza[5], and $\Gamma$ ἐπιδημία, year 3 of Hadrian's grand tour of the East (fig. 2). Hadrian was in Gaza in the late spring or early summer of 130, but he may have already started on his tour in 129. The underlying coin was struck in 131/132 or – as is more likely – in 132. It follows that the coin must have been overstruck and the Bar Kokhba War must have begun after that date. On the 9th of August 1949, the London Times published the first news of the discovery of the documents found in the Judaean desert. Thus it happened that a second primary source – original papyri – confirmed the chronology established in 1947/1948 on the basis of a first primary source, the Rogers coin. The evidence obtained from the coins has been fully confirmed by sales contracts, leases, and the Bar Kokhba letters contained in the papyri, which were published between 1955 and 1962[6].

G. KENNETH JENKINS has recently dealt with an overstrike of a quite different kind. In the first part of his «Coins of Punic Sicily», he attributed the first series of these issues to the Punic mint of Lilybaion in Sicily, established on the site of Motya after this city had been destroyed by Dionysios I in 397[7]. In the following year a tetradrachm of Akragas appeared in the Bank Leu auction sale catalogue, obviously overstruck, as was duly noted (fig. 3)[8]. In Part 2 of his monograph, published in 1974, JENKINS revealed a spectacular and far-reaching discovery: just as the underlying Gaza coin of the overstrike discussed above had determined the chronology of the Bar Kokhba issue, so the overstriking Akragas coin had determined the chronology of the underlying Punic issue (fig. 4)[9]. The Akragas coin was obviously minted before 406, when the city was destroyed by the Carthaginians, and the Punic coin must, therefore, be earlier. In addition, to quote JENKINS: «it now seems, therefore, with the starting date firmly placed about 410 B.C., that we are driven after all to the conclusion that the QRTḤDŠT legend must be read in a perfectly literal sense, that is that the mint, as well as the minting authority, for the first tetradrachm series was at Carthage itself»[10]. Thus, surprisingly, the first Punic coins found in Sicily were struck in about 410 and not after 397.

---

[5] Not the era of Ascalon, as stated by error in BMC Palestine 144.

[6] See especially Discoveries in the Judaean Desert, Vol. 2 by P. BENOIT, J.T. MILIK, and R. DE VAUX, Oxford 1961, and Vol. 3 by M. BAILLET, J.T. MILIK, and R. DE VAUX, Oxford 1961; Y. YADIN, The Expedition to the Judean Desert, 1960, Expedition D, IEJ 11 (1961) 36-52; id., The Expedition to the Judean Desert, 1961, Expedition D – The Cave of the Letters, IEJ 12 (1962) 227-257.

[7] SNR 50 (1971) 25-78.

[8] Bank Leu Auction Sale Catalogue 2 (1972) no. 69.

[9] Coins of Punic Sicily: Part 2, SNR 53 (1974) 23-41.

[10] Ibid., 26. Hoard evidence and coining procedure indicate, however, that even the first Siculo-Punic coins were struck on the island and not at Carthage, cf. L. MILDENBERG, Sikulo-punischen Münzlegenden, SNR 72 (1993) 5-21 [hier S. 150-160].

## 2. Die Links

In 1949, in a study of the Eleazar coins of the Bar Kokhba rebellion, I published two plates which for the first time applied the die-comparison method to ancient Jewish coins[11]. The die links were correctly rendered and the alternative use of the grape-obverse G-1 for the production of the small silver and bronze denominations, an astounding phenomenon, was clearly indicated. In my Bar Kokhba corpus of 1984 the die links, although presented differently, are in fact identical[12]: the same structure appeared in 1984 as in 1949. There was nothing to change or to add after 35 years. The reason is obvious: then and now, a system of order of a coinage can only be obtained by the application of the die comparison method which is based on the examination of technical criteria, such as the gradually increasing detorition of a single die and the interlinking of all dies. Since in an ancient mint one obverse die was often used together with several reverse dies, the state of preservation of the obverse die indicates which die couple was struck first and which last. Thus, by determining the condition of the dies throughout the striking process, the structure of a coinage with its internal chronology emerges. In the case of the Bar Kokhba coinage, this internal chronology, too, was confirmed by the documents found in the Judaean desert.

At the Rome International Congress of Numismatics in 1961 I presented a paper entitled «Mithrapata und Perikles», a preliminary survey of some unusual Lycian coins from the Podalia-Elmali hoard of 1957[13]. The known Mithrapata dies with his portrait and name as presented in my paper are reproduced here (fig. 5). The evidence from the entire hoard shows a homogeneous issue with obverses and reverses linked together. The late OTTO MØRKHOLM combined the materials collected by several hands in the 1950s and 1960s with coins from this hoard, now in the Istanbul Archaeological Museum, and published in 1971, together with NEKRIMAN OLÇAY, all the specimens then known[14]. In the space of only ten years numismatic research had firmly established an entirely new portrait coinage, issued about 380 by a Lycian ruler of whom only some silver money without any effigy had previously been recorded. This proved to be important for the understanding of the origin and development of early coin portraiture, of the circulation of money in Asia Minor in the first quarter of the fourth century, and of the coinage policy of the Achaemenids within the Persian empire. We have still to deal with the three facing Perikles heads from the hoard. The engravers, following the example of Kimon of Syracuse, put the facing head on the obverse die, which would protect their fine and delicate work better than the reverse die, which had to support the stroke of the hammer. To our surprise the three die-combinations were not linked together, but it was noted that the first head showed a wreath, the second a quasi-wreath (leaves above and locks below), and

---

[11] Hist. Jud. 11 (1949) 71-108 [hier S. 183-201].
[12] The Coinage of the Bar Kokhba War (Typos 6), Aarau – Frankfurt a.M. – Salzburg 1984; for a brief account of the die-comparison method see pages 18-20.
[13] Congresso Internazionale di Numismatica Roma 1961, 2. Atti, Rom 1965, 45-55 [hier S. 105-109].
[14] The Coin Hoard from Podalia, NC 11 (1971) 1-29.

the third no wreath at all (fig. 6). «Der Durchbruch zum Portrait ist erfolgt» was my conclusion[15]. WILLY SCHWABACHER, like MØRKHOLM a scholar of outstanding merit, was not at all pleased with this statement. In a truly splendid paper, he argued on purely stylistic grounds in favor of a 3-2-1 order of striking rather than the order 1-2-3 which I had proposed[16]. He was, however, soon proven utterly wrong by a single die link which MØRKHOLM – OLÇAY published for the first time. As MØRKHOLM politely put it: «the sequence A2-A3 is now securely established. As the sequence A2-A3-A I would be very awkward (wreathed head – head without wreath – wreathed head) it seems preferable to return to the order first proposed by Mildenberg»[17]. A die link has to be taken as convincing evidence, while stylistic analysis remains subjective and therefore questionable.

## 3. Hoards

Further details of the Podalia-Elmali find are worth discussing, as they show the importance of hoard evidence for determining authenticity. In contrast to the Mithrapata portrait staters, the Perikles facing heads were already known from two specimens that had been struck from the same dies (fig. 6 center). The first one, pierced, housed in the Hermitage since the nineteenth century, appeared suddenly at a Berlin sale in 1935, a time when the Soviets were selling treasures from their museums[18]. The second specimen was illustrated in the Warren collection catalogue of 1906, but its authenticity was seriously doubted at the time by the compiler, KURT REGLING[19]. This fine piece reached the British Museum in 1927, but on the basis of REGLING's verdict it was condemned to the forgery trays. The unfortunate coin remained there until 1958, when the fresh Perikles material, especially five specimens from the same die couple and two others from the same obverse but a different reverse die, proved the authenticity of the Warren and Hermitage pieces beyond any doubt. Thus justice was finally done. The whereabouts of the Hermitage piece, withdrawn as a forgery from the sale in 1935, are unknown; perhaps it returned to Leningrad.

Generally scholars do not pay due attention to small change, the tiny silver coins and bronze issues of ancient times. This has been particularly true for the monetary history of Syria-Palestine in the fourth century B.C. It had been assumed that gold darics, large silver denominations struck in the Phoenician coastal cities and in Cilicia, and Athenian tetradrachms circulated in the huge fifth Persian satrapy, but no scholar had even speculated about the money of daily life. Fifteen years ago, a hoard was found just south of Jerusalem which was enlightening in many respects. Struck in Judaea, it contained obols, hemiobols, and tetratemoria, with weights from half a

---

15 Congresso Internazionale di Numismatica Roma 1961, 2. Atti, 1965, 48 [hier S. 107].
16 W. SCHWABACHER, Lycian Coin Portraits, in: C.M. KRAAY / G.K. JENKINS (ed.), Essays in Greek Coinage Presented to St. Robinson, Oxford 1968, 111-124.
17 O. MØRKHOLM / N.OLÇAY, NC 11 (1971) 16.
18 Auction sale F. Schlessinger 13 (1935) no. 1372.
19 K. REGLING, Die griechischen Münzen der Sammlung Warren, Berlin 1906, 189-190, no. 1231, formerly in the Naue collection.

gram to one-tenth of a gram. These tiny silver coins dating from about 360 to about 290 B.C. bear the name of the province: «Yehud» (Aramaic) or «Yehuda» (Hebrew)[20]. Even the Podalia hoard has not filled the gaps in our knowledgelge in such a spectacular way. Here we find coins of small denomination, used in a transit region during Persian, Macedonian, and Ptolemaic rule, displaying new and astounding issues, fresh numismatic evidence in an exemplary setting. Still more discoveries were to follow. From Lycia after Podalia nothing substantially new in portrait coinage had appeared. The Jerusalem hoard, however, was soon supplemented by the Nablus hoard, discovered in 1968, buried just before or during Alexander's campaign. This find contained not only tiny silver issues of the Cilician and Phoenician mints, but also the local Samarian currency, again with the name of that province: «Shamrayin» or «Samaria»[21]. Thus we now know the currency used in daily life in the Persian provinces of Samaria and Judaea and recognize at the same time its close political, economic, and cultural connections with the neighboring countries.

## 4. Types and Legends

The contemporary image of the first Berenike from the Jerusalem hoard, like the portrait of Mithrapata, yields new and indisputable numismatic evidence constituting a primary historical source of decisive importance in several respects. Berenike's head is the first extant female coin portrait with the face of a living woman (fig. 7). It demonstrates, furthermore, that not only Ptolemaios II Philadelphos but also Ptolemaios I Soter (fig. 8) had reason to emphasize the importance of the part played by the queen in his kingdom, at least in the province of Judaea[22]. The discovery of this hitherto unknown Ptolemaic small silver issue indicates that in about 305, when Ptolemy I finally dared to call himself $\beta\alpha\sigma\iota\lambda\epsilon\acute{u}\varsigma$ on his coins and the codification of the Egyptian monetary system began, the administration in Alexandria consented to the continued production of small local silver currency that had been introduced into the fifth Persian satrapy long ago. The officials also allowed the name of the province of Judaea to appear in semitic letters on these coins, a practice which indicates some degree of provincial autonomy[23]. Recently our knowledge of this Ptolemaic coinage in Judaea was enriched by some hitherto unknown

---

[20] L. MILDENBERG, Yehud: a preliminary study of the provincial coinage of Judaea, in: O. MØRKHOLM / N. WAGGONER (ed.), Greek Numismatics and Archaeology: Essays in Honor of M. Thompson, Wetteren 1979, 183-196 [hier S. 67-76].

[21] Y. MESHORER, Ancient Jewish Coinage I, Dix Hills/NY 1982, 160; A. SPAER, A coin of Jeroboam, IEJ 29 (1979) 218.

[22] Y. MESHORER, ibid., 17-18 and 184 attributed the Ptolemaic Yehud coinage to Ptolemy II Philadelphos (283-240 B.C.). It is, however, unlikely that the province of Judaea was left without an everyday money supply for nearly half a century. Moreover, in the third century bronze coinage had definitely replaced the tiny silver issues as small change.

[23] The name of the province is usually written in Aramaic as «Yehud», but occasionally also in Hebrew as «Yehuda». In the inconsistent scripts, however, the Hebrew letter forms prevail.

hemidrachms from the same issue (fig. 9)[24]. The interpretation of any of this numismatic evidence may be questioned, but the essential facts provided by the coins have to be accepted and accounted for.

In 1973, in a Bank Leu sale catalogue, a previously unpublished tetradrachmon appeared (fig. 10)[25]. Until that time only a drachm and a diobol from the Pergamon city coinage under the Attalids had been known. Many points are now open for discussion. Why did the kingdom allow the city to mint these large coins? When did this happen? On the occasion of the peace agreement of Apameia in 188, or at the games introduced in 183 after the completion of the temple of Athena Nikephoros, destroyed by Philip V of Macedonia in 202? Does the coin legend favor the first or the second proposal? Does the obverse still show the influence of the facing head of Athena created for Syracuse at about 410[26]? Why is there a marked difference in workmanship between the head and the cult image? These details need not concern us here. We wish, rather, to stress the following facts: (1) This is a tetradrachm, that is, a large silver coin, hitherto unknown; (2) On the reverse the type and the legend indicate Athena Nikephoros, a specific cult image, hitherto unknown; (3) On the obverse a facing head is depicted, also previously unknown; (4) The weight standard is the same as the contemporary Pergamene royal tetradrachm coinage with portraits, obviously because the new city coin had to be accepted at the same value as the current large portrait issues. Thus, apart from the weight standard, the whole issue is new and unparalleled. These four facts constitute the essential numismatic evidence for numismatists and historians alike.

A legend on an ancient coin has to be taken at face value. On some Bar Kokhba bronze coins (figs. 19-21) one reads «Shim'on, Prince of Israel». The man's name was Simon and he was prince of Israel. That is it. In the past, however, many scholars, myself included, had speculaled about who this Simon was: a spiritual leader, or perhaps the Messiah[27]? Then the aforemenitioned Hebrew, Aramaic, and Greek documents from the Judaean desert revealed that his name in fact was Shim'on ben (or bar) Kosiba and that he was indeed a prince, a stern ruler, and a warlord and landlord who exercised the emperor's prerogatives, which included not only striking coins, but even leasing crown land to the Jewish peasants, his comrades in arms[28].

As to the types, even a small detail can be highly important, as the following example will show. It concerns an ornament on the coin portrait of young Vabalathus (*Wahb'allāt*), son of Septimius Odenathus, the Romanized king of

---

24 Y. MESHORER, Ancient Jewish Coinage I, 1982, 184.
25 Bank Leu Auction Sale Catalogue 7 (1973) no. 207 and frontispiece.
26 The coin is the work of the die-engraver Eukleidas: L.O.TH. TUDEER, Die Tetradrachmenprägung von Syrakus, Berlin 1913, 58; G.E. RIZZO, Le Monete Greche della Sicilia, Rome 1946, Pl. 43:22.
27 Hist. Jud. 11 (1949) 92 [hier S. 193f]. There I understood «Shim'on» as the name of a patriarch. I did not, however, accept the Messiah-thesis.
28 See L. MILDENBERG, The Coinage of the Bar Kokhba War, 1984, 90-94; also Bar Kokhba Coins and Documents, HSCP 84 (1980) 313-315 [hier S. 223-225].

Palmyrene, and Septimia Zenobia (*Bat Zabbai*), his second queen[29]. In December 270 A.D., after the Palmyrene armies in an unprecedented sweeping campaign had conquered the entire Roman East, special antoniniani were struck in Syria. On these coins, as DELBRÜCK pointed out in 1940[30], Vabalathus wears not only a laurel but also a diadem, which stresses his position as king, rather than emperor or co-emperor (fig. 12). The abbreviated legend around Vabalathus' head must be read as *Vir Consularis Rex Imperator Dux Romanorum* , that is, with titles his father had received during and after his victorious battles as defender of the Roman Eastern frontier against the Parthians between 261 and 267 A.D. Here *imperator* does not mean «emperor», but «high commander». The same titles appear on the Palmyrene billon coins of Alexandria and in several Egyptian papyri[31]. The emperor Aurelianus' portrait and titles still appear on these coins, but they are not emphasized. Obviously Zenobia was well aware of the implications of all these highly compromising details of coin types and legends. Hence the guardian-queen's extremely cautious coinage policy, designed to avoid the blatant illegality of this Palmyrene money. In May 272, however, a dramatic and decisive change occurred, the origin and reason for which remain unclear: suddenly Vabalathus and Zenobia declared themselves on the coins as σεβαστός and σεβαστή in Alexandria and as *Augustus* and *Augusta* in Syria (fig. 13). Just as the diadem on Vabalathus' head had meant that the Palmyrene kingdom remained a loyal outpost within the Roman empire, so the supreme titles on the new coins signify Vabalathus' and Zenobia's self-proclamation as emperor and empress. Aurelian either had to accept what had been promulgated on the Palmyrene issues, thus recognizing Vabalathus and Zenobia as co-rulers, or remove the bold and dangerous pretenders once and for all. He chose the second solution and destroyed their vast realm. Thus the queen and her son paid dearly for their failure to seek timely, effective, and lasting consent from the powerful Pannonian emperor.

## 5. Imitations

The imitation copies the original which, therefore, is earlier. A commonplace, perhaps, but one that can become important when applied to coinage. An excellent example is the unique Segesta in the manner of Kimon illustrated here (fig. 14). The Segestan engraver cut his die as he saw the original, not knowing the basic rules of his trade. As a result his facing head is bent slightly to the right, whereas the original is bent to the left (figs. 15-16). The significance of this imitation was first pointed out at the New York-Washington International Congress of Numismatics in

---

[29] L. MILDENBERG, Aufstandsprägungen im Römischen Kaiserreich, in: Numismatics – Witness to History (AINP Publication No. 81), Wetteren 1986, 41-50 [vgl. hier S. 163-169].

[30] R. DELBRÜCK, Die Münzbildnisse von Maximinus bis Carinus, Berlin 1940, 161.

[31] V. PICOZZI, Le monete di Vaballato, Numismatica (Rome) September-December 1961, 123-128.

1973, and a date of 405-400 was proposed for the coin[32]. Only in recent years, however, has it become a cornerstone in Sicilian numismatics and history. CHRISTOF BOEHRINGER, in his publication of the Ognina hoard[33] and his arrangements of the late Syracusan tetradrachms in the Dewing catalogue[34], has shown that the two Kimonian facing heads were not·struck in 413-410, but rather about 405. KENNETH JENKINS has proven that the last Segestan didrachm which is die-linked with the facing head tetradrachm cannot have been struck before 405[35], because the Pennisi specimen of these Segestan didrachms is overstruck on one specimen of the latest didrachms of Camarina, dated about 406 (the city was evacuated in 405). This chain of numismatic evidence leads to the following important conclusions: the mint of Segesta was not closed around 409, as LEDERER thought[36], and Segesta did not lose her autonomy, as is generally believed, but was still a Carthaginian ally when Dionysios I of Syracuse campaigned in the west of Sicily in the years 397-396.

## 6. «Negative» Numismatic Evidence

The fact that no coins of a certain issue were found in a given excavation at a given time may be of great significance, but one can never be absolutely certain. On several occasions I have stressed that no Bar Kokhba coins were found on the site of Jerusalem[37] – not one single coin among the tens of thousands unearthed in extensive excavations. This is one of the reasons for the assertion that the high city remained in Roman hands during the three-and-a-half years of the war. It is unlikely that future excavations will have different results, but the possibility cannot be excluded a priori . Every collector and student of the Bar Kokhba coins knows that the rebels had struck silver tetradrachms and drachms-denarii and bronzes of large, medium, and small size (figs. 17-22). It is also generally known that the tetradrachms of the Syrian-Phoenician provincial coinage, issued from Augustus through Hadrian, and their quarters, drachms with Greek legends and denarii with Latin legends from different Roman mints, served as flans to be overstruck by the Jewish administration. The same was true for other bronzes of foreign origin. No scholar, however, has stressed in this connection that Roman didrachms also existed in the Syrian-Phoenician provincial coinage. The reason is simple: these didrachms are extremely

---

[32] L. MILDENBERG, Kimon in the manner of Segesta, in: Actes du 8ème Congrès International de Numismatique, New York -Washington 1973, Paris 1976, 113-121, Pl. 10-11 [hier S. - ].

[33] Rekonstruktion des Schatzfundes von Ognina 1923, SNR 57 (1978) 102-143, esp. 137-138.

[34] The Arthur S. Dewing Collection of Greek Coins, ed. L. MILDENBERG and S. HURTER (ACNAC 6), New York 1985, 54, nos. 846-848.

[35] U. WESTERMARK U. / K. JENKINS, The Coinage of Kamarina, London 1980, 65, Pl. 22a.

[36] P. Lederer, Die Tetradrachmenprägung von Segesta, München 1910, 43.

[37] Bar Kochba in Jerusalem?, SM 105 (1977) 1-6 [hier S. - ].

rare, having been issued only once[38]. In May 1985, however, a mixed hoard of Bar Kokhba silver and bronze coins, bronze city coins, and Roman silver coins was published[39]. The group of Roman silver issues consisted of 17 denarii-drachms, 4 tetradrachms, and 1 didrachm, none overstruck or hammered flat. At almost the same time, a heavily encrusted coin with the weight of a didrachm appeared in Jerusalem. When this piece of metal was cleaned, a Bar Kokhba didrachm appeared (fig. 23)! I have published a short study of the cleaned coin[40] and will summarize the meaning of this numismatic evidence here. The Bar Kokhba didrachm was struck at the very end of the war with regular lettering of the legend on the obverse, but irregular lettering on the reverse. The temple façade shows only two columns; the reverse has the usual lulav, but without the etrog. Clear traces of the underlying didrachm from the single issue of 100 A.D. are visible: Trajan's head, part of the eagle's leg, and considerable remains of the legends. And so the lesson about «negative» numismatic evidence is learned: the fact that no Bar Kokhba didrachms had previously been published does not mean that they did not exist. Shortly after my study appeared, my attention was directed to the following note in G.F. HILL's introduction to his masterly «Catalogue of the Greek coins of Palestine in the British Museum»: «... I may note here that I have also recently seen a coin professing to be a half-shekel or didrachm of the Second Revolt, with types similar to those of the tetradrachms (save that on the obv. the ark has no arch, and there are but two pillars, while on the rev. there is no citron). The inscriptions are šmʿwn and yrwšlm lḥrwt ; but they show such a confusion of forms that in themselves they suffice to make the authenticity of the piece extremely doubtful»[41]. HILL had a plaster cast made from the coin, but, since he had marked it «False», this cast was relegated to the forgery trays of the British Museum. It now turns out that HILL's coin was, in fact, struck from the same dies as the newly found specimen[42]! Thus, 72 years[43] had to pass before fuller numismatic evidence proved beyond a shadow of doubt that Bar Kokhba didrachms did indeed exist and that the great English scholar was wrong not to accept the piece

---

[38] Under Trajan in the year 100 B.C. See BMC Galatia, etc. no. 58; D.K. WALKER, The Metrology of the Roman Silver Coinage 2 (British Archaeological Reports, Suppl. Ser. 22), London 1977, 93; W. WRUCK, Die Syrische Provinzialprägung von Augustus bis Trajan, Stuttgart 1931, no. 145.

[39] Y. MESHORER, A coin-hoard of Bar-Kokhba's time, IMJ 4 (1985) 43-50.

[40] A Bar Kokhba Didrachm, INJ 8 (1984-1985) 33-36, Pl. 28 [hier S. - ].

[41] BMC Palestine (1914) p. CV, mentioned in D.P. BARAG, New Evidence for the Identification of the Showbread Table on the Coins of the Bar Kokhba War, in: 10th International Congress of Numismatics, London 1986 (abstract of paper).

[42] The British Museum plaster cast was retrieved by D.P. BARAG. It thus became obvious that the die break at the first letter shīn of Shim'on's name was still shorter on HILL's coin than on the 1985 specimen.

[43] It is noteworthy that a year before HILL's BMC publication, S. RAFFAELI, Coins of the Jews, Jerusalem 1913 (in Hebrew) had already recorded «one half with two columns» and hinted at two other specimens. Unfortunately, RAFFAELI could not illustrate any of these three pieces (communication from A. Spaer and D.P. Barag). Recently D.P. BARAG found HILL's coin in the trays of the Rockefeller Museum in Jerusalem. The piece is now exhibited in the Israel Museum in Jerusalem.

he had seen as genuine[44]. Obviously numismatic evidence itself does not fail or fade away, we numismatists, however, do.

---

[44] Fortunately we still have - in addition now to the coin itself - the plaster cast made by HILL and the two good photographs of the two Perikles pieces described above in the Warren and Schlessinger catalogues. In retrospect one is relieved that the eminent numismatist K. REGLING did not exclude the Warren piece in his publication of the collection.

# «Those Ridiculous Arrows»
## On the Meaning of the Die Position

### (Tf. LXX - LXXI)

In another context I have stressed the decisive importance of each of the elements of numismatic evidence as hard facts in a logical, mathematical and physical sense: overstrikes, die links, hoards, types and legends, imitations and the so-called negative evidence[1]. Here I shall deal with another element of numismatic evidence: the fabric, and specifically with one of its details, the die position. It is usually indicated either by the hours clockwise or by arrows indicating the position on the dial. It determines how the obverse die was placed on the reverse die for striking, either fixed (12 h or 6 h) or loose (1-12 h). Dies could be fixed by hinges or guides or by clamps. Striking from loose dies was carried out by placing the reverse die on the inserted obverse die at random.

The die position was indicated for the first time by G.F. HILL in his British Museum Catalogue of Greek Coins of Phoenicia in 1910; there were no arrows in his BMC of Cyprus, published in 1904. In my view, the importance of this revolutionary innovation is not adequately appreciated even today.

The arrows appeared in an auction sale catalogue for the first time, so far as I know, in the Hess-Leu 1, 14th April 1954, conceived by me. At the time a renowned dealer asked sarcastically: «Are these ridiculous arrows worth the printing expenses?». They were and are indeed. Two reasons for this firm opinion will suffice:

## 1. The location of the mint

Were the major issues of the Carthaginian coinage produced in Carthage proper or in Sicily? In the first instalment of his masterly corpus «Coins of Punic Sicily» in the SNR of 1971, G.K. JENKINS attributed the Siculo-Punic tetradrachms to Sicily. He had already done so in JENKINS-LEWIS, Carthaginian gold and electrum coins, in 1963. In his second corpus instalment of 1974 he demonstrated, on the evidence of an overstruck coin of Akragas[2], that the very first tetradrachms were issued as early as about 410 B.C. Here he was indeed right but concluded «that the mint, as well as the minting authority for the first tetradrachm series was at Carthage itself»[3]. Here he was wrong, as is proved first and foremost by the die position. The first coins of

---

[1] Numismatic Evidence, HSCP 91 (1987) 381-392 [hier S. 253-262].

[2] Leu 2, 1972, 69.

[3] G.K. JENKINS, SNR 54 (1971) 26.

Punic Sicily, as well as later ones, were exclusively struck from loose dies following the example of all Greek coins of Sicily. One has only to turn the specimens in any collection of Sicilian coins back to front[4], to have the proof of the pudding. Needless to say, the protuberances, another unique feature of the Sicilian minting technique[5], and the hoard evidence[6] confirm without a shadow of doubt what the die position has already revealed.

All electrum staters[7], all gold and electrum tristaters and all later coins of Carthage in gold, electrum, silver, billon and bronze have been exclusively struck from fixed dies at 12 h. They come from the metropolis in Africa and have nothing to do with Sicilian coins of the Carthaginian Empire[8]. Thus the die position invariably pinpoints the location of the mint.

## 2. Genuine and false

Fortunately, the master counterfeiters of the past seem not to have been aware of this instructive detail. «Dubious silver staters of Karystos in Euboea have haunted the numismatic market for decades. They were probably made in the 1930's»[9]. This cunning craftsman, whenever and wherever he worked, struck from loose dies, whereas the corresponding genuine coins were struck from dies firmly fixed at 12 h.

The Beirut forgeries of the Ptolemaic gold octodrachms with the legends $A\Delta E\Lambda\Phi\Omega N$ $\Theta E\Omega N$ and the portraits of Ptolemaios II with Arsinoe II and Ptolemaios I with Berenike I have also been struck from loose dies whereas the genuine pieces again come from dies fixed at 12 h[10].

The lessons of the numismatic evidence are simple and obvious. Woe betide anyone who disregards them!

---

[4] See, for instance, H. CAHN – L. MILDENBERG – R. RUSSO – H. VOEGTLI, Griechische Münzen aus Grossgriechenland und Sizilien, Basel 1988.

[5] Protuberances are the two metal protrusions, facing each other, which remained from the casting procedure. The craftsmen in the Sicilian mints did not bother cut them off, either before or after striking. With gold and electrum flans they were more careful.

[6] The Siculo-Punic coins are found on the island. In any case, not one single specimen from the first silver tetradrachm issue has an African origin or is believed to come from the continent.

[7] The Carthaginian gold staters struck around 300 B.C. are anepigraphic and show the same types and dot marks as the later Metropolitan issues. They have therefore been attributed to the mint of Carthage. This abundant and beautiful money was, however, struck from loose dies which hints at Sicily. Were the gold staters produced on the island, and the somewhat later electrum staters in Carthage after the Syracusan king Agathokles had landed on the continent?

[8] In the second half of the third century a massive bronze coinage was issued in Sardinia; silver and bronze money in Barkid Spain.

[9] S. HURTER, IAPN Bulletin on Counterfeits, Vol. 12,1, 1987, 1.

[10] There are other points which betray these forgeries: the flans are too large and incuse on both sides, the dotted grenetis is incomplete on obverse and reverse. See S. HURTER, preceeding footnote, vol. 9, No. 3.

# Florinus Mildenbergensis

## (Tf. LXXII)

Es ist schon einige Jahre her, daß ich Herbert Cahn mitteilte, ich besäße jetzt eine Münze[1], auf der mein Name stünde – nämlich einen Goldgulden des Mainzer Erzbischofs Gerlach von Nassau aus der Münzstätte Miltenberg am Main. Er hatte dies damals amüsant gefunden und gemeint: «Schicken Sie mir doch eine kurze Notiz für die Münzblätter». Ich hatte mir vorgenommen, die Anregung aufzunehmen, aber der kleine Artikel blieb ungeschrieben. Jetzt kommt nach der letzten der vielen von Herbert Cahn so ausgezeichnet redigierten Nummern der Schweizer Münzblätter auch schon das ihm gewidmete Heft und damit für mich die allerletzte Möglichkeit, mein Versprechen einzulösen.

Daß ich mich jetzt so sputen muß, daran ist nicht nur die berufliche Beanspruchung, sondern auch ein anderer Umstand schuld: Die Münze stammt aus einer Periode, in der ich mich nicht gut auskenne. Außerdem erfuhr ich noch von Kennern der Materie, daß mein Stück ein uneditiertes Unicum sei und besonders schwierige Probleme aufwerfe. Es sei heute noch verfrüht, diese Probleme zu lösen; eine kurze Publikation des Stückes hingegen sei sehr erwünscht.

Die Hauptschwierigkeit liegt darin, daß es über die Prägung der Erzbischöfe von Mainz noch kein Corpus und nur wenige Einzelstudien gibt[2]. Glücklicherweise liegt aber eine vorbildliche Publikation des einzigen bisher bekannten unter Gerlach von Nassau geprägten Miltenberger Goldguldens vor[3]. Er kommt aus dem wohl um 1370 vergrabenen Fund von Idstein und wird heute in Wiesbaden aufbewahrt[4]. Das Stück zeigt im Avers eine Lilie mit der vollen Legende ꟿILTᘓ NBᘓRᘜ, also dem Stadtnamen in der heutigen Form, und im Revers Johannes den Täufer in Bild und Legende mit dem Mainzer Rad links oben im Feld als Beizeichen.

Mein Goldgulden ist grundverschieden und muß einer anderen Emission angehören, wie die folgende Beschreibung zeigt:

---

[1] Die Münze verdanke ich der Güte meiner Kollegin Mme N. Kapamadji. Für wertvolle Hinweise bin ich verbunden P. Berghaus, W. Hees, E. Nau, B. Peus, D. Schwarz und H. Schoppa. Ohne die Hilfe von Fräulein E. Nau und Herrn P. Berghaus hätte die vorliegende Anzeige nicht erscheinen können.

[2] W. DIEPENBACH, Der Rheinische Münzverein, Mainz 1949, 89-120, id., Die Tätigkeit der mainzischen Münzstätten, Deutsche Münzbl. 54 (1934) 137-144.

[3] San.Rat Dr. HESS, Goldgulden- und Turnosenfund in Idstein, Mitteilungen für Münzsammler 4 (1927) 88ff, genaue Beschreibung 105, Taf. 3,1.

[4] Sammlung Nassauische Altertümer, Wiesbaden.

Vs. ◦ FLOKI MILDÊB' Lilie nach Florentiner Typ; Rs. ST IOHA NNES·B·

Nach links sitzender Hund oben links im Feld. Johannes der Täufer mit Kreuzstab in der Linken von vorn. Stempelstellung 12h. Gewicht 3,51 g. Auffällig die Schreibung *Florinus* statt *Florenus.*

Wir finden also statt des einfachen Stadtnamens *MILTENBERG* in der üblichen gotischen Schreibung die Bezeichnung *FLORI(nus) MILDE(n)B(ERGENSIS)* in gedrungenen Buchstabenformen. Diese Legende schließt sich enger an das Florentiner Vorbild an, und die Schreibung des Stadtnamens noch mit D dürfte älter sein.

Was hat es nun mit dem Beizeichen des hockenden Hundes auf sich? Üblich sind die Reichssymbole (Doppeladler, Adler, Krone). Das Rad ist das Wappen von Mainz und bezeichnet den Goldgulden mit der Legende *MILTENBERG* aus dem Idsteiner Fund deutlich als eine Prägung des Mainzer Erzbischofs als Landesherrn. Der hokkende Hund ist dagegen viel schwerer zu deuten. Parallelen scheinen sehr selten[5]. Vermutlich handelt es sich nicht um das Zeichen eines Münzmeisters oder gar eines Stempelschneiders, sondern um das eines Münzpächters oder Pfandinhabers[6] der Miltenberger Münze, der vielleicht in den Mainzer Archiven festzustellen wäre.

Der *terminus post quem* für die Datierung des Stückes ist die Bestallung des Münzmeisters Henselin von Straßburg in Miltenberg am 22.Januar 1354 durch Erzbischof Gerlach von Nassau, der beauftragt wird, Silbermünzen und einen kleinen Gulden von 23 Karat zu schlagen[7].

Der *terminus ante quem* dürfte um 1365 liegen, als in Köln die letzten Liliengulden geprägt wurden. Unser Stück hat wohl auch nichts mehr mit der Emission zu tun, die nach der 1370 erfolgten Weisung von Erzbischof Gerlach unter seinem Münzpächter Fritz Ergensheimer in Miltenberg erfolgten[8].

Die Reichssymbole dürften erst nach 1356, also nach der Regelung der Goldprägung in der Goldenen Bulle, häufig geworden sein. Vermutlich kommen die privaten Beizeichen etwas früher vor als die Reichssymbole und wohl auch die Zeichen der Landesherren[9]. Die Münze, auf der ich meinen Namen fand, müßte also – vor dem Stück aus dem Idsteiner Fund – wohl zwischen 1355 und 1360 geprägt worden sein.

Deutung und Datierung des neuen Miltenberger Goldguldens stehen also noch nicht endgültig fest. Diese vorläufige Anzeige und der Versuch, die wichtigsten Probleme aufzuwerfen und die Lösungsmöglichkeiten anzudeuten, fallen aber gewiß in den Aufgabenbereich der Schweizer Münzblätter.

---

[5] Helm auf einem Eltviller Goldgulden des Erzbistums Mainz und auf einem Goldgulden Walrams von Jülich, Erzbischofs von Köln, Noss 92, 93f (Hinweis von E. Nau).

[6] Hinweis von P. Berghaus.

[7] HESS, op.cit., 95.

[8] WÜRDTWEIN, Dipl. Mag. II 153.

[9] In München liegt – nach Mitteilung von P. Berghaus – ein Goldgulden mit dem Rad als Beizeichen und der Legende *FLORENTIA* aus dem Fund von Willanzheim – eine Nachahmung der Mainzer Gepräge, vielleicht der Münzstätte Miltenberg?

# Tafeln und Abbildungen

# Über das Münzwesen im Reich der Achämeniden* (S. 3-29) – Taf. I

## A. Frühes Elektron-Geld in Ionien und Lydien (zum Vergleich)

1. Stater Anfang 6.Jh. 13,42 g. Schildförmige, gerippte Fläche / Zwei vertiefte Rechtecke mit Strichmuster. Hess-Leu 31, 444.
2. Stater Anfang 6.Jh., 16,43 g. Löwin nach rechts, den Kopf umgewendet / Zwei vertiefte Quadrate, verschieden groß. Leu und MMAG, Kunstfreund, 28.5.1974, I. Unikum.
3. Erste Hälfte 6.Jh., 14,02 g. Stier, nach rechts stoßend, auf gewölbter Fläche / Längliches Rechteck zwischen zwei Quadraten, alle vertieft und verziert. Leu 28, 143.
4. Erste Hälfte 6.Jh., 14,05 g. Zwei Löwenvorderteile miteinander verbunden, oben Lotusblume / Rechteck zwischen zwei Quadraten, alle vertieft und mit den gleichen gepunzten Mustern verziert. Classical Numismatic Group, New York sale, 9.12.1992, 292A. Unikum.
5. Lydien. Anfang 6.Jh., Elektron-Drittelstater, Sardis, 4,72 g. Leu 45, 237.

## B. Die lydische Doppelwährung, Sardis, Mitte 6.Jh. (zum Vergleich)

6. «Schwerer» Goldstater, 10,78 g. Die Vorderteile eines Löwen und eines Stieres, einander gegenüber / Vertieftes Rechteck, gebildet aus zwei verschieden großen Quadraten. Leu 54, 147.
7. «Leichter» Goldstater, 8,03 g. Leu 38, 124.
8. Gold-Drittelstater, 3,57 g. Leu 54, 148.
9. Gold-Sechstelstater, 1,33 g. Leu 50, 179.
10. Silberstater, 10,72 g. Leu 30, 190.
11. Silber-Halbstater, 5,38 g. Leu 22, 138.
12. Silber-Sechstelstater, 1,67 g. Hess-Leu 45, 307.

---

* AV Gold, EL Elektron, Æ Bronze, alles andere Silber.

# Tafel I

1 EL    2 EL    3 EL    4 EL

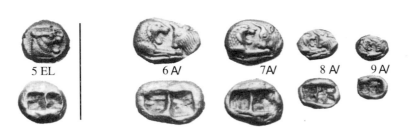

5 EL    6 A/    7 A/    8 A/    9 A/

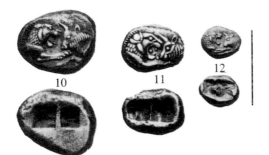

10    11    12

# Über das Münzwesen im Reich der Achämeniden (S. 3 -29) – Taf. II

## 1. Das Reichsgeld

13. 1. Typ. Silber-Siglos um 500 v.Chr., 5,39 g. Halbfigur des Großkönigs mit der Zackenkrone, den Bogen haltend. London, British Museum, 1948 (7-12.15).
14. 2. Typ. Gold-Dareike, 1. Hälfte 5.Jh., 8,28 g. Großkönig mit der Zackenkrone im Mantel, den Bogen spannend. Leu 20, 168.
15. 2. Typ. Siglos, 1. Hälfte 5.Jh. Wie vorher Nr. 14, 5,37 g. SKA Zürich, Liste 55, Frühjahr 1991, 119.
16. 3. Typ. Golddareike, Mitte 5.Jh., 8,33 g. Der Großkönig von gedrungener Gestalt in der Zackenkrone und Mantel mit Bogen und Speer. Leu 45, 283.
17. 3. Typ. Golddareike, um 400, 8,36 g. Der Großkönig wie vorher 16, nur Gestalt länglich. Hess-Leu 49, 289.
18. 3. Typ. Silbersiglos um 400, 5,38 g. Wie vorher 16-17. SKA Zürich, Liste 55, Frühjahr 1991, 122.
19. 3. Typ. Silber-Achtelsiglos um 400, 0,71 g. Wie vorher 16-18. Hess-Leu 45, 386.
20. 4. Typ. Silbersiglos, 1. Hälfte 4.Jh., 5,47 g. Der Großkönig wie vorher 16-19, aber mit Dolch statt Speer. Numismatica Ars Classica, 11.3.1993, 197.
21 4. Typ. Gold-Dareike, Mitte 4.Jh., 8,33 g. Wie vorher 20. Hess-Leu 49, 288.

## 2. Die sogenannten Satrapenmünzen

22. Kyzikos. Tetradrachme Ende 5.Jh., 14,62 g. *ΦAP-N-ABA* Kopf des Granden Pharnabazos in der Tiara / Schiffsbug mit Greifen nach links zwischen Delphinen, unten Thunfisch, das Stadtwappen, nach links. Leu 45, 199.
23. Kyzikos, Hemidrachme. Wie vorher Nr. 22, 1,72 g. Legende [*ΦAP*]-*N-A*. Leu 42, 279.
24. Lykien. Stater mit dem Namen des Granden Tissaphernes, Anfang 4.Jh., 8,41 g. *aruna* Perser zu Pferd im Schritt nach r. / *zis..na* Behelmter Kopf der Pallas Athene nach r. S. HURTER, in: FS M. Thompson, 1979, Nr. 6.

# Tafel II

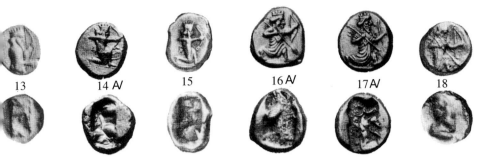

13    14 A/    15    16 A/    17A/    18

19    20    21 A/

22    23    24

# Über das Münzwesen im Reich der Achämeniden (S. 3 -29) – Taf. III

25. Astyra in Mysien. Kleinbronze mit dem Namen des Granden Tissaphernes, Anfang 4. Jh., 1,53 g. [*T*] *IΣ* [*ΣA*] Bärtiger Kopf nach r. / *AΣTΥPH*. Kultbild der Artemis von vorn. F. Sternberg 26, 90.

26. Westliches Kleinasien. Tetrobol mit dem Namen des Satrapen *ΣΠIΘPI* - Spithridates, um 334, 2,63 g. Bärtiger Kopf mit der Tiara nach links / Pegasus-Protome r. Berlin, E. BABELON, Traité, 2$^e$ partie, 1910-1912, 69, Pl. 89,1.

## 3. Das Provinzialgeld (Vergrößerungen 3 x 1)

### 3.1. Samaria

27. Obol um 345 mit den Namen der Provinz, 0,68 g. Weiblicher Kopf von vorn in der Art der Arethusa des Kimon von Syrakus / Behelmter, bärtiger Kopf links davor *šmryn*. Aus dem Samaria-Fund, Y. MESHORER / S. QEDAR, Coinage of Samaria, 1991, Nr. S-H 74 auf Pl. 23.

28. Obol unter Mazaios um 340, 0,78 g. Der thronende Großkönig in hoher Zackenkrone mit Blume und Zepter in der Art des Baal von Tarsos. Dahinter *š* - *n*, als Abkürzung für *šmryn* (Samaria) gedeutet / Ahuramazda nach r., dahinter *mz*, die ersten zwei Buchstaben von *mzdy* - Mazaios. Aus dem Nablus Hoard, Oxford. Y. MESHORER / S. QEDAR, Coinage of Samaria, 1991, 21.

29. Obol mit einem sonst unbekannten Personennamen um 340, 0,77 g. Der Großkönig wie vorher Nr. 28, aber als *ZEΥΣ* bezeichnet / Perser mit gezückter Lanze auf nach r. sprengendem Pferd. Unten *yhw'nh*. Aus dem Nablus Hoard, Oxford. Y. MESHORER / S. QEDAR, Coinage of Samaria, 1991, 38.

30. Hemiobol mit dem Provinznamen um 335, 0,28 g. Sidonische Galeere über Wellen nach links, oben *šmryn* / Der Großkönig mit Bogen und Lanze in der Art des späten Reichsgeldes nach r. Sammlung Sofaer. Y. MESHORER / S. QEDAR, Coinage of Samaria, 1991, 17.

### 3.2. Iudaea

31. Hemiobol mit dem Provinznamen um 345, 0,29 g. Lilie / Falke mit gespreizten Schwingen, Kopf nach r. Oben r. *yhd*. F. Sternberg 26, 131.

32. Hemiobol mit dem Provinznamen um 340, 0,35 g. Kopf des Großkönigs in der Zackenkrone nach r. / Bild und Inschrift wie vorher Nr. 31. F. Sternberg 26, 133.

33. Hemiobol, mit dem Namen des Gouverneurs Yeḥezqiah um 335 sowie Titel. Gewicht ca. 0,20 g. Weiblicher Kopf von vorn in der Art der Arethusa des Kimon von Syrakus / Eule mit leicht gespreizten Flügeln. Links von unten nach oben *yḥzqyh*, rechts von oben nach unten *hpḥh* über A. Erstveröffentlichung L. MILDENBERG, in: FS M. Thompson, 1979, Pl. 22, 15.

34. Viertelobol mit dem Provinznamen im ptolemäischen Königreich 292-283, 0,19 g. Kopf des Ptolemaios I. Soter nach r. in der Königsbinde / Kopf der Berenike I. nach r., davor *yhd*. F. Sternberg 26, 140.

# Tafel III

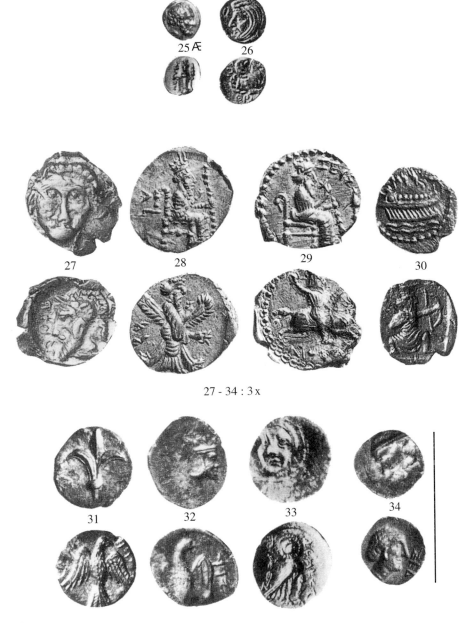

25 Æ  26

27  28  29  30

27 - 34 : 3 x

31  32  33  34

# Über das Münzwesen im Reich der Achämeniden (S. 3-29) – Taf. IV

## 4. Der Münzimport

35. Die Ichnaier in Makedonien. Oktadrachme um 480, 29,14 g. Nackter Mann, zwei nach links gehende Ochsen führend. Im Feld *I-X-NAI[-ON]* / Vierspeichenrad. Aus dem Asyūṭ-Fund, verborgen um 475, M. PRICE - N. WAGGONER, Archaic Greek Silver Coinage. The «Asyut» Hoard, 1975, 41 = Leu 54, 69.

36. Stagira, Makedonien. Tetradrachme um 480, 17,25 g. Löwe nach links über Eber nach r. / Vertieftes, viergeteiltes Quadrat. Einhieb. Aus dem Asyūṭ-Fund, verborgen um 475. M. PRICE - N. WAGGONER, Archaic Greek Silver Coinage. The «Asyut» Hoard, 1975, 191 = Leu 54, 80.

37. Delphi. Tridrachme um 478, 18,31 g. Zwei Widderkopf-Rhyta gegeneinander, oben zwei Delphine / Vertiefte Kassettenquadrate mit je einem Delphin. Aus dem Asyūṭ-Fund, M. PRICE - N. WAGGONER, Archaic Greek Silver Coinage. The «Asyut» Hoard, 1975 = Leu 54, 100.

38. Athen. Tetradrachme um 500, 17,31 g. Behelmter Kopf der Pallas Athene nach r. / Eule nach r. sitzend in vertieftem Quadrat. Aus dem Antilibanon-Fund, verborgen um 475. S. HURTER / E. PÁSZTHORY, in: FS L. Mildenberg, 1984, 115, Nr. 15.

## 5. Das Lokalgeld
### 5.1. Die Eulen des Ostens

39. Gaza. Tetradrachme um 400, 16,81 g. Behelmter Kopf der Pallas Athene, eine gekonnte Nachahmung der athenischen Vorbilder von der Mitte des 5. Jh.s / Sitzende Eule von vorn zwischen Ölzweigen, rechts Θ, links Volute, beides als *'ayin-zayin* für Gaza zu lesen. Berlin 468/1891.

40. Tetradrachme, östliche Imitation in der Levante nach 400, 16,59 g. Kopf der Pallas Athene mit übertrieben langer Nase, unkenntliche Zeichen auf dem Helm / *AΘH* Eule nach r. in noch deutlich vertieftem Quadrat. F. Sternberg 26, 82.

41. Tetradrachme. Levante, 4. Jh., nur 13,82 g. Kopf der Pallas Athene mit *ankh*-förmigen Zeichen auf der Wange / Eule nach r. in angedeutetem vertieftem Quadrat. Leu 54, 183.

42. Palästina. Obol, Mitte 4. Jh., 0,69 g. Kopf der Pallas Athene / *AΘH* Eule. Aus dem Samaria-Fund. Y. MESHORER / S. QEDAR, Coinage of Samaria, 1991, Nr. S-H 290, auf Tafel 47. Vergrößerung 3 x.

# Tafel IV

35

36

37

38

39

40

41

42 : 3 x

# Über das Münzwesen im Reich der Achämeniden (S. 3-29) – Taf. V

5.2. Die Prägungen der Herrscher

Die Hekatomniden in Karien:

43. Hekatomnos, 395-377, Tetradrachme, 14,90 g. Zeus Labrandeus nach r. stehend / *EKA TOMNΩ* Löwe nach r. in vertieftem Rund. Leu 28, 169.
44. Mausolos, 377-353, Tetradrachme, geprägt um 367 in Halikarnassos, 15,15 g. Kopf des Apollon von vorn / *MA ΥΣΣΩΛΛO* Zeus Labrandeus wie oben Nr. 43. Leu 25, 161.
45. Hidrieus, 351-344, Tetradrachme, Halikarnassos, 15,17 g. *IΔPIEOΣ* Zeus Labrandeus wie vorher. Leu 45, 231.
46. Pixodaros, 340-334, Gold-Halbstater, Halikarnassos, 4,15 g. [*ΠI*]*ΞΩΔAPO* Kopf des Apollon in Lorbeerkranz nach r. / Zeus Labrandeus wie vorher. Leu 45, 232.
47. Pixodaros, 340-334, Didrachme, Halikarnassos, 6,92 g. *ΠIΞΩΔAPOΥ* Apollon mit Zeus Labrandeus wie vorher, Leu 28, 172.
48. Rhoontopatos, Perser, Schwiegersohn des Pixodaros, 334-333, Tetradrachme, Halikarnassos, 15,11 g. *POONTOΠA TOΥ*. Wie oben die Nummern 44, 45 und 47. Leu 50, 177.

Die lykischen Dynasten:

49. Limyra, unbestimmter Dynast, Tetrobol um 420, 2,81 g. Löwenkopf mit geöffnetem Rachen / Triskelis, im Feld der Stadtname und *ankh*- förmiges Zeichen. Leu 54, 154.
50. Kherei 425/420-400, Stater, 8,37 g. Pallas Athene in der Art der athenischen Tetradrachmen / Kopf des Herakles in gutem, griechischem Stempelschnitt, links Telmessos, die Münzstätte, und Kherei, der Name des Dynasten, auf lykisch. Leu 50, 182.
51. Kherei, Stater, 8,48 g. Wie vorher / Tiarakopf mit Diadem nach links statt des Herakleskopfes (!), davor der Name des Kherei. Leu 45, 242.
52. Vekhssere, Tetrobol Anfang 4.Jh., 2,85 g. Löwenkopf nach links, oben der abgekürzte Name des Dynasten / Kopf der Pallas Athene von vorn, ganz in der Art des Eukleidas von Syrakus. Aus dem Fund von Podalia. Leu 30, 192.

# Tafel V

43       44       45

46 A/     47     48     49

50     51     52

# Über das Münzwesen im Reich der Achämeniden (S. 3-29) – Taf. VI

53. Mithrapata, Stater um 375, 9,89 g. Löwenkopf nach r. / Bärtiger Kopf des Dynasten nach links, im Feld sein Name und Triskelis. Aus dem Fund von Podalia. Leu 20, 143.
54. Perikles, Stater um 370, 9,88 g. Bärtiger Kopf mit Lorbeerkranz von vorn, angeregt von der Arethusa des Kimon von Syrakus / Bis auf den Helm nackter Krieger mit Schild nach r. Im Feld der Name des Perikles und Triskelis. Aus dem Fund von Podalia. Leu 50. 183.

Die Herrscher auf Zypern:

55. Münzstätte unbestimmt, Stater um 480, 11,32 g. Löwenkopf mit geöffnetem Rachen nach links / Stiervorderteil mit Zeichen auf dem Hals nach links, davor Zweig, unten die zyprischen Zeichen für die Silben *ba-ka*. Einhieb. Aus dem Fund von Asyūṭ (M. PRICE - N. WAGGONER, Archaic Greek Silver Coinage. The «Asyut» Hoard, 1975), nicht verzeichnet. Leu 28, 187.
56. Salamis. König Euanthes, Stater um 400, 11,02 g. Liegender Widder nach links / Widderkopf nach r., darüber Lorbeerzweig. Leu 28, 190.
57. Kition. König Baalmelek II., ca. 425-400, Stater, 10,92 g. Herakles nackt mit Löwenfell, Bogen und geschwungener Keule nach r. schreitend / Löwe über Hirsch, oben die phönizische Inschrift *lb'lmlk* = dem Baalmelek. Leu 28, 188.
58. Salamis. König Pnytagoras, 351-332, Goldstater, 8,30 g. Frauenkopf mit Diadem nach links dahinter BA / Frauenkopf mit Mauerkrone nach links, dahinter *ΠN*. Leu 28, 191.

# Tafel VI

53

54

55

56

57

58 A/

# Über das Münzwesen im Reich der Achämeniden (S. 3-29) – Taf.VII

## 5.3. Lokale Elektron- und Goldprägungen

Kyzikos

59. Elektronstater um 520, 16,00 g. Kopf der Athena in korinthischem Helm nach links, dahinter Thunfisch / Vertieftes Quadrat mit Balkenkreuz. Leu 20, 111.

60. Elektronstater um 520, 16,15 g. Kopf einer Löwin nach links, dahinter Thunfisch / Wie vorher Nr. 59. Leu 33, 354.

61. Elektronstater des späten 6.Jh.s, 16,08 g. Löwe nach links über Thunfisch / Wie vorher Nr. 59 und 60. Leu 52, 83.

62. Elektronstater um 480, 16,14 g. Ungeheuer als nackter, geflügelter Mann mit Wolfskopf und -Schweif nach links im Knielauf, Thunfisch in der Rechten / Vertieftes Quadrat mit Fadenkreuz. Leu 45, 196.

63. Silber-Diobol, Mitte 5. Jh. (als Vergleichstück), 0,86 g. Ebervorderteil nach links, umgekehrtes E auf der Schulter / Löwenkopf nach links in vertieftem Quadrat. Leu 28, 131.

64. Elektronhekte um 450, 2,63 g. Stier, sich legend, auf Thunfisch nach links / Wie vorher Nr. 62. Leu 25, 135.

65. Elektronstater 450, 16,00 g. Nackter Silen auf Thunfisch nach r. kniend mit großer Amphora und Kantharos / Wie vorher Nr. 64. Leu 42, 278.

66. Elektronstater um 430, 14,98 g. Skylla mit erbeutetem Thunfisch nach links, unten das Thunfisch-Wappen / Wie vorher Nr. 65. Leu 45, 198.

67. Elektronstater Mitte 4. Jh., 16,06 g. Adler mit gespreizten Schwingen auf runder Scheibe, unten Thunfisch / Wie vorher Nr. 66, aber jetzt mit körnigen Feldern. Leu 48, 217.

# Tafel VII

59 EL          60 EL          61 EL

63

62 EL

64 EL

65 EL

66 EL

67 EL

# Über das Münzwesen im Reich der Achämeniden (S. 3-29) – Taf. VIII

68. Stater, Bündnisprägung, um 400, 11,39 g. Herakles als Kind im Kampf mit den Schlangen, im Feld *Σ-Υ-N* / Löwenkopf nach links über Thunfisch, im Feld *K Υ-Z* für den in der Elektronprägung nie genannten Stadtnamen. British Museum.
69. Tetradrachme 390-387, 15,25 g. Kopf der Kore Soteira im Schleier nach links, oben *Σ-Ω-T-EIPA* / Löwenkopf nach links über Thunfisch, im Feld *K ΥΖΙ KHN-ΩN*, rechts Biene. Leu 42, 283.

### Lampsakos

70. Elektronstater 2. Hälfte 5. Jh., 15,38 g. Pegasus-Vorderteil nach li., unten *Ξ* / Vertieftes Quadrat mit Fadenkreuz. Leu 42, 284.
71. Silber-Hemidrachme, Ende 5. Jh. (als Vergleichsstück), 2,08 g. Weiblicher Januskopf / Kopf der Athena mit korinthischem Helm nach r., im Feld *Λ AM-ψ-A*, der in der Goldprägung nie genannte Stadtname. Leu 33, 362.
72. Goldstater um 360, 8,40 g. Kopf des Helios auf strahlender Sonnenscheibe nach links / Pegasus-Vorderteil nach r. in noch deutlich vertieftem Quadrat. Leu 45, 202.
73. Goldstater, Mitte 4. Jh., 8,45 g. Bärtiger Tiarakopf mit Diadem nach links / Pegasus-Vorderteil nach r. Leu 30, 167.
74. Goldstater, Mitte 4. Jh., 8,41 g. Bärtiger Zeus-Kopf mit Lorbeerkranz nach links / Wie vorher Nr. 73. Leu 54, 123.
75. Goldstater, Mitte 4. Jh., 8,40 g. Kopf des Aktaion mit Hirschgeweih / wie vorher Nr. 74. Leu 50, 155.
76. Goldstater, Ende 4. Jh., 8,41 g. Kopf einer Göttin mit Blütenkranz nach links / Wie vorher Nr. 75. Leu 54, 124.

### Phokaia

77. Elektronhekte um 530, 2,56 g. Greifenkopf mit geöffnetem Rachen, dahinter kleiner Seehund / Vertieftes Quadrat. Leu 52, 93.
78. Elektronhekte um 420, 2,55 g. Kopf des Hermes nach links / Vertieftes Quadrat mit Fadenkreuz. Leu 42, 300.

### Lesbos - Mytilene

79. Elektronhekte um 500, 2,55 g. Widderkopf nach r., darunter Hahn nach links / Vertiefter Löwenkopf nach r., dahinter längliches Rechteck, zweigeteilt. Leu 42, 292.
80. Elektronhekte um 450, 2,55 g. Kopf eines bärtigen Silens mit Tierohren und Binde im Haar / Zwei Widderköpfe, gesenkt, einander gegenüber im vertieften Quadrat. Leu 45, 208.

# Tafel VIII

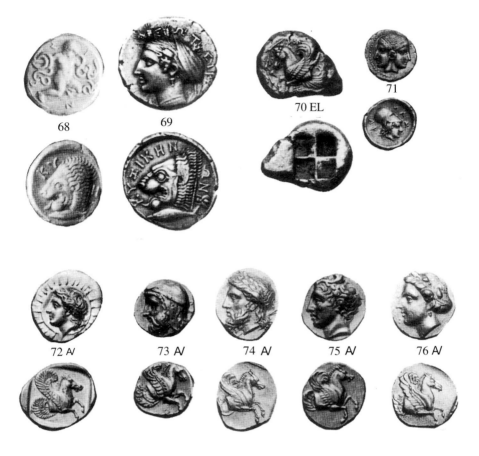

68

69

70 EL

71

72 AV     73 AV     74 AV     75 AV     76 AV

 77 EL     78 EL     79 EL     80 EL

# Über das Münzwesen im Reich der Achämeniden (S. 3-29) – Taf. IX

### 5.4. Das Silbergeld der Städte
Knidos

81. Drachme um 455, 6,21 g. Löwenkopf, geöffneter Rachen / Kopf der Aphrodite mit Binde, Kette und Haar, im Zopf. MMAG-Leu, Katalog Kunstfreund, 163.
82. Drachme um 450, 6,03 g. Wie vorher Nr. 81, aber nun *K-N-I* auf Rückseite. Leu 36, 163.
83. Didrachme, anfangs 4. Jh., 7,40 g. Großer Löwenkopf nach r., im Feld *ΠΕΙΣΙΣΤΡΑΤΟΣ* / Kopf der Aphrodite mit Ohrring, das Haar aufgebunden. Dahinter Schiffsbug. Kat. der Slg. R. Jameson, Paris 1913-1932, 1536.
84. Tetradrachme um 390, 15,26 g. Vorderteil eines Löwen nach r. / Kopf der Aphrodite mit Ohrring und Perlenkette, das Haar in Haube, links Eichel, unten *K-NI*. Numismatica Ars Classica 4, 148.
85. Tetradrachme um 360, 14,77 g. Kopf der Aphrodite mit Binde, Ohrring und Perlenkette nach links, dahinter Schiffsbug / Löwenvorderteil nach links, unten *KNIΔ*. Leu 52, 96.

Nagidos

86. Silberstater, 1.Viertel des 4. Jh.s, 9,91 g. Aphrodite mit Schale und Lotosblume auf Sphingen-Thron nach r. sitzend, dahinter *NAΓΙΔΙΚΟΝ* / Kopf eines bärtigen, behelmten Kriegers nach links, davor *prnbzw-klk*   Pharnabazos - Kilikien. SNG Paris, Cilicie, 1993, 23.
87. Silberstater um 350, 10,05 g. Thronende Aphrodite mit hohem Hut, in der Rechten Schale, unten Maus / Dionysos mit Thyrsos und Traube an Ast nach links stehend, hinten *NAΓΙΔΙΚΟΝ*, vorne Monogramm, Löwenkopf nach links und *ΠΟΛ*. Leu 45, 249.

# Tafel IX

81

82

83

84

85

86

87

# Über das Münzwesen im Reich der Achämeniden (S. 3-29) – Taf. X

Tarsos

88. Silberstater um 410, 10,49 g. Reiter nach r. / Nergaltars mit Speer und Bogen auf Löwen von vorn stehend. Rechts im Feld steht, in dem Tarsos schon damals eigenen Duktus der aramäischen Schrift in zwei Linien, *nrgl* - *trz*. British Museum. L. MILDENBERG, in: FS H. Bloesch (AK.B 9), 1972, Taf. 28, 4 [= Taf. XIVB 4].

89. Silberstater um 400, 10,63 g. Mann in persischer Tracht mit Treibstab pflügt mit Ochsen nach links, oben *trz* / Kuh nach links säugt ihr Kalb, darüber geflügelte Sonnenscheibe. Leu 45, 250.

90. Silberstater für Pharnabazos, 379-374, 10,72 g. Baaltars, Oberkörper nackt, nach links thronend, dahinter *bʿltrz*, davor *ankh*-artiges Zeichen / Bärtiger behelmter Kriegerkopf nach links, davor *prnbzw*, dahinter *klk*. L. MILDENBERG, INJ 11 (1990-1991) 1 [hier Taf. XVII 1)]; Hess-Leu 31, 497.

91. Silberstater für Datames, 378-372, 10,86 g. Weiblicher Kopf von vorn, ganz in der Art des Stempelschneiders Kimon von Syrakus / Kriegerkopf wie vorher Nr. 90, aber nach r., davor *trdmw*. L. MILDENBERG, INJ 11 (1990-1991) 2 [hier Taf. XVII 2]; Leu 42, 340.

92. Silberstater für Datames, 10,47 g. Baaltars mit Ähre und Traube nach r., hinten Thymiaterion, unter dem Sitz Stierkopf, im Zinnenrund *bʿltrz* / *trdmw*. Persischer Krieger nach r. sitzend, einen Pfeil prüfend. Im Feld Bogen und geflügelte Sonnenscheibe. Leu 50, 189.

93. Silberstater für Datames, 10,72 g. Wie vorher, aber Stern im Feld, Baaltars blickt nach vorne / Der mit seinem Namen r. im Feld bezeichnete *trdmw* -Datames steht mit erhobener Rechter vor dem die Rechte ausstreckenden nackten Gott Ana, dessen Namen *ʾnʾ* verzeichnet ist. Leu 48, 253.

94. Mazaios, Silberstater nach 361, 10,71 g. Baaltars mit Ähre und Traube nach links sitzend, unter dem Thron Ankh / Löwe über Hirsch nach links unten Kreis, oben *mzdy*-Mazday-Mazaios. L. MILDENBERG, INJ 11 (1990-1991) No. 4 [hier Taf. XVII 4]; Leu 30, 197.

95. Mazaios, Silberstater, Mitte 4.Jh., 10,79 g. Baaltars mit Ähre, Traube und Adler (!) nach links sitzend / Löwe über Stier nach links, oben in gepunkteten Schriftzeichen *mzdy*, unten *z* und *m*. Hess-Leu 31, 500.

# Tafel X

88  89  90  91

92  93  94  95

## Über das Münzwesen im Reich der Achämeniden (S. 3-29) – Taf. XI

96. Mazaios, Silberstater um 340 mit Namen und Titel des Granden, 11,02 g. Baaltars wie oben Nr. 93, aber aramäisches *mēm* unter dem Sitz und Monogramm links / Löwe über Stier, unten zwei parallele Turmbefestigungen, oben *mzdy zy ʿl ʿbr nhrʾ wḥlk* «Mazday, der über Transeuphratesien und Kilikien ist». Liste SKA 59, 1993, 87.

97. Balakros, Statthalter unter Alexander, Silberstater um 332, 10,65 g. Baaltars wie vorher. Im Feld Helm und griechisches B, unter dem Sitz *Σ* / Büste der Athena im Helm mit 3 Kämmen. Hess-Leu 31, 501.

98. Mazaios, «Löwen»-Stater um 333, 10,49 g. Baaltars wie vorher, links im Feld Adler (!) und Thymaterion / Löwe auf felsigem Gelände nach links, oben *mzdy* - Mazaios. Numismatica Ars Classica 6, 185 (dort unter Myriandros).

### Babylon

99. Mazaios als Statthalter Alexanders, «Löwen»-Tetradrachme 331-328, 16,90 g. Baaltars mit Stab und Zepter nach links sitzend / Löwe auf Bodenlinie nach links, oben *mzdy*. Einhieb. L. MILDENBERG, INJ 11 (1990-1991) 19; Gorny 58, 492.

### Sidon

100. Silber-Didrachme um 430, 7,07 g. Sidonische Galeere mit gerefften Segeln auf 2 Reihen stilisierter Wellen nach links / Der Großkönig den Bogen spannend nach r. Unten r. vertiefte Tierdarstellung. BMC Phoenicia Pl. 42, 11. Berlin.

101. Oktodrachme auf dickem Flan. Ende 5. Jh., 28,06 g. Sidonische Galeere vor drei Festungstürmen, unten zwei Löwen nach links und r. / Der Großkönig im Wagen nach links, die Pferde im Galopp, der Lenker mit Treibstab, unten springender Stier mit nach hinten gedrehtem Kopf, vertieft. Leu 15, 352.

102. Didrachme, Ende 5. Jh., 6,68 g. Sidonische Galeere wie vorher Nr. 101 / Der Großkönig mit Dolch in der Rechten packt einen aufrecht stehenden Löwen am Kopf. Einhieb. BMC Phoenicia Pl. 18, 7. British Museum.

103. Oktodrachme unter Mazaios, 341 (18. Jahr von Artaxerxes III.), 25,79 g. Sidonische Galeere über vier stilisierten Wellen nach links, oben Zahl 18. / Der Großkönig im Wagen auf doppelter Bodenlinie nach links, die Pferde im Schritt, der Lenker hält je drei Zügel, dahinter Diener mit Krummstab. Oben *mzdy* - Mazaios. L. MILDENBERG, INJ 11 (1990-1991) 15 [hier Taf. XVIII 15]; Hess-Leu 28, 263.

# Tafel XI

96      97      98      99

100      101      102      103

# Über das Münzwesen im Reich der Achämeniden (S. 3-29) – Taf. XII

## 6. Das späte Reichsgeld

104. Tetradrachme um 400. 15,31 g. Bärtiger Tiarakopf mit Stirnbinde, die vorn mit Schleife gebunden ist / Leier, im Feld *BAΣ*. British Museum.

105. Wie vorher Nr. 104, 16,96 g. Rückseite Eule in Athener Art, r. im Feld *BAΣ*. Gegenstempel (aramäisches *z* ?). British Museum.

106. Wie vorher, 14,92 g. Der Großkönig mit Speer und Bogen im Knielaufschritt in der Art des Reichsgeldes der 2.Hälfte des 5. Jh.s. Dahinter Galeere sidonischer Form nach links. Oben *BAΣIΛΕ⁻Ω[Σ]*. Berlin.

107. Lokale Prägung von Kyzikos. Tetradrachme Ende 5. Jh., 14,82 g. Wie oben Nr. 22, aber von anderem Stempel. Bildnis des Pharnabazos und die Buchstaben seines Namens *[ΦAP]N⁻A⁻B⁻A* in besonders feiner Art geschnitten (hier als Vergleichsstück). Berlin.

108. Tetradrachme um 340, 15,01 g. Der nach r. stehende Großkönig in der Zackenkrone, den Bogen spannend, oben r. aramäisches *m* / Zeus Labrandeus mit Doppelaxt und Speer nach r. stehend. Leu 25, 166.

109. Stater, Mallos, Mitte 4.Jh., 10,39 g. Der Großkönig in der Zackenkrone im Knielaufschritt mit Speer und Bogen nach r., dahinter Korn. Stempelbruch / Herakles, auf Basis stehend, im Kampf mit dem nemeischen Löwen ganz in der Art des Meisters KAL im süditalienischen Herakleia (der Stadtname *MAΛ* steht an der gleichen Stelle wie die Signatur *KAΛ*). Leu 30, 195 (hier als Vergleichsstück).

110. Tetradrachme um 340, 14,43 g. Ähnlich wie vorher Nr. 109 / Voluten und Punkte, teils verziert, als Landkarte gedeutet. Leu 30, 213.

111. Tetradrachme um 340, 14,95 g. Der Großkönig mit Zackenkrone in weitem, wallendem Gewand, im Feld *[ΠΥ]ΘΑΓ⁻Ο⁻ΡΗ[Σ]* / Ähnlich wie vorher Nr. 110. Leu 25, 165.

# Tafel XII

104

105

106

107

108

109

110

111

# Über das Münzwesen im Reich der Achämeniden (S. 3-29) – Taf. XIII

112. Kleinbronze um 340, 2,38 g. Wie vorher Nr. 111. F. IMHOOF-BLUMER, Kleinasiatische Münzen, 1901-1902, Taf. 19,22.

113. Gold-Doppeldareike, schon unter makedonischer Herrschaft, 340-335, 16,62 g. Der Großkönig im Mantel mit Speer und Bogen, Köcher hinter der Schulter, im Knielaufschritt nach r. wie vorher und nachher / Wellenförmiges Ornament vertieft. Leu 48, 263 (hier als Vergleichsstück).

114. Stater um 340, 10,56 g. Der Großkönig in der Zackenkrone mit Speer und Bogen im Knielaufschritt nach r. / Der Großkönig mit Bogen, den Pfeil aus dem Köcher nehmend, im Knielaufschritt nach r. Dahinter Gegenstempel (Stier). HEAD, Historia Nummorum, 47 vermutet Kilikien. De Luynes 2827 in Paris.

115. Stater um 340, 10,56 g. Wie vorher Nr. 114, aber zwei Gegenstempel (Vogel vor Dreizack und Stier) auf der Vorderseite. München, Staatliche Münzsammlung.

116. Tetradrachme 340-335, 14,95 g. Der Großkönig wie vorher / Reiter in der Tiara und persischem Kriegsgewand mit gezücktem Speer auf nach r. galoppierendem Pferd. F. IMHOOF-BLUMER, Kleinasiatische Münzen II, 1901-1902, 518,1 mit Taf. 19,23, sowie id., SNR 1906, 266, Nr. 12. Winterthur.

117. Tetradrachme um 335, 14,80 g. Der Großkönig mit Zackenkrone, seinen großen Bogen spannend, den Köcher hinter der linken Schulter, im Knielaufschritt nach r. auf Bodenlinie / Reiter wie vorher Nr. 116. Irreguläre Prägung wie nächstes Stück 118. Leu 15, 315.

118. Tetradrachme um 335, 15,04 g. Wie vorher Nr. 117, nur Blitzbündel r. Irregulärer Prägevorgang, da das Königsbild vom Unterstempel geprägt wurde. Leu 28, 206.

119. Tetradrachme um 335, 14,59 g. Wie vorher, aber r. neben dem Großkönig Speerspitze. Reguläre Prägung. Leu 30, 214.

120. Tetradrachme um 335, 1461 g. Wie vorher, aber *MO* im Feld links auf der Rückseite. Hess-Leu 45, 304.

# Tafel XIII

112 Æ

113 A/

114

115

116

117

118

119

120

# Über das Münzwesen im Reich der Achämeniden (S. 3-29) – Taf. XIV

121. Drachme um 335, 3,51 g. Wie vorher, aber hinter dem Großkönig die Bezeichnung *BA*. Leu 2, 255.

122. Tetradrachme um 335, 16,78 g. Wie vorher mit *BA*, aber bärtiger Herakleskopf links im Feld der Rückseite. F. IMHOOF-BLUMER, Kleinasiatische Münzen II, 1901-1902, Taf. 19,24.

123. Tetradrachme um 335, 15,11 g. Wie vorher Nr. 122, aber die Bezeichnung *BA* im Abschnitt und *P* hinter dem Großkönig. MMAG-Leu, Niggeler, 508. Sammlungen Warren, Regling 1310; Kat. der Slg. R. Jameson (Paris 1913-1932) 1630.

124. Artaxerxes III. Ochos als Pharao von Ägypten, 343-338. Tetradrachme, wohl Memphis um 342-340, 16,78 g. Kopf der Pallas Athene im Helm, das Auge im Profil / Die Eule in der Art der Athener Prägungen des 4. Jh.s, rechts die demotische Legende «Artaxerxes Pharao». M. PRICE, in: FS R. Carson - K. Jenkins, 1993, 153 (dies Ex.). Leu 52, 125.

# Nergal in Tarsos (S. 31-34) – Taf. XIV

1. Tarsos (Kilikien) Drittelstater «phökäisch» um 420 v. Chr. Paris, Cabinet des Médailles. Pegasusprotome nach rechts. Rv. *NeRGaL* in aramäischer Schrift. Nach r. schreitende bärtige Gestalt des Gottes im Mantel mit senkrecht gestellten Stab in der Rechten und Bogen in der Linken. Grenetis. Quadratum incusum. AR, 3.25 g.

2. Tarsos (Kilikien). Drittelstater um 420 v. Chr. Istanbul, H. von Aulock. Gleiche Legende und Darstellung wie Taf 28, 1. AR, 2.57 g.

3. Tarsos (Kilikien). Drittelstater um 420 v. Chr. London, Britisches Museum. Protome eines geflügelten und gehörnten Löwen nach links. Rv. *LeNeRGal*. Gleiche Darstellung wie Taf. 28,1. Grosser mittlerer Mantelzipfel. AR, 3.40 g.

[4. = Taf. X 88] Tarsos (Kilikien). Stater um 420 v. Chr. London, Britisches Museum. Reiter in Kappe und Mantel auf im Schritt gehenden Pferde n.r. Er hält in der Linken eine Blume. Die Bogentasche ist am Sattel befestigt. Unten *ankh*. Rv. *NeRGaL* und darunter *TaRZ* r. im Feld. Kultbild des Nergal von vorn mit Zepter und Bogen auf n.r. kauerndem Löwen. Links im Feld Baum. Grenetis. Quadratum incusum. AR, 10.49 g.

5. Tarsos (Kilikien). Stater um 390 v. Chr. Tessin, Privatsammlung. Bellerophon auf n.l. fliegendem Pegasus mit der Lanze nach unten stossend (auf die Chimaira?). Kreisende Grenetis. Rv. *NeRGaL-TaRZ*. Das Kultbild des Gottes in persischer Tracht n.l. mit Doppelaxt in der Rechten, den Bogen geschultert. Links grosse, schmale Ähre und rechts grosse Staude. Grenetis. Quadratum incusum. AR, 10.35 g.

# Tafel XIV

121
122
123
124

1
2
3

4
5

5

# Baana (S. 35-42) – Taf. XV

The Baana Series - end of 5th century BCE. Persian Standard (all coins silver)

1. Stater, 10.54 gr. 9 h, Leu 38, 155. Obv. Cow standing r., head turned back, suckling calf which stands l. Rev. Melqart r., club in r. hand, grasps a small lion by the tail. The lion's head turned upwards. The whole in incuse square.
2. Stater, 10.64 gr. Glasgow, HUNTER III, Pl. 77:15; SIX, p. 152,2; BMC Phoenicia, p. CXLV,3. From same dies as Ill. 1. Thorn-like die flaws now appearing r. in field of rev. and l. in field of obv.
3. Stater, 10.62 gr. Paris, Traité, 804. From same dies as Ill. 1-2; heavily corroded.
4. Stater, 11.07 gr. Paris. Traité, 805. Obv. Melqart r. as above, but with quiver at waist. The lion's head downwards. Several die flaws in field. Rev. Cow standing l. on dotted exergual line, suckling calf which stands r. Above, monogram with *bēt* clearly visible. The whole in dotted incuse square.
5. Stater, 10.72 gr. Glasgow, HUNTER III, Pl. 77:16; SIX, 152,3; BMC Phoenicia, p. CXLIV, 2. From same dies as Ill. 4. The flaws on obv. more developed.
6. Third-stater, 3.46 gr., 12 h, London, BM Inv. No. 10-9.8, acquired 1952. From de Nanteuil Coll., Cat. (Paris 1925), 506. As Ill. 4 and 5, but no monogram.
7. Stater, 10.72 gr. Glasgow, HUNTER III, Pl. 77:17; SIX, 152,3; BMC Phoenicia, p. CXLIV, 1. Obv. Persian Great King in *kandys* , wearing *kidaris* , dagger in r. hand, marching r., about to stab a large lion, standing l. on hind legs. Rev. Cow standing l. on dotted exergual line, suckling calf which stands r. between the cow's forelegs. Above: Baana (*b'n'* ). The whole in dotted incluse square.
8. Stater, 10.65 gr. Paris, Traité, 806. Obv. Similar to Ill. 7. Rev. From same dies as Ill. 7.
9. Third-stater, 3.49 gr. 1 London, BM Inv. No. 6-13.3, acquired 1910. From the Philipsen Coll. Cat. (by J. HIRSCH, 25, Munich 29.11.1909), 3060; BMC Phoenicia, p. CXLV, 4 (not illustrated). Obv. Similar to Ills. 7-8. Rev. Bull standing l., above: *bēt* - *'ayin* (the frist two letters of the name Baana). The whole in dotted incuse square.

Sidonian City Coins - Phoenician Standard (all coins silver)

10. Didrachm, ca. 430 BCE, 6.88 gr. MMAG, Cat. 37, 271. Obv. Sidonian galley with four sails to l. Rev. Persian Great King in *kandys*, wearing *kidaris*, as archer r. In field r., incuse goat protome, l. incuse Bes head.
11. Octadrachm, end of 5th century BCE, 27.19 gr. London, BMC Phoenicia, Pl. 18:2; Traité, 892. Obv. Sidonian galley to l. lying before fortifications with five high, square towers, in exergue two lions rampant tail to tail. On exergual line at r.: *'ayin* and probably *tāw* (letter form indistinct). Rev. Persian Great King, as on Ill. 10, standing in chariot drawn by three galloping horses, before King charioteer; below incuse goat l.; below goat: *mēm* or *šīn* and *'ayin* .
12. Didrachm, ca. 400 BCE, 5.97 gr., 12 h, New York, ANS, ex Newell Coll., acquired ca. 1927. BETLYON, Pl. 2:3. Obv. Galley as Ill. 11. Rev. Persian Great King as on Ill. 7 obv., grasping large lion by the mane. Below in field: *bēt* - *'ayin* (see here, n. 29).

# Tafel XV

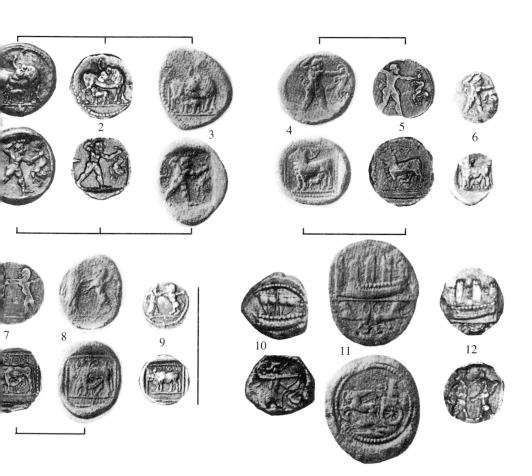

## Baana (S. 35-42) – Taf. XVI

13. Didrachm, ca. 400 BCE, 6.36 gr., 6 h, Hess-Leu 28, 262. From the Carfrae Coll. (London, May 1894), 332. Similar to Ill. 12, but no letters on rev.
14. Octadrachm, ca. 380 BCE, 28.43 gr., 12 h, Leu 33, 410; Leu 2, 295. Obv. Sidonian galley l. over double zigzag wave, above: bet. Rev. Similar to Ill. 11, but horses in slow pace and attendant (Sidonian king?) following on foot.
15. Obol, ca. 350 BCE, 0.79 gr. Munich Cabinet. From the Philipsen Coll., Cat. (by J. HIRSCH, 25, Munich, 29.11.1909), 305. Obv. As Ill. 14, but numeral 3 above galley. Rev. As Ill. 12-13, but letters ʿayin - bēt upwards in field.

Comparable Coin Types (All coins Silver)

16. Kition (Cyprus). Stater, ca. 425 BCE, 11.03 gr., 12 h, Hess-Leu 24, 226. Obv. Herakles with club and bow marching r. Rev. Lion fighting with stag r. Above, in neat Phoenician letters: «To ʿAzbaʿal» (Phoenician king of Kition).
17. Dyrrhachion (Illyria). Stater, ca. 380 BCE, 10.94 gr., 12 h, Leu 15, 209. Obv. Cow and calf, similar to Ill. 1-3, 20. Rev. Two floral designs, each in rectangle. The whole within doube line square, club on l.

Baana Images on Other Glyptic Artefacts

18. Cylinder-seal impression (detail). Achaemenian, 5th century BCE (from FURTWÄNGLER, Pl. 1:14). Persian Great King with dagger, in kandys and with kidaris, grasping the r. hind-leg of a large lion. The feline turns his head outward.
19. Engraved scarab impression. Graeco-Persian, 5th century BCE (from FURTWÄNGLER, Pl. 7:54). Melqart-Herakles with small lion, similar to Ills. 1-3. In field l., small fox running downwards.
20. Engraved scaraboid impression. Greek, 5th century BCE (from FURTWÄNGLER, Pl. 8:46). Cow suckling calf, similar to Ill. 1-3 and 17.
21. Ivory plaque from Arslan Tash, ca. 800 BCE; length 10.2 cm (from Cat. N. Schimmel Coll., Mainz 1978, 144). Cow suckling calf, similar to Ills. 1 - 3, 17 and 20.

# Tafel XVI

13

14

15

16

17

8

19

20

21

# Notes on the Coin Issues of Mazday (S. 43-53)* – Taf. XVII

I. Pharnabazus (379-374) and Datames (378-372 B.C.) at the mint of Tarsus

1. Pharnabazus. Baaltars I., legend 1. Rev.: Bearded, helmeted head l.; legend 2. Hess-Leu 31, 97, 10.72 gr.
2. Datames. Female head, facing, in the manner of Kimon. Rev.: Bearded, helmeted head r.; legend 3. Leu 42, 3430, 10.86 gr.
3. Datames. Baaltars r. in mural circle, below Greek M (for Mallos?). Rev.: Nobleman in Persian attire with bow and arrow, above winged solar disk; legend 3. Leu 15, 335, 10.43 gr.

II. The Coinage of Mazaeus 361-328 B.C.

**Tarsus**
A. The early coinage 361-335 B.C.

4. Baaltars l., below Greek *thēta*; legend 1. Rev.: Lion l. attacking stag. Below large circle; legend 4. Leu 30, 197, 10.71 gr.
5. Baaltars-Zeus, facing, holding grape, wheat and large eagle (!), below *mēm*, l. *tāw - nūn* ; legend 1. Rev.: Lion l. attacking bull, below *ankh* -like monogram; legend 4. Gorny 58, 453, 10.87 gr.
6. Baaltars l. Rev.: Bull butting r.; above legend 4. Paris, BABELON, Traité 718, 2.92 gr.
7. Baaltars l.; legend 1. Rev.: Lion l. attacking bull r., below the Cilician Gates; above legend 5. Paris, BABELON, Traité 709 a., 10.92 gr.

B. The Tarsus mint around 333 B.C.

8. Baaltars l., below Greek I (for Issus?); legend 1. Rev.: Lion l. attacking bull r. below the Cilician Gates, above l. club. London. SIX, p. 130, Pl. VI:2, 11.02 gr.
9. Baaltars l.; legend 1. Rev.: as above 8, Greek B in field. Paris, ex de Luynes 2863, BABELON, Traité 712, 9.53 gr. Test cut.
10. Balacrus. Baaltars l, in field r. *BAΛAKPOϒ*. Rev.: Bust of Pallas Athene facing. Leu 45, 251, 10.73 gr.

C. The «lion» staters

11. Baaltars l.; legend 1. Rev.: Lion striding l., below half-moon, above star; legend 4. Gorny 58, 448, 10.74 gr.
12. As above 11. Below Baaltars *yōd* , l. *mēm*. Test cut. Paris, BABELON, Traité 744, 10.82 gr.

---

* Staters: 1-5, 7-14; Bronze: 6; Four Shekels: 15; Obols: 16-17; Tetradrachms: 18-19; Didrachms: 20-24. For the legends see p. 53. Auction Sales: Gorny München; Hess-Leu Luzern; Leu Zürich; MMAG Basel; NFA Los Angeles.

# Tafel XVII

1

2

3

4

5

6

AE

7

8

9

10

11

12

# Notes on the Coin Issues of Mazday (S. 43-53) – Taf. XVIII

13. As above 11. Below Baaltars bull's head, l. *yōd*, above lion a «2»-shaped symbol. NFA 25, 188, 11.04 gr.
14. Baaltars r. on throne, the back with swan's head final. He wears Phrygian cap and holds small lotus flower and lotus sceptre; legend 1. Rev.: Crouching lion, above bow. NFA 25, 186. 10.86 gr.

**Sidon 345-331 B.C.**
15. War galley on stylized waves l. Above date 18 (341 B.C.), Rev.: The Great King in chariot to l. The charioteer holds three reins in each hand. Behind servant with jug and staff. Above l. *mzdy* - legend 6. Hess-Leu 28, 263, 25.79 gr.

**Samaria 345-331 B.C.**
16. The Great King on biga with charioteer r. Rev.: The Great King r. fighting lion l., in field *mz* - legend 7. Oxford. Samaria 48c, 0.88 gr.
17. The Great King with flower and scepter on throne, the back with swan's head finial as on No. 14 above; left in field *šn* - legend 8. Rev.: Bearded figure with wings and fish tail, l. *mz* - legend 7. Oxford, Samaria 21, 0.78 gr.

**Babylon 331-328 B.C.**
The «lion» tetradrachms

18. Baaltars l.; legend 1. Rev.: Striding lion on serpent, above *mzdy* - legend 4, Paris, ex de Luynes 2871, BABELON, Traité, 752, 17.20 gr. Test cut.
19. As above No. 18, but lion on horizontal line, above *mzdy* - legend 4. Gorny 58, 492, 16.90 gr. Test cut.

III. Didrachms struck under Mazaeus in Northern Syria 334-330 B.C.

**Incertum**
20. Baaldagon ('Lord of the Grain') in the manner of Baaltars facing, as above, No. 5; legend 9. Rev.: Lion seated r., head facing, *mēm* r. and «2»-shaped symbol, as above, No. 13. Dagon Museum, Haifa, 8.15 gr. Small test cut.

**Hierapolis-Bambyce**
21. Zeus-Baaltars l., plough l. in field. Legend *hdd mnbg* (Hadad of Manbog) r. in field. Rev.: Female head facing, in the manner of Kimon of Syracuse, l. *ʿth* (Atah). H. SEYRIG, Monnaies hellénistiques, le monnayage de Hierapolis de Syrie à l'époque d'Alexandre, RN 6ᵉ sér. 13 (1971) 6a (same dies).
22. Atargatis enthroned with long pigtails and cup in her r. hand, thymiaterion r. in field, l. *ʿtrʿth* (Ataratah) - legend 10. Rev.: Lion crouching l. as above, No. 14; below two concentric circles, above *ʾlksndr* (Alexander) - legend 11. Paris, ex MMAG 32, 139. H. SEYRIG, RN 6ᵉ sér. 13 (1971) 13a, 8.37 gr.
23. As above No. 22, but careless lettering. H. SEYRIG, RN 6ᵉ sÈr., 13 (1971) 13b, 8.14 gr.
24. Bust of Atargatis r., the hair in strands, l. in field *ʿth* (Atah) and spade-like symbol. Rev.: Lion l. attacking bull l., below *d* or *r* . See above, No. 5; legend 11. Paris, ex de Luynes 2685. H. SEYRIG, RN 6ᵉ sér. 13 (1971) 10. 8.38 gr.

# Tafel XVIII

13

14

15

16

(3:1)

17

18

19

20

(3:1)

21

MAZDAY

22

23

24

# Palestine from Artaxerxes II till Ptolemy I (S. 59-66) – Taf. XIX

1-4 From *Tell el-Mashūṭa*. Athenian originals or Eastern imitations?

1. Y. BERRY, Numismatic Bibliography (Luzern 1971), no. 416.
2. Ibid., no. 418.
3. Ibid., no. 420.
4. Ibid., no. 422.


5-8 Eastern Owls.

5. Berlin, Staatliche Museen, Münzkabinett; ʿ*ayin* – *zayin* (retrograde) for Gaza.
6. Paris, Cabinet des Médailles; ʿ*ayin* – *zayin* countermarked on obverse for Gaza.
7. New York, SNG ANS, Palestine, no. 2.
8. Ibid., no. 3.


9-12 Gaza Fractions

 9. Los Angeles, Private Collection; *mēm* for Marnas on reverse; 3:1.
10. Ibid.; ʿ*ayin* – *zayin* above horse protome; 3:1.
11. Ibid.; ʿ*ayin* – *zayin* right and left of small facing head; 3:1.
12. Sternberg sale 24, no. 167; ʿ*ayin* – *zayin* right in field; 3:1.

# Tafel XIX

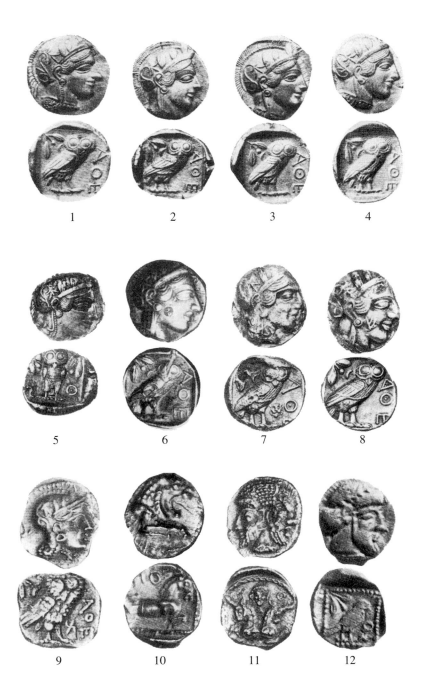

1

2

3

4

5

6

7

8

9

10

11

12

## Palestine from Artaxerxes II till Ptolemy I (S. 59-66) – Taf. XX

13-15 Ashdod

13. Los Angeles, Private Collection, see MESHORER-QEDAR, op. cit. (n. 8), 9; *'āleph – šīn – dālet – dālet* on reverse; 2:1.
14. Abū Shūsheh Hoard, LAMBERT, loc. cit. (n. 17), no. 53; *'āleph – šīn* on reverse; 3:1.
15. Los Angeles, Private Collection; *'āleph – šīn – dālet – dālet* on reverse; 3:1.

16-20 «Ascalon» Drachms with inscription ( *'āleph – nūn* )

16. Jerusalem, Department of Antiquities.
17. Scardale, Private Collection.
18. Paris, Cabinet des Médailles. E. BABELON, Catalogue (1893), no. 1041.
19. London, BMC Palestine, no. 9.
20. Paris, Cabinet des Médailles; BABELON, op. cit., no. 1040.

21-24 Southern Border Region Fractions

21. Abū Shūsheh Hoard, LAMBERT, loc. cit. (n. 17), no. 16; 3:1.
22. Los Angeles, Private Collection; 3:1.
23. Abū Shūsheh Hoard, LAMBERT, loc. cit. (n. 17).
24. Los Angeles, Private Collection, 3:1; cf. MESHORER-QEDAR, op. cit. (n. 8), 27.

# Tafel XX

13             14             15

16       17       18       19       20

21             22             23             24

# Yehud* (S. 67-76) – Taf. XXI

## Yehud Drachm

1. Obv.: Bearded head with Corinthian helmet, face three quarter r. Border of dots. Rev.: *yhd.* Bearded deity on winged wheel seated r., holding falcon in l. hand. Head of Bes l. in right corner. Incuse square with cable pattern border. Drachm, 12 h, 3.29 g. 15 mm. London, BMC Palestine Pl. 19,29. Unique.

## Yehud Minute Silver Coins under Persian Rule

Group One

2. Obv.: Feline protome r. (?). Rev.: Blundered Yehud legend. Bird walking r., head turned back. Obol. 9 h, 0,36 g. 6.5 mm. Jerusalem, Y. Sasson coll. Unpublished.
3. Obv.: Head of Pallas Athene r. in fifth century Athenian manner. Rev.: Legend and type as no. 2. Obol. 7 h, 0.41 g. 6-7 mm. Jerusalem, Y. Sasson coll. Cp. MESHORER, 3.
4. Obv.: Head of Pallas Athene, with earring and -pendant r., in helmet with crest and three leaves. Rev.: Yehud legend retrograde l., owl (*Athena noctua*) l., large olive twig r. Obol. 9 h, 0.50 g. 7 mm. Zurich, private coll. 1.
5. Obv.: Similar head of coarser style, no crest visible. Rev.: Blundered Yehud legend r., owl r., smaller olive twig with fruit and half moon l. Obol. 11 h, 0.68 g. 7 mm. Photograph: Y. MESHORER.
6. Obv.: Head of Athene in expressive local style r., helmetlike headgear with three pointed leaves and oliveshaped pendant. Rev.: Good legend: *yhd,* owl right. Obol. 5 h, 0.515 g. 7 mm. Photograph: Y. MESHORER.
7. Obv.: Similar, but ivy leaves on helmet. Rev.: Similar legend and type, but olive twig and fruit transformed into lily. Obol. 3 h, 0.50 g. 8.5 mm. Zurich, private coll. 2.
8. Obv.: Similar. Large die-break below head. Rev.: Similar. Obol. 11 h, 0.39 g. 7 mm. Location unknown, formerly Jerusalem, M. Salzberger coll. MESHORER 1 (obv.: «male head, oriental style, r.»). A larger piece from the same dies, Zurich, private coll. 1, 5 h. 0.50 g., clearly shows leaves on helmet of Pallas Athene.
9. Obv.: Head of Pallas Athene as on no. 4. Rev.: *y - hd* legend retrograde, with the y blundered. Owl as on no. 8. Obol. 5 h, 0.43 g. 7-8 mm. Jerusalem. A. Spaer, coll. SPAER 1.

Group Two

10. Obv.: Lily. Rev.: No legend. Seated owl, wings almost closed. Tetartemorion. 7 h, 0.13 g. 4.5-6 mm. Jerusalem, A. Spaer, coll. SPAER 2.
11. Obv.: Lily. Rev.: *yhd* (other specimens show full, flawless legend). Falcon with wide spread wings, head r., seen from above. Hemiobol. 6 o'clock, 0.33 g. 8 mm. Zurich, private coll. 1. Compare MESHORER, p. 116 X.
12. Obv.: Head of Persian Great King in *kidaris* r. Rev.: Similar legend and type. The falcon has the wings half-spread. Obol. 7,5 mm. Photograph: Y. MESHORER.
13. Obv.: Similar. Rev.: Similar. Hemiobol. 9 h, 0.315 g. 6-7 mm. Zurich, private coll. 1

---

* 1. Metal: Silver. – 2. Diameter: Drachm 15 mm; Yehud coins between 5 and 8 mm. – 3. Weight: Drachm 3.29 g. Yehud coins between 0.70 g. and 0.10 g. approx. - Weights indicated if known. – 4. Axis: The positions vary considerably within and between the groups in Persian time, much less in later periods. – 5. Provenance: All but nos. 1. 4. 7 allegedly come from the recent Hebron hoard (cp. n. 12 above). – 6. Rarity: No. 1 is still unique; nos. 4. 10. 19-23 seem to be rare; nos. 11. 27-28 are scarce. However, well-informed people have indicated that the recent hoard contained at least 100 specimens of the Yeḥezqiyah coins nos. 14-18 and even about 150 items of the Ptolemy I issue nos. 24-28. – 7. Collections: When the location of a coin illustrated here remains uncertain, the name of the person who supplied the photograph is given.

# Tafel XXI

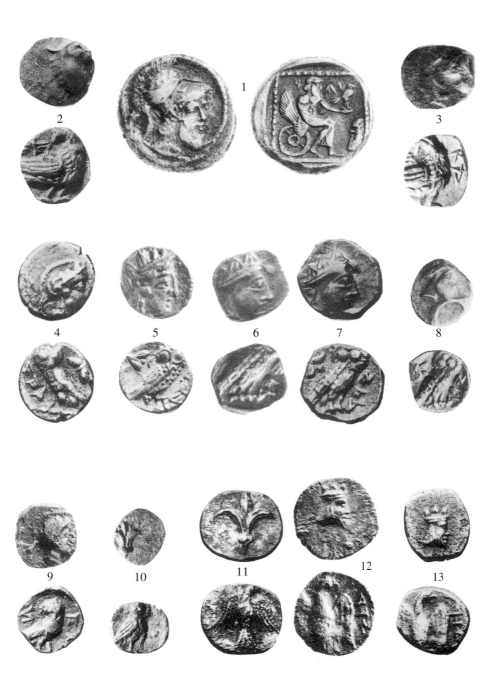

# Yehud (S. 67-76) – Taf. XXII

Group Three

14. Obv.: Female head facing. Border of dots. Rev.: *yhzqyh hphh* - Yehezqiyah hap-pehāh. Owl with wings half spread. Greek A r. in field. Hemiobol. 5 h, 0.22 g. 7 mm. Zurich, private coll. 1.
15. Obv.: Similar. Rev.: Similar, but uncertain sign above A. Hemiobol. 7,5 mm. Jerusalem, Sh. Qedar coll.
16. Obv.: Similar. Rev.: Similar, but name Yehezqiyah r., title *hap-pehāh* l. Hemiobol. 0.20 g. 7 mm. Jerusalem, Sh. Qedar coll.
17. Obv.: Similar. Rev.: Similar, but careless lettering. Hemiobol (?). 1 h, 0.165 g. 8 mm. Zurich, private coll. 2.
18. Obv.: Same type, but completely blundered. Rev.: Legend and type blundered. Hemiobol. 6 to 8 mm. Photograph: Y. MESHORER.

## Yehud Minute Silver Coins during the Macedonian Occupation

19. Obv.: Youthful male head l., in field the Yehezqiyah legend and part of lynx's wing in mirror impression (freak). Rev.: *Yehezqiyah* in straight line, protome of winged lynx, the typical tufts above ear clearly visible. Hemiobol. 1 h, 0.25 g. 6.5-8 mm. Jerusalem, Y. Sasson coll.
20. Obv.: Similar head as on no. 19, neck thin and stretched. Rev.: Similar lynx as on no. 19, but legend in bended line. Hemiobol. 3 h, 0.28 g. 7 to 7.5 mm. Jerusalem, A. Spaer, coll. SPAER 3a.

## Yehud Minute Silver Coins in the Ptolemaic Kingdom
Group One

21. Obv.: Youthful male head l., very similar to no. 20. Rev.: *yhd* – Yehud. Ptolemaic eagle l., wings spread. Tetartemorion. 9 h, 0.12 g. 6 to 8 mm. Jerusalem, A. Spaer coll. SPAER 4.
22. Obv.: Similar. Rev.: Similar. Hemiobol. 3 o'clock, 0.22 g. 7.5 mm. Photograph: Y. MESHORER.

Group Two - portrait of Ptolemy I

23. Obv.: Head of Ptolemy I r. Rev.: Protome of lynx as on nos. 19 and 20. Hemiobol. 9 h, 0.21 g. 7 mm. Zurich, private coll. 1. Unpublished.
24. Obv.: Portrait of Ptolemy I with diadem, veristic style. Rev.: *yhdh* – Yehudah. Ptolemaic eagle as on nos. 21 and 22, but on fulmen. Tetartemorion. 12 h, 0.177 g. 7 mm. Jerusalem, D. Jeselsohn coll. JESELSOHN 1.
25. Obv.: Similar, of good style. Rev.: Similar, legend and type of good style. Die break. Tetartemorion. 11 h, 0.185 g. 6.5 mm. Zurich, private coll. 1. Several specimens from these dies known.

Group Three - portraits of Ptolemy I and Berenike I

26. Obv.: Portrait of Ptolemy I of good style. Rev.: Traces of legend. Portrait of Berenike I, hair in parallel curls combed up at neck. Tetartemorion. 11 h, 0.19 g. 7 mm. Jerusalem, A. Spaer coll. SPAER 5a.
27. Obv.: Similar portrait of King. Rev.: Legend Yehudah (not fully clear on this specimen). Similar portrait of queen. Tetartemorion 11 h, 0.155 g. 6 mm). Edge damaged. Zurich, private coll. 1 SPAER 5b.
28. Obv.: Portrait of Ptolemy I in coarse style, diadem heavy. Rev.: Legend and portrait of Berenike I, coarsely executed, hair of queen held by double pearl diadem and in chignon at neck. Tetartemorion. 12 h, 0.15 g. 6.5 mm. Photograph: Y. MESHORER.

# Tafel XXII

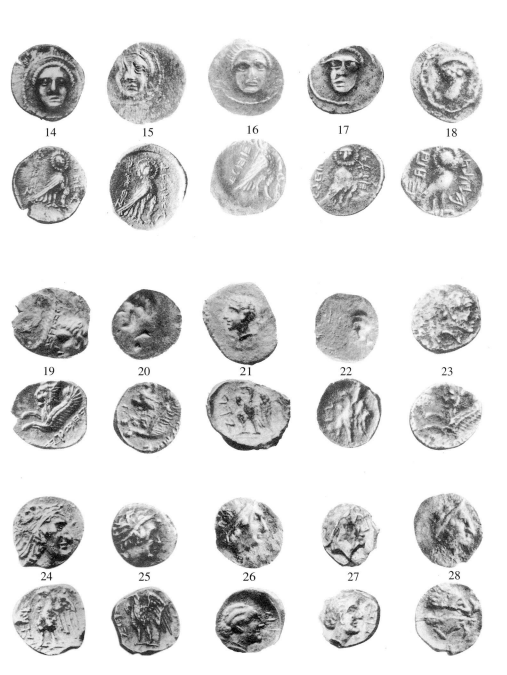

14  15  16  17  18

19  20  21  22  23

24  25  26  27  28

# Gaza von 420 bis 332 nach den Sachquellen (S. 77-78) – Taf. XXIII

Drachmen aus der Lohnmünzstätte Gaza

1. Athena / Januskopf, 3,78 g. Auktion Leu 18,378.
2. Januskopf / Eule, 3,13 g. Privatslg. Los Angeles.
3. Bärtiger Kopf in athenischer Manier / 2 sitzende Löwen über 2 Delphinen, oben Löwenkopf r. und *bēt* links, 3,25 g. Auktion Leu 2,297.
4. Behelmter, bärtiger Herrscherkopf links / Löwe nach r., dahinter Lotusszepter, 3,93 g. Privatslg. Los Angeles.
5. Bärtiger Herrscherkopf r. / Januskopf, 3,85 g. Paris, Traité 1061.
6. Bärtiger Kopf eines Scheichs in flacher Kappe / Kamelreiter r., 3,44 g. Paris, De Luynes, Traité 1068.
7. Zwei Besköpfe unter Löwenprotomen / Januskopf, links Beskopf von vorn, 3,55 g. Paris, Traité 1658.
8. Gehörnter Beskopf / Kauernder Löwe r. mit Hörnern und Flügeln, 3,35 g. Privatslg. Los Angeles.

Abb. 1: Gaza am Meer und an den Straßen

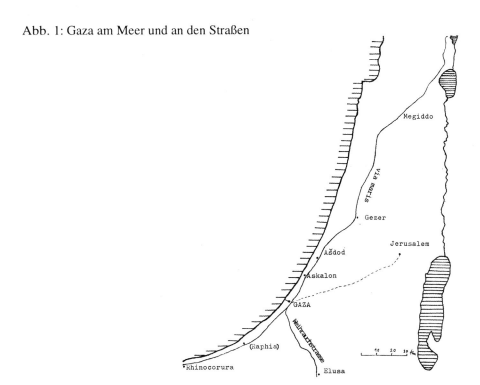

# Tafel XXIII

# Tafel XXIV

## Gaza Mint Authorities in Persian Times (S. 79-87)
Gaza municipal coinage. Unscribed imitations of Athenian tetradrachms.

# Tafel XXV

Gaza Mint Authorities in Persian Times (S. 79-87)

Gaza municipal coinage. Unscribed local drachma and fractions.

# Tafel XXVI

Gaza Mint Authorities in Persian Times (S. 79-87)
Coinage from Gaza for external authorities.

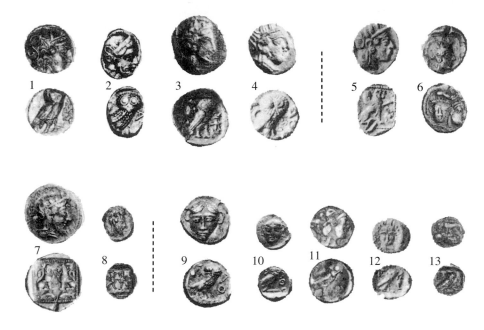

# Tafel XXVII

## Gaza Mint Authorities in Persian Times (S. 79-87)
Athenian influence. Coinage from Gaza for external authorities. Local varieties.

# The Philisto-Arabien Coins (S. 88-94)* – Taf. XXVIII

## 1. Yehud minute silver coins, scale: 4:1

a: Under Persian rule. Obol 360-350 B.C. Palaeo-Hebrew legend *yhd* = «Yehud» for Judaea on reverse. Private coll. Zurich.

b: Under Persian rule. Obol 340-331 B.C. Palaeo-Hebrew legends on reverse r. from above *yhzqyh*, l. from below *hphh* = «Yeḥezkiyah the governor». Private coll. Zurich.

c: During the Macedonian occupation. Obol 300-282 B.C. Palaeo-Hebrew legend in beautiful lettering «Yeḥezkiyah». On obverse same legend in mirror impression (freak). MILDENBERG, Yehud, 19 [hier Taf. XXIII]. Private coll. Jerusalem.

## 2. Kimon's facing Arethusa heads and some imitations 406/5-310 B.C.

a: Syracuse. Tetradrachm, 406/405 B.C. Marked $APE\Theta OY\Sigma A$ above and signed $KIM\Omega N$ on ampyx. First die. Hess-Leu 28, 89.

b: As a. Second die. The masterpiece. Pennisi coll. Acireale.

c: Segesta. Tetradrachm, 405-400 B.C., MILDENBERG, in: ICN 1973/1976, 120, no. 13.

d: Camarina. Didrachm, 405 B.C., the earliest copy existing. L. de Hirsch coll., Brussels.

e: Fistelia Campaniae. Nommos, 400/390 B.C., an imitation of excellent local style. Gulbenkian coll. Lisbon.

f: Chersonessos, Tauric Chersones. Didrachm, c. 310 B.C. Ars Classica 13,666.

g: Larisa. Drachm, c.360 B.C. Leu 2,172.

h: Larisa. Didrachm, c.370 B.C., a copy in fine style. Hess-Leu 36,183.

i: Tarsos. Stater. Datames, 378-372 B.C. Hess-Leu 24,224.

k: Tarsos. Tetrobol. Pharnabazos? First decade of $4^{th}$ century B.C. Hess-Leu 24,223.

l: Philisto-Arabian. Obol, c. 350 B.C. Numismatic Fine Arts 5,221.

## 3. The origin of the Gaza Janus-head type

a: Lampsakos [recte Tenedos]. Stater, 460-450 B.C. Leu 30, 164.

b: Gaza. Drachm, 430-420 B.C. Hess-Leu 1962, 368.

---

* Photographs: ANS, New York; Dept. of Antiquities and Museums, Jerusalem; British Museum, London; Estate J. Hirsch, Hirmer-Verlag, München; S. Hurter; Israel Museum, Jerusalem; D. Jeselsohn, Y. Meshorer, A. Spaer, Z. Radovan.

# Tafel XVIII

1 a

1 b

1 c

2 a

2 b

2 c

2 d

2 e

2 f

2 g

2 h

2 i

2 k

2 l

3 a

3 b

## The Philisto-Arabien Coins (S. 88-94) – Taf. XXIX

**4 . The beginning of the coinage at Gaza 430-420 B.C.** Janus head l. bearded mail head, r. female head in Athenian manner within framed incuse square. Legend 'zh – Gaza.

**5. The Yehud coinage in the Ptolemaic kingdom 300-283/82 B.C.**

a: Head of Ptolemy I with diadem, a veristic, contemporary portrait / Ptolemaic eagle l., legend *yhdh* – Yəhūdā. Obol. Private coll. Zurich. MILDENBERG, Yehud, 24 [hier Taf. XXIII].

b: Head of Ptolemy I / head of Berenike I. Traces of legend. Obol. Private coll. Jerusalem. MILDENBERG, Yehud, 26 [hier Taf. XXIII].

c: Head of Ptolemy I / head of Berenike I. Traces of legend. Tetartemorion. Private coll. Jerusalem. MILDENBERG, Yehud, 27 [hier Taf. XXIII].

**6 . Philisto-Arabian.** Drachm, mid 4th century B.C. Female head r. / Owl with wings spread widely, legend *'n* – Ascalon (MESHORER) – Persepolis [Heliopolis] (LIPINSKI). ANS, New York.

**7 . Philisto-Arabian?** Head of Pallas Athena r. / Owl and Greek legend *A? E*, between: Aramaic legend which has been read from below as *tdnm*, alledgedly *Tadanmu* – Datames, or from above *mnpt* «Memphite» for Memphis. Obol. Dept. of Antiquities and Museums, Jerusalem, from Abū Shūsheh.

4

5 a          5 b          5 c

6

7

## The Philisto-Arabien Coins (S. 88-94) – Taf. XXX

**8. Philisto-Arabian Drachms in Athenian manner, 4$^{th}$ century B.C.**

a: Helmeted head r. / Owl in incuse square. Legend *b'm*. Israel Museum Jerusalem.
b: Head of Pallas Athena r. / Owl and Greek legend *A*? *E*, between legend *'bd'l* – Ebedel or Abdiel. Israel Museum Jerusalem.

**9. Philisto-Arabian drachms,** c. 380-330 B.C., with varied local types, partially imitating Athenian and other foreign models. Publication in preparation.

**10.Philisto-Arabian.** Drachm. Female head / camel rider. BMC Pl. 19:25. British Museum, London.

# Tafel XXX

8 a                8 b

9

10

# Bes on Philisto-Arabien Coins (S. 95-97) – Taf. XXXI

1. Drachm. Winged Bes facing. / Incuse square. 2,84 g. Paris, private collection.
2. Hemiobol. Bes head facing, above bar, in round braided border. / Same image in dotted square. 0,32 g. Los Angeles, private collection.
3. Drachm. Two bearded Bes heads, facing, winged lion protome r. and l., above letter *bēt* . Dotted border. / Janus head composed by bearded, nearly facing Bes head l. and profile female nead r., both wreathed, in dotted border. Die break r. below in field. 3,72 g. Numismatic Fine Arts 5, 220.
4. Obol. Same images and letter *bēt* as on preceding. 0,58 g. Los Angeles, private collection.
5. Drachm. Large horned Bes head, facing, in braided square. / Winged lion griffin, squatting r., in incuse square. Above l. *dālet.* 3,35 g. Cuts on border r. Los Angeles, private collection.
6. Obol. Similar images and letter *dālet* as on preceding. 0,56 g. Jerusalem, private collection.
7. Obol. Bes head facing, with large feather trimming. / Owl with hook and flail, in the manner of Tyre, seated l. Round dotted border. 0,61 g. Los Angeles, private collection.
8. Obol. Bes head facing, in dotted border. / Lion protome r., straight in dotted square. 0,72 g. SNG ANS 42. New York, ANS.
9. Tetartemorion. Same type, but lion protome l. 0,15 g. Los Angeles, private collection.
10. Obol. Bes head facing, between two standing lions with heads turned back. / Lion r. over ram l. 0,75 g. Abu Shusheh hoard (IGCH 1507, C. LAMBERT, QDAP 2, 1932, no. 48). Jerusalem, Department of Antiquities.
11. Hemiobol. Puffy Bes head facing. / Crouching human figure r. Legend *yrb*ʿ [*m* ] l. upwards. The coin attributed to Samaria (an item with this legend was in the Nablus hoard, IGCH 1504) by Y. MESHORER – SH. QEDAR, The coinage of Samaria, 1991. 0,27 g. Los Angeles, private collection.
12. Drachm. Female head r. / Lion head, looking outwards, l. and r. in upper field. 3,65 g. BABELON, Traité 1071. Paris, Cabinet des Medailles.
13. Drachm. Bearded head in fez like headgear r. / Large Bes head facing. Letters *ʾāleph* (?) r. and *dālet* (or *rēsh* r?) in dotted square. Paris, Cabinet des Medailles.
14. Obol. Female head facing, in the manner of the Syracusan master Kimon's Arethusa. / Bes head facing, quite similar to the obverse image of no. 7. 0,68 g. SNC Delepierre 2999. Paris, Cabinet des Medailles.
15. Obol. As 14. 0,75 g. Los Angeles, private collection.
16. Drachm. Janus-head, female l. and bearded head r., in the manner of Tenedos. / Bes facing as «Lord of the Animals» in dotted square. 2,66 g. Jerusalem, private collection.
17. Drachm. Lion r. over ram r. / Bes facing as «Lord of the Animals», holding a lion with head down l. and r. 3,77 g. Hole in field above l. 3,77 g. SNG ANS 39. New York, ANS.
18. Obol. As 17. 0,62 g. London, British Museum acquired 1936.
19. Drachm. Pegasus protome r. / Bes head r., the hair in rays. Dotted square. 3,37 g. Attribution still not certain. Hess-Leu Auction 31, no. 531.

1    2    3    4    5    6

7    8    9    10    11    12    13

14    15    16    17    18    19

2    9    11    15

3 x

# Kunst der griechischen Kleinmünzen[*] (S. 101-104) – Taf. XXXII

1. Rhegium. Litra gegen 400. Löwenmaske. Rückseite: Olivenzweig mit Früchten und *PH* (für Rhegium). Gewicht 0,77 g. Durchmesser 9 mm. Slg. Mildenberg.

2. Agrigentum. Litra 413-406. Zwei Adler mit Hasen in den Fängen. Rückseite: Krabbe, darunter Stachelfisch. Gewicht 0,74 g. Durchmesser 12 mm. Aus Auktionen ArsClassica XVII, 128; U. LOCKETT I, 600. Schweizer Privatsammlung.

3. Corinth. Trihemiobol um 430. Pegasus n. l. Rückseite: Springender Pegasus, von vorn gesehen. Gewicht 0,95 g. Durchmesser 14/10 mm. Aus Auktion Consul Weber 1784 und Coll. Tameson 1208. Rückseite abgebildet. Slg. Mildenberg.

4. Tarentum. Diobol um 340. Kopf des Herakles in der Löwenhaut von vorn. Rückseite: Herakles, den nemeischen Löwen erwürgend. Gewicht 0,98 g. Durchmesser 19 mm. Vorderseite abgebildet. Schweizer Privatsammlung.

5. Catana. Litra um 476. Kopf eines bärtigen Silen. Rückseite: Blitz und Stadtnamen. Gewicht 0,71 g. Durchmesser 10 mm. Aus Coll. Sir A. J. Evans und Jameson 536. Vorderseite abgebildet. Schweizer Privatsammlung.

6. Tarsos. Obol der Satrapenzeit (396-333). Kopf eines persischen Satrapen (Mazaios?) n.r. Rückseite: Pegasusprotome. Gewicht 0,71 g. Durchmesser 11 mm. Vorderseite abgebildet. Slg. Mildenberg.

7. Stiela (Sizilien). Litra um 400. Kopf eines jugendlichen Flußgottes n.l. Rückseite: Protome eines Stiers mit Menschenkopf. Gewicht 0,83 g. Durchmesser 11,5 mm. Vorderseite abgebildet. Slg. Mildenberg.

---

[*] Aufnahmen (alle Vergrößerungen ca. 3fach): Schweizer. Landesmuseum, Zürich: 5. 12. 13. 15; Prof. Dr. Max Hirmer, München: 1. 3. 4. 6. 8-11. 14; Ganz & Co., Zürich: 2. 7.

# Kunst der griechischen Kleinmünzen (S. 101-104) – Taf. XXXIV

8. Stymphalos (Peleponnes). Obol anfangs 4. Jh. Kopf des Herakles in der Löwenhaut n.r. Rückseite: Kopf eines stymphalischen Vogels. Gewicht 0,98 g. Durchmesser 11,5 mm. Rückseite abgebildet. Slg. Mildenberg.

9. Ephesus. Trihemiobol nach 387. Biene, Rückseite: Zwei Hirschköpfe. Gewicht 0,94 g. Durchmesser 10 mm. Vorderseite abgebildet. Slg. Mildenberg.

10. Celenderis (Cilicia). Obol um 420. Pegasusprotome n.r. Rückseite: Kniender Ziegenbock mit umgewendetem Kopf. Gewicht 0,88 g. Durchmesser 9 mm. Rückseite abgebildet. Slg. Mildenberg.

11. Argos (Peloponnes). Obol Ende 5. Jh. Wolfskopf n.l. Rückseite: Großes A in vertieftem Quadrat. Gewicht 0,88 g. Durchmesser 9 mm. Vorderseite abgebildet. Slg. Mildenberg.

12. Camarina (Sizilien). Litra um 410. Frauenkopf. Rückseite: Schwan über Wellenkamm, unten Fisch. Gewicht 0,82 g. Durchmesser 12,5 mm. Aus Coll. Philipsen 952 und Jameson 529. Rückseite abgebildet. Schweizer Privatsammlung.

13. Tarentum. Litra Mitte 4. Jh. Muschel. Rückseite: Delphin, darunter Fackel. Gewicht 0,68 g. Durchmesser 11 mm. Rückseite abgebildet. Schweizer Privatsammlung.

14. Pharae (Böotien). Trihemiobol 387-374. Böotischer Schild. Rückseite: Volutenkrater, daneben Ähre. Gewicht 0,95 g. Durchmesser 10 mm. Rückseite abgebildet. Slg. Mildenberg.

15. Naxos (Sizilien). Litra um 420. Kopf des Dionysos n.l. Rückseite: Traube. Gewicht 0,77 g. Durchmesser 10 mm. Aus Coll. de Ciccio 248 und Jameson 684. Rückseite abgebildet. Schweizer Privatsammlung.

# Tafel XXXIII

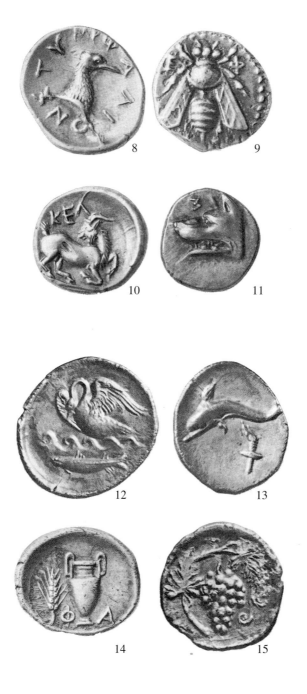

8

9

10

11

12

13

14

15

# Mithrapata und Perikles (S. 105-109) – Taf. XXXIV

Statere des Mithrapata mit Portrait

Av.: a) Löwenprotome nach r. (1-6); b) Löwenmaske, darunter Triskelis (7-12)
Rv.: Bärtiger Kopf des Mithrapata n.l. Triskelis hinter dem Kopf. Name in lykischen
Buchstaben *MITHRAPATA*. Das Ganze in vertieftem Quadrat. Silberstatere.

1. Av. 1. Kleine Protome in hohem Relief. Rv. 1. Kleiner Kopf mit sehr spitzem
   Bart. Die Haare sind im Nacken hochgebunden. Sehr tiefes quadratum incusum.
   Photographie: Hess-Leu 1959, 269. 9.77 g. 6 h. Registriert: 4 Ex.
2. Av. 1. Gleicher Stempel in schlechterem Zustand. Rv. 2. Idealisiertes Portrait
   von feinem Stil. Photographie: Privatsammlung (ex Hess-Leu 1959, 268).
   9.69g. 2 h. Registriert: 1 Ex.
3. Av. 2. Größere Protome in weniger hohem Relief. Rv. 2. Gleicher Stempel,
   verbrauchter. Photographie: Handel 1959. 9.84 g. Registriert: 11 Ex., deren
   Prägefolge an Hand der Stempelbrüche leicht festzustellen ist. Der größte
   Stempelbruch in entwickeltem Zustand deckt das *T* der Legende zu.
4. Av. 2. Gleicher Stempel, verbraucht. Rv. 3. Ähnlich, aber größere Triskelis.
   Ausgezeichnetes Portrait von sehr feinem Stil. Photographie: Boston 9.71 g.
   Registriert: 5 Ex.
5. Av. 3. Etwas kleinere Protome. Rv. 4. Sehr ähnlich, aber kräftigeres Portrait.
   Photographie: Handel 1958. 9.83 g. Registriert: 3 Ex.
6. Av. 3. Sehr verbrauchter Stempel. Rv. 5. Älteres Portrait von realistischer
   Auffassung. Photographie: Handel 1958. 9.78 g. Registriert: 7 Ex.
7. Av. 4. Rechteckige Löwenmaske. $\Sigma$ unter dem linken Ohr. Rv. 5. Gleicher
   Stempel mit langem Stempelriß im r. Feld. Photographie: Santamaria 1961,
   133. 9.87 g. 7 h. Registriert: 1 Ex.
8. Av. 4. Gleicher Stempel mit dem $\Sigma$. Rv. 6. Ähnlich wie vorher, aber der Kopf
   ist größer und von weniger feinem Stil. Die Legende endet mit *E*. Photographie:
   Privatsammlung. Registriert: 1 Ex.
9. Av. 5. Löwenmaske (ohne $\Sigma$). Rv. 6. Stempel in ähnlichem Zustand wie no. 8.
   Photographie: Handel 1961. 9.85 g. Registriert: 5 Ex.
10. Av. 6. Löwenmaske mit runderer Mähne. Rv. 7. Herrliches Portrait, das beste,
    das wir von diesem Herrscher kennen. Photographie: Kopenhagen, publiziert von
    MØRKHOLM 1961. Registriert: 8 Ex.
11. Av. 6. Gleicher Stempel, verbrauchter. Rv. 8. Realistisches Portrait von
    ungewöhnlichem Stil. Photographie: Boston. 9.77 g. Registriert: 2 Ex.
12. Av. 7. Löwenmaske mit sehr großer Mähne. Rv. 8. Gleicher Stempel mit
    Stempelbrüchen im Feld. Photographie: Handel 1958. 9.78 g. Registriert: 4 Ex.

# Tafel XXXIV

1          2          3          4

5          6          7          8          9

10          11          12

# Mithrapata und Perikles (S. 105-109) – Taf. XXXV

## Statere des Mithrapata ohne Portrait

Av.: Löwenmaske. Rv.: Große Triskelis. Im Feld verschiedene Symbole, besonders unten links. Legende in den gleichen tadellosen lykischen Buchstaben wie auf den Portrait-Stücken: *MITHRAPATA*. Silberstatere.

13. Av. 8. Löwenmaske. Rv. 9. Delphin in der Gegenrichtung der Triskelis schwimmend. Photographie: Kopenhagen, 1960 von MØRKHOLM publiziert. Registriert: 3 Ex.
14. Av. 9. Löwenmaske. Rv. 10. Kleiner Kopf des jungen Herakles in der Löwenhaut von vorn, leicht n.r. gewendet; r. daneben die stehende Keule. Photographie: British Museum, publiziert von JENKINS in NC 1959, 18. 9.92 g. 3 h. Registriert: 4 Ex.
15. Av. 10. Löwenmaske. Rv. 11. Im oberen Feld l. Kopf der Pallas Athene n.l. Photographie: Privatsammlung. 9.79 g. Registriert: 1 Ex.
16. Av. 11. Löwenmaske. Rv. 12. Kopf des Hermes in geflügeltem Petasos von vorn; l. daneben der Caduceus. Photographie: British Museum, publiziert von JENKINS in NC 1959, 13. 9.50 g. 7 h. Registriert: 3 Ex.
17.    Av. 12. Gleicher Stempel, verbrauchter. Rv. 13. Ähnlich wie vorher, aber Caduceus r. Photographie: Kopenhagen, 1960 von MØRKHOLM publiziert. Registriert: 1 Ex.
18. Av. 12. Löwenmasken von grobem Stil. Rv. 14. Gerstenkorn. Die beiden letzten Buchstaben der Legende fehlen. Photographie: Privatsammlung. 9.53 g. Registriert: 2 Ex.
19. Av. 13. Löwenmaske von sehr grobem Stil. Rv. 14. Kein Symbol. Photographie: Privatsammlung. 9.77 g. Registriert: 1 Ex.

## Perikles: Silberstatere mit Portrait

Av.: Büste von vorn, leicht n.r. gewendet. Rv.: Nackter bärtiger Krieger in Ausfallstellung n.r. Er trägt korinthischen Helm, hält Schwert und Schild am l. Arm. Im Feld Triskelis und Name in lykischen Buchstaben *PÄRIKLÄ*.

20. Av. 14. Bekleidete Büste. Der Lorbeerkranz, aus dem seitlich ein großer Zweig herauswächst, ist nur auf der l. Seite des Kopfs sichtbar. Im Feld r. ein nach unten schwimmender Delphin. Rv. 15. Kleine Triskelis im Feld l. Zweite Legende *VÄHNTÄZÄ* = Antipellus r. Photographie: Av. siehe no. 22; Rv. Handel 1960. 9.83 g. Registriert: 7 Ex.
21. Av. 14. Gleicher Stempel. Rv. 16. Große Triskelis im Feld oben r. Stark entwickelte Stempelrisse auf allen registrierten Exemplaren. Die Legende *VÄHNTÄZÄ* l. im Feld. Photographie: Rv. = Handel 1958. 9.85 g. Registriert: 4 Ex.
22. Av. 14. Gleicher Stempel. Rv. 17. Triskelis im Feld unten r. Legenden wie bei 21. Photographie: Handel 1958. 9.70 g. Registriert: 10 Ex.
23. Av. 14. Gleicher Stempel. Rv. 18. Im Feld r. nach unten schwimmender Delphin. Legende *VÄHNTÄZÄ* rechts. Photographie: Handel 1959. Registriert: 1 Ex.

# Mithrapata und Perikles (S. 105-109) – Taf. XXXVI

24. Av. 15. Bekleidete Büste. Der Kopf ist größer und von kräftigerem Stil. Der Lorbeerkranz ist nur durch die obere Reihe der Blätter angedeutet, während Locken die untere Reihe ersetzen. Beidseitig wächst ein Zweig aus dem Kranz nach oben. Rv. 19. Triskelis im Feld unten r. Legende *VÄHNTÄZÄ* fehlt. Photographie: Av. und Rv. = Handel 1960. 9.78 g. Registriert: 6 Ex., darunter British Museum (ex Naue und Warren 1231) und Schlessinger (Auktion Ermitage) 1372.

25. Av. 15. Gleicher Stempel in verbrauchtem Zustand. Mehrere Stempelrisse; der stärkste befindet sich über dem l. Auge. Rv. 20. Im Feld unten r. große Triskelis, deren l. stehendes Bein von Stempelriß deformiert ist. Photographie: Rv. = Handel 1958. Registriert: 2 Ex.

26. Av. 16. Gänzlich unbekleidete Büste. Kein Kranz oder «Halb-Kranz» in den wehenden Haaren. Herrliches Portrait von außergewöhnlich feinem Stil. Rv. 21. Im Feld r. achtstrahliger Stern und darunter kleine Triskelis. Der bärtige Kopf des Kriegers ist größer. Photographie: Av. = Privatsammlung (aus Hess-Leu 1959, 270). 9.85 g. Ausgestellt in Basel «Meisterwerke griechischer Kunst» 1960, Kat.No. 508. - Rv. = Handel 1960. 9.87 g. Registriert: 2 Ex.

27. Av. 16. Gleicher Stempel, aber mit mehreren Stempelbrüchen in den Augen. Rv. 22. Siebenstrahliger Stern links im Feld. Photographie: Rv. = Handel 1960. 9.71 g. Registriert: 6 Ex.

28. Av. 16. Gleicher Stempel in ähnlichem Zustand. Rv. 23. Ähnlich, nur kleine Triskelis rechts im Feld. Photographie: Rv. = ANS. Registriert: 2 Ex.

29. Av. 16. Gleicher Stempel. Rv. 24. Ähnlich, aber der Körper des Kriegers ist schlanker. Photographie: Rv. = Oxford. 9.75 g. Registriert: 2 Ex.

## Perikles: Tetrobole und Triskelis

30. Av. 17. Löwenmaske mit 6 großen Stirnlocken. Rv. 25. Große Triskelis. Legende *PÄRIKLÄ*. Photographie: Privatsammlung. Registriert: 3 Ex.

31. Av. 18. Löwenmaske von schlechterem Stil. Rv. 26. Buchstaben der Legende flüchtig. Photographie: Handel 1958. 2.55 g. Registriert: 1 Ex.

## Perikles: Diobole mit dem Kopf der Athena von vorn

32. Av. 19. Löwe einen Stier reißend. Der Löwe ist im Profil dargestellt. Der Stier, links ins Knie gesunken, hebt den Kopf. Sehr feine Bodenlinie. Typus der Tetradrachmen von Akanthus (DESNEUX D 113!). Legende *VÄDÄVIÄ*. Rv. 27. Bekleidete Büste der Pallas Athene im Helm von vorn, mit wehenden Haaren. Rechts auf dem Stirnschutz des Helmes eine kleine Harpienprotome nach links. Typus des Meisterwerkes des Eukleidas mit dem schmalen Kopf (RIZZO pl. 46,3). Triskelis links im Felde. Legende *PÄRIKLÄ*. Photographie: Boston. 1.23 g. Registriert: 16. Ex.

# Tafel XXXVI

Mithrapata und Perikles (S. 105-109)

# Kimon in the Manner of Segesta* (S. 110-115) – Taf. XXXVII

## Some Related Heads *de face* preceding Kimon

1. Segesta. Sizilian litra c. 425. 6 h, 0.81 g. London, SNG Lloyd 1193; cf. G.K. JENKINS, The Coinage of Gela, 1970, Pl. 38:13 and 84f. Obverse: Head of Aigeste, facing three-quarters left.
2. Gela. Attic tetradrachm c. 425. 7 h, 16.31 g. London, SNG Lloyd 985, cf. JENKINS, The Coinage of Gela, 1971, 465 and 84 f. Reverse: Head of river-god, facing three-quarters right.
3. Amphipolis. Ligth Thraco-Macedonian tetradrachm c. 420. 12 h, 14.27 g. Sale Catalogue Bank Leu AG - MMAG, 1974, Kunstfreund, 138. Obverse: Head of Apollo, facing slightly left.
4. Kyzikos. Phokaian stater c. 410. 16.02 g. Sale cat. above no. 3, 160. Obverse: Head of Apollo facing slightly right. 5. Syracuse. Attic tetradrachm c. 410. 7 h, 16.59 g. Sale cat. above no. 3,120. Reverse: Head of Pallas Athene, facing slightly left, signed *Eϒ-KΛEIΔ*/A on helmet.

## Kimon's Facing Arethusa Group

Obverse: Head of Arethusa, facing slightly left, inscribed *APEΘOΣA*, signed *KIMΩN* on ampyx. Reverse: Fast quadriga left.

6. Syracuse. Attic tetradrachm c. 406. 9 h, 16.85 g. Paris, Catalogue de Luynes 1226. Obverse die 1: Fuller head, thicker hairlocks. Earring with 3 pearls. Reverse die 1: Nike flying, signed *KIMΩN* between the two exergual lines. TUDEER 80 e.
7. Syracuse. Attic tetradrachm c. 406. 1 h, 17.40 g. Sale Catalogue Hess-Leu 28, 89. Obverse die 1: Flaw right, below chin. Reverse die 2: Nike standing, no signature. TUDEER 81 j.
8. Syracuse. Attic tetradrachm c. 406. Acireale, Pennisi Collection. Obverse die 2: Head smaller, hairlocks thinner. Lower dolphin right on its back. Reverse die 1: Flaw over the right arm of the auriga. TUDEEr 78 e.
9. Syracuse. Attic tetradrachm c. 406. 12 h. 16.94 g. Ticino collection. Obverse die 2: Flaws between Arethusa's lips. Reverse die 2: Flaw above left wheel. TUDEER 79.

## Kimon's Followers in Sicily

10. Camarina. Attic drachm 406-405. 10 h, 4.03 g. Brussels. Catalogue de Hirsch 328. Obverse: Female head facing three-quarter left, close copy of Kimon's Arethusa die 1, but no dolphins.
11. Motya. Attic didrachm c. 400. 7.30 g. Ticino Collection. G.K. JENKINS, SNR 50 (1971) 32, Pl. 5:50. Obverse: Facing Arethusa head; around, six dolphins.
12. Motya. Sicilian litra c. 400. 9 h. 0.71 g. London. SNG Lloyd 1144. Obverse: Facing head.

## Kimon in the manner of Segesta

13. Segesta. Attic tetradrachm 405-400. 7 h, 17.35 g. Ticino collection. Unpublished. Unique. Obverse: *EΓEΣTAIΩN* The hunter Aigestes with two Lakonian hounds, small ithyphallic herm right in field. Reverse: *ΣEΓEΣTA‡IB* Head of Aigeste, facing slightly to the right, close copy of Kimon's Arethusa-die 1, but no dolphins. Enlarged 2:1.

---

* No. 4 EL, all others AR.

# Tafel XXXVII

1

2

3

4

5

6

7

8

9

10

11

12

13

# Kimon in the Manner of Segesta (S. 110-115) – Taf. XXXVIII

**The Revised Chronology of the Tetradrachms of Segesta**
Attic standard.

The first series c. 415
Aigeste in slow quadriga / Aigestes as hunter.

14. LEDERER 1a. *ΕΓΕΣΤΑΙΟ*[N] / *ΣΕCΕΣΤΑ*-‡-I-B 17.10 g. Berlin.
15. LEDERER 2. *ΣΕLΕΣΤΑ*‡IB / *ΣΕCΕΣΤΑ*-‡-I-B 16.46 g. Cat. Sir H. Weber Collection 1519. Unique.
16. LEDERER 3a. *ΣΕLΕΣΤΑ*‡[IB] / *ΕΓΕΣΤΑΙ-ΟΝ* 7 h, 16.76 g. Sale cat. quoted above, no. 3, 100.

The trial-piece c. 410

17. LEDERER 4. *ΕΓΕΣΤΑΙΟΝ* (sic!) / No legend. 17.25 g. Paris. Catalogue de Luynes 1121. Unique.

The related didrachm: c. 410-405
Lakonian hounds / Head of Aigeste.

18. LEDERER s.n. *ΣΕΓΕΣΤΑ*‡IB (retrograde) / No legend. 6 h, 8.28 g. Sale catalogue Leu 2,100. Same reverse-die as no. 22.

The second, central series c. 405-400
Aigestes as hunter / Head of Aigeste.

19. Unpublished. *ΕΓΕΣΤΑΙΩΝ* / *ΣΕΓΕΣΤΑ*‡IB For description and enlarged photograph see above no. 13. Unique.
20. LEDERER 5. *ΕΓΕΣΤΑΙΩΝ* / *ΣΕΓΕΣΤΑ*‡IB 17.00 g Berlin. Unique.
21. LEDERER 6a. *ΕΓΕΣΤΑΙΩΝ* / *ΣΕΓΕΣΤΑ*‡IA 16.85 g. London. BMC 32.
22. LEDERER 7. *ΕΓΕΣΤΑΙΩΝ* / No legend. 5 h, 17.41 g. Sale Cat. Leu 2,99. Same reverse-die as no. 18.

The third series c. 400-398
Fast quadriga / Aigestes as hunter.

23. LEDERER 9. *ΣΕLΕ̄-ΣΤΑ*‡IA / No legend. 16.80 g. Berlin.
24. LEDERER 10b. *ΣΕLΕ̄-ΣΤΑ*‡IA / No legend. 17.13 g. London. BMC 33.
25. LEDERER 11b. *ΣΕLΕ̄-ΣΤΑ*‡IA / No legend. 17.15 g. Catalogue R. Jameson Collection 716.

The «Punic» piece: c. 398-397
Aigestes as hunter left / Head of Aigeste.

26. LEDERER 8. No legend / no legend. 17.00 g. Naples. Unique.

14

15

16

18

19

20

21

22

17

23

24

25

26

# Tafel XXXIX

## Kimon und Euainetos in Funde von Naro (S. 116-126)

*Katalog*

| Lfde. Nr. gleiche Vs./Rs. | Signatur Vs./Rs. | Gewicht | Stempel-Stellung | Literatur | Standort |
|---|---|---|---|---|---|
| 1 | – | 43.50 | ↓ | Seltman 10a (dies Ex.) | Gulbenkian 168 |
| 2 | KIMΩN/KIM | 43.19 | ↖ | Jongkees 1i (dies Ex.) | SNG Lloyd 1409 |
| 3 | » | 43.30 | ↙ | Jongkees 1f (dies Ex.) | Gulbenkian 301 |
| 4 | KIMΩN/K/KIMΩN | 43.36 | ? | Jongkees 3 | AC 17, 236 |
| 5 | » | 43.17 | ↘ | Jongkees 3 | Gulbenkian 303 |
| 6 | » | 43.17 | ? | Jongkees 3t (dies Ex.) | AC 13, 335 |
| 7 | KIMΩN/KI | 43.34 | ↑ | Jongkees 6d (dies Ex.) | Dewing 870 ex Gallatin coll. |
| 8 | KI | 43.35 | ? | Jongkees 7k (dies Ex.) | AC 17, 766 ex AC 13, 336 |
| 9 | KI | 42.99 | ↘ | Jongkees 7f (dies Ex.) | SNG Lloyd 1410 |
| 10 | – | 43.04 | ↖ | Jongkees 10 | Gulbenkian 306 |
| 11 | – | 42.86 | ↘ | Jongkees 11 | Gulbenkian 307 |
| 12 | -/EY AINE | 43.16 | ← | Gallatin Vs. 4/Rs. C7 : 5 (dies Ex.) | SNG Lloyd 1412 |
| 13 | » | 43.26 | ↗ | Gallatin Vs. 4/Rs. C9 : 1 (dies Ex.) | Dewing 884 ex Gallatin coll. ex AC 13, 345 |

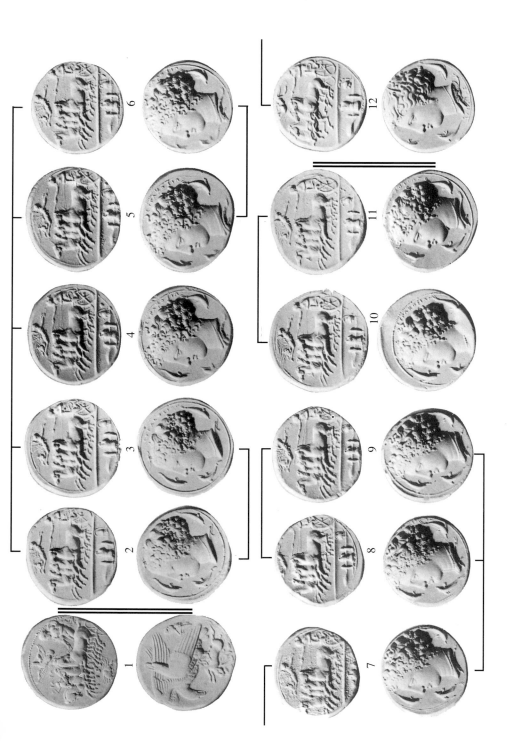

# Tafel XL

## Kimon und Euainetos in Funde von Naro (S. 116-126)

*Katalog*

| Lfde. Nr. gleiche Vs./Rs. | Signatur Vs./Rs. | Gewicht | Stempel- Stellung | Literatur | Standort |
|---|---|---|---|---|---|
| 14 | » | 43.05 | ↙ | Gallatin Vs. 2/Rs. C8 : 1 (dies Ex.) | Dewing 875 ex Gallatin coll. |
| 15 | » | 43.17 | ↘ | Gallatin Vs. 2/Rs. C8 : 2 (dies Ex.) | Gulbenkian 311 |
| 16 | » | ? | ? | Gallatin Vs. 2/Rs. C8 | ? |
| 17 | -/Δ EY AINE | 43.17 | ↗ | Gallatin Vs. 9/Rs. D1 : 1 (dies Ex.) | Gulbenkian 314 |
| 18 | -/Δ EY AINE | ? | ? | Gallatin Vs. 9/Rs. D2 | ? |
| 19 | » | ? | ? | Gallatin Vs. 9/Rs. D2 | ? |
| 20 | » | 43.37 | ↗ | Gallatin Vs. 9/Rs. D2 : 1 (dies Ex.) | SNG Lloyd 1413 |
| 21 | » | 43.19 | ? | Gallatin Vs. 9/Rs. D2 | AC 13, 340 |
| 22 | » | 43.29 | ? | Gallatin Vs. 9/Rs. D2 | AC 13, 342 |
| 23 | » | 43.33 | ? | Gallatin Vs. 9/Rs. D2 | AC 13, 341 |
| 24 | » | 43.30 | ? | Gallatin Vs. 9/Rs. D2 | AC 13, 343 |

# Tafel XL

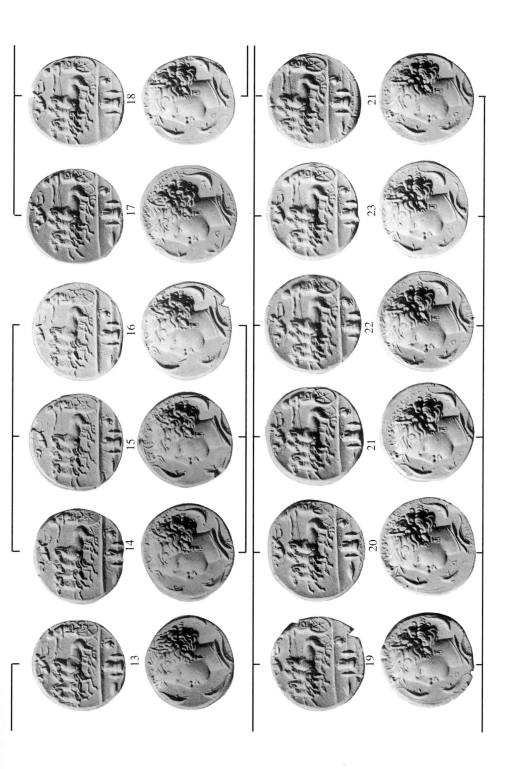

# The Cyzikenes: A Reappraisal (S. 127-135) – Taf. XLI

## Cyzicus' Own Images

1. Hecte, mid-6th century. Tunny head l. with fish in mouth. Rev., incuse square with thick crossbars. FRITZE 2. Hess-Leu 28, 219, 2.67 g.
2. Stater, ca. 500 B.C. Hercules with bow and club r., behind, large tunny. FRITZE 107. Kunstfreund 6, 16.09 g.
3. Stater, ca. 500 B.C. Helmeted, winged sphinx protome l. over tunny. FRITZE 71. Leu 36, 143, 16.04 g.
4. Stater, ca. 470 B.C. Winged demon holding large tunny l. FRITZE 123. Leu 45, 196, 16.14 g.
5. Hecte, ca. 470 B.C. As 4. FRITZE 123 and 124. NFA 5, 136, 2.69 g.
6. Stater, ca. 460 B.C. Naked warrior with Corinthian helmet, kneeling l. on large tunny. FRITZE 115. Leu 42, 277, 15.87 g.
7. Stater, ca. 450 B.C. Naked Selinos kneeling r. on tunny, pours wine from amphora into cantharus. FRITZE 134. Leu 42, 278, 16.00 g.
8. Stater, ca. 450 B.C. Perseus with gorgon kneeling r. on tunny, head turned back. FRITZE 162. NFA 4, 250, 16.00 g.
9. Stater, ca. 390 B.C. Young Hercules and Iphicles fighting serpents on large tunny. FRITZE 208. Leu 42, 280, 16.14 g.
10. Stater, ca. 350 B.C. Head of bearded man laureate, l., tunny below neck. FRITZE 199. Kunstfreund 212, 16.07 g.

## Imitations

11. Stater, ca. 460 B.C. Naked youth on dolphin l., holding tunny; below, another tunny. FRITZE 110. Leu 50, 149, 16.14 g. A charming variation by an excellent engraver of the Tarentine model, struck around 480-470 B.C.
12. Stater, ca. 375 B.C. Head of bearded Hercules in tightly fitting lion skin headgear. FRITZE 140. Hess-Leu 45, 242, 16.00 g. Conceived after the Hercules heads of the Macedonian king Amyntas, 389-369 B.C.
13. Stater, ca. 370 B.C. Kekrops with an olive branch l. on tunny. FRITZE 158. Hess-Leu 31, 394, 16.00 g. An imitation of the Triton-Glaucus issues of Cretan Itanos around 380 B.C.
14. Stater, ca. 400 B.C. Bearded Achelous swimming r. FRITZE 174. Leu 22, 119, 16.04 g. A close imitation of the classic Gela tetradrachm struck in Sicily around 430 B.C.
15. Stater, ca. 360 B.C. Cow to l., head turned to suckling calf which kneels on tunny. FRITZE 219. NFA 4, 252, 16.06 g. A skillfully engraved image of the time-honored oriental motif popular in the ancient minor arts, also appears on the coins of Dyrrachiun, Caristus, and Eretria on Euboea.

# Tafel XLI

# The Cyzikenes: A Reappraisal (S. 127-135) – Taf. XLII

**Not in FRITZE**

16. Stater, ca. 520 B.C. Fox biting tail of big, long tunny. Hess-Leu 45, 238, 16.25 g. Only a hemihecte was known to FRITZE, 35.
17. Hecte, ca. 490 B.C. Youthful warrior in Ionian helmet l., tunny behind neck. Kunstfreund 7, 2.65 g.
18. Hecte, ca. 480 B.C. Head of Athena in Corinthian helmet to l., behind, tunny. Leu 45, 195, 2.64 g. This is a new fine die. The stater FRITZE 64 is earlier and of different conception.
19. Stater, ca. 470 B.C. Presumably rape of Thetis by Perseus; below, tunny. Leu 33, 356, 15.99 g. Known to FRITZE, 109, as hecte only. «Masterly composition: the back of the tunny is formed as a domed hill and gives a tridimensional plasticity to the scene», Leu 33.
20. Hecte, ca. 370 B.C. Nike sacrificing bull; below, tunny. Leu 30, 161, 2.68 g.
21. Stater, ca. 370 B.C. Sphinx with straight wing, seated l. on tunny. Glendining 1963, 296, 15.95 g.
22. Hemihecte, ca. 360 B.C. Athena in helmet with shield and spear attacking. Leu 50, 133, 1.30 g.
23. Stater, ca. 360 B.C. Large, bearded head of old man l., tunny below neck. Ars Classica 10, 644, ex Ars Classica I (POZZI), 2718, 16.03 g. This impressive head, a masterpiece of glyptic art, seems to be known by this large specimen only.
24. Stater, ca. 350 B.C. Head of young girl l., within disk over tunny. NFA 2, 170, 15.77 g.
25. Stater, ca. 350 B.C. Head of Artemis in corymbus r. Leu 50, 152, 15.95 g.
26. Stater, ca. 340 B.C. Lion attacking deer l., below, tunny. MMAG 19, 471, 15.95 g. The animal fight, a popular image in eastern Greek and Scythian art, appeared on Cyzicus electrum only in the late period, as shown by the Prinkipo hoard with several specimens (ZfN 41, 1931: see 138, p. 22 and pl. 3; and 139, p. 23, and pl. 3).
27. Stater, ca. 340 B.C. Dionysos seated on panther l.; below, tunny. Leu 52, 85, 15.98 g.
28. Stater, ca. 340 B.C. Youth kneeling on tunny throwing astragalus. Leu 52, 84, 15.93 g.

16      17      18      19

20      21      22      23      24

25      26      27      28

# Tafel XLIII

Punic Coinage on the Eve of the First War (S. 139-143)

1. The Provincial Coinage in Sicily.
From F. Sternberg sale 1988, the arrows added.

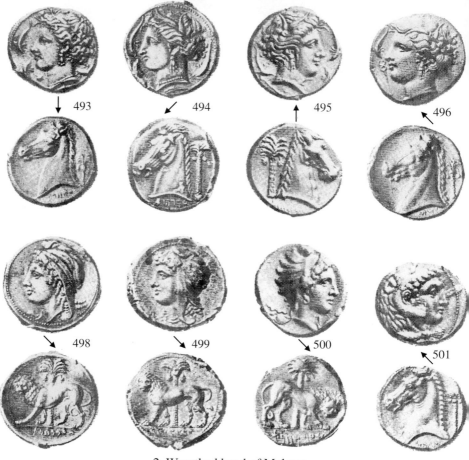

2. Wreathed head of Melqart,
the first reverse die for the issue of the army unit "Roš Melqart".
From G.K. Jenkins, *RSN* 50 (1971), pl. 15 and 21.

# Tafel XLIV

Punic Coinage on the Eve of the First War (S. 139-143)

Coinage struck *c.* 300-260 B.C., the gold staters from loose dies, the gold trihemistaters and the electrum stater from fixed dies.

### GOLD TRIHEMISTATERS CARTHAGE

1 Leu 15, 150, 12.48 g.      3 Hess-Leu 45, 86, 12.48 g.
2 Leu 42, 144, 12.49 g.      4 Leu 36, 85, 12.46 g.

### GOLD STARTERS           ELECTRUM STARTER CARTHAGE

 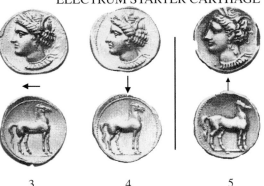

1 Leu 36, 84, 9.29 g.      5 Leu 7, 105, 7.55 g.
2 Leu 45, 78, 9.44 g.
3 Leu 2, 125, 9.24 g.
4 Leu 42, 142, 9.02 g.

# Tafel XLV

Punic Coinage on the Eve of the First War (S. 139-143)

High denominations in gold, electrum and silver, struck in the years 265-250 B.C. from fixed dies in Carthage, from loose dies in Sicily

CATHAGE

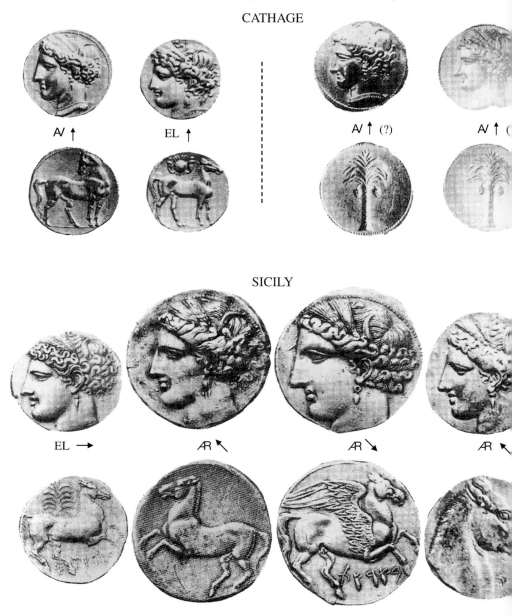

SICILY

# Sikulo-punische Münzlegenden (S. 150-160)

|  | |  |
|---|---|---|
| 1 | 𐤀𐤔𐤂𐤇𐤕𐤓𐤒 | qrtḥdšt |
| 2 | 𐤀𐤍𐤇𐤌 | mḥnt |
| 3 | 𐤀𐤍𐤇𐤌𐤌𐤏 | ʿmmḥnt |
| 4 | 𐤀𐤍𐤇𐤌𐤌𐤏 | ʿmhmḥnt |
| 5 | 𐤀𐤍𐤇𐤌𐤌𐤏𐤔 | šʿmmḥnt |
| 6 | 𐤌𐤔𐤇𐤁𐤌 | mḥšbm |
| 7 | 𐤌𐤌 | mm |
| 8 | 𐤁𐤀𐤓𐤑𐤕 | bʾrṣt |
| 9 | 𐤓𐤔𐤌𐤋𐤒𐤓𐤕 | ršmlqrt |
| 10 | 𐤓𐤀𐤔𐤌𐤋𐤒𐤓𐤕 | rʾšmlqrt |
| 11 | 𐤑𐤉𐤑 | ṣyṣ |
| 12 | 𐤌𐤈𐤅𐤀 | m ṭwʾ |
| 13 | 𐤇𐤁 | ḥb |

# The Mint of the First Carthaginian Coins (S. 144-146) – Taf. XLVI

Fig. 1 The «JENKINS-overstrike»: The details on the Akragas tetradrachm ex Leu 2.69 and on the early Carthaginian coin JENKINS II 6 ex Jameson 907 = NIGGELER I 538 are identical: the date bunch is visible on the front horse's flank and parts of the mane, the bridle and the topknot from the Carthaginian horse and of the Nike's belt appear on the front eagle.

Fig. 4 The exclusive denomination: The Carthaginian institutional coinage in Sicily consists of the «Siculo-Punic» tetradrachms exclusively, lasting from 410 till 290 B.C.

Fig. 5 The Institutional inscriptions: *qrthdšt, mhnt, mhšbm, b'rst, ršmlqrt* in Punic writing.

# Tafel XLVI

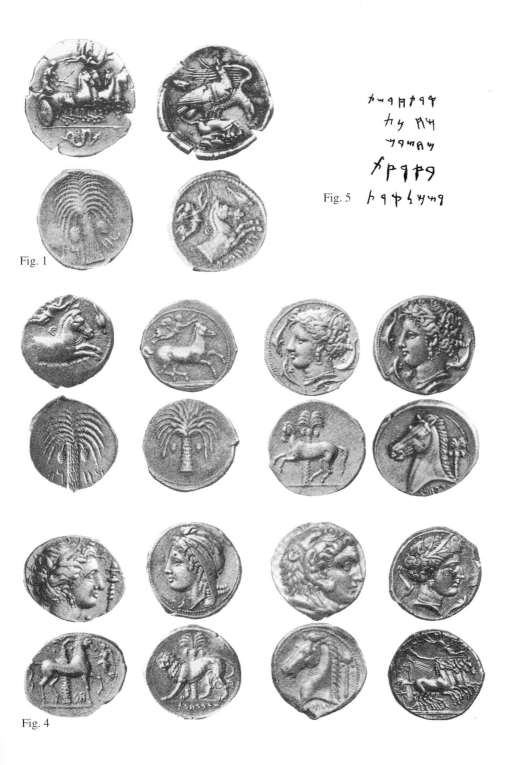

Fig. 1

Fig. 4

Fig. 5

# The Mint of the First Carthaginian Coins (S. 144-146) – Taf. XLVII

Fig. 2 Die axis and protuberances: The arrows indicate the different positions of obverses and reverses in the Sicilian striking process from loose dies. Distinct protuberances are visible on the illustrated specimens.

Fig. 3 Die axis and round flans: The coins produced in the metropolis in Africa come from fixed dies, as the arrows on 12 h demonstrate. The flans are round.

# Tafel XLVII

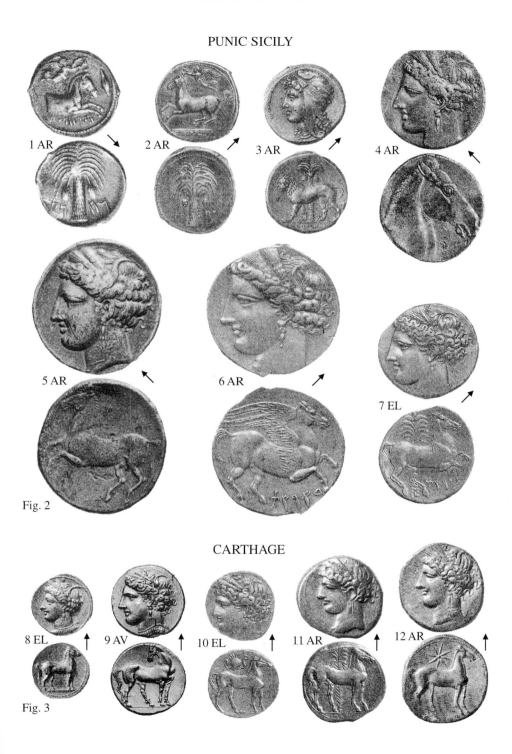

PUNIC SICILY

1 AR

2 AR

3 AR

4 AR

5 AR

6 AR

7 EL

Fig. 2

CARTHAGE

8 EL

9 AV

10 EL

11 AR

12 AR

Fig. 3

# Sikulo-Punische Münzlegenden (S. 150-160)[1] – Taf. XLVIII

## Sikulo-punische Münzstätten[2]

1. Ca. 409. 17.24 g. Vs. Gezäumte Pferdeprotome im Galopp n.r., von Nike bekränzt; rechts Korn. Unten Legende I «Neustadt». Rs. Breite Palme mit zwei Fruchtständen. Unten Legende 2 «Lager». JENKINS II, 14 (Ex. I, auf Taf. 2 abgebildet). Ex Ars Classica 13 (1926) 379, und Montagu 807.
2. Ca. 400. 16.80 g. Vs. Ungezäumtes Pferd im Galopp n.l., von Nike bekränzt. Auf Abschnittleiste, in kleinen Buchstaben, Legende 1 var. Außen feiner Perlkreis. Rs. Palme; unten Legende 2 var. JENKINS II, 38 (Ex. 2, auf Taf. 5 abgebildet). British Museum (PCG Taf. 26,40).
3. 2.Hälfte des 4.Jahrhunderts. 17.16 g. Vs. Quadriga im Galopp n.l.; oben Nike. Im Abschnitt Legende 9 «Haupt des Melqart». Rs. Kopf der Kore-Persephone n.r.; außen vier Delphine. JENKINS I, 54. Ex MMAG 38 (1968) (Voirol), 21, und Schlessinger 13 (1935) (Eremitage), 244.
4. 2.Hälfte des 4.Jahrhunderts. 16.58 g. 12 h. Vs. Kopf der Kore-Persephone n.r.; außen vier Delphine. Rs. Quadriga im Galopp n.r.; keine Nike. Unter der doppelten Bodenlinie Legende 10 (mit 'ālef) «Haupt des Melqart». JENKINS I, 71 (Ex. 3, auf Taf. 21 abgebildet). ANS, SNG ANS 734, aus den Auktionen Bourgey, 29. Mai 1911, 39 und Sotheby, April 1909 (White King), 55.
5. Ca. 320. 17.09 g. 10 h. Arbeit eines nicht-punischen, wohl griechischen Stempelschneiders. Vs. Kopf der Tanit-Artemis mit phrygischer Tiara n.l. Außen Perlkreis. Rs. Löwe n.l., dahinter Palme. Im Abschnitt Legende 5 «des Lagervolkes». JENKINS III, 270 (Ex. 1). Gulbenkian 376, aus Auktion Naville 10 (1925) 358.
6. Ca. 320. 17.49. 5 h. Ähnlich wie Nr. 5. Die Legende 5 «des Lagervolkes» ist mit spiegelverkehrten Buchstaben wiedergegeben, was zusätzlich für einen nicht-punischen Stempelschneider spricht. JENKINS III, 271. Ex Leu 57 (1993) 43, und Numismatic Fine Arts 14 (1985) 65.
7. Ca. 315. 16.95g. 5 h. Vs. Kopf der Kore-Persephone n.l.; außen vier Delphine. Rs. Pferdekopf n.l., dahinter kleine Palme. Unten Legende 3 «Lagervolk». JENKINS III, 172 (Ex. 5). Ex Leu 57 (1993) 42 und MMAG 43 (1970) 28.
8. Ca. 315. 16.94 g. 6 h. Vs. Kopf der Kore-Persephone n.l., Delphin und Kerykeion. Rs. Grosser Pferdekopf n.l.,, dahinter kleine Palme. Unten Legende 7 «mm». JENKINS III, 225 (Ex. 2, auf Taf. 17 abgebildet). Antikenmuseum Basel (Slg. Tessin) 563.
9. Ca. 300. 17.01 g. 1 h. Vs. Kopf des Melqart-Herakles mit der Löwenhaut n.r., vom Typ der Tetradrachmen Alexanders des Großen. Rs. Pferdekopf n.l., dahinter Palme. Unten Legende 4 «das Lagervolk». JENKINS IV, 277 (=). Ex Leu 30 (1981) 53.
10. Ca. 285. Vs. Kopf des Melqart-Herakles n.r. Rs. Pferdekopf n.l., dahinter Palme; links Astragal. Unten Legende 6 «Rechnungsführer». JENKINS IV, 366 (Ex. 3, auf Taf. 9 abgebildet). Slg. Tessin.

---

[1] Die Fotografien stammen aus dem Fotoarchiv Leu Numismatik, Zürich, oder sind der jeweilig zitierten Publikation entnommen.

[2] Die Nrn. 1-10 sind Tetradrachmen von attischem Gewicht in Silber. (=) bedeutet stempelgleich. Die uneinheitlichen sizilischen Stempelstellungen sind durch Stellung im Uhrzeigersinn angegeben.

1

2

3

4

5

6

7

8

9

10

# Sikulo-Punische Münzlegenden (S. 150-160) – Taf. XLIX

11. Ca. 260. Silber-Dekadrachmon, Sizilien, 37.40 g. 12 h. Vs. Kopf der Kore-Persephone mit zwei Kornähren und Blatt im Haar n.l.; einfacher Ohrring. Rs. Pegasos n.r.; unten, in elegantem Duktus, Legende 8 «in den Ländern». JENKINS IV, 431 (=). Ex Leu 38 (1986) 49, und Schlessinger 13 (1935) (Eremitage), 1631.

**Vergleichsmaterial**

12. Panormos. AR Didrachmon vom Typ Segesta, ca. 400. 8.49 g. Vs. Jagdhund n.r., am Boden schnüffelnd; oben kleiner Frauenkopf n.r. Rs. Kopf einer Nymphe n.r.; außen drei Delphine und Legende 11 ṣyṣ. JENKINS I, Z 1 (auf Taf. 2 abgebildet). Berlin.

13. Akragas. AR Teradrachmon, ca. 410. 17.30 g. 5 h. Vs. Quadriga im Galopp n.r., darüber Nike, den Auriga bekränzend. Im Abschnitt Ketos n.r. Rs. Zwei Adler über einem Hasen; links oben Zikade. Publiziert in JENKINS II, Taf. 6 E und 7. Ex Leu 48 (1989) 35, und Leu 2 (1972) 69. Überprägt auf ein frühes sikulo-punisches Teradrachmon vom Typ Taf. XLVI1 (JENKINS Vs. O 3); auf dem Flügel des vorderen Adlers sind die Pferdemähne und die Zügel noch deutlich zu erkennen.

14. Panormos. AR Litra, ca. 410 mit Bilingue. 0.75 g. 3 h. Vs. Poseidon mit Dreizack n.r. sitzend; rechts Delphin und pun. Legende ṣyṣ. Rs. Jüngling seitlich auf einem n.r. springenden Ziegenbock sitzend; rechts die griechische Legende ΠΑΝΟΡΜΟΣ. JENKINS I, Taf. 2, Y und Taf. 24,6, sowie JENKINS IV, Taf. 24 A. Glasgow. Hunter Collection S. 208, 2, Taf. 15,10.

15. – AR Litra, Mitte des 4. Jahrhunderts. 0.54 g. Vs. Kopf eines Flussgottes n.l. Rs. Stier mit Menschenkopf n.l.; oben Legende ṣyṣ. JENKINS I, Taf. 24, 14. British Museum. BMC 27

16. Motya. AR Tetradrachmon um 410. 17.19 g. Vs. Adler n.r.; links Legende 12 hmṭw' (mit zusätzlichem h). Rs. Krabbe vom agrigentischen Typ, darunter Fisch n.r. JENKINS I, Taf. 5,42 (=; vermutlich Ex. 3). Gulbenkian 228.

17. – AR Litra, ca. 405. 0,74 g. Vs. Gorgoneion. Rs. Palme; im Feld Legende 12 mṭw'. JENKINS I, Taf. 23,4a. Aus Auktion Ars Classica 16 (1933) 580.

18. – AR Tetradrachmon, ca. 400. 17.19 g. 11 h. Vs. Frauenkopf n.r., eine enge, gelungene Kopie des Arethusakopfes auf dem zweifach signierten syrakusischen Dekadrachmon des Kimon (JONGKEES 3) unter Weglassung der Delphine. Links Legende 12 mṭw'. Rs. Krabbe. JENKINS I, 45 (Ex. 2, auf Taf. 5 abgebildet). Gulbenkian 229 (vorher de Ciccio, vermutlich aus dem Contessa-Fund).

19. – Bronze, ca. 400. 2.35 g. Vs. Frauenkopf n.r., das Haar in Ampyx und Sphendone. Rs. Krabbe, darunter Legende mṭw'. Ex MMAG 76 (1991) (Lafaille), 184 (inédit).

20. Thermai. AR Tetradrachmon, ca. 340. 17.29 g. 7 h. Vs. Quadriga im Galopp n.l.; Nike bekränzt den Lenker. Im Abschnitt Altar mit zwei Hörnern. Rs. Frauenkopf n.l., das Haar in Netz; außen drei Delphine. JENKINS I, Taf. 22,1. Ex Leu 22 (1979) 44.

21. ryx. AR Tetradrachmon, 1.Hälfte des 4. Jahrhunderts. 17.24 g. 3 h. Vs. Quadriga n.r., Nike bekränzt den Lenker. Rs. Aphrodite mit Taube n.l. sitzend, vor ihr Eros; rechts (hier nicht auf Schrötling) griechische Legende. British Museum. SNG Lloyd 943.

22. – AR Stater, ca. 335 vom Typ Korinth. 8.53 g. Vs. Pegasos n.l. fliegend; unten die punische Legende 'rk. Rs. Kopf der Athena mit korinthischem Helm n.r. JENKINS I, Taf. 24,25. Ex Leu 57 (1993) 19, und Lanz 48 (1989) 67.

# Tafel XLIX

11

12

14

13

15

16

17

18

19

20

21

22

# Sikulo-Punische Münzlegenden (S. 150-160) – Taf. L

23. Panormos. AR Tetradrachmon, ca. 320. 17.20 g. 1 h. Vs. Quadriga im Galopp n.l., Nike bekränzt die Pferde. Oben Stern, im Abschnitt Legende 11 ṣyṣ . Rs. Kopf der Kore-Persephone n.l., der Arethusa der syrakusischen Dekadrachmen des Euainetos fein nachempfunden. Unter dem Kinn Hakenkreuz; außen vier Delphine. JENKINS I, 70 (Ex. 7). Ex Leu 25 (1980) 84, und MMAG 43 (1970) 53.

24. Sikulo-punisch. AR Tetradrachmon einer Sonderemission, ca. 340. 17.09 g. 9 h. Vs. Kopf der Kore Persephone n.l. Griech. Stempelschnitt in der Art des Euainetos. Rs. Hengst in hochgetriebenem Galoppsprung n.r., dahinter Palme. JENKINS III, 127. Ex Leu 42 (1987) 138, und MMAG 43 (1970) 21.

25 – AR Tetradrachmon, ca. 330. 17.30 g. 11 h. Vs. Kopf der Kore-Persephone n.r., davor Thymiaterion. Rs. Pferde vor Palme n.r.; rechts Nike über Kerykeion. Über der Bodenlinie die Buchstaben ḥb (Legende 13). Jenkins III, 94 (Ex. 2). Gulbenkian 367.

26. – AR Tetradrachmon, ca. 330. 17.13 g. Vs. Kopf der Kore-Persephone n.r., rechts Thymiaterion, unter dem Kinn Kugel. Rs. Pferd vor Palme n.r.; rechts Nike und Kerykeion. Über der Bodenlinie die punischen Buchstaben ḥb, links oben die griechischen Buchstaben ΣΩ. JENKINS III, 100 (Ex. 4). British Museum. SNG Lloyd 1623, aus Auktion Naville 10, 1925, 362.

27. Ršmlqrt . AR Tetradrachmon, ca. 340. 16.32 g. Vs. Quadriga im Galopp n.l., oben, anstelle der Nike, querliegendes Kerykeion. Im Abschnitt Legende 9 ršmlqrt . Rs. Bärtiger Kopf des Melqart-Herakles mit rundem Ohrring und Kranz n.r. JENKINS I, 1. Taf. 21 (Erstpublikation). British Museum.

28. Sikulo-punisch. EL Tristater, ca. 260. 22.68 g. 1 h. Vs. Kopf der Kore-Persephone mit Ährenkranz und einfachem Ohrring n.l. Rs. Pferd im Galopp n.r., dahinter Palme. Unten die Legende 8 «in den Ländern». JENKINS-LEWIS 371 (Ex. 1=2). JENKINS IV, Appendix S. 54 (0 1/R 5). Gulbenkian 377, aus den Auktionen Ars Classica 13, 1926, 393, und Sotheby, Mai 1905, 183, sowie aus Sammlung Warren 1370. JENKINS' Liste der Tristatere (IV, 54) zeigt die unregelmässigen, für Sizilien typischen Stempelstellungen.

29[3]. Karthago. AV Zehntelstater, ca. 330. 0.74 g. 12 h. Vs. Palme mit zwei Fruchtständen. Rs. Pferdekopf n.r. JENKINS-LEWIS 168. Ex Hess-Leu 36 (1968) 122.

30. – EL Fünftelstater, ca. 320. 1.54 g. 12 h. Vs. Kopf der Kore-Persephone n.l. Rs. Pferd mit umgewendetem Kopf n.r. JENKINS-LEWIS 240. Aus Auktion Glendining 1955 (Lockett I), 963 (SNG Lockett 1058).

31. – EL Stater, ca. 280. 7.48 g. 12 h. Vs. Kopf der Kore-Persephone n.l. Rs. Pferd n.r. JENKINS-LEWIS 353. Aus Auktion Ars Classica 16 (1933) 943.

32. – AV Trihemistater, ca. 260. 12.49 g. 12 h. Vs. Kopf der Kore-Persephone n.l. Rs. Pferd mit umgewendetem Kopf n.r. JENKINS-LEWIS 390. Ex Leu 52 (1991) 38.

33. – EL Trihemistater, ca. 250. 10.70 g. 12 h. Vs. Kopf der Kore-Persephone n.l. Rs. Pferd n.r., auf der Bodenlinie fünf Kugeln; oben Uräusschlange. JENKINS-LEWIS 423. Ex Leu 57 (1993) 48.

---

[3] NB: Man beachte die einheitliche, regelmäßige Stempelstellung dieser fünf karthagischen Edelmetallprägungen (Nrn. 29-33), die alle anepigraphisch sind.

# Tafel L

23        24        25        26

27        28

29        31        32        33

30

# Rebel Coinage in the Roman Empire (S. 163-169) – Tf. LI

## Vindex
1. SALUS GENERI - HUMANI. Victoria, holding wreath and palmbranch on globe to left; Rev. SPQR in oak wreath.(Leu 2, 1972, 374).
2. AUGUSTUS - DIVI - F. Head of Augustus, laureate, r.; Rev. IMP XII, Bull butting r. (Hess-Leu 49, 1971, 342).

## Clodius Macer
1. L. CLODI - MACER / SC. Bust r. Rev. PRO-PRAE-AFRICAE. War galley with standard and aplustre r. (Sternberg, 29.11.1974, 47).
2. CLOD - MACRI SC. Libertas with wreath and Phrygian cap to left. Rev. LEG-I-MAC-RIANA-LIB(eratrix). Legionary eagle between standards (Leu 20, 1978, 246).

## Vabalathus and Zenobia
1 - 3. Obv. Ἰ(ούλιος) Α(ὐρήλιος) Σ(επτίμιος) Ου<α>βάλλαθος Ἀθηνόδωρος) Ὑ(πατος) Αὐ[τ(οχράτωρ) Σ(τρατηγὸς) Ῥ]ωμαίων). Rev. Αὐτ(οχράτωρ) Κ(αῖσαρ) Λ(ούκιος) Δ(ομίτιος) Αὐρηλιανὸς Σεβαστός)
1. Year 4 of Vaballathus, Year I of Aurelian (270/271). Legends 1-3: Bust of Vaballathus with diadem, laurel wreath, cuirass and paludamentum r. In field L-Δ; Rev. Bust of Aurelianus with laurel wreath, cuirass and paludamentum r. Date L-A (Geissen-Weiser 3055).
2. Year 5 and Year 2 (271/272). Legends 1-3: As 1, but date on obv. L-E and on rev. L/Br. (Geissen-Weiser 3059).
3. Year 5 and Year 2. As 2, but date on rev. L-B. (Geissen-Weiser 3063).
4. Obv. Αὐτ(οχράτωρ) Κ(αῖσαρ) Οὐαβάλλαθος Ἀθηνόδωρος) Σεβαστός). Year 5 of Vaballathus as Emperor (272). Legend 4: Bust with laurel wreath, cuirass and paludamentum, but without royal diadem; Rev. Homonia left in chiton and peplos with cornucopiae. Date L-E. (Geissen-Weiser 3064).
5. Obv.Σεπτιμία Ζηνοβία Σεβαστή). Year 5 of Zenobia as Empress (272). Legend 5: Bust of Zenobia with drapery and stephane r., Rev. Elpis l. with chiton and peplos, holding flower. Date L-E. (Geissen-Weiser 3065).
6. Obv. Αὐτ(οχράτωρ) Κ(αῖσαρ) Λ(ούκιος) Α<ὐ>ρηλιανὸς Σεβαστός). Year 3 of Aurelian (272, after the victory over Vaballathus and Zenobia). Legend 6: Bust of Aurelian r. with laurel wreath, cuirass and paludamentum. Rev. Roman she-wolf suckling Romulus and Remus. Date L-Γ. (Geissen-Weiser 3071).

## Money in circulation in Iudaea before and during the Jewish Revolt
1. Tyrian Shekel. First Century BCE (Private collection, Zürich).
2. Tyrian Half-shekel. First Century BCE (MMAG 32, 1966, 156).
3. Nero. Tetradrachm, Antiochia, 63 CE (Photo-File Leu).
4. Nero. Denarius, Rome. 68 CE (Hess-Leu 36, 1985, 445).
5. *Bellum Iudaicum.* Shekel. Year 3. (Leu 33, 1983, 420).
6. *Bellum Iudaicum.* Half-shekel. Year 3. (Leu 28, 1988, 281).

[Zur Bar-Kochba-Prägung vgl. Tf. LII - LXVI]

# Tafel LI

Rebel Coinage

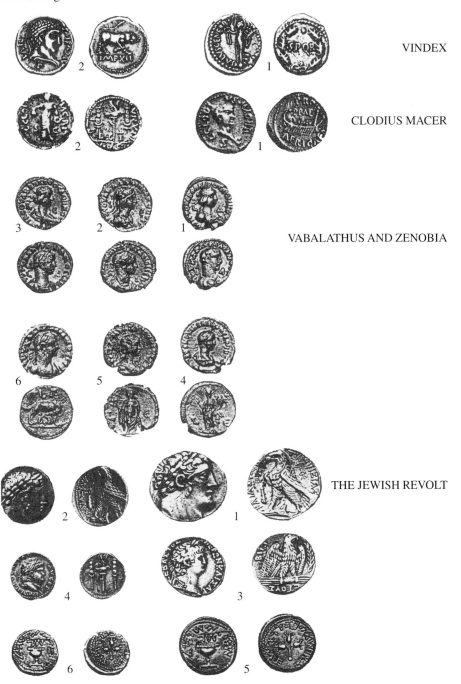

VINDEX

CLODIUS MACER

VABALATHUS AND ZENOBIA

THE JEWISH REVOLT

# Zur Chronologie der Bar-Kochba-Erhebung (S. 176-182) – Taf. LII

1. AR Jüdischer Denar. Av.: Traube am Rebast (SIM)EON; [HADRIANUS, Reste v. Knoten und Schleifen des Stirnbandes]. Rv.: Dreisaitige Leier, DER FREIHEIT (JERUSALEMS); [IUSTITIA, CO(S III) in ex., Unterarm m. Patera, Knie]. Aukt. Kat. Florange-Ciani, Paris. 17.II.1925 (Coll. du Col. Alotte de la Fuye), Nr. 1131, 20 mm, 3,45 gr.

2. AR Hadriandenar. Aus sehr ähnlichen Stempeln wie die unterliegende Prägung bei Nr. 1. Basel. Historisches Museum, Nr. 1903.2775.

3. AE Jüdische Mittelbronze. Aus denselben Stempeln wie Nr. 6. Av.: Weinblatt, DER FREIHEIT JERUSALEMS. Rv.: Dattelpalme, SIMEON. München. Staatliche Münzsammlung.

4. AE Gaza-Mittelbronze Hadrians. Sehr schön erhaltenes Ex. dieser seltenen Münzen, deutliche Typen und Inschriften. Datenvermerke: 192 und 3. Jahr. Wien. Bundessammlung für Münzen, Medaillen und Geldzeichen.

5. AE Gaza-Mittelbronze Hadrians. Aus denselben Stempeln wie die unterliegende Prägung bei Nr. 6. Datenvermerke: 192 und 3. Jahr. Paris. Bibliothèque Naionale, Cabinet des Médailles, No. 160, 11 gr.

6. AE Jüdische Mittelbronze. Av.: Weinblatt, DER (FREIHEIT JER)USALEMS; [.. I.TPA., Hinterkopf Hadrians mit Resten von Knoten und Enden des (von den Juden nach der Überprägung abgefeilten!) Stirnbandes]. Rv.: Dattelpalme, SIM(EON); [BYP, rechter Arm der Stadtgöttin mit aufgestütztem Speer, Reste von Kopf und Haarschmuck – sowie Füllhorn und Schleppe derselben. Starke Abfeilungen]. Coll. Rev. E. ROGERS, A handy quide to Jewish Coins, 1914, 91, Pl. VII, no. 3. Neben Av. sowie Rv. von Nr. 6: Nachzeichnung der Spuren.

7. AE Jüdische Mittelbronze. Gleiche Typen sind Inschriften wie Nr. 6. Auf dem Av. hat sich ebenfalls TPA erhalten, auf dem Rv. aber traf die jüdische Legende SIMEON auf Füllhorn, Schleppe und das Beizeichen von Gaza (semit. Buchstabe *mēm* , mit dem der Name Marnas – Zeus von Gaza ? – beginnt, das *EΠI* aber blieb deutlich stehen. London. BM, BMC Palestine, 312, no. 81, ca. 27 mm, 10,78 gr.

8. AE Jüdische Mittelbronze. Gleiche Typen und Inschriften wie Nrn. 6 und 7. Auf dem Holzschnitt sind die stehengebliebenen Legendenteile sowie der Umriß des Kaiserkopfes mit Bandschleifen getreulich nachgezeichnet. F.W. MADDEN, Coins of the Jews, 1881, no. 22 («Formerly in the Coll. of the late Mr. Wigan». - Heute: ?).

9. AE Jüdische Mittelbronze. Gleiche Typen und Inschriften wie Nrn. 6-8. Sehr späte Notprägung: Flüchtiger Perlkranz des Av. – Auf Rv. SIM(E)ON in retrograder Schreibung bereits irregulärer Buchstabenformen. Im Zentrum des Av.: die deutlichen Umrisse des Kaiserkopfes mit dem für die Gaza-Bronzen charakteristischen Profil Hadrians. London. British Museum, BMC Palestine, 313, no. 89, 28 mm, 10,93 gr.

# Tafel LII

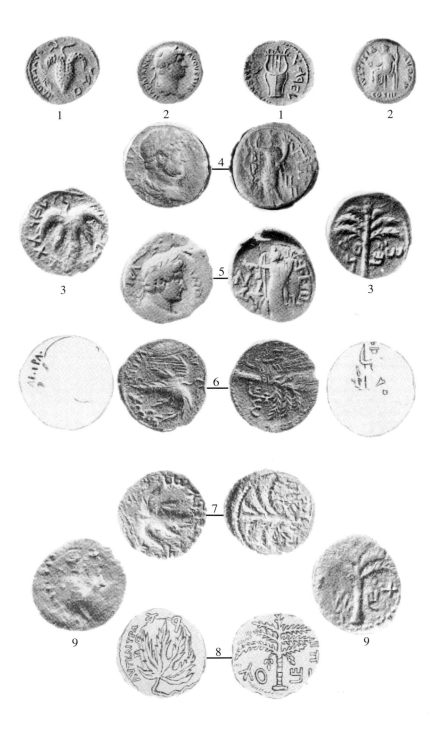

# Eleazar Coins of the Bar Kochba Rebellion (S. 183-201) – Taf. LIII

**Explanations to Plate L - The System of Interlinking Dies**

A. Eleazar Coins

1    AE: Obverse: G 1. Type: Bunch of grapes with one small, chased leaf to left on a curved, cut branch. Inscr.: «Year One of the Redemption of Israel». Reverse: E 1. Type: Palm tree with erect top, one bunch of three small fruits left. Inscr.: «Eleazar the Priest» (mirror-writing, retrograde). 16 specimens examined: 1. Coll. REIFENBERG, Ancient Jewish Coins, [2]1947, Pl. XIV, 189a (Plate); 2-5. London. 4 spec.: BMC Palestine, 302, 3-6 (3 spec. from Coll. Hamburger). 6,7. Paris. 2 spec.: 333; 334, 6.5 gr., large flan; 334, 6.S gr., reverse worn. 8. Vatican. Coll. «Feu Grégoire», donated in 1932; 43, 5.0 gr., 18 mm; 9. Glasgow. Hunter Coll., small flan, 16 mm; 10. Coll. Hecht. 5, 1 gr., 17 mm; 11. Cat. Naville XV, 1119 = Cat. Baranovski IV, 1931, 767 = Cat. Ratto, Monete Ebraiche, 1931-1932, 84. Cast in Berlin; 12. Cat. L. Hamburger 96, 25. X. 1932, 5.67 gr., 18 mm; 13. Cat. Ratto, Monete Ebraiche (1931-1932), 85, large oval flan, 20 x 16 mm; 14. Cat. L. Hamburger, 16. 12. 1907, 545; 15. For sale in 1947, MMAG, Basel, 5.99 gr., 20 mm; 16. Coll. Reifenberg, new acquisition in 1948, 17 mm.

2    AE: Obverse: G 1. Type: as above; Inscr.: as above. Reverse: E 2. Type: Palm tree with top inclined to left, two bunches of three very small fruits. Inscr.: «Eleazar the Priest» (mirror-writing, retrograde, var.). 1 0 specimens examined: 1. Jerusalem, Hebrew University, 3494, 18 mm. (Plate); 2-3. London. 2 spec.: BMC 302, 7 and 8 (No. 8 with traces of overstrike). 4: Vatican, Coll. «Feu Grégoire», 42, 4.70 gr., 18 mm; 5-7. Paris. 2 spec.: 538 Inv. Vogüé, 6.5 gr.; 332, 6.1 gr.; 334; 8. Coll. ROGERS, A Handy Guide, 95, p. 89, Pl. V, 1; 9. Cat. Sotheby, 19. I. 1914, 302; 10. Cat. Cahn 60, 2. VII. 1928, 1103, very fine spec. on large flan, 22.5 mm.

3    AE: Obverse: G 1. Type: as above. Inscr.: as above. Reverse: E 3. Type: Palm tree with trunk stout up to the top, two bunches of three large fruits. Inscr.: «Eleazar the Priest» (scattered legend). 9 specimens examined: 1. Cat. Egger XLV, 12. XI. 1913, 786, 7.22 gr., 19 mm. Cast in Berlin. Early, very fine coin (Plate); 2. Paris. 1839, 4.6 gr., 16 mm. Early, fine specimen; 3. Coll. REIFENBERG, Ancient Jewish Coins, [2]1947, 189, 17 mm. Very early and excellent specimen; 4. Coll. Werner. 21 mm. Fine reverse. Very large flan; 5. Cat. L. Hamburger 96, 25. X. 1932, 191, 6.32 gr., 19 mm; 6. Cat. Cahn 68, 26. XI. 1930, 1671 (erroneously described as an Eleazar coin of year 2), 19 mm; 7. For sale in 1947, A. Hess A.G., Luzern, 19 mm; 8. Cat. Cahn 66, 6. VI. 1930, 420 = Cat. H. Seligmann, VI, 1. IX. 1930, 1039. Very large flan, 21,1 mm. Worn; 9. Jerusalem, Hebrew University, 3703, 18 mm.

4    AE:Obverse: G 1. Type: as above. Inscr.: as above. Reverse: E 4. Type: Palm tree, high trunk, top a little to left, two bunches of very large fruits; Inscr.: «Eleazar the Priest» (usual script, but last letter *nūn* in the second line, to the right of trunk).16 specimens examined: 1. Jerusalem, Hebrew University, 675, 18 mm. Very fine reverse (Plate); 2-3. London. 2 spec.: BMC Palestine, 302, 1. and 2; 4. Jerusalem, Bezalel National Museum: M. NARKISS, Coins of Palestine, I, Pl. VII, 2. Early and very fine specimen; 5-6. Coll. Hecht. 2 spec.: 5.9 gr., 17 mm 4.5 gr., 16 mm; 7-8. Vienna. 2 spec. Both on oval flan, one worn; 9. Vatican. Coll. «Feu Grégoire», 41, 6.30 gr., 18 m; 10. Coll. Klagsbald. Early specimen, 17 mm; 11. For sale at MMAG Basel, in 1948/1949 = Cat. Naville XV, 1118 = Cat. Ratto, Monete Ebraiche, 83). Cast in Berlin. 5.6 gr., 1 8 mm; 12. Cat. Ratto, Monnaies Grecques (1926), 2687 = Cat. Baranovski IV, 766 = Cat. Ratto, Man. Ebr., 82; 19 mm; 13. Cat. Cahn 66, 6. VI. 1930, 421, 19,5 mm; 14. Cat. Cahn 71, 620, 5.65 gr., 18 mm; 15. Cat. Münzhandlung Basel 4, 1935, 905, 18,07 mm, 6.09 gr.; 16. Berlin. Coll. Prokesch: MERZBACHER, ZfN (1876-1877) 350s. (woodcut).

5    AE:Obverse: G 2. Type: Bunch of grapes with small, circular leaf left and thin tendril r. On a stright cut branch. Inscr.: «Y[ear] 2 of the Freedom of Israel» (beginning with second letter left of stem). Reverse: E 4. Type: as above. Inscr.: as above. 1 specimen examined: 1. Jerusalem, The Palestine Museum: C. LAMBERT, QDAP 1 (1931) 71, Pl. XXXVII,8 (Plate).

6    AE: Obverse: G 3. Type: Bunch of grapes, no leaf, waved tendril to r., long stem. Inscr.: «To the Freedom of Jerusalem». Reverse: E 4a. Type: as E 4, only first branch r. lower. Inscr.: as E 4, but form of all letters slightly altered. 6 specimens examined: 1. Jerusalem, Hebrew University, 642, 19 mm. (Plate); 2. Coll. REIFENBERG, Ancient Jewish Coins, [2]1947, 203. Large flan with edge hammered-up before overstriking; 3. London, British Museum, acquired in 1927, 6.04 gr.; 4. Paris. Inv. Vogüé 537, 5.70 gr.; 5. Coll. ROGERS, A Handy Guide, Pl. V, 2; 3542 grain = 2,3 gr. Very light weight; for the flan is small and the upper part of obverse filed off; 6. Coll. ROGERS, A Handy Guide, 56, n. 1.

7    AR: Obverse: G 1. Type: as above Nos. 1-4. Inscr.: as above Nos. 1-4. Reverse: E 5. Type: One-handled jug with lip to r., small straight palm branch r. Inscr.: «Eleazar the Priest» (only two letters [2. and 4.] retrograde). 1 specimen examined: 1. Cat. L. Hamburger, 16. XII. 1907, 544 (Plate).

8    AR: Obverse: G 1. Reverse: E 5. From same dies as No. 7: the worn, pierced Paris specimen, described first b y DE VOGÜÉ, RN 1860, 290s. 1. Paris. Inv. Vogüé 536, 2.20 gr. (weight much reduced) (Plate).

9    AR: Obverse: ,G 1 a. Type: very similar to G 1, but smaller and less chased leaf to left, cut branch less curved and not joining the border of dots. Inscr.: as G 1, but with more acute-angled form of the letter *lāmed* ; the last letter *rēsh* still closer to the stem. Reverse: E 5. Type: as above Nos. 7-8. Inscr.: as above Nos. 7-8.1 specimen examined: 1. Vatican. Coll. «Feu Grégoire», 10, 3.20 gr., 18 mm. (remaining outline of back of emperor's [Vespasianus?] head, laureate, and four letters) (Plate).

# Tafel LIII

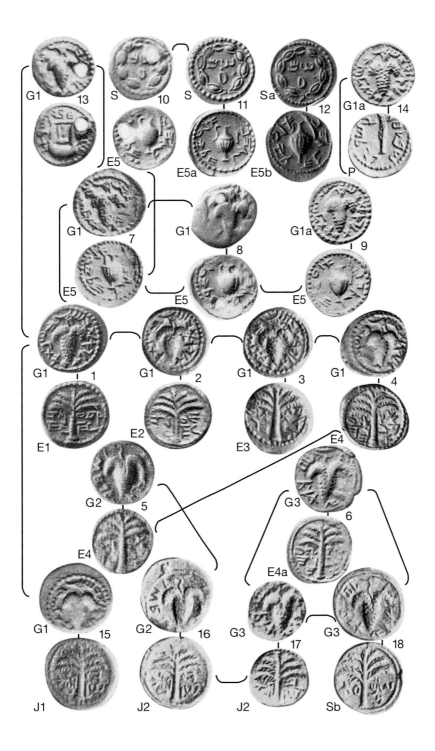

# [Eleazar Coins of the Bar Kochba Rebellion (S. 183-201) – Taf. LIII]

B. The Simon / Eleazar Coins

10  AR: Obverse: S. Type: Wreath placed around eight olives, fifth link above empty, not closed below.  Inscr.: The first three of the five letters of the name, Simon, within the olive-wreath and in a triangular arrangement around a dot.Reverse: E 5. Type and inscription as above Nos. 7-9. 1. Paris. 551: 18 mm., pierced (cast after an authentic coin?) (Plate). (From the same dies: Vatican, 11; London: BMC Palestine, 288, No. 2).

11  AR: Obverse: S. Type and inscription as above No. 10.Reverse: E 5a. Type: Smaller jug, very fine style. Inscr.: as E 5, but all letters smaller and thinner. 1. Paris. 1837, 320 gr. Superb specimen (Plate). (From the same dies: the London overstruck specimen, BMC Palestine, 288, No. 3).

12  AR: Obverse: S a. Type: Similar to S (Nos. 10-11), but no dot in center and altered ends of wreath.  Inscr.: very similar to S. Reverse: E 5 b. Type: Large jug, palm branch more inclined. Inscr.: Large letters, differently placed in circle. 1. Coll. REIFENBERG, Ancient Jewish Coins, $^2$1947, 169. Superb specimen. (Plate).

C. Interlinking Coins of Other Series

13  AR: Obverse: G 1. Type: as above Nos. 1-4, 7, 8.  Inscr.: as above Nos. 1-4. 7-8: «Year One of the Redemption of Israel».Reverse: L. Type: Lyre with three strings.  Inscr.: «Y[ear] 2 of the Free[dom] of Israel» (three abbreviations). 1. London. BMC Palestine, 289, No. 5 (pierced) (Plate).

14  AR: Obverse: G 1a. Type: as above No. 9. Inscr.: as above No. 9: «Year One of the Redemption of Israel». Reverse: P. Type: Palm branch straight. 1. Vatican. Coll. «Feu Grégoire», 12, 3.30 gr. Very fine specimen. Inscr.: «Y[ear] 2 of the Free[dom] of Israel» (three abbreviations). (Plate). (From the same dies: the London specimen; BMC Palestine, 289, No. 4).

15, AE: Obverse: G 1. Type: as above Nos. 1-4, 7-8, 13.  Inscr.: as above 1-4, 7-8, 13. Reverse: J 1. Type: Palm tree with erect top, two bunches of fruits. Inscr.: «Jerusalem». 1. Cat. L. Hamburger 1914. Cast in Berlin (Plate). (From same dies: Coll. REIFENBERG, Ancient Jewish Coins, $^2$1947, Pl. XIV, 195).

16  AE: Obverse: G 2. Type: as above No. 5.  Inscr.: as above No. 5: «Y[ear] 2 of the Free[dom] of Israel».Reverse: J 2. Type: very similar to J 1. Inscr.: as J 1, but form of letter *shīn* acute-angled instead of round. 1. Cat. Naville XV, 1127. Cast in Berlin. (Plate).

17  AE: Obverse: G 3. Type: as above No. 6.  Inscr.: as above No. 6: «To the Freedom of Jerusal[em]». Reverse: J 2. Type: as above No. 16. Inscr.: as above No. 16: «Jerusalem». 1. Cat. Egger, 7.1. 1908, 679. (Plate). (Many other specimens from the same dies, or from the same obverse die and different reverse dies are known).

18  AE: Obverse: G 3. Type: as above Nos. 6 and 17.  Inscr.: as above Nos. 6 and 17: «To the Freedom of Jerusal[em]». Reverse: S b. Type: Palm tree with top inclined to r., two bunches of fruits. Inscr.: Simon. 1. Cat. Cahn 60, 2. VII. 1928, 1101. Early and fine specimen. (Plate).

# The Eleazar Coins of the Bar Kochba Rebellion (S. 183-201) – Taf. LIV

The Eleazar Inscriptions – The Alphabet of the Eleazar Inscriptions – The Position of G1 in the System of  Interlinking Dies.

# Tafel LIV

THE ELEAZAR INSCRIPTIONS

| E1 | E2 | E3 | E4 | E5 |

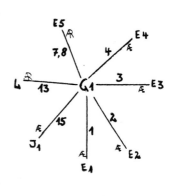

| MODERN | Æ E4, E2 | Æ E3, E4 | Æ E5, E5a | E |
|---|---|---|---|---|
| א | ‎ | | ‎ | |

# Monetary System of the Bar Kochba Coinage (S. 202-207) – Taf. LV

Some die-sequences of the Bar Kokhba tetradrachms

| No | Corp. | Obv. | Rev. | gr. | Provenance No. |
|---|---|---|---|---|---|
| 1 | 3 | V.1 | R.3 | 12.37 | ANS, ex Newell |
| 2 | 6 | V.1 | R.6 | 14.39 | ANS, ex Newell and Hebron Hoard |
| 3 | 9 | V.3 | R.6 | 14.15 | Schonwalter, ex Pozzi 3082 |
| 4 | 10 | V.3 | R.8 | 14.80 | Montagu sale, London 1896, 756 |
| 5 | 11 | V.4 | R.8 | 4.35 | Allotte sale, Paris 1925, 1090 |
| 6 | 14 | V.4 | R.11 | 4.68 | Egger XIV, Wien 1913, 800 |
| 7 | 16 | V.4 | R.13 | 13.60 | Allotte sale, Paris 1925, 1105 |
| 8 | 19 | V.6 | R.13 | 14.72 | Ars Classica XII, 2022 |
| 9 | 22 | V.7 | R.11 | 14.45 | Allotte sale, Paris 1925, 1098 |
| 10 | 28 | V.9 | R.20 | 14.21 | Hess-Leu 1963,59 ex Cahn 66,4407 |
| 11[*] | 29 | V.10 | R.21 | - | De la Tour sale, Paris 1911, 81 |
| 12 | 30 | V.7 | R.22 | - | Neumayer sale, New York 1960 |

# Monetary System of the Bar Kochba Coinage (S. 202-207) – Taf. LVI

| No | Corp. | Obv. | Rev. | gr. | Provenance No. |
|---|---|---|---|---|---|
| 13 | 33 | V.10 | R.25 | 14.40 | Allotte sale, Paris 1925, 1092 |
| 14 | 39 | V.10 | R.31 | 14.32 | Mildenberg, acquired 1950 |
| 15 | 50 | V.13 | R.41 | 14.10 | Ars Classica XII, 2025 |
| 16 | 33 | V.14 | R.41 | 14.42 | Baranowsky 1931, 765 ex Ratto 1926, 2685 |
| 17 | 59 | V.14 | R.45 | 14.41 | Glendining 1955, 617 ex Sotheby 1914, 307 and J. Hirsch 1906, 3055 |
| 18 | 60 | V.14 | R.46 | 14.35 | ANS ex Newell and Hebron Hoard |
| 19 | 61 | V.14 | R.47 | - | Hebrew University |
| 20 | 62 | V.15 | R.47 | 14.15 | Allotte sale, Paris 1925, 1104 |

[*] On the plate the number of the reverse of this specimen is 31, it should be 21.

# Tafel LV

I

V 1 ———————— V 1        V 3 ———————— V 3

1-3        2-6        3-9        4-10

R 3        R 6 ———————— R 6        R 8

V 4 ———————— V 4 ———————— V 4        V 6

5-11        6-14        7-16        8-19

R 8        R 11        R 13 ———————— R 13

V 7        V 9        V 10        V 7

9-22        10-28        11-29        12-30

R 11        R 20        R 31        R 22

# Tafel LVI

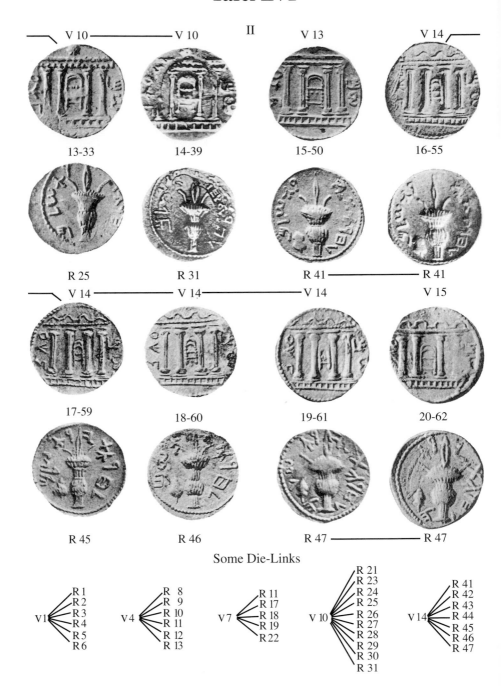

II

# Tafel LVII

A Bar Kochba Didrachm (S. 208-211)

1. Bar Kokhba didrachm, uncleaned; 7.85 gr. 12 h.

2. Bar Kokhba didrachm, cleaned; 7.62 gr. 12 h.

3. Bar Kokhba didrachm, scale 2:1

4. Trajan, didrachm, Syria-Phoenicia, BMC Galatia, No. 58, 7.80 gr., 6 h.

5. Bar Kokhba didrachm, traces from the underlying coin ( observe turned upside down).

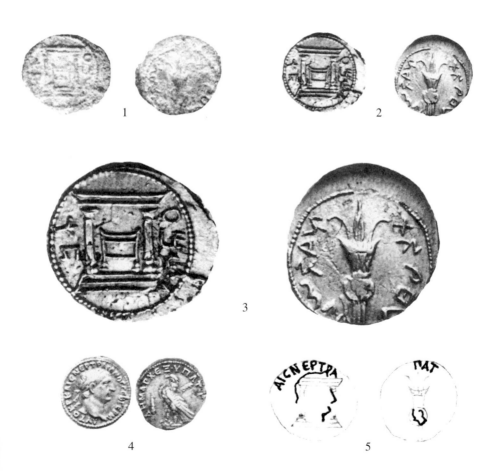

## Bar Kochba in Jerusalem? (S. 212-216) – Taf. LVIII

### Tetradrachmen

Vs. *Tempel*
1 Jerusalem
2 Gleicher Stempel
3 Jerusalem
4 Simon

Rs. *Lulab und Ethrog*
Jahr Eins der Befreiung Israels
Jahr 2 der Freiheit Israels
Jahr 2 der Freiheit Israels
Jahr 2 der Freiheit Israels

### Denar

Vs. *Traube*
5 Jahr 1 der Befreiung Israels

Rs. *Krug*
Eleazar der Priester

### Kleinbronzen

Vs. *Traube*
6 Gleicher Stempel wie 5
7 Gleicher Stempel
8 Jahr 2 der Freiheit Israels
9 Für die Freiheit Jerusalems

Rs. *Palme*
Eleazar der Priester
Jerusalem
Jerusalem
Jerusalem

### Mittelbronze

Vs. *Palmzweig im Kranz*
10 Simon Fürst Israels

Rs. *Leier*
Jahr 1 der Befreiung Israels

Vs. *Palme*
11 Simon Fürst Israels

Rs. *Weinblatt*
Jahr 1 der Befreiung Israels

### Großbronze

Vs. *Ölkranz*
12 Simon Fürst Israels

Rs. *Amphora*
Jahr 1 der Befreiung Israels

Standort: Privatsammlungen in Jerusalem und Zürich. Photos: 2-4 und 6-12 S. Hurter; 1 und 5 Sammler.

# Tafel LVIII

1 Æ      2 Æ      3 Æ      4 Æ

5 Æ      6 Æ      7 Æ      8 Æ      9 Æ

10 Æ      11 Æ

12 Æ

# A Bar Kochba Coins and Documents (S. 217-234)

Map 3. Judaea.

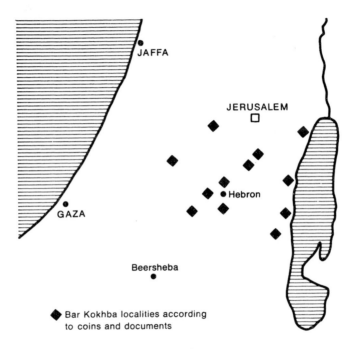

JAFFA

JERUSALEM

GAZA

Hebron

Beersheba

◆ Bar Kokhba localities according
to coins and documents

# Tafel LIX

A Bar Kochba Coins and Documents (S. 217-234)

# Tafel LX

A Bar Kochba Coins and Documents (S. 217-234)

Map 1. Palestine.

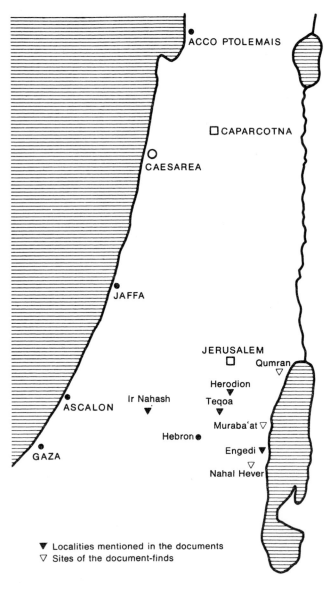

# Tafel LXI

A Bar Kochba Coins and Documents (S. 217–234)

Map 2. Palestine.

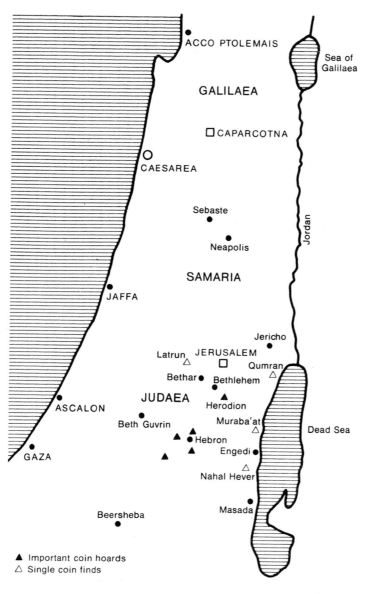

# Der Bar-Kochba-Krieg (S. 241-249) – Tf. LXII

Standort s. MILDENBERG 1984 (= M).

## Struktur regulär

1. Tempel / Lulav mit Etrog. Legenden 7 und 3. Tetradrachme. M 82.14.
2. Traube / Zwei Trompeten. Legenden 7 und 3. Denar-Drachme. M 167.54.
3. Schrift im Kranz / Amphora. Legenden 5 und 2. Großbronze. M 18.6.
4. Palmzweig im Kranz / Chelys-Leier. Legenden 3 und 2. Mittelbronze. M 29.2.
5. Weinblatt / Palme. Legenden 3 und 7 var. Mittelbronze. M 135.1.
6. Traube / Palme. Legenden 3 und 8. Kleinbronze. M 160.4.

## Struktur irregulär

7. Tempel / Lulav mit Etrog. Legenden 4 und 2. Tetradrachme. M 97.1.
8. Traube / Zwei Trompeten. Nachahmung von 2 oben. Denar-Drachme. M 253.1.
9. Weinblatt / Palme. Nachahmung von 5 oben. Mittelbronze. 207.1.
10. Traube / Palme. Nachahmung von 6 oben. Kleinbronze. M 229.1.

# Tafel LXII

Regulär

1     AR

2     AR

3     Æ

4     Æ

5     Æ

6     Æ

Irregulär

7     AR

8     AR

9     Æ

10     Æ

# Der Bar-Kochba-Krieg (S. 241-249) – Tf. LXIII

**Bilder**

Tempel und Tempelutensilien

1. Tempelfassade mit Umschrift JERUSALEM. Legende 4. Tetradrachme, V. M 11.3.
2. Krug, hier mit Palmzweig. Legende 2. Denar-Drachme, R. M 22.1.
3. Amphora. Legende 1. Großbronze, R. M 1.14.

Musikinstrumente

4. Zwei Trompeten. Legende 2. Denar-Drachme, R. M 25.1.
5. Chelys-Leier mit 3 Saiten. Legende 2. Denar-Drachme, R. M 13.16.
6. Chelys-Leier mit 4 Saiten. Legende 1. Mittelbronze, R. M 24.2.
7. Kithara-Leier. Legende 3. Denar-Drachme, R. M 101.8.
8. Kithara-Leier. Legende 7. Mittelbronze, R. M 32.3.

Pflanzen – Früchte

9. Lulav (Feststrauß aus Palmzweig, Weiden- und Myrtenzweigen) und Etrog (Citrusfrucht). Legende 2.Tetradrachme, R. M 82.14.
10. Kranz, um acht Oliven geflochten. Legende 8 var. Denar-Drachme, V. M 65.6.
11. Kranz aus Palmzweigen. Legende 6. Großbronze, V. M 1.14 (für R s. o. 3).
12. Kranz aus Ölzweigen. Legende 8 var. Großbronze, V. M 19.6.
13. Palmzweig. Legende 3. Denar-Drachme, R. M 136.7.
14. Palmzweig mit Lorbeerkranz. Legende 6. Mittelbronze, V. M 26.25.
15. Traubendolde, an Ast hängend. Legende 7. Denar-Drachme, R. M 161.11.
16. Traubendolde mit großem Blatt links. Legende 1 var. Kleinbronze, V. M 151.2.
17. Weinblatt mit zwei Ranken. Legende 3. Mittelbronze, V. M 116.1.
18. Palme mit drei Früchten r. und links. Legende 8 var. Mittelbronze, R. M 112.12.
19. Palme wie vorher. Legende 8 var. Kleinbronze, R. M 159.3.

# Tafel LXIII

# Der Bar-Kochba-Krieg (S. 241-249) – Tf. LXIV

## Übersetzung der abgebildeten Legenden

1. Jahr Eins der Erlösung Israels.

2. Jahr 2 der Freiheit Israels.

3. Für die Freiheit Jerusalems.

4. Jerusalem (in einer Zeile).

5. Jerusalem (in zwei Zeilen).

6. Šimʿōn Fürst Israels.

7. Šimʿōn (in einer Zeile).

8. Šimʿōn (in zwei Zeilen).

9. Šimʿ[ōn] (abgekürzt).

10. Eleazar der Priester.

1

2

3

4

5

6

7

8

9

10

# Der Bar-Kochba-Krieg (S. 241-249) – Tf. LXV

## Überprägungen

Römische und frühere Silber- und Bronzemünzen aus Bar-Kochba-Funden, zum Überprägen flachgehämmert, aber noch nicht überprägt, sowie noch unberührte Stücke aus gleichen Emissionen.

1. Tetradrachme der syrischen Provinzialprägung vom Jahre 70. Vespasian / Titus. M ill. E.
2. Römische Republik. Denar 82-80 v. Chr. M ill. G.
3. Römische Republik. Gleiche Emission wie vorher. Nach Verformung und Riss des Schrötlings durch Flachhämmern wurde das Stück für die Überprägung unbrauchbar. M ill. H.
4. Gaza. Großbronze, teilweise flachgehämmert. Hadrian 131/132. Doppeldatierung im Abschnitt. M ill. M.
5. Provinzialprägung Trajans im Osten. Stehende Arabia mit Kamel. Drachme 111/112. M il. I.
6. Gleiche Emission wie vorher, teilweise flachgehämmert. M ill. K.
7. Bar-Kochba 134/5. Überprägung einer Trajan-Drachme. M. 159.24.
8. aza. Mittelbronze Hadrians von 131/132, da doppelt datiert: Jahr 192 (Ära von Gaza) links im Feld und Jahr 3 (seit dem Besuch von Hadrian 130) r. von oben nach unten. L. MILDENBERG, Numismatische Evidenz zur Chronologie der Bar-Kochba-Erhebung, SNR 34 (1948/49), Tf. 3,4 [hier Tf. LII 4].
9. Bar-Kochba. Mittelbronze, regulär. Weinblatt und Palme kaum sichtbar. Überprägung auf Gaza wie vorher. Das Datum 192 links von der Stadtgöttin blieb noch deutlich sichtbar stehen. M ill. S.
10. Bar-Kochba. Mittelbronze mit dem gleichen Datum an der gleichen Stelle wie hier 8 und 9. M 120.3 und ill. T.
11. Bar-Kochba. Kleinbronze. Überprägung auf einem seleukidischen *serratus*. Starke Spuren der Feile, welche die stehengebliebenen Reste von Bild und Schrift der unterliegenden Münze entfernte. M ill. Q.
12. Bar-Kochba. Mittelbronze mit deutlichen, waagrechten Feilspuren. M 136.1.

# Tafel LXV

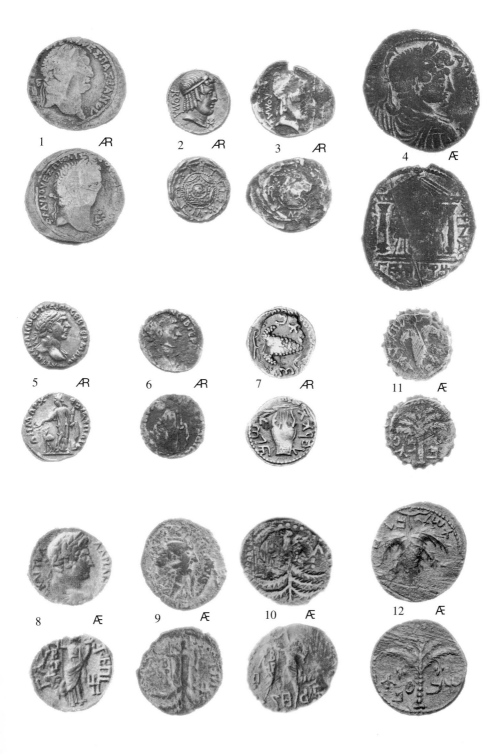

1  Æ

2  Æ

3  Æ

4  Æ

5  Æ

6  Æ

7  Æ

11  Æ

8  Æ

9  Æ

10  Æ

12  Æ

# Der Bar-Kochba-Krieg (S. 241-249) – Tf. LXVI

## Stempelverbindungen

Koppelung eines Vorderseitenstempels mit 29 Rückseitenstempeln, zuerst in der zweiten und dann in der dritten Prägeperiode.

V1 Vorderseitenstempel M V 14, verbunden in frischem Zustand mit dem Rückseitenstempel M R 31 zu Nr. 56 (oben links).

1.         Erster Rückseitenstempel in der Reihe (M R 31).

2.- 5.     Abfolge mit den Rückseitenstempeln der zweiten Prägeperiode (M 57-60).

6.-28.     Abfolge bis zum vorletzten Stück in der dritten Prägeperiode (M 61-83).

V 1 Vorderseitenstempel M V 14 in verbrauchtem Zustand (unten r.).

29.       Letzter Rückseitenstempel, verbunden mit Vorderseitenstempel M 14 zu Nr. 84.


–––––––    unmittelbare Stempelverbindung

·········     unmittelbare Verbindung zwischen einem nachgeschnittenen Stempel und dem gleichen Stempel in unberührtem Zustand

<–––––    Stempelverbindung mit einem früheren Stück

–––––––>   Stempelverbindung mit einem späteren Stück

# Tafel LXVI

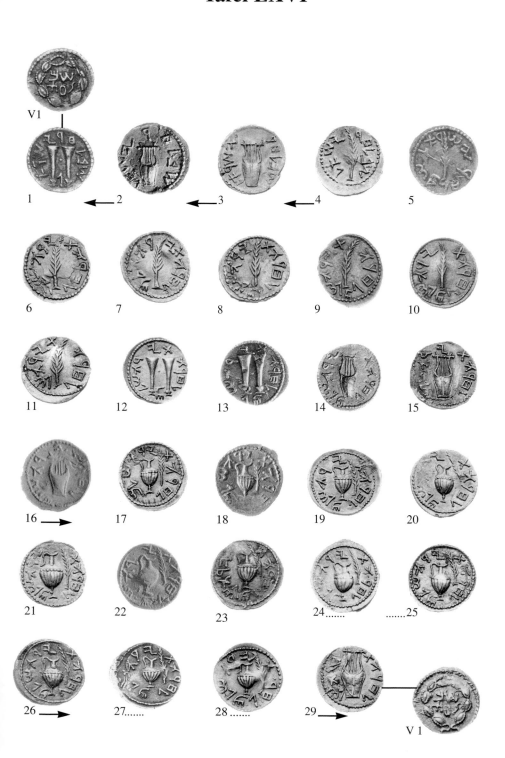

V1

1  2  3  4  5

6  7  8  9  10

11  12  13  14  15

16  17  18  19  20

21  22  23  24 .......  ....... 25

26  27 .......  28 .......  29  V 1

Numismatic Evidence (S. 381-395) – Taf. LXVII

Figs. 1-4, 7-9, 12-13

# Tafel LXVII

Numismatic Evidence (S. 381-395) – Taf. LXVIII

Figs. 5-6

# Tafel LXVIII

Figs. 5-6

Numismatic Evidence (S. 381-395) – Taf. LXIX

Figs. 10-11, 14-24

# Tafel LXIX

10

11

10

14

15

16

17

18

22 AE

20 AE

19 AE

21 AE

23

24

23

# «Those ridiculous arrows» (S. 263-264) – Taf. LXX

## 1. Punic Sicily

Coins struck from loose dies, often with distinct protuberances.

1. Tetradrachmon, ca. 409 A.D., 16.72 g. 5 h, Hess-Leu 1956, 227. Forepart of bridled horse r., above Nike, corn grain r., below legend qrtḥdšt «New City». Rev. Palm tree below legend mḥnt «Camp»[4].
2. Tetradrachmon, ca. 400, 16.92 g. 1 h. Basel catalogue 556. Free horse cantering left, below legend on triple line qrtḥdšt [5] «New City». Rev. Palm tree, below mḥnt «Camp».
3. Hexadrachmon, ca. 320-310, 17.23 g. 2 h. Basel catalogue 561. Head of Tanit left. Rev. Lion left, behind Palm tree, below legend š 'mmḥnt «The money of the People of the Camp».
4. Hexadrachmon, ca. 265[6], 21.94 g. 10 h. Basel catalogue 566. Head of Kore-Persephone left. Rev. Horse's head.
5. Dodekadrachmon, ca. 265. 44.13 g. 10 h. Basel catalogue 565. Head of Kore-Persephone left. Rev. Stallion prancing left.
6. Dekadrachmon, ca. 260, 37.88 g. 11 h. Basel catalogue 567. Head of Kore-Persephone left. Rev. Pegasus prancing r., below legend b'rṣt «In the Territories».
7. Electrum-Tristater, ca. 260. 21.83 g. 1 h. Basel catalogue 568. Head and legend as No. 6. Rev. Stallion prancing r., behind Palm tree.

## 2. Carthage

Coins struck from fixed dies, Obv.: Head of Kore-Persephone left.

8. Electrum-Stater, ca. 300. 7.64 g. 12 h. Sternberg 20, 505. Stallion standing r.
9. Gold Trihemistater, ca. 260. 12.46 g. 12 h. Leu 36,85. Stallion standing r. head reverted.
10. Electrum-Trihemistater, ca. 255-250, 10.87 g. 12 h. Basel catalogue 570. Stallion standing r., above uraeus-cobra.
11. Tetradrachmon, debased silver, ca. 245, 10.19 g. 12 h.Basel catalogue 571. Stallion, behind palm tree.
12. Tetradrachmon, debased silver, ca. 245, 14.69 g. 12 h. Sternberg 20, 514. Stallion, above star.

---

[4] See H. CAHN et al., Griechische Münzen aus Grossgriechenland und Sizilien, 1988.

[5] «Carthago» in Latin. The legends on obverse and reverse have to be read together and understood as «Carthaginian Military Administration».

[6] The high denominations, described here under Nos. 4-7 and 8-10, are war issues struck simultaneously in Sicily and Carthage to finance the struggle with Rome in the years 264-241 B.C.

# Tafel LXX

PUNIC SICILY

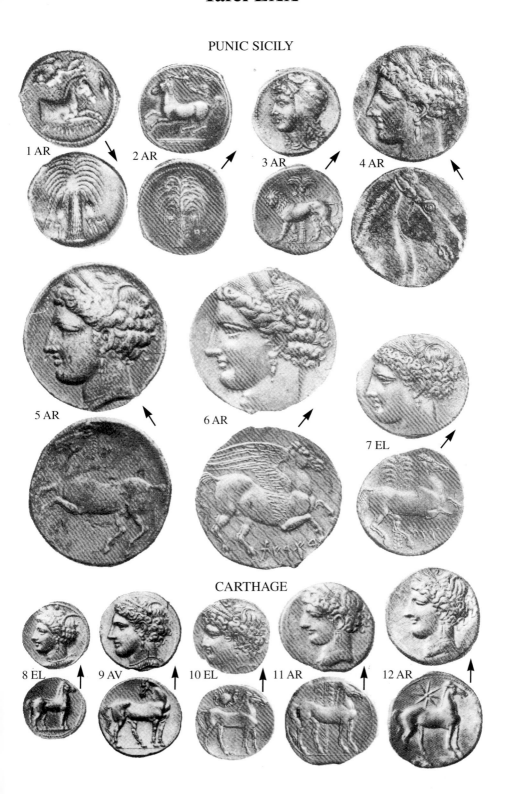

1 AR

2 AR

3 AR

4 AR

5 AR

6 AR

7 EL

CARTHAGE

8 EL

9 AV

10 EL

11 AR

12 AR

# «Those ridiculous arrows» (S. 263-264) – Taf. LXXI

### 3. Carystus
Silver staters ca. 300 B.C.[7]. Legends *KAPYΣ* and *KAPYΣTIΩN*.
Obv.: Cow standing r., head turned to nuzzle sucking calf.
Rev.: Rooster standing r.

13.      Hess-Leu 31, 314, 7.53 g. 10 h. HURTER[8] I c. Forgery.
14.      Hess-Leu 45, 183, 7.22 g[9]. 9 h. HURTER 3b. Forgery[10]
15.      Niggeler 1 (1965), 290, 7.84 g. 12 h.
16.      Hess-Leu 1958, 169, 7.86 g. 12 h.
17.      SNG Lockett 1782 = Pozzi 1465, 7.52 g (Corroded).
18.      Hess-Leu 1962, 222, 7.72 g. 12 h.
19.      Hess-Leu 36, 199, 775 g. 12 h.
20.      Hess-Leu 24, 158 = J. Hirsch 24 (1914), 331, 7.78 g. 10 h[11].

### 4. Ptolemaic Egypt
Gold Octodrachms, Second quarter of the third century.
Obv.: Jugate busts of Ptolemy II and Arsinoe II, behind shield.
Rev.: Jugate busts of Ptolemy I and Berenike I.

21.      Hess-Leu 1958, 265, 27.73 g. 10 h. Forgery. S. HURTER, IAPN Bulletin, vol. 9,1 (1984), Pl. 3,3.
22.      Hess-Leu 1957, 320, 27.77 g. 12 h.
23.      Hess-Leu 28, 313, 27.76 g. 12 h.
24.      Hess-Leu 49, 294, 27.75 g. 12 h.

---

[7] O. PICCARD, Chalcis et la Confédération Eubéenne, Paris 1979, 177-178, has placed this series as late as first half of the third century, probably underestimating the long duration of the circulation of single coins on the island of Euboea.

[8] See S. HURTER, IAPN Bulletin on Counterfeits, Vol. 12,1, 1987, 1.

[9] The average weight of the forgeries is about half a gram lower than that of the genuine coins.

[10] The other forgeries can be added to those published by S. HURTER, ibid., 1: Bourgey June 1959, 325, 7.51 g (short legend) and Dewing 1530, 6.99 g with the completely wrong die position 7 h and the provenance «Acq. Athens 1937» (full legend). See S. HURTER's hint p. 1 of specimen No. 19 in D.M. ROBINSON, A Hoard of Silver Coins from Carystus, ANSNNM 124 (1952).

[11] Some additional published specimens with the die position 12 h are: SNG Copenhagen 415 and 416, SNG Delepierre 1753, SNG Berry 610 and ACNAC Dewing 1529. The specimen SNG Berry 611 with the entirely wrong die position 5 h shows the incomplete legend placed in exactly the same manner as piece No. 20, illustrated here. It is difficult to explain either irregularity of the SNG Berry piece 611.

# Tafel LXXI

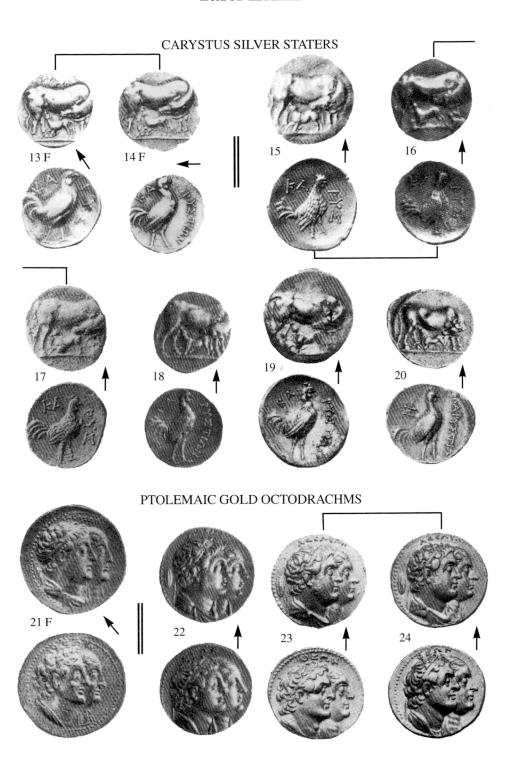

CARYSTUS SILVER STATERS

13 F   14 F   15   16

17   18   19   20

PTOLEMAIC GOLD OCTODRACHMS

21 F   22   23   24

# Tafel LXXII

Florinus Mildenbergensis (S. 265-266)

Goldgulden des Erzbischofs Gerlach von Nassau aus Miltenberg 1:1 und vergrößert.

Goldgulden des Erzbischofs Gerlach von Nassau aus Miltenberg (Vergr.)

Gleiches Stück (1:1)

Bd. 1    MAX KÜCHLER, Schweigen, Schmuck und Schleier. Drei neutestamentliche Vorschriften zur Verdrängung der Frauen auf dem Hintergrund einer frauenfeindlichen Exegese des Alten Testaments im antiken Judentum. XXII+542 Seiten, 1 Abb. 1986. [vergriffen]

Bd. 2    MOSHE WEINFELD, The Organizational Pattern and the Penal Code of the Qumran Sect. A Comparison with Guilds and Religious Associations of the Hellenistic-Roman Period. 104 Seiten. 1986.

Bd. 3    ROBERT WENNING, Die Nabatäer – Denkmäler und Geschichte. Eine Bestandesaufnahme des archäologischen Befundes. 360 Seiten, 50 Abb., 19 Karten. 1986. [vergriffen]

Bd. 4    RITA EGGER, Josephus Flavius und die Samaritaner. Eine terminologische Untersuchung zur Identitätsklärung der Samaritaner. 4+416 Seiten. 1986.

Bd. 5    EUGEN RUCKSTUHL, Die literarische Einheit des Johannesevangeliums. Der gegenwärtige Stand der einschlägigen Forschungen. Mit einem Vorwort von Martin Hengel. XXX+334 Seiten. 1987.

Bd. 6    MAX KÜCHLER/CHRISTOPH UEHLINGER (Hrsg.), Jerusalem. Texte – Bilder – Steine. Im Namen von Mitgliedern und Freunden des Biblischen Instituts der Universität Freiburg Schweiz herausgegeben... zum 100. Geburtstag von Hildi + Othmar Keel-Leu. 238 S., 62 Abb.; 4 Taf.; 2 Farbbilder. 1987.

Bd. 7    DIETER ZELLER (Hrsg.), Menschwerdung Gottes – Vergöttlichung von Menschen. 8+228 Seiten, 9 Abb., 1988.

Bd. 8    GERD THEISSEN, Lokalkolorit und Zeitgeschichte in den Evangelien. Ein Beitrag zur Geschichte der synoptischen Tradition. 10+338 Seiten. 1989.

Bd. 9    TAKASHI ONUKI, Gnosis und Stoa. Eine Untersuchung zum Apokryphon des Johannes. X+198 Seiten. 1989.

Bd. 10   DAVID TROBISCH, Die Entstehung der Paulusbriefsammlung. Studien zu den Anfängen christlicher Publizistik. 10+166 Seiten. 1989.

Bd. 11   HELMUT SCHWIER, Tempel und Tempelzerstörung. Untersuchungen zu den theologischen und ideologischen Faktoren im ersten jüdisch-römischen Krieg (66–74 n. Chr.). XII+432 Seiten. 1989.

Bd. 12 DANIEL KOSCH, Die eschatologische Tora des Menschensohnes. Untersuchungen zur Rezeption der Stellung Jesu zur Tora in Q. 514 Seiten. 1989.

Bd. 13 JEROME MURPHY-O'CONNOR, O.P., The Ecole Biblique and the New Testament: A Century of Scholarship (1890–1990). With a Contribution by Justin Taylor, S.M. VIII + 210 Seiten. 1990.

Bd. 14 PIETER W. VAN DER HORST, Essays on the Jewish World of Early Christianity. 260 Seiten. 1990.

Bd. 15 CATHERINE HEZSER, Lohnmetaphorik und Arbeitswelt in Mt 20, 1–16. Das Gleichnis von den Arbeitern im Weinberg im Rahmen rabbinischer Lohngleichnisse. 346 Seiten. 1990.

Bd. 16 IRENE TAATZ, Frühjüdische Briefe. Die paulinischen Briefe im Rahmen der offiziellen religiösen Briefe des Frühjudentums. 132 Seiten. 1991.

Bd. 17 EUGEN RUCKSTUHL/PETER DSCHULNIGG, Stilkritik und Verfasserfrage im Johannesevangelium. Die Johanneischen Sprachmerkmale auf dem Hintergrund des Neuen Testaments und des zeitgenössischen hellenistischen Schrifttums. 284 Seiten. 1991.

Bd. 18 PETRA VON GEMÜNDEN, Vegetationsmetaphorik im Neuen Testament und seiner Umwelt. Eine Bildfelduntersuchung. 558 Seiten. 1991.

Bd. 19 MICHAEL LATTKE, Hymnus. Materialien zu einer Geschichte der antiken Hymnologie. XIV + 510 Seiten. 1991.

Bd. 20 MAJELLA FRANZMANN, The Odes of Solomon. An Analysis of the Poetical Structure and Form. XXVIII + 460 Seiten. 1991.

Bd. 21 LARRY P. HOGAN, Healing in the Second Temple Period. 356 Seiten. 1992.

Bd. 22 KUN-CHUN WONG, Interkulturelle Theologie und multikulturelle Gemeinde im Matthäusevangelium. Zum Verhältnis von Juden- und Heidenchristen im ersten Evangelium. 236 Seiten. 1992.

Bd. 23 JOHANNES THOMAS, Der jüdische Phokylides. Formgeschichtliche Zugänge zu Pseudo-Phokylides und Vergleich mit der neutestamentlichen Paränese XVIII + 538 Seiten. 1992.

Bd. 24 EBERHARD FAUST, Pax Christi et Pax Caesaris. Religionsgeschichtliche, traditionsgeschichtliche und sozialgeschichtliche Studien zum Epheserbrief. 536 Seiten. 1993.

Bd. 25 ANDREAS FELDTKELLER, Identitätssuche des syrischen Urchristentums. Mission, Inkulturation und Pluralität im ältesten Heidenchristentum. 284 Seiten. 1993.

Bd. 26    THEA VOGT, Angst und Identität im Markusevangelium. Ein textpsychologischer und sozialgeschichtlicher Beitrag. 288 Seiten. 1993.

Bd. 27    ANDREAS KESSLER/THOMAS RICKLIN/GREGOR WURST (Hrsg.), Peregrina Curiositas. Eine Reise durch den orbis antiquus. Zu Ehren von Dirk Van Damme. X + 322 Seiten. 1994.

Bd. 28    HELMUT MÖDRITZER, Stigma und Charisma im Neuen Testament und seiner Umwelt. Zur Soziologie des Urchristentums. 344 Seiten. 1994.

Bd. 29    HANS-JOSEF KLAUCK, Alte Welt und neuer Glaube. Beiträge zur Religionsgeschichte, Forschungsgeschichte und Theologie des Neuen Testaments. 320 Seiten. 1994.

Bd. 30    JARL E. FOSSUM, The Image of the invisible God. Essays on the influence of Jewish Mysticism on Early Christology. X + 190 Seiten. 1995.

Bd. 31    DAVID TROBISCH, Die Endredaktion des Neuen Testamentes. Eine Untersuchung zur Entstehung der christlichen Bibel. IV + 192 Seiten. 1996.

Bd. 32    FERDINAND ROHRHIRSCH, Wissenschaftstheorie und Qumran. Die Geltungsbegründungen von Aussagen in der Biblischen Archäologie am Beispiel von Chirbet Qumran und En Feschcha. XII + 416 Seiten. 1996.

Bd. 33    HUBERT MEISINGER, Liebesgebot und Altruismusforschung. Ein exegetischer Beitrag zum Dialog zwischen Theologie und Naturwissenschaft. XII + 328 Seiten. 1996.

Bd. 34    GERD THEISSEN / DAGMAR WINTER, Die Kriterienfrage in der Jesusforschung. Vom Differenzkriterium zum Plausibilitätskriterium. XII + 356 Seiten. 1997.

Bd. 35    CAROLINE ARNOULD, Les arcs romains de Jérusalem. 368 pages, 36 Fig., 23 Planches. 1997.

Bd. 36    LEO MILDENBERG, Vestigia Leonis. Studien zur antiken Numismatik Israels, Palästinas und der östlichen Mittelmeerwelt. – XXII + 266 Seiten, Tafelteil 144 Seiten. 1998.

UNIVERSITÄTSVERLAG FREIBURG SCHWEIZ
VANDENHOECK & RUPRECHT GÖTTINGEN

# ORBIS BIBLICUS ET ORIENTALIS (eine Auswahl)

Bd. 25/1 MICHAEL LATTKE: Die Oden Salomos in ihrer Bedeutung für Neues Testament und Gnosis. Band I. Ausführliche Handschriftenbeschreibung. Edition mit deutscher Parallel-Übersetzung. Hermeneutischer Anhang zur gnostischen Interpretation der Oden Salomos in der Pistis Sophia. XI–237 Seiten. 1979.

Bd. 25/1a MICHAEL LATTKE: Die Oden Salomos in ihrer Bedeutung für Neues Testament und Gnosis. Band Ia. Der syrische Text der Edition in Estrangela Faksimile des griechischen Papyrus Bodmer XI– 68 Seiten. 1980.

Bd. 25/2 MICHAEL LATTKE: Die Oden Salomos in ihrer Bedeutung für Neues Testament und Gnosis. Band II. Vollständige Wortkonkordanz zur handschriftlichen griechischen, koptischen, lateinischen und syrischen Überlieferung der Oden Salomos. Mit einem Faksimile des Kodex N. XVI–201 Seiten. 1979.

Bd. 25/3 MICHAEL LATTKE: Die Oden Salomos in ihrer Bedeutung für Neues Testament und Gnosis. Band III. XXXIV–478 Seiten. 1986.

Bd. 76 JOŽE KRAŠOVEC: La justice (Ṣdq) de Dieu dans la Bible hébraïque et l'interprétation juive et chrétienne. 456 pages. 1988.

Bd. 90 JOSEPH HENNINGER: Arabica varia. Aufsätze zur Kulturgeschichte Arabiens und seiner Randgebiete. Contributions à l'histoire culturelle de l'Arabie et de ses régions limitrophes. 504 Seiten. 1989.

UNIVERSITÄTSVERLAG FREIBURG SCHWEIZ
VANDENHOECK & RUPRECHT GÖTTINGEN

*Zum Buch:*

Die Numismatik ist neben der Archäologie und der Epigraphik die dritte und am wenigsten beachtete «Hilfswissenschaft», die sich den Primärquellen der Geschichte Israels/Palästinas seit der Perserzeit widmet. Leo Mildenberg hat wie kein anderer die numismatische Evidenz Palästinas/Israels von der Perserzeit (5.Jh.v.Chr.) bis zum zweiten jüdischen Krieg (135 n.) in höchst bedeutsamen Untersuchungen aufgearbeitet. Die Sammlung der wichtigsten seiner Aufsätze, die zum Teil in sehr entlegenen Publikationen erschienen sind, bilden ein eindrückliches Dokument nicht nur für die Schaffenskraft von Leo Mildenberg, der dieses Jahr 85 Jahre alt wird, sondern auch für die Nützlichkeit numismatischer Forschung im Bereich der Geschichtswissenschaften, der Bibelwissenschaft, der Judaistik und der jüdischen und christlichen Theologie.

Together with students of archaeology and epigraphy, numismatists provide the field of Biblical, Israelite, and Palestinian history with a constant flow of new primary evidence for the period from Cyrus to Bar Kochba. No living specialist in coins and their history contributed more to the study of the Holy Land in the Persian, Hellenistic and Roman periods than did Leo Mildenberg, who celebrates his 85th birthday this year. His collected essays demonstrate the meaning and the relevance of numismatic research to the historian, the biblical scholar and the student of Jewish and Christian religion alike.

ISBN 3-7278-1155-2 (Universitätsverlag)
ISBN 3-525-53907-X (Vandenhoeck & Ruprecht)

Nachdem Sie das Diplom oder Lizentiat in Theologie, Bibelwissenschaft, Altertumskunde Palästinas/ Israels, Vorderasiatischer Archäologie oder einen gleichwertigen Leistungsausweis erworben haben, ermöglicht Ihnen ab Oktober 1997 ein Studienjahr (Oktober – Juni), am Biblischen Institut in Freiburg in der Schweiz ein

## Spezialisierungszeugnis
# BIBEL UND ARCHÄOLOGIE
(Elemente der Feldarchäologie, Ikonographie, Epigraphik,
Religionsgeschichte Palästinas/Israels)

zu erwerben.

Das Studienjahr wird in Verbindung mit der Universität Bern (25 Min. Fahrzeit) organisiert. Es bietet Ihnen die Möglichkeit,

☞ eine Auswahl einschlägiger Vorlesungen, Seminare und Übungen im Bereich "Bibel und Archäologie" bei Walter Dietrich, Othmar Keel, Ernst Axel Knauf, Max Küchler, Silvia Schroer und Christoph Uehlinger zu belegen;

☞ diese Veranstaltungen durch solche in Ägyptologie (Hermann A. Schlögl, Freiburg), Vorderasiatischer Archäologie (Markus Wäfler, Bern) und altorientalischer Philologie (Pascal Attinger, Esther Flückiger, beide Bern) zu ergänzen;

☞ die einschlägigen Dokumentationen des Biblischen Instituts zur palästinisch-israelischen Miniaturkunst aus wissenschaftlichen Grabungen (Photos, Abdrücke, Kartei) und die zugehörigen Fachbibliotheken zu benutzen;

☞ mit den großen Sammlungen (über 10'000 Stück) von Originalen altorientalischer Miniaturkunst des Biblischen Instituts (Rollsiegel, Skarabäen und andere Stempelsiegel, Amulette, Terrakotten, palästinische Keramik, Münzen usw.) zu arbeiten und sich eine eigene Dokumentation (Abdrücke, Dias) anzulegen;

☞ während der Sommerferien an einer Ausgrabung in Palästina / Israel teilzunehmen, wobei die Möglichkeit besteht, mindestens das Flugticket vergütet zu bekommen.

Um das Spezialisierungszeugnis zu erhalten, müssen zwei benotete Jahresexamen abgelegt, zwei Seminarscheine erworben und eine schriftliche wissenschaftliche Arbeit im Umfange eines Zeitschriftenartikels verfaßt werden.

Interessenten und Interessentinnen wenden sich bitte an den Curator des Instituts:

Prof. Dr. Max Küchler, Biblisches Institut, Universität, Miséricorde

CH-1700 Freiburg / Schweiz        Fax +41 – (0)26 – 300 9754

INSTITUT BIBLIQUE DE L'UNIVERSITÉ DE FRIBOURG EN SUISSE

L'Institut biblique de l'Université de Fribourg en Suisse offre la possibilité d'acquérir un

## certificat de spécialisation
# CRITIQUE TEXTUELLE ET HISTOIRE DU TEXTE ET DE L'EXÉGÈSE DE L'ANCIEN TESTAMENT
### (Spezialisierungszeugnis Textkritik und Geschichte des Textes und der Interpretation des Alten Testamentes)

en une année académique (octobre à juin). Toutes les personnes ayant obtenu une licence en théologie ou un grade académique équivalent peuvent en bénéficier.

Cette année d'études peut être organisée

☞ autour de la critique textuelle proprement dite (méthodes, histoire du texte, instruments de travail, édition critique de la Bible);

☞ autour des témoins principaux du texte biblique (texte masorétique et masore, textes bibliques de Qumran, Septante, traductions hexaplaires, Vulgate, Targoums) et leurs langues (hébreu, araméen, grec, latin, syriaque, copte), enseignées en collaboration avec les chaires de patrologie et d'histoire ancienne, ou

☞ autour de l'histoire de l'exégèse juive (en hébreu et en judéo-arabe) et chrétienne (en collaboration avec la patrologie et l'histoire de l'Eglise).

L'Institut biblique dispose d'une bibliothèque spécialisée dans ces domaines. Les deux chercheurs de l'Institut biblique consacrés à ces travaux sont Adrian Schenker et Yohanan Goldman.

Pour l'obtention du certificat, deux examens annuels, deux séminaires et un travail écrit équivalent à un article sont requis. Les personnes intéressées peuvent obtenir des informations supplémentaires auprès du Curateur de l'Institut biblique:

Prof. Dr. Max Küchler, Institut biblique, Université, Miséricorde
CH-1700 Fribourg / Suisse       Fax +41 – (0)26 – 300 9754